Barr

W9-DBD-773

THE LAW OF TORTS

FOURTH EDITION

ESSENTIALS OF
CANADIAN LAW

THE LAW OF
TORTS

FOURTH EDITION

PHILIP H. OSBORNE
Faculty of Law
The University of Manitoba

IRWIN
LAW

Published in 2011 by

Irwin Law Inc.
14 Duncan Street
Suite 206
Toronto, ON
M5H 3G8

www.irwinlaw.com

ISBN: 978-1-55221-212-7
e-book ISBN: 978-1-55221-213-4

Library and Archives Canada Cataloguing in Publication

Osborne, Philip H.
    The law of torts / Philip H. Osborne. — 4th ed.

(Essentials of Canadian law)
Includes bibliographical references and index.
Issued also in electronic format.
ISBN 978-1-55221-212-7

    1. Torts—Canada. 2. Liability (Law)—Canada. I. Title. II. Series: Essentials of
Canadian law

KE1232.O83 2011   346.7103   C2011-902785-2
KF1250.O83 2011

The publisher acknowledges the financial support of the Government of Canada
through the Canada Book Fund for its publishing activities.

We acknowledge the assistance of the OMDC Book Fund, an initiative of
Ontario Media Development Corporation.

Printed and bound in Canada.

1 2 3 4 5   15 14 13 12 11

SUMMARY
TABLE OF CONTENTS

DETAILED
TABLE OF CONTENTS

CHAPTER 2:
NEGLIGENCE: BASIC PRINCIPLES   25

PREFACE
To the First Edition

This book has been written primarily to assist students in Canadian law schools to understand the essential principles of the Canadian law of torts and the social policies that support them. It does not seek to categorize and organize the multitude of Canadian tort cases. It does not explore the subtleties of exceptional cases. It does not delve into fine distinctions among relevant provincial statutes. It explains the basic framework and nature of Canadian tort law from which a more advanced study of the law may proceed.

I am mindful of the fact that in most Canadian law schools the law of torts is a first-year course. I have, therefore, tried to make the law accessible to someone coming to the subject for the first time. I have also included an extensive glossary. A happy consequence of this is that the book may have some appeal to members of the public who seek some understanding of this fascinating corner of Canadian law. I also hope that the book will hold some interest for members of the practising bar, if only as a reminder of the basic principles underlying judicial policies and current trends.

My attempt to find the path of reliable generality through the thicket of tort cases and legislation has been assisted by the works of all the writers on Canadian tort law who have gone before me. I am indebted to them all.

I am most appreciative of the support I received from the Legal Research Institute of the University of Manitoba and its director, Professor Alvin Esau. This allowed me to benefit from the fine work done by my research assistant, James Mercury, who conscientiously and cheerfully did much of the research for this book.

I am grateful to Professor Lee Stuesser and Professor John Irvine for reading an early draft of this book and providing useful comments and support. Thanks also to Professor Linda Vincent, who read a number of parts of the draft text and made useful comments. I am grateful, as well, to John Osborne, who proofread the final draft and improved the text. None of these fine people is, however, responsible for any deficiencies that may remain.

The final draft of this book was written while I was on research and study leave at the University of Auckland, New Zealand. I am grateful to Dean Bruce Harris and all the members of the Faculty of Law for their warm collegiality and support.

My thanks to Sue Law, who patiently and expertly attended to and polished my word-processing.

Finally, but most important, I thank my wife, Judy, and my daughter, Becky, whose love and support are constant.

PREFACE
To this Edition

My thanks to my colleague Professor John Irvine who read some of the changes in this edition and made useful comments.

My thanks also to Pat Power for her patience, diligence, and expertise in the word-processing of this edition.

The Canadian law of torts is described as it was on 1 January 2011.

CHAPTER 1

INTRODUCTION

Every day in Canada some of its citizens suffer harm as a consequence of personal, social, business, and governmental activities. The harm may be to their person, dignity, property, or wealth. Tort[1] law determines when the person who causes the harm must pay compensation to the person who suffers it. The answer to that question depends upon the nature of the conduct of the person who caused the harm, the nature of the harm suffered by the victim, and the circumstances in which the harm was inflicted.

This chapter addresses six matters. First, a typical torts case is considered to illustrate some of the characteristics of tort law and the nature of the civil litigation process. Second, reference is made to the origins of tort law. Third, consideration is given to the foundation elements of tort law. Fourth, reference is made to the objectives of tort law. Fifth, special attention is given to personal injury and fatality claims and how the remedies provided by the law of torts relate to other compensatory systems. Finally, consideration is given to the organization of tort law for the purposes of this book.

---

1   The word is not used colloquially. It comes from the French word meaning "wrong," and its use is restricted to the legal system.

A. AN EXEMPLARY TORTS CASE

Evaniuk v. 79846 Manitoba Inc.[2] is not a well-known torts case. It is not referred to in any of the treatises on Canadian tort law.[3] It does not make any special contribution to the development of the law of torts. It is, however, a good example of the kind of cases that Canadian lawyers routinely deal with and it provides a useful starting point for understanding the torts system.

The *Evaniuk* litigation arose from an incident in a Winnipeg bar. Ms. Evaniuk was sitting in the bar with her girlfriend. She noticed that her brother, who was sitting at an adjacent table, was kissing Ms. Fuerst, a waitress at the bar. Ms. Evaniuk warned her brother that he had better watch what he was doing because his wife would be arriving in a few minutes. Ms. Fuerst responded by throwing a full glass of liquid over Ms. Evaniuk. A heated exchange took place between the two women until two bouncers, employed by the bar, intervened. They took hold of Ms. Evaniuk, forcibly removed her from the premises, and threw her into the parking lot. She fell heavily and was injured.

1) Criminal Law and Tort Law Contrasted

Ms. Evaniuk's first response to this incident was to go to the local police station to lodge a complaint. The bouncers may well have committed the crime of assault causing bodily harm. A criminal prosecution is, however, independent of any tort litigation,[4] and the characteristics of the criminal process are distinct from those of the tort process in three important ways.

First, the main function of the criminal law is to punish those who have committed offences under the *Criminal Code*.[5] The punishment is designed to prevent a repeat offence by the defendant and to deter other citizens from similar antisocial conduct. Consequently, the criminal process focuses primarily on the offender, his conduct, and, if he is found guilty, an appropriate punishment. Tort law provides a signifi-

---

2   (1990), 68 Man. R. (2d) 306 (Q.B.).

3   See, for example, G.H.L. Fridman, *The Law of Torts in Canada*, 3d ed. (Toronto: Carswell, 2010); L.N. Klar, *Tort Law*, 4th ed. (Toronto: Carswell, 2008); and A.M. Linden & B. Feldthusen, *Canadian Tort Law*, 8th ed. (Toronto: Butterworths, 2006).

4   Probably the most famous illustration of the independence of the criminal process from the tort process arose from the deaths of Nicole Brown Simpson and Ronald Goldman. O.J. Simpson was acquitted of all criminal charges relating to their deaths but was found liable in tort and ordered to pay substantial damages.

5   R.S.C. 1985, c. C-46.

cant contrast. The focus of tort law is primarily on those who have suffered injury or damage as a consequence of either criminal or non-criminal conduct and their interest in receiving compensation for their losses.

Second, the administration of the criminal justice system is a community responsibility. Prosecutions are brought, almost exclusively, by a branch of government. Tort litigation is brought at the initiative, and at the expense,[6] of the person who has suffered the loss. The reason for governmental involvement in the administration of the criminal law is that the maintenance of public order and safety has a much higher social priority than the compensation of persons who have suffered injuries or damage.

Third, the burden of proof in criminal law is a heavy one. The prosecutor must establish the guilt of the accused beyond a reasonable doubt.[7] This high standard of proof is appropriate given the emphasis of the criminal law on punishment and the accused person's possible loss of freedom upon conviction. The emphasis on compensation in tort law supports the use of the civil burden of proof that requires the plaintiff to prove her case on the balance of probabilities. The plaintiff must show only a 51 percent likelihood that the facts of the case are as she alleges.[8]

It is not known whether the two bouncers in the *Evaniuk* case were prosecuted criminally but, in any event, a criminal prosecution could not provide a compensatory remedy to Ms. Evaniuk.[9] That must be sought under the law of torts.

2) The Tort Litigation

The most serious of the injuries that Ms. Evaniuk suffered were an aggravation to an existing back injury and an injury to her wrist. She retained a lawyer to assist her in recovering compensation for these injuries.

---

6   The successful litigant in tort litigation is normally awarded legal costs against the other party, but legal costs are normally insufficient to cover the full cost of the litigation.

7   For this reason a criminal conviction may be used in a torts case as evidence of that wrongdoing.

8   The civil burden of proof also applies where the alleged tortious conduct would also be a crime. See *F.H. v. McDougall*, [2008] S.C.J. No. 54.

9   The *Criminal Code,* above note 5, contains provisions empowering a court to make a restitutionary order in favour of a victim but such orders are rarely made. See Klar, above note 3 at 43.

The first step in that process was to identify the particular tort that had been committed. Tort law is made up of a number of discrete wrongs with their own definitions and requirements.[10] When the bouncers threw Ms. Evaniuk out of the bar, they committed the tort of battery. Battery is defined as any direct and intentional interference with the person of another which is either harmful or offensive to a reasonable sense of dignity.[11] The bouncers' conduct clearly fits that definition. Moreover, there was no legal justification or defence for the conduct of the bouncers. A bar owner does have the right to ask a patron to leave a bar, and, if the patron does not leave within a reasonable time, she is deemed to be a trespasser and reasonable force (a battery) may be used to eject her. In this case, however, the bouncers did not ask Ms. Evaniuk to leave before they ejected her, and, in any event, they used more than reasonable force when they threw her to the ground. They committed a battery that could not be justified on any lawful basis.

It is useful to note, in a preliminary way, that the function of a tort action such as battery is not exclusively to provide compensation to the plaintiff (Ms. Evaniuk). A successful lawsuit against the two bouncers incidentally inflicts some measure of punishment for their wrongful conduct and that punishment may not only deter them from similar conduct in the future but may also deter other members of society from acting in a similar manner. To some extent, therefore, tort litigation complements the criminal law and seeks to influence the conduct of citizens. Tort liability also serves to identify and remedy the individual wrongdoing of the bouncers to Ms. Evaniuk and correct the personal injustice suffered by her. It serves, also, to mollify Ms. Evaniuk's anger and resentment over the humiliating way that she was treated and provides a civilized vehicle for her to secure a degree of vengeance against the bouncers. In addition, the tort action has an educational dimension, teaching litigants about requisite standards of conduct and the need to recognize and accommodate the legitimate interests of other persons. These various functions are commonly referred to as *compensation, punishment, deterrence, accountability, corrective justice, appeasement, vengeance,* and *education.* They are all legitimate functions of tort law.[12] Nevertheless, it is important not to lose sight of the fact that the

---

10   Each tort has its own formula of essential requirements that must be established by the plaintiff to prove her case. The metaphor of a recipe has been used to explain the need for the plaintiff to fit her case within the formula of a particular tort. All the ingredients must be established to secure success. See P. Cane, *The Anatomy of Tort Law* (Oxford: Hart Publishing, 1997) at 2–10.

11   Battery is discussed in chapter 4.

12   The objectives of tort law are discussed at greater length later in this chapter.

dominant motivation of most plaintiffs is to secure financial compensation. It is not likely that Ms. Evaniuk would have commenced tort litigation without the expectation of receiving financial compensation for her injuries. It was, therefore, incumbent upon her lawyer at an early stage to address this most practical of issues. Would the two bouncers be able to pay an award of damages[13] to the plaintiff?

Defendants in tort litigation must be worth suing. Defendants worth suing fall into three categories: people or institutions with liability insurance[14] that permits the cost of the judgment to be spread among all of those who purchase liability insurance from the defendants' insurers (*insured defendants*); large corporations or governmental institutions that are able to absorb the cost of judgments by spreading it through the price of the goods and services they produce or, in the case of government, by spreading it through taxation (*self-insured defendants*); and uninsured persons or corporations who have personal wealth or assets sufficient to pay the judgment (*defendants with means*). As a rule, employees such as bouncers do not fall into any of these categories. They are not financially viable defendants. Consequently, although the bouncers committed the tort of battery, they were not sued by Ms. Evaniuk. Tort litigation is influenced as much by practical realities as it is by legal principles.

The only potential defendant involved in the incident worth suing was the bouncers' employer, the corporation that owned the bar. A corporation is much more likely to fall into one or more of the three categories of financially viable defendants.[15] Consequently, although its involvement was indirect, the sole defendant in the *Evaniuk* case was the employer/corporation.

---

13 It is important to distinguish between the words "damage" and "damages" in the context of tort law. Damage is the harm or loss that the defendant has caused the plaintiff. In most torts, damage is an essential element of liability. Damages refers to the amount of money awarded by the court to remedy the harm or loss suffered by the plaintiff.

14 Liability insurance is a contract in which the insurer, in exchange for the payment of premiums by the insured, undertakes to protect the insured from the adverse consequences of legal liability to third parties. The nature and extent of the liability insured against and the monetary limits of the protection are controlled by the terms of the policy. The Supreme Court discussed the scope of protection provided by an automobile insurance policy in *Citadel General Assurance Co. v. Vytlingam*, [2007] 3 S.C.R. 373 and *Lumbermens Mutual Casualty Co. v. Herbison*, [2007] 3 S.C.R. 393.

15 The corporation's liability insurance policy may have covered its potential liability arising from the incident. It would depend upon the precise wording of the policy.

A corporation can be found liable for the wrongdoing of its employees (the bouncers) on two grounds. First, if the corporation, as employer, fails to select, train, supervise, or control its employees with due care, it may be found *personally* liable to those who suffer loss as a consequence of that failure to exercise care. Second, the corporation may be found liable on the basis of *vicarious liability*.[16] It is well established that an employer who is free from personal fault, is, nevertheless, vicariously liable for the torts of its employees, if the torts are committed within the scope of their employment. It was on this latter principle of vicarious liability that Ms. Evaniuk's lawyer chose to base her claim. There was, however, a dispute between the parties as to whether or not the principle of vicarious liability was applicable to the case. The contentious point was whether or not the battery was committed within the scope of the bouncers' employment. The arguments were nicely balanced. On the one hand, the bouncers were responsible for the safety and security of the premises and for dealing with the kind of dispute that arose, and they handled their responsibilities poorly. On the other hand, the employer never expressly or impliedly authorized its employees to literally throw people out of its bar. In doing so, they, arguably, were going beyond their role as employees and were acting out of personal hostility to the plaintiff. It was this legal argument that, in all likelihood, prevented the case from being settled before trial.[17] The trial was held before a judge alone. Tort trials before civil juries, where the judge resolves issues of law and the jury resolves issues of fact, are now common only in Ontario and British Columbia.

The judge resolved the case in favour of Ms. Evaniuk. He found that the bouncers had committed an unjustifiable battery against her and the corporation was vicariously liable for the battery because the bouncers were carrying out tasks that they were employed to do, albeit in a wrongful manner. They were, therefore, acting within the scope of their employment. The judge awarded $450 in special damages[18] for Ms. Evaniuk's pretrial expenses and losses and $10,000 in general compensatory damages[19] for the injuries that she suffered. The judge then considered the propriety of awarding punitive damages. Punitive damages are an additional sum of money designed to punish the defendant when his conduct has been particularly vicious, premeditated, high-handed, or disgraceful. It is a power that is exercised with some

16   Vicarious liability is discussed in chapter 5.
17   Over 90 percent of tort litigation is settled by agreement between the litigants.
18   Special damages compensate the plaintiff for losses arising before the trial. In most cases they are susceptible of precise arithmetic calculation.
19   General damages compensate the plaintiff for future losses.

caution, but it does clearly recognize the punitive and deterrent aspects of tort law. In this case, an award of punitive damages may have been appropriate against the bouncers personally but legal liability was imposed exclusively on the corporation. Since the management of the corporation had not encouraged or condoned the conduct of the bouncers, the judge declined to make an award of punitive damages.

This snapshot of the tort process not only describes some of the characteristics of tort law, but it also illustrates an unresolved tension that pervades a great deal of modern tort law. That tension is between the compensatory aspect of tort law, which emphasizes the plaintiff and her need for recompense, and the aspect of tort law that stresses the personal responsibility of wrongdoers and tries to integrate compensatory concerns with notions of deterrence, punishment, and accountability. The compensatory function of tort law is promoted by allocating the plaintiff's loss to the best loss distributor (an insured or a self-insured defendant). Personal responsibility for wrongdoing is promoted by allocating the loss to the primary wrongdoer. This tension is illustrated by the way in which the *Evaniuk* case was resolved by the tort system. Compensatory and loss distribution objectives were achieved by imposing liability on the corporation, but the attainment of other goals was thwarted because the primary wrongdoers, the bouncers, were left unaccountable.

B. THE ORIGINS OF CANADIAN TORT LAW

The origins of Canadian tort law lie in the thousand-year evolution of the English common law of torts.[20] The common law was received in all provinces other than Quebec[21] and it has given Canadian tort law its language, concepts, and system of classification. Canada, along with the United States, Australia, and New Zealand, are all part of the common law tradition. This explains why Canadian judges continue to cite landmark English cases and are influenced to an increasing extent by American cases and, to a lesser extent, by Australian and New Zealand cases. Canada has, however, created a unique law of torts. It continues to reflect its origins and traditions but it is increasingly an

---

20 For a brief summary of the history of English tort law, see R.M. Solomon, B.P. Feldthusen, & R.W. Kostal, *Cases and Materials on the Law of Torts*, 7th ed. (Toronto: Carswell, 2007) at 5–9. A detailed account can be found in C.H.S. Fifoot, *History and Sources of the Common Law: Tort and Contract* (London: Stevens, 1949).

21 For a useful summary of the Quebec law of torts, see J.L. Baudouin & A.L. Linden, *Tort Law in Canada* (The Netherlands: Kluwer Law International BV, 2010).

independent product of Canada's societal values and attitudes to the allocation of losses.

C. THE ELEMENTS OF CANADIAN TORT LAW

As noted earlier, tort law is made up of a number of discrete, nominate (named) torts that provide remedies for some of the losses generated by a myriad of societal activities. These torts dictate when the loss will be allocated by an award of damages to the defendant and when it will be left where it has fallen—on the shoulders of the plaintiff. There is, nevertheless, a certain similarity to the structure of all torts. Most torts are formulated on the basis of the nature of the defendant's conduct and the nature of the plaintiff's loss that has been caused by that conduct.[22] Tort law is about both conduct and consequences. The tort of battery, the basis of liability in the *Evaniuk* case, is illustrative. It requires *intentional* conduct that causes *bodily interference*. In combination, they are actionable. Tort law is, in large part, constructed on various combinations of these two elements and the causal link between them. These ideas of *conduct* and *loss* are the building blocks of the law of torts and, as such, they deserve some further preliminary attention.

1) The Nature of the Defendant's Conduct

The Canadian law of torts reflects an intuitive sense of fairness that a defendant should be held liable only for loss caused by a wrongful act, not for loss caused by an accident, an error of judgment, or bad luck. Tort law, therefore, classifies the conduct of defendants in a way that permits a line to be drawn between wrongful and innocent conduct. In general, three concepts perform this task: *intention, negligence,* and *accident.*[23] Each term describes the defendant's conduct with reference to its consequences.

Conduct is intentional when the defendant desires its consequences.[24] The professional hit man who assassinates a politician, the arsonist who sets fire to a building, the political candidate who falsely calls his rival a racist, and the person who discloses intimate and em-

---

22 See J.G. Fleming, *The Law of Torts*, 9th ed. (Sydney: LBC Information Services, 1998) at 5–7.

23 The concepts of *gross negligence, recklessness,* and *malice* play a more minor role in Canadian tort law.

24 This is known as actual intent. The concepts of constructive and transferred intent are described in chapter 4.

barrassing information about a former friend *intentionally* cause damage to person, property, reputation, and privacy, respectively.

Conduct is negligent when the defendant creates a reasonably foreseeable and substantial risk of its consequences. The homeowner who fails to clear ice from the steps to his house, causing a visitor to fall and injure herself; the operator of a public swimming pool who fails to post a warning of the shallow depth of the pool and contributes to the injury of a swimmer who dives in; and the driver of a car who drives in excess of the speed limit and hits another vehicle *negligently* cause damage to either person and property.

Conduct is accidental when the defendant neither desires its consequences nor creates a foreseeable and substantial risk of its consequences.[25] The hunter who discharges a firearm in an unpopulated area and wounds a person whom she has no reason to believe was in the vicinity; the person who leaves a dog locked in an automobile, which leads to a passing pedestrian losing the sight of her eye from a glass splinter when the dog breaks a window in the vehicle;[26] and the owner of a car driving within the speed limit who hits a child when she darts out from between two parked vehicles into his path cause personal injuries *accidentally*.

The nature of the defendant's conduct is a vital element in the Canadian law of torts. As a general rule, proof of intentional or negligent conduct is an essential component of tort liability. "No liability without fault" is a maxim that continues to command substantial judicial and public support. There are only a few torts where liability extends to accidental conduct. These torts are known as torts of *strict liability*. They impose liability solely on causation of damage. Courts normally feel obliged to provide some special justification for dispensing with the usual requirement of wrongful conduct.

2) The Nature of the Plaintiff's Loss

Tort law cannot compensate everyone for all the losses generated by the intentional or negligent conduct of others. That would exceed the financial capacity of defendants and their insurers and exhaust the capacity of the legal system to adjudicate the multitude of claims. Consequently,

---

25 The word "accident" in this context is given a technical meaning of innocent, not wrongful. This must be distinguished from the more common use of the word, meaning an unexpected and untoward event causing loss, which covers both injury caused by fault and injury without fault.

26 If this example seems unrealistic, see *Fardon v. Hardon-Rivington*, [1932] All E.R. Rep. 81 (H.L.).

scrutiny of the nature of the defendant's conduct is matched by a consideration of the nature of the plaintiff's loss or damage. Awarding compensation for personal injury is, for example, more easily justified than awarding compensation for a person's public embarrassment or humiliation. Consequently, tort law must draw lines between compensable and non-compensable damage. This is a difficult and contentious task upon which opinions may differ. The cases of *Hinz v. Berry*[27] and *Star Village Tavern v. Nield*[28] provide good illustrations of the kind of line-drawing that is an essential part of the law of torts.

In *Hinz*, a family of ten went for a drive in the countryside in the family van. They parked on the side of the road to have a picnic. The plaintiff mother and one of her children crossed the road to pick bluebells growing in a nearby field. While they were picking the flowers there was a terrible accident. A car, driven negligently by the defendant, crashed into the van, killing the plaintiff's spouse and injuring all of her other children. The claims by the family for the loss of financial support resulting from the death of the breadwinning spouse and by the children for their personal injuries posed little difficulty and they were settled without the need of a trial. A number of additional claims brought by the plaintiff were more problematic. They included claims for her grief and sorrow at the loss of her spouse, for her anxiety about the welfare of her children, for her financial stress generated by the death of the family's primary breadwinner, for her stress in adjusting to her future life circumstances, and for the nervous shock she suffered from witnessing the accident. These claims were hotly contested by the defendant. Eventually, the Court allowed only the claim for nervous shock suffered as a result of witnessing the accident. It was allowed because the immediate shock of the accident caused her to suffer a clinical depression, which is a *recognizable psychiatric illness*. The line between compensable and non-compensable psychiatric injury was drawn between psychiatric illness and the more transient and minor emotional distress that formed the basis of the other claims. Some people may disagree with the Court and feel that some or all of the plaintiff's other claims should have been allowed. There is, of course, no right or wrong answer to this issue. It is a matter of judicial wisdom and social policy. In cases of psychiatric injury, judges have been influenced by a variety of factors that have caused them to adopt a cautious and conservative approach. One important factor is the realization that recovery for men-

---

27   [1970] 2 Q.B. 40 (C.A.). This English decision reflects Canadian law on the point discussed.

28   (1976), 71 D.L.R. (3d) 439 (Man. Q.B.) [*Star Village Tavern*].

tal distress (as opposed to psychiatric illness) would widen the range of potential plaintiffs considerably and could impose a burden on defendants which might be severe and disproportionate to their degree of negligence. Mental distress claims may also present special difficulties in respect of proof and causation. There may also be a larger number of fraudulent claims than in respect of other kinds of losses. In deciding an individual case, a judge must always keep in mind the broader consequences of her decision, and the factors outlined have, rightly or wrongly, led courts to deny claims for mental distress.[29]

Another example of this line-drawing is *Star Village Tavern*. In that case, the defendant negligently drove his car into the side of a bridge spanning a river. The bridge, which was owned by the government, was closed for repairs for a number of weeks. The plaintiff owned a bar that drew patrons from a small town on the other side of the river. When the bridge was closed, many of the patrons declined to make the much longer trip to the bar by an alternative route and the bar lost patronage and profits. The bar sued the negligent driver for its loss of profits. The defendant was clearly liable for the property damage to the bridge but should he be liable for the plaintiff's pure economic loss? Courts have approached claims for pure economic loss[30] with a great deal of caution. There are a number of reasons for this. A common concern is the sheer volume and magnitude of financial losses that can arise from damage to property upon which many people, other than the owner, may rely for their financial well-being. Liability for all of these claims may be grossly disproportionate to the degree of the plaintiff's negligence. There are also concerns in respect of the proof of economic losses and causation. Additionally, there is doubt about the wisdom of collecting widespread, moderate, pure economic losses and shifting them to the defendant whose insurer will distribute them in a slightly different, but similarly widespread, manner to all of those who purchase liability insurance. Where to draw the line in respect of economic losses is a continuing problem in the law of torts and it remains to be finally resolved. The plaintiff in *Star Village Tavern* did not recover its economic losses.[31]

One might imagine that, given the central role of these two elements (the defendant's conduct and the plaintiff's loss), the law of torts

---

29   The liability for the negligent infliction of psychiatric injury is discussed in more detail in chapter 2.

30   It should be noted that the plaintiff had suffered no property damage and no personal injury. The only loss was a loss of business profits, hence the term pure economic loss.

31   The liability for the negligent infliction of economic loss is canvassed in greater detail in chapter 3.

might be contained within several general principles matching the required conduct to the particular kind of loss caused by that conduct. Canadian tort law is, however, made up of a collection of many discrete, unrelated torts which reflects the *ad hoc* and incremental nature of the historical development of English tort law. Some of the individual torts are named after the kind of loss to which they relate (*defamation, privacy, nuisance*), some emphasize certain kinds of wrongful conduct (*negligence, intentional infliction of nervous shock, intimidation*), some are named after the piece of litigation that gave rise to the tort (the rule in *Rylands v. Fletcher*), and some refer to the activity from which the wrongful conduct arises (*cattle trespass, conversion, false imprisonment, occupiers' liability*). An analysis of each tort will, nevertheless, indicate that an evaluation of both the nature of the defendant's conduct and the nature of the plaintiff's loss caused by it plays a central role in formulating tort liability.

D. THE OBJECTIVES OF TORT LAW

In recent years, there has been a great deal of debate about the purpose of tort law in Canadian society. There are two contrasting approaches to this issue. The first approach perceives tort law as primarily an ethical system promoting the personal responsibility of wrongdoers for the harm that they have caused to others. The function of tort law is, therefore, primarily to correct individual injustices that have arisen between citizens. The contrasting approach suggests that tort law is a legal construct designed to achieve a number of identifiable functions, all of which are in the public interest. Therefore, emphasis is placed on identifying the full range of the objectives of tort law and on evaluating the degree to which these objectives are met. It may loosely be described as a contest between the approach of the "moralists" and that of the "instrumentalists."

1) The Moralist View

The moralist approach explains tort law as a system of corrective justice based on the ethical principle of personal responsibility for damage caused by wrongdoing.[32] Tort law is designed primarily to rectify an imbalance between the litigants caused by the wrongful conduct of the

---

32   See E.J. Weinrib, "The Special Morality of Tort Law" (1989) 34 McGill L.J. 403; Cane, above note 10; and Klar, above note 3 at 13–15.

defendant. Tort law is, on this view, grounded in a simple and elegant moral imperative: personal accountability for the consequences of one's wrongful actions. It is a reflection and embodiment of intuitive ethical and moral principles that are the foundation of a stable, civilized, and humane society. Like all deeply held cultural attitudes and values, the ideas of accountability for wrongdoing and the reparation of harm caused by wrongdoing are so ingrained that they tend to be taken for granted. It is for that reason that many tort principles feel "right" on a visceral and emotional level. Tort law is, consequently, to be valued for itself. It does not need to be justified by what it may or may not achieve in respect of other pragmatic public or private functions. It is a repository of societal values that speak to us about how to live in a crowded community with mutual respect for the interests of others. It protects individual liberty by defining our rights against the wrongful interference of others with our person, property, and other recognized interests. That is enough to explain its appeal, its strength, and its importance to Canadian society.

2) The Instrumentalist View

The instrumentalist approach to tort law is less romantic and idealistic. It identifies the multiplicity of desirable functions of tort law, it evaluates the degree to which these goals are achieved, and it contemplates alternative legal and non-legal vehicles that may attain those goals more effectively and efficiently.[33] These questions generate a great deal of heated debate but there is some agreement on the aspirations and objectives of tort law, which are set out below.

a) Compensation
The most important function of tort law is to provide compensation for losses caused by conduct that the courts regard as below societal standards. Tort law is designed to restore the plaintiff to the position that she would have been in if the tort had not been committed. Compensation is, therefore, tailored to the particular loss that the individual plaintiff has suffered. It seeks to provide a full indemnity for the plaintiff's losses.

The compensatory power of tort law has been enhanced dramatically by liability insurance. Liability insurance not only protects the defendant from the adverse financial consequences of being held liable in

---

33   A more detailed description of the functions of tort law is found in Linden, above note 3 at 1–32 and Klar, *ibid.* at 9–19.

tort, but it also guarantees, to the great advantage of successful plain-tiffs, that judgments and settlements within the scope of the defend-ant's policy will be paid. Almost all defendants in tort cases either carry liability insurance or are self-insurers. To a large degree, therefore, the tort process does not shift loss from the plaintiff to the defendant. The loss is spread or distributed broadly throughout the community to those who purchase liability insurance and to the consumers of goods and services of self-insurers.[34]

b) Punishment

Tort law also aspires to express society's disapproval of the conduct of wrongdoers who cause harm to other citizens. An award of damages is not only designed to compensate the plaintiff. It also acts as a sanc-tion on the defendant. The punitive power of tort law is diminished to a large degree by liability insurance but there are circumstances where it continues to operate with some vigour. Liability insurance does not normally apply to intentional wrongdoing and, even if the wrongdoer is only negligent, a judgment may exceed the terms of the policy, leaving the balance to be paid by the defendant personally.

c) Deterrence

Tort law aspires to influence the conduct of citizens in order to secure a safer society. By imposing liability for wrongful conduct it hopes to deter both the defendant and other members of society from acting in a similarly dangerous manner in the future. Three theories of deterrence contribute to the accident prevention role of tort law: specific deter-rence, general deterrence, and market deterrence.

i) Specific Deterrence

Specific deterrence operates against the individual defendant and is an aspect of the punitive function of tort law. The award of damages oper-ates to alert the defendant that his conduct is wrongful and unacceptable. The defendant is thereby encouraged to change his future behaviour in a way that will reduce the chance of causing similar future losses. Tort liability has a powerful deterrent effect when the judgment is a charge on the defendant's personal wealth, but its force is dissipated when a liability insurer pays the judgment. However, there may be some resid-ual deterrent impact on insured defendants. The cost of the defendant's

---

34 This has been referred to as a hidden tax levied on virtually all goods, services, and activities: see P.W. Huber, *Liability: The Legal Revolution and Its Conse-quences* (New York: Basic Books, 1988) at 3.

liability insurance may rise after a successful claim. The defendant's deductible may be increased. The insurer may refuse future coverage. The insurer may pressure the defendant to adopt better risk-management practices. The defendant may also be particularly sensitive to a publicized finding of liability. Professionals and manufacturers are unlikely to welcome further judicial findings of wrongful conduct on their part even if they are insured. Nevertheless, the specific deterrence of insured defendants is unlikely to play a major role in accident prevention.

ii) General Deterrence

There is a great deal of debate about the general deterrent effect of tort law. The theory is that the general threat of tort liability encourages citizens to adopt safe practices and avoid conduct likely to cause damage to others. The general deterrent effect of tort law may be powerful in exceptional circumstances. Uninsured persons with a good understanding of tort law may adjust their planned conduct and behaviour to avoid tort liability. Defendants who are hypersensitive to a finding of liability, such as health-care professionals, may also be encouraged to take steps to prevent accidents. In other situations, however, the general deterrent effect of tort law is at best weak.[35] Many people have little or no understanding of tort law; a great deal of tort litigation arises from spontaneous, unreflective conduct; few people ever contemplate the possibility of injuring others; and most people whose activities carry a risk of injury to others are protected by liability insurance. In general, our conduct and our concern for others probably reflect psychological traits, attitudes, habits, and a personal code of conduct rather than a pervasive concern to avoid tort liability. In some activities, general deterrence would seem to be marginal. Those individuals who are not deterred from bad driving by a concern for their own safety, or by a desire to avoid a criminal prosecution, the possible loss of their driver's licence, or damage to their own vehicle, are unlikely to be deterred by the prospect of their liability insurer having to pay for any damage they may cause to others.

iii) Market Deterrence

The theory of market deterrence[36] is one that is most applicable to selected activities such as the manufacture of goods and the commercial

---

35   See E.P. Belobaba, *Products Liability and Personal Injury Compensation in Canada: Towards Integration and Rationalization* (Ottawa: Consumer and Corporate Affairs Canada, 1983), and S.D. Sugarman, "Doing Away with Tort Law" (1985) 73 Cal. L. Rev. 558.

36   G. Calabresi, *The Costs of Accidents: A Legal and Economic Analysis* (New Haven, CT: Yale University Press, 1970).

supply of services. The central premise is that tort liability allocates accident costs flowing from substandard conduct to the defendant producer, and the consequential increase in the price of the defendant's goods or services will encourage both the defendant and consumers to respond in a way that will reduce accidents. First, the defendant is encouraged to reduce its liability costs by making a safer product in order to remain competitive with other producers who have better accident records. If the defendant does not respond and reduce liability costs, consumers will purchase the cheaper, safer products from the defendant's competitors and the defendant may be forced out of business. Second, if all the suppliers of a line of goods or services have uncontrollably high liability costs or refuse to reduce liability costs, consumers may spend their money on other products or activities that are cheaper and safer. One way or another, dangerous products and activities will be replaced by safer ones. The effectiveness of market deterrence depends to some degree upon sophisticated consumers, an efficient tort liability process (preferably strict liability), and a sufficient price differential to affect consumer choice.

d) Psychological Dimensions

There are psychological dimensions to tort liability. The infliction of injury can generate an intense psychological response from the victim. Even a minor "fender-bender" can give rise to lost tempers and harsh language. Anger and a desire for vengeance and retribution may not be the most admired of human traits, but they are a reality. Tort law provides a civilized and non-violent way to allow the victims of wrongdoing to secure some appeasement, retribution, and accountability for their suffering.

e) Education

Tort law has both a general and a specific educational role. The tort system speaks *generally* to citizens of the importance of compliance with reasonable standards of conduct in the interests of the safety of others. This general educative role may operate directly on litigants and others involved in tort litigation and it may influence indirectly those who have some knowledge of the tort system or are informed of its operation by the media.

Tort law also has a *specific* educational role. From time to time, litigation arises that is of particular interest to a segment of society. A court may be called upon to address a particularly contentious issue affecting a small group, to rule on the current practices of a profession or industry, to determine liability in a novel circumstance, or to rule on a test case that challenges the behaviour of a public or private institution. In these cases, the educational function of tort law may not extend to the public at large, but it does extend beyond the litigants and may profoundly affect conduct that has an impact on the public's well-being and safety. The coverage in professional journals, trade publications, and the popular media given to the Supreme Court cases dealing with the need for physicians to secure an informed consent to medical treatment,[37] the obligation of bar owners to their intoxicated patrons,[38] the responsibility of manufacturers to tell consumers about dangers arising from their use of products,[39] the obligations of boat owners to their passengers, the obligation of police officers to those suspected of committing crimes,[40] and the potential liability of government for services it provides to the public[41] was informative and educational for all persons involved in those activities.

f)   The Ombudsperson Role

The role of tort law as ombudsperson has been identified and promoted by Mr. Justice Linden.[42] He has pointed out that tort law is well placed to challenge the wrongful and harmful behaviour of the most powerful persons and institutions in Canada. From time to time, concern is expressed about the accountability of the rich and powerful in society and the effectiveness of public law controls on their activities. In these situations, the accountability and sanctions of tort law may be advantageous because tort litigation can be initiated by private individuals and it is adjudicated by judges who are independent of political control. All that a person needs is a valid tort claim and the money to press that claim and the most powerful can be made to account for their wrongful conduct.[43] Litigation in North America by consumers against the manufacturers of tobacco, asbestos, firearms, silica, lead paint, and fast food for harm caused by their products; against governments for their failure to act expeditiously and effectively against the spread of SARS and West Nile Virus; against airlines by passengers experiencing deep vein thrombosis on long-haul flights; and against casinos for the

---

37   *Reibl v. Hughes*, [1980] 2 S.C.R. 880.

38   *Jordan House Ltd. v. Menow* (1973), [1974] S.C.R. 239.

39   *Lambert v. Lastoplex Chemicals Co.* (1971), [1972] S.C.R. 569.

40   *Hill v. Hamilton-Wentworth Regional Police Services*, [2007] S.C.J. No. 41.

41   *Just v. British Columbia*, [1989] 2 S.C.R. 1228.

42   Linden, above note 3 at 22–30.

43   Mr. Justice Linden identifies governmental officials, including the police, manufacturers, polluters, and professionals, as potential targets for this supervisory and regulatory role of tort law.

economic hardship suffered by those addicted to gambling are illustrative of this aspect of tort law. Much of this litigation was unsuccessful but it has had a significant political and social impact, leading to safer products and practices. The decades of tobacco litigation, for example, resulted in very few individual litigants receiving compensation but information disclosed in the litigation process and the attention drawn to the conduct of the defendant corporations has contributed to a societal and political shift in attitudes towards smoking.

There is little agreement as to the relative importance of the various functions of tort law and there is little empirical evidence on the extent to which tort law achieves its objectives. Much depends upon the particular area of tort law and the prevalence of liability insurance.

E. PERSONAL INJURY, TORT LAW, AND OTHER COMPENSATORY VEHICLES

It has been noted that the law of torts deals with a wide range of damage and losses. It is, however, personal injury and fatality claims that have presented the most significant challenge to the Canadian law of torts. The twentieth century witnessed a rising tide of accidental[44] personal injury and death and an associated public demand for security from the personal and economic consequences of it. The law of torts responded to this challenge. The concept of fault-based liability was expanded to cover the widest range of societal activities, and virtually every citizen is subject to a duty of care to prevent foreseeable injuries to others. Moreover, in the course of the twentieth century, the principles of tort law were liberalized to facilitate claims and expand the range and quantum of personal injury compensation. Tort law was stretched to its conceptual limits by a humane and sympathetic judiciary to provide as generous a protection from the consequences of injury and death as is possible in a fault-based system. This process was encouraged and facilitated by the prevalence of liability insurance and by an acute judicial awareness of the power of liability insurance to spread accident costs throughout society.

In spite of these efforts, tort law has proved incapable of providing the degree of security from personal injury losses that the public has demanded. This is largely due to the inherent conceptual limitations of fault as a compensatory mechanism. A fault system can never provide

---

44   The word "accidental" in this context means unexpected. The word is not used to contrast innocent from wrongful conduct of a defendant.

universal coverage and compensation for all accident victims. It is designed to compensate only those who have been injured as a result of wrongdoing. Those who suffer personal injury as a result of a defendant's innocent conduct, their own carelessness, or bad luck are beyond the scope of conventional tort remedies. In addition to the inherent limitations of tort coverage, there has been criticism about the manner in which tort law processes personal injury claims. As a compensatory mechanism, tort litigation is slow, expensive, and unpredictable and some actions fail because of procedural obstacles, a lack of evidence of the defendant's fault, a lack of resources, or a lack of will to embark on the difficult adversarial process of civil litigation.

The limitations and shortcomings of the tort process have led to two contrasting developments. First, there were a number of governmental initiatives throughout the course of the twentieth century creating alternative or supplementary compensatory vehicles designed to provide compensation to a broader range of accident victims. These initiatives were prompted by public demand for broader and improved protection from random accident losses and by ideas of collective security which lie at the heart of the social welfare system. Second, the incomplete coverage of both tort and social welfare systems has led to a much greater use of private sector first-party insurance instruments[45] tailored to individual circumstances for the protection of personal financial security. The limitations of the social welfare state and the uneven scope of tort liability have spawned a trend towards greater personal responsibility for the security of one's self and family from accidental injury and death. A brief description of these two developments provides some perspective on the place and role of tort law in the overall societal response to personal injury and fatality losses.

1) Governmental Initiatives

The first governmental initiative was the introduction early in the twentieth century of workers' compensation schemes that replaced tort law in respect of workplace accidents and industrial disease. This development was prompted by the inadequate coverage and compensation provided by tort law to disabled workers. Workers gave up their tort remedies[46] in return for guaranteed no-fault compensation. The

---

45   First-party insurance is a contract under which the insurer promises to pay a sum of money on the occurrence of a particular event, such as accidental death, injury, or property damage, in return for the payment of premiums by the insured.

46   A tort claim may still be available to an injured worker against a person other than an employer or employee covered by the scheme.

provincial schemes, which are administered by a public body and funded by levies paid by employers, provide compensation for lost income, rehabilitation expenses, and other associated losses.

Later in the century, in spite of the *compulsory* third-party liability insurance of drivers and owners of cars, similar concerns were expressed about the adequacy of tort law to compensate the victims of automobile accidents. The response of the various provincial governments has not been uniform. Most provinces have introduced either *add-on* no-fault schemes that pay moderate no-fault benefits to all the victims of automobile accidents while preserving the right to sue in tort, or *modified* no-fault plans that restrict injured persons to no-fault benefits unless their injuries or losses exceed a certain threshold of seriousness. Manitoba and Quebec have completely replaced the tort system with a *pure no-fault* system paying income replacement benefits, other associated costs or expenses, and compensation for permanent disability. Saskatchewan uniquely provides a choice between pure no-fault coverage and a tort option combined with lower no fault benefits.[47] Some of these plans are delivered by the private sector. Others are delivered through public corporations. Their unifying characteristic is the desire to expand the number of victims of automobile accidents receiving compensation and to deliver that compensation more efficiently.[48]

There has also been legislative activity in respect of criminal violence. The victims of crime have a notoriously difficult time securing compensation from the perpetrators of criminal violence. Often the offender is not known and when he is known and sued, it is unlikely that a tort judgment will be paid. The victims of crime almost always have a tort claim but rarely receive any compensation from it. Consequently, all provinces have introduced criminal injury compensation schemes that provide compensation to the victims of crime on a no-fault basis. They are funded by general tax revenues and normally provide income replacement benefits, reimburse various expenses arising from the injury, and compensate pain and suffering. The tort action remains available to those victims who wish to pursue it.

There are also a number of federal and provincial social welfare programs such as Employment Insurance, the Canada Pension Plan, health-services insurance, and social allowances that assist accident victims. These programs were not initiated primarily to assist the victims of accidents but they often provide important financial support for them.

---

47   The Saskatchewan Government Insurance (SGI) indicated that as of 30 April 2010, 6,069 or one half of one percent of the population selected the tort option.

48   General information about each of the provincial automobile insurance plans is available on the Insurance Bureau of Canada website, online: www.ibc.ca.

Most recently, there have been a number of discrete governmental initiatives designed to settle claims of various categories of persons who have suffered loss from alleged wrongdoing. Special arrangements have been made to assist persons who contracted HIV and hepatitis C from the Canadian blood supply, persons sterilized without their consent under Alberta's old eugenics law, persons harmed by physical and sexual abuse in residential institutions in Nova Scotia, persons injured by the unsafe water supply in Walkerton, Ontario, and Aboriginal persons who suffered physical and sexual abuse in residential schools.[49] Although these various initiatives are unrelated, they do seem to be prompted by similar circumstances. First, they all relate to tragic events or episodes that damaged large numbers of utterly innocent persons. Second, the mass claimants have potential tort actions, but these actions are so difficult, uncertain, and expensive to litigate that a global settlement is an attractive option. Third, these persons suffered harm as a consequence of governmental activities or activities in which there was strong governmental involvement, and either federal or provincial governments face potential tort liabilities. Fourth, there is very strong public sympathy and support for these people and a political consensus that they should be directly compensated by public money without the need to litigate the matter.

The foregoing governmental initiatives, collectively, are responsible for the distribution of a huge amount of money to vast numbers of injured persons. They have intruded into the traditional realm of tort law and have eroded its significance — most dramatically in respect of workplace accidents and automobile accidents, the two activities that generate most personal injury. At one time it was expected by some that this growing tide of governmental intervention would ultimately lead to the replacement of tort law and the other compensatory schemes with a universal governmental no-fault accident compensation scheme.[50] However, the lack of political will and the entrenched interests of the insurance industry and the legal profession make that unlikely in the foreseeable future.

---

49   In 2006, after more than a decade of individual and class action lawsuits and various settlement proposals, a comprehensive settlement was reached in favour of an estimated 80,000 former students of the Aboriginal residential school system. It includes a common experience pain award of $10,000 per claimant for the first year in a residential school and $3,000 for each additional year; additional awards under an independent assessment process for those students who suffered serious sexual or physical abuse; and funds for an Aboriginal healing foundation and commemoration, for a truth and reconciliation process, and for legal fees.

50   New Zealand is the only common law jurisdiction to implement a universal no-fault accident compensation scheme.

2) Private Sector First-Party Insurance

Currently, there is greater interest in the potential of the private sector insurance industry to provide more complete and affordable first-party insurance instruments covering all kinds of personal disability. The trend towards more private protection is one that is likely to accelerate in this century. Life insurance is the most established and common form of first-party insurance. Disability insurance is less common, particularly on an individual basis, but there has been considerable growth in group plans for employees, school children, participants in organized sport, holders of credit cards, and members of professional, alumni and other organizations. In 2008, the members of the Canadian Life and Health Insurance Association reported that more than twenty million Canadians owned life insurance, ten million were covered by disability insurance protection, and twenty-two million had extended health and dental care coverage. Payments under these policies were almost thirty billion dollars.[51] One respected academic[52] has even suggested that both tort and most governmental compensation plans for accidental injury and death might be abolished, leaving citizens to make their own financial security arrangements against physical disability with private insurers on a first-party basis. That is unlikely to occur in Canada in the foreseeable future but it indicates renewed interest in the private sector as an engine for greater disability protection.

The result of these various developments is that the current Canadian system of compensation for accidental personal injury and death is an amalgam of tort liability, no-fault schemes, and first-party insurance. In terms of the number of persons compensated and the amount of money provided, the no-fault plans and private insurance dwarf the tort process. This is a perspective that may not be immediately apparent in the conventional study of tort law. Lawyers tend to regard tort law as having central importance in the field of accident compensation. It is in fact a minor player whose importance continues to diminish. This perspective is essential to understanding and evaluating the place, role, and future of tort law in the field of personal injury and fatality compensation.

---

51 "Industry Information," Canadian Life and Health Insurance Association, online: www.clhia.ca/e4.htm.

52 P.S. Atiyah, "Personal Injuries in the Twenty-First Century: Thinking the Unthinkable" in P. Birks, ed., *Wrongs and Remedies in the Twenty-First Century* (Oxford: Clarendon Press, 1996) at 1.

F. THE ORGANIZATION OF TORT LAW

It was noted earlier that tort law is made up of a somewhat disorganized congregation of individual torts. Not surprisingly, there is no conventional way of describing this area of the law. One may describe tort law in its historical context and trace its development chronologically. One may identify the interests that tort law protects, such as personal safety, privacy, and property interests, and describe the torts that address those interests. One may focus on conduct and arrange torts in groups of intentional torts, negligent torts, and torts of strict liability. The choice is largely arbitrary. This book adopts the third option, but it begins with negligence and then deals with the intentional torts before it turns to the torts of strict liability. This approach recognizes the dominance of the tort of negligence in the landscape of Canadian tort law.[53] It is not only of central importance in its own right, but it also exerts a powerful influence on all other areas of tortious liability. Consequently, the Canadian law of torts can best be understood by considering the tort of negligence before the other bases of tort liability. Although the torts of nuisance and defamation may be considered torts of strict liability, they are given discrete consideration. Nuisance is, in fact, a confusing mixture of negligence and strict liability concepts, and defamation, the most technical of all the torts, is replete with unique concepts and principles.

We are now ready to embark on a discussion of the essential principles of the Canadian law of torts and the social policies that support it.

FURTHER READINGS

ATIYAH, P.S., *The Damages Lottery* (Oxford: Hart Publishing, 1997)

KLAR, L.N., *Tort Law*, 4th ed. (Toronto: Carswell, 2008) at 1–25

LAWTON, D. & P. HINDMARCH, "Some Insurance Basics: What Every Lawyer Should Know" Parts I and II, (2004), 62 The Advocate 567 and 661

LINDEN, A.M. & B. FELDTHUSEN, *Canadian Tort Law*, 8th ed. (Toronto: Butterworths, 2006) at 1–32

---

53   Klar, above note 3 at 157.

WEINRIB, F.J., "Corrective Justice in a Nutshell" (2002) 52 U.T.L.J. 349

WILLIAMS, G.L. & B.A. HEPPLE, *Foundations of the Law of Tort*, 2d ed. (London: Butterworths, 1984)

CHAPTER 2

NEGLIGENCE: BASIC PRINCIPLES

A. INTRODUCTION

The tort of negligence is composed of a number of components or ele-ments, most of which must be proved by the plaintiff. These elements are not all self-evident. They are conventional concepts that the courts have found of assistance in clarifying, organizing, and analysing the various issues that present themselves in negligence litigation.

There are three core elements: the *negligent act*, *causation*, and *dam-age*. It is, indeed, difficult to conceive of negligence liability without proof of these three core elements. The negligent act is determined by identifying the appropriate standard of care and applying it to the facts of the case. Causation is established by showing a link between the defendant's negligent act and the plaintiff's damage. Damage is the vital element that triggers the claim and launches the litigation process.

In Canadian negligence law, however, a defendant is not respon-sible for every consequence of his negligent act. Important and conten-tious issues in respect of the extent of liability, the range of plaintiffs, the nature of the loss, and the nature of the defendant's activities must be addressed. Consequently, control devices have been developed to keep negligence liability within appropriate boundaries. There are two critically important control devices in negligence law: *duty of care* and *remoteness of damage*. Negligence liability cannot be established unless the judge recognizes that the defendant owes the plaintiff a duty of care in respect of the plaintiff's interests. This concept allows judges to regulate the application and extent of negligence liability, excluding it from certain activities, denying its applicability to certain kinds of losses, and excluding certain persons from the scope of the defendant's responsibility.[1] Remoteness of damage plays a similar role. A negligent act may have utterly improbable consequences that are entirely removed in time and place from the defendant's act. Causation cannot be denied, but fairness may dictate that the defendant should be sheltered from responsibility for some or all of the consequences of his negligent conduct. In such circumstances, the court may hold that the consequences are too remote and not compensable by the defendant. The manner in which the courts apply the concepts of duty of care and remoteness of damage reflect social policy and current judicial attitudes to the extent of liability for negligent conduct. Throughout the twentieth century, there was an unrelenting, incremental relaxation of the boundaries of negligence liability and a dramatic expansion in the scope of the tort of negligence. In this century the pace of expansion has slowed but the control devices continue to play an important role, particularly in cases of nervous shock and pure economic loss, and they are of central importance when novel claims are made involving the application of negligence law to new activities, persons, or kinds of damage.

Once the plaintiff has established these elements, the defendant may assert any of four defences. *Contributory negligence* by the plaintiff is a partial defence leading to a proportionate reduction in the quantum of damages. *Voluntary assumption of risk* is a complete defence that arises where the plaintiff consents to the defendant's negligence and its consequences. *Illegality* operates to deny a claim, such as one for future illegal earnings, that would subvert the integrity of the legal system. Finally, a defendant may assert that, in spite of indications to the contrary, the loss was caused, not by his fault, but by an *inevitable accident*. This, too, is a complete defence.

Once liability has been established upon a consideration of the aforementioned elements, damages must be assessed. Damages are tailored to the plaintiff's individual losses and are made in a lump sum

---

1   Some judges and commentators begin their analysis of the tort of negligence with the issue of the duty of care. Nothing of importance turns on the order in which the essential elements of the negligence action are considered. There was, however, some debate on the sequencing of analysis with respect to breach of the standard of care and causation in medical malpractice litigation. It now seems settled that the standard of care issue must be resolved before causation is considered. See *Bafaro v. Dowd*, [2010] O.J. No. 979 (C.A.) and *McCardle Estate v. Cox*, [2003] A.J. No. 389 (C.A.).

award. Assessment of pecuniary and non-pecuniary losses arising from personal injuries creates particularly difficult problems.

This framework of negligence law is typical of a fault-based civil liability system. In its underlying theory, its terminology, and its concepts, negligence law appears to be a loss-shifting system based upon the moral imperative that wrongdoers should be individually liable for the damage they cause. In practice, the negligence system operates quite differently. It is predominantly a negligence/insurance system that spreads or distributes losses caused by negligent conduct to a broad segment of the community. This reality has had a profound effect on the development and application of negligence law. In the course of the twentieth century, it promoted a dramatic growth in the scope of liability, an increase in the size of awards of damages in personal injury and fatality claims, and a reformulation of some of the principles of negligence law to provide much greater protection of the interests of plaintiffs. Nevertheless, the public face and theoretical framework of negligence law do not reflect this reality. They continue to reflect a loss-shifting system that is based on personal accountability and is focused on the issue of interpersonal justice between the litigants. Consequently, negligence law is imbued with an unresolved tension between loss-shifting rules and loss-spreading realities. Modern Canadian negligence law continues to seek an appropriate balance between these two competing visions of its ultimate purpose.

B. THE STANDARD OF CARE: THE REASONABLY CAREFUL PERSON

The primary element of negligence liability is the negligent act — a failure to take care for the safety of the plaintiff. In determining the appropriate degree of care, it is useful to have some standard against which to measure the conduct of the defendant. One could suggest a number of possible standards such as the degree of care shown by a parent to a child, the care of a compassionate and humane person, or the care friends exhibit to each other.[2] The common law has, however, typically resorted to the *reasonable person* when it is in need of a normative standard of conduct, and negligence law is no exception. The standard of care that must be met in the tort of negligence is that of the reasonably careful person in the circumstances of the defendant.

---

2   Some other standards, including that of the reasonable woman, are alluded to in L. Bender, "An Overview of Feminist Torts Scholarship" (1993) 78 Cornell L. Rev. 575.

The standard of the reasonably careful person was authoritatively established in the English case of *Vaughan v. Menlove*.[3] In that case, the defendant built a haystack close to the boundary between his land and that of the plaintiff. The haystack was so poorly constructed that it gave rise to a risk of spontaneous combustion. The defendant was warned of the danger but he did not take adequate steps to deal with it. In due course, the haystack caught fire and the fire spread to the plaintiff's property where it destroyed some cottages. At issue was the appropriate measure of the defendant's conduct. It was argued that the defendant was not negligent because he had acted honestly, in good faith, and to the best of his judgment. To impose liability would punish him, unfairly, for not being of a higher intelligence. Chief Justice Tindal rejected that argument and held that the defendant must "adhere to the rule which requires in all cases a regard to caution such as a man [person] of ordinary prudence would observe."[4] The defendant was held liable.

The standard of care of the reasonable person is an objective standard. It focuses on the defendant's conduct and its sufficiency with reference to that of a reasonable person. No consideration is given to the defendant's thought process or his subjective awareness of the danger that his conduct poses to others. Therefore, it is not necessary to show that the defendant was a conscious risk taker. Indeed, the test of the reasonable person excludes all the psychological and physical traits that make each person different. A person's ability to apprehend and avoid danger may well depend, in part, on his intelligence, reaction time, strength, courage, memory, coordination, maturity, wisdom, temperament, confidence, dexterity, and many other personal attributes. The objective test excludes all of these individual characteristics in its determination of reasonable care.[5]

The reasonable person is not, therefore, any single person. It is not appropriate for a judge or juror to evaluate the defendant's conduct on the basis of what she would have done in similar circumstances.[6] Neither is the average person the reasonable person. The average person may fail to exercise sufficient care in some circumstances. For example, the average driver is prone to frequent acts of negligence. In truth, the reasonable person is an abstract legal construct, used to set appropriate standards of conduct in society. That standard of conduct is determined by taking into account both the practical realities of what ordinary

---

3   (1837), 3 Bing. N.C. 468, 132 E.R. 490 (C.P.).

4   *Ibid.* at 493 (cited to E.R.).

5   Exceptions are made for children and mentally or physically incapacitated persons. They are discussed later in this chapter.

6   *Arland v. Taylor*, [1955] O.R. 131 (C.A.).

people do and what judges believe they ought to do.[7] It is not, however, a standard of perfection. The reasonable person may make mistakes and errors of judgment for which there is no liability. Nevertheless, the reasonable person is more alert to risk, and cautious by nature, than most of us.

The standard of the reasonably careful person has displayed surprising resilience and longevity. It is rarely questioned. There are a number of reasons for this. First, an objective standard presents fewer problems in respect of the proof of negligence. It is much easier for a plaintiff to establish the words and actions of the defendant as required by an objective test than to establish the defendant's thought process that accompanied that conduct as required by a subjective test. Administrative convenience and expedience are, therefore, served by an objective standard. Second, it is good policy to require a uniform standard of safety and security in society. Citizens may then anticipate and expect a reasonable degree of care from others and may act in reliance on the fact that these standards have legal recognition and are enforceable. Third, the adoption of an objective standard more efficiently promotes the compensatory functions of negligence law. The use of a subjective standard of care, which imposes liability only on conscious risk takers, would significantly reduce the number of persons compensated by negligence law.[8] Most defendants in negligence cases are not conscious risk takers. They are people who have done their best but have failed to reach the normative standard of care by reason of mental or physical characteristics, momentary distractions, inadvertence, oversight, and other morally blameless reasons. Finally, the objective standard of the reasonably careful person *in the circumstances* has provided judges and juries with an abstract and malleable concept that can be applied to all activities, in all circumstances, at any time. Indeed it is capable of perpetual application as society evolves in this century.

1) Application of the Standard of Care

When applying the standard of care to the facts of a case, courts have found it useful to review a number of factors that guide a reasonable person in the regulation of her conduct.[9] The most significant of these

---

7   See M.A. Millner, *Negligence in Modern Law* (London: Butterworths, 1967) at 18.

8   F. James Jr. & J.J. Dickinson, "Accident Proneness and Accident Law" (1950) 63 Harv. L. Rev. 769.

9   The *application* of the standard of care to the facts of the case is a matter of fact to be decided by a judge trying a case alone, or for the jury in a jury trial. Even in non-jury trials, the distinction between issues of fact and law is important

is the concept of a reasonably foreseeable risk. Conduct is negligent only if it carries a risk of damage that a reasonable person would contemplate and guard against. In addition, courts routinely consider the likelihood of the damage occurring, the seriousness of the threatened harm, the cost of preventive measures, the utility of the defendant's conduct, any circumstances of emergency, compliance by the defendant with approved practice or custom, and the defendant's post-accident precautions. Other more controversial and elusive factors such as judicial policy, economic factors, the equity of the individual case, and the psychological phenomenon of hindsight bias may also be influential.

a) Foreseeable Risk

The central element in applying the standard of reasonable care is the concept of a reasonably foreseeable risk. The reasonably careful person avoids creating a foreseeable risk of injury to others. The concept of foreseeability may not, in itself, be sufficient to support a finding of negligence because other factors must be considered, but it is an *essential* component of liability. Four decisions of the Supreme Court illustrate the pivotal role of reasonable foreseeability. All four cases involved children who were injured when they came into contact with high-voltage electric wires under the control of the defendant power corporations. The defendant was found to be negligent in two of them.

In *Gloster v. Toronto Electric Light Co.*,[10] a boy aged eight-and-a-half years was injured when he reached out and touched a live wire that was just fourteen to twenty inches away from the public bridge on which he was standing. The danger was obvious to a reasonable person and the defendant was held to be negligent. In *Amos v. New Brunswick (Electric Power Commission)*,[11] the defendant had allowed a poplar tree to grow up through electricity lines so that they were obscured from sight. Children were known to play in the area. The plaintiff was nine. He climbed to the top of the tree and was severely injured when the trunk or a branch of the tree swayed into the high-tension wires. The Court imposed liability. The risk was clearly foreseeable and a reasonably careful person would have trimmed the tree.

In the other two cases, the plaintiffs were unable to establish a foreseeable risk of injury. In *Shilson v. Northern Ontario Light & Power*

---

for the purposes of appeal. An appellate court will not reverse a finding of fact unless there has been "palpable and overriding error." In reviewing the interpretation and application of the law, the standard is "correctness." *Housen v. Nikolaisen* (2002), 211 D.L.R. (4th) 577 at paras. 7–37 (S.C.C.).

10   (1906), 38 S.C.R. 27.

11   (1976), [1977] 1 S.C.R. 500.

Co.,[12] a twelve-year-old boy was electrocuted as he walked across a narrow pipe stretching three hundred feet across a ravine that was twenty feet deep. When he got to the middle of the ravine, he reached out and touched a live wire four feet above the pipe. Warnings and barricades at each end of the pipe had not dissuaded him from venturing across. Given these unusual circumstances, the Court concluded that the defendant had "no reason to apprehend that children might find an opportunity of making the company's high voltage wire . . . a source of danger."[13] In *Moule v. New Brunswick Electric Power Commission*,[14] the ten-year-old plaintiff was injured when he climbed a maple tree and came into contact with the defendant's power lines. The defendant had taken some steps to reduce the danger. The maple tree had been trimmed of branches on the side facing the power lines and it was not possible to climb the tree directly from the ground. The plaintiff had initially scrambled into an adjacent spruce tree with the help of some boards nailed onto its trunk in the form of a makeshift ladder. From there he crossed over to the maple by way of a wooden platform. He then climbed the maple with the help of more nailed boards and straps. All of this "construction" appears to have been the work of children in the area. When he was high up in the maple, he stepped on a rotten branch and fell in such a way as to come into contact with the tree and the live wires at the same time. The Court held that a reasonable person could not have foreseen such an extraordinary concatenation of events. It agreed with the words of Ritchie J.A. in Court of Appeal, who stated: "The defendant should not be held guilty of negligence for not having foreseen the possibility of the occurrence of such an unlikely event as happened in this case and provided against it by the removal of the maple tree."[15]

These four cases indicate the need for a scrupulous consideration of the facts to determine if the defendant's conduct created a reasonably foreseeable risk of harm. It is not always an easy task. The looseness and highly discretionary nature of the concept of reasonable foresight provides a great deal of freedom for the judge or jury. Nevertheless, its importance is unquestioned. It is the essence of negligence.

b) The Likelihood of Damage

Consideration is to be given not only to the foreseeability of damage but also to the likelihood of it occurring. The reasonable person takes

---

12   (1919), 59 S.C.R. 443.
13   *Ibid.* at 446.
14   (1960), 24 D.L.R. (2d) 305.
15   *Ibid.* at 309.

greater care where there is a strong likelihood of damage and takes lesser care when the chance of damage is minimal. The leading case on this point is *Bolton v. Stone*.[16] The plaintiff was struck by a cricket ball while she was standing in the street outside her house. The ball was hit out of the defendant's nearby cricket ground in the course of a match. In the past thirty years, approximately six balls had been hit onto that street. The plaintiff argued that, once a single ball had been hit there, it was foreseeable that it might happen again and that someone might be injured. It was, therefore, negligent to continue to play cricket on that ground. The House of Lords disagreed. To demand that the conduct of citizens be entirely free of all foreseeable risk would be not only excessively burdensome but, in the light of human nature, impractical. The Court drew a distinction between foreseeable risks that are substantial and material and foreseeable risks that are highly unlikely or mere possibilities. Reasonable people avoid creating material and substantial risks of foreseeable harm. They cleanse their conduct of unreasonable risks, not every foreseeable risk. While the case was close to the borderline, it was not, in the opinion of the Court, negligent to expose the plaintiff to such a small risk of being hit. This is not an easy line to draw at the margins and much will depend on the other factors influencing the application of the standard of care.

c)   The Seriousness of the Threatened Harm
The reasonable person also regulates his conduct with reference to the severity of the threatened harm. The leading case illustrating the need to take greater care when the threatened harm is serious is *Paris v. Stepney Borough Council*.[17] In that case, the plaintiff was, in the course of his employment, removing bolts from the chassis of a motor vehicle with a steel hammer. Although the plaintiff had previously lost his sight in one eye, he was not given protective eyewear to protect himself from the foreseeable risk of steel splinters flying off the bolts. While he was carrying out this task, a splinter entered his good eye and he became totally blind. The defendant employer argued that, because the risk of any eye injury was low, and because it was not customary to provide protective eyewear to fully sighted employees, it was unnecessary to provide protective eyewear to the plaintiff. His risk of an eye injury was no greater than that of the other workers. A majority of the House of Lords rejected this argument. While there may have been no *greater*

---

16   [1951] A.C. 850 (H.L.) [*Bolton*].
17   [1951] A.C. 367 (H.L.).

risk of injury to the plaintiff, there was a *risk of greater injury to him*,[18] and a reasonable employer would have taken greater care for an employee who had already lost his sight in one eye.[19]

The severity of the threatened harm was also a factor in favour of the defendant in *Bolton*. A cricket ball does not present a risk of serious injury or death. A laceration or a bruise is the most that one might anticipate. If the ground had been used as a training facility for track-and-field athletes and it was a discus or javelin that was occasionally thrown into the street, the decision would probably have gone against the defendant.

d) The Cost of Preventive Measures

Consideration of the magnitude of the risk (the likelihood of the damage multiplied by the seriousness of the threatened harm) must be balanced by a consideration of the cost of the measures needed to reduce or neutralize the risk. It is neither good policy nor good sense to demand extravagantly expensive and impractical measures to remove minimal risks. On the other hand, where reasonable, affordable, and practical safety measures are available to combat foreseeable risks, they must normally be taken.

The Supreme Court addressed this issue in *Ware's Taxi Ltd. v. Gilliham*.[20] The defendant taxi company transported young children to and from school in a four-door car. In the course of a journey, the plaintiff, a five-year-old girl, was playing with the push-button lock on the back door. The driver admonished the plaintiff, she told her to move away from the door, and she checked that the door was locked. In spite of these precautionary measures, the door opened and the plaintiff was injured when she fell out. The Court noted that childproof locks were available at a cost of ten dollars per lock and that some other taxi companies either positioned older children in the back seat to guard the doors or used two-door vehicles. The Court evaluated the sufficiency of the defendant's care in the light of these available preventive measures. A majority held that the defendant was negligent. The suggested precautionary measures, including the use of the childproof locks, were inexpensive, feasible, and would not interfere unduly with the transportation of children to and from school.

---

18   J.G. Fleming, *The Law of Torts*, 9th ed. (Sydney: LBC Information Services, 1998) at 128.

19   The work-related accident litigated in this case would not give rise to a tort claim in Canada. It would fall within the scope of the workers' compensation scheme. In England, workers retain the right to sue in tort.

20   [1949] S.C.R. 637.

A useful contrast is provided by the House of Lords decision in *Latimer v. A.E.C. Ltd.*[21] In that case, a factory was flooded during a sudden and severe rain storm. The flood water mixed with oil and when it receded the floor was left in a very slippery state. An extensive clean-up took place but the only way to make the floor completely safe was to close the factory temporarily. The defendant chose not to do so and the plaintiff slipped and injured his ankle. The House of Lords held that the defendant was not negligent. On balance, the small risk to the employees was insufficient to justify the expense and inconvenience of completely interrupting the defendant's business, even on a temporary basis.[22]

Bolton also provides a useful illustration. The Court appears to have decided the case on the assumption that the only way to remove the risk of personal injury to those outside the cricket ground was to stop playing cricket at that location. This significant economic and social cost probably supported the Court's decision in favour of the defendant. The decision might have been different if, for example, the plaintiff was able to establish that a minor realignment of the cricket pitch or a small increase in the height of the boundary fence would have prevented balls from being hit out of the ground.

e) The Utility of the Defendant's Conduct

The utility of the defendant's conduct is also a relevant factor in the application of the standard of care. This factor, however, appears to be *directly* relevant to only a few cases. Those cases usually involve governmental services where the inevitable price of direct and necessary benefits to the public is an increased risk of injury to innocent persons. A good example is found in cases involving plaintiff bystanders who are injured as a result of high-speed police chases designed to apprehend suspected criminals.[23] Police officers in such circumstances are permitted to expose the public to a degree of risk that would not be tolerated from private citizens. Police officers and other emergency personnel do not, however, have carte blanche in respect of their conduct. The standard of conduct remains one of reasonable care in the light of all the relevant factors including the danger created, the nature and purpose of the defendant's conduct, the urgency of the situation, any alternative means of achieving the laudable purpose, and the surrounding circumstances of time and place. A majority of the Newfoundland Court of

---

21   [1953] A.C. 643 (H.L.).

22   In England, a worker may sue his employer in tort. In Canada, the plaintiff in this case would be compensated under the workers' compensation scheme.

23   *Priestman v. Colangelo*, [1959] S.C.R. 615.

Appeal in *Hammond v. Wabana (Town of)*[24] did, however, introduce a degree of subjectivity into the standard of care of volunteer firefighters. The Court was sensitive to the fact that a volunteer fire department may be burdened by a lack of training resources and experience in delivering services. It held that the difficulty of their task, the utility of their conduct, and the interest of the community in supporting and maintaining a volunteer firefighting service dictated a subjective standard of care. The Court held that they must, in the light of the available resources, do their *best* to put out fires. *Bona fide* decisions or actions are not open to question unless they worsen the situation or amount to a substantial departure from basic principles of firefighting.[25]

The utility of the defendant's conduct also has a *general*, pervasive influence in all negligence cases. Judges are acutely aware that most defendants in negligence cases are, at the time of the accident, pursuing legitimate activities of personal, commercial, or public utility and that these activities inevitably carry some degree of risk.[26] The task of the courts is to decide society's current degree of risk tolerance by labelling risks as either reasonable (no liability) or unreasonable (liability). In drawing this distinction, courts must be sensitive to current attitudes to risk and the importance of facilitating the legitimate activities, needs, and aspirations of citizens. Transportation must move at an adequate speed, new medications must be released to the public on a timely basis, aircraft in landing patterns over Toronto's Pearson Airport must be in close proximity to each other, millions of consumer items must be put on the market without individual safety checks, and physicians must limit the time that they spend with each patient. Many foreseeable risks must be tolerated because they are integral to the kind of society that we have chosen to create and live in.

Conversely, there appears to be no reason why the courts should not also take into account the disutility of the defendant's conduct. This has not been directly acknowledged by the courts but there is no reason

---

24 (1998), [1999] 170 Nfld. & P.E.I.R. 97 (Nfld. C.A.) application for leave to appeal to S.C.C. dismissed, [1999] S.C.C.A. No. 104 [*Hammond*].

25 In *Killip's Television Service Ltd. v. Stony Plain (Town)*, [2000] 3 W.W.R. 702 (Alta. Q.B.), Smith J. preferred to accommodate the pragmatic considerations expressed in *Hammond* by utilizing the more objective formulation of a reasonable volunteer fire department in like circumstances and with like resources. See also *Schouten v. Rideau (Township)*, [2009] O.J. No. 2812 (C.A.).

26 See *The Scout Association v. Barnes*, [2010] EWCA Civ 1476 for a discussion of the significance of the social value of scouting in applying the standard of care to the defendant Association.

to tolerate even minimal risks arising from antisocial conduct of no redeeming value.

f) Emergency Situations

Sometimes a defendant must act in an emergency that is not of his making. Emergencies tend to breed excitement, confusion, and anxiety, which may rob the defendant of his usual power to exercise prudent judgment and due care. In retrospect, he may make a poor choice, perform badly, or exacerbate the situation. Courts are sympathetic to the defendant's plight and some leniency is shown to defendants who have done their best in the "agony of the moment." This leniency is particularly pronounced where the defendant is acting in the capacity of a rescuer. In *Horsley v. McLaren*,[27] the Supreme Court considered the actions of the defendant owner of a pleasure boat when a passenger fell overboard and died in the frigid water. The defendant attempted a rescue by backing the boat towards the passenger. Expert evidence established that this was an improper rescue technique. A bow-on procedure was indicated. A majority of the Court held that the defendant may, in the heat of the moment, have made a mistake but he had acted in good faith and had done his best to rescue the deceased. He was not negligent. Justice Laskin (as he then was) rejected this lenient standard of care. He found negligence on the ground that it was not a case of carrying out the appropriate procedure badly because of the pressure and stress generated by the emergency. It was a case of not putting into action standard procedures that are required in an emergency and which the defendant knew of and had practised. He would have imposed liability.

g) Custom and Approved Practice

The application of the standard of care is also influenced by proof that the defendant's behaviour was consistent with the established practices and customs of other citizens carrying out similar activities and tasks. It is not uncommon, for example, for a defendant who is a member of a business, trade, or profession to seek to avoid a finding of negligence on the ground that she had acted in accordance with a well-established custom or practice of the group to which she belongs. There are good reasons for the court to consider such evidence. It establishes a concrete, defined course of conduct that reflects the accumulated wisdom of those involved in the activity. It indicates a course of conduct that has been found in the past to be acceptable and affordable. Furthermore, in situations where the courts have little expertise, evidence that

---

27   (1971), [1972] S.C.R. 441 [*McLaren*].

crystallizes the abstract standard of the reasonable person into actual practices and procedures is of significant assistance.

The more difficult question relates to the weight that should be given to the evidence that the defendant complied with established practice. Early in the twentieth century, courts treated compliance with approved practice as conclusive of due care. That view has been discredited partly on the grounds that it is the responsibility of the judge or jury to decide whether there has been negligence, not the particular profession or occupation, and partly because it threatened to be an impediment to legitimate innovation and progress. The current approach is to view proof of compliance with approved practice as providing some evidence of due care. The strength of that evidence depends upon the longevity of the practice, its universality, the status and reputation of the profession or occupation and its members, the degree of technical difficulty of the task at issue, and any evidence of additional precautions that may have been available.

Proof of compliance with approved practice is particularly influential in medical malpractice cases. Courts pay great deference to the practice and customs of the medical profession. This is explained by the high social status of physicians, their reputation for integrity and competence, and the technical nature of much of the practice of medicine. The Supreme Court decision in *ter Neuzen v. Korn*[28] is illustrative. The plaintiff patient participated in an artificial insemination program run by the defendant physician. As a result of a procedure performed before 1985, the plaintiff was infected with HIV. Expert evidence indicated that the defendant had complied with approved medical practice in screening sperm donors at the time of the procedure. The trial judge, nevertheless, instructed the jury that it could find the practice negligent and the jury so found. The Supreme Court held that the instruction was incorrect. It held that "where a procedure involves difficult or uncertain questions of medical treatment or complex, scientific or highly technical matters that are beyond the ordinary experience and understanding of a judge or jury, it will not be open to find a standard medical practice negligent."[29] The Court also recognized, however, that, conversely, where a standard practice is fraught with obvious risks that any layperson could understand, a finding of negligence may be made. The facts of *Anderson v. Chasney*[30] illustrate this latter situation. In that case, a child suffocated after a tonsillectomy. A sponge had been

28 [1995] 3 S.C.R. 674 [*ter Neuzen*].
29 *Ibid.* at 701.
30 (1949), 57 Man. R. 343 (C.A.), aff'd [1950] 4 D.L.R. 223 (S.C.C.).

inadvertently left in his throat. The Court held that it was appropriate to find that the failure to perform a sponge count and have tapes on the sponges was negligent even though the approved practice at that time was not to do so.[31]

The case of *Girard v. General Hospital of Port Arthur*,[32] however, indicates that the principle in *ter Neuzen* is not always easy to apply. In the course of a neurological examination of the plaintiff, the defendant physician performed a gait assessment. It involved following the patient from behind while she walked across the examination room. The plaintiff, who had experienced dizziness and a loss of balance for some weeks, fell before the defendant could catch her. The defendant argued that the test had been performed in accordance with approved and standard practice. The trial judge held that, in spite of this, the defendant was negligent. There was an obvious risk, apparent to the ordinary person, that the plaintiff might fall, and it was negligent not to have a nurse or an orderly present to prevent that eventuality. The Ontario Divisional Court disagreed. It noted that the expert evidence, accepted by the trial judge, was that the defendant's actions were consistent with approved practice and that there was no reason to suspect that the plaintiff would fall. It was not open to the court to reject that professional opinion even though the presence of a nurse might be considered to be a reasonable precaution by a lay observer.

Approved practice and custom is also a relevant factor when the defendant is not in compliance with it. A deviation from customary standards is not conclusive of negligence but it is likely to be given significant weight by the court, and the defendant is wise to negate this evidence by giving some explanation for the deviation or by showing that her conduct was no more dangerous than the standard practice.

h) Post-Accident Precautions
When an accident occurs, risks that may not have been contemplated by the defendant before the accident become known. Subsequently, he may adopt additional safety measures to make sure that a similar accident does not happen again. At trial, a plaintiff may seek to use these post-accident precautions as indicative of the defendant's negligence.

---

31   See also *Canadian Red Cross Society v. Walker Estate*, [2001] 1 S.C.R. 647 where expert evidence approving of the Red Cross's screening procedures to prevent blood donations from groups at high risk of carrying HIV was rejected. A judicial evaluation of the procedures was appropriate because no assessment of complex, scientific, or highly technical matters was involved. The primary question was how a lay person would respond to the donor-screening questions.

32   [1997] O.J. No. 2666 (Gen. Div.), rev'd [1998] O.J. No. 6137 (Div. Ct.).

The use of post-accident precautions in this way advances the compensatory function of negligence law by facilitating a finding of liability, but it may have an adverse impact on accident prevention goals by discouraging potential defendants from taking additional precautionary measures for fear that they will conclusively foreclose the issue of fault in favour of the plaintiff. The courts have attempted to steer a middle path between these competing policy objectives. Evidence of post-accident precautions may not, *in itself*, be construed as an *admission of liability* but it may be admitted to establish a fact that supports a finding of negligence where the evidence would not be unduly prejudicial to the defendant. This distinction, which is not an easy one to draw in practice, is illustrated by *Anderson v. Maple Ridge (District of)*.[33] In that case the British Columbia Court of Appeal approved the use of evidence that a stop sign was moved by the defendant municipality after a car accident and that there was a subsequent reduction in accidents to show that the sign was difficult to see in its original location. This treatment of post-accident conduct may lack precision and certainty but it does allow the courts to deal with the issue sensitively and to promote one or other of the competing policies as the circumstances of the individual case warrant.

i) Judicial Policy

There is a great deal of unevenness in the way the standard of care is applied to different activities. This unevenness, which is facilitated by the abstract and malleable nature of the reasonable person standard, is reflective of judicial policy. In respect of some activities, the courts have exercised their discretion to impose high standards of care approaching strict liability. In other cases, a more relaxed standard has been favoured. A stringent standard of care has been imposed on the drivers of automobiles, common carriers of passengers such as airlines, bus companies, shipping lines and railways,[34] and the manufacturers of consumer products. High standards of care are also imposed

---

33 [1993] 1 W.W.R. 172 (B.C.C.A.). See also *Jetz v. Calgary Olympic Development Association*, [2002] A.J. No. 1470 (Q.B.) where evidence that there were no further bicycle accidents after better warnings signs of a dangerous speedbump were adopted was admitted to establish that the speedbumps were difficult to see at the time of the accident.

34 Until 1999, railways were treated with some leniency. The *McKay/Barclay* rule dictated that unless there were exceptional dangers or extraordinary circumstances, railways could not be held liable in negligence if they were in compliance with statutory safety rules and regulations. The rule, which evidenced the historical power, influence, and importance of the railways in Canada, was abolished by the Supreme Court in *Ryan v. Victoria (City of)*, [1999] 1 S.C.R. 201

in respect of fire hazards and on those who carry out other dangerous activities such as the handling of gasoline, blasting operations, or
the bulk distribution of electricity. This may reflect a coincidence of
loss distribution and deterrence policies. On the other hand, there are
situations where the standard of care is applied in a way that is more
protective of defendants. The standard of care has not been applied
rigorously in respect of players in sporting events who injure other
players. This may reflect judicial concern about a lack of liability insurance and the difficulty in setting a standard of care for robust body
contact sports. Courts are also slow to impose liability on professional
persons, particularly physicians, even though liability insurance is virtually guaranteed. This reflects the courts' sensitivity to the importance
of a professional's reputation. There is a reluctance to label errors, mistakes, and misadventure as malpractice in order to promote the compensatory function of negligence law. Judicial policy is rarely addressed
openly in written judgments dealing with standard of care issues, but
general patterns of liability are apparent and are increasingly identifiable through computer searches of judgments in various fields of activity. They may be useful, albeit imprecise, predictors of the manner in
which the standard of care is applied.

j) Economic Analysis

It is difficult to estimate the degree of influence that the economic analysis of law has on decision making in Canadian negligence cases.
The courts have not openly embraced the concept but it is likely that
economic theories developed and popularized in the United States[35] influence some judicial thinking. Of particular relevance is the view that
the dominant purpose of negligence law is not compensation but accident prevention. The standard of care should, therefore, be set to reflect
the economically efficient level of accident prevention. Consequently,
if the cost of precautionary measures is less than the likelihood of the
injury multiplied by the magnitude of the loss, it is negligent to fail to
take the precautionary measures. If, on the other hand, the cost of precautionary measures is more than the likelihood of the injury multiplied by the magnitude of the loss, it is not justifiable, economically,
to take those measures, and the failure to take them is not negligent.
This approach is consistent with much of the decision making in negligence cases, and the weighing of factors similar to those used in the

---

[Ryan]. It is now likely that railways will be treated in the same way as other
    common carriers.

35 R.A. Posner, *Economic Analysis of Law*, 6th ed. (New York: Aspen Law & Busi-
    ness, 2002).

economic analysis of the standard of care has been approved by the Supreme Court.[36] Nevertheless, most Canadian judges appear reluctant to reduce the standard of care to an economic cost-benefit analysis.[37] The factors in that equation are difficult to quantify, and Canadian judges appear to be more comfortable with the conventional analysis with its impressionistic assessment of all the relevant considerations.

k) The Equity of the Case

Judges are reluctant to recognize their personal influence on the outcome of individual cases. The conventional wisdom is that judges find the facts and apply the law in a dispassionate and even-handed manner. The result is dictated by the law, not by the judge. Most people, however, recognize that, inevitably, other factors such as an intuitive sense of fairness and a visceral response to the facts of the case exert some degree of influence. Consciously or unconsciously, facts may be emphasized or marginalized and principles may be interpreted broadly or narrowly to accommodate the demands of justice in a particular case. It should not be overlooked that negligence law presents special pressures and opportunities for a judge (and a jury) to accommodate the equity of the case. The pressures are created by the serious plight of many plaintiffs, particularly those who have suffered catastrophic personal injuries, and the acute awareness of the trier of fact that almost all defendants are insured and will not be personally burdened by a finding of liability against them. The opportunities are provided by the open-textured, discretionary nature of the standard of reasonable care. The extent to which the equity of the case influences decision making depends in large part on individual judges and juries but it is a factor that should not be ignored.

l) Hindsight Bias

The judge or jury in a negligence case is asked to assess the risk that a reasonable person would have foreseen at the time of the accident and to determine how a reasonable person would have acted in the light of that foreseeable risk. The defendant must be judged by the foresight and care of a reasonable person when the act or omission at issue took place, not by the hindsight of the trier of fact. The judge or jury, however, knows, with certainty, that the foresight and precautions of the

---

36   See, for example, *Jordan House Ltd. v. Menow* (1973), [1974] S.C.R. 239 at 247 [*Jordan House*].

37   The leading American decision championing the economic analysis of the standard of care, *United States v. Carroll Towing Co.*, 159 F.2d 169 (2d Cir. 1947), has rarely been cited in Canadian judgments.

defendant have proven to be inadequate. This knowledge may operate substantially to the advantage of the plaintiff. Psychological studies have shown that people "overstate the predictability of past events"[38] and consistently overestimate what could have been foreseen before an event occurred. This is known as *hindsight bias*. There are some rules of negligence law which seek to minimize the risk of hindsight bias in applying the standard of care. The use of approved practice and custom in setting the standard of care is a moderating influence, and the trier of fact must not treat post-accident precautions as an admission of liability. Nevertheless, an elusive concept such as reasonable foreseeability, which is so integral to the determination of negligence liability, is highly susceptible to hindsight bias and may lead to a *de facto* strict liability in some borderline cases. It may also explain the almost prophetic foreseeability of some judges and the visceral discomfort that may be felt in making one's own assessment of what a reasonable person could have foreseen in marginal cases.[39]

2) Special Standards of Care

There are certain situations where the standard of the reasonably careful person is not applied to the defendant. This may have the effect of either lowering or elevating the standard of care. It is lowered in respect of some defendants who are incapable of discharging the normative standard of care, such as persons who are mentally ill, children, and persons with significant physical disabilities. The standard of care is raised when the defendant is a professional or in some other way represents herself as having an ability to exercise special care and skill.

a) Mental Disability

Few issues so starkly spotlight the tension between the ethical foundation of negligence law and its compensatory goals than that of a defendant's mental incapacity to appreciate and discharge her obligation of care. Considerations of fairness and justice suggest that mentally incapacitated defendants should be free of liability. It does not seem right to punish or deter those who are incapable of acting with reasonable care. Compensation and loss distribution policies, however, favour the

---

38   J.J. Rachlinski, "A Positive Psychological Theory of Judging in Hindsight" (1998) 65 U. Chi. L. Rev. 571. Rachlinski provides an excellent description of hindsight bias and its influence on decision making in negligence.

39   One American judge has quipped that "there are clear judicial days on which a court can foresee forever." *Thing v. La Chusa*, 771 P.2d 814 at 830 (Calif. S.C. 1989), Eagleson J.

application of the objective standard of reasonable care and the imposition of liability. Canadian law has traditionally resolved this conflict in
favour of mentally impaired defendants.

The issue of a defendant's mental disability operates on two levels in
negligence cases. It may render the defendant's actions involuntary or it
may prevent a volitional defendant from complying with the normative
standard of care. In both situations there is no liability in negligence.

Volition is an essential requirement for all legal liability. An involuntary act is one where the defendant's bodily movement is not directed
by the defendant's conscious mind. A good example of an involuntary
act is found in the American case of *Stokes v. Carlson*.[40] The defendant
was asleep in the back seat of a two-door car driven by the plaintiff.
While asleep, the defendant pushed the driver's seat forward, causing
the plaintiff to lose control of the car. The defendant was not held liable
for the plaintiff's injuries because his actions lacked volition. The judge
stated that

> a contraction of a person's muscles which is purely a reaction to some
> outside force, . . . or the convulsive movements of an epileptic, are
> not acts of that person. So too, movements of the body during sleep
> when the will is in abeyance are not acts . . . Nowhere in cases deal-
> ing with the subject of torts do we find the suggestion that a person
> should be held responsible for injuries inflicted during periods of
> unconsciousness.[41]

There are few Canadian negligence cases dealing with the volition of
the defendant. The best-known is *Slattery v. Haley*.[42] In that case, the
defendant driver of a car was suddenly taken ill and lost consciousness.
The automobile left the road and killed a person on the sidewalk. The
defendant was not held responsible for the death because of his lack of
volition.

The landmark case dealing with the impact of mental disability
on the application of the standard of care to volitional defendants is
the Ontario Court of Appeal decision in *Buckley v. Smith Transport
Ltd*.[43] Taylor, an employee of the defendant Smith Transport, crashed
his truck into a tram and injured the plaintiff. It was established that
Taylor, at the time of the accident, suffered from advanced syphilis of
the brain. He was labouring under the delusion that his truck was re-
motely controlled by an electrical beam and that he was incapable of

---

40   240 S.W.2d 132 (Mo. 1951).
41   *Ibid.* at 135–36.
42   (1922), 52 O.L.R. 95 (C.A.).
43   [1946] O.R. 798 (C.A.) [*Buckley*].

controlling the truck or stopping it. The Court held that, since Taylor's mental illness was such as to prevent him both from understanding the duty of care that rested upon him and from discharging that obligation, he could not, in fairness, be found negligent.

The final decades of the twentieth century witnessed some shift in judicial attitude away from *Buckley*. It was noted by some that *Buckley* was decided before compulsory third-party liability insurance of motor-vehicle owners and operators was introduced, before the power of liability insurance to spread accident losses among all the drivers and owners of motor vehicles was fully appreciated, and before the compensation of accident victims was regarded as the primary purpose of tort law. One Alberta trial judge wrote:

> I see no reason why a person whose mental state is such that he does not appreciate that he owes a duty of care to others while operating his motor vehicle, by reason of which he caused loss or damage to others, should not be subjected to the same criteria for establishing civil liability as anyone else, namely the objective standard of the reasonable driver.[44]

This view is reflective of much American jurisprudence and promotes more vigorously the compensatory policies that predominantly drive modern Canadian negligence law.[45]

Nonetheless, in 1999 the Alberta Court of Appeal followed *Buckley*. In *Fiala v. Cechmanek*[46] the defendant, who was suffering from a severe manic episode, violently attacked the driver of a car stopped at an intersection. In the course of the attack, the driver unintentionally hit the gas pedal, causing the car to accelerate into the intersection where it hit the plaintiff's vehicle. The Court characterized tort law as a system of corrective justice that should not be distorted by a robust pursuit of compensatory goals. The defendant was robbed of his capacity to understand or appreciate his duty of care by the sudden onset of a serious mental illness and he could not be found liable in negligence.

---

44 *Wenden v. Trikha* (1991), 116 A.R. 81 at 115, additional reasons at (1992), 1 Alta. L.R. (3d) 283 (Q.B.), aff'd (1993), 135 A.R. 382 (C.A.). The trial judge in *Hutchings v. Nevin* (1992), 9 O.R. (3d) 776 (Gen. Div.) also suggested that it is time for a re-examination of *Buckley* in the light of legislative and societal developments since that case was decided. See also G. Robertson, *Mental Disability and the Law in Canada*, 2d ed. (Toronto: Carswell, 1994) at 240.

45 A useful discussion of whether or not the standard of care should be relaxed in favour of mentally disabled defendants is found in L.N. Klar, *Tort Law*, 4th ed. (Toronto: Carswell, 2008) at 338–39.

46 (1999), 71 Alta. L.R. (3d) 72 (C.A.).

b) Children

Children do not have the same knowledge, experience, or wisdom as adults to foresee danger and act accordingly. Mental capacity and the ability to perceive risk develop gradually at a child's own pace. The courts have been sensitive to the diminished capacity of children to take care and have developed a special standard of care applicable to them. A number of approaches were available. An objective standard of care would require a child to display the same degree of care as a reasonable child of like age. Alternatively, a subjective standard could be used, imposing liability only where the defendant child was aware of the danger she created. Canadian courts have rejected both of these approaches and have adopted a mixed objective/subjective test of liability. In *McEllistrum v. Etches*,[47] the Supreme Court held that the standard of care applicable to a child was that of a child of similar age, intelligence, and experience as the defendant. The latter two elements are clearly subjective and a careful evaluation of the child and the circumstances surrounding her conduct is required. The Manitoba Court of Appeal decision in *Joyal v. Barsby*[48] is illustrative. The Court applied the test to determine whether or not a six-year-old girl was guilty of contributory negligence. She was seriously injured when she failed to observe the defendant's oncoming motor vehicle when crossing a busy rural highway. The majority of the Court refused to find any contributory negligence on her part. It emphasized that she was not of above-average intelligence, she was not a city child who would have had more experience with motor vehicle traffic, and she was distracted by a fog horn sounded by a large semi-trailer truck that had passed a few seconds earlier in the opposite direction from which she was hit. She had acted no differently from other children of her age, intelligence, and experience. The dissenting judge was influenced by the facts that she had been carefully instructed by her parents on how to cross the highway, she had successfully crossed it on previous occasions, and she lived close to it.

There is no fixed age below which a finding of negligence cannot be made, but children of tender years (under five) have little capacity to appreciate danger and there is virtually no chance that children of that age will be held to be negligent. If an older child is undertaking an activity normally carried on only by adults, however, it is likely that the adult standard of care will be applied to her.[49] There is a good reason for this exception to the lower standard of care. When children are

---

47   [1956] S.C.R. 787.
48   (1965), 55 D.L.R. (2d) 38 (Man. C.A.).
49   See, for example, *Ryan v. Hickson* (1974), 7 O.R. (2d) 352 (H.C.J.) and *McErlean v. Sarel* (1987), 61 O.R. (2d) 396 (C.A.).

performing activities typical of children, members of the public have notice of the presence of children and can protect themselves from any potential danger arising from their immaturity. When children are performing adult activities, such as driving a power boat, a sea-doo, a dirt bike, or an all-terrain vehicle, members of the public reasonably expect it to be under the control of an adult and they adjust their conduct accordingly. The courts protect that reasonable expectation by applying the standard of the reasonably careful adult.

Careful consideration must be given to a variety of factors before any decision is made to sue a child. A child is unlikely to have sufficient assets to discharge a judgment. A child may, however, have coverage under her parents' liability insurance policy, and there is the option of keeping the judgment alive by periodic re-registration until the child is an earner or acquires assets. There is also a possibility that parents may volunteer to pay off the award.

Parents are not vicariously liable for the torts of their children. But they are under a personal duty to take reasonable care to supervise and control their minor children and they may be liable for loss caused by a failure to discharge that obligation. There is, however, renewed interest in the idea of vicarious liability of parents. It has been prompted by a rise in juvenile gang activity and by an increase in juvenile crime, such as car theft, shoplifting, and the defacement of private and public property with graffiti. It is argued by some that vicarious liability may provide an incentive for parents to exercise more control and supervision over their children. Some provinces have taken a step in that direction. The Manitoba Parental Responsibility Act,[50] for example, imposes civil liability on parents for the intentional destruction, damage, or taking of property by their children up to a maximum sum of $10,000. This is, however, not a true vicarious liability. Proof by the parents that they exercised reasonable supervision over their child and that reasonable efforts were made in good faith to discourage the child from the kind of activity that gave rise to the property loss amounts to a complete defence. The Act, therefore, imposes a rebuttable presumption of parental fault in respect of deliberate property damage caused by their child.[51]

---

50   S.M. 1996, c. 61. See also Parental Responsibility Act, S.B.C. 2001, c. 45; Parental Responsibility Act, S.O. 2000, c. 4. A useful discussion of this legislation is found in E. Adjin-Tettey, "Significance and Consequences of Parental Responsibility Legislation" (2002) 17 Sup. Ct. L. Rev. (2d) 221.

51   Some provinces have legislation that imposes vicarious liability in narrow circumstances. The British Columbia School Act, R.S.B.C. 1996, c. 412, s. 10, for example, makes parents liable for damage to school property; see Coquitlam, School District No. 43 v. D.(T.W.) (1999), 170 D.L.R. (4th) 107 (B.C.C.A.).

c) Physical Disability

The law accommodates those persons who suffer from a serious physical disability with a standard of care that is compatible with their condition. The blind are not required to see, the deaf are not required to hear, and paraplegics are not required to walk.[52] This advances the policy of encouraging the full integration of disabled persons into the mainstream of community activity. Public safety is not unduly compromised because there is a corresponding obligation on the part of disabled or ill persons to adjust their conduct so that no avoidable risk is created and to refrain from activities that are beyond their capacity to perform safely.

This adjustment of the standard of care appears to be applicable only to major physical disabilities. No dispensation from the usual standard of care is provided to persons who are short-sighted, poorly coordinated, slow, elderly, or arthritic. It is not easy to discern the principle underlying this distinction. It may be good policy to draw a line between, on the one hand, obvious physical disabilities that alert members of the public to the fact that a person has a physical limitation affecting her ability to take care and, on the other, concealed physical disabilities of which members of the public have no notice. This does not, however, explain the courts' willingness to adjust the standard for the deaf and their reluctance to adjust the standard of care for elderly persons.

There are also obligations to take precautions to prevent foreseeable injuries to the disabled. For example, those persons who are responsible for public sidewalks and commercial buildings to which members of the public are admitted must take care that there are no defects that would present a special danger to blind persons.[53]

d) Superior Skill and Knowledge

When applying the standard of care, a court must attribute a reasonable amount of knowledge, skill, and life experience to the reasonable person. It is assumed, for example, that reasonable people know that propane gas is highly inflammable, that worn tires are dangerous, that children are mischievous, that alcohol impairs judgment, and that acid

---

52   A.M. Linden & B. Feldthusen, *Canadian Tort Law*, 8th ed. (Toronto: Butterworths, 2006) at 149.

53   *Haley v. London Electricity Board* (1964), [1965] A.C. 778 (H.L.). But see *Ryall v. Alsa Road Construction Ltd.*, [2004] A.J. No. 627 (Prov. Ct.), no liability to a visually impaired jogger who while running prior to sunrise fell over a wooden barrier warning of sidewalk repairs. The construction company was not required to install flashing lights sufficient to have alerted her to the danger.

burns. Through the course of the twentieth century, increased access to information and skill, rising literacy rates, and the increasing sophistication of modern consumer goods and services probably raised the level of knowledge and skill of the reasonable person. Nevertheless, it is not always easy to determine the normative information and skill that should be attributed to the reasonable person. In *Cone v. Welock*,[54] for example, the defendant guest at a hunting lodge felt and smelled fuel before using it to start a fire in his room. He mistook gasoline for fuel oil and the lodge was damaged by fire. The Supreme Court held that a reasonable person cannot readily distinguish fuel oil from gasoline and that reasonable care had been taken by the defendant.

A higher standard of care is applied to those persons who represent themselves as having special skill and knowledge that allow them to perform tasks that are normally beyond the capacity of the ordinary person. The public may reasonably expect such people to exercise a degree of skill and knowledge commensurate with that representation. An elevated standard of care applies not only to members of the professions but also to business, commercial, and trades people such as automobile mechanics, builders, and electricians. The standard of care is that of the reasonably prudent and competent member of the particular profession or vocation to which the defendant belongs.

Many of the rules relating to professional liability have arisen from malpractice litigation between physicians and their patients. This is not surprising. The practice of medicine is one of the oldest professions, and medical accidents and unsuccessful treatments are a regrettable, but inevitable, feature of health care. The family physician is, predictably, held to the standard of the reasonably competent and prudent member of that branch of the medical profession. This standard of care is probably uniform across Canada. There is little support for a *locality rule* that would permit variations in the standard of care according to the location of the physician's practice. There is no good reason to tolerate a disparity of *care*, *skill*, and *knowledge* between family physicians in rural or remote areas of the country and those in urban centres. The university-based medical education of physicians is reasonably consistent across the country, there are opportunities for continuing education, and modern communication systems facilitate the appropriate updating of medical knowledge and consultation. A physician in Toronto may have more immediate access to sophisticated hospitals, more specialist support, and more treatment options than a physician in rural Saskatchewan, but the uniform standard of care is sensitive to

---

54   [1970] S.C.R. 494.

these variations, being a standard that is applied to the circumstances of each case. Circumstances may vary greatly but the *care*, *skill*, and *knowledge* of family physicians should be the same.

Courts are similarly unwilling to excuse poor medicine on the ground of inexperience. Inexperienced professionals cause more than their fair share of accidents but that is no reason to depart from the normative standard of care. The public's expectation of competent medical care from all qualified persons must be protected.

Like many professions, medicine has its areas of specialist practice. Specialists must comply with the elevated knowledge, skill, and care of the reasonable member of their specialty whether it is orthopedic surgery, cardiology, or obstetrics. This medical hierarchy also requires lesser-qualified physicians to be sensitive to their own limitations and to refer patients to specialists and to consult in a manner that is consistent with good medical practice.

Courts have been careful not to set unrealistically high standards for physicians. The standard is that of *reasonable* care and judges are sensitive to the fact that medical practice carries no guarantee of success. Mistakes are made, inherent risks manifest themselves, and treatments fail. Error of judgment, misadventure, and the failure of treatment are not inconsistent with due care. It is, nevertheless, often difficult for a judge or jury to determine whether or not reasonable care was taken by a physician. Consequently, considerable reliance is placed on expert witnesses (highly qualified and experienced physicians who have no involvement in the litigation) to assist the trier of fact in understanding technical matters and in identifying the accepted and approved practice of the profession. As was noted earlier, compliance with standard medical practice in complex, scientific, and technical matters is conclusive of due care in medical cases.

Many of the principles that have been developed in medical malpractice cases are, with appropriate adjustments, readily transferable to other professions and vocations.

3) Proof of Negligence: Direct and Circumstantial Evidence

Whether or not there has been a breach of the standard of care is a question of fact to be decided by a judge sitting alone or by a jury. The burden of proof is on the plaintiff to establish on the balance of probabilities that the defendant was negligent. This standard of proof is sometimes expressed as requiring a finding that there is a preponderance of the evidence in favour of the plaintiff's allegations. There may be direct evidence of negligence, as when a number of witnesses observe the failure of the defendant to stop at a red light. Sometimes, however, there is no direct evidence of how the accident occurred. In those cases, the plaintiff must rely on circumstantial evidence. Circumstantial evidence may support an inference or conclusion that the defendant was negligent.

The use of circumstantial evidence with respect of the breach of the standard of care was, traditionally, controlled by the Latin maxim *res ipsa loquitur* (the thing speaks for itself). In 1998, however, the Supreme Court declared in *Fontaine v. British Columbia (Official Administrator)*[55] that this Latin maxim had outgrown its usefulness and should no longer be used in negligence cases. The Court did not, however, disagree with the general process of proving negligence by circumstantial evidence that had taken place under the rubric of *res ipsa loquitur* for over a hundred years.[56] Some general understanding of that process, therefore, remains useful.

Res ipsa loquitur created an inference of negligence when the accident or event that caused the damage was something that in ordinary human experience does not happen without negligence, and the situation and circumstances from which the accident arose were under the sole management and control of the defendant. In the absence of direct evidence of how the accident happened, proof of these two factors created an inference that it was the negligence of the defendant that caused the loss. This circumstantial evidence was said to "speak" of the defendant's negligence and a *prima facie* case was made out.

Kirk v. McLaughlin Coal & Supplies Ltd.[57] and *Clayton v. J.N.Z. Investments Ltd.*[58] illustrate the operation of the maxim. In *Kirk*, the oil furnace in the plaintiff's home exploded. It had been serviced by the defendant for twelve years. Within a period of one month there was a cycle of repair work followed by an explosion, followed by further repairs and then a final explosion that gave rise to the loss that was the subject matter of the litigation. The cause of the explosion was never established. The Court applied *res ipsa loquitur*. Oil furnaces in houses do not normally explode unless there has been some negligence, and the furnace was under the effective control and management of the de-

---

55   [1998] 1 S.C.R. 424 [*Fontaine*].

56   In *Marchuk v. Swede Creek Contracting Ltd.*, [1998] B.C.J. No. 2851 (C.A.), Mackenzie J.A. noted at para. 10 that "the underlying principles governing the use of circumstantial evidence in determining liability in negligence were not modified" by *Fontaine*.

57   [1968] 1 O.R. 311 (C.A.) [*Kirk*].

58   [1969] 1 O.R. 89 (C.A.) [*Clayton*].

fendant since the plaintiff testified that no one else had touched it. The circumstantial evidence pointed strongly to the defendant's negligence as the probable cause of the explosion. The Court in *Clayton* reached an opposite conclusion. The plaintiff in that case leased an apartment in a recently completed building. A lead pipe leading to a radiator in the apartment inexplicably burst, causing water damage to the plaintiff's furnishings and fixtures. The plaintiff relied on the maxim to establish the liability of the company that had installed the pipe. The Court held that it may have been reasonable to infer that someone's negligence caused the failure of the pipe, but it was not reasonable to infer the negligence of the installer. The pipe was not under his sole control and management. The occurrence could equally point to the negligence of the owner of the block, maintenance personnel, or the manufacturer of the pipe, none of whom gave evidence.

Application of the maxim did not provide conclusive proof of the defendant's negligence. It created a rebuttable inference of negligence, often described as a *prima facie* case of negligence. There was some judicial inconsistency in formulating the burden that rested on the defendant to rebut this inference. This was explained to some degree by the varying strength of circumstantial evidence and the strength of the inference in any given case. The dominant view was that the defendant was required to provide an explanation of how the accident happened that was consistent with due care on his part. Such an explanation neutralized the inference of negligence raised by the plaintiff's evidence. The explanation must have some evidential foundation. Mere theorizing, conjecture, or speculation of how the accident might have happened without negligence was normally insufficient.

In the *Fontaine* case the Supreme Court reconsidered the utility and role of *res ipsa loquitur*. The case dealt with a single motor vehicle accident. A truck left the highway in severe weather conditions and crashed into a swollen stream. Both the driver and his passenger were killed. The family of the deceased passenger sued the driver. There was no direct evidence as to how the accident occurred. The Supreme Court held that it was no longer appropriate to resort to the maxim of *res ipsa loquitur* in cases of circumstantial evidence. The Court appeared to be concerned that some courts were treating the maxim as a doctrine of law involving the application of rules and principles. It sought to emphasize that the maxim merely described the process of using circumstantial evidence to establish the negligence of the defendant. To give that process a Latin description created confusion and difficulty. The Court held that the trier of fact must simply weigh the circumstantial evidence with any available direct evidence and determine if the plaintiff has established a *prima facie* case of negligence. Once the plaintiff has done this, the defendant must present evidence negating the inference of negligence or the plaintiff will win. On the facts, it was held in *Fontaine* that there was insufficient circumstantial evidence to create an inference of negligence against the driver of the vehicle.

A good illustration of the use of direct and circumstantial evidence to create a *prima facie* case of negligence is found in *Hassen v. Anvari*.[59] In that case the defendant surgeon severed the plaintiff's aorta while performing a repair of a hiatus hernia. It was severed by a surgical cutting instrument known as a trocar. The statistical risk of such an injury was 1 in 5,000 and the defendant had performed 700 such procedures without cutting an aorta. The trial judge held that these circumstances warranted an inference that the defendant's feel and touch had let him down and he had either pushed the trocar too far, with too much pressure and speed, or at the wrong angle. The defendant attempted to rebut this inference of negligence with two explanations. First, the plaintiff's aorta might have been unusually close to her abdominal wall. Second, the engaging of the safety shield on the trocar might have been delayed. Both explanations were dismissed as speculative and without evidentiary foundation.[60]

---

59   [2001] O.J. No. 6085, appeal dismissed, [2003] O.J. No. 3543 (C.A.). See also *Lemaire v. Ashabi*, [2003] B.C.J. No. 2438 (C.A.) where a *prima facie* case of negligence was established against the owner of a truck by proof that a wheel flew off the truck a few days after he had tightened a wheel nuts and *Michel (Litigation Guardian of) v. Doe*, [2009] B.C.J. No. 1021 (C.A.) where proof that a rock flew off a loaded logging truck did not create a *prima facie* case of negligence against the driver who inspected his load before beginning his journey.

60   There are some discrete situations where there is a legal presumption of negligence that shifts the burden of proof to the defendant. A defendant bailee carries the burden of proof that loss of, or damage to, the bailed goods was not caused by her negligence (*National Trust Co. Ltd. v. Wong Aviation Ltd.*, [1969] S.C.R. 481) and a defendant public carrier must prove due care and skill if an accident injures a passenger (*Day v. Toronto Transportation Commission*, [1940] S.C.R. 433). In these situations the bailee or carrier is normally in the best position to explain what happened. If, on the facts of the case, this is not so, the presumption will not be applied. But see *Whelan v. Parsons & Sons Transportation Ltd.*, [2005] N.J. No. 264 at para. 21 where the Court of Appeal of Newfoundland and Labrador concluded that in light of *Fontaine* "it is not helpful to speak of shifting the onus of proof to require a common carrier to prove it was not negligent. The ordinary principles of proof are sufficient to the task."

C. CAUSATION

The plaintiff must prove that the defendant's negligence caused his loss. This is known as *cause-in-fact*. It should not to be confused with the control device *remoteness of damage*, sometimes known as *proximate cause*, which may excuse a defendant from liability for loss caused to the plaintiff on the ground of fairness. Cause-in-fact focuses on the factual issue of the sufficiency of the connection between the defendant's wrongful act and the plaintiff's loss. It is this connection that justifies the imposition of responsibility on the negligent defendant. That is the issue canvassed here together with some related problems of multiple tortfeasors.

1) Cause-in-Fact

The conventional test to determine cause-in-fact is the *but for* test. One must ask the question "would the plaintiff's damage have occurred *but for* the defendant's negligence?" If the answer is "no," the defendant's negligence is a cause-in-fact of the damage. If the answer is "yes," indicating that the damage would have occurred whether or not the defendant was negligent, his negligence is not a cause-in-fact. The test is grammatically awkward but it does have the merit of focusing on the defendant's role in producing the damage to the exclusion of other legally extraneous causes.

The application of the *but for* test rarely calls for close or precise analysis. Most frequently, courts merely identify the test and draw a conclusion. It has recently been pointed out, however, that clarity, accuracy, and certainty are enhanced by recognizing that the application of the *but for* test involves a number of discrete steps.[61] First, the harm that is alleged to have been caused by the defendant must be identified. Second, the specific act or acts of negligence by the defendant must be isolated. Third, the trier of fact must mentally adjust the facts so that the defendant's conduct satisfies the standard of care of the reasonable person, being sure to leave all other facts the same. Fourth, it must be asked if the plaintiff's harm would have occurred if the defendants had been acting with reasonable care. The fifth step is to answer the question.

The burden of proof in respect of cause-in-fact is on the plaintiff. The trier of fact must be persuaded that the defendant's negligence probably caused the plaintiff's loss. Courts have warned against sheer

---

61   This step-by-step process is outlined by D.W. Robertson, "The Common Sense of Cause in Fact" (1997) 75 Tex. L. Rev. 1765 at 1769–73.

speculation, theorizing, and guessing, but there is always some degree of speculation in determining cause-in-fact. It is inevitably a hypothetical inquiry. One can never be assured of what would have happened if the defendant had exercised reasonable care. The trier of fact is assisted by the evidence of the circumstances of the accident, but ultimately, the determination of cause-in-fact depends upon a generous application of common sense, experience, and intuition.

The operation of the *but for* test is usefully illustrated by two contrasting American decisions. In *Marek v. Southern Enterprises, Inc.*[62] some unknown persons began throwing firecrackers around a movie theatre. Several minutes after this began, one of the firecrackers exploded close to the plaintiff's head, causing him a loss of hearing in one ear. The defendant owner of the theatre was found negligent for failing to deal with this dangerous situation more promptly. The Court was also persuaded that, if the defendant had immediately turned on the lights and interrupted the movie, the plaintiff's injury would not have occurred. The *but for* test was satisfied. The opposite conclusion was drawn in *East Texas Theatres, Inc. v. Rutledge.*[63] The plaintiff was hit in the head by a bottle when she was leaving the defendant's movie theatre at the end of the show. The bottle was thrown from the balcony by some unidentified person. During the performance of the movie, there had been a good deal of rowdiness in the theatre and paper cups had been thrown about. The jury found that the defendant was negligent. He ought to have intervened and ejected the rowdy persons. In its opinion, the bottle would not have been thrown if he had taken these steps. The Texas Court of Appeal disagreed. In its view, it had not been established on the balance of probabilities that the bottle thrower was one of the rowdy persons who would have been ejected if due care had been taken. The injury, therefore, might have occurred even if such steps had been taken. An alternative argument that some timely and lesser measures of crowd control would have prevented the bottle-throwing incident was dismissed by the Court as purely speculative.

It is not necessary to prove that the defendant's negligence was the sole cause or the predominant cause of the plaintiff's damage. There may be a number of causes both tortious and non-tortious. So long as the defendant's act is *a* cause of the plaintiff's damage, the defendant is fully liable for that damage. The Supreme Court decision in *Athey v. Leonati*[64] is illustrative. The plaintiff, who had a long history of back prob-

---

62   99 S.W.2d 594 (Tex. Comm'n App. 1936).

63   453 S.W.2d 466 (Tex. 1970).

64   [1996] 3 S.C.R. 458.

lems, suffered back injuries as a result of the defendants' negligence. In the course of his rehabilitation, he suffered a herniated disc. The trial judge found that his herniated disc was caused by a combination of the pre-existing problems and the defendants' negligence. In her view, the defendants' negligence was 25 percent responsible for the herniated disc and she awarded 25 percent of her assessment of the plaintiff's damages. The Supreme Court held that this was incorrect. On the balance of probabilities, the trial judge had found that the defendants' negligence was a cause of the loss and consequently the defendants were 100 percent liable for that loss.

The *but for* test has proved to be an effective one in determining cause-in-fact but there are circumstances where it is unworkable and leads to clear injustice. The classic example is where two defendants negligently light separate fires, each of which is sufficient to spread and destroy a neighbour's premises. The fires, however, converge and a single conflagration destroys the premises. Application of the *but for* test sequentially to each of the defendants results in each defendant being exonerated because the loss would still have occurred if either one, but not both, had been careful. Clearly, in fairness, both defendants should be held responsible. To achieve this result the courts developed the *material contribution* test. Under this test the conduct of both defendants is regarded as a cause-in-fact because it materially contributed to the loss.

In the latter part of the twentieth century, there was a good deal of debate about cause-in-fact and the sufficiency of the *but for* test to handle sophisticated medical malpractice cases; "toxic torts" cases dealing with the negligent testing, manufacture, and distribution of products and compounds that are suspected of causing cancer or other illnesses; and cases dealing with the exposure of persons to illness-causing micro-organisms. These are situations where the plaintiff may be able to prove that the defendant was negligent and that the harm she suffered was within the scope of the risk created by the defendant's negligence, but she cannot prove a causal link on the balance of probabilities. It was argued that in such cases it was appropriate to ease the conventional burden of proof on the plaintiff by applying an augmented risk theory. An *augmented risk* rule would require a plaintiff to prove that the defendant was negligent and that the harm suffered by the plaintiff was within the scope of the risk created by the defendant's negligence. This would be sufficient to establish a *prima facie* case of cause-in-fact and liability would be imposed unless the defendant was able to prove on the balance of probabilities that his conduct was not a cause-in-fact of the plaintiff's loss.

The augmented risk theory was considered by the House of Lords in *McGhee v. National Coal Board*.[65] In that case the plaintiff worker suffered dermatitis as a consequence of working in dusty brick kilns. There was no negligence in having a dusty work site. The only negligence was in failing to provide the worker with adequate shower facilities to remove the dust at the end of his shift. The expert scientific/medical evidence could not determine if the delay in removing the dust caused the dermatitis. All that could be said was that exposure to dust increased the risk of getting dermatitis. A majority of the House of Lords held that in these circumstances, a material increase in the risk of the disease may be *equated* with a material contribution to the disease, and it concluded that the defendant's act was a cause of the dermatitis. Lord Wilberforce, however, was willing to go further and more fully embrace an augmented risk theory. In his view, proof by the plaintiff that the defendant was negligent, coupled with proof that the plaintiff's loss was within the scope of the risk created by the defendant's negligence, was sufficient to reverse the burden of proof of causation. To escape liability, the defendant would have to prove on the balance of probabilities that the lack of washing facilities was not a cause of the dermatitis. *McGhee* gave rise to a sustained academic and judicial debate about cause-in-fact and the scope and merit of an augmented risk rule. The Canadian courts initially embraced Lord Wilberforce's approach in *McGhee* but they became more ambivalent about it when the House of Lords insisted in *Wilsher v. Essex Area Health Authority*[66] that no new principle of law had been established in *McGhee*. It was construed as no more than a robust and pragmatic application of conventional cause-in-fact principles. Eighteen years after *McGhee*, the Supreme Court joined the debate in *Snell v. Farrell*.[67]

In *Snell*, the defendant surgeon continued cataract surgery on the plaintiff in spite of the fact that an anaesthetizing injection had caused some bleeding behind her eye. The prudent course of action was to discontinue the surgery. Bleeding threatens the optic nerve and a continuation of the surgery could exacerbate the bleeding and increase

---

65   (1972), [1973] 1 W.L.R. 1 (H.L.) [*McGhee*].

66   [1988] A.C. 1074 (H.L.). Lord Bridge stated that in his view, *McGhee* was consistent with traditional principles, albeit applied pragmatically and robustly. This interpretation was, however, repudiated in *Fairchild v. Glenhaven Funeral Services Ltd.*, [2002] UKHL 22 [*Fairchild*]. In that case, the defendant employers materially increased the risk of mesothelioma by negligently exposing the plaintiff employees to asbestos dust. The House of Lords applied the "new" principle in *McGhee* to find causation.

67   [1990] 2 S.C.R. 311 [*Snell*].

the risk of damaging the patient's sight. Some months later it was discovered that the plaintiff had lost her sight in that eye. At the trial, the medical experts were unable to give a firm opinion that the nerve damage was caused by a continuation of the surgery. It may have resulted from natural causes, including the plaintiff's high blood pressure or her diabetes. The plaintiff argued that the defendant's negligent act had certainly increased the risk of damage to the optic nerve and the loss of sight was within the scope of that risk. The lower courts found for the plaintiff on the basis of *McGhee*. The Supreme Court upheld their ruling but did not adopt the *McGhee* approach. In a unanimous decision, the Court reasserted the conventional *but for* test and the traditional burden of proof. The Court was not convinced that a change in the law was necessary. In its view, the traditional rules had not prevented plaintiffs with valid claims from proving their cases. Furthermore, the adoption of *McGhee* would create the risk of defendants being held responsible for loss that they had not in fact caused. It might also lead to an undesirable increase in medical liability, placing pressure on the liability insurance system. The Court, however, emphasized that causation rules must not be applied in a strict or rigid manner. It called for a flexible, pragmatic, and common-sense approach. It also noted that, where facts lie particularly within the knowledge of the defendant, little affirmative evidence of cause-in-fact is required of the plaintiff and, in the absence of evidence to the contrary, it is fair to make an inference of cause-in-fact. It is not appropriate, however, to reverse the burden of proof. The ultimate burden remains on the plaintiff. The Court also addressed the issue of expert evidence in medical malpractice cases. It is not necessary to secure a firm expert opinion in favour of the plaintiff's assertion of cause. Medical experts tend to speak in terms of scientific certainty rather than the lower standard of the balance of probabilities favoured by tort law. In the Court's view, the plaintiff had presented sufficient evidence to permit an inference of causation to be drawn.

Snell provided some needed stability to the law by establishing the primacy of the *but for* test and providing guidance as to how it should be applied. This stability was, however, shaken by later decisions of the Supreme Court in *Athey v. Leonati*[68] and *Walker Estate v. York Finch General Hospital*,[69] which appeared to favour a more expansive role for the *material contribution* test. In those cases, the Court confirmed that the *material contribution* test was applicable where the *but for* test was unworkable and that a contribution was material if it was not *de minimis* (trivial).

---

68   Above note 64.
69   [2001] 1 S.C.R. 647 [*Walker*].

The cases, however, produced some uncertainty about the scope of the test and its relationship to the *but for* test. First, it was not clear when the *but for* test would be considered to be "unworkable." The Court, for example, stated that the test was applicable in both *Athey* and *Walker* albeit that in both cases the plaintiff also satisfied the *but for* test. Second, there was no discussion of the meaning of either *material* or *de minimus*. Third, there was some doubt about whether the test required proof of a material contribution to the harm (similar to *but for*) or a material contribution to the risk of harm (similar to *augmented risk*). The conventional view was that the Court intended the former since it did not indicate that it was departing from its decision in *Snell*. After *Athey* and *Walker* the jurisprudence was uneven, but there was a growing consensus that the *material contribution* test was a more lenient test of causation and it was resorted to (more by name than by exposition) when deserving plaintiffs fell short of establishing the *but for* test on the balance of probabilities.

In 2007, a full bench of the Supreme Court sought to clarify the nature and applicability of the *material contribution* test in *Resurfice Corp. v. Hanke*.[70] The Court declined to review the extensive judicial and academic commentary on the issue, preferring instead to assert a few general principles. It confirmed that the "basic" and "primary" test of causation is the *but for* test. The *material contribution* test is applicable only in exceptional circumstances where two pre-conditions are met. First, it must be impossible, because of factors beyond the plaintiff's control (such as the limits of scientific knowledge) for the plaintiff to prove that the defendant's negligence caused the plaintiff's loss on the *but for* test. Second, the harm suffered by the plaintiff must be of a kind that is within the scope of the *risk* generated by the defendant's negligent conduct. In such circumstances *liability* may be imposed because to deny it would offend basic notions of fairness and justice. The Court gave two examples where the *material contribution* test applied. The first is where it is impossible to say which of two simultaneous negligent acts caused the harm.[71] The second is where it is impossible to prove what

---

70   [2007] S.C.J. No. 7 [*Hanke*]. The case involved an allegation of the negligent design of an ice making machine which led to hot water being poured into the gasoline tank rather than the water tank. Vapourized gasoline which escaped from the over-filled gasoline tank was ignited by an overhead heater. The resulting explosion burned the operator of the machine. The Court upheld the trial judge's conclusions that the design was not negligent and in any event cause-in-fact was not established. The accident resulted entirely from operator error.

71   This example, drawn from *Cook v. Lewis*, [1957] S.C.R. 830 [*Cook*] is described in more detail below as a case of alternative liability. See section C(2), below in this chapter.

a particular person in a causal chain would have done had the defendant not been negligent.[72] These two situations have been characterized, respectively, as *"circular causation"* and *"dependency causation."*[73]

Hanke did not, however, fully settle the confusion that has plagued the *material contribution* test. This was due in part to the Court's retention of the label *material contribution* while defining it as a limited *augmentation of risk* test. The language used by the Supreme Court in *Hanke* is, indeed, more reflective of Lord Wilberforce's opinion in *McGhee* than that of its own decision in *Athey*. Furthermore, the *material contribution* test as defined in *Hanke* was capable of both a broad and a narrow interpretation. On the one hand, it could be interpreted as introducing an augmented risk theory capable of evolving in an expansionary and pro-plaintiff manner. On the other hand, it could be interpreted as displacing the *Athey* version of material contribution with a very narrow and closed exception to the *but for* test. While some of the language in *Hanke* may encourage the former interpretation, the intent of the Court seems clearly to have been the latter. This has led to jurisprudence which is not uniform and is at times confusing. Nevertheless it is now possible to draw some general conclusions. First, there are two tests of causation in negligence law; the *but for* test as described in *Snell* and the *material contribution* test as defined in *Hanke*. Second, most causation issues are argued and resolved on the *but for* test and it is not uncommon for cases to fail because of the plaintiff's inability to satisfy that test. Third, the most restrictive element of the *material contribution* test is the need to show that proof of causation under the *but for* test is impossible. Impossibility, in this context, appears to mean scientific impossibility, not impossibility caused by the inadequacy of evidence, the unavailability of witnesses, or other common impediments to the forensic process. Moreover, there is recent authority which suggests that the *material contribution* test applies exclusively to the kind of impossibility found in circular and dependency causation.[74] Fourth, the patterns of decision making, including that in medical malpractice litigation, remain largely unchanged from those before *Hanke*. Fifth, the courts have not, as yet, had an opportunity to consider the toxic tort cases of the kind that have been decided by the English courts during the last decade. The toxic tort cases present the kind of facts that may satisfy the elements of the *Hanke* test including the scientific impossibility of satisfying the *but for* test, the possibility of a causal link, and the dictates of justice and fairness. An illustrative decision

---

72 This example is drawn from *Walker*, above note 69.

73 See E.S. Knutson, "Clarifying Causation in Tort" (2010) 33 Dal. L.J. 153.

74 See *Clements (Litigation Guardian of) v. Clements*, 2010 BCCA 581.

is *Fairchild v. Glenhaven Funeral Services Ltd.*[75] In that case employees suffered a signature disease caused by asbestos fibres. They had worked for a number of employers who had negligently exposed them to asbestos fibres. They were not, however, able to prove cause-in-fact against any one employer because the disease may be caused by one or more exposures to asbestos. Nevertheless, the House of Lords rehabilitated its decision in *McGhee* and imposed joint and several liability on the employers on the grounds that their negligence had increased the risk of an asbestos-related disease and the harm suffered was within the scope of that risk.[76]

Finally it should be noted, as observed by the Supreme Court in *Snell*, that causation principles are not immutable. They are subject to change to reflect societal needs and justice. The Court has in the past recognized certain exceptions and a number of special challenges lie ahead. Some are canvassed below.

2) Alternative Liability

In *Cook v. Lewis*,[77] the Supreme Court adopted the American principle of alternative liability. It applies where it is clear that only one of a small number of negligent persons caused the plaintiff's loss, but the plaintiff is unable to establish which person it was. If *all* the negligent persons are joined as defendants, the burden of proof of causation is reversed and each defendant is held jointly and severally liable (each defendant is fully liable for the plaintiff's losses) unless he can establish on the balance of probabilities that he did not cause the loss to the plaintiff. In *Cook*, for example, two hunters fired simultaneously in the direction of the plaintiff. The plaintiff was hit by shotgun pellets discharged by a single gun. Both hunters were clearly negligent, but the plaintiff was unable to prove which of them shot him. Each hunter claimed that the other caused the injury. The requirements of alternative liability were met and, in the absence of exonerating evidence from either one of them, they were held jointly and severally liable. Alternative liability is normally justified on the grounds that all of the defendants are wrongdoers, they normally have better information of the circumstances of the accident than the plaintiff, they may have impaired the plaintiff's power to prove cause-in-fact, and, given the small number of defendants, there is a high likelihood that any one of them caused the loss.

---

75   Above note 66.

76   See also *Barker v. Corus*, [2006] UKHL 20.

77   Above note 71. *Cook* was referred to in *Hanke* as a case where the *material contribution* test of causation was satisfied.

3) Joint Tortfeasors (Concerted Action)

In some circumstances, a number of people may be responsible for the single tortious act of one of them. In those circumstances, proof of a single tort suffices to establish liability against them all. Broadly speaking, this arises where the defendants have some special relationship or they participate in a common venture or joint enterprise involving tortious conduct. These defendants are known as *joint tortfeasors* and they are jointly and severally *liable* for the plaintiff's loss.

There are four categories of joint tortfeasors. First, one who instigates or encourages another to commit a tort and the person who commits it are joint tortfeasors. Second, an employer and an employee are joint tortfeasors in respect of a tort committed by the employee within the scope of his employment. Third, a principal and agent are joint tortfeasors in respect of torts committed by the agent within the actual or apparent authority of the agent. Fourth, there is a residual fact-specific category covering other instances of concerted action by two or more involving the commission of a tortious act. The basis of joint responsibility in this residual category is guilt by participation, not guilt by association. The hunters in *Cook v. Lewis*, for example, were not joint tortfeasors. It was a case of independent and parallel tortious conduct. That situation may be contrasted with those of a driver of a towed vehicle and the driver of the vehicle doing the towing, who were held to be joint tortfeasors in respect of damage arising from safety violations in the towed vehicle,[78] and highway workers who were held to be joint tortfeasors when they threw sand at a passing bus and thereby injured the eye of a passenger who was sitting by an open window.[79]

4) Market Share Liability

American law developed the theory of market share liability to address the special challenges presented by DES litigation. DES is a drug that was prescribed to pregnant women between the years 1951 and 1971. It was banned for use during pregnancy when it was discovered that it caused a signature cancer in some of the adult daughters of those women who had taken it. The responsibility of the manufacturers of DES and the link between the DES and the cancer were never at issue. However, the latent nature of the injury prevented many plaintiffs from identifying which of approximately 300 drug companies manufactured the DES taken by their mothers. The plaintiffs could not rely

---

78 *Harpe v. Lefebvre* (1976), 1 C.C.L.T. 331 (Alta. Dist. Ct.).
79 *Beecham v. Henderson & Houston*, [1951] 1 D.L.R. 628 (B.C.S.C.).

on alternative liability because that principle is normally restricted to a small number of defendants all of whom can be brought before the court. Some of the manufacturers of DES had gone out of business. The defendant companies were not joint tortfeasors because they were not involved in concerted action and there was no joint venture to market DES. At best, there was parallel tortious conduct.

A solution was found in market share liability. It was first recognized in California in *Sindell v. Abbott Laboratories*.[80] Since then it has been developed and modified in a variety of ways by other states. A robust version of this theory was adopted by the New York Court of Appeal in *Hymowitz v. Eli Lilly & Co*.[81] In that state, it is necessary to join, as defendants, manufacturers who collectively enjoyed a *substantial share* of the *national* DES market at the time that the prescription for DES was filled for the plaintiff's mother. Liability may then be imposed on each defendant in proportion to its share of the national DES market at that time. The culpability of each defendant is, consequently, measured by the risk each defendant created to the American public at large. Therefore, it is no excuse that an individual defendant did not market DES in New York where the plaintiff's mother lived.[82] Proof that the defendant did not market DES to pregnant women is, however, exculpatory because the defendant did not contribute in any way to the risk to children. Each defendant is severally (individually) liable for its proportionate share of the plaintiff's loss. A defendant who had a 30 percent share of the national market is liable for 30 percent of the plaintiff's damages. There is no joint and several liability of all defendants for all of the plaintiff's loss. Indeed, if the defendants sued collectively had an 85 percent of the national market, the plaintiff will not be able to recover more than 85 percent of her damages.

Although the market share doctrine is generally restricted to DES cases in the United States, it is capable of being applied to other mass product liability litigation involving indeterminate defendants. It may be applied to a wide range of toxic products and compounds such as asbestos and Agent Orange where the significant time between exposure and illness makes it difficult to determine which manufacturer caused the plaintiff's loss. The idea of a collective liability of this nature has not been addressed by Canadian courts as yet. Consequently, market share liability has neither been accepted nor rejected. It does, however, provide a vivid illustration of the inherent power of judges to fashion

---

80 607 P.2d 924 (Cal. 1980).

81 539 N.E.2d 1069 (N.Y. 1989).

82 Most other states that have accepted market share liability permit a defendant to prove the absence of causation.

innovative solutions to new problems where the demands of justice and fairness are sufficiently compelling.

5) Loss of a Chance

The law relating to claims for the loss of a chance of avoiding damage is not in a satisfactory state. The issue arises, most often, in medical malpractice cases. The Ontario Court of Appeal decision in *Cottrelle v. Gerard*[83] is illustrative. In that case, the plaintiff, who had suffered from diabetes for thirty years, developed an infected sore between the toes of her left foot. The sore became gangrenous and her left leg had to be amputated. The trial judge found that the defendant attending physician was negligent. He should have been more vigilant from the outset and he should have ordered more aggressive treatment. There was, however, no evidence that proper care would on the balance of probabilities have saved her leg. At best she could establish that she was robbed of a less than 50 percent chance of saving her leg. That, in the view of the Court of Appeal, was insufficient. It applied traditional causation rules which focus not on the loss of a chance but on the ultimate harm (the loss of her leg). On the balance of probabilities (at least 51 percent) the defendant did not cause the harm. If the plaintiff lost a 60 percent chance of salvaging her leg liability would be imposed because on the balance of probabilities the defendant's negligence did cause the harm.

This rigid, all-or-nothing approach may be avoided by acceptance of *loss of a chance* as a discrete and independent head of damage in itself. Once loss of a chance is defined as a distinct injury, the causation problem disappears (there is no doubt that the physician did cause the loss of a chance of full recovery), and damages may be assessed on a probabilistic basis.[84] Many American states have adopted this view, arguing that the loss of an opportunity for improved outcome is something of real value, and that loss of a chance liability is particularly attractive in medical malpractice cases since reliable statistics to measure the chance of a better outcome are more available in these cases and the physician's primary role is to maintain her patient's health and to

---

83   (2003), 233 D.L.R. (4th) 45, leave to appeal to S.C.C. refused, [2003] S.C.C.A. No. 5472.

84   Once all the *elements* necessary to establish a cause of action in negligence (including causation of damage) are established, the court in assessing *damages* takes into account future uncertainties and awards damages on a probabilistic basis.

secure the best possible outcome.[85] Nonetheless, neither the Supreme Court[86] nor other Commonwealth jurisdictions[87] have followed the American lead.[88]

6) Multiple Tortfeasors Causing Indivisible Damage

At common law, multiple tortfeasors causing the same (indivisible) damage were either joint tortfeasors or several concurrent tortfeasors. The four categories of joint tortfeasors were described earlier. Defendants who commit a series of discrete, independent torts, each of which is a cause-in-fact of the plaintiff's damage, are several concurrent tortfeasors. This distinction is still one of some importance. For example, to secure the liability of joint tortfeasors, it is necessary to prove only a single tortious act by one of the joint tortfeasors. On the other hand, liability must be established individually against each of several concurrent tortfeasors. The importance of the distinction, however, has been minimized by legislative reform that now controls the responsibility of multiple tortfeasors. The legislation is not uniform[89] and there continue to be many technical issues that are not fully or uniformly resolved. Nevertheless, the general approach to multiple tortfeasors is not significantly different from that of the Manitoba *Tortfeasors and Contributory Negligence Act*.[90]

Under that Act, all tortfeasors may be sued by the plaintiff in the same action and the defendant may third party any potential tortfeasor overlooked by the plaintiff. The *liability* of multiple tortfeasors (both

---

85   For example, *Matsuyama v. Birbaum*, 890 N.E. 2d 819 (Mass. 2008) commented on in "Tort Law: Recent Cases" (2008–09) 122 Harv. L. Rev. 1247.

86   *Laferriere v. Lawson*, [1991] 1 S.C.R. 541.

87   See *Gregg v. Scott*, [2005] 2 A.C. 176 (H.L.) and *Tabett v. Gett*, [2010] HCA 12.

88   Some courts are not as resolutely opposed to loss of a chance recovery in cases of financial loss arising from the loss of adjudication or negligent misrepresentation: see S.M. Waddams "The Valuation of Chances" (1998) 30 Can. Bus. L.J. 86.

89   In some provinces and territories the legislation also deals with apportionment for contributory negligence: see British Columbia *Negligence Act*, R.S.B.C. 1996, c. 333; Manitoba *Tortfeasors and Contributory Negligence Act*, R.S.M. 1987, c. T90; Newfoundland and Labrador *Contributory Negligence Act*, R.S.N.L. 1990, c. C-33; Northwest Territories *Contributory Negligence Act*, R.S.N.W.T. 1988, c. C-18; Ontario *Negligence Act*, R.S.O. 1990, c. N.1; Prince Edward Island *Contributory Negligence Act*, R.S.P.E.I. 1988, c. C-21; Saskatchewan *Contributory Negligence Act*, R.S.S. 1978, c. C-31; Yukon Territory *Contributory Negligence Act*, R.S.Y. 2002, c. 32. Other jurisdictions have separate Acts: see Alberta *Tort-Feasors Act*, R.S.A. 2000, c. T-5; New Brunswick *Tortfeasors Act*, R.S.N.B. 1973, c. T-8; and Nova Scotia *Tortfeasors Act*, R.S.N.S. 1989, c. 471.

90   *Ibid.*

joint tortfeasors and several concurrent tortfeasors) is joint and several, which means that all of the defendant tortfeasors are liable for the full amount of the damages awarded and each defendant is individually responsible for that amount. The plaintiff may, therefore, opt to fully execute her judgment against any one of the defendants. Joint and several liability is designed to maximize the plaintiff's chance of having the judgment paid. Full satisfaction (payment) by one defendant of a settlement or judgment discharges the liability of all other defendants to the *plaintiff*. Double recovery is not permitted. If satisfaction has not been made by the judgment debtors, further actions against tortfeasors not initially sued may be brought. Any subsequent judgment may not, however, exceed the quantum of the first. This is designed to prevent court shopping to secure a more generous award from a subsequent judge. Furthermore, unless there are reasonable grounds for bringing the later action, costs may be awarded against the plaintiff. This acts as an incentive for the plaintiff to join all potential tortfeasors in the initial proceedings.

As noted earlier, joint and several liability permits the plaintiff to execute a judgment against any one of multiple defendants. The possible unfairness of a plaintiff executing a judgment fully against only one of several defendants has been mitigated by the rules of contribution among defendants. Courts are now directed to apportion the responsibility for the plaintiff's loss among the defendants in accordance with the degree to which each is at fault. This apportionment does not affect the plaintiff, who may continue to seek 100 percent of the judgment against any of the defendants, but it does provide an enforceable framework for the allocation of losses among the defendants themselves. Consequently, when two defendants are held equally responsible for the plaintiff's loss and the plaintiff chooses to execute the judgment against the first defendant, the first defendant may in turn seek contribution from the second defendant for half of the award of damages. Contribution can also be sought from a defendant who was not joined in the action if, had he been sued, he would have been found liable. In exceptional circumstances, the court may require a defendant to indemnify fully the other defendants and thereby allocate the loss ultimately to the dominant wrongdoer.

D. DAMAGE

It is axiomatic that no liability can arise in negligence unless the plaintiff suffers damage as a result of the defendant's wrongful act. Proof of negligent conduct without consequences will not do. This is not a matter of debate or contention in negligence law. It is true that the punitive and deterrent functions of negligence law would support the idea of liability for merely exposing another to a significant risk of injury, but the compensatory rationale of the tort is so dominant and the flood of litigation would be so great that such a notion has not received serious consideration.

There is little authority on the seriousness of harm to satisfy this requirement since the cost of the torts process excludes many minor and marginal claims. Occasionally, difficult questions about the scope and definition of personal injury and property loss have arisen. Two English cases are illustrative. In *Rothwell v. Chemical & Insulation Co. Ltd.*[91] the House of Lords held, in a controversial decision, that pleural plaques in the lungs of plaintiffs who had been negligently exposed to asbestos were not "personal injury" sufficient to support a negligence action since pleural plaques do not create any symptoms and do not cause other asbestos-related illnesses.[92] In *Yearworth v. North Bristol NHS Trust,*[93] the plaintiffs required chemotherapy which threatened their fertility. Before the treatment, they chose to freeze samples of their semen at the defendant hospital. When the semen was destroyed by the negligence of the defendant, the plaintiffs were robbed of their chance for future fatherhood. The Court of Appeal held that the loss of semen was "damage" sufficient to support a negligence action. It was, however, in its opinion, a type of property loss rather than personal injury.[94]

There has been considerable debate about whether other categories of damage should be recoverable in negligence. There is a good deal of caselaw, for example, defining the scope of recovery for psychiatric damage and economic losses. But this debate has not taken place under the rubric of damage. It has taken place in a discussion of one or other of the control devices: *duty of care* and *remoteness of damage*. The element of *damage* has therefore been largely marginalized from any policy debate about the scope of negligence liability.

---

91   [2007] UKHL 39 [*Rothwell*].
92   The Scottish Parliament subsequently departed from *Rothwell*. It enacted the *Damages (Asbestos-related Conditions) Scotland Act 2009* allowing liability for pleural plaques.
93   [2009] 2 All E.R. 986 (C.A.).
94   See *Lam v. University of British Columbia*, [2010] B.C.J. No. 1259 (C.A.), where a class action by 161 men, whose frozen semen was compromised when a freezer at the University of British Columbia sperm bank shut down without triggering the alarm, was certified.

E. THE DUTY OF CARE

The establishment of a duty of care is an essential element of liability in negligence. It is a question of law which requires the judge to determine if the defendant is under a legal obligation to exercise reasonable care in favour of the plaintiff This has proved to be a difficult and contentious task and in the course of the last hundred years a variety of approaches have been utilized.

Prior to the decision in *Donoghue v. Stevenson*,[95] courts approached this task by examining the particular relationship between the defendant and the plaintiff in the light of prior authority and the surrounding circumstances, and by declaring whether or not a duty of care was owed by the defendant. This incremental process of examination and classification provided guidance in respect of those relationships that had been the subject of judicial consideration, but it provided no underlying or unifying principle for application to future cases.

In 1932 the famous case of *Donoghue v. Stevenson* was decided. The plaintiff, Mrs. Donoghue, alleged that she visited a café with a friend who purchased for her an opaque bottle of ginger beer manufactured by the defendant, Stevenson. She poured some of it into a glass with ice cream and drank it. When the remainder of the ginger beer was poured into the glass, the decomposed remains of a snail floated out. She became ill as a consequence of drinking the adulterated ginger beer. The plaintiff had no claim for breach of contract because she had not purchased the ginger beer. She sued in negligence. The defendant argued that he owed no duty of care to the plaintiff.[96] The House of Lords disagreed. In a majority decision, it held that a manufacturer of products does owe a duty to the ultimate consumer to take reasonable care to prevent defects in its products which are likely to cause damage to person or property. This finding alone was sufficient to establish *Donoghue* as a products' liability case of first importance.[97] Its fame was secured

---

95 *M'Alister (or Donoghue) v. Stevenson*, [1932] A.C. 562 (H.L.) [*Donoghue*].

96 The case was litigated on this preliminary question of law. After this litigation, the case was settled. There was no trial to determine the truth of the plaintiff's allegations. It is not uncommon in novel cases for the defendant to attempt to derail the plaintiff's case by means of a pretrial motion attacking the plaintiff's pleadings on the ground that the defendant did not owe the plaintiff any duty of care. The plaintiff will not, however, be "driven from the judgment seat" if she has some chance of success. The defendant must establish that it is "plain and obvious" that the statement of claim discloses no cause of action, see *Hunt v. Carey Canada Inc.*, [1990] 2 S.C.R. 959.

97 After *Donoghue*, for example, a defendant (manufacturer) could not argue that a *contract* with a third party (retailer) was the exclusive repository of its civil obligations.

by a passage of Lord Atkin's judgment where he attempted to formulate a general conception of relationships which gives rise to a duty of care. It is known as the *neighbour* principle. He stated:

> The rule that you are to love your neighbour becomes in law, you must not injure your neighbour; and the lawyer's question, Who is my neighbour? receives a restricted reply. You must take reasonable care to avoid acts or omissions which you can reasonably foresee would be likely to injure your neighbour. Who, then, in law is my neighbour? The answer seems to be — persons who are so closely and directly affected by my act that I ought reasonably to have them in contemplation as being so affected when I am directing my mind to the acts or omissions which are called in question.[98]

In the last sentence of this passage, two intersecting ideas are identified as pertinent to establishing a duty of care. There is the notion of a *close and direct relationship*, which is captured by the word *proximity* used later in Lord Atkin's judgment, and the idea of *contemplation* or *foreseeability* of damage to the plaintiff. It is not immediately apparent from the judgment if the concept of close and direct relationship (from which foreseeability of harm is an ancillary consequence) is the ultimate touchstone of a duty of care or whether the reasonable foreseeability or contemplation of damage is the defining criterion of a sufficiently close and direct relationship. This ambiguity is reflected in many subsequent judgments addressing the duty issue. Lord Atkin probably wished to emphasize the former, but after *Donoghue* the tendency of Canadian courts was to interpret the neighbour principle as requiring the foreseeability of harm to the plaintiff as the primary touchstone of duty of care. The terms *neighbourhood*, *foreseeability*, and *proximity* were seen as largely interchangeable.

The neighbour principle ushered in an unprecedented expansion of negligence liability which, in the course of the twentieth century, drew a wide range of persons, activities, and kinds of damage within the scope of the obligation of care. The duty of care was not, however, resolved simply on the issue of foreseeability. If that was the case, there would be little to distinguish it from the standard of care analysis, in which foreseeability plays such a central role. Duty of care plays a much more sophisticated role in negligence law. It is the primary instrument of control over the extent of negligence liability. Consequently, consideration must be given to public policy and whether or not the recognition of a legal obligation to exercise care in favour of the plaintiff is

---

98   *Donoghue*, above note 95 at 580.

in the best interests of society. Quite simply, a court must be convinced that the imposition of a duty of care on the defendant is a good idea. For example, the incompetence of a judge may cause foreseeable damage to a litigant and poor parenting may foreseeably contribute to a person's lack of self-esteem, but the courts have not recognized an actionable duty of care in either situation. Factors such as the independence of the judiciary, the integrity of the appeal structure, and the discretionary nature of judicial decision making all support a judicial immunity from a suit in negligence, and the potentially adverse impact on family relationships, the lack of a societal consensus over the way in which children should be raised, and causation and loss assessment problems caution against imposing liability on parents for the personality impairments of their children.

Until the latter part of the twentieth century, however, the assessment of policy factors was often hidden behind a façade of conclusionary statements about foreseeability. Judges were reluctant to openly acknowledge the controlling function of policy analysis and their role in evaluating the needs of society.

In 1977 Lord Wilberforce in *Anns v. Merton London Borough Council*[99] changed all of this. He called for a two-stage analysis of the duty of care issue, which separated the consideration of foreseeability from the policy assessment of societal need. He stated:

> First one has to ask whether, as between the alleged wrongdoer and the person who has suffered damage there is a sufficient relationship of proximity or neighbourhood such that, in the reasonable contemplation of the former, carelessness on his part may be likely to cause damage to the latter—in which case a prima facie duty of care arises. Secondly, if the first question is answered affirmatively, it is necessary to consider whether there are any considerations which ought to negative, or to reduce or limit the scope of the duty or the class of person to whom it is owed or the damages to which a breach of may give rise.[100]

The Supreme Court of Canada adopted the *Anns* dictum in *Neilson v. Kamloops (City of)*[101] and applied it consistently in a number of important cases from 1984 to 2001.

The first stage of the *Anns/Kamloops* test was interpreted as requiring no more than reasonable foreseeability of damage to the plaintiff

---

99 [1978] A.C. 728 (H.L.) [*Anns*].
100 *Ibid.* at 751–52.
101 [1984] 2 S.C.R. 2 [*Kamloops*].

and rarely created problems for the courts. The second branch of the test invited a full and open debate about the societal costs and benefits of recognizing a duty of care. It not only allowed the *prima facie* duty of care to be negated on policy grounds, but also allowed the duty to be restricted or modified to meet policy concerns. For example, before a duty would be recognized, the courts could demand that some additional element be found in the relationship, such as reliance by the plaintiff, an assumption of responsibility by the defendant, a specially close relationship, or some other element that defined the relationship more closely than foreseeability.

The *Anns/Kamloops* test reinvigorated the expansionary trends in negligence law in two ways. First, it created a presumption of a duty of care in all relationships giving rise to a reasonable foreseeability of damage to the plaintiff. Second, it placed on the defendant the unenviable, and sometimes considerable, burden of persuading the court that the plaintiff did not deserve to be protected from his negligent conduct. Because of its expansionary tendencies, the *Anns* dictum quickly fell out of favour with the English courts. They adopted a much more conservative, incremental approach that relies on the gradual extension of prior authority and an assessment of whether the proposed duty is fair, just, and reasonable.

It was not until the beginning of the twenty-first century that the Supreme Court of Canada turned away from *Anns/Kamloops* and reformulated the test of duty of care in a manner that was reflective of the concerns that motivated the English courts. The leading decision is *Cooper v. Hobart*.[102] The issue was whether the defendant Registrar of Mortgage Brokers in British Columbia was under a duty of care to investors who had suffered financial losses caused by the wrongdoing of a mortgage broker. The plaintiffs argued that the defendant was aware of serious wrongdoing on the part of the broker in August 1996, but failed to notify the plaintiffs that the broker was under investigation, and failed to suspend the broker's license until October 1997. According to the plaintiffs, if the defendant had acted more expeditiously, their losses would have been avoided or lessened. The Supreme Court held that the defendant did not owe a private duty of care to the investors. In a unanimous judgment, the Court outlined the correct approach to the duty of care issue. First, it is necessary to decide if the case falls within any recognized category of relationships where a duty

---

102 [2001] 3 S.C.R. 537 [*Cooper*]. The Court adopted the same approach in the companion decision *Edwards v. Law Society of Upper Canada* (2001), 206 D.L.R. (4th) 211 (S.C.C.).

of care has previously been recognized or if it is closely analogous to a recognized category. In those circumstances, a *prima facie* duty of care may be posited. If the case falls outside an established category, a modified *Anns/Kamloops* test is to be applied. The Court articulated a three-stage test for the "novel" case. First, foreseeability of damage to the plaintiff remains an essential element of a duty of care but it is not sufficient in itself to establish a *prima facie* duty of care. Second, there must be a proximate relationship between the parties. For Lord Wilberforce, foreseeability and proximity were one and the same. The Supreme Court now views them as distinct concepts. Proximity focuses on both the "closeness and directness" of the relationship between the parties and on *broad* policy factors to determine, overall, whether it is fair and just to impose a duty of care. A *prima facie* duty of care is established when foreseeability *and* proximity have been established. The third stage (stage two in *Anns*) involves a consideration of *residual* policy factors. Residual policy factors are not concerned with the relationship between the parties. They are concerned with the impact of the proposed duty of care on other legal obligations, the legal system, and on society generally.[103] The Court concluded that in *Cooper* there was insufficient proximity between the defendant and the plaintiffs to find a *prima facie* duty of care and that conclusion was supported by residual policy factors, including the nature of the defendant's statutory function and the risk of indeterminate liability.[104]

The Court anticipated that the new *Anns/Cooper* test would not lead to any significant change in Canadian negligence law. Indeed, no prior decision of the Supreme Court was reversed or criticized and the Court approved the incremental extension of those authorities to analogous circumstances. Nevertheless, *Cooper*, with its emphasis on relational proximity, has had a chilling effect on the expansionary tendencies of modern negligence law. Consequently, some further discussion of the various stages of the *Anns/Cooper*[105] test may be useful.

---

103 For a very useful discussion of *Cooper*, see L. Klar, "Foreseeability, Proximity and Policy" (2002) 25 Advocates' Q. 360.

104 *Cooper* is discussed in more detail in chapter 3.

105 There is a great deal of unevenness in both the name given to the current test for a novel case and the number of steps involved. The names include *Anns*, *Anns/Kamloops*, *Cooper*, and *Cooper/Anns*. It is sometimes described as a two-stage test, sometimes as a two-stage test in which stage one has two elements and sometimes as a three-stage test. None of this is of any substantive consequence. In a series of cases decided since *Cooper* (*Odhavji Estate*) v. *Woodhouse*, [2003] 3 S.C.R. 263, *Young v. Bella*, [2006] 1 S.C.R. 108, *Childs v. Desormeaux*, [2006] 1 S.C.R. 643 [*Childs*], *Hill v. Hamilton-Wentworth Regional Police Services Board*, [2007] S.C.R. No. 41 [*Hill*], *Design Services Ltd. v. Canada*, [2008] S.C.J. No. 22

1) Categories

The Supreme Court recognized that there are certain categories of cases where the courts have recognized a duty of care. Several were listed in *Cooper*. If the posited duty falls within a recognized category or is closely analogous to a recognized category, a *prima facie* duty of care is owed. This reflects the conventional common law process of incremental extension of the law to new situations that are "legally proximate" to earlier authorities. *Cooper* emphasizes the need for a more rigorous examination of the existing authorities and a more careful examination of the extent to which the law must be changed in order to accommodate the plaintiff's claim. It is only where the posited duty is clearly "novel" that the further three-step analysis is called for.

2) Foreseeability

The foreseeability requirement of a duty of care is more narrowly focused than the similar inquiry in respect of the standard of care. The essence of negligent conduct is foreseeability of some damage. The essence of a duty of care is foreseeability of damage *to the plaintiff*. Negligence in the common law is a relational concept. A duty of care is not owed to the world. It is owed only to those whom the defendant might reasonably foresee as being adversely affected by his failure to take care. It is not, however, necessary that the particular individual be foreseen so long as he belongs to a *class* of persons who might foreseeably be harmed if care is not taken. Nevertheless, it is an unusual fact situation where the defendant has been guilty of negligent conduct but the plaintiff was not within the scope of the risk created. The famous American case of *Palsgraf v. Long Island R. Co.*[106] is illustrative. In that case, a passenger, carrying a parcel wrapped in newspaper, ran to catch one of the defendant's trains as it was pulling out of the station. He succeeded in scrambling aboard with the help of a guard on the train pulling him in and a guard on the platform pushing him in. Unfortunately, his parcel, which contained fireworks, fell onto the track and exploded. The plaintiff, who was standing many feet away at the other end of the platform, was injured when the force of the explosion knocked over some weigh

---

and *Fullowka v. Pinkerton's of Canada Ltd.*, [2010] S.C.J. No. 5 [*Fullowka*]). The Supreme Court has confirmed that in a novel case consideration of reasonable foreseeability of harm to the plaintiff, a proximate relationship between the parties, and residual policy factors is essential.

106 162 N.E. 99 (N.Y. 1928).

scales that fell onto her.[107] The Court held that the defendant owed no duty of care to her. The guards may have been negligent, and they may reasonably have perceived some risk to the passenger and his parcel, but the plaintiff was beyond the range of foreseeable danger.[108]

3) Proximity

Proximity requires a consideration of *factual* closeness and *policy* factors.

Factual proximity focuses on the nature of the relationship between the defendant and the plaintiff. It was noted earlier that the term "proximity" as initially used by Lord Atkin in *Donoghue* was open to more than one interpretation. The Supreme Court in *Cooper* favoured an interpretation that emphasizes the closeness and directness of the relationship. It invites a consideration of factors that differentiate the relationship between the defendant and the plaintiff from that of the defendant and the rest of the world. Duty is a relational concept and factors which speak to the closeness of the relationship include physical closeness, social closeness, circumstantial closeness, causal closeness, and closeness created by a representation, an assumption of responsibility, reliance, and reasonable expectations.[109] In *Cooper*, proximity in this sense was weak. The registrar had a general statutory power to promote an efficient operation of the mortgage marketplace and to act in the public interest but there was no close and direct relationship with any individual investor.

---

107 The suggestion that fireworks created sufficient force to throw down a weigh scale some considerable distance away imbues the case with an air of unreality. Although these were the facts on which the case was decided, it has been suggested that the more likely scenario was that the exploding fireworks caused a panic and the weigh scale was knocked down in the ensuing stampede. For a useful discussion of *Palsgraf*, see W.L. Prosser, "*Palsgraf* Revisited" (1953–54) 52 Mich. L. Rev. 1.

108 See also *Childs*, above note 105, where the Supreme Court held that a social host of a BYOB party could not have foreseen that a user of the highway might be harmed by a guest driving home from the party and *Newton v. Newton*, [2003] B.C.J. No. 1546 where the British Columbia Court of Appeal held that a reasonable mother could not have foreseen that her two-year-old child would uncharacteristically and unexpectedly jump from the top of an unguarded flight of stairs into the arms of his grandmother, who was ascending the stairs, causing her to fall.

109 Some further guidance as to the meaning of factual proximity can be found in the judgment of McLachlin J. (as she then was) in *Canadian National Railway v. Norsk Pacific Steamship Co.*, [1992] 1 S.C.R. 1021.

Proximity also depends upon policy considerations. These might be referred to as micro-policy factors because they relate to the relationship under consideration rather than broader societal interests. They assist in determining if it is fair and just that the defendant owe a duty of care to the plaintiff. In *Cooper*, for example, it was held that it would not be fair and just to impose a duty of care to a wide range of anonymous investors with whom the registrar had no direct communication.

There can be no doubt that proximity has a central role in the *Anns/ Cooper* test and that most cases will be decided at this stage. Nevertheless, there is no disguising the fact that proximity is an elusive concept which provides little principled guidance as to when in novel cases a *prima facie* duty will be recognized.

4) Residual Policy Factors

Policy considerations also operate on a macro level. These are referred to as residual policy factors, which may negate or limit a *prima facie* duty of care. They include the overall needs and interests of the community at large and the impact of the posited duty of care on other legal obligations and the legal system generally. The defendant carries the burden of persuading the court that the negative policy considerations are not merely speculative. They must be compelling and raise a real potential for negative consequences.[110] Although *Cooper* was decided at the proximity stage, the Court identified the residual policy factors that supported its conclusion that the Registrar owed no duty of care to the plaintiff investors. The public policy and quasi-judicial nature of many of the registrar's functions, the spectre of indeterminate and extensive liability, and the undesirability of allocating private investment losses ultimately to the tax-paying public all dictated caution.

5) Three Categories

Some further insight into the role of duty of care can be gained by a consideration of three of the existing categories of duty of care: the duties of affirmative action, the duty of care owed to rescuers, and the duty to avoid causing psychiatric harm. Such an analysis illustrates the incremental extension of duty of care and exposes the powerful role played by the judicial assessment of the needs of society.

---

110 *Hill*, above note 105 at para. 48.

a) Duties of Affirmative Action

The primary role of negligence law is to oblige people to act in a manner that is not dangerous to others. As a general rule, negligence law does not oblige a person to provide assistance to others, or to confer benefits on them, or to rescue them from situations of danger not of the person's own making. Negligence law dictates that you must not expose people to the risk of injury, not that you must help them. This dichotomy is captured by the terms misfeasance (dangerous conduct) and nonfeasance (the omission to confer a benefit). It is a dichotomy that is deeply rooted in the common law and reflects nineteenth-century judicial policy, which valued individualism, self-sufficiency, minimal governmental intervention in the affairs of its citizens, and the maximization of personal freedom. Affirmative duties to act for the benefit of others in peril were regarded as exclusively within the realm of moral and religious precepts.

Early in the twentieth century, the dichotomy between misfeasance and nonfeasance was applied with considerable rigour. The American case of *Osterlind v. Hill*[111] is illustrative. Osterlind, who was in a state of visible intoxication, rented a canoe from Hill. Shortly afterwards, the canoe overturned. Osterlind clung to the canoe and shouted for help for thirty minutes before he drowned. Hill, who was aware of the situation, ignored Osterlind's cries for help. He was held to have no legal duty to take reasonable steps to rescue the deceased. He had not contributed to the perilous situation in which Osterlind found himself and he was not responsible for his safety. The case is mirrored by the Ontario Court of Appeal decision in *Vanvalkenburg v. Northern Navigation Co.*[112] The Court held that a captain of a ship had no legal duty to rescue an employee who had fallen overboard. In each case, there was reasonable foreseeability of harm if the defendant failed to act but judicial policy was firmly opposed to legal duties of affirmative action.

In the latter part of the twentieth century, judicial policy changed. A heightened concern for personal security, a greater acceptance of collectivist principles evidenced by the development of the welfare state, a greater willingness to translate social and moral obligations into legal obligations, and changing public attitudes and expectations in an increasingly dangerous society encouraged courts to recognize a growing range of duties of affirmative action to assist others in danger and in need of help. Nevertheless, the courts have continued to assert that there is no *general* duty to rescue a person who finds herself in danger

---

111 106 N.E. 301 (Mass. 1928).
112 (1913), 30 O.L.R. 142 (C.A.).

from a source completely unrelated to the defendant. To this extent, the parable of the Good Samaritan continues to portray an ideal standard of conduct for the moral person, not the legal obligation of a reasonable person. The growing number of duties of affirmative action continue, therefore, to be characterized as exceptions to the general principle of no liability for nonfeasance.

The main conceptual vehicle used to extend the range of duties of affirmative action is that of a *special relationship*. A defendant is under a duty of affirmative action if she stands in a special relationship to the plaintiff. The virtue of the concept of a special relationship is that it facilitates an incremental and controlled expansion of the range of affirmative duties on a case-by-case basis. It also allows a judge to answer the "why pick on me?"[113] question. That question is likely to be posed by a defendant who finds herself under an obligation of affirmative action that does not apply to others who knew of the plaintiff's perilous circumstances and were also in a position to help. The answer is, "you [the defendant] are under a duty of affirmative action because, unlike other persons, you have a special relationship with the plaintiff."[114]

A number of special relationships have been recognized for the purposes of establishing a duty of affirmative action. They include contractual and quasi-contractual relationships such as employer and employee; fiduciary relationships such as parent and child; professional relationships such as doctor and patient; relationships of authority, control, and supervision, such as teacher and pupil or custodian and prisoner; the relationship of occupier and visitor; and the relationship between professional rescuers such as firefighters, police, and emergency personnel and citizens in danger. This catalogue of relationships is not exhaustive and it is not closed. In novel cases, courts undertake a scrupulous examination of the relationship under consideration to determine if it exhibits the characteristics that are typical in previously recognized special relationships. These characteristics include any voluntary assumption of responsibility by the defendant for the plaintiff; any authority, control, and supervision the defendant has over the plaintiff; commercial benefits derived by the defendant from the relationship with the plaintiff; close family or personal bonds; any reasonable reliance or dependence by the plaintiff on the defendant; any special expertise the defendant may have in emergency services or rescue operations; the extent of the burden that would be imposed on

---

113 *Stovin v. Wise*, [1996] A.C. 923 (H.L.) at 944, Lord Hoffmann.
114 Tony Weir has captured the point noting, "You may ignore an infant drowning in a pond unless it is your infant, your pond or you are a lifeguard." T. Weir, *Tort Law* (Oxford: Oxford University Press, 2002) at 1.

the defendant; any direct or indirect contribution by the defendant to
the plaintiff's peril; statutory obligations resting on the defendant; and
a comparison of the cost of affirmative action to the defendant with
the extent of the *benefit* it would bestow on the plaintiff. The court will
consider if there is a sufficient number of these factors to differentiate the defendant from other members of the public and to justify the
recognition of a special relationship and the imposition of a duty of
protective care.

A series of Supreme Court decisions illustrates the Court's approach to duties of affirmative action. In *Horsley v. McLaren*[115] the
Court overruled *Vanvalkenburg v. Northern Navigation Co.*[116] and held
that the defendant owner-operator of a pleasure boat is under a legal
duty to take reasonable steps to rescue a passenger who fell overboard
through no fault of the defendant. A number of factors made the relationship special. They included the authority and control that a boat
owner has over his passengers, the implied assumption of responsibility of the boat owner for the safety of his passengers, the trust and reliance that his passengers place in the boat owner, and the expertise and
competence that passengers may reasonably expect of a boat owner.
These factors made the relationship between the boat owner and the
passenger who fell overboard quite different from the relationship between that passenger and fellow passengers or casual observers from
the shore or other vessels. In *Jordan House Ltd. v. Menow*,[117] the Court
began to explore the affirmative duties that bar owners owe to patrons
who become intoxicated on their premises. In that case, the Court imposed a duty of protective care on a defendant bar owner who ejected
an intoxicated patron. The plaintiff patron was hit by an automobile
when he was walking home on a wet, dark, rural highway. The Court
identified a number of factors which supported its conclusion that the
relationship between the defendant and the plaintiff was sufficient to
generate a duty to take reasonable steps to protect the plaintiff from
injury. They included the relationship of commercial host and patron,
the defendant's personal knowledge of the plaintiff, his propensity to
drink to excess, his intoxication when he was ejected, the special dangers that the plaintiff would face when he left the bar, and the fact
that the plaintiff was served alcohol beyond the point of intoxication in
contravention of provincial liquor control legislation and the defendant's own house rules. The bar owner was clearly in a different position

---

115　Above note 27.
116　Above note 112.
117　Above note 36.

from patrons in the bar and members of the public observing an intoxi-cated person in the street. The decision was a narrow one that turned on its unusual facts, but it heralded more extensive responsibilities of affirmative action. In *Crocker v. Sundance Northwest Resorts Ltd.*,[118] the defendant owned a ski resort. He organized a contest involving racing down mogulled ski slopes on large inflated inner tubes. The plaintiff, who was visibly intoxicated, took part in the race and was rendered a quadriplegic when he fell off his tube. The Court imposed a duty to take reasonable steps to prevent the plaintiff from participating in the contest even though the defendant had supplied only a small amount of the liquor consumed by him. It stressed the authority and control that the defendant had over the race, the inherent danger in the contest, the defendant's knowledge of the plaintiff's incapacity, the defendant's commercial and promotional interest in the contest, and the height-ened danger of racing when intoxicated. These factors made the rela-tionship sufficiently special to generate a duty of affirmative action on the defendant. Both *Jordan House* and *Crocker* were cases where the in-toxicated person was injured. It was not, therefore, surprising that the Supreme Court extended the duty of care to an innocent third person who was injured by an intoxicated person after he left the defendant's drinking establishment. In *Stewart v. Pettie*,[119] the Court recognized a duty to third parties in respect of the conduct of a person who had drunk to excess on the defendant's premises. The duty arises from the relationship of commercial host and customer and the foreseeability of harm to innocent third persons such as users of the highway. The duty is to take reasonable steps to control the conduct of the intoxi-cated customer or, in some other way, to protect innocent persons.[120] In *Childs v. Desormeaux*,[121] however, the Court held that the *social* hosts of a private BYOB party do not owe a duty of care to members of the public injured as a consequence of an intoxicated guest's operation of a motor vehicle on leaving the party. The Court utilized, for the first time in the field of duties of affirmative action, the *Anns/Cooper* test. It found that the posited duty was novel being insufficiently analogous to the duty of a commercial host established in *Stewart*[122] and, since neither

---

118 [1988] 1 S.C.R. 1186 [*Crocker*].

119 [1995] 1 S.C.R. 131 [*Stewart*].

120 In *Stewart*, the Court found that reasonable care had been taken.

121 *Childs*, above note 105.

122 The Court pointed out that social hosts are not subject to statutory regulations and responsibilities, that they have a limited capacity to monitor their guests' consumption of alcohol and that there is no contractual link between hosts and their guests.

the foreseeability nor proximity elements of the *Anns/Cooper* test were established, there was no duty of affirmative action. The Court was not willing to find on the facts that a reasonable person hosting a party at which liquor is consumed ought reasonably to have foreseen danger to users of the highway,[123] and in the absence of any reliance upon the social hosts to control their guests, or any reasonable expectation that they would do so, there was no special relationship or nexus to create the degree of proximity between the parties necessary to give rise to a duty of affirmative action.[124]

Although the Court held that there was no duty in *Childs* it did offer the opinion that the existing cases recognizing duties of affirmative action fall into three broad classes. First, there are those cases such as *Crocker* where the defendants intentionally invite third parties to an inherent or obvious risk that they have created or to which they have contributed. Second, there are cases where there are paternalistic relationships of supervision and control producing an imbalance of power and vulnerability, as in the parent-child relationship. Third, there are cases such as *Jordan House* where the defendants offer services to the general public that include attendant responsibilities to act with special care to minimize risk to the users of those services. The Court clarified the role of this classification of cases in *Fullowka v. Pinkerton's of Canada Ltd.*[125] In that case the defendant Pinkerton's had been retained by a mine owner to maintain security and to protect replacement workers during a bitter, and at times violent, strike of its miners. A rogue striker trespassed into the mine and planted a bomb which exploded, killing nine replacement miners. The Court held that the defendant owed a duty of affirmative action to the deceased miners.[126] The Court indicated that the three classes of cases identified in *Childs* are not strict legal categories. They provide some synthesis of the cases at a high level

---

123 On this point the Court gave weight to the special facts of the case rather than merely asking if the reasonable host of a party ought to foresee harm to the plaintiff if care is not taken, a question that would appear to beg for a positive answer.

124 It is likely that the Court would extend the immunity in *Childs* where the plaintiff is a guest rather than an innocent third party but there will be both exceptions and borderline cases where a duty of affirmative action will be imposed. One possible exception is where the host continues to serve a visibly intoxicated guest knowing that he will drive home. Borderline cases include situations where employers hold office parties, see *Hunt (Guardian of) v. Sutton Group Incentive Realty Inc.*, [2002] O.J. No. 3109 (C.A.), and social hosts supply alcohol to minors, see *Dryden (Litigation guardian of) v. Campbell Estate*, [2001] O.J. No. 829 (S.C.J.).

125 *Fullowka*, above note 105.

126 The Court found that the defendant was not in breach of the standard of care.

of abstraction and they identify relevant factors in determining if there is sufficient proximity to support a duty of care. In *Fullowka*, the Court relied on a wide range of factors to support a duty of affirmative action including the reasonable expectation of the miners that the defendant would take reasonable care to secure their safety, the undertaking by the defendant to protect persons and property and control the danger posed by the strikers, the reliance of the replacement workers on the defendant, and that they were a well defined and identifiable group.[127] *Fullowka* is, therefore, consistent with the conventional approach of carefully scrutinizing the nature of the relationship between the parties to determine if it is sufficiently special or proximate to warrant a duty of affirmative action.

There are two further situations that are likely to generate duties of affirmative action. The first relates to defendants who are under no initial or threshold duty to rescue but who, nevertheless, voluntarily embark on a course of conduct designed to assist a person in danger. There is little direct Canadian authority on the nature of the defendants' obligations in such circumstances. Three views compete for recognition. The first suggests that it is inappropriate to impose any obligation. To do so would place a person who has acted in a selfless and altruistic way in a worse position than a person who was heedless of another's distress and did nothing. The second view is that the defendant's liability should be restricted to circumstances where he has made the plaintiff's position worse, either by causing additional damage or by abandoning a rescue attempt after the commencement of it led other potential and willing rescuers to turn away. The third view is that the usual duty of care attaches to the defendant as soon as he commences a rescue. There is some judicial support for the second view,[128] but the third view, calling for the imposition of a duty of care once the voluntary actions have commenced, is more consistent with modern trends of negligence law.[129] This certainly appears to be the as-

---

127 The Court also held that the government mine inspectors were under a duty of care to the deceased miners.

128 See, for example, *Zelenko v. Gimbel Bros. Inc.*, 287 N.Y.S. 134 (Sup. Ct. 1935), aff'd 287 N.Y.S. 136 (App. Div. 1935).

129 This is particularly so where there is an established pattern of protective conduct on which others have placed reasonable reliance, such as the operation of railway crossing gates, aircraft landing lights, and marine and freshwater beacons. See also *Goodwin v. Goodwin*, [2007] B.C.J. No. 242 (C.A.). In that case the defendant highway contractor was informed by the RCMP that there was black ice on a section of a particular road. The defendant undertook to send out a crew to deal with it but failed to do so. The plaintiff was injured when a truck in which she was a passenger slid on the black ice and left the road. Albeit that the defendant's

sumption or premise underlying the spate of Good Samaritan statutes that have been passed in most provinces.[130] The statutes address the concern that the imposition of a duty of care on voluntary rescuers may create a significant disincentive to altruistic conduct. Particular concern was expressed about the reluctance of health-care professionals to stop and assist at roadside accidents for fear of legal liability. The Good Samaritan legislation seeks to remedy this impediment to rescue by restricting the potential liability of a volunteer to acts of gross negligence or recklessness, thereby removing any inhibitions they may have about rescuing because of the fear of legal liability. Some Acts apply to certain health-care professionals. Some apply to all rescuers.

The second situation arises where the defendant, *without fault*, has created a dangerous situation. It is not unreasonable to expect the creator of the peril to take reasonable steps to abate it, to warn of the danger, or to alert the appropriate authorities of it. For example, a danger may be created on a highway without negligence. Quite apart from statutory obligations, the creator of a danger has a special responsibility to protect other users of the highway.[131]

The significant development and expansion of affirmative duties of care have given rise to some debate and criticism. On the one hand, it is argued that the growth of affirmative duties unduly restricts personal freedom, unduly de-emphasizes personal self-sufficiency and responsibility, improperly substitutes legal compulsion for moral duties, and imprudently creates a slippery slope towards enforcing charitable conduct in favour of those who suffer misfortune. On the other hand, there are those who believe that the current law does not go far enough and that a humane and compassionate society should, at a minimum,

---

contractual obligation to maintain certain highways did not extend to the road in question it had voluntarily assumed responsibility to abate the danger and owed a duty of care to the plaintiff as a member of the driving public.

130 See Alberta *Emergency Medical Aid Act*, R.S.A. 1980, c. E-9; British Columbia *Good Samaritan Act*, R.S.B.C., 1996, c. 172; Manitoba *Good Samaritan Protection* Act, S.M. 2006, c. 38. Newfoundland and Labrador *Emergency Medical Aid Act*, R.S.N.L. 1990, c. E-9; Northwest Territories *Emergency Medical Aid Act*, R.S.N.W.T. 1988, c. E-4; Nova Scotia *Volunteer Services Act*, R.S.N.S. 1989, c. 497; Nunavut *Emergency Medical Aid Act*, R.S.N.W.T. (Nu.) 1988, c. E-4; Prince Edward Island *Volunteers Liability Act*, R.S.P.E.I. 1994, c. 65; Saskatchewan *Emergency Medical Aid Act*, R.S.S. 1978, c. E-8; and Yukon Territory *Emergency Medical Aid Act*, R.S.Y. 1986, c. 52. This legslation is discussed in M. McInnes, "Good Samaritan Statutes: A Summary and Analysis" (1992) 26 U.B.C.L. Rev. 239.

131 A common situation is where a motorist without negligence hits and kills a moose or deer. If the body of the animal is blocking the highway reasonable steps must be taken to protect other highway users. See *Fajardo v. Horianopoulos*, 2006 BCSC 147.

impose a duty of risk-free rescue on every citizen to fellow citizens in situations of acute physical danger.[132]

The courts have used the concept of a special relationship to pursue a middle path that is reflective of the unresolved tension in Canadian society between rugged individualism and self-sufficiency and collect-ive security and compassionate responsibility for fellow citizens.

b) The Duty Owed to Rescuers

The issue of liability to a rescuer arises where the defendant, A, has negligently placed B or herself in a position of danger and C, the plain-tiff, is injured or killed in the course of a rescue attempt. The changing judicial attitude to rescuers vividly illustrates the profound influence of judicial policy on the duty of care issue. At the turn of the twenti-eth century, the courts had little sympathy for rescuers. The policies of laissez-faire liberalism and personal self-sufficiency that supported the misfeasance/nonfeasance dichotomy also supported the view that rescuers were meddlesome interlopers and authors of their own misfor-tune. A variety of legal reasons could be produced to reject the claims of rescuers, including that there was no duty of care on the grounds that the rescuer was unforeseeable, that the chain of causation was broken by the wilful act of the rescuer, or that the rescuer had consented to the injury. The twentieth century witnessed a spectacular reversal in judi-cial attitudes to rescuers. The courts now encourage altruistic conduct by protecting rescuers from virtually all losses arising from the rescue attempt. The rescuer has become one of the heroes of the common law and an action brought by a rescuer rarely fails.[133]

The modern view has been captured by the words of Lord Den-ning in *Videan v. British Transport Commission*.[134] In a passage that has received the approval of the Supreme Court,[135] he said:

> It seems to me that, if a person *by his fault* creates a situation of peril, he must answer for it to any person who attempts to rescue the person who is in danger. He owes a duty to such a person above all others.

---

132 In Quebec, for example, s. 2 of the *Charter of Human Rights and Freedoms*, R.S.Q., c. C-12 states: "Every person must come to the aid of anyone whose life is in peril, either personally, or calling for aid, by giving him the necessary and immediate physical assistance, unless it involves danger to himself or a third person, or has another valid reason."

133 This is not merely a legal phenomenon. Rescuers routinely are featured sym-pathetically in any media coverage of the event and often receive medals from government.

134 [1963] 2 Q.B. 650 (C.A.) [*Videan*].

135 *McLaren*, above note 27 at 444.

The rescuer may act instinctively out of humanity or deliberately out of courage. But whichever it is, so long as it is not wanton interference, if the rescuer is killed or injured in the attempt, he can recover damages *from the one whose fault has been the cause of it*.[136]

This policy is promoted by a generous interpretation of reasonable foreseeability in favour of finding a duty of care to rescuers. In *Corothers v. Slobodian*,[137] for example, a rescuer who left the site of an automobile accident caused by the defendant's negligence and ran down the highway seeking assistance was held to have a good claim against the defendant when she was hit by an oncoming vehicle. The rescuer of a trespassing child on a railway track has been held to be foreseeable,[138] although the Court admitted that the child rescued was unforeseeable,[139] and in *Urbanski v. Patel*[140] the defendant surgeon, who negligently removed the only kidney of the plaintiff's daughter, was held liable for the damage arising from the unsuccessful kidney transplant from the plaintiff to his daughter on the ground that the plaintiff donor was a rescuer. It is, indeed, hard to imagine a situation where a rescuer would not be held to be foreseeable. It is true that conventional principles suggest that a wanton, rash, or reckless rescue may be outside the scope of reasonable foresight, but there appears to be no case where a plaintiff's claim has failed solely on that ground.

It has also been held that the rescuer's claim is independent from that of the imperilled person. Consequently, the claim of a rescuer cannot be denied because the defendant owes no duty of care to the imperilled person or because the defendant has a valid defence against any claim made by the imperilled person. Furthermore, persons who, as a consequence of their own negligence, place themselves in positions of peril owe a duty of care to their rescuers.

The generosity of the courts to rescuers does not, however, extend to dispensing with the requirement of fault on the part of the defendant. In the Supreme Court decision in *Horsley v. McLaren*,[141] the defendant was the owner-operator of a pleasure boat. A passenger, Matthews, fell overboard. After an unsuccessful attempt by the defendant to rescue

---

136 *Videan*, above note 134 at 669 [emphasis added].

137 (1974), [1975] 2 S.C.R. 633.

138 *Videan*, above note 134.

139 Lord Justice Denning finessed this lack of consistency on the grounds that it was not necessary to foresee the actual emergency as long as it was foreseeable that some sort of an emergency might arise and that someone might come to the rescue.

140 (1978), 84 D.L.R. (3d) 650 (Man. Q.B.).

141 Above note 27.

Matthews, another passenger, Horsley, dived to the rescue. Both passengers died. The action by the Horsley family raised the unusual scenario of a first rescuer being sued by the family of a second rescuer. It was argued that the defendant had prolonged or exacerbated the danger to Matthews, thereby inducing Horsley to attempt a rescue. The Court was of the view that liability could be imposed only if the first rescue was conducted *negligently*. The majority held that the defendant had made a mistake in his choice of rescue technique but he was not negligent.[142]

It should also be noted that arguments by the defendant based on the ultimate futility of the rescue or on the contributory negligence of the plaintiff are not likely to succeed. The futility of the rescue is not a defence. It is the reasonable perception of the rescuer that is important, not the certainty of hindsight that the imperilled person was beyond help. Consequently, liability may be imposed even though the person being rescued was already dead. Contributory negligence is difficult to establish because rescue usually involves instinctive and spontaneous action where risk to one's own safety is unavoidable. That is the reason why rescuers are held in such high regard. In *McLaren*, for example, the dissenting judge, who would have imposed liability, declined to find contributory negligence even though Horsley had worn no life jacket and did not use a lifeline.[143]

In all probability, rescuers are statistically neither more nor less likely to intervene today than they were early in the twentieth century. The change that has taken place in the law of negligence reflects changes in judicial policy, not in the factual foreseeability of rescuers.[144]

---

142 There is no Canadian authority on whether or not "professional rescuers" such as firefighters and paramedics may sue if they are harmed attending an emergency arising from the defendant's negligence. American jurisprudence rejects such claims under the aptly named "fireman's rule." The contrary view has been adopted by the House of Lords in *Ogwo v. Taylor*, [1988] A.C. 431 (H.L.). The dearth of claims in Canada may be due to the fact that professional rescuers are covered by the provincial workers compensation schemes, although tort claims may be made against defendants who are not employers or employees covered by the scheme.

143 A duty may also be owed to those who rescue property imperilled by the defendant's negligence. There may, however, be a greater willingness to find that a rescuer of property has acted wantonly or rashly or has been guilty of contributory negligence.

144 One policy underlying and uniting both the duties of affirmative action and the duty of care owed to a rescuer is the judicial approval and desire to promote altruistic conduct. Negligence law uses both the carrot (protection of rescuers from harm arising in a rescue attempt) and the stick (duties to rescue).

c) Psychiatric Injury (Nervous Shock)

The courts have used the concept of duty of care to keep liability for psychiatric injury on a tight rein. The judicial approach to psychiatric injury is cautious and conservative and reflects a pro-defendant inclination that seems out of step with the expansionary trends of modern negligence law. The primary reason for the slow recognition of psychiatric injury claims is the fear of unleashing a flood of litigation. This concern may be illustrated with reference to a car accident caused by the defendant's negligence. So long as liability is confined to losses arising from death, bodily injury, and property damage, the pool of potential plaintiffs is kept within tolerable limits. A recognition of psychiatric injury expands the pool of potential plaintiffs significantly. It may include bystanders who witnessed the accident, persons rendering assistance to the injured persons, and family members, friends, and acquaintances who suffer some degree of emotional trauma upon learning of the death or injury of a loved one or friend. Entertaining large numbers of minor and remote psychiatric claims threatens to impose an unreasonable burden on defendants and increase liability insurance premiums, particularly in the rate-sensitive field of motor-vehicle insurance. Judicial apprehension about large numbers of claims is intensified by the prospect of mass disasters such as aircraft crashes, train disasters, massive chemical fires, nuclear accidents, and the failure of crowd control at major sporting events, all of which may generate, in addition to personal injury and death, extensive psychiatric injury.

The cautious approach to psychiatric injury is not, however, explained solely by the fear of opening the floodgates. The processing of psychiatric injury claims also presents some technical challenges. It has been suggested, for example, that psychiatric injury claims may be more easily fabricated, thus requiring special vigilance against fraud. Furthermore, there are difficulties sorting out whether or not a psychiatric injury or illness arises from the life experience and the constitutional make-up of the plaintiff or from the conduct of the defendant. These arguments, however, probably underestimate the acumen of judges and the reliability of expert psychiatric evidence.

There may also be cultural reasons contributing to the resistance to claims for psychiatric injury. The stigma of mental illness has not been removed from society. Mental illness can produce a visceral discomfort, born of ignorance and anxiety, which may result in a lack of compassion and sensitivity to the serious and debilitating consequences of it. The judicial process cannot be totally immunized from stubborn cultural biases.

All of these factors contribute to the current state of the law of negligence in respect of psychiatric injury, which limits recovery to the most serious kinds of psychiatric damage in narrow circumstances. This conservative judicial policy towards psychiatric claims is implemented both by a narrow definition of recoverable psychiatric loss and by heavy restrictions on the scope of the duty of care to avoid such loss.

There is no liability for any psychiatric injury unless it satisfies the legal concept of *nervous shock*. Nervous shock is defined as a severe emotional trauma that manifests itself in a physical disorder or in a recognizable psychiatric illness such as clinical depression or post-traumatic stress disorder. It does not include emotional upset, mental distress, grief, sorrow, anxiety, worry, or other transient and more minor psychiatric injury. Consequently, the severe emotional distress caused to surviving passengers on a ferry that sank after hitting a reef,[145] and the grief and sorrow of family members following the death of a loved one[146] were not sufficient to ground liability. The line between nervous shock as conventionally defined and severe emotional distress is not an easy one to draw, and there is some unevenness in the judicial interpretation of nervous shock. Some additional uncertainty was introduced by the Supreme Court decision in *Mustapha v. Culligan of Canada Ltd.*[147] In that case, the Court departed from the conventional terminology and spoke of the need for proof of harm which is "*serious and prolonged* and rise[s] above . . . ordinary annoyances, anxieties and fears."[148] It is unlikely, however, that the Court intended to modify conventional doctrine since the seriousness of the harm was not at issue, the point was not dealt with directly or fully, and conventional authority was cited with approval.[149] In its recent decision in *Healey v. Lakeridge Health Corp.*,[150] the Ontario Court of Appeal was not persuaded that any change in the law was intended. In its view, a modification of the requirement of a recognizable psychiatric illness was not to be

---

145 See *Kotai v. Queen of the North (The)*, [2009] B.C.J. No. 2022 (S.C.). [*Kotai*] where the judge conducted a scrupulous examination of the claims of a number of passengers and concluded, on the basis of extensive expert psychiatric testimony, that most of the plaintiffs had not suffered a recognizable psychiatric illness.

146 *Devji v. Burnaby (District of)* (1999), 129 B.C.A.C. 161 (C.A.) [*Devji*].

147 2008 SCC 27 [*Mustapha*].

148 *Ibid.* at para. 9 [emphasis added].

149 One advantage of retaining the need to prove a recognizable psychiatric illness is that the issue is resolved largely on the evidence of expert witnesses rather than judicial opinion of what is "serious and prolonged."

150 [2011] O.J. No. 231.

assumed in the absence of an extensive consideration of the long line of consistent authority and the pertinent policy factors.[151]

The defendant must also be responsible for an event that would foreseeably produce nervous shock in the person of average psychological resilience. No recovery is permitted if the injury is triggered by an abnormal sensitivity on the part of the plaintiff or a predisposition to psychiatric harm. In *Vanek v. Great Atlantic & Pacific Co. of Canada*[152] an eleven-year-old girl suffered a minor stomach upset as a consequence of drinking contaminated grape nectar manufactured by the defendant. She made a quick and complete recovery. Nevertheless, her parents became obsessed with the incident, unreasonably feared for their child's health, and suffered psychiatric injury. The Ontario Court of Appeal held that the parents were particularly hypersensitive and lacked reasonable fortitude. This requirement was also a central issue in *Mustapha*.[153] In that case the plaintiff suffered nervous shock when he discovered a dead fly in a bottle of water supplied by the defendant even though he discovered the fly before he or other members of his family consumed any of the water. The Supreme Court concluded that it could not be foreseen that such harm would be suffered by "a person of ordinary fortitude."[154]

The main control device on the extent of recovery for psychiatric injury is, however, the duty of care.[155] The cases can be loosely divided between those where the conduct of the defendant had a direct and primary impact on the plaintiff's psychological well-being and those cases where the plaintiff is a secondary or relational victim of conduct that causes death or injury to a third person.

As a general rule, there is less difficulty in dealing with cases where the defendant's conduct has a direct consequence on the plaintiff. The close and direct relationship between the parties allays indeterminacy

---

151 See also *Kotai*, above note 145.

152 [1999] O.J. No. 4599 (C.A.).

153 Above note 147.

154 *Ibid.* at para. 18.

155 Some courts have adopted a remoteness analysis for nervous shock claims. A remoteness analysis may be adopted where the duty of care to the plaintiff can be established independently of any foreseeability of nervous shock. This may arise in two situations. First, the defendant may owe a duty of care because the plaintiff is within the zone of foreseeable personal injury or property loss (*Healey*). Second, the relationship between the parties may fall comfortably within a previously recognized nominate category of duty of care such as manufacturer/consumer (*Mustapha*). The choice of analysis is not likely to produce a different outcome since proof of the foreseeability of nervous shock lies at the heart of both the duty and remoteness rules.

concerns sufficiently to permit the imposition of a duty of care where nervous shock is the reasonably foreseeable consequence of the defendant's conduct.[156] A duty of care may be owed, for example, where the defendant negligently causes nervous shock by directly threatening the plaintiff's safety[157] by supplying grossly adulterated food to the plaintiff;[158] by causing the death of the plaintiff's baby in the course of labour;[159] by exposing the plaintiff (without injury) to phenol, a toxic chemical;[160] or by giving false and shocking information such as a report that the plaintiff or a close family member has died or has been diagnosed with a fatal illness.[161] Public officials may also be liable for nervous shock caused by their negligence. In *Odhavji Estate v. Woodhouse*,[162] for example, the Supreme Court refused to strike out the claim of family members of the deceased who was killed in a police shooting. They alleged that they had suffered nervous shock as a consequence of the failure of the chief of police in Toronto and some of his officers to co-operate and facilitate the work of the Special Investigative Unit whose task it was to investigate the shooting.[163] A more cautious approach has been taken by some courts where the plaintiff has suffered nervous shock as a result of the defendant's negligently or wilfully self-inflicted injuries. In *Nespolon v. Alford*,[164] for example, the Ontario Court of Appeal was not persuaded that the plaintiff's nervous shock was a foreseeable consequence of the defendants' negligence. In that

---

156 In *Page v. Smith*, [1996] 1 A.C. 155, the House of Lords adopted a strict dichotomy between primary and secondary victims. Primary victims, who are characterized as those who were in the range of foreseeable physical harm, do not have to establish a foreseeability of nervous shock. Foreseeability of physical harm is sufficient. The Ontario Court of Appeal in *Mustapha v. Culligan of Canada Ltd.*, [2006] O.J. No. 4964, gave cogent reasons for rejecting this view, preferring to maintain foreseeability of nervous shock as a necessary element in all cases.

157 *Dulieu v. White & Sons*, [1901] 2 K.B. 669 (D.C.).

158 *Curll v. Robin Hood Multifoods Ltd.* (1974), 14 N.S.R. (2d) 252 (S.C.T.D.).

159 *Martin v. Mineral Springs Hospital*, [2001] A.J. No.78 (Q.B.).

160 *Sant v. Jack Andrews Kirkfield Pharmacy Ltd.*, [2002] M.J. No. 30 (Q.B.).

161 See *Drage v. Page*, [2003] B.C.J. No. 64 (S.C.) (erroneous report of pancreatic cancer). But see *Guay v. Sun Publishing Co.*, [1953] 2 S.C.R. 216.

162 [2003] 3 S.C.R. 263.

163 See also *W. v. Essex County Council*, [2001] 2 A.C. 592 where the House of Lords refused to strike out pleadings which alleged that foster parents had suffered nervous shock as a consequence of officials of the local authority, contrary to the express prohibition of the foster parents, placing a fifteen-year-old foster child in their home who had a history of sexual misconduct and who sexually assaulted their biological children.

164 (1998), 40 O.R. (3d) 355 (C.A.). See also *Greatorex v. Greatorex*, [2000] 4 All E.R. 769 (Q.B.).

case, the plaintiff suffered nervous shock when he ran over the defendant, a grossly intoxicated youth who had collapsed on a highway after being let out of a car occupied by two of his friends. It was held that, in the circumstances of the case, the deceased could not reasonably have foreseen the post-traumatic stress suffered by the plaintiff as a consequence of his driving over the deceased.[165]

Courts have also exhibited caution in the "fear of future illness" cases. These are cases where the plaintiff has been negligently exposed to either toxic substances such as asbestos or disease-causing microorganisms such as HIV or Hepatitis C. The harm complained of is not, however, that the plaintiff has contracted an illness, but that she has suffered psychiatric harm from the fear of developing a serious or fatal illness in the future. In *Grieves v. FT Everard & Sons Ltd.*,[166] a case dealing with the exposure to a toxic substance (asbestos), the House of Lords rejected such claims on the basis that there is no liability for anxiety and distress and that claims by those who suffer a recognizable psychiatric illness are unsustainable on the ground that it is not reasonably foreseeable that persons of normal mental fortitude would suffer such harm. A fear of future illness claim was recently addressed by the Ontario Court of Appeal in *Healey*.[167] The case dealt with allegations that the defendant health care facility had negligently exposed the plaintiffs to patients suffering from a contagious disease (tuberculosis). The Court upheld a summary judgment dismissing the claims. It held that a duty of care was owed to the plaintiffs since they were within the range of foreseeable personal injury. The claims failed because none of the plaintiffs suffered any recognizable psychiatric illness.

Many of the cases on nervous shock, however, deal with relational or secondary victims of the defendant's negligence. These cases present more difficult issues and raise severe indeterminacy problems. A relational victim suffers nervous shock as a result of seeing, hearing, or being told of a horrifying and tragic event that was caused by the defendant's negligence and which led to the death or injuries of third persons. The relational victim is usually outside the zone of foreseeable physical injury. In the early part of the twentieth century, the courts did not recognize relational nervous shock claims. This gradually changed, and by the middle of the century the courts declared that a duty of care was owed to those relational claimants that the defendant could reasonably have foreseen might suffer nervous shock as a result of his ac-

---

165 The court also held that the deceased's companions owed no duty of care to the plaintiff.

166 [2007] 4 All E.R. 1047.

167 Above note 150.

tions. It soon became apparent, however, that foreseeability was being interpreted restrictively in these situations. This narrow interpretation of foreseeability suggested, but did not disclose, that some additional arbitrary restraints were at work. A good illustration of the phenomenon is *Abramzik v. Brenner*.[168] In that case, the defendant, who was driving the plaintiff's young children to church, negligently collided with a train. The plaintiff suffered nervous shock when her husband told her about the accident and that two of their children had been killed. The Saskatchewan Court of Appeal concluded that the defendant could not be expected to have foreseen that the plaintiff would suffer nervous shock in such circumstances. This implausible conclusion was asserted without any acknowledgment that factors other than foreseeability were operating to determine whether or not the defendant owed a duty of care to the plaintiff.

Gradually, courts began to articulate that, indeed, a closer proximity than that supplied by foreseeability of shock was needed to establish a duty of care to relational nervous shock victims of the defendant's negligence. The courts began to articulate a number of control mechanisms, including *relational* proximity, *locational* proximity, and *temporal* proximity, and to emphasize the importance of the *nature* and *intensity* of the *horrifying event* that caused the shock. These factors provide an evidential foundation for a finding of a duty of care. Relational proximity emphasizes the bond between the plaintiff and the person who was injured or killed in the accident. Normally, a close family relationship is essential, but other relationships of love and affection may be sufficient.[169] The courts have, however, permitted a claim by a rescuer who suffers nervous shock as a consequence of rescuing strangers injured in a mass disaster.[170] Mere bystanders, friends, and acquaintances are normally not regarded as having sufficient relational proximity and are not owed a duty of care. Locational proximity demands either that the plaintiff was at or close to the scene of the accident or, in what is known as the *aftermath* doctrine, that the plaintiff arrived at the accident site soon after the event. The aftermath doctrine has even been extended by the House of Lords in *McLoughlin v. O'Brian*[171] and by the High Court of

---

168 (1967), 65 D.L.R. (2d) 651 (Sask. C.A.) [*Abramzik*].

169 A great deal of emphasis was given to the importance of close ties of love and affection by the House of Lords in *Alcock v. Chief Constable of the South Yorkshire Police*, [1992] 1 A.C. 310 (H.L.).

170 *Chadwick v. British Transport Commission*, [1967] 1 W.L.R. 912 (Q.B). The House of Lords in *White v. Chief Constable of South Yorkshire*, [1998] 3 W.L.R. 1509 sought to restrict *Chadwick* to situations where the rescuer is in physical danger.

171 [1983] 1 A.C. 410 (H.L.).

Australia in *Jaensch v. Coffey*[172] to cover shock caused when the plaintiffs attended at a hospital and saw members of their immediate family being treated for serious injuries.[173] Generally, there is no recovery for *distant shock* where the plaintiff is informed of the tragic event rather than experiencing it with his own unaided senses. This factor may have been the unarticulated reason for the decision in *Abramzik*, because the plaintiff mother learned of her tragic loss when her husband returned home and told her what had happened. Temporal proximity, which is sometimes known as causal proximity, identifies the need to show that the nervous shock arose directly from the traumatic and tragic event produced by the defendant's negligence and not from a subsequent reaction to the consequences or circumstances that flowed from the event. It seeks to draw a distinction between psychiatric injury caused by the manner in which a person was injured or killed and that which flows from the fact of the injury or death. *Beecham v. Hughes*[174] is illustrative. The plaintiff and his wife were involved in a car accident caused by the negligence of the defendant. The plaintiff's wife suffered serious brain damage. The plaintiff suffered a reactive depression, not from seeing his wife injured, but from his inability to accept and adjust to his wife's permanent disability. The defendant was not liable because the nervous shock did not arise from the direct emotional impact of the accident. The courts are also influenced by the intensity of the event that gave rise to the nervous shock. Foreseeability of nervous shock increases in relationship to the horror of the occasion. No one of these factors is conclusive but they are critically important in establishing the strong proximity necessary to support a duty of care in respect of relational nervous shock.

The leading Canadian decision illustrating the modern approach to the duty of care in relational nervous shock cases is *Rhodes v. Canadian National Railway*.[175] The plaintiff's twenty-three-year-old son was killed in the Hinton train disaster of 1986. She heard about the train crash on the radio at her home in British Columbia. She then travelled to Alberta to discover what had happened to her son, who she knew was on the train. During the next few harrowing days, she came to the realization that her son was dead. She visited the accident site eight days after the crash. The whole experience led to a severe clinical depression. The

---

172 (1984), 155 C.L.R. 549 (H.C.A.).

173 The "aftermath" doctrine was not applied in *Devji* above note 146, where close relatives were summoned to a hospital some hours after the accident to view and identify an appropriately prepared body.

174 (1988), 52 D.L.R. (4th) 625 (B.C.C.A).

175 (1989), 75 D.L.R. (4th) 248 (B.C.C.A.).

British Columbia Court of Appeal concluded that the defendant was not liable. The defendant did not owe her a duty of care. The relational proximity was strong (mother and son) but locational proximity was weak since the plaintiff did not see the accident or its immediate aftermath. Temporal or causal proximity was also weak. The plaintiff's depression did not arise directly from the shock of the accident but from the subsequent grief and sorrow flowing from the death of her child.

Although *Rhodes* preceded *Cooper v. Hobart*[176] the emphasis on proximity is consistent with the *Anns/Cooper* test. *Joudrey v. Swissair Transport Co.*[177] is illustrative. The plaintiff, a member of the Canadian Armed Forces, suffered psychiatric harm as a consequence of his involvement in the recovery of aircraft debris and human remains after the crash of Swissair Flight 111 off the coast of Nova Scotia. The Court characterized the case as novel and concluded that the Swissair did not owe a duty of care to the plaintiff. There was neither foreseeability that a member of the Armed Forces would suffer psychiatric harm nor sufficient proximity since the plaintiff had no personal relationship with any of the deceased passengers nor was he near the crash site when the aircraft crashed.

Few observers would claim that negligence law in respect of psychiatric injury is in a satisfactory state. The policies driving the law in this area are clear but there has been a failure to translate that policy into principles that are clear, fair, and rational. The use of largely arbitrary proximity devices to limit recovery by relational victims is bound to produce unpredictable and uneven adjudication. The current law may also reflect an over-reaction to the dangers of psychiatric injury claims. So long as the requirement of nervous shock, or even serious emotional distress, is maintained, liability is not likely to explode exponentially if conventional negligence doctrine is applied.[178]

---

176 Above note 102.

177 [2004] N.S.J. No. 268 (S.C.).

178 The High Court of Australia expanded liability in *Tame v. New South Wales* and *Annetts v. Australian Stations Pty. Ltd.* (2002), 76 A.L.J.R. 1348. In these cases the Court discounted the importance of some of the conventional control devices and favoured a more expansive approach to liability for nervous shock. Most interesting, the Court held that neither a direct perception of the horrifying event nor sudden shock are preconditions of liability to secondary victims. In *Annetts*, for example, a duty of care was recognized in a case of distant shock. In that case, the plaintiffs, parents of a sixteen-year-old boy, let their son go to work on a remote cattle station in Western Australia on condition that he would be constantly supervised and well looked after by the defendant. In fact, he was sent to a remote outpost on the station by himself. Subsequently, the plaintiffs received reports by telephone, first that their son was missing and, some months later,

It is apparent from the cases on duties of affirmative action, duty of care owed to rescuers, and duty of care to avoid psychiatric injury that the legal reasoning does not always articulate or reflect either the *Anns/ Kamloops* or the *Anns/Cooper* test of duty of care. This is explained by the tendency, approved by the Supreme Court in *Cooper*, to focus on the particular category of case under consideration and the existing authorities within that category. The three-stage approach in *Cooper* is reserved for those cases that are characterized as "novel" and not falling within an existing category. Nevertheless, consideration of foreseeability, proximity, and policy factors is implicitly or explicitly a feature of all duty of care cases.

6) Formulating the Duty of Care

There is a great deal of variation in how judges formulate or express the duty of care resting on the defendant. Normally, the focus is exclusively on the relationship that existed between the litigants and whether that *relationship* generated an obligation to exercise the care of a reasonable person to the plaintiff. No consideration is given, at that stage, to the manner in which that duty should be discharged in the circumstances of the case. That is a standard of care issue dependent upon the facts of the case and the application of the variety of factors that influence the conduct of the reasonable person. Sometimes, however, judges define the duty of care, not merely in the abstract but in a way that encompasses and describes the conduct required to discharge that duty. This tends to blur the distinction between duty and standard. The inconsistency is explained to some extent by the decline in the use of civil juries, which makes it less important to distinguish between issues of law (duty of care) and issues of fact (standard of care). Another reason is the ease with which the standard of care issue can be expressed in duty language, such as stating that a driver of a motor vehicle has a duty to have good brakes, stop at stop signs, and remain sober. These are examples of the manner in which the standard of care may be broken. They do not have anything to do with the general issue of the duty of care that drivers owe to other users of the highway. A final reason for the blurring of duty and standard questions is that it allows appellate courts to maintain greater control over the extent of the duty being established by describing the kind of conduct it has in mind.

---

that his body had been found in the desert where his vehicle had bogged down. The Court emphasized the strong relational proximity and the reasonable foreseeability of nervous shock.

The Supreme Court decision in *Galaske v. O'Donnell*[179] provides a useful illustration of this phenomenon. In that case, the defendant driver of a truck was accompanied by an adult passenger and the passenger's six-year-old son. The defendant took no steps to make sure that the plaintiff child was using an available seat belt. In the subsequent collision with another vehicle, which was not caused by the defendant's negligence, the plaintiff suffered injuries that would have been less severe if he had been wearing his seat belt. The Supreme Court held that the defendant owed a duty of care to the plaintiff. The members of the Court expressed the duty of care in different ways. Justice Cory formulated the duty in a way that foreshadowed and included some aspects of the standard of care issue. He said, "[T]here is a duty of care resting upon a driver . . . to ensure that the seat belts of young passengers are in place. That duty exists whether or not a parent of the child is in the car."[180] Justice LaForest stated that "the . . . driver owed a duty of care to take some action concerning the [plaintiff's] use of a seat belt."[181] Justice McLachlin, as she then was, and Major J., the latter of whom dissented, more clearly separated the two concepts, stating simply that a driver is under a duty of care to his passengers, leaving all questions of the appropriate conduct to be decided by an application of the standard of care.

In *Ryan v. Victoria (City)*[182] the Supreme Court endorsed the approach of McLachlin and Major JJ. and called for a more disciplined approach to this issue. It recognized that occasionally courts have framed the duty issue in terms of its degree and content and that this complicates the duty inquiry with matters that are more properly handled in the standard of care inquiry. The Court emphasized that the duty of care is determined by an application of the *Anns* test (now the *Anns/ Cooper* test) and the standard of care issue involves a separate determination of the conduct of a reasonable person charged with that duty. A clear distinction should be maintained between the two inquiries.

F. REMOTENESS OF DAMAGE

The courts have consistently held that a defendant is not liable for every consequence of a breach of a duty of care. There are situations where the loss is so different from what one might have expected, so dispro-

---

179　[1994] 1 S.C.R. 670 [*Galaske*].
180　*Ibid.* at 689.
181　*Ibid.* at 675–76.
182　Above note 34.

portionate to the magnitude of the fault, or so fluky or bizarre that it is unfair to hold the defendant legally responsible for it. In such cases, the courts may resort to the second control device of negligence law and hold that the loss is too *remote* from the negligent act to warrant liability. The role of remoteness of damage, like that of duty of care, is to contain liability within fair and reasonable boundaries. A variety of concepts might be used to perform this task. Liability could be restricted to damage that is a natural, direct, probable, possible, immediate, foreseeable, or close consequence of the negligent act. All of those terms indicate the need for some proximate connection between the negligent act and the damage. No single concept, however, can easily or fairly resolve the many difficult issues that arise in litigation. The true determinants of decision making are more likely to be current judicial policy and an intuitive and impressionistic sense of fairness about where to draw the line on the defendant's responsibility than any single rule. Nevertheless, a great deal of judicial energy has been expended over the choice and interpretation of the rule of remoteness of damage in negligence.

1) The Reasonable Foreseeability Rule

Early in the twentieth century, the courts adopted the *directness* rule.[183] Under that rule a defendant was liable for all the direct consequences of her negligence. Reasonable foreseeability was relevant to culpability (breach and duty) but not to the extent of liability. The directness rule tended to favour plaintiffs. By mid-century, however, directness had fallen into judicial disfavour. It was perceived as being too difficult to interpret and apply. This led to a reassessment of the rule of remoteness by the Privy Council in *Overseas Tankship (U.K.) Ltd. v. Morts Dock and Engineering Co. Ltd., The Wagon Mound (No. 1).*[184] In that case, the defendant, who was the charterer of the ship *The Wagon Mound*, negligently discharged furnace oil into Sydney harbour. Eventually it spread under the plaintiff's wharf where welding equipment was being used by the plaintiff's employees. Molten metal from the welding operations dropped onto and ignited cotton waste floating on the water. This in turn ignited the oil and the plaintiff's wharf was damaged by fire. At trial, the fire was found to be unforeseeable. The Australian courts, however, applied the directness rule and imposed liability on the defendant. In the Privy Council the directness rule was repudiated and the defendant's appeal was allowed. The Court held that the defendant was liable only for the

---

183 *Re Polemis & Furness Withy & Co.*, [1921] 3 K.B. 560 (C.A.).
184 [1961] A.C. 388 (P.C.) [*Wagon Mound No. 1*].

reasonably foreseeable consequences of its negligence. The foreseeablity test was favoured on the grounds of fairness and justice to the defendant, its simplicity of application, and the logic of synthesizing breach, duty, and remoteness under the single concept of foreseeability. After a brief period of indecision the Supreme Court adopted the foreseeability test and it is now well entrenched in Canadian negligence law.

It was not, however, immediately clear how the foreseeability test would be interpreted in the context of remoteness of damage. The judgment in *Wagon Mound No. 1* suggested a relatively strict approach. It was, in policy, a pro-defendant decision that treated negligence law as predominantly a loss-shifting system grounded in notions of corrective justice between individuals. This approach was at odds with the emerging pro-plaintiff trends of negligence law that emphasized compensation and loss distribution policies. Today, it is apparent that *Wagon Mound No. 1* did not unduly hamper the pro-plaintiff drift of negligence law. In a series of decisions the courts have indicated a desire to promote a broad and robust interpretation of foreseeability in the context of remoteness of damage.

2) The Interpretation of Reasonable Foreseeability

The courts have used a variety of interpretive techniques and stratagems to apply reasonable foreseeability in a generous manner. In combination, they give a great deal of discretion to the trial judge and permit an extensive responsibility for the consequences of a negligent act.

a) The Mechanics of the Accident
In *Wagon Mound No. 1* the Court spoke of the need to establish both foreseeability of *damage* and foreseeability of the consequences of the accident. This left some uncertainty about what, precisely, had to be foreseen, and, in particular, whether the nature of the accident and the manner in which it occurred must be foreseen. This issue was resolved in *Hughes v. Lord Advocate*.[185] In that case, employees of the defendant Post Office negligently left a manhole open and unattended while they took a tea break. The manhole had a canvas tent over it and paraffin lamps surrounding it. The plaintiff, a young boy, took one of the lamps and climbed down a ladder to explore the manhole. As he was emerging, he accidentally dropped the lamp down the hole where it exploded violently. He fell back into the hole and suffered serious burns. The defendant argued that the explosion, which was caused by the

---

185 [1963] A.C. 837 (H.L.).

vapourization of some of the paraffin, was entirely unforeseeable and, consequently, the plaintiff's loss was too remote. The House of Lords held that the defendant was liable. It decided that there was no need to establish the foreseeability of the explosion. It was sufficient that the plaintiff had suffered a kind of harm (burns) that was foreseeable. The Court's decision that it was not necessary to foresee the manner in which the accident occurred, the mechanics of the accident, or the precise concatenation of events that led to the accident has contributed significantly to the expansive interpretation of the remoteness rule.[186]

b) The Likelihood of Damage

In *Wagon Mound No. 1*, the Privy Council held that the defendant must foresee that the damage was a probable consequence of the negligent act. Some years later, however, in companion litigation arising out of the same incident, the Privy Council held that foreseeability that the damage was a *possibility* was sufficient. In *Wagon Mound No. 2*[187] the plaintiff owned a ship that was tied up at the wharf where the fire occurred. It also suffered considerable damage. The evidence adduced at trial, on behalf of the plaintiff shipowner, was different from the first case[188] and it supported a conclusion that while damage by fire was not probable, it was a possibility that in exceptional circumstances could become an actuality. The risk of fire was low, but it was not so far-fetched as never

---

186 See also *Jolley v. Sutton London Borough Council*, [2003] 3 All E.R. 409 (H.L.), where a fourteen-year-old boy was rendered a paraplegic when a rotten boat he had jacked up fell on him. The boy was trying to repair the boat in the hope that he could restore it to a seaworthy state. The defendant municipality, on whose land the abandoned boat rested, admitted that it should have removed it since someone might stand on it and fall through its rotten timber. It argued, nonetheless, that it was entirely unforeseeable that children would embark on such a task in such a dangerous manner. The House of Lords disagreed holding that it was sufficient that harm to children was foreseeable.

187 *Overseas Tankship (U.K.) Ltd. v. Miller Steamship Co. Pty. Ltd., The Wagon Mound (No. 2)*, [1967] 1 A.C. 617 (P.C.) [*Wagon Mound No. 2*].

188 The difference in the evidence is explained by the rule of contributory negligence in New South Wales at the time of the accident. Contributory negligence was a complete defence to an action in negligence. Consequently, it was not in the interests of the plaintiff in *Wagon Mound No. 1* to prove the foreseeability of fire in the circumstances because their employees continued welding after they were aware of the furnace oil below the wharf. This could be construed as contributory negligence, and their claim would fail. They, therefore, relied on the directness rule, a winning formula until they reached the Privy Council. The plaintiff in *Wagon Mound No. 2* was not troubled by this issue and was in a position to present a strong case based on expert testimony that ignition of the furnace oil was foreseeable.

to occur to the mind of a reasonable person. This was held to be sufficient to satisfy the foreseeability test and liability was imposed. After *Wagon Mound No. 2*, Canadian courts adopted the view that the harm needed only to be reasonably foreseeable as a possibility rather than a probability.[189] This further dissipated the pro-defendant sentiment of *Wagon Mound No. 1*.

In its recent decision in *Mustapha v. Culligan of Canada Ltd.*,[190] however, the Supreme Court expressed dissatisfaction with the "possibility of damage" test, claiming that it was not a meaningful standard for the application of reasonable foreseeability since any harm that has actually occurred is possible.[191] The Court preferred to use other language also found in *Wagon Mound No. 2*, and framed the question as being "whether it [the harm] is a 'real risk' i.e. one which would occur to the mind of a reasonable man in the position of the defendant and which he would not brush aside as far-fetched?" It is not clear that this language will change the patterns of decision making in favour of defendants. The terms reasonably foreseeable as a "possibility," "real risk," and "not far-fetched" would appear to be of uniform imprecision and inexactness and are all equally unlikely to reverse the general pro-plaintiff trend in remoteness analysis.

c) Linkage

A common technique to bridge a substantial gulf between the negligent act and the ultimate damage is to divide the causal sequence into a number of discrete steps, each of which is a readily foreseeable consequence of the preceding step. A narrative from step to foreseeable step allows the gulf to be spanned in a persuasive way with apparent fidelity to the foreseeability principle. The technique was used in *Assiniboine South School Division No. 3 v. Greater Winnipeg Gas Co.*[192] In that case, the defendants' failure to start a snowmobile with reasonable care resulted in fire damage to the plaintiff's school. The risk inherent in the starting procedure was that the snowmobile might take off without its rider to the peril of persons and property in the vicinity. The chain of events that led to the fire was broken down into a series of foreseeable occurrences. They included the foreseeability of impact with a building, foreseeability of gas-riser pipes on buildings in that area of Win-

---

189   See *Assiniboine South School Division No. 3 v. Greater Winnipeg Gas Co.* (1971), 21 D.L.R. (3d) 608 at para. 11 (Man. C.A.), aff'd [1973] S.C.R. vi [*Assiniboine*].

190   Above note 147.

191   The Court appears to have overlooked the fact that the test was not the mere possibility of harm but the *reasonably foreseeable* possibility of harm.

192   Above note 188.

nipeg, foreseeability of impact with a gas-riser pipe, foreseeability of the escape of gas from the impact with a pipe, and foreseeability that gas might find its way into the school where it might be ignited by a foreseeable pilot flame in the boiler room. Foreseeability was thereby established and liability was imposed. This technique of building fore-seeability on foreseeability is not uncommon in remoteness cases.[193]

d) The Demarcation of Damage

Courts seeking to impose a broad responsibility for negligence may also exploit the inherent ambiguity of the term *damage*. It may be defined broadly or narrowly for the purposes of applying the remoteness rule. The broader the definition, the more likely it is that the damage will be found to be foreseeable. Imagine a circumstance where a plaintiff's drinking supply is polluted by the defendant's negligence. The plaintiff is so traumatized when he discovers this that he has a non-fatal heart attack. The damage that the deceased suffered can be classified as coronary disease, illness, or bodily damage. Clearly, the way the question is framed can influence the answer given. Foreseeability of coronary disease may seem implausible but foreseeability of illness or bodily damage seems more reasonable. Judges are not unaware that the characterization of damage can influence the outcome of a case.

e) The Elasticity of Foreseeability

In remoteness cases the courts have been particularly adept at exploiting the inherent flexibility of foreseeability. Foreseeability is an undefinable concept that can be construed in as myopic or prophetic a manner as circumstances demand. In remoteness cases, courts are not normally receptive to arguments that the loss was unforeseeable. After all, the plaintiff has proved duty of care, negligence, causation, and damage, and there is an understandable reluctance to dismiss the plaintiff's claim unless there are compelling reasons to do so.[194] In most

---

193 Perhaps the best example of this process, of which courts do not always appear to be conscious, is *Falkenham v. Zwicker* (1978), 32 N.S.R. (2d) 199 (S.C.T.D.). The defendant driver on a rural highway was held liable for causing illness to the plaintiff farmer's cows. The links included the defendant's negligent driving; the automobile leaving the highway; the automobile hitting the fence surrounding the plaintiff's farm; the fence being a wire fence; staples being ejected from the damaged wire fence into the farmer's field; cows being in the field; cows ingesting the staples; and the cows becoming ill from hardware disease.

194 See, for example, *Trevison v. Springman* (1995), [1996] 4 W.W.R. 760, aff'd [1997] B.C.J. No. 2557 (C.A.). In that case, the defendant's son had a known propensity for breaking and entering and theft of the contents of houses. The defendant negligently failed to prevent her son from gaining access to the key to a neigh-

cases an imposition of liability on the defendant is fair, and foreseeability can accommodate that decision with ease.

The conventional view today is that, through the use of these techniques of construction and modification, the foreseeability rule is no more protective of defendants than the directness rule and, indeed, it may be less protective since foreseeable indirect damage[195] is now within the scope of recovery. The pro-defendant sympathies of *Wagon Mound No. 1* have been subverted by a pro-plaintiff judiciary.

3) Special Remoteness Issues

There are some remoteness issues that tend to arise frequently. Cases dealing with these common issues have been categorized under descriptive labels. The advantage of this approach is that common problems are identified, the pertinent policy concerns can be addressed, and a greater consistency of decision making may be achieved. The three categories of cases considered here are the thin-skull cases, cases of intervening acts, and cases involving suicide.

a) The Thin-Skull Rule

The thin-skull rule has played a pivotal role in personal injury litigation since the beginning of the twentieth century. It states that, as long as some physical injury to the plaintiff was foreseeable, the defendant is liable for all the consequences of the injury arising from the plaintiff's unique physical or psychological make-up whether or not those consequences were foreseeable. The consequences of a minor accident may, for example, be unexpectedly severe because the plaintiff suffers from a pre-existing vulnerability or condition such as a thin-skull, particularly brittle bones, or a weak heart. Nevertheless, the defendant must take her victim as she finds him and must compensate him for the full extent of his losses.

Shortly after the decision in *Wagon Mound No. 1*, the thin-skull rule was challenged on the ground that it was inconsistent with the foreseeability test adopted in that case. The issue was resolved in *Smith v. Leech Brain & Co. Ltd.*[196] The defendant's negligence in that case caused one of its employees to suffer a burn on his lip. The burn became malignant

---

bour's house that had been entrusted to her. The son not only stole from the house (an entirely foreseeable event), but the following night, he returned to the house and, to cover his tracks, he set it alight. The arson was not, in the Court's opinion, a foreseeable consequence of the defendant's negligence.

195 See, for example, *Assiniboine*, above note 189.

196 [1962] 2 Q.B. 405 (C.A.) [*Smith*].

and he died from the cancer some years later. A claim was brought by his family. The Court recognized that the deceased was predisposed to cancer and the burn was a promoting agent. Nevertheless, the Court reaffirmed the thin-skull rule and imposed liability. It was sufficient that the burn was foreseeable. It was not necessary to foresee the cancer or death.

The thin-skull rule can operate harshly on defendants. In *Smith*, for example, the ultimate consequence of death was grossly disproportionate to the threshold injury. Other relatively minor injuries may lead to chronic pain, trigger illnesses such as multiple sclerosis and chronic fatigue syndrome, or lead to psychiatric conditions.

In spite of its potentially harsh consequences, however, the rule is well entrenched in Canadian negligence law and there are good policy reasons supporting it. First, it promotes the compensatory goals of negligence law in the field of personal injury and is consistent with the strong protection given to the plaintiff's interest in personal security. Second, it relieves the courts from the unenviable and difficult task of determining the normal and foreseeable consequences of trauma in the context of the uniqueness of individual persons. In this way it contributes to the efficient administration of personal injury litigation.

Some of the harshness of the thin-skull rule is mitigated by the *crumbling-skull* rule. The former is a rule of liability; the latter relates to the assessment of damages. The general principle of tort damages is that the plaintiff must be returned to the position that she would have been in if the accident had not happened. The defendant, however, is not required to place the plaintiff in a better position than she would have been in. A wrongdoer is liable only for the damage that she has caused. Consequently, if the plaintiff's existing condition (a thin skull) is one that has caused no debilitating effects before the accident and was not likely to cause adverse consequences in the future, full damages for the complete loss are awarded. If the pre-existing condition (a crumbling skull) has, however, produced some debilitating effects prior to the accident or is, independently of the accident, likely to cause some disability in the future, the defendant is not liable for the full extent of the damage. The defendant is liable only for what she has caused and damages are calculated to compensate the plaintiff to the extent that the defendant has worsened the plaintiff's underlying condition. *Smith* is illustrative. The thin-skull rule was used to impose liability for the employee's death but damages were significantly discounted to recognize the fact that the deceased probably would have died prematurely of cancer in any event.[197]

---

197 A more recent illustration of the operation of the thin-skull/crumbling-skull rules is found in *Wallace v. Thibodeau*, [2008] N.B.J. No. 417 (C.A.). The plaintiff

b)   Intervening Acts (*Novus Actus Interveniens*)

An intervening act is one that arises after the defendant's negligent act and either precipitates or worsens the plaintiff's damage. The intervening act may be a culpable or non-culpable act of a third person or an act of nature. A legally operative intervening act, sometimes called a *novus actus interveniens*, relieves the defendant of responsibility for the damage precipitated or aggravated by it.

Early in the twentieth century, courts were sympathetic to defendants in these situations and they were not reluctant to protect them when an intervening event arose between the negligent act and the occurrence of the damage. This was particularly so in respect of the intervening culpable acts of third persons. This was often explained on the basis of causation. It was suggested that the intervening act broke the chain of causation between the defendant's act and the plaintiff's damage and it was, therefore, the intervening act, and not the defendant's negligence, that was the "real" or "ultimate" cause of the loss. The issue, however, is not one of cause-in-fact. In these cases, the defendant's act is always a cause-in-fact of the damage. The damage would not have occurred *but for* the defendant's negligence. The issue is one of remoteness of damage and the potential unfairness of holding the defendant liable when an intervening act triggers or worsens the plaintiff's loss.

Modern courts are not as eager to protect defendants from the consequences of their negligence as they were in the past and they are less likely to regard an intervening act as exculpatory. Since the issue is one of remoteness of damage, it is not surprising that the foreseeability test has been adopted to determine if the defendant is liable for the loss triggered or worsened by the intervening act. If the intervening act was broadly within the scope of the foreseeable risk created by the defendant's negligence, he remains liable for the damage caused by it. This has, to some extent, lessened the importance of the kind of intervening act under consideration. The cases do, however, continue to reflect the old classification to the extent that the more culpable the intervening act is, the more likely it is to be found to be unforeseeable.

The central role of reasonable foreseeability in deciding if an intervening act curtails the defendant's responsibility was confirmed by the

---

suffered acute temporo-mandibular joint disfunction as a consequence of the defendant's negligence. The severity of the harm was due to a pre-existing misalignment of his jaw. The pre-existing condition was, however, stable and asymptomatic before the defendant's negligence and was unlikely to have become symptomatic absent the negligence. It was, therefore, in the opinion of the Court, a classic thin-skull case and the unexpectedly high dental expenses were recoverable in full.

Supreme Court in *Bradford v. Kanellos*.[198] The plaintiff was a customer at the defendant's restaurant. An employee of the defendant negligently caused a minor grease fire on the cooking grill, which triggered the automatic fire extinguisher. The hissing sound of the extinguisher caused an unidentified person to shout that gas was escaping and that an explosion might occur. The customers panicked and in the rush to get out of the restaurant, the plaintiff was knocked down and injured. Justice Martland, who spoke for the majority of the Court, held that the intervening act was unforeseeable and the defendant was not liable to the plaintiff. In his view, the actions of the third person were hysterical and idiotic and were beyond the contemplation of a reasonable person. Justice Spence, writing for the minority, agreed that foreseeability was the appropriate test but disagreed with the majority's application of it. In his view, the intervening negligence was a usual and normal human response to the situation that occurred and, in the circumstances, was utterly foreseeable.

The contrasting judgments in *Bradford* are reflective of the uneven handling of intervening negligent acts. In spite of the decision in *Bradford*, courts today are much more likely to treat intervening negligence as an opportunity to impose joint and several liability on both wrongdoers than as a reason to protect the initial wrongdoer. To that extent, the judgment of Spence J. may be more reflective of current attitudes than that of Martland J.[199]

Nevertheless, there are circumstances where older, more conservative authorities continue to be influential. A good example is where the plaintiff is initially injured by the defendant's negligence and his injuries are worsened by an intervening act of medical malpractice. In 1941 the Ontario Court of Appeal held, in *Mercer v. Gray*,[200] that, unlike medical error or mistake, medical *negligence* is an intervening act that

---

198 (1973), [1974] S.C.R. 409 [*Bradford*].
199 See, for example, *Bingley v. Morrison Fuels*, [2009] O.J. No. 1576 (C.A.). In that case the defendant, Stanzell, converted the plaintiffs' home heating system from an oil furnace to natural gas. He decommissioned the old system by tightening the cap on the exterior oil fill pipe so that it could not be removed without using a wrench and turning the pipe towards the ground. Twenty years later the defendant oil supplier, Morrison, misread the address of a customer and prepared to deliver oil to the plaintiffs' home. He turned the intake pipe back up and, using a wrench, removed the cap. He pumped a large quantity of oil into the tank which by this time had rusted. The basement was flooded with oil. The court held that Stanzell should have permanently plugged the pipe and a mistaken delivery was reasonably foreseeable. The defendants were jointly and severally liable.
200 [1941] O.R. 127 (C.A.).

exonerates the first wrongdoer from responsibility for the loss caused by the attending physician. This not only is unfortunate for plaintiffs, given the difficulty of suing physicians, but it is also difficult to defend on grounds of foreseeability or policy. The case has not, however, been applied when the first tortfeasor is herself a physician,[201] and there are indications that it may soon be reconsidered.[202]

The most difficult cases of intervening acts are those involving the *intentional* conduct of a third person. Courts are reluctant to hold a defendant liable when the loss is triggered by the deliberate and often criminal act of a third person over whom the defendant has no control. Initially, however, care must be taken to separate those situations where the defendant is under a duty of affirmative action to prevent a third person from inflicting intentional damage on the plaintiff.[203]

Duties of affirmative action to prevent third persons from deliberately injuring others arise out of special relationships where the defendant has voluntarily assumed some responsibility for controlling the conduct of another person or preventing damage to third persons. They may be imposed, for example, on the custodians of prisoners who are a threat to other inmates or, if they escape, to members of the public, on the caregivers of mentally ill patients who are a danger to society, on personal bodyguards hired to keep celebrities safe from stalkers or overenthusiastic fans, on the operators of security systems designed to prevent theft, on tradespersons who fail to lock the homes of their customers when they leave in order to prevent theft, and on referees in body-contact sports to prevent violence from breaking out or escalating unduly. In these cases, the defendant is negligent because he has failed in his duty of care to prevent third persons from inflicting injury on the plaintiff. It would make no sense to exonerate the defendant on the ground of an intervening act.

The intervening act cases tend to deal with situations where the defendant's negligence has created an opportunity or occasion for a stranger to carry out intentional and sometimes criminal acts against the plaintiff which are not broadly related to the risk created by the defendant. Consider, for example, a variation on the facts of *Bradford*. Imagine that when the customers panicked and ran out of the restaurant, one customer seized on the opportunity to steal the plaintiff's abandoned handbag. Should the negligent defendant restaurant owner be held liable for this property loss? The usual answer given by the

---

201 *Price v. Milawski* (1977), 18 O.R. (2d) 113 (C.A.).
202 See Linden, above note 52 at 417; and Klar, above note 45 at 504.
203 See Klar, *ibid.* at 495–99.

courts is "no." The thief has taken advantage of an opportunity presented by the defendant's negligence but it is not fair to hold the defendant responsible for a risk so different from that which he created. One
situation that arises quite frequently is the liability of an owner of an
unlocked motor vehicle for damage caused by the bad driving of a thief
who steals the vehicle. An action may be brought against the owner
on the grounds that it was negligent not to lock the motor vehicle and
that the plaintiff would have suffered no loss but for that negligence.
In this situation, there are two culpable intervening acts to contend
with—the deliberate act of stealing the vehicle and the negligent driving by the thief. Some courts have approached the issue as one of duty
while others have seen the issue as one of remoteness. The former may,
indeed, be more technically correct, but on either view decisions have
been based on foreseeability and the results have been quite consistent.[204] In most cases, the courts have refused to impose liability on the
negligent owner of the motor vehicle on the ground that the actions of
the thief are not foreseeable. Like most remoteness issues, however, the
situation presents a choice between competing policies rather than a
demand for a factual conclusion about foreseeability. The current position protecting the defendant owner can be supported on the grounds
that it is unfair to hold a defendant liable for the criminal acts of those
over whom he has no control, that the owner has assumed no responsibility to protect the plaintiff, that the potential responsibility of the
owner may extend to a series of culpable acts by the thief resulting in
heavy losses, that the act of negligence is relatively minor, and that the
imposition of liability adds further insult to the injury of having one's
motor vehicle stolen in the first place. This position is, however, becoming more difficult to defend. Both the deterrent and compensatory
objectives of tort law support the imposition of liability on the insured
owner of the motor vehicle. Furthermore, there are legislative provisions in most provinces making it an offence to leave a motor vehicle
unattended on a highway without first stopping the engine, locking
the ignition, and removing the key,[205] and the rise in juvenile car theft,
the increasing amount of damage to person and property caused by juvenile car thieves, the popularity of the "club" security device, and the

---

204 See, for example, *Hewson v. Red Deer (City of)* (1976), 63 D.L.R. (3d) 168 (Alta.
    S.C.T.D.), rev'd (1983), 146 D.L.R. (3d) 32 (Alta. S.C.A.D.); *O'Reilly v. C.* (1979),
    99 D.L.R. (3d) 45 (Man. C.A.); *Hollett v. Coca-Cola Ltd.* (1980), 37 N.S.R. (2d)
    695 (S.C.T.D.); *Spagnolo v. Margesson's Sports Ltd.* (1983), 41 O.R. (2d) 65 (C.A.);
    and *Werbeniuk v. Maynard*, [1994] 7 W.W.R. 704 (Man. Q.B.). Contra, *Kalogerop-
    oulos v. Ottawa (City)*, [1996] O.J. No. 3449 (Gen. Div.).
205 See, for example, Manitoba *Highway Traffic Act*, S.M. 1985–86, c. 3, s. 221(1).

strenuous efforts of the manufacturers of motor vehicles to make their vehicles theft-proof seem to contradict the conventional judicial wisdom that the theft and bad driving by the thief are not broadly within the risk of leaving a motor vehicle unlocked.

In the latter part of the last century the House of Lords proposed an alternative approach to the intentional intervening acts of third parties. It held in *Smith v. Littlewoods Organisation Ltd.*[206] that the defendant should only be held liable if the intentional intervening act was "very likely" to happen. Some Canadian courts have followed *Smith.*[207] Others have been content to resolve the issue under the conventional concept of reasonable foreseeability, albeit a foreseeability that is interpreted in a manner quite protective of defendants. This uncertainty has been exacerbated by the recent repudiation of *Smith* in the House of Lords decision in *Mitchell v. Glasgow City Council*[208] and the express refusal of the Supreme Court in *Fullowka v. Pinkerton's of Canada Ltd.*[209] to address the issue.

c) Suicide

The suicide of an accident victim presents difficult challenges for negligence law. It arises most commonly where a person, who is permanently disabled by the negligence of a defendant, is unable to adjust to and accept his post-accident situation, becomes clinically depressed, and subsequently commits suicide. There are policy reasons both for and against imposing liability on the defendant for the death. The imposition of responsibility can be supported on the grounds that the defendant's death would not have occurred but for the defendant's negligence and that a finding of liability furthers the compensatory and deterrent goals of negligence law. The denial of liability can be supported on the grounds that the direct cause of the death is the deliberate act of the deceased, that the defendant had no control over or responsibility for the conduct of the deceased, that suicide is a rare consequence of traumatic injury, and that there is a general societal discomfort with, and disapproval of, suicide. A judicial reluctance to hold a defendant, whose negligent act may have been relatively minor, publicly accountable for the death of a person should also not be discounted.

Legal principles can accommodate either view with relative ease and the cases are not consistent. Liability can be imposed on the basis

---

206 [1987] A.C. 241 [*Smith*].

207 For example, *Garratt v. Orillia Power Distribution Corp.*, [2008] O.J. No. 2090 (C.A.).

208 [2009] A.C. 874.

209 Above note 105 at para. 24.

of the thin-skull rule.[210] It can be avoided on the ground that the deceased's act was an unforeseeable intervening act.[211] There is also support for the view that liability should be imposed only if the defendant's negligent act directly impaired the deceased's rationality and that impairment led to his suicide.[212] This might arise where the defendant's negligence caused brain damage that impaired the deceased's sanity and ultimately led him to take his own life. This line between "sane" and "insane" suicide is, however, a difficult one to draw.

Overall, the weight of authority is against liability for the suicide of an accident victim. The few decisions going the other way may reflect sympathy for the family of the deceased and its compensatory needs and may anticipate a more generous approach in the future.[213]

G. DEFENCES

There are four defences to an action in negligence: contributory negligence, voluntary assumption of risk (*volenti non fit injuria*), illegality (*ex turpi causa non oritur actio*), and inevitable accident. Contributory negligence is a partial defence that leads to a reduction in the damages payable by the defendant. Voluntary assumption of risk, illegality, and inevitable accident are complete defences to the plaintiff's action. The evolution of these defences mirrors the evolution of negligence from a system emphasizing the concept of shifting loss between individuals on the basis of clearly established moral culpability to one that is significantly influenced by the loss-spreading power of liability insurance systems and compensatory concerns. In a loss-shifting system of corrective justice, defences are integral to achieve a fair result between the litigants. When compensatory and loss distribution goals predominate, defences tend to be perceived as impediments to addressing the compensatory needs of plaintiffs. Consequently, there has been a progressive restriction in the definition, scope, and application of the defences

---

210 *Gray v. Cotic*, [1983] 2 S.C.R. 2.

211 *Wright Estate v. Davidson* (1992), 88 D.L.R. (4th) 698 (B.C.C.A.).

212 *Swami v. Lo (No. 3)* (1980), 105 D.L.R. (3d) 451 (B.C.S.C.).

213 See *Corr v. IBC Vehicles Ltd.*, [2008] UKHL 13, where the deceased suffered severe depression following a serious work-related accident caused by the negligence of the defendant. Six years after the injury, the deceased committed suicide. The defendant was held liable for his death since he owed the deceased a duty of care embracing both physical and psychological injury. His suicide would not have occurred but for the injury and it was a reasonably foreseeable consequence of the wrongdoing.

in negligence law. While contributory negligence continues to show some vitality, voluntary assumption of risk, illegality, and inevitable accident have been so successfully marginalized as to be of little practical consequence.

1) Contributory Negligence

Contributory negligence is the failure of the plaintiff to take reasonable care for her own safety which contributes to the accident or her loss. Under the old common law, contributory negligence was a complete defence to an action in negligence. The plaintiff was viewed as undeserving, a wrongdoer who did not warrant protection from the negligence of another. The allocation of the loss to the negligent plaintiff was also consistent with the tendency of the old common law to seek out a single cause of an accident. However, the injustice of placing all the loss on the plaintiff soon became apparent, particularly in cases where the plaintiff's negligence was comparatively trivial and preceded the defendant's negligence. The courts responded to these situations by developing the rule of *last clear chance*, which held that, in cases where the defendant had the last clear opportunity to avoid the accident, the defendant was the sole cause of the accident and fully responsible for the plaintiff's losses. This provided the courts with some discretion to allocate 100 percent of the loss either to the plaintiff or to the defendant as justice demanded. Yet the common law proved incapable of developing the intuitively correct rule of splitting the loss between the two wrongdoers.

Eventually, apportionment of the loss between the parties was introduced in all provinces by legislation.[214] The legislation is not uniform and each Act must be carefully analysed to determine its scope and application and the extent to which remnants of the old common law doctrines such as the rule of last clear chance survive. There is, however, a great deal of consistency in the way the legislation deals with the issue of contributory negligence in the typical negligence ac-

---

214 See Alberta *Contributory Negligence Act*, R.S.A. 2000, c. C-27; British Columbia *Negligence Act*, R.S.B.C. 1996, c. 333; Manitoba *Tortfeasors and Contributory Negligence Act*, R.S.M. 1987, c. T90; New Brunswick *Contributory Negligence Act*, R.S.N.B. 1973, c. C-19; Newfoundland and Labrador *Contributory Negligence Act*, R.S.N.L. 1990, c. C-33; Northwest Territories *Contributory Negligence Act*, R.S.N.W.T. 1988, c. C-18; Nova Scotia *Contributory Negligence Act*, R.S.N.S. 1989, c. 95; Nunavut *Contributory Negligence Act*, R.S.N.W.T. (Nu.) 1988, c. C-18; Ontario *Negligence Act*, R.S.O. 1990, c. N.1; Prince Edward Island *Contributory Negligence Act*, R.S.P.E.I. 1988, c. C-21; Saskatchewan *Contributory Negligence Act*, R.S.S. 1978, c. C-31; and Yukon Territory *Contributory Negligence Act*, R.S.Y. 2002, c. 42.

tion. If the negligence of the plaintiff contributed to her loss, the court must determine the degree to which the plaintiff is responsible for that loss and reduce the damages accordingly.[215] If a court is not able to determine the respective degrees of fault of the parties, they are deemed to be equally at fault and the defendant is liable for 50 percent of the damages. In this way the legislation provides the courts with a flexible loss allocation mechanism and avoids the all-or-nothing approach of the common law.[216]

Contributory negligence can arise in three ways.[217] First, the plaintiff's negligence may be a cause of the accident. In *Cork v. Kirby Mac-Lean Ltd.*,[218] a worker suffered an epileptic fit and fell from an unsafe scaffolding on which he was standing. He had imprudently failed to tell his employer that he suffered from epilepsy. The Court held that, if he had told his employer of his illness, he would not have been assigned to work on the scaffold and the accident would probably not have occurred.[219] The loss was allocated equally between the defendant, whose failure to provide a safe scaffolding was also a cause of the loss, and the plaintiff. Second, contributory negligence may arise where the plaintiff's negligence is not a cause of the accident but he has put himself in a position of foreseeable harm from the defendant's negligence. A passenger who chooses to get into a car with a driver whom she knows to be intoxicated will be found to be contributorily negligent. Third, a plaintiff may fail to take protective measures in the face of foreseeable danger such as a failure to use an available seat belt in an automobile

---

215 See, for example, Ontario *Negligence Act*, R.S.O. 1990, c. N.1, s. 3: "In any action for damages that is founded upon the fault or negligence of the defendant if fault or negligence is found on the part of the plaintiff that contributed to the damages, the court shall apportion the damages in proportion to the degree of fault or negligence found against the parties respectively."

216 The apportionment statutes do not cover some situations such as maritime negligence. In *Bow Valley Husky (Bermuda) Ltd. v. Saint John Shipbuilding Ltd.*, [1997] 3 S.C.R. 1210, the Supreme Court finally changed the common law to permit an apportionment of the loss.

217 The three categories of contributory negligence are listed in Klar, above note 45 at 511, citing N.P. Gravells, "Three Heads of Contributory Negligence" (1977) 93 Law Q. Rev. 581.

218 [1952] 2 All E.R. 402 (C.A.).

219 It is always necessary for the defendant to prove that the plaintiff's contributory negligence was a cause-in-fact of the accident or the loss. Furthermore, contributory negligence is inoperative if the damage suffered by the plaintiff is not within the scope of foreseeable risk that made her conduct negligent. For example, the failure to look both ways before crossing the road is not contributory negligence in respect of being injured by a baseball hit by the defendant from a nearby sports field onto the road.

or aircraft. If the plaintiff's loss would have been less severe if the precautions had been taken, damages will be reduced for contributory negligence.

Contributory negligence is determined by applying the objective standard of the reasonably prudent person. Consideration is given to the same factors as are influential in deciding a defendant's negligence. The foreseeability of harm, the likelihood of damage, the seriousness of the threatened damage, the cost of precautionary measures, the exigencies of emergency situations, and the utility of the plaintiff's conduct are all taken into account. The utility of the plaintiff's conduct is particularly influential in respect of police officers and rescuers where the task undertaken demands a selfless disregard for one's own safety. Courts are reluctant to reduce damages in such cases.

The plaintiff's negligence must contribute to the harm, but the assessment of contributory negligence is not made on the degree to which the conduct of each party caused the harm. It is made on the basis of the comparative blameworthiness of the conduct of the parties. Consequently, proof that a plaintiff would have suffered no injuries in a motor vehicle accident if she had been using her seatbelt does not warrant a large reduction for contributory negligence. The character of the comparative wrongdoing is different. The defendant has breached his duty of care to users of the highway and has caused the accident. The plaintiff has failed to protect herself from the consequences of the defendant's wrongdoing. The defendant, consequently, must bear the greater share of the loss.[220]

Overall, the apportionment process in cases of contributory negligence tends to be conventional, arbitrary, and lenient. It is conventional in the sense that in many cases courts either reduce damages by 20 to 30 percent or they utilize the option of splitting the loss either because of a rough equality of fault between the parties or because it is not possible to allocate the respective degrees of fault of the parties. This permits contributory negligence to play some role in accident prevention without unduly affecting the compensatory functions of negligence law. It is arbitrary in the sense that, although courts are required to make an assessment of blameworthiness, they are often not particularly sensitive to degrees of culpability. For example, the same 25 percent reduction in damages has been made where a passenger failed to wear her seat belt[221] and where a grossly intoxicated person participated in

---

220 *Snushall v. Fulsang*, [2005] O.J. No. 4069 (C.A.) [*Snushall*] (failure to use seatbelt 5 percent). See also *Heller v. Martens*, [2002] A.J. No. 638 (C.A.) (failure to use seatbelt 25 percent).

221 *Stewart*, above note 119.

a tube-racing competition down a mogulled ski hill after he had been warned of the extreme danger of doing so.[222] It is lenient in respect of both the degree of reduction in the damages (not often in excess of 50 percent and often less than 30 percent), and the manner in which the standard of care is applied. This leniency is largely due to the patterns of insurance. Judges are acutely aware of the harsh consequences of a finding of contributory negligence, particularly in personal injury litigation. Plaintiffs who suffer personal injury often do not carry first-party disability insurance. A 25 percent reduction of a large award will, therefore, result in a harsh penalty and significant undercompensation. Defendants, on the other hand, are normally covered by liability insurance and are largely immune from personal hardship when liability is imposed. Courts are therefore more indulgent of plaintiffs than they are of defendants. This attitude is even evidenced in some cases of damage to property where first-party insurance is more common. The New Brunswick Court of Appeal decision in *Walls v. Mussens Ltd.*[223] provides a splendid illustration of a lenient application of the standard of care. The plaintiff owner of a service station was faced with a small gasoline fire on his premises. It was caused by the negligence of the defendant's employees who were using the plaintiff's facilities to repair a timber-jack. The plaintiff failed to use available fire extinguishers to control the fire. He joined with the defendant's employees in throwing snow on it. The fire, however, was being fed by a disconnected fuel line and it spread and destroyed the plaintiff's premises. A strong argument can be made that the plaintiff did not exercise the skill and knowledge of a reasonably careful owner of a service station in protecting his property. Nevertheless, the Court held that there was no contributory negligence. In doing so, it applied the standard of a reasonable person rather than the standard of the reasonable service station operator, it invoked the "agony of the moment" rule even though the fire was initially small, and it concluded that the plaintiff's actions were consistent with what an ordinarily prudent man might (not ought) to have done. It is difficult to imagine such indulgence if the plaintiff was named as a *defendant* in respect of damage to a neighbouring property or injuries to persons by a further spread of the fire.

One issue to which courts have given great attention is the plaintiff's failure to use available seat belts in automobiles. The courts, in fact, took a lead in this area and in most provinces the failure to wear a seat belt was regarded as contributory negligence before legislation

---

222 *Crocker*, above note 118.
223 (1969), 2 N.B.R. (2d) 131 (S.C.A.D.).

mandating the use of seat belts was passed. This was, at the time, a heavily debated issue. That debate subsided after the legislation was passed. Now courts routinely make a moderate reduction (5 to 25 percent) in damages for the failure to wear an available seat belt so long as there is proof that the plaintiff's injuries would have been less severe if the seat belt had been used.[224] Nevertheless, the pre-legislation seat belt cases raise some interesting issues in respect of the increasing range of protective clothing, equipment, and devices that are readily available in the marketplace but are not as yet required by legislation. A court may find that there has been such wide public acceptance of affordable and effective safety equipment such as helmets for cycling (in those provinces that do not as yet have legislation), roller-blading, or ice-skating, protective eyewear for a variety of sports and activities, and possibly smoke detectors in private residences that the failure to use them is negligent. The independent purchase of protective equipment is not necessarily a sufficient distinguishing feature from manufacturer-installed seat belts. Current trends indicate that judicial policy is reflective of an increasingly risk-sensitive public that expects people to take precautionary measures. A modest reduction in an award of damages for contributory negligence is likely to be made when the protective measures are common practice, common sense, affordable, and effective.[225] Whether or not the extension of contributory negligence principles to an increasing range of safety measures is good policy depends upon which of the conflicting policies and functions of negligence law are favoured. Deterrence and fairness suggest that the defendant should not bear the whole loss. Compensatory policies favour the plaintiff and suggest that deterrence and accident prevention concerns should be left to the introduction and strict enforcement of penal legislation.

2) Voluntary Assumption of Risk (*Volenti Non Fit Injuria*)

The defence of voluntary assumption of risk arises where a plaintiff has indicated that she consented (*volenti non fit injuria*)[226] to the risk of harm generated by the defendant's negligence. In the early part of the twentieth century, the courts interpreted the defence broadly and merely exposing oneself to a known and wrongful risk was often sufficient to establish a willing assumption of that risk.[227] This pro-defend-

---

224 *Galaske*, above note 179 at 682. See also *Snushall*, above note 220.

225 A good example is the use of life jackets: see *Chamberland v. Fleming* (1984), 54 A.R. 291 (Q.B.). Life jackets were not mandatory when the case was decided.

226 No injury can be done to a willing person.

227 Fleming, above note 18 at 333.

ant interpretation yielded gradually to the increasing judicial emphasis on the compensatory role of negligence law, to the desire to maintain some deterrent effect on the defendant, and to the popularity of the apportionment regime of the contributory negligence legislation. The current position is that the defence is limited in scope and difficult to establish.

The modern test of voluntary assumption of risk was developed by the Supreme Court in a single genre of cases. They dealt with drunk drivers whose negligence injured their willing passengers.[228] The plaintiff passengers were clearly guilty of contributory negligence in accepting a ride with a driver whom they knew to be intoxicated. The issue was whether or not this amounted to a voluntary assumption of risk. It was the Court's view that it was only in extreme circumstances that the plaintiff should be denied a remedy. In most situations it was preferable, from a policy point of view, that the loss be apportioned between the defendant and the plaintiff. This would achieve some degree of deterrence on both parties and secure for the plaintiff some degree of compensation from a compulsorily insured defendant. The use of the defence of voluntary assumption of risk in these cases was not, therefore, an attractive option. It would free the defendant from all responsibility and allocate the loss totally to the plaintiff. Consequently, the modern test of voluntary assumption of risk was formulated in narrow terms.

The defendant must prove an *express or implied agreement* between the parties whereby the plaintiff has consented to accept both the *physical* and the *legal risk* of injury from the defendant's negligence. The *physical* risk is the danger of being injured in fact. Proof that the plaintiff has consented to the physical risk is often not difficult to establish. The passenger of a drunk driver, for example, knowingly places herself in a position of danger and implicitly assumes the chance of being injured by the driver's negligence. The plaintiff must also, however, *agree* to accept the *legal* risk of injury, which requires an agreement to abandon her right to sue the defendant in negligence. This is very difficult to prove. The difficulty is compounded both by the artificiality of the notion of an agreement about legal rights in these situations and by the fact that it is not uncommon for both the driver and the passenger to be intoxicated when the alleged agreement was entered into.

That this stringent test has proved highly effective in marginalizing the defence was underlined in the most recent of the Supreme Court's

---

228 *Car & General Insurance Corp. v. Seymour*, [1956] S.C.R. 322 (no consent); *Miller v. Decker*, [1957] S.C.R. 624 (consent); *Stein v. Lehnert*, [1963] S.C.R. 38 (no consent); *Eid v. Dumas*, [1969] S.C.R. 668 (no consent).

drunk driver–willing passenger cases, *Dubé v. Labar.*[229] Both the plaintiff and the defendant were involved in a joint venture of heavy drinking and driving. At the time of the accident, both were very intoxicated. The jury decision that the plaintiff had voluntarily assumed the risk of the defendant's bad driving which caused the accident was challenged on the ground that erroneous directions had been given to the jury by the presiding judge. The Court confirmed the test of voluntary assumption of risk that had been established in its earlier decisions. It stressed that the defence is inapplicable in the great majority of drunk driver–willing passenger cases, and, more generally, that it is rare for a plaintiff to consent genuinely to the risk of the defendant's negligence. Nonetheless, the Court was ultimately unwilling to interfere with a jury decision, which was reached following appropriate instructions, and, given the particular circumstances of the case, was not manifestly unreasonable.

There is a diminishing residue of extreme cases where the courts continue to apply the defence against the passengers of drunk drivers. A frequent characteristic of these cases is the joint planning and participation of both the plaintiff and the defendant in an evening of heavy drinking and driving or the active encouragement of the plaintiff in the defendant's excessive use of alcohol or other wrongful conduct. In some of these cases, the necessary agreement can be found when the litigants, at a time of sobriety, plan a course of reckless drunken conduct. At that point they are at least in a position to understand the degree of risk that they are about to incur and might, more plausibly, be releasing each other from all adverse legal consequences of the venture. In the vast majority of cases, however, contributory negligence is the rule.[230]

Although the modern test of voluntary assumption of risk was developed in a single genre of cases, it is applicable in all negligence cases. It was, for example, considered by the Supreme Court in *Crocker v. Sundance Northwest Resorts Ltd.*[231] The Court refused to find a voluntary assumption of risk on the part of a grossly intoxicated participant in a tube race down a mogulled ski hill who ignored advice from the defendant to withdraw from the race. Justice Wilson expressed doubt that the plaintiff, given his degree of intoxication, could even be seen as appreciating and accepting the physical risk of injury. Proof of an

---

229 [1986] 1 S.C.R. 649.
230 The demise of the defence of consent is also evidenced by the Supreme Court decision in *Hall v. Hebert*, [1993] 2 S.C.R. 159 [*Hall*], a case of joint participation in an evening of heavy drinking and driving. Damages were reduced by 50 percent for contributory negligence.
231 Above note 118.

agreement to accept the legal risk was, on the facts, well-nigh impossible. The plaintiff was found 25 percent contributorily negligent.

The defence of voluntary assumption of risk does have greater viability in respect of express agreements to consent to the defendant's negligence. The most common form of express consent is a written waiver or release of liability. Waivers are used frequently in commercial and non-profit sporting and recreational events and activities. The validity of these documents is controlled primarily by contract principles. A waiver, for example, is normally not enforceable unless reasonable notice of its restrictive terms has been given to the plaintiff. Any misrepresentation of the terms of that waiver may render it unenforceable. A waiver that is *prima facie* enforceable is subject to the *contra proferentem* rule, which requires that the waiver be given the narrowest possible interpretation against the interests of the defendant. The rules of privity of contract are also pertinent to waivers. A strict application of privity rules restricts the operation of the waiver to the contracting parties. Recent cases, however, point to a relaxation of privity rules and, in certain circumstances, the negligent employees of the contracting party may be protected by an appropriately worded waiver.[232]

The approach of the Supreme Court to waivers has been uneven. In *Dyck v. Manitoba Snowmobile Assn. Inc.*[233] the Court interpreted a signed waiver as protecting both the Snowmobile Association and a volunteer whose negligence caused the plaintiff snowmobiler to crash his machine at the end of a race organized by the association. In *Crocker v. Sundance Northwest Resorts Ltd.*[234] the Court refused to enforce a signed waiver because the plaintiff did not read it and did not understand that it was anything more than an entry form to the race. The *Dyck* case was distinguished on the ground that the plaintiff, in that case, had read the waiver and had a better understanding of its nature and purpose. It is, however, doubtful that the difference in the plaintiffs' degree of comprehension of the waiver was sufficient to justify such disparate legal results.[235]

The use of the concept of an express or implied agreement to resolve the consent issue has created some incoherence and inequity in the law. The courts, on the one hand, will not find an implied agreement unless the plaintiff was fully informed of the risk and had a complete

---

232 See, for example, *London Drugs Ltd. v. Kuehne & Nagel International Ltd.*, [1992] 3 S.C.R. 299.

233 [1985] 1 S.C.R. 589.

234 Above note 118.

235 See D. Vaver, "Developments in Contract Law: The 1984–85 Term" (1986) 8 Sup. Ct. L. Rev. 109 at 160 and J.J. Neumann, "Disclaimer Clauses and Personal Injury" (1991) 55 Sask. L. Rev. 312.

willingness to abandon his right to protective care. On the other hand, voluntary assumption of risk can be established with much greater ease by the use of a standard form signed waiver. Reasonable notice of its restrictive terms must be given but that does not ensure that the plaintiff had either a good understanding of the risk[236] or an understanding of the true nature of the document.[237]

3) Illegality (*Ex Turpi Causa Non Oritur Actio*)

Ex turpi causa non oritur actio is a long-established maxim of the common law. Loosely translated it means that no action may arise from a base cause. It embodies an intuitive reaction that plaintiffs who are involved in illegal conduct and other serious wrongdoing when they suffer damage should not be permitted to engage the legal system to pursue a remedy.

The scope and application of the illegality or *ex turpi* defence in negligence law has been the subject of much debate and uncertainty. Initially it played a minor role, operating to deny a claim by a plaintiff whose injuries arose from joint criminal activities undertaken with the defendant. For a brief period of time, the defence gained greater prominence. This coincided with the restriction of the defence of voluntary assumption of risk. *Ex turpi* was seen as a vehicle that could be used, in some cases, to outflank the restrictive interpretation of that defence and fully deny a claim where a judge strongly disapproved of the plaintiff's wrongful conduct. Some judges began to suggest that the defence was not restricted to situations of joint criminal enterprise but might be available wherever "the conduct of the plaintiff giving rise to the claim is so tainted with criminality or culpable immorality that as a matter of public policy the Court will not assist him to recover."[238] This revitalization of the defence was, however, short-lived.

---

236 Consumers may be confused, for example, by the fundamental dichotomy between the inherent (non-negligent) risks of the activity and the risks created by negligent conduct. Consumers may interpret waivers as applying to the former and not the latter, without recognizing that no liability arises from inherent risks and that the sole purpose of the waiver is to protect the provider of the activity from liability for his negligent conduct.

237 The Report of the Manitoba Law Reform Commission on *Waivers of Liability for Sporting and Recreational Injuries* (Winnipeg: Manitoba Law Reform Commission, 2009) contains an extensive discussion about the use of waivers in respect of personal injury and death and recommends that waivers protecting the providers of commercial and non-profit sporting and recreational activities from liability be invalid.

238 *Hall v. Hebert* (1991), 6 C.C.L.T. (2d) 294 at 302 (B.C.C.A.), Gibbs J.A.

The Supreme Court restricted the scope and application of the *ex turpi* maxim in *Hall v. Hebert*.[239] In that case, the litigants, two young men, spent the evening drinking to excess and driving around in the defendant's car. When the car stalled, the plaintiff passenger asked if he could drive. The defendant agreed, and in the course of roll-starting the powerful manual-shift car, the plaintiff lost control of it and was injured. The defendant was held liable because he surrendered control of his car to a grossly intoxicated driver. The primary issue was the applicability of the defence of illegality since the plaintiff's conduct in driving while intoxicated was both negligent and illegal. The Court interpreted the defence in a very restrictive manner. It held that the defence can operate only when the integrity of the legal system is threatened by allowing the claim. This normally arises in only two narrow situations. A plaintiff is not permitted to use a tort action to make a direct profit from illegal conduct, and a tort action may not be used to circumvent, subvert, or negate a criminal penalty.[240] In *Hall* the Court held that the defence was inapplicable to the case under appeal. An award of damages to the plaintiff for injuries caused by the defendant's negligence did not amount to profiting from an illegal activity. Its purpose was to compensate the plaintiff for his loss and there was no suggestion that any criminal penalty was being avoided. The plaintiff was, however, found to be 50 percent contributorily negligent.

The *Hall* decision, for all practical purposes, makes the defence of illegality inapplicable to negligence actions. The Court has shown a clear preference to apportion damages in cases dealing with undeserving plaintiffs. This approach is compatible with the restrictive interpretation of the defence of voluntary assumption of risk and secures a degree of deterrence on both parties and some degree of compensation for the plaintiff. The Court's commitment to this view may, however, be severely tested in more extreme cases. It is hard to imagine that the Court would hold a manufacturer of a firearm liable for a negligent defect that injured the plaintiff when he was in the act of shooting another person or that a municipality would be liable to a person who slipped on a dangerous sidewalk while running away after committing a violent sexual assault. Even less exaggerated situations will test the Court's resolve to maintain the defence within the narrow boundaries set by *Hall*.

---

239 *Ibid.*

240 See *British Columbia v. Zastowny*, [2008] 1 S.C.R. 27, a case of intentional wrong-doing, where the Supreme Court denied an award of damages for the plaintiff's loss of earnings while he was in prison because it would undermine the punishment for his illegal acts and create an inconsistency between principles of tort and criminal law.

4) Inevitable Accident

Reference can be found in Canadian negligence law to the defence of inevitable accident.[241] It arises most often in cases of automobile accidents caused by brake or other mechanical failure. These situations present strong circumstantial evidence of the defendant's negligence and the defendant may feel obliged to respond in the strongest manner. This gives rise to an argument that the loss was caused by an inevitable accident, and evidence may be offered by the defendant to show that the motor vehicle was kept in good repair and regularly inspected. It is doubtful, however, if this is a defence in the true sense of the word. The debate is over whether the defendant took reasonable care. If the loss was caused by an accident, inevitable or otherwise, there is no liability. On the issue of reasonable care, the ultimate burden of proof is on the plaintiff. The defence of inevitable accident is, therefore, something of a legal curiosity, neither helpful nor particularly harmful. It merely emphasizes the centrality of fault and indicates that a defendant may try to rebut the plaintiff's case by adducing evidence of his own showing that reasonable care was taken and the accident was unavoidable.

H. REMEDIES

The remedy for plaintiffs who suffer loss as a consequence of the defendant's negligence is an award of damages. Damages may be compensatory, aggravated, or punitive. In negligence actions, the primary focus is on compensatory damages. They are essentially restitutionary in nature, being designed to place the plaintiff in the position she would have been in if the negligent conduct had not taken place. Aggravated and punitive damages play a very modest role in negligence law. Aggravated damages are also compensatory in nature. They are awarded for the humiliation, embarrassment, or distress caused by the nature and gravity of the defendant's wrongdoing. Punitive or exemplary damages are awarded when a defendant's conduct is so outrageous, vicious, malicious, or despicable that it warrants a severe reprimand and punishment. It is in the nature of a civil fine payable to the victim. The conduct of defendants in negligence cases rarely warrants either aggravated or punitive damages[242]. They are most commonly awarded in cases of intentional injury.

---

241 Rintoul v. X-Ray & Radium Industries Ltd., [1956] S.C.R. 674.
242 But see McIntyre v. Grigg, [2006] O.J. No. 4420, where the Ontario Court of Appeal upheld a jury award of punitive damages in a negligence action against

The general restitutionary principle of compensatory damages is applicable to personal injury, fatality, and property claims but most judicial energy is expended on personal injury and fatality cases. Not only has tort law always given high priority to personal security, but personal injury and fatality claims present the most technically difficult assessment issues. The patterns of insurance also dictate that courts are primarily concerned with personal injury and fatality claims. Property, both real and personal, is normally insured on a first-party basis. Consequently, when property is damaged, destroyed, or stolen, its owner is more likely to turn to her first-party loss insurer than to commence a tort action. Insurers do have a right of subrogation which allows them to recoup payments they have made to the insured by exercising the insured's tort rights against the wrongdoer who caused the loss, but that right is not always exercised. First-party insurance against death and disability is much less common and it may be inadequate to cover catastrophic losses. Much greater reliance must therefore be placed on the fault/liability insurance system to secure adequate compensation. Emphasis will accordingly be given to the assessment of compensatory damages for personal injury and for losses arising out of fatal accidents.[243]

1) Personal Injury

The calculation of damages for personal injuries has undergone a dramatic change in the last thirty years. Prior to 1978, judges tended to make an impressionistic global award for all the plaintiff's past and future losses. No explanation, justification, or itemization of the lump sum award was given. This assessment process was unscientific and unreliable and probably led to the undercompensation of many plaintiffs. In a trilogy of cases[244] in 1978, however, the Supreme Court reformulated the principles upon which damages for personal injuries are assessed. In these cases the Court called for, among other things, the full compensation of all probable future pecuniary losses, the math-

---

a defendant driver whose "choice to drink excessively and drive indicated a conscious and reckless disregard for the lives and safety of others" including the plaintiff pedestrian.

243 The authoritative treatise on personal injury and fatality damages is K.D. Cooper-Stephenson, *Personal Injury Damages in Canada*, 2d ed. (Toronto: Carswell, 1996). See also C. Brown, *Damages: Estimating Pecuniary Loss*, looseleaf (Aurora, ON: Canada Law Book, 2001–) vols. 1 & 2.

244 *Andrews v. Grand & Toy Alberta Ltd.*, [1978] 2 S.C.R. 229 [*Andrews*]; *Thornton v. Prince George School District No. 57*, [1978] 2 S.C.R. 267; *Arnold v. Teno*, [1978] 2 S.C.R. 287.

ematical calculation of future economic losses based on the expertise of actuaries, economists, and other professionals (the actuarial method of assessment), and the itemization of the lump sum award to explain its manner of calculation and the use to which it is intended. The leading decision is *Andrews v. Grand & Toy Alberta Ltd.*[245] In that case, the plaintiff was a twenty-one-year-old man who suffered catastrophic physical injuries, including permanent quadriplegia. He did not, however, suffer mental or psychological damage. Occasional reference will be made to the *Andrews* case as the elements of the assessment process are described.

a) Lump Sum Award

At common law, damages must be awarded in a single lump sum award. The common law knows nothing of periodic payments or of any system for reviewing and varying the lump sum as future circumstances might warrant. The lump sum award has certain advantages, including finality, certainty, and administrative efficiency, but a high price is paid in terms of the accuracy of the award and the time it takes either to settle or to adjudicate the appropriate quantum. That delay may be detrimental to the rehabilitation process of the plaintiff and may create heavy pressure to settle her claim for less than is due. A judicial initiative to introduce a modest system of periodic payments was unsuccessful[246] and it is now clear that systemic reform of the judicial assessment process requires legislative intervention. A few provinces including Ontario,[247] Manitoba,[248] and British Columbia[249] have legislation that permits or requires periodic payments to be ordered in limited circumstances.

Some flexibility has been introduced into the system through the settlement process by the use of structured settlements. Structured settlements are used to provide a stream of periodic payments to cover future losses. This requires the purchase of an annuity by the defendant to provide payments tailored to the particular circumstances and needs of the plaintiff. The significant advantage of a structured settlement is that the payments are not taxable in the hands of the plaintiff. This provides some efficiencies over the lump sum since the interest earned on the lump sum, although not the lump sum itself, is classified as taxable income. These potential tax savings can be shared between the parties, providing an incentive for both to use a structured settlement. Struc-

---

245 *Ibid.*
246 *Watkins v. Olafson*, [1989] 2 S.C.R. 750.
247 *Courts of Justice Act*, R.S.O. 1990, c. C.43, ss. 116 and 116.1.
248 *The Court of Queen's Bench Act*, S.M. 1988–89, c. 4, s. 88.1.
249 *Insurance (Motor Vehicle) Act*, R.S.B.C. 1996, c. 231, s. 55.

tured settlements are particularly advantageous in cases of serious injuries to children. Payments may be delayed until the age of majority,
which permits an accumulation of investment income to the ultimate
advantage of the plaintiff. Structured settlements also guard against the
risk of large sums being dissipated by seriously disabled plaintiffs who
may then be forced to fall back on the social welfare system.

b) Special and General Damages

Special damages compensate the plaintiff for all pretrial losses. These
include loss of income, nursing and personal attendant costs, medical
expenses, any travel costs necessitated by the injury, and other out-of-
pocket expenses. In many situations, these damages are susceptible of
precise arithmetic calculation.[250]

General damages compensate future losses. They are assessed
under three broad heads of damage: *future care costs* and *loss of earning
capacity*, which cover the plaintiff's pecuniary losses, and *non-pecuniary losses* such as pain and suffering, permanent disability, and loss of
expectation of life. The awards of damages in each category of pecuniary loss must be itemized and explained to the extent that it is feasible.
This permits a meaningful review on appeal and informs the plaintiff
of the way in which the lump sum was calculated and how it is intended that it be invested and spent.

c) Guidelines

The function of compensatory damages is to provide full compensation
for the plaintiff's pecuniary losses (future care and loss of earning capacity) and moderate compensation for non-pecuniary losses. Neither
undue sympathy for the plaintiff nor a punitive approach to the defendant is appropriate. The defendant's ability to pay the damages awarded
and the existence and limit of any liability insurance are not relevant and
should not be alluded to at trial. The plaintiff must not make excessive or
unreasonable demands but mitigation principles play a more minor role
than in cases of property damage. Damages may, however, be reduced
on the ground of a failure to mitigate loss if the plaintiff has refused remedial medical treatment that has a substantial chance of success.[251]

---

250 Special damages may also be awarded in the form of an "in trust" sum for
family members who have provided special care to the plaintiff before trial. The
assessment is based on the reasonable cost of securing such care-giving services. In Ontario some family members have a direct right of action for pecuniary
losses arising from an injury to a family member, See *Family Law Act*, R.S.O.
c.F.3, ss. 61–63.

251 *Janiak v. Ippolito*, [1985] 1 S.C.R. 146.

d) Future Care Costs

General damages for future care include the costs of all care necessitated by the injury, including nursing and personal attendant services, home or motor-vehicle modifications, medical, dental, and pharmaceutical expenses, transportation expenses, the purchase of prosthetic devices and other necessary equipment, and other expenses incurred because of the plaintiff's disability. This head of damage is of central import-ance to claimants who are seriously and permanently incapacitated, and courts strive to achieve full compensation for these costs and ex-penses. This standard of full compensation was established in *Andrews*. In that case, the plaintiff required twenty-four-hour attendant care. A central issue in the case was the location of that care. His future care costs in a home setting were assessed at $4,135 per month. The only alternative presented to the Court was institutional care, which would cost $1,000 per month. Arguably the most important decision made by the Court in the *Trilogy* was to choose home care as the appropriate level of care for the plaintiff. The decision was clearly consistent with the general rule that the plaintiff is to be put in the position he would have been in if the accident had not occurred and, therapeutically, it was the best option for him. The Court was not influenced by the high cost of that care.[252] It noted that future care costs must be given the first priority and that the potential burden on defendants is almost always dissipated by liability insurance.

Once the basic monthly expense is established, a variety of other factors are considered in order to calculate the required lump sum to pay for this level of care. First, actuarial tables are used to determine how long such care will be required. Second, the controversial process of the contingency assessment must be addressed. Events may occur in the future that reduce the need for, or the cost of, home care. The plaintiff may, for example, require periods of hospitalization, or benefit from expanded social services, or be unable to secure necessary servi-ces or equipment. These contingencies suggest that $4,135 will not be needed for every month of the plaintiff's life. There may, on the other hand, be events that increase the cost of future care. Social services may be restricted, user fees may be introduced for services that are currently free, or the plaintiff's condition may deteriorate necessitating additional care or costs. These contingencies suggest that more than $4,135 per month will be needed. The conventional approach at the

---

252 If various levels of care are available such as home, group home, or institutional care, the general guide is the amount that a reasonable person with adequate means would be willing to spend to meet the plaintiff's needs.

time of *Andrews* was to reduce the award by an arbitrary 20 percent on the assumption that the negative contingencies (those that will reduce the loss) will outweigh the positive ones. Now courts are more willing to review the probabilities in the individual case and they are more likely to make a very moderate reduction or to conclude that no deduction should be made because the negative and positive contingencies are likely to cancel each other out. Third, it is assumed that the lump sum award will be prudently invested, that both capital and interest will be applied to future care costs, and that, at the end of the plaintiff's life, the future care fund will be exhausted. It is also anticipated that inflation will erode the purchasing power of money. Consideration must, therefore, be given to the real rate of return that can be expected on the investment of the lump sum. This is known as the capitalization or discount rate. It represents the difference between long-term investment rates and the long-term rates of inflation. In most provinces it is now set by legislative provision at between 1 and 3 percent. These factors allow the future care award to be arithmetically calculated. Fourth, the lump sum for future care costs must be "grossed up" to cover tax liabilities on the interest earned on the lump sum. Otherwise, there will not be sufficient funds to provide the required care. There are wide variations on the extent of the gross-up in individual cases but an increase of 30 to 40 percent is most common. The future care award may also include the cost of necessities of life such as accommodation, clothing, and food. In those circumstances, an appropriate adjustment must be made in the calculation of the loss of earning capacity award to avoid double compensation.

e)   Loss of Earning Capacity

The second head of pecuniary loss discussed in *Andrews* is the plaintiff's loss of earning capacity. There are two ways of calculating that loss. The first attempts to calculate what the plaintiff would *in fact* have earned but for the accident. The second seeks to assess the *capacity* of the plaintiff to earn but for the accident whether or not he would have chosen to exercise it. The Supreme Court in *Andrews* appeared to favour the second approach by referring to a person's earning capacity as a capital asset and suggesting that the task of a court is to value that asset and determine the degree to which it had been damaged. The loss of a capital asset approach is attractive in theory but its evaluation presents added difficulty and speculation. The plaintiff's past work history and anticipated employment are more reliable considerations in reaching a reasonable assessment. Indeed, in the final analysis in *Andrews* the Court applied the first approach and made a determination of the gross income that Andrews would have earned if he had not been permanently and totally incapacitated.[253]

The first step in making the loss of earnings calculation is to determine the future earnings that the plaintiff would have made and to deduct from them the amount that the plaintiff is still capable of earning. This task was relatively straightforward in *Andrews*. The plaintiff was earning $830 per month as an apprentice for the Canadian National Railways at the time of his accident. The maximum amount payable in this line of work was $1,750 per month. The Court accepted that his average future earnings would probably be $1,200 per month. After the accident, Andrews could not work at all. Consequently, his average future gross income per month ($1,200) was used as a base figure to calculate his loss of earning capacity. The use of gross income rather than after-tax or net income is justified by the difficulty of predicting future tax liability and by the fact that income tax must be paid on the income generated by investment of the non-taxable lump sum award.

Not all calculations of the plaintiff's lost future earnings are as straightforward as that in *Andrews*. The calculation of the future earnings of disabled children presents special difficulties. The court must undertake the unenviable task of determining the probable future earnings of the individual child. Older children may have displayed their potential ability, aptitude, and interest for a particular profession or vocation. A young child presents even greater difficulties. Reference may be made to the educational level of the parents, the expectations and plans that the parents had for the child, and the educational level or vocational circumstances of older siblings. This will assist a court in determining the level of education the child would have attained and then reference can be made to income tables indicating the average level of earnings for persons with that level of education.

There is a great deal of debate about the calculation of the future earnings of women. The reliance on pre-accident earnings in respect of adult women already in the workplace and the reliance on income tables indicating the average earnings of women in respect of girls and young women leads to awards that reflect and sustain the historic wage discrimination of women in the workplace. Courts are now sensitive to the fact that the gap between male and female incomes is gradually nar-

---

253 Since *Andrews*, lip service continues to be paid to the capital asset approach but the weight of authority indicates that all relevant evidence is used to calculate what the plaintiff would have earned but for the accident.

rowing and this must be taken into account in calculating likely future earnings of women.[254]

The next step in assessing damages for loss of earning capacity is to determine the length of time that the plaintiff would have earned income. Reference is made to statistical tables of pre-accident working life expectancy to make this calculation. Sometimes the accident reduces the plaintiff's life expectancy below her pre-accident working life expectancy. Compensation for the *lost years* of employment is allowed but the award is subject to a deduction for income that would have been expended on the plaintiff's living expenses during those years.

Finally, consideration is also given to the contingencies that might have affected the earning capacity of the plaintiff. Negative contingencies include the possible interruption of employment because of illness, accident, or periods of unemployment. Positive contingencies include improved employment opportunities, promotions, and increases in the productivity of the economy. Rule-of-thumb deductions of around 20 percent that were common at the time of *Andrews* have now been replaced with a more realistic evaluation of contingencies in the individual case. The lump sum is calculated, in the same way as the future care award, on the basis of an exhausting fund of capital and interest, discounted to current value.

Since the decision in *Andrews*, special attention has been paid to two other heads of pecuniary damage associated with the loss of capacity to work. The first is the plaintiff's claim for the loss of capacity to carry out homemaking services. This is of particular importance to stay-at-home spouses but it is not restricted to them. The homemaking services include those that are for the benefit of all members of the family. Damages for the incapacity to perform both service and managerial homemaking functions are calculated on the basis of cost of replacement services.[255] The second is the claim for pecuniary loss arising from the inability to establish a permanent relationship with another person. Recoverable losses include both the economies derived from shared expenses and homemaking and the benefits of shared income.[256]

---

254 For a good discussion of this issue, see M. McInnes, "The Gendered Earnings Proposal in Tort Law" (1998) 77 Can. Bar Rev. 152 and E. Adjin-Tettey, "Contemporary Approaches to Compensating Female Tort Victims for Incapacity to Work" (2000) 38 Alta. L. Rev. 504.

255 *Carter v. Anderson* (1998), 168 N.S.R. (2d) 297 (S.C.A.D.) and *McIntyre v. Docherty*, [2009] O.J. No. 2185 (C.A.). See Cooper-Stephenson, above note 243 at 312–36.

256 *Reekie v. Messervey* (1989), 59 D.L.R. (4th) 481 (B.C.C.A.). See Cooper-Stephenson, *ibid.* at 336–49.

f) Non-pecuniary Loss

Non-pecuniary loss includes pain, suffering, permanent impairment of physical or mental capacity, and loss of expectation of life. It is a difficult task to determine an appropriate quantum of compensation for these losses. In *Andrews*, the Supreme Court rejected any approach that called for the valuation of what the plaintiff had lost. There is no market in human capabilities and no normative or personal value can be assigned to them. Moreover, any attempt to evaluate the plaintiff's losses risks an extravagant escalation in the quantum of awards for non-pecuniary loss, something that the Court clearly wished to avoid. This led the Court to choose a *functional* approach based on the plaintiff's need for solace. The purpose of a non-pecuniary award based on solace is to allow the plaintiff to purchase goods and services that will provide some entertainment, enjoyment, or comfort to replace some of the pleasure and enjoyment of life that has been lost as a result of the accident. In a case of catastrophic injury, for example, money might be spent on sophisticated sound- and video-entertainment equipment, entertaining friends, or attending the theatre or sporting events.

The Court was not convinced, however, that the choice of a functional approach to non-pecuniary loss was, in itself, sufficient to prevent an undue escalation of awards based on sympathy for the plaintiff and, possibly, an uneradicable subconscious tendency on the part of judges and juries to *evaluate* the plaintiff's losses. Consequently, the Court set an upper limit or cap on non-pecuniary damages of $100,000. In *Andrews*, a case of a mentally alert but catastrophically disabled young person, the maximum amount was awarded. The maximum amount increases with inflation and it is now set at $340,000. In making the award, courts will consider the gravity of the injury, the age of the plaintiff, and the need for solace in the particular case.[257]

Not all of the ramifications of a functional approach have been authoritatively resolved. There does not seem to be any role for solace in respect of *pretrial* non-pecuniary loss or for plaintiffs in a state of permanent unconsciousness. Nevertheless, damages are routinely awarded for pretrial non-pecuniary loss and small amounts are awarded to unaware plaintiffs if there is any residual awareness or any prospect of awareness.

---

257 A number of provinces including Alberta, New Brunswick, Nova Scotia, and Prince Edward Island have caps on non-pecuniary damages for minor automobile-related injuries such as sprains, strains, or whiplash-associated disorders that leave no long-term impairment or pain. The caps do not exceed $10,000.

g) Collateral Benefits

Most accident victims are not totally reliant on tort actions for compensation of their injuries. The accident may trigger a number of benefits from a variety of sources, including governmental schemes such as employment insurance, Canada Pension Plan, social allowances, and no-fault automobile insurance plans, private employment-related schemes such as sick pay and group insurance protection, personal first-party insurance instruments such as disability and accident insurance, charitable organizations, and friends and family. There is no uniformity in the way these benefits are treated in the assessment of damages against the defendant.[258] Some benefits are deducted from the overall award of damages (*deduction*). Some benefits may be accumulated with a full award of damages (*double recovery*). In some cases a full award of damages is made but the collateral fund must be reimbursed in the amount of the benefit received by the plaintiff (*readjustment*). The common law generally favours double recovery on the ground that a deduction of the benefit would operate solely to the advantage of a wrongdoer. This justification, however, operates on the assumption that negligence law is a loss-shifting system and defendants, individually, pay damage awards. The recognition of both the loss-spreading capacity of the negligence/insurance process and the fact that the public directly or indirectly funds the tort system and the collateral benefits has led to some resistance to double recovery. In spite of this, the idea of deduction of benefits has not generally been adopted other than in respect of no-fault automobile benefits, past welfare payments and employee benefits that are not directly or indirectly contributed to by the employee. There has, however, been an increase in readjustment mechanisms that result in no lessening of the defendant's burden but do prevent double recovery by forcing repayment of the benefit to the collateral source. Nevertheless, careful consideration must be given to the details of each collateral source to determine its relationship to the tort system.

h) Management Fees

Damage awards for future care and loss of earning capacity are intended to be prudently invested so as to ensure a stream of income that, together with a gradual drawing down of capital, will provide sufficient compensation during the plaintiff's lifetime. Some plaintiffs do not, however, have the capacity, education, or sophistication to handle large capital sums. In such circumstances, the court may award a man-

---

258 See *Bloomer v. Ratych*, [1990] 1 S.C.R. 940 and *Cunningham v. Wheeler*, [1994] 1 S.C.R. 359.

agement fee to pay for professional advice in the administration and the investment of the fund.

i)   The Impact of the *Trilogy*

Since the *Trilogy*, the assessment of damages for personal injuries has become a much more sophisticated and reliable process. There remains an unavoidable degree of speculation but the use of actuaries and other experts allows the courts to achieve a much greater degree of accuracy than before. The *Trilogy* has also led to an increase in the quantum of damages awarded in personal injury litigation. Lawyers are particularly diligent in ensuring that all potential pecuniary losses are identified and claimed because, unlike the award of non-pecuniary damages, the awards for pecuniary losses are not subject to a cap on quantum. This increase in damage awards is clearly advantageous to plaintiffs but it has exacerbated the gap between the compensation available to the victims of fault-based accidents and that available to those who suffer disability from other causes (for example, workplace accidents) and it has increased the pressure on the liability insurance system, particularly in respect of medical malpractice claims.

j)   An Illustrative Case of Personal Injury Damages Assessment

The recent decision of the British Columbia Supreme Court in *Danicek v. Alexander Holburn Beaudin & Lang*[259] provides a useful example of the damages assessment process for personal injuries.[260] In April of 2001, the plaintiff, an articling student, attended a social event organized by her employer's law firm. After the event the plaintiff and some members of the firm moved on to a nightclub. The plaintiff was injured when a colleague negligently stumbled and fell on her when they were dancing. She lost consciousness briefly and was absent from work for eight months with very severe headaches and other post-concussion symptoms. In December 2001 she returned to work but continued to suffer from severe headaches and other debilitating symptoms. She left the firm in 2004 and did not practice law again. At the trial, nine years later, she continued to suffer from what was characterized as a "mild traumatic brain injury," manifesting itself in chronic severe headaches together with physical, cognitive, and emotional difficulties, all of

---

259   [2010] B.C.J. No. 1575 (S.C.).

260   The case is discussed here solely on the assessment of damages for the "dance accident." The plaintiff also suffered a motor vehicle accident which caused separate and divisible loss. Other issues relating to additional defendants and insurance coverage remain to be resolved.

which had a profound effect on her life. There was no evidence that there would be any future improvement in her health. At the time of the accident the plaintiff was thirty-one years old.

The calculation of *special damages* fell into two categories. First, there was an award for pretrial medical expenses, including acupuncture and chiropractic treatments, kinesiology, massage and rehabilitation therapy, prescription medications, and psychological counselling. Damages were assessed at $22,563.54. Second, there was an award for pretrial loss of income. The award for the period between the accident and leaving the law firm was $34,220. From the time she left the firm until the trial she was not employed but she was not totally unable to work. The award of income loss during this time was based on the finding that the plaintiff, given her aptitude, strong motivation, and high performance evaluations would probably have been at the high end of the salary range for lawyers, would have received bonuses, and would have become a partner. The Court assessed the loss of past income for this period at $950,000. This sum was reduced by the amount she was capable of earning ($425,000) for a final award of $525,000.

The *general damages* award covered the cost of future care, loss of earning capacity, and non-pecuniary loss. *Future care costs* included all that was necessary to promote the physical and emotional health of the plaintiff. This included a continuation of the kinds of medical expenses that were a part of the special damages award. Claims for housekeeping services and yard-work services were not allowed on the grounds that she would have paid for such services even if she had not suffered the injury. Other claims for a pain program, ergonomic seating, and for memory and organizational aids were also disallowed on the grounds that they would not be used or were not needed. The future care quantum was $48,000. The largest award was for *loss of future earning capacity*. The Court held that she would have stayed in legal practice but for the accident and that she would have achieved a substantial income as a successful commercial solicitor. The Court was assisted by a report of an economist which assumed that the plaintiff would have earned $492,000 per annum until the age of sixty-five. Although the plaintiff would not be able to resume the kind of sophisticated legal work she was doing before leaving her firm she did, however, have some residual earning capacity that had to be taken into account. The plaintiff's work history and the age of her children suggested that no deduction should be made on the basis that women lawyers commonly take time off for child-rearing and that any reduction for other contingencies should be modest. The Court determined that a fair and reasonable assessment of her loss of earning capacity was $5.1 million. The Court considered the claim for *non-pecuniary loss* on the basis that in 2010 the upper limit of such an award was $330,000. The Court found that the injury and its associated chronic and severe headaches had a very serious impact on the plaintiff's life. It affected her physical and mental abilities and her relationships with her partner and friends. Many recreational activities that she enjoyed prior to the accident were no longer available to her. Furthermore, the loss of her career affected her feelings of self worth and emotional well-being. None of these problems was likely to be resolved in the future. The Court awarded $185,000 for her non-pecuniary loss. The total award of special and general damages was $5,913,783.54.

2) Death

At common law the death of either the plaintiff or the defendant terminated existing and contemplated tort litigation. The death of the defendant extinguished all liability and no action could be brought or continued against the deceased's estate by those who had suffered losses as a result of the defendant's wrongdoing. Equally, any cause of action the deceased enjoyed at the time of his death could not be brought or continued by the deceased's estate against the wrongdoer. Moreover, the family of the deceased could not sue for their pecuniary and non-pecuniary losses where death was caused by the wrongful act of another.

This state of affairs, which gave rise to the bleak observation that at common law it was "cheaper to kill than to maim," did not outlast the nineteenth century. The increase of fatal accidents associated with rail travel and industrialization led to the initial legislative reform that allowed family members to sue in respect of a wrongful death. Later, legislation permitted the deceased's estate to sue and be sued in tort. These legislative initiatives terminated all impetus for judicial reform and, even today, reference must be made to the appropriate *fatal accidents* or *survivorship* legislation to determine the impact of death on tort litigation. Fatal accidents legislation deals with the rights of the family of a person killed by the defendant's wrongful act. Survivorship legislation deals with the rights and duties of the deceased's estate.

a) Fatal Accidents Legislation
Fatal accidents legislation[261] in all provinces provides a remedy for family members in respect of their losses arising from the wrongful

---

261 See Alberta *Fatal Accidents Act*, R.S.A. 2000, c. F-8; British Columbia *Family Compensation Act*, R.S.B.C. 1996, c. 126; Manitoba *The Fatal Accidents Act*,

death of a relative. The legislation is not uniform but some degree of generalization is possible.[262]

This statutory cause of action arises where the deceased, if he had survived the accident, would have had a valid cause of action against the defendant. The cause of action is, therefore, a derivative one and is subject to any defences that the defendant would have been able to raise against the deceased. Although the death of a person may have significant adverse financial and personal consequences for a wide range of persons and corporations, the legislation restricts the claimants to a narrow band of family members. Normally, only spouses (including common law spouses and same sex spouses[263]), children (including stepchildren and adopted children), and parents (including grandparents) are included. Siblings are included in some provinces. All of the legislation provides for the recovery of the claimants' pecuniary losses arising from the death of a family member and some also permit recovery of their non-pecuniary losses.

The primary purpose of the legislation is to allow claimants to recover their pecuniary losses arising from the death of a family member. The cause of action is particularly important to dependent spouses and children but a dependency is not required. Claimants may recover all financial benefits that they might reasonably have expected to receive from the deceased in her lifetime. Damages may be awarded for pretrial pecuniary losses, the loss of future financial support of the claimants, the value of future domestic work that the deceased would have undertaken for the claimants, and the loss of future wealth. Although one action is brought on behalf of all the claimants by the executor of the deceased's estate, each claimant's loss is assessed individually.

The most important claim is for the loss of the future financial support of the claimants. This demands a difficult calculation of both the

---

R.S.M. 1987, c. F50; New Brunswick *Fatal Accidents Act*, R.S.N.B. 1973, c. F-7; Newfoundland and Labrador *Fatal Accidents Act*, R.S.N.L. 1990, c. F-6; Northwest Territories *Fatal Accidents Act*, R.S.N.W.T. 1988, c. F-3; Nova Scotia *Fatal Injuries Act*, R.S.N.S. 1989, c. 163; Nunavut *Fatal Accidents* Act, R.S.N.W.T. (Nu.) 1988, c. F-3; Ontario *Family Law Act*, R.S.O. 1990, c. F.3, ss. 61–63; Prince Edward Island *Fatal Accidents Act*, R.S.P.E.I. 1988, c. F-5; Saskatchewan *Fatal Accidents Act*, R.S.S. 1978, c. F-11; and Yukon Territory *Fatal Accidents Act*, R.S.Y. 2002, c. 86.

262 For a full discussion of damages in fatal accident actions, see Cooper-Stephenson, above note 243, c. 11.

263 *M. v. H.*, [1999] 2 S.C.R. 3. Amendments have been made to provincial legislation as a consequence of this decision. See, for example, Ontario *Amendments Because of the Supreme Court of Canada Decision in M. v. H. Act*, 1999, S.O. 1999, c. 6, s. 25.

deceased's future earnings and the proportion of it that would have been available to the family if the deceased had lived. A variety of deductions must be made to the future gross earnings of the deceased to determine how much of it would have been spent on the claimants. Deductions must be made for income taxes, insurance premiums, personal costs and living expenses, work-related expenditures, personal expenditures, and savings. A wide range of negative and positive contingencies that might have affected both the deceased's future financial situation and the claimant's receipt of financial benefits from the deceased must be taken into account, and the length of time that each claimant would have received pecuniary benefits must be calculated with the assistance of actuarial tables. The lump sum is then calculated in a manner similar to that used in respect of personal injuries. That sum is then grossed up to cover future tax liabilities on income generated by investment of the lump sum. The claim for future domestic work includes all household tasks that the deceased would probably have provided in his lifetime. The usual method of valuation is the cost of replacement services converted to a lump sum in the standard manner. The loss of future wealth includes not only the loss of potential inheritance but also any gifts that the deceased would probably have made during his lifetime.

As a general rule, collateral benefits such as private insurance, public benefits, and private largesse are not deducted from the award. There are, however, deductions made for benefits that result from the wrongful death that would not have accrued to the claimants if the deceased had lived. These include the benefits of remarriage, the benefits of an accelerated inheritance, and any damages awarded to the estate in a survival action that the claimant inherits provided that the damages are a real gain to the claimant, not merely a sum that she would have received in any event.[264]

Claims by parents in respect of the wrongful death of young children present special difficulties and arguably some injustice. The award of damages for the parents' pecuniary losses depends upon proof of a reasonable expectation of gaining some financial benefit from the child in the future. The value of anticipated domestic work provided by the child and an expectation of future financial support during the parents' retirement years may qualify but these amounts are discounted by the parental savings in child-raising costs. Contingencies may further diminish the award. It is a fact of life that children are predominantly the recipients of financial support from their parents rather than the

---

264 Cooper-Stephenson, above note 243 at 718–20.

providers of financial support to their parents. Unless there are special circumstances, the award for pecuniary loss is likely to be low. The low awards for financial loss to the parents of young children was one of the factors that prompted some provinces to amend their fatal accidents legislation to allow recovery for some of the non-pecuniary loss suffered by members of the family.

Non-pecuniary loss includes the grief, loss of companionship, and emotional distress that arise from the death of a family member. Fatal accidents legislation, as originally drafted, did not expressly provide for recovery of non-pecuniary loss, and a narrow and constrained judicial interpretation of the legislative language restricted recovery to pecuniary loss. Today, public policy favours some recognition and compensation of the family's non-pecuniary loss. Fatal accidents legislation in all provinces, except British Columbia and Newfoundland and Labrador, has therefore been amended to permit the recovery for non-pecuniary losses. The amendments are not uniform but a common formula is to allow claims for the loss of *care, guidance,* and *companionship* of the deceased. There is little interprovincial consistency in the quantum of damages for non-pecuniary loss. Overall, the awards to individual family members are moderate, ranging from $10,000 to $75,000.[265] This is not surprising. The main priority is the future financial security of the family members and there is a limit to which the public, through the fault/liability system, can be expected to compensate a significant number of family members in respect of non-pecuniary losses. Nevertheless, these modest awards play a useful role in recognizing the intangible losses arising from the tragic and unexpected death of a close family member, especially where there are no pecuniary losses.

b) Survivorship Legislation

Survivorship legislation[266] controls the liability of the deceased's estate for torts committed by the deceased and the rights of the deceased's estate, as an entity distinct from individual family members, to bring

---

265 In those jurisdictions without an amending formula, some recovery of non-pecuniary losses has been achieved by characterizing the loss of a parent's care and guidance as a pecuniary loss to the child.

266 See Alberta *Survival of Actions Act*, R.S.A. 2000, c. S-27; British Columbia *Estate Administration Act*, R.S.B.C. 1996, c. 122, s. 66; Manitoba *The Trustee Act*, R.S.M. 1987, c. T160, s. 53; New Brunswick *Survival of Actions Act*, R.S.N.B. 1973, c. S-18; Newfoundland and Labrador *Survival of Actions Act*, R.S.N.L. 1990, c. S-32; Northwest Territories *Trustee Act*, R.S.N.W.T. 1988, c. T-8, ss. 31–32; Nova Scotia *Survival of Actions Act*, R.S.N.S. 1989, c. 453; Nunavut *Trustee* Act, R.S.N.W.T. (Nu.) 1988, c. T-8; Ontario *Trustee Act*, R.S.O. 1990, c. T.23, s. 38; Prince Edward Island *Survival of Actions Act*, R.S.P.E.I. 1988, c. S-11; Saskatch-

an action on behalf of the deceased where his death was caused by a tortfeasor.[267]

i) Actions against the Estate

Survivorship legislation in all provinces allows actions to be brought against the estate of a deceased tortfeasor. The defendant's death has little effect on the plaintiff's claim or the assessment of damages.

ii) Actions by the Estate

Survivorship legislation also allows the estate to commence or continue tort actions available to the deceased at the time of his death. In some provinces, claims for personal torts such as defamation and malicious prosecution are barred but claims in negligence for personal injury or property damage that have arisen before the plaintiff's death, and claims arising from wrongful death, continue in the estate. These are derivative claims. The estate acquires the rights of the deceased and any defences that the defendant may have had against the deceased if he had lived apply to the estate.

The most difficult assessment problems arise where the estate is suing in respect of a wrongful death. The heads of damage that the estate may recover are controlled by the pertinent legislation. Unhappily, there is no consistency among the provincial legislation but some broad generalizations are possible. All provinces allow the recovery of funeral expenses and, where death is not instantaneous, recovery is allowed for the deceased's pecuniary losses such as medical expenses, lost income, and the cost of personal care incurred before death. There is significant inconsistency in respect of the deceased's pre-death non-pecuniary losses. There is no recovery for future care costs and most jurisdictions do not permit recovery of the deceased's loss of future earnings or expectation of life. Punitive damages are generally not recoverable even though the need to deter the defendant may be particularly compelling given the harm caused.

3) Property Damage

The general principle is that the plaintiff is entitled to an award of damages that will restore her to the position she was in before the property was damaged, destroyed, or lost. This principle is applicable both to the

---

ewan *Survival of Actions Act*, S.S. 1990–91, c. S-66.1; Yukon Territory *Survival of Actions Act*, R.S.Y. 2002, c. 212.

267 A full discussion of damages in survival actions is found in Cooper-Stephenson, above note 243 at 721–46.

loss, destruction, or damage of chattels and to the damage or destruction of realty.

a) Chattels

When a chattel is lost, destroyed, or damaged beyond repair, the normal measure of damages is the value of the chattel. The measure of that value is the market value of the chattel at the time of the tort rather than the replacement cost of a new one. When a chattel is damaged, the measure of damages is the diminution of the value of the chattel calculated by subtracting its post-accident market value from its pre-accident value. The cost of repairs is, however, often an appropriate measure when it is no higher than the reduction in the chattel's value. Repair costs that are higher than the diminution in the value of the chattel and, indeed, replacement costs in excess of market value may be awarded in respect of antique or rare chattels when there is evidence that the money will be spent to repair or replace them.

Damages may also be given for the loss of use of chattels such as an award for loss of profits or temporary replacement costs while a chattel is repaired. The general restitutionary principle, tempered by the duty to act reasonably in mitigation of one's losses, determines the appropriate quantum. Occasionally, small awards are made for non-pecuniary losses such as mental distress and frustration. The killing of a pet or damage to a bride's gown on her wedding day may warrant such an award.

b) Realty

The assessment principles that apply to chattels also apply to realty. The general measure of damages is the diminution in the value of the property. The cost of repair or replacement of damaged or destroyed premises is an appropriate measure where that cost is less than the diminution of value. However, the overriding principle is the restoration of the plaintiff to her pre-accident position and the costs of repair or replacement of premises in excess of its diminution in value may be allowed in special circumstances. A more generous award may, for example, be made in respect of the repair and restoration of a personal residence or to replace premises that are an essential component of successful business. Sometimes, rebuilt or repaired premises have a higher value than the pre-accident structure. In those situations a deduction may be made to prevent the plaintiff from being in a better position than before the defendant's negligence. Consequential losses such as loss of profits and the cost of securing temporary premises during the repair period are recoverable. Non-pecuniary losses may also be awarded when damage to realty has caused special frustration or emotional distress.

FURTHER READINGS

Standard of Care

GREEN, E., "The Reasonable Man: Legal Fiction or Psychosocial Reality?" (1968) 2 L. & Soc'y Rev. 241

JAMES JR., F. & J.J. DICKINSON, "Accident Proneness and Accident Law" (1950) 63 Harv. L. Rev. 769

LINDEN, A.M. & B. FELDTHUSEN, *Canadian Tort Law*, 8th ed. (Toronto: Butterworths, 2006) at 128–222

Causation

BROWN, R., "The Possibility of 'Inference Causation': Inferring Cause-in-Fact and the Nature of Fact-Finding" (2010) 55 McGill L.J. 1

FLEMING, J.G., "Probabilistic Causation in Tort Law" (1990) 68 Can. Bar Rev. 661

KING JR., J.H., "Causation, Valuation, and Chance in Personal Injury Torts Involving Preexisting Conditions and Future Consequences" (1981) 90 Yale L.J. 1353

KNUTSEN, E.S., "Clarifying Causation in Tort" (2010) 33 Dal. L.J. 153

MCINNES, M., "Causation in Tort Law: Back to Basics at the Supreme Court of Canada" (1997) 35 Alta. L. Rev. 1013

MCLACHLIN, B.M., "Negligence Law: Proving the Connection" in *Torts Update Materials* (Vancouver: Continuing Legal Education Society of British Columbia, 1988) at c. 5

WADDAMS, S.M., "The Valuation of Chances" (1998) 30 Can. Bus. L.J. 86

Damage

LEE, J., "The Fertile Imagination of the Common Law: *Yearworth v. North Bristol NHS*" (2009) 17 Torts Law Journal 130

NOLAN, D., "New Forms of Damage in Negligence" (2007) 70 Mod. L. Rev. 59.

Duty of Care

BOHLEN, F.H., "The Moral Duty to Aid Others as a Basis of Tort Liability" (1908) U. Pa. L. Rev. 217

DENTON, F.E., "The Case Against a Duty to Rescue" (1991) 4 Can. J. Law & Jur. 101

MCINNES, M., "The Question of a Duty to Rescue in Canadian Tort Law: An Answer from France" (1990) 13 Dal. L.J. 85

MULLANY, N.J., "Fear for the Future: Liability for Infliction of Psychiatric Disorder" in N.J. Mullany, ed., *Torts in the Nineties* (North Ryde, NSW: LBC Information Services, 1997)

MULLANY, N.J. & P.R. HANDFORD, *Tort Liability for Psychiatric Damage: The Law of "Nervous Shock"* (London: Sweet & Maxwell, 1993)

SYMMONS, C.R., "The Duty of Care in Negligence: Recently Expressed Policy Elements" (Parts 1 & 2) (1971) 34 Mod. L. Rev. 394 & 528

WEINRIB, E., "The Disintegration of Duty" (2006) 31 Advocates' Q. 212

Remoteness of Damage

COVAL, C., J.C. SMITH, & J. RUSH, "'Out of the Maze': Towards a 'Clear Understanding' of the Test Remoteness of Damages in Negligence" (1983) 61 Can. Bar Rev. 559

Defences

GRAVELLS, N.P., "Three Heads of Contributory Negligence" (1977) 93 L.Q. Rev. 581

HAMZO VENTRESCA, Y.S., P.W. KRYWORUK, & S.D. CHAMBERS, "With Patients' Rights Come Patient Responsibilities: Contributory Negligence in Medical Negligence Actions" (2007) 33 Advocates' Q. 207

HERTZ, M., "*Volenti Non Fit Injuria*: A Guide" in L.N. Klar, ed., *Studies in Canadian Tort Law* (Toronto: Butterworths, 1977) 101

KOSTAL, R.W., "Currents in the Counter-Reformation: Illegality and Duty of Care in Canada and Australia" (1995) 3 Tort L. Rev. 100

WEINRIB, E.J., "Illegality as a Tort Defence" (1976) 26 U.T.L.J. 28

Damages

BERRYMAN, J., "Accommodating Ethnic and Cultural Factors in Damages for Personal Injuries" (2007) 40 U.B.C.L. Rev. 1

CASSELS, J. & E. ADJIN-TETTEY, *Remedies: The Law of Damages*, 2d ed. (Toronto: Irwin Law, 2008)

COOPER-STEPHENSON, K.D., *Personal Injury Damages in Canada*, 2d ed. (Toronto: Carswell, 1996)

FLEMING, J.G., "The Collateral Source Rule and Loss Allocation in Tort Law" (1966) 54 Cal. L. Rev. 1478

MCINNES, M., "The Gendered Earnings Proposal in Tort Law" (1988) 77 Can. Bar Rev. 152

WADDAMS, S.M., *The Law of Damages*, 2d ed., looseleaf (Aurora, ON: Canada Law Book, 1991)

CHAPTER 3

SPECIAL TOPICS IN NEGLIGENCE

A. INTRODUCTION

Negligence law is not static. It is constantly in flux, adjusting to new activities, unusual fact situations, shifts in societal attitudes, unusual losses, and the public's increasing demands for protection from risk-laden conduct. In the past few decades, imaginative and innovative lawyers have pushed the envelope of negligence liability to secure greater and greater protection of their clients. In this chapter, a number of special and topical issues are considered in more depth. Most illustrate the moulding of negligence principles to new claims, new situations, new losses, or new defendants. Some concern the interaction between legislative regulation and negligence principles and the accountability of governmental institutions. Another involves the legislative codification of negligence principles that has taken place in the field of occupiers' liability. Others relate to the manner in which negligence law has addressed the unique aspects of various professional activities. Collectively they illustrate the inherent flexibility of negligence law, the influence of social policy, and the dynamism of the fault concept, and they point to the future development of the law of negligence in this century.

B. PRODUCTS LIABILITY

The mass production and consumption of consumer products in the twentieth century presented a considerable challenge to tort law. Negligence law responded to this challenge, and the initial duty to take reasonable care to manufacture products that are free of dangerous defects—recognized in *Donoghue v. Stevenson*[1]—has been complemented by a duty to warn of the inherent dangers of products and a duty to design products with reasonable care. Courts have, however, proceeded more cautiously in respect of the duty to warn and to design with care. The reason is that manufacturing defects normally arise in isolated rogue products. The defect is the result of a mistake or malfunction in the defendant's manufacturing or quality control systems. In practice, therefore, the extent of liability will not normally be unmanageable or overly burdensome. In contrast, liability arising from a failure to warn of inherent dangers or a failure to use reasonable care to design a safe product may condemn a complete line of the defendant's products and may place undue burdens on manufacturers. This differentiation among the obligations of manufacturers is also reflected, in a different way, in American product liability law. Strict liability is the norm for manufacturing defect cases but, in cases of design flaws and a failure to warn, fault is often required.

1) Manufacturing Defects

The modern law of products liability began with a defective bottle of ginger beer and the case of *Donoghue v. Stevenson*. Lord Atkin stated:

> [A] manufacturer of products, which he sells in such a form as to show that he intends them to reach the ultimate consumer in the form in which they left him with no reasonable possibility of intermediate examination, and with the knowledge that absence of reasonable care in the preparation or putting up of the products will result in an injury to the consumer's life or property, owes a duty to the consumer to take reasonable care.[2]

This passage outlines the primary obligation of manufacturers. It is to take reasonable care that their products are manufactured in compliance

---

1   *M'Alister (or Donoghue) v. Stevenson*, [1932] A.C. 562 (H.L.) [*Donoghue*].
2   *Ibid.* at 599.

with their intended specifications and design and that they are not dangerously defective.

Lord Atkin's formulation of this duty of care was expressed in cautious and guarded terms. His language reflected both the novelty of the case and the state of negligence law at that time. His expression of the scope of the manufacturer's duty has now been loosened and broadened in almost every conceivable way.

The duty of care extends to all consumer and commercial products, including buildings. The requirement in *Donoghue* that the product must reach the consumer in the same form in which it left the manufacturer initially gave rise to suggestions that the product must be in a sealed package or bottle. Now it is taken to reflect the normal requirement of cause-in-fact and the need to show that the damage was caused by the manufacturer's negligence and not by the negligence of some other person or by the normal deterioration of the product through wear and tear. The suggestion, in the case, that the defendant would be protected from liability if the defect could be discovered by an intermediate examination of the product by a third party or the plaintiff reflected the prevailing judicial attitude to intervening acts and to contributory negligence. Today, the failure of a third party, such as a retailer, to discover a defect by reasonable inspection is unlikely to exonerate the defendant. It is more likely that the manufacturer and the third party will be held jointly and severally liable.[3] A failure by the plaintiff to inspect the product suggests contributory negligence, which was a complete defence when *Donoghue* was decided. Now damages may be reduced on account of the plaintiff's fault but the defendant will not be exonerated from all liability.

The duty of care currently extends beyond the manufacturers of products. It rests on the makers of component parts, assemblers, installers, repairers, and building contractors. Liability is restricted to those who may foreseeably be injured by the defective product but it is difficult to imagine a situation where a consumer, a user, or even a non-user of a defective product who is injured by it would not satisfy that test. In his dissenting judgment in *Donoghue*, Lord Buckmaster feared

---

3   But see *Viridian Inc. v. Dresser Canada Inc.*, [2002] A.J. No. 937 (C.A.), where it was held that a defendant supplier of a component part was not under a duty of care to the plaintiff purchaser of a product manufactured by a third party. An intermediate examination of the component part by the third party was anticipated and it would have revealed the defect. However, the defendant did not know the use to which the component would be put and it needed further engineering by the third party before it could be used.

that if one step was taken fifty would follow. That has proved to be a conservative estimate.

As yet, however, Canadian courts have resisted the temptation of imposing strict liability on manufacturers of defective products.[4] This has created a technical inconsistency in product liability law because under contract law the *retailer* of goods normally gives to the purchaser an implied warranty (guarantee) that the goods are free from defect.[5] This strict liability of the seller to a purchaser contrasts with the standard of reasonable care of the manufacturer to all those who may foreseeably be injured by his goods. This theoretical disparity between the intensity of the obligations of retailers and manufacturers is, however, minimized in practice by the application of high standards of care against manufacturers, the use of circumstantial evidence (formerly known as *res ipsa loquitur*), and the principle of vicarious liability of employers for the torts of their employees, all of which conspire to allocate most accident losses caused by defective products to the manufacturers of them.

The expansion of liability that followed *Donoghue* was fuelled by policies of accident prevention, compensation, and loss distribution. Negligence liability provides some deterrence against the manufacture of dangerously defective products. The liability costs may eventually be passed on to customers but there may be some market deterrence, and manufacturers prefer to avoid the bad publicity that may accompany a finding of liability. The compensatory concerns of plaintiffs also favour the extensive liability of manufacturers who are well placed to spread the loss through the price of the product or liability insurance.

2) The Duty to Warn

Manufacturers are also under a duty to warn consumers of dangers inherent in the use of their products. The leading decision on the duty to warn is that of the Supreme Court in *Lambert v. Lastoplex Chemicals Co.*[6] In that case, the plaintiff was using a highly volatile and inflammable lacquer sealer to seal his basement floor. Writing on the can warned of the danger of using the product near an open flame but it did not direct the plaintiff to extinguish all pilot lights, the very peril over-

---

4   Some form of strict liability for defective products is found in the United States, the European Community (including Great Britain), and Australia.

5   A.M. Linden & B. Feldthusen, *Canadian Tort Law*, 8th ed. (Toronto: Butterworths, 2006), has a very useful discussion of the contractual liability of sellers for defective products at 600–20.

6   (1971), [1972] S.C.R. 569 [*Lambert*].

looked by the plaintiff. The open can of sealer exploded when fumes were ignited by a pilot light. The plaintiff was injured. The product was not defective. Nevertheless, the Supreme Court found the defendant manufacturer liable because the warnings provided were insufficient to allow the product to be used safely. It held that a duty to warn arises where the product is placed on the market for use by the general public, the product is dangerous when used for its intended purpose, the manufacturer knows or ought to know of the danger, and the public does not have the same awareness of the danger as the manufacturer.[7]

The applicable standard of care is to take reasonable steps to provide warnings that permit the product to be used safely. The nature and extent of the warning required depends upon all the surrounding circumstances. Consideration is given to the nature and degree of the danger, the size, distinctiveness, intensity, clarity, and extent of any written warning, and the practice of the manufacturers of similar products. Attention is also paid to whether the warning is on the product itself, on the packaging, or in accompanying literature. What is reasonable depends in part on the nature of the product, the manner in which the product is marketed, commercial practice, and the habits of reasonable consumers. Compliance with statutory rules and regulations pertaining to the safety of products may not be sufficient to discharge the common law duty to warn. In *Lambert*, the Supreme Court held that compliance with the statutory standards did not sufficiently protect the plaintiff from the known risk of pilot lights.

Some product dangers do become sufficiently well known to the general public to permit manufacturers to dispense with warnings. There is no need, for example, to warn of the danger of knives, gasoline, hammers, or matches. It may reasonably be assumed that consumers fully appreciate and assume the risk arising from the use of such products. There is, however, good reason to continue warnings on many familiar products such as aerosol cans, domestic cleaning products, and small electrical appliances because consumers may not have complete knowledge or a reliable memory of all the risks. Furthermore, there is always someone such as a young adult, an immigrant, or a tourist who is using the product for the first time.

Generally, there is no need to warn of dangers arising from the abuse of products unless the defendant knows or ought to know that there

---

7   This duty to warn also rests on others involved in the production and distribution of products who know or ought to know of the product's inherent dangers. See *Hutton v. General Motors of Canada Ltd.*, [2010] A.J. No. 1077 (Q.B.) (distributor) and *Walford (Litigation guardian of) v. Jacuzzi Canada Inc.*, [2007] O.J. No. 4053 (C.A.) (retailer).

is some history of abuse of the product by a segment of the public or if abuse of the product may reasonably be anticipated. Furthermore, knowledge that the particular product is going to be used by a purchaser in an improper and dangerous way may oblige a retailer to refuse to sell it to that person. This situation arose in a case where the purchaser expressed a determination to use the wrong tires on his gravel truck.[8] The retailer, who nevertheless sold them to the owner of the truck, was held liable for the death of innocent users of the highway who were hit by the truck when the tires blew out. The Court held that the defendant retailer ought not to have sold the tires. The issue may also arise in respect of the sale of solvents or glue to a known or suspected abuser of the product.

Less detailed warnings may be required where products are supplied for professional, commercial, or industrial purposes. The users of these products often have greater expertise and knowledge of the product than members of the general public. Much will depend upon the length of time that the product has been on the market, the extent of knowledge and use of the product in the particular trade or industry, the feasibility of warnings, and the practice of other manufacturers.

Causation is often a crucial element in duty to warn cases. The plaintiff must establish that he would have read and complied with a warning had it been given. If the product was used by the plaintiff without checking it for instructions or warnings, the accident would have happened even if a warning had been given and cause-in-fact cannot be established.

The manufacturer's duty to warn does not terminate on the sale of the product. It is a continuing one that requires the manufacturer to warn the consumer of inherent risks and dangers that are discovered after the product is on the market. Warnings must also be given of manufacturing defects and design flaws when they become known to the manufacturer. The manner in which the warning is given depends upon the product, the number in circulation, and the power to locate and contact the consumers.[9]

a) Medical Products and the Learned Intermediary Rule
The *Lambert* principle is equally applicable to the manufacturers of medical products such as pacemakers, heart valves, breast implants, artificial joints, and prescription drugs, and to the suppliers of biological products such as blood and semen. Manufacturers and suppli-

---

8   *Good-Wear Treaders v. D. & B. Holdings Ltd.* (1979), 31 N.S.R. (2d) 380 (S.C.A.D.).
9   The situation that the public is most familiar with is the recall of automobiles with defects that come to light after the automobile is released onto the market.

ers of these products are under a heavy obligation to provide clear, complete, and current information concerning the dangers inherent in the ordinary use of these products. There are, however, obstacles to the direct communication of that information to patients. These products are normally provided to health-care professionals, and there is no practical way for the manufacturer to inform the individual patient.

The Supreme Court had an opportunity to address this issue in *Hollis v. Dow Corning Corp.*[10] In that case, the plaintiff sued the defendant manufacturer in respect of a silicone breast implant that had ruptured and caused her damage. The crux of her case in the Supreme Court was that the manufacturer had failed to inform her or her physician of a small but known risk that the implant could rupture from normal, everyday activity. The Court recognized the obstacles to direct communication between the manufacturer and the patient and the primary reliance of the patient on her physician and held that it was sufficient for the manufacturer to provide the requisite information to a *learned intermediary* (normally the attending physician) who is then in a position to pass it on to the patient. The Court stated that disclosure could be made to a learned intermediary where a product is highly technical in nature and is intended to be used only under the supervision of experts (for example, breast implants, artificial joints, and pacemakers) or where the nature of the product is such that the consumer will not realistically receive a direct warning from the manufacturer before using the product (for example, prescription drugs).[11] In the circumstances of the *Hollis* case, the manufacturer had not informed the learned intermediary of a material risk of rupture. The physician was not, therefore, in a position to tell the patient and the defendant was liable.

The Court also addressed two further issues arising in the *Hollis* case. Both related to aspects of the proof of causation.

The first dealt with establishing that the plaintiff would have declined to have had the breast implant surgery if she had been told of the material risk of rupture. If the plaintiff would have agreed to proceed with the implant surgery with knowledge of the risk of rupture, the defendant's fault was not a cause-in-fact of the plaintiff's loss. The contentious issue was the choice between the modified objective test, which would ask what a reasonable person in the plaintiff's position would have done if she had known of the risks, and a subjective test which would ask what the individual plaintiff would have done. A majority of the Court chose

---

10   [1995] 4 S.C.R. 634 [*Hollis*].
11   *Ibid.* at 660.

a subjective test and concluded that the plaintiff would not have had the implant surgery if she had been given appropriate warnings.

The second issue dealt with the lack of evidence in *Hollis* that the learned intermediary, the plaintiff's attending surgeon, would have passed on information about the risks of the implant rupturing to the plaintiff if it had been provided to him by the defendant. The defendant argued that such proof was essential to the plaintiff's case. Without it, cause-in-fact was not established. However, a majority of the Court held that it was not necessary to delve into such a hypothetical question and the defendant manufacturer could not exonerate itself on the ground that the physician might have been delinquent in his duty of disclosure.[12] To hold otherwise could lead to the anomalous result of the manufacturer escaping responsibility on the ground that the learned intermediary would not have passed on the information to the patient and the learned intermediary escaping responsibility on the ground that she was not given the information by the manufacturer. The majority's decision on this point may also be justified on the ground that a manufacturer, who is given the convenience and indulgence of giving information to the learned intermediary rather than the consumer, must accept the risk of the learned intermediary defaulting on her obligation. Nevertheless, it does appear that the policies of deterrence and loss distribution have trumped the conventional need for the proof of cause-in-fact.

The learned intermediary rule does not apply to all medical products. Sometimes the manufacturer can give information and warnings directly to the consumer. This is the case with over-the-counter medications and some prescription medications such as oral contraceptives. The packaging of oral contraceptives, their long-term usage, the influence of socio-economic factors in deciding to use them, and, in some cases, the limited ongoing medical involvement and supervision of the patient by the prescribing physician, all support the desirability of direct warnings from the manufacturer.[13] The packaging and marketing of other prescription medications, such as inhalants, also facilitate direct communication of information to the consumer. Another vehicle for a manufacturer to provide information to consumers of the risks and side effects of prescription medications is "direct-to-consumer advertising." "Full product" advertisements which contain both the name of

---

12   A physician must disclose the material risks of treatment to her patient under the doctrine of informed consent to medical treatment, which is discussed later in this chapter.

13   See *Buchan v. Ortho Pharmaceuticals (Canada) Ltd.* (1986), 54 O.R. (2d) 92 (C.A.).

the drug and its intended purpose are not permitted in Canada.[14] However "reminder" advertisements which refer to the name of the drug, but not its intended use,[15] and "illness" advertisements that encourage persons with a particular illness to see their physician are allowed. A manufacturer may be liable to a consumer for a failure to warn in "reminder" advertisements.

3) Reasonable Care in Design

The duty of manufacturers to design products with due care is well established in Canadian product liability law.[16] Manufacturers have a duty to make reasonable efforts to design products that are reasonably safe for their intended purpose. American courts have identified two tests to determine if the design of a product is defective. The first focuses on the *reasonable expectations* of the consumer. If the product is not as safe as a consumer might reasonably expect, the design is defective. This test has, however, proved to be very difficult to apply in a fair and predictable manner. The reasonable expectations of consumers in respect of some products may be unrealistically high and in respect of others it may be unduly low. The test also fails to consider if there is an alternative and safer design available. The second test, which is favoured in Canada, is a *risk-utility* analysis that seeks to determine if the utility of the product's design outweighs the foreseeable risks of the design.[17]

The risk-utility test was applied in *Rentway Canada Ltd. v. Laidlaw Transport Ltd.*[18] The case involved a head-on collision between two trucks when both of the headlights of one of the trucks failed. The defendant had designed the lighting system of that vehicle. Flying rubber from a tread separation of a tire knocked out one headlight and, because both headlights were on the same circuit, the other one also failed. The plaintiff claimed that the two headlights should have been

14 *Food and Drug Regulations*, C.R.C., c. 870, s. C.01.044(1). These advertisements are permitted in the United States.
15 Some "reminder" advertisements use context and images to hint at its intended use.
16 *Resurfice Corp. v. Hanke*, [2007] S.C.J. No. 7.
17 The utility-risk analysis is favoured by the American courts and has recently been adopted by the American Law Institute in its *Restatement of the Law: Torts—Products Liability* (St. Paul, MN: American Law Institute, 1998).
18 (1989), 49 C.C.L.T. 150 (Ont. H.C.J.). See also *Mayburry v. Ontario Liquor Control Board*, [2001] O.J. No. 1494 (S.C.J.), appeal dismissed (*sub nom. Mayburry v. Ontario (Minister of Consumer and Commercial Relations)*) [2002] O.J. No. 1177 (C.A.).

on independent circuits, in which case one headlight would have remained on. The trial judge assessed the safety of the design on a risk-benefit analysis and decided the design was defective. Consideration was given to the degree of danger arising from the design, the nature of the product, the utility of the design, the availability of a safer design, and the functionality, the cost, and the risks of that alternative design. The ultimate question was whether or not, in the light of these factors, the product was reasonably safe. The Court held that the danger of having both headlights on a single circuit and the availability of a functional and affordable alternative design outweighed the utility of the single circuit system used by the defendant.[19]

Sometimes a poor design does not cause an accident but it either increases the harm or fails to effectively minimize the harm suffered by the plaintiff if an accident takes place. This issue arises in cases dealing with the "crashworthiness" of products such as motor vehicles and aircraft and with the protective qualities of safety equipment such as football and ice hockey helmets.[20] The same kind of risk-benefit analysis is called for to decide if reasonable care has been taken to minimize the seriousness of injuries caused in an accident. A balance must be drawn among a number of factors, including the foreseeable danger, the gravity of the danger, the expense and availability of measures to improve the crashworthiness or protective quality of the product and the impact of those measures on the utility of the product, and its attractiveness to consumers.

C. THE DOCTRINE OF INFORMED CONSENT TO MEDICAL TREATMENT

In the latter part of the twentieth century, the nature of the relationship of physician and patient evolved from an authoritarian or paternalistic model to a more egalitarian and participatory one. The authoritarian model is characterized by a physician who, while acting in what she perceives to be the best interests of her patient, largely dictates the appropriate treatment to an uninformed and acquiescent patient.[21] The

---

19   The plaintiff's claim failed on an absence of proof of cause-in-fact. It was affirmed on that basis by the Ontario Court of Appeal: *Rentway Canada Ltd. v. Laidlaw Transport Ltd.*, [1994] O.J. No. 50 (C.A.).

20   See *More v. Bauer Nike Hockey Inc.*, [2010] B.C.J. No. 1954 (S.C.) (hockey helmet).

21   The very use of the word "patient," rather than client or customer, captures the nature of the paternalistic physician-client relationship.

participatory model treats the relationship between the physician and the patient as a partnership in which the patient plays an active role in understanding and controlling the course of her medical treatment. It promotes the patient's right of self-determination. Current medical practice is probably more subtle than either of these models, but the trend towards a participatory model is clear and it has been fostered and promoted by the courts by the doctrine of informed consent to medical treatment.

The key to a more balanced physician-patient relationship is to increase the information that the patient has about his illness, the alternative treatments that are available, and the risks and benefits of those options. A patient's right to self-determination cannot be exercised wisely unless he has sufficient information to determine what is in his own interests. The courts have, therefore, recognized that physicians not only have an obligation to diagnose and treat with due care, but they also have an obligation to inform their patients of the nature of their illness and the nature, risks, and benefits of the proposed treatment.

The landmark decision is *Reibl v. Hughes*.[22] In that case, the plaintiff was not told that surgery designed to unblock his carotid artery carried a significant risk of a stroke, a risk that manifested itself and left him partially paralysed. The Supreme Court imposed liability on the defendant surgeon for his failure to secure the plaintiff's informed consent. Liability was based on the tort of negligence. Consequently, the extent of the physician's obligation is controlled by an application of principles relating to the duty of care, the standard of care, and causation.[23]

1) The Duty of Care

A physician is under a duty of care both to answer the patient's questions and to volunteer information about the patient's health and treatment options.[24] The patient's questions must be answered in a full, frank, and honest manner. There must be no evasion or equivocation. Information must be volunteered in respect of the nature and gravity of the patient's

---

22 [1980] 2 S.C.R. 880 [*Reibl*].

23 There was some discussion before *Reibl* that a failure to secure an informed consent may lead to liability in battery on the theory that the consent to treatment was invalidated by the lack of information. The Court rejected this theory and confined battery in medical cases to situations where there is no consent at all or the nature and character of the treatment is misrepresented by the physician.

24 Some provinces have legislatively codified the obligation to secure an informed consent to medical treatment. See, for example, *Health Care Consent Act, 1996*, S.O. 1996, c. 2, Schedule A, s. 11.

illness, the risks and benefits of the proposed treatment, the risks and benefits of any alternative treatment, the consequences of inaction, any mishaps and accidents occurring in the course of treatment, and the results of the treatment. The extent and detail of the information to be provided is determined on a case-by-case basis by an application of the standard of care.

2) The Standard of Care

The standard of care adopted by the Supreme Court in *Reibl* is the *full disclosure* standard. This may be contrasted with the *professional* standard that measures the defendant's disclosure of information against current professional custom and practice. The professional standard, which is the conventional way to judge the conduct of a physician, was rejected in *Reibl* on the grounds that it was controlled largely by the medical establishment and it might not protect sufficiently the patient's right to be informed. It should be noted, however, that the term *full disclosure* is something of a misnomer. It does not require the disclosure of every known risk of the proposed treatment. Sufficient information must be given to allow a reasonable person in the particular circumstances of the patient to make a decision in her best interests. All material risks must be disclosed. A material risk is one to which a reasonable person in the circumstances of the patient would attach some significance in determining the course of her health care. They include low risks of serious consequences and high risks of minor consequences. Special and unusual risks that are not common, ordinary, or everyday occurrences but do occur occasionally must also be disclosed. The courts have not been reluctant to label risks as material. Even extremely low risks of death or paralysis must be disclosed, but remote risks of minor consequences and risks that are common knowledge such as bleeding, scarring, and pain after surgery do not normally need to be discussed.

The standard of disclosure is tailored to the particular circumstances of the patient. The physician must take account of what she knows about the patient and her lifestyle. Account must also be taken of any information supplied by family members. There continues to be some uncertainty over the degree to which a physician must actively inquire about the patient's personal circumstances. This may vary according to the nature of the physician-patient relationship. A long-time family physician or one who has been involved in the treatment of a chronic illness may be expected to have more extensive knowledge than a consultant, a physician working in a walk-in clinic, or a physician in an emergency department of a hospital.

The physician must take reasonable steps to assure himself that the patient understands the information presented, particularly if the physician is not using the patient's first language or the patient, for reasons of anxiety, illness or incapacity, appears to have difficulty comprehending the information. Consequently, it is dangerous for a physician to rely exclusively on pamphlets or videos to explain the treatment and to identify the risks. Not only is there no opportunity to test the degree of understanding of the patient but also the information is not tailored to the individual. *Byciuk v. Hollingsworth*[25] is illustrative. The patient underwent an elective gastroplasty. He claimed that the surgeon had not informed him of the risks of the surgery. The patient, however, had been given a videotape and literature outlining the risks and benefits of the procedure and the surgeon asked him if he had read the material and had any questions. There was no further discussion of risks. The Court concluded that the standard of care was not met. While the use of remote communication was not wrong, there must be some additional personal dialogue which addresses the personal circumstances of and risks to the patient and allows the physician to judge the degree of understanding of the patient. The Court also noted that even less credence will be given if the remote communication glosses over risks, is promotional in nature or is designed primarily to achieve office efficiency.

The courts have imposed particularly stringent standards of disclosure in respect of certain kinds of health care. Cosmetic surgery that carries only minor therapeutic benefits and any innovative, experimental, or research procedures necessitate the fullest disclosure of all pertinent information. Any risk to reproductive capacity also demands a full and frank disclosure.

Patients must also be given information about any available alternative treatment. In *Haughian v. Paine*[26] a surgeon was held to be negligent for not explaining to the patient that a conservative course of treatment involving medications, rest, and exercise was an alternative to back surgery that carried a risk of paralysis. In *Van Mol (Guardian ad litem of) v. Ashmore*[27] the British Columbia Court of Appeal took this obligation one step forward, holding that a surgeon is obliged to discuss any alternative surgical procedures. The patient, who was operated on to relieve a narrowing of her aorta, was not given an opportunity to choose the less risky of three possible procedures and thereby avoid the resulting paraplegia.

---

25   [2004] A.J. No. 620 (Q.B.).
26   (1987), 37 D.L.R. (4th) 624 (Sask. C.A.).
27   (1999), 168 D.L.R. (4th) 637 (B.C.C.A.).

The concept of therapeutic privilege was recognized by the Supreme Court in *Reibl*. It permits a physician to withhold or generalize information relating to the risks of treatment where its disclosure may cause *psychological* harm to the patient. The privilege has received a narrow interpretation and there is no Canadian case in which it has been applied. In *Meyer Estate v. Rogers*[28] the Court refused to apply it where a deliberate decision not to disclose a small risk of paralysis and death arising from an invasive diagnostic test was defended on the ground that the risk of adverse physical consequences was increased by any anxiety suffered by the patient. The trial judge doubted that the privilege was part of Canadian law and stated that, in any event, it could be justified only to avoid psychological harm to the patient, not to minimize physical harm. In these situations, some way, other than keeping the patient in the dark, must be found to allay a patient's fears and anxiety. It is unlikely that other Canadian judges will have greater enthusiasm for the privilege. It has the potential to undermine seriously the patient's right to self-determination and will, therefore, be kept on the tightest of reins.

A patient may waive his right to be informed. He may, for example, make it clear that he has total confidence in the physician and does not wish to talk about risks or dangers associated with the treatment.

Information does not normally have to be repeated throughout the course of treatment or where treatment is temporarily interrupted. In *Ciarlariello v. Schacter*[29] the Supreme Court considered a case in which the plaintiff patient had undergone two cerebral angiograms to locate a brain hemorrhage. The Court held that the plaintiff was fully informed of all the material risks including the risk of paralysis. During the course of the second procedure, she experienced some discomfort and she withdrew her consent. When she calmed down, she agreed to the completion of the procedure. Shortly after the resumption of the angiogram, she suffered an allergic reaction to the dye and was rendered a quadriplegic. It was argued that a further explanation of the risks was called for before the resumption of the second test. The Court held that this was not necessary. The interruption of the test had introduced no new risks and the risk-benefit ratio of the procedure had not changed. The patient was sufficiently informed to decide whether or not the test should continue.

The physician's obligation under the informed consent doctrine extends only to providing information. The physician is not obliged

---

28   (1991), 2 O.R. (3d) 356 (Gen. Div.).
29   [1993] 2 S.C.R. 119.

to advise a patient of what she believes to be the patient's best course of action. That would be inconsistent with the favoured participatory model of the physician-patient relationship which seeks to empower the patient to make her own decisions. This does not, of course, prevent the physician from offering or giving advice in response to a patient's request for it.

The duty to inform patients has been described with reference solely to physicians since they are the primary source of information for most patients. The duty, however, rests on all health care professionals within their area of expertise and practice. This includes not only dentists, physiotherapists, and diagnostic technicians but also those who work on the fringes of conventional medicine such as chiropractors, acupuncturists, and non-traditional healers. Nurses can usually rely on physicians to inform patients but they may have some duty to inform a patient in respect of particular techniques or treatment that are within their sphere of responsibility.

The restructuring of the health-care system and the financial constraints on public health care have raised new issues in respect of informed consent. Physicians may now be obliged to inform patients of the inadequacies of the health-care system and of the availability of better diagnostic or treatment options elsewhere in Canada or in the United States. Information may also need to be given in respect of superior medications that may be unavailable to the patient because of their expense.

A further, and largely unexplored, issue is the extent to which a surgeon must disclose her own track record in terms of infection rates, failure rates, any adverse disciplinary or peer review findings, and her health status, such as being HIV positive. In these situations the risks arise not from the proposed treatment but from the professional and personal characteristics of the physician. In *Halkyard v. Mathew*[30] it was held that a surgeon did not have to disclose to his patient that he suffered from epilepsy. In that case, however, the epilepsy was well controlled by medications and there was no risk of harm to the patient. More difficult cases will require a delicate balance to be drawn between the physician's interest in privacy and the patient's interest in safety.

3) Causation (Cause-in-Fact)

In order to establish cause-in-fact it must be proved that the patient would not have consented to the procedure if the defendant physician

---

30   [2001] A.J. No. 293 (C.A.).

had performed her duty to inform the patient of the material risks of the treatment. If the patient would have made the same decision in any event, causation is not proved. In *Reibl*, the Court had to choose between a subjective test of causation and an objective one. A subjective test asks what the patient would have done if the appropriate information had been provided. An objective test asks what the reasonable person would have done. Each has its weakness. A subjective test may cause the trier of fact to place too much emphasis on the self-serving testimony of the plaintiff, thereby causing unfairness to the defendant. An objective test risks the conclusion that a reasonable person normally follows her physician's advice, thereby compromising the patient's right to self-determination. In *Reibl*, the Supreme Court resolved the conundrum by adopting a *modified objective* test that asks what the reasonable person in the plaintiff's particular circumstances would have done.

It soon became apparent, however, that the modified objective test posed some difficulties. First, there was no consistent approach as to the range or kind of particular circumstances of the plaintiff that were to be taken into account. This created some uncertainty and unpredictability in the application of the test. Second, causation proved to be a substantial obstacle to plaintiffs in informed consent cases. Most informed claims failed and most failed on the causation issue.

In 1997 the Supreme Court revisited the causation issue in *Arndt v. Smith*.[31] In that case, the plaintiff contracted chickenpox in the course of her pregnancy. The defendant physician chose not to tell her patient that this posed a small risk of serious birth defects to her child. The child was born with serious disabilities and the plaintiff argued that if she had been told of this risk, she would have terminated her pregnancy. The trial judge applied the modified objective approach, and, after noting that the plaintiff had a particular desire for children and a suspicion of mainstream medicine, he concluded that a reasonable person in her particular circumstances would not have terminated her pregnancy. The British Columbia Court of Appeal ordered a new trial, ruling that the modified objective test had not been applied properly. A majority of the Supreme Court affirmed the modified objective test and held that the trial judge had applied it appropriately. The Court indicated that a wide range of personal factors may be included to modify the reasonable person test. A court may take into account all the objectively ascertainable circumstances of the patient such as her age, income, and marital status, any special considerations affecting the patient, including those that she raised with her physician, and all of the patient's

---

31   [1997] 2 S.C.R. 539 [*Arndt*].

reasonable beliefs, fears, desires, expectations, and concerns. The modified objective test eliminates consideration only of the patient's idiosyncratic, unreasonable, and irrational beliefs and subjective fears that are unrelated to the material risks of the medical treatment. In the opinion of the majority, therefore, it was appropriate to ask what the reasonable pregnant woman who had a particular desire for children, who was sceptical of mainstream medicine, and who had expressed no particular fears of having a disabled child would have done had she been told of the small risk of a birth defect. This is what the trial judge had done and his conclusion that the reasonable woman in these circumstances would not have terminated her pregnancy was upheld.

Although the Court reaffirmed the modified objective test, it has approved the use of so many personal factors that it may not, in practice, be significantly different from the subjective test favoured by the minority of the Court. The decision does, however, present a new challenge. In an ethnically and religiously diverse society, it is difficult to draw a line between beliefs and concerns that are reasonable and those that are not. This difficulty would be avoided and the patient's right to self-determination would be strengthened by a subjective test tempered by a careful judicial assessment of the plaintiff's credibility.

An intriguing causation issue arises where the appropriate disclosure of information would have led the patient to delay surgery but not refuse it. The House of Lords considered the point in *Chester v. Afshar*[32] The patient consented to back surgery without being told of the risk of paralysis. The surgery was conducted skilfully but she suffered severe permanent disability. The patient's evidence, accepted by the trial judge, was that if she had been told of the risks involved she would have delayed the surgery to make further inquiries and considered other options.[33] She would, however, likely have had the same surgery, carrying the same risks, at a later date. The majority of the Court emphasizing the importance of patient autonomy and the right of free choice found for the patient. The minority held that the risk of the surgery did not change because the surgery took place at a different time and that to establish causation it was necessary to show that she would not have had the surgery at all.[34]

---

32   [2004] 4 All E.R. 587 (H.L.).

33   In England a subjective test of causation is used but that is not determinative of the point at issue.

34   See *Martin v. Capital Health Authority*, [2007] A.J. No. 446 (Q.B.) rev'd on other grounds [2008] A.J. No. 462 (C.A.) which favours the majority decision in *Chester*.

It is difficult to judge whether the informed consent doctrine has influenced or reflected a change in the relationship of physician and patient. The safest conclusion is that the law, medical practice, and changing public attitudes have conspired to transform the relationship into one that is more participatory and egalitarian and more responsive to the patient's right of self-determination.

D. HUMAN REPRODUCTION

The expansion of the tort of negligence into the field of human reproduction was heralded by the case of *Duval v. Seguin*.[35] The plaintiff in that case sued in respect of prenatal injuries suffered when her mother was involved in a car accident caused by the negligence of the defendant. The Court held that the defendant owed a duty of care to the fetus which was actionable by the child as soon as she was born alive. The attention that this case brought to the issue of liability to the unborn, the expansionary trends of negligence law, and the lack of any intrafamily immunity from tort liability have sparked both interest and litigation on a variety of issues relating to human reproduction. Some of the issues present profound policy dilemmas and have tested the limits of negligence liability. Four kinds of cases are canvassed below: cases involving prenatal injuries, wrongful birth cases, wrongful life cases, and wrongful pregnancy cases.

1) Prenatal Injuries

A child who is born alive may sue in respect of prenatal injuries caused by the defendant's negligence. This is the cause of action that was recognized in *Duval*.[36] No tort is committed while the child is a fetus. In Canadian law a fetus is not a human person and, therefore, has no legal rights. Consequently, if a child is stillborn because of the defendant's negligence, the mother may sue for her personal losses, but there is no right of action in the fetus that might survive to the benefit of his estate and no right of action is available to family members under fatal accidents legislation.[37] Once the child is born alive, however, he is a human

---

35   [1972] 2 O.R. 686 (H.C.J.), aff'd (1973), 1 O.R. (2d) 482 (C.A.).

36   It is also confirmed by legislation in Ontario. See Ontario *Family Law Act*, R.S.O. 1990, c. F.3, s. 66: "No person is disentitled from recovering damages in respect of injuries for the reason only that the injuries were incurred before his or her birth."

37   *Martin v. Mineral Springs Hospital*, [2001] A.J. No. 78 (Q.B.).

person and may sue in respect of physical or mental disabilities that were caused by the defendant's prenatal negligence. Liability may be imposed, for example, on the manufacturers of drugs who fail to do sufficient testing of new products in respect of dangers to the fetus or fail to warn doctors that a medication should not be prescribed for pregnant women. A physician may also damage the fetus by prescribing medications that are not recommended for pregnant women, by injuring the fetus in the course of an unsuccessful abortion,[38] or by failing to take appropriate care in the course of a Caesarean section or a difficult labour. Physicians do not, however, owe a duty of care to *future* children not as yet conceived when treating women of child-bearing age. The issue arose in *Paxton v. Ramji*.[39] The alleged negligence was the failure of the defendant physician to follow stringent advisory protocols emphasizing the importance of the patient not getting pregnant while on the drug Accutane because of the risk of fetal harm. The woman became pregnant while on the drug and her child suffered serious disabilities. The Ontario Court of Appeal concluded that a duty of care to the child should not be recognized on public policy grounds including the potential for a conflict between the duty to the mother and future children.[40]

A duty of care is not, however, owed by a mother to her unborn child. The issue arose in *Dobson (Litigation guardian of) v. Dobson*.[41] The plaintiff child sued his mother for prenatal injuries caused allegedly by her negligent driving. A majority of the Supreme Court held that she owed no duty of care either to her fetus or to her subsequently born child. This maternal immunity in respect of prenatal injuries was justified on policy grounds. The recognition of a duty of care in *Dobson* could not, in the majority's view, be constrained or tailored to the operation of motor vehicles. It would, therefore, lead to the judicial scrutiny and assessment of all maternal conduct that carried a risk of injury to the unborn child including the mother's lifestyle choices such as her use of alcohol, tobacco, drugs and solvents, her recreational activities, her sexual practices, and her dietary regime. This in turn could lead to

---

38   *Cherry (Guardian at litem of) v. Borsman* (1992), 94 D.L.R. (4th) 487 (B.C.C.A.).

39   [2008] O.J. No. 3964 (C.A.) [*Paxton*]. See also *Bovingdon v. Hergott*, [2008] O.J. No. 11 (C.A.).

40   A conflict of duties may arise after conception in both maternal/fetal care and in labour and delivery but the ruling in *Paxton* has not impaired a long line of authority holding that a physician owes a duty of care both to the mother and her fetus. Any conflict must be resolved by looking at how a reasonable physician would handle such a scenario. See *Liebig (Litigation Guardian of) v. Guelph General Hospital*, [2010] ONCA 450 and *Ediger (Guardian at litem of) v. Johnston*, [2009] B.C.J. No. 564 (S.C.).

41   [1999] 2 S.C.R. 753 [*Dobson*].

unacceptable restrictions on the bodily integrity, liberty, privacy, and autonomy of pregnant women. Moreover, the articulation and application of an appropriate standard of care in these circumstances is fraught with difficulty. The minority favoured the recognition of a duty of care in cases like *Dobson* where the duty at issue (to drive safely) is owed not only to the unborn child but also to third parties. In those circumstances the recognition of a duty of care to the unborn child does not place any additional restrictions on the mother's freedom of action.[42]

2) Wrongful Birth

Wrongful birth refers to the claim brought by the parents of a congenitally disabled child against a health-care professional on the ground that her negligent advice or treatment prevented them from avoiding conception or of terminating the pregnancy. Some cases involve preconception negligence in the course of genetic testing or counselling. In *H.(R.) v. Hunter*,[43] for example, the defendant physician failed to inform the plaintiff that there was a genetic risk that her male children might develop Duchenne muscular dystrophy. Both of her sons developed the disease. Other cases involve post-conception negligence such as the failure to warn mothers of the risk of fetal abnormality from post-conception illnesses, the failure to test for fetal abnormalities, or the failure to interpret test results accurately. A good illustration of post-conception negligence is found in *Arndt*,[44] discussed above, where the defendant physician failed to tell the plaintiff of the risk that chickenpox contracted after conception posed to her fetus. *Arndt* also addressed the importance of causation in these cases. The plaintiff must establish that, if the defendant had not been negligent, a reasonable person in her particular circumstances (the modified objective test) would have prevented the pregnancy or terminated it as the case may be. The plaintiff's action in *Arndt* failed on that ground.[45]

---

42   The "*Dobson* immunity" has been limited in Alberta by the *Maternal Tort Liability Act*, S.A. 2005, c. M-7.5. A mother is liable for prenatal injuries to her child caused by her negligent operation of a motor vehicle. The liability is restricted to the limits of her liability insurance.

43   (1996), 32 C.C.L.T. (2d) 44 (Ont. Gen. Div.).

44   Above note 31.

45   See *Mickle v. Salvation Army Grace Hospital* (1998), 166 D.L.R. (4th) 743 (Ont. Gen. Div.) for a discussion of the difficulties of determining cause-in-fact in wrongful birth cases.

The primary head of damage in wrongful birth cases is the increased costs and special expenses of caring for a handicapped child,[46] but the award may also include the loss of income suffered by the parental caregiver and general damages to both parents for emotional suffering. The claim of the father is wholly derivative, standing or falling with that of the mother.

3) Wrongful Life

The wrongful life action has not been recognized by any Canadian court.[47] It is the companion action of the child to the parents' wrongful birth claim. The plaintiff child's contention is that, had the defendant health care professional given his mother timely warning of the risk of congenital abnormality, she would have chosen either not to have had a child or, if the negligence was after conception, to have terminated her pregnancy. In either case, the plaintiff would not have been born and he would have been spared a life burdened by physical or mental incapacity, pain, and suffering. As in the case of wrongful birth, there is no suggestion that the defendant *caused* the plaintiff's disability. The plaintiff never had a chance of being born free of congenital disability. The plaintiff's claim is that he should never have been born at all. Claimants in wrongful life actions in the United States have commonly sought recovery for future care costs and non-pecuniary damages for pain and suffering and for an impaired childhood flowing from the chronic sorrow and psychological grief suffered by some parents upon the birth of a handicapped child.[48]

The only Commonwealth court of last resort to consider the wrongful life action is the High Court of Australia. In *Harriton v. Stephens*[49] a majority of the Court relied on a number of technical objections and policy concerns in rejecting the wrongful life action. The primary technical problem related to the assessment of damages. Damages in negli-

---

46   It is not yet clear if a claim for ordinary child-raising costs can also be made; see section D(4), "Wrongful Pregnancy," below in this chapter. For claims by parents relating to future care costs after the age of majority, see *Krangle v. Briscoe*, [2002] 1 S.C.R. 205.

47   See *Lacroix (Litigation guardian of) v. Dominique*, [2001] M.J. No. 311 (C.A.), leave to appeal to the S.C.C. refused, [2001] S.C.C.A. No. 477. Some courts have declined to strike out claims for wrongful life, for example, *McDonald-Wright (Litigation guardian of) v. O'Herlihy*, [2005] O.J. No. 135 (S.C.J.), appeal dismissed [2007] O.J. No. 478 (C.A.).

48   Only a few American states have recognized the wrongful life action, see *Procanik v. Cillo*, 478 A.2d 755 (N.J. 1984).

49   [2006] HCA 15 and *Waller v. James; Waller v. Hoolihan*, [2006] HCA 16.

gence are designed to restore the plaintiff to the position that he would have been in if the negligence had not taken place. In wrongful life claims this gives rise to a profound and unanswerable philosophical and theological conundrum. If the defendant had exercised care, the plaintiff would not be in existence. A comparison between the state of non-existence and the plaintiff's current state was clearly not justiciable on conventional principles. Policy factors also dictated great caution. There is a risk that the recognition of a wrongful life claim will devalue the sanctity of life in general, and the plaintiff's life in particular. A finding of liability may be interpreted as a finding that the plaintiff's life is a legally recognized loss and that he would be better off dead. Recognition of the action would also produce some uncertainty. It is not clear, for example, if the plaintiff's claim depends upon the manifestation of catastrophic disabilities or whether more minor disabilities may also give rise to the action. Only Kirby J. favoured imposing liability. He avoided the pejorative term "wrongful life," preferring "wrongful suffering," and he emphasized competing policy factors including the need for deterrence against the negligence of health care professionals, the plaintiff's need for adequate compensation and the desirability of allocating the loss to the better loss distributor. In his view the lack of a "comparator" against which the plaintiff's position could be assessed should not deter the courts from awarding general damages for pain and suffering and special damages for needs caused by the defendant's negligence.

The fundamental motivation for actions for prenatal injuries, wrongful birth, and wrongful life actions is the financial need of those born with severe disabilities. Until those needs are adequately met by government the plaintiffs' bar will continue to attempt to utilize the tort system to secure some compensation.

4) Wrongful Pregnancy

This action arises where the defendant's negligence is a cause of the plaintiff's pregnancy. It arises most commonly from negligently performed sterilization, but it may also be brought in respect of an unsuccessful abortion and defective contraceptive products. On learning of her unplanned pregnancy, the plaintiff has three options: to terminate the pregnancy, to continue the pregnancy and raise her child, or continue her pregnancy and put her child up for adoption. Each of these options may generate losses, such as a loss of income during the pregnancy, expenses associated with terminating a pregnancy, non-pecuniary losses, and, in cases of failed sterilization procedures, expenses associated with remedial procedures. These kinds of losses are normally recoverable. The single contentious issue is whether or not a mother who chooses to raise her child can recover child-raising costs and expenses.

There are a number of competing approaches to this issue. The first approach rejects all claims for child-rearing expenses because the birth of a child is a blessing and a source of joy. It ought, therefore, not to be characterized as a harm or loss necessitating compensation. Moreover, such a claim is for pure economic loss, the recovery of which is subject to severe restraints.[50] The second approach applies conventional tort principles and awards full child-rearing costs.[51] The third approach avoids a personalized assessment of child-rearing costs based on the socio-economic circumstances and the lifestyle of the family by making a "one size fits all" conventional sum.[52] The final approach characterizes the claim, not as one for child-rearing expenses, but as a claim by the parents for their *non-pecuniary* losses. The quantum of damages depends upon their reasons for choosing sterilization, and any adverse impact the child has had on their lives such as emotional and relational stresses, disrupted vocational plans, and foregone lifestyle activities and choices.[53] There is as yet no Canadian appellate authority on the point but the current trend is in favour of compensation on one basis or another.[54]

E. OCCUPIERS' LIABILITY

Occupiers' liability determines the care that is owed by those persons who control land (occupiers) to visitors who enter onto that land. The most common case is that of a visitor who slips and falls because of a

---

50 This was the initial approach of the House of Lords in *McFarlane v. Tayside Health Board*, [1999] 4 All E.R. 961 (H.L.). It later reversed its approach, favouring an award of a conventional sum, in *Rees v. Darlington Memorial Hospital N.H.S. Trust*, [2004] 1 A.C. 309 (H.L.) [*Rees*].

51 This approach was adopted by the High Court of Australia in *Cattanach v. Melchior*, [2003] HCA 38, but note that *Cattanach* has been legislatively reversed in some Australian States.

52 In *Rees*, above note 50, the House of Lords adopted this approach awarding a conventional sum of 15,000 pounds to be adjusted for inflation.

53 This approach has been favoured by the British Columbia Supreme Court in *Bevilacqua v. Altenkirk*, [2004] B.C.J. No. 1473 and *Roe v. Dabbs*, [2004] B.C.J. No. 1485. Although the courts did not make a conventional award of damages the quantum in each case was around $50,000.

54 See *Stockford v. Johnson Estate*, [2008] N.B.J. No. 122 (Q.B.).

dangerous defect on the premises. It might be assumed that the tort of negligence is adequate to the task of deciding the liability of an occupier of land. The relationship between an occupier and a visitor is a relationship of proximity, and the duty of care would appear to impose an appropriate standard of reasonable care in the circumstances. Negligence law, however, is not applicable in these situations. Occupiers' liability continues to be a discrete area of tort law, albeit one that is increasingly indistinguishable from the tort of negligence.

The explanation for this state of affairs is that the rules of occupiers' liability crystallized in the late nineteenth and early twentieth centuries before the generalizing and rationalizing influence of *Donoghue v. Stevenson*[55] made itself felt. The rules, which reflected Victorian attitudes to land ownership and civil liability for personal injury, proved to be remarkably resistant to the generalized duty of care and it was only in the latter part of the twentieth century that judicial activism in some provinces and statutory reform in others modernized what is known as the classical law of occupiers' liability. A brief description of the classical law will be useful in understanding the language and concepts used in this area of tort law and the current state of occupiers' liability.

1) The Classical Common Law of Occupiers' Liability

By the early part of the twentieth century, the classical common law doctrine of occupiers' liability, which continues to be the basis of occupiers' liability law in those provinces without reforming legislation, could be stated, if not applied, with a great deal of confidence. This area of tort liability was marked off from the law of negligence by two concepts. First, it applied only to the occupier of land. The concept of occupier included not only those who had exclusive possession of land, such as owners in possession and lessees, but also those who had control of the land. Control provides the opportunity to be aware of dangerous conditions and the power to do something about them. Second, the rules of occupiers' liability applied only to injuries arising from static defects in the premises. Liability for injuries caused by the occupier's activities was controlled by the tort of negligence.

Within these boundaries the occupier's liability was determined by a graduated standard of care tied to the status of the visitor who was injured. This approach called for the classification of the injured visitor as either a trespasser, a licensee, an invitee, or a contractual entrant, and for the application of the correlative standard of care. A trespasser

---

55   Above note 1.

was defined as an entrant who had no express or implied permission to be on the land. The occupier owed no duty to make the premises safe for a trespasser. The only duty was not to intentionally or recklessly injure a trespasser whom the occupier knew to be on the land. A licensee was defined as a visitor who had express or implied permission to be on the land. The occupier's duty was to prevent injury from hidden dangers of which the occupier had actual knowledge. If the occupier not only gave permission to the visitor but also had some economic interest in her presence, the visitor was an invitee. The classic example of the dichotomy between a licensee and an invitee is that between a social guest, in whom the occupier normally has no economic interest, and a customer in a retail store, in whom the occupier does have an economic interest. The standard of care owed to an invitee was substantially the same, in substance, if not in language, as the standard of reasonable care in negligence. The occupier was required to take reasonable care to prevent injuries caused by unusual dangers of which the occupier knew or ought to have known. The term contractual entrant referred to those visitors who entered into a contract, the primary purpose of which was to gain entry onto the land. It included, for example, those who paid to attend concerts and sporting events. In the absence of contractual terms to the contrary, the contract contained an implied warranty that the premises were as safe as reasonable care and skill could make them.

This classical scheme of responsibility faithfully reflected nineteenth-century judicial attitudes to land ownership and personal safety. Overall, it was protective of the occupier by maximizing his interest in freedom of land use at the expense of the visitor's interest in personal security. It reflected the idea that obligations of care are primarily generated by contractual or pseudo-contractual relationships such as the invitor/invitee relationship. It also reflected the traditional common law dichotomy between misfeasance and nonfeasance. The low standard of care to licensees and trespassers was justified on the ground that the injury arose from the occupier's failure to act rather than from his dangerous conduct. It also promoted the idea that no obligation should normally arise where the visitor knew of the danger. Modern Canadian tort law has rejected almost all of these ideas. The interest in personal safety is given much greater priority than property interests. Obligations of care roam free of contractual relationships. The misfeasance/nonfeasance dichotomy no longer applies to special relationships such as exist between an occupier and a visitor, and the defences of voluntary assumption of risk and contributory negligence, which address the issue of the plaintiff's knowledge of the danger, are, in the case of voluntary assumption of risk, held on a tight rein, and, in the case of contributory negligence, no longer bar recovery. As the twentieth century unfolded, the classical doctrine became increasingly inconsistent with modern negligence principles. This unsatisfactory situation was exacerbated by the diversity of land use, the variety of visitors, and new divisions between the ownership and the control of land, which made the application of the classical doctrine increasingly problematic. This prompted two responses. First, the common law, which is applied in Newfoundland and Labrador and Saskatchewan, gradually evolved towards more general principles of reasonable care. Second, in the other provinces statutory intervention swept away the old common law and replaced it with either a legislative regime of responsibility or, in the case of New Brunswick, with negligence principles.

2) The Modern Common Law of Occupiers' Liability

The twentieth century witnessed the development of both covert and open judicial reform of the classical common law of occupiers' liability. These measures have ameliorated some of the harsh pro-defendant bias of the classical doctrine. Covert reform includes a number of techniques which allow the law to be applied in a more pro-plaintiff manner. A judge may, for example, take advantage of the inexactness of the classification system of visitors and assign a visitor to a higher category of entrant in order to apply a more favourable standard of care. Child trespassers may, in some instances, be categorized as licensees on the basis of the implied consent of the occupier. Licensees such as visitors to health care facilities, public libraries, educational institutions, and parks may be categorized as invitees on the basis of some tenuous economic interest of the occupier. There is also a sufficient degree of flexibility in the conventional standards of care to allow them to be applied in a generous pro-plaintiff manner. Occupier's liability rules can also be circumvented by a finding that the defendant was not an occupier or that the injury arose from the occupier's activities rather than a static defect, thereby permitting negligence rules to apply. These stratagems provide greater justice in individual cases but are productive of much uncertainty and unpredictability. Covert activity has been supplemented by an open adjustment of some of the more draconian aspects of classical doctrine. Not surprisingly, particular attention was paid to the low standard of care owed to trespassers and licensees. The main problem in respect of the low standard of care owed to trespassers under the classical doctrine was that it treated all trespassers alike. No differentiation was made between persons who entered the property for criminal purposes, children who lost their way, and adults who mistakenly had exceeded the terms of their licence. The Supreme Court addressed this problem by adopting a more generous standard of care.[56] An occupier who knows of the presence of a trespasser or knows that the presence of a trespasser is likely must act with *common humanity* to prevent injury from dangers of which he is aware. The obligation is not an onerous one. There is no duty on the occupier to inspect his property for dangers, and the very discretionary standard of common humanity allows the courts to tailor the standard of care with reference to the degree of danger on the land, the age of the trespasser, the reason why the trespasser came onto the property, the knowledge and resources of the occupier, and the cost of preventive measures. Often, a warning of the dangers on the property will be sufficient to discharge this obligation to adults. Greater precautions may be necessary to protect children. The standard of common humanity has the advantage of permitting the courts to discriminate between deserving and undeserving trespassers without imposing an intolerable burden on occupiers.

The key problem in respect of licensees was that the classical doctrine dictated a low standard of care to a wide range of visitors to public places and non-commercial private property to whom an obligation of reasonable care seemed more appropriate. Gradually, the standard of care was reformulated in a way that, to a large extent, closed the gap between the standard of care owed to licensees and that owed to invitees. The conventional wisdom now is that an occupier must take reasonable care to protect a licensee from an unusual danger of which the occupier knows or ought to know because he is aware of the circumstances.[57] It appears that the one remaining difference is that an occupier is under an obligation only to invitees to inspect his land for unknown dangers. This gradual coalescence of the standard of care to lawful visitors has recently been completed in Newfoundland and Labrador. In *Stacey v. Anglican Church of Canada (Diocesan Synod of Eastern Newfoundland and Labrador)*,[58] the Court of Appeal swept away the common law rules of occupiers' liability in respect of *lawful visitors*. The Court held that an occupier, in respect of both the condition of the property and his activities on the property, owes a duty to all lawful visitors[59] to take such care as is reasonable, in the circumstances, to see that they are

---

56   *Veinot v. Kerr-Addison Mines Ltd.*, [1975] 2 S.C.R. 311.
57   *Bartlett v. Weiche Apartments Ltd.* (1974), 7 O.R. (2d) 263 at 267 (C.A.).
58   [1999] N.J. No. 275 (C.A.).
59   The position of the trespasser has yet to be resolved definitively.

reasonably safe while using the premises for the purposes for which they are permitted to be there.

3) Legislative Reform

Six provinces—Alberta,[60] British Columbia,[61] Manitoba,[62] Nova Scotia,[63] Ontario,[64] and Prince Edward Island[65]—have opted for a fresh start in occupiers' liability law by replacing the common law with occupiers' liability acts. Only New Brunswick[66] has taken the more radical step of abolishing a discrete occupiers' liability tort, thereby permitting the general principles of negligence to apply.

The occupiers' liability acts are not identical but the central purpose of each is to replace the common law with a duty of reasonable care to almost all visitors. Brief consideration is given here to a representative Act, that of British Columbia. It illustrates the general approach of the other Acts and flags the kind of issues that the legislation of the other provinces address. Each Act, however, requires careful and independent analysis.[67]

The British Columbia *Occupiers Liability Act* was passed in 1974 and was modelled on the Uniform Occupiers' Liability Act proposed by the Conference of Commissioners on the Uniformity of Legislation in Canada.

The scope of the Act and the boundary between occupiers' liability law and negligence law are drawn by the definitions of "occupier" and "premises." "Occupier" is defined as a person with physical possession of the premises or responsibility for, and control over, the condition of the premises, the activities conducted on the premises, and the persons allowed on the premises. The central idea is that with control comes responsibility. Where control rests with more than one person, there may be more than one occupier. "Premises" is given an extended meaning and includes not only land and buildings but also ships, mobile homes, trains, vehicles, and aircraft when they are not in operation. There is quite a lot of consistency among the various Acts on these definitions.

---

60 *Occupiers' Liability Act*, R.S.A. 2000, c. O-4.
61 *Occupiers' Liability Act*, R.S.B.C. 1996, c. 337.
62 *Occupiers' Liability Act*, R.S.M. 1987, c. O8.
63 *Occupiers' Liability Act*, S.N.S. 1996, c. 271.
64 *Occupiers' Liability Act*, R.S.O. 1990, c. O.2.
65 *Occupiers' Liability Act*, R.S.P.E.I. 1988, c. O-2.
66 *Law Reform Act*, S.N.B. 1993, c. L-1.2, s. 2.
67 See Linden, above note 5 at 726–50 for a discussion of the occupiers' liability acts.

The centrepiece of the British Columbia Act is section 3, which replaces the common law with a general standard of reasonable care. The occupier owes a duty of reasonable care to see that visitors, their property, and the unaccompanied property of visitors on the premises is reasonably safe. The Act also removes the static defect limitation of the common law, extending the occupier's obligation of care to his activities on the premises and to the conduct of third parties on the premises. The effect of this language, which is consistent with other Acts, is to impose the same standard of care as that found in the tort of negligence. It increases the level of care owed to trespassers and licensees and reduces that owed to contractual entrants. The standard of care is applied with reference to the foreseeability of damage, the degree of risk of injury, the gravity of the threatened injury, the kind of premises, the burden of preventive measures, the practice of other occupiers, and the purpose of the visit. The cases deal with a range of situations, including "slip and fall," walking or running into structures, falling objects, barroom brawls, and swimming-pool accidents. Occupiers continue to be subject to other Acts or rules of law that impose a higher standard of care in respect of any particular class of person or kind of premises.

A difficult issue in occupiers' liability law is whether or not certain classes of visitors should be excluded from the protection of the general duty of care. The issue arises primarily in respect of trespassers. In British Columbia, the general duty of care is not owed to trespassers with criminal intent or to trespassers on certain agricultural and rural land. The only duty owed to them is not to injure them intentionally and not to act in reckless disregard for their safety. This, of course, is the old common law standard of care in respect of trespassers. The exception for rural and agricultural trespassers may be justified on the ground that they often enter land at unpredictable times, at remote locations, and with varying degrees of frequency. A duty of reasonable care may, therefore, impose too great a burden on landowners. Most of the other Acts also lower the standard of care for certain categories of trespassers. In British Columbia, the same low standard is applied to some lawful entrants on certain agricultural and rural land for recreational purposes and to those visitors who have willingly accepted risks on the land. Most of the other Acts treat the assumption of risk as a complete defence.[68] The partial defence of contributory negligence is available under all the Acts.

---

68 The defence has been interpreted in a manner that is consistent with the narrow definition of the defence of voluntary assumption of risk in negligence law. See

Section 4 of the British Columbia Act allows occupiers to extend, restrict, modify, or exclude the statutory duty by express agreement or notice. There are several qualifications to this power. Reasonable notice must be given of any alteration of the normative standard. An occupier may not restrict, modify, or exclude the statutory obligations in respect of either a visitor not privy to the express agreement or a visitor who is empowered to enter the premises without the consent of the occupier. Finally, the duty of care may not be restricted, modified, or excluded where the occupier is bound by contract to permit persons who are not privy to the contract to enter the premises. These specific qualifications are unique to the British Columbia Act but all of the Acts have similar provisions. Some also require restrictions or exclusions to be reasonable.

At common law, there was some uncertainty about the liability of an occupier for the negligence of independent contractors such as those employed to maintain or repair premises. Section 5 of the Act clarifies the situation in British Columbia. The occupier is not liable for the negligence of an independent contractor provided that it was reasonable to have retained an independent contractor to do the work in question and reasonable care was taken in the selection and supervision of the independent contractor. This provision is common to the other Acts.

At common law, the landlord was immune from liability to the visitors of his tenants. There was no contractual liability because the visitors were not parties to the lease, there was no occupiers' liability because the landlord (an owner out of possession) was not the occupier of the leased premises, and no duty of care was owed in negligence since it was an occupier's liability issue. Section 6 of the Act changed this position in respect of landlords who have a duty to repair and maintain the premises under the lease. The landlord, in those circumstances, is treated as an occupier in respect of all persons on the premises. It must, however, be shown that the plaintiff was injured by the landlord's failure to repair under the terms of the lease.

The remaining provisions further fine-tune the scope of the Act. It does not apply to, or affect, the liability of an employer to an employee, a person subject to the *Hotel Keepers Act*, a person subject to a contract of bailment, or persons subject to a contract for the hire of, or for the carriage of persons or property in, any vehicle, vessel, aircraft, or other means of transportation. The provincial Crown is bound by the Act but it does not apply to public highways and roads or to some private roads.

Waldick v. Malcolm, [1991] 2 S.C.R. 456.

The Act is clearly an improvement on the common law but it produces its own set of problems including the interpretation of statutory language and the construing of the boundaries between occupiers' liability, negligence, and other areas of the law. In retrospect, it may have been better to adopt the New Brunswick reform and simply to abolish the common law rules of occupiers' liability and allow negligence principles to govern.

F. BREACH OF STATUTORY DUTY

One unfortunate consequence of the technological and social progress that Canada enjoyed throughout the twentieth century was a rising tide of personal accident losses. This increase in accident rates led to a much greater emphasis on personal safety and the need for effective accident prevention mechanisms. Both negligence law and statutory regulatory schemes play complementary roles in this important task.

Accident prevention is a legitimate and important aspiration of negligence law. The deterrent power of negligence law, however, probably diminished throughout the course of the twentieth century. The widespread use of liability insurance, the vicarious liability of employers for the wrongdoing of employees, the haphazard application of the tort system to dangerous conduct, and the failure to promote the deterrent power of negligence law by tying damages to the degree of fault or broadening the use of punitive damages, all had an adverse impact on the power of tort law to prevent accidents. Nevertheless, negligence law probably has some residual power to affect the behaviour of certain classes of defendants such as the manufacturers of products who make planned cost-benefit decisions, professionals who may suffer adverse consequences from publicity surrounding successful litigation, uninsured defendants, and defendants whose legal liability may affect the continuation or price of liability insurance coverage.

The erratic and indirect deterrent influence of negligence liability has, however, been supplemented and strengthened by a massive increase in legislative safety regulation and controls. These direct legislative controls promote the safety of citizens in respect of the manufacture and distribution of products and services, the workplace, the environment, transportation, health care, public buildings, public health, and virtually every other societal activity that carries a significant risk of damage to person or property. This legislation is largely independent of the tort system. It normally provides for the adoption of specific safety measures and describes a range of penalties for the failure to comply with them. These legislative instruments are administered by governmental officials, and a scheme of inspection, informal and formal enforcement procedures, and sanctions is normally established. These regulatory schemes have further diminished the importance of negligence as a deterrent device and have led to a heavy reliance on governmental controls to protect the health and safety of citizens. Although the tort of negligence and statutory regulatory schemes are discrete legal phenomena, there are situations where they intersect. Of particular importance are those situations where a person has been injured by a breach of a statutory duty arising from conduct that may or may not be a breach of the common law standard of reasonable care. There has been much debate about the relationship between statutory duties and the tort of negligence in these situations.

There are good reasons to integrate the statutory breach into negligence law in some way. It allows courts to support and reinforce the accident prevention initiatives of government, it offers the courts concrete standards of conduct which have often been set with the assistance of expert advice, policy debate, and the input of those involved in the relevant activities, and it permits courts to add the deterrent clout of tort law to enhance the effectiveness of the legislation.

Most of the debate has, therefore, focused on the legal analysis best suited to accommodate breach of statute within negligence law. Two situations must be kept separate. There are a few statutes that directly address the issue of civil liability for loss caused by their breach. The statute may, for example, expressly state that a breach does not, under any circumstances, give rise to an action in damages. This will be a defence to any tort action. Conversely, the statute may expressly provide that a person damaged by a breach of statute has an action for damages for loss caused by the breach. This creates a discrete statutory cause of action independent of the negligence action. The plaintiff's claim depends solely on proof of the breach of the statute, causation, and damage. Statutes containing an express declaration of legislative intent are, however, the exception.

Most regulatory legislation is, however, silent on the subject of civil liability for loss caused by statutory breach. Its language is directed solely to the duty to be obeyed and the penal consequences of delinquency. The manner in which evidence of statutory breach is to be handled in a negligence action is left to the courts. There are a number of competing views about how to accommodate breach of statute and negligence law where the statute is silent as to its relationship to civil liability. The English theory is based on the fact that some legislation contains an express statutory cause of action. It is reasoned from that premise that the legislature may *impliedly intend* a cause of action in favour of those injured by a breach of a statute. The controlling concept, therefore, is the intention of the legislature as divined from the statutory language and legislative policy. This pursuit of an elusive, and often non-existent, intent of the legislature has been criticized as promoting a great deal of arbitrary decision making and producing considerable uncertainty. If the requisite intent to provide a civil action is discovered, an independent statutory cause of action arises and liability is determined in the same way as an express statutory cause of action.

The American courts have chosen to accommodate the breach of statute within the tort of negligence. The statutory standard is adopted as the standard of care in the negligence action. There has, however, been a disagreement among American courts in respect of the procedural effect of adopting a statutory standard of care. The majority view is that a breach of the standard is negligence *per se*. The setting of the standard of care is taken away from the judge and jury and is set conclusively by the legislation. The minority view is that proof of a breach of a statutory standard is merely another relevant factor in determining if the defendant has met the common law standard of reasonable care.

Canadian courts had shown no fidelity to any one of these theories until the Supreme Court addressed the issue in *Saskatchewan Wheat Pool v. Canada.*[69] In that case, the defendant Wheat Pool delivered infested grain to the plaintiff Wheat Board in breach of section 86(c) of the *Canada Grain Act.*[70] The plaintiff sought to recover the cost of fumigating the grain to make it fit for export. The defendant had not been negligent. Consequently, the plaintiff relied on the English statutory tort theory and the majority American theory of negligence *per se*, neither of which required the proof of negligence in the conventional common law sense. A unanimous Court rejected the plaintiff's contentions and adopted the minority American position. The Court held that the statute may afford a specific and useful standard of conduct, and the breach of it may provide evidence of negligence. The ultimate issue, however, is whether or not the defendant failed to act with reasonable care, something that the plaintiff had not even attempted to prove. The Court rejected the competing views because of their potential to lead to the imposition of strict liability. That potential was well illustrated by the *Wheat Pool* case itself. The Court reasoned that the imposition of a strict civil liability for a minor breach of statute, the remedy for which

---

69   [1983] 1 S.C.R. 205 [*Wheat Pool*].
70   S.C. 1970-71-72, c. 7.

would normally be a small fine, would be unduly burdensome to the defendant and productive of unfairness.

There is no doubt that the *Wheat Pool* case has settled the Canadian debate about the place of breach of statutory duty in tort law.[71] Ultimately, liability depends on fault and the application of negligence principles. The choice of negligence as the controlling basis of liability may have been influenced by the unusual facts of the *Wheat Pool* case. First, the issue of statutory breach most commonly arises in respect of safety statutes and personal injury litigation. The statutory provision under consideration in the *Wheat Pool* case dealt with the quality of a commercial commodity. It did not raise the issues of deterrence and compensation of personal accident losses, which may have led to a greater sympathy for the English or majority American theories. Second, the loss was essentially economic and the courts are notoriously reluctant to allow recovery of economic loss in negligence. Any theory that might lead to the imposition of a strict liability for economic loss was not likely to succeed. Third, on the facts of the case and in the absence of negligence, there does not appear to be any compelling reason to shift the loss from the shoulders of one excellent loss distributor to those of another. These factors clearly support the choice of fault rather than the statutory breach as the touchstone of civil liability in the *Wheat Pool* case. Nevertheless, they also indicate that the case was atypical and that the Court might have found the majority American theory more attractive if the case had been one of statutory breach causing personal injuries.

The later Supreme Court decision in *Galaske v. O'Donnell*[72] provides a useful perspective. In that case, the defendant driver failed to ensure that an eight-year-old passenger was securely fastened in an available seat belt in direct contravention of section 217(6) of the British Columbia *Motor Vehicle Act*,[73] which prohibits the driving of an automobile unless children between the ages of six and sixteen are wearing a seat belt. The Court held that the defendant owed the plaintiff a duty of care and then applied its decision in *Wheat Pool* to the standard of care issue. The breach of the statute was not conclusive of the issue of due care. It could be taken as an indication that the defendant's conduct was unreasonable but it was necessary to consider all the relevant factors to determine if, in the circumstances of the individual case, the defendant

---

71   The Supreme Court confirmed its decision in *Wheat Pool* in *Holland v. Saskatchewan*, [2008] S.C.J. No. 43 [*Holland*] where the Court held that the breach of a statutory duty by government does not in itself constitute negligence.

72   [1994] 1 S.C.R. 670 [*Galaske*].

73   R.S.B.C. 1979, c. 288.

had failed to take due care. Since the defendant had clearly taken no steps to ensure that the seat belt was fastened, negligence was readily found. It was recognized that, in other cases, it might be more difficult to determine the issue of reasonable care and that it might depend upon the age of the driver, the relationship among the passengers, and other relevant circumstances.

It is in this kind of case that the American negligence *per se* theory is most attractive. The result in *Galaske* would be the same, but the adoption of the statutory standard as the controlling standard of care leads to much greater certainty and predictability. It shows a strong commitment to the safety initiatives of government. It promotes the deterrent and compensatory functions of tort law. Moreover, there is, arguably, no great injustice in imposing strict liability where personal injury arises from dangerous activities that are conducted in violation of statutory regulations.

It was open to the Supreme Court to distinguish *Galaske* from the *Wheat Pool* case on the ground that *Wheat Pool* dealt with the quality of a commercial product, not the safety of children on the highway. This would have allowed the Court to impose a more stringent liability in respect of dangerous activities such as the operation of motor vehicles. A stricter liability would also have been consistent with the conventional treatment of industrial safety statutes, which the Court isolated for special mention in *Wheat Pool*. The Court did not disapprove of the strict liability that historically has been imposed for a breach of those statutes.[74] Yet it declined to make these distinctions and it now seems fully committed to a global approach to breach of statutory duty on the basis of the tort of negligence. There is, however, room in this approach to take into account the nature of the statute and the interest it is designed to protect, and to give special emphasis to the evidence of breach of the statute. In appropriate cases, courts are not uncomfortable with a covert strict liability under the cover of negligence law.

The approach taken by the Supreme Court in respect of the breach of statutory obligations is mirrored in its approach to evidence that the defendant was *in compliance* with statutory duties. The issue arose in *Ryan v. Victoria (City of)*.[75] In that case, the plaintiff motorcyclist attempted to cross the defendant's railway track, which ran down the centre of a street. The front wheel of the motorcycle wedged into the flangeway gap running along the inside edge of the tracks. He was thrown off his

---

74   There is, however, little scope in Canada for a tort action based on the breach of an industrial safety statute because of the workers' compensation schemes. The Court appears to have been referring to the English experience.

75   [1999] 1 S.C.R. 201 [*Ryan*].

motorcycle and injured. The defendant argued that it was not negligent because it was in compliance with all statutory rules and regulations in respect of its track. The Supreme Court held that compliance with statutory obligations was not a complete defence to an action in negligence. It provides evidence of reasonable conduct but the controlling standard is the common law standard of reasonable care. The weight to be given to statutory compliance depends upon the kind of case before the court. More weight is given to it where the legislation prescribes specific statutory standards of conduct and the case falls comfortably within the scope of the legislation. Less weight will be ascribed to it where the legislation prescribes general and discretionary standards of conduct and the case does not fall comfortably within the scope of the legislation. In *Ryan* the legislation gave significant discretion as to the width of the flangeway gap and the case did not fall comfortably within its scope because the regulations were designed primarily to deal with railway crossings. The Court held that the standard of reasonable care dictated a narrower flangeway gap, which, on the facts, would have prevented the accident.

G. PURE ECONOMIC LOSS

The expansion of negligence law prompted by *Donoghue v. Stevenson* has provided a broad protection of personal security and property interests. It was not until the case of *Hedley Byrne & Co. Ltd. v. Heller & Partners Ltd.*,[76] however, that the courts began to extend the tort of negligence to provide a remedy for pure economic loss. The word *pure* is used to exclude those situations where the economic loss is consequential upon damage to the person or property. Injured earners have always been able to recover their loss of income, and the owner of a damaged chattel may recover repair costs and any unavoidable loss of profits. The distinguishing characteristic of those situations is that the plaintiff has suffered some threshold damage to her person or property and the economic loss flows from that initial damage. The pure economic loss cases deal with plaintiffs whose sole loss is economic or financial.

There are a number of reasons for the delayed and cautious recognition of pure economic loss claims. First, there is the fear that a recognition of liability for economic loss might trigger a flood of litigation. The damage caused to person or property as a result of negligence is, in most circumstances, confined to a handful of people. The

---

76   [1964] A.C. 465 (H.L.) [*Hedley Byrne*].

diversity and wealth of interrelating economic relationships in a market economy suggest that an act of negligence that causes damage to the economic interests of one person may have a ripple effect causing related economic harm to many other persons. This concern has been captured by the evocative words of Cardozo C.J. in *Ultramares Corp. v. Touche*.[77] He warned that economic loss cases present the potential for "liability in an indeterminate amount for an indeterminate time to an indeterminate class."[78] These words have become something of a mantra for judges in all common law jurisdictions. Worst-case scenarios include negligent acts that sever the supply of electricity to a city, close major transportation routes, disable communication networks, or disseminate erroneous investment advice to the world via the Internet. The conventional control devices, as they have been interpreted in personal injury and property cases, could not prevent a multitude of claims that might result in a burdensome liability totally disproportionate to the degree of the defendant's negligence. Second, economic interests have not traditionally been assigned the same value or importance as personal or property interests. The priority of personal safety is obvious. It is more difficult to explain why property has been assigned greater value than wealth. There may be reasons other than the historical emphasis on property interests in the common law. It may, in part, be because property is the tangible result of a person's work and effort and it is selected by the owner to serve her personal needs and tastes. There is, therefore, a degree of emotional attachment to property and a sense of personal violation when it is damaged or destroyed. In contrast, wealth, which is independent of property, is not only a luxury that relatively few people enjoy, but is also suggestive of corporate and commercial interests disassociated from the ordinary person. Third, economic loss has conventionally been seen as the subject matter of contract law. Generally, financial interests and expectations have been secured by contractual relationships, and the recognition of tort liability for economic losses inevitably affects traditional ideas about the boundaries between the two regimes of civil responsibility. Contractual liability has been carefully constrained by the doctrines of consideration and privity of contract. In combination, they have, in the main, restricted contractual liability to those who are parties to an exchange transaction. There has been some reluctance to subvert traditional boundaries by unleashing tort law and allowing it to intrude

---

77   174 N.E. 441 (N.Y. 1931).
78   *Ibid.* at 444.

into the citadel of contract law.[79] Fourth, the high cost of liability insurance in comparison to first-party insurance has supported the traditional reluctance to reallocate economic losses from those who suffer them to those who cause them. Finally, in a free market economy it is generally permissible to intentionally inflict economic loss on rivals and competitors. There is, therefore, a certain disassociation from the normal tort principles that provide broader protection of interests from intentional conduct than from negligent conduct.

In spite of these reservations, the House of Lords in *Hedley Byrne*[80] launched negligence law into the field of economic loss by recognizing that in certain circumstances liability may be imposed for pure economic loss caused by a negligent misrepresentation. It was the first step in extending the reach of negligence law to economic losses. Since that decision, the courts have been involved in the as yet unfinished task of defining the scope and extent of liability for economic loss in negligence law. In this process they have been assisted by the insight of Professor Feldthusen,[81] who has pointed out that economic loss cases can best be analysed by grouping them into categories that give rise to similar policy concerns and similar solutions. These categories include negligent misrepresentation, negligent performance of a service, relational economic loss, and claims for economic loss arising from the supply of poor quality goods and structures.[82] The Supreme Court has relied on both this framework of analysis and the general test of a duty of care to define the appropriate scope of negligence liability for pure economic loss.

1) Negligent Misrepresentation

The landmark case on liability for pure economic loss caused by a negligent misrepresentation is *Hedley Byrne*. In that case, the defendant

---

79 See *Martel Building Ltd. v. Canada*, [2000] 2 S.C.R. 860, where the Supreme Court held that a party to arm's length commercial contractual negotiations does not owe a duty of care to the other party. The Court reasoned that such a duty would be inconsistent with the beneficial process of bargaining in a free market and that existing contractual and tortious remedies exercised sufficient control on the negotiation process. See also *Design Services Ltd. v. Canada*, [2008] S.C.J. No. 22 and *Exploits Valley Air Services Ltd. v. College of the North Atlantic (Board of Governors of)*, [2005] N.J. No. 274 (C.A.).

80 Above note 76.

81 B. Feldthusen, *Economic Negligence*, 5th ed. (Scarborough, ON: Carswell, 2008).

82 There is a fifth category dealing with loss caused by the negligent exercise of statutory powers by public bodies. This issue is given separate consideration because the relevant principles cover personal injury, property damage, and pure economic loss.

bank negligently provided a positive credit report to the plaintiff in respect of one of the plaintiff's customers. The plaintiff relied on the information and took a personal responsibility for some of its customer's business liabilities. It suffered economic loss when the customer went into receivership and was unable to discharge those liabilities. The bank had sought to insulate itself from any potential liability by including in the credit report a written disclaimer of responsibility for its accuracy.

The plaintiff was forced to argue its case in negligence because the established causes of action for economic loss caused by words (contract, deceit, and fiduciary law) were not applicable. There was no contract between the plaintiff and the defendant because the plaintiff provided the credit report free of charge. The plaintiff could not, therefore, rely on an implied warranty that reasonable care would be taken in the preparation of the credit report. The plaintiff also had no action in the tort of deceit. Deceit requires proof of fraud. A fraudulent misrepresentation is one that the representor either knows is untrue or is consciously reckless as to whether it is true or false. The common thread uniting these alternative definitions is that the defendant has no honest belief in the truth of the statement. The defendant bank was not guilty of fraud because it had an honest belief in the truth of its credit report. At most, there was a failure to take care in its preparation. There was also no basis for arguing that the relationship between the defendant and the plaintiff was a fiduciary relationship giving rise to stringent obligations of good faith, loyalty, and care. The relationship between a bank and its customer is typically an arm's length commercial relationship and there must be special circumstances giving rise to a high degree of trust, reliance, and confidence by the customer in the bank before the relationship is transformed into one that requires fiduciary care. Consequently, the plaintiff's case depended on the tort of negligence and a willingness of the House of Lords to recognize a duty of care.

The House of Lords accepted that in certain circumstances a duty of care may arise in providing "information, opinion or advice."[83] The Court was, however, cautious in defining those circumstances. It made it clear that the duty of care could not be defined solely by the foreseeability of economic loss. Foreseeability, as interpreted in cases of personal injury and property damage, could not keep liability for economic loss caused by words within reasonable and appropriate boundaries. Particular concern was expressed about the wide range of situations in

---

83   *Hedley Byrne*, above 76 at 482.

which advice and information is given and the need to avoid imposing liability where words are spoken on social, family, and other informal occasions. A constant obligation to be careful in all that one says would not only be burdensome and a threat to one's freedom of speech, but would also be unrealistic in the light of human nature. Unless the occasion demands it, people often speak without reflection or prudence and they rarely ponder their words for accuracy or parse them for various connotations. It is not reasonable to expect care to be taken unless the nature of the occasion or the words of the inquirer signal the importance of the information and the likelihood of reliance on it by the plaintiff.

The Court was also influenced by the fact that information can circulate quickly and spread to large numbers of persons. Moreover, the power of information to cause economic loss to many persons is not exhausted by its initial causation of economic loss to one person. When a defective product causes personal injury, it is discarded or repaired. Defective information may continue to circulate unabated and uncorrected long after the initial loss has been caused.

The solution to these concerns was found in the limiting concept of a *special relationship* that could be used on a case-by-case basis to identify the occasions on which a duty of care may arise. The concept of a special relationship is, of course, not a guiding principle. It is a vehicle to express a judicial conclusion that on the facts of the case the speaker was obliged to exercise care. The factors in *Hedley Byrne* that supported a finding of a *special relationship* included the plaintiff's request for the credit report, the expertise of the bank in such matters, the seriousness of the occasion on which the report was given, and the reasonable and foreseeable reliance of the plaintiff. On the other hand, an important factor that pointed to the opposite conclusion was that the credit report was accompanied by a disclaimer. It signalled that no responsibility was being taken for the accuracy of the report and that no reliance should be placed on it. The Court concluded that the disclaimer was the most compelling factor and it concluded that the defendant owed no duty of care to the plaintiff.

The general principle in *Hedley Byrne* was immediately adopted by Canadian courts and most cases have been decided with reference to the notion of a special relationship. In due course it became apparent that the most compelling factors in deciding whether or not there was a special relationship were the defendant's voluntary assumption of responsibility for the accuracy of her words and the plaintiff's foreseeable and reasonable reliance on the information. In most cases, it was unnecessary to determine which was the true determinant of a duty of care, and the Supreme Court avoided choosing one or the other until its decision in *Hercules Management Ltd. v. Ernst & Young.*[84] In that case, the court de-emphasized the language of special relationship and the importance of an assumption of responsibility and stressed the importance of the concept of *foreseeable and reasonable reliance* by the plaintiff. The Court also noted that the negligent misrepresentation cases should not be isolated from the general law of negligence. As far as possible, the *Anns* test, as it was then constituted, should be used to determine if a duty of care is owed by the defendant to the plaintiff. Few cases will be decided differently after *Hercules* but it does provide an authoritative framework for the development of liability for negligent misrepresentations in Canada.

a) Duty of Care

The Supreme Court in *Hercules* recognized that some modification of the *Anns* test was necessary to accommodate the special features of negligent misrepresentation cases. To establish the *prima facie* duty of care under the first branch of the *Anns* test, it is not sufficient to show that the defendant might reasonably foresee damage to the plaintiff. In negligent misrepresentation cases, the plaintiff must establish that the representor "ought reasonably to have foreseen that the plaintiff would rely on his representation and that reliance by the plaintiff, in the circumstances, would be reasonable."[85] It is then necessary, under the second branch of the test, to determine if the *prima facie* duty creates sufficient concerns of indeterminate liability that it must be negated on the grounds of public policy.[86]

i) *Foreseeable Reliance/Reasonable Reliance: The* Prima Facie *Duty of Care*

The foreseeable and reasonable reliance necessary to establish a *prima facie* duty of care is not a precise or certain concept. It is highly fact-sensitive and dependent on a number of factors, none of which is, in itself, conclusive. There are a number of general indicia, most of which were mentioned in *Hercules*.[87]

---

84   [1997] 2 S.C.R. 165 [*Hercules*].

85   *Ibid.* at 200 [emphasis added].

86   There is nothing in *Cooper v. Hobart*, [2001] 3 S.C.R. 537 [*Cooper*] to indicate any disagreement with the analysis of duty of care for negligent misrepresentation adopted in *Hercules*.

87   See also Feldthusen, above note 81 at 34–86.

aa. The Expertise and Knowledge of the Representor

The duty of care is not restricted to professional persons or those who are in the business of giving advice to others. Nevertheless, a duty of care most commonly arises where the defendant has some special expertise, knowledge, skill, information, or access to information that is not possessed by the ordinary person. The cases indicate that a duty of care has been placed on a wide range of professionals, those in trades and businesses, and those who work for private and public institutions including governmental officials. It is both readily foreseeable and reasonable that ordinary persons and business entities will rely on those with superior knowledge or special skills in accessing and evaluating information. An imbalance of information between the defendant and the plaintiff is, therefore, a reliable indicator of a *prima facie* duty of care.

A duty will also be placed on those who represent themselves as having a greater expertise than they, in fact, have. They cannot be heard to complain when the reliance that they have invited occurs. Conversely, it is normally unforeseeable and unreasonable for persons to rely on those who do not enjoy or represent themselves as having any special expertise. Everyone knows of people who have an answer for everything and an opinion on everyone, but, if it is clear that they have no special expertise, few of us rely on them.

bb. The Seriousness of the Occasion

The nature of the occasion is an important factor in establishing a duty of care. Reliance on information is foreseeable and reasonable when it is given on a business, professional, formal, or serious occasion. It is not normally reasonable to rely on information that is given in a casual, recreational, social, or informal setting. There is a world of difference between giving legal advice under a retainer and giving it in reply to a casual inquiry at a boisterous party. There may, however, be exceptional cases. An inquirer at a social event may put the defendant on guard by indicating the seriousness of the matter and her intention to rely on the advice. In such circumstances, there is no duty to reply, but, if the defendant does, he is likely to be held to be under a duty of care.

cc. An Initial Request for Information

It is probably more reasonable to rely on information that was, at least initially, given at the request of some person. A request indicates to the defendant that the inquirer, and possibly others, have a real interest in receiving the information and that they are likely to rely on it. Like all factors, however, a request is not conclusive. If information is volunteered without a prior request to a person or to a small targeted group of persons who have special interest in the information and are likely to rely on it, there is no impediment to finding a duty of care. This situation may, however, be contrasted with information that is volunteered to the public at large through modern systems of mass communication. Reliance on information distributed by the media, supplied by governments to the public, or posted on the Internet may not be foreseeable or reasonable unless it is deliberately tailored to the special circumstances of individual persons or a special class of persons. In *Premakumaran v. Canada*,[88] for example, the Federal Court of Appeal held that the Government did not owe a duty of care to prospective immigrants in respect of general informational brochures and documents prepared for their use.

dd. Pecuniary Interest

Any direct or indirect financial benefit received by the representor, or anticipated by the representor, increases the cachet of the information and encourages reliance on it. The pecuniary interest of the defendant is, therefore, an influential factor in establishing a duty of care. This is particularly so where the information is provided under contract. Information and advice that is purchased is reasonably perceived as being more reliable than information that has been given gratuitously, and that probably holds true in respect of non-privity third parties such as those who rely on the financial reports that auditors prepare under contract for client corporations.[89] Even an indirect pecuniary interest may have some bearing on the issue of duty. It is not uncommon for businesses to provide assistance and information without payment as a public promotions gesture. There may be the hope of future business or a desire to cultivate relationships with existing customers. In those cases, it is not at all unreasonable for the recipients to expect that reasonable care has been taken to ensure the accuracy of the information provided.

ee. The Nature of the Statement

There is some difference in opinion about the importance of the nature of the statement on which the plaintiff relied. At one extreme, it is said that liability for a negligent statement is restricted to erroneous statements of fact, and that statements of prediction, opinion, forecast, and advice are never actionable under *Hedley Byrne*. The alternative view is

---

88   [2006] F.C.J. No. 893 (C.A.).

89   The *prima facie* duty of care to third parties may, however, be restricted or negated on policy grounds because of indeterminacy concerns.

that reliance upon facts may be more foreseeable and reasonable than reliance on more subjective and speculative statements, but there is no hard and fast rule about it.[90] This is an issue that does seem to call for a flexible approach. First, it is not easy to categorize representations. Many communications are an amalgam of fact, opinion, and conclusions. The credit report in *Hedley Byrne*, for example, would appear to contain as much opinion and prediction as fact. Second, many professionals and other experts are not relied on primarily to collect and communicate facts. Their essential task is to analyse facts and, on the basis of their expert skill and knowledge, provide advice, opinions, and projections to assist people and businesses to make informed decisions that are in their financial interests. This is the work of investment advisers, lawyers, accountants, real estate appraisers, and many more. To restrict the duty of care to factual statements unduly restricts the scope of responsibility. The issue is better resolved by a determination of whether or not the reliance was, in the circumstances, foreseeable and reasonable. The courts can then discriminate between, on the one hand, the responsibility of an investment adviser who recommends the purchase of shares in a corporation that he has not investigated and knows nothing about and, on the other, the responsibility of a fortune-teller informing the plaintiff of his financial destiny.

ff. Disclaimers

As a general rule, a disclaimer of responsibility for the accuracy or reliability of the representation will prevent the establishment of a duty of care. It is normally not foreseeable that a person will rely on information for which the defendant has disclaimed responsibility and any reliance on it is likely to be regarded as unreasonable. Nevertheless, there may be exceptional circumstances where disclaimers will not be operative. First, insufficient notice may have been given of the disclaimer and the plaintiff may, reasonably, have acted in ignorance of it. Second, there is no judicial enthusiasm for disclaimers and it can be expected that courts will construe them severely against the defendant.[91] Third, it may, occasionally, be reasonable to rely on information in spite of a known disclaimer. The information may not, for example, be available from any other source and it may not be possible to verify the information. A court may be sympathetic to the plaintiff when he had no choice but to rely on the information. The decision of the Brit-

---

90   This issue was recognized, but left unresolved, by the Supreme Court in *Queen v. Cognos Inc.*, [1993] 1 S.C.R. 87 [*Cognos*].

91   *Cognos, ibid.*

ish Columbia Court of Appeal in *Micron Construction Ltd. v. Hong Kong Bank*[92] is illustrative. In that case, the defendant bank made negligent misrepresentations to the contractor that financing was secured for a large construction project. The bank knew that the information would be passed on to the plaintiff sub-trades. The Court held that the bank could not rely on its written disclaimer because the bank was making a significant profit from the loan, it generally did not use a disclaimer when giving a construction loan confirmation letter, and there was no other way for the sub-trades to secure the information. In those circumstances, the reliance of the plaintiffs was reasonable and justifiable. This case brings into question the actual decision in *Hedley Byrne*. In that case, the defendant bank had unique access to the requested information and reliance was placed on the bank's expertise and its general reputation for accuracy and integrity. If *Hedley Byrne* was decided today, the formulaic words of a disclaimer might not be sufficient to protect the defendant from liability.

Disclaimers may also be embodied in written contracts between the defendant and the plaintiff. As a general rule, a contractual relationship between the parties does not negate tort liability for statements that are made before the contract is entered into or during the performance of the contract. Tort and contract liability is concurrent, not mutually exclusive. The plaintiff generally, therefore, has a full and free choice to choose the most advantageous cause of action. Tort liability may not, however, subvert or contradict the terms of the contract, and if an exemption clause negates tort liability for a negligent misrepresentation, the contractual provision governs.[93] At points of inconsistency and contradiction, the contract "trumps" tort.[94]

ii) Policy Concerns: The Issue of Indeterminacy
The *prima facie* duty of care may be negated where a problem of indeterminacy arises. This occurs most acutely in respect of information that is initially prepared for a client under a contract but is subsequently circulated to a broad range of non-privity third parties who use it for a variety of purposes. This was the central issue in *Hercules*. The defendant was a firm of chartered accountants who prepared the annual audited financial statements for corporations in which the plaintiffs were shareholders and investors. The plaintiffs argued that they had relied

---

92   (2000), 184 D.L.R. (4th) 75 (B.C.C.A.).
93   Disclaimers in contracts are, however, subject to strict interpretation under the *contra proferentum* rule. See *Cognos*, above note 90.
94   The relationship between tort and contract is covered more extensively in chapter 8.

on the negligently prepared audited statements and had made financial decisions relating to their shareholdings and investments based on them. In due course the companies went into receivership and the plaintiffs suffered financial loss.

The Supreme Court had no difficulty in finding a *prima facie* duty of care. It was readily foreseeable that the shareholders and investors would rely on the financial statements and it was reasonable for them to do so since the statements were prepared by professional persons under contract with the corporations. There were, however, in the Court's opinion, severe indeterminacy problems in the area of auditors' liability. A corporation's audited financial statements may be used by many different persons, including customers, creditors, shareholders, investors, employees, and takeover bidders, for a wide variety of purposes. The losses generated by an auditor's negligence may, therefore, be extravagant and disproportionate to the fault of the defendant. A flood of claims would lead to a heavy expenditure of time and money by accounting firms in defensive practices and in defending litigation. This would ultimately increase the cost of accounting services and possibly lead to a decrease in the availability of those services. These consequences would be detrimental to the profession and disadvantageous to the public. The Court held that factors of this kind are sufficient to negate the *prima facie* duty of care to non-privity third parties unless the factual matrix of the case is such as to allay the fears of indeterminacy. This arises where the defendant knows that identifiable plaintiffs or members of an identifiable class of plaintiffs are going to rely on the information and the information is used by them for the precise or specific purpose for which it was prepared. In *Hercules*, the defendant knew the identity of the plaintiffs, since they had been the auditors of the corporations for many years, but the Court held that the audited statements were prepared solely for the statutory purpose of allowing the shareholders, as a collective, to supervise and oversee the management of the corporations, not to assist the plaintiffs in making personal investment decisions. This negated the *prima facie* duty of care owed to the plaintiffs.

Two earlier Supreme Court decisions provide illustrations of situations where the *prima facie* duty of care to non-privity third parties does not raise indeterminacy problems. In *Haig v. Bamford*,[95] the defendant auditors were requested by their client, a private corporation, to prepare an audited financial statement for the purposes of attracting equity investment. The plaintiff was one of a limited class of potential

---

95   [1977] 1 S.C.R. 466.

investors that the defendant knew would be relying on the statement to make that investment decision. The financial statement was prepared negligently and the plaintiff lost the equity investment that he made in reliance on it. The defendant was held liable for the plaintiff's investment loss. In *Edgeworth Construction Ltd. v. N.D. Lea & Associates Ltd.*,[96] the defendant engineering firm contracted with the British Columbia government to design and provide drawings and specifications for the construction of a highway. The government incorporated the drawings and specifications in the information provided to tenderers for the construction contract. The plaintiff, Edgeworth, who was the successful tenderer, relied on the information that was incorporated into the construction contract with the government. The plaintiff suffered financial loss because of negligent errors in the drawings and specifications. Concerns about an indeterminate liability were allayed by the defendant's knowledge that a limited class of construction companies would rely on the information for the precise purpose for which it was prepared and, in the long run, only the successful tenderer could suffer any loss.

The *Hercules* decision will, nevertheless, keep liability to non-privity third parties in tight check. Some will regret that the Court did not entertain a more generous scope of liability for negligent advice and information. There are policy factors that support a more consumer-friendly approach. It may be argued, for example, that the indeterminacy concerns in the area of negligent statements are overstated and that reliable and accurate information is such an important component of a fair and efficient marketplace that negligence law ought not to be unduly restrained in an information age from providing consumer protection to a wider range of users.

b) Standard of Care, Causation, and Contributory Negligence
The importance and attention paid to the duty of care in negligent misrepresentation cases must not overshadow the other equally important components of the negligence action.[97] It must not be overlooked, for example, that the liability for misrepresentations is not based solely on the inaccuracy of the information. The defendant is not a guarantor of the truth of the information he provides. The defendant is obliged

---

96   [1993] 3 S.C.R. 206.

97   In their joint judgment in *Cognos*, above note 90, Sopinka and Iacobucci JJ. provided a useful list of all the elements of a negligent misrepresentation action: (1) a duty of care between the representor and representee; (2) an untrue, inaccurate, or misleading misrepresentation; (3) negligence; (4) reasonable reliance; and (5) detrimental reliance in the sense that harm was suffered.

only to take reasonable care to ensure that the information is accurate. The appropriate standard of care was discussed at some length by the Supreme Court in *Cognos*,[98] which dealt with an employer's misrepresentation about the nature and existence of an employment opportunity for which the plaintiff successfully applied. The employer suggested that the only obligation was one of common honesty. The employee argued that the employer was under an obligation to make complete disclosure of all relevant information. The Supreme Court rejected both arguments, affirming the traditional standard of the care of a reasonable person. The defendant must "exercise such reasonable care as the circumstances require to ensure that representations made are accurate and not misleading."[99]

There is little difficulty with the common case of an express statement made with a lack of care. The more difficult situations involve implied misrepresentations and the failure to volunteer information that, in the circumstances of the case, is highly relevant to the plaintiff. Courts have had no hesitation in imposing liability for implied misrepresentations. They are acutely aware of the possibility that statements which are technically accurate may, nevertheless, create a false impression because of the delicate choice of words, the relationship between the parties, or the surrounding circumstances. There may also be special circumstances where there is a duty to volunteer information that is highly relevant to the plaintiff. This involves considerations similar to those that are relevant to the duty of affirmative action. It all depends on the relationship between the parties and the circumstances of the case. Disclosure has been required, for example, in the context of insurance and employment contracts. An insurance broker has special expertise and information on which the average citizen is particularly dependent for guidance in respect of risk and coverage. A full discussion of insurable risks and available coverage may be necessary.[100] An employer has also been required to provide highly relevant information to a prospective applicant about the nature and existence of the employment opportunity.[101] The central importance of employment, the monopoly of information enjoyed by the employer, and the power differential between prospective employers and many job applicants all underline the importance of such disclosure.

The concept of reliance plays a dual role in negligent misrepresentation cases. In order to establish a duty of care under *Hercules*, it must

---

98 Above note 90.
99 *Ibid.* at 121.
100 *Fletcher v. Manitoba Public Insurance Corp.*, [1990] 3 S.C.R. 191.
101 *Cognos*, above note 90.

be established that reliance by the plaintiff is foreseeable and reasonable in the particular circumstances of the case. The second role relates to causation. It must be shown that the plaintiff did, in fact, rely on the misrepresentation. Prior to *Hercules*, the common formulation of the cause-in-fact requirement was that the plaintiff must prove that the plaintiff did in fact *reasonably* rely on the representation. After *Hercules*, the issue has been narrowed to whether there was actual reliance. The reasonableness question has been subsumed within the duty issue since it must now be shown that the reliance would have been reasonable *on the facts of the particular case* to impose a duty of care. The proof of actual reliance, however, remains essential to show causation.

A final point of some debate is the applicability of the defence of contributory negligence in negligent misrepresentation cases. The current emphasis on reasonable reliance suggests that the plaintiff has acted prudently and that the defence will be difficult to establish. The issue was considered by the Ontario Court of Appeal in *Avco Financial Services Realty Ltd. v. Norman*.[102] The Court held that if the claim of contributory negligence is based on the contention that the plaintiff acted unreasonably in relying on the misrepresentation it is unsustainable because reasonable reliance is an essential element of the cause of action. It recognized, nevertheless, that there may be situations where the circumstances surrounding the event that occasioned the loss are different or wider from those which surrounded the making of the misrepresentation. A finding of contributory negligence in those situations may not be inconsistent with the finding of liability. A prudent plaintiff may, for example, have heeded some subsequent information or advice from a third party or made some further inquiries before acting.[103] Contributory negligence will also be available where the plaintiff has negligently exacerbated his losses or unreasonably failed to mitigate them.

2) Negligent Performance of a Service

Pure economic loss may also be caused by the negligent failure to perform a service. In most situations, services are provided pursuant to a contract between the service supplier and the plaintiff. That contract will, in the absence of exempting provisions to the contrary, contain a warranty that the services will be performed with reasonable skill and care. A failure to perform that obligation will give rise to an action

---

102 [2003] O.J. No. 1255 (C.A.).

103 See *S. Maclise Enterprises Inc. v. Union Securities Ltd.*, [2009] A.J. No. 1405 (C.A.) (failure to conduct proper diligence with respect to matters outside the representations).

for breach of contract. The nature of the loss presents no obstacles to a contract action. Contract law, however, provides incomplete protection in respect of the negligent performance of services in two situations. First, contract law provides no remedy for economic loss caused by the negligent performance of a gratuitous service. If the service is free, there is no consideration, and an essential element of a contract is absent. Secondly, the negligent performance of a contractual service may cause economic loss to a third person who stands to benefit directly or indirectly from the promised performance. The rule of privity of contract prevents the third party from suing on the contract. Third parties who stand to gain from the performance of gratuitous services are doubly disadvantaged in contract law because of the absence of both consideration and the lack of privity. One answer to this problem is to reform contract law and free it from the constraints of consideration and privity doctrine. In due course, this may occur but the reform of traditional contract law has proved to be a slow, incremental, and conservative process. Consequently, innovative lawyers have sought to outflank the narrow and rigid law of contract by turning to the dynamism and flexibility of negligence law to broaden liability for the negligent performance of services.

It will be apparent that the problem with expanding the duty of care into this area is less one of indeterminacy and more one of finding criteria to identify relationships that, while not contractual, are sufficiently *equivalent to contract* to warrant the imposition of liability. The courts have, therefore, been influenced by the ideas of an *assumption of responsibility* by the service provider to the plaintiff and a *reasonable and justifiable reliance* by the plaintiff on the service provider. A relationship evidencing these characteristics is often sufficient to support a duty of reasonable care to avoid economic loss to the plaintiff in the performance of a service.

a)   The Negligent Performance of a Gratuitous Service to the Plaintiff

The negligent performance of a gratuitous service directly to the plaintiff will often give rise to a duty of care. An assumption of responsibility and foreseeable reliance, coupled with proof of negligence and damage generated by the plaintiff's reliance, is normally sufficient to impose liability.[104] This may be illustrated by some situations arising from the

---

104 Feldthusen, above note 81 at 128.

placement of insurance.[105] A defendant may gratuitously undertake to secure insurance for the plaintiff. The defendant may carry out that task negligently by, for example, making misrepresentations to the insurer which invalidate the insurance policy, by failing to insure fully the plaintiff's interests, or by failing to ensure compliance with some condition of the insurer on which the coverage depends. The willingness to undertake an important task such as this is often not only indicative of an assumption of responsibility by the defendant, but it also generates reasonable and foreseeable reliance by the plaintiff. The defendant will be liable for uninsured losses resulting from his negligence.

An allied and more difficult issue arises where the defendant has promised to perform a gratuitous service but has failed to carry it out at all. Courts are more cautious in this situation because a more direct attack is being made on the contract rule that there is no obligation to perform a gratuitous promise, and on the negligence rule that there is no general duty of affirmative action. Nevertheless, there would seem to be no significant difference between a person who, for example, gratuitously undertakes to secure insurance for another person and does it negligently and another who undertakes the same task and does not do it at all. An assumption of responsibility and reasonable reliance may also be found in the latter situation and a duty may well be imposed.

It can, however, be expected that, where there has been a failure to commence the performance of a gratuitous promise, compelling evidence of assumption of responsibility and reliance will be required. *Maxey v. Canada Permanent Trust Co.*[106] is illustrative. The defendant mortgagee was concerned that the plaintiff mortgagor had not properly insured the mortgaged property, thereby placing the mortgagee's security interest in jeopardy. The defendant threatened to take out the necessary insurance at the plaintiff's expense if the plaintiff did not secure adequate coverage. The bank placed insurance to cover its own interest for a year but it did not, at any time, insure the mortgagor's interest. The house was uninsured when it burned down. The plaintiff attempted to recover his loss on the grounds that he relied on the defendant's assurance that it would insure the property in a way that would protect his interest. The Manitoba Court of Appeal reversed the trial judgment and held that the defendant was not liable. The defendant had not clearly assumed a responsibility to protect the plaintiff's interests and it was not reasonable for the plaintiff to rely on the defendant to protect his interest.

---

105 See, for example, *Fine's Flowers Ltd. v. General Accident Assurance Co.* (1977), 17 O.R. (2d) 529 (C.A.).

106 (1984), 9 D.L.R. (4th) 380 (Man. C.A.).

Canadian courts have yet to deal with cases involving the failure of gaming operators to perform gratuitous self-exclusion agreements with self-identified problem gamblers. Under such agreements the gaming operator promises to deny the gambler access to its gaming facilities. The operator may be sued for betting losses caused by a failure to perform the agreement or for its negligent performance. It may be argued that liability should be imposed since the operator undertakes responsibility for a vulnerable person and the gambler relies on the operator to enforce the agreement. The counter-argument is that the loss has been triggered by the gambler's deliberate and evasive conduct and the operator should not be liable for failing to protect an autonomous adult from the consequences of his poor decision making.[107]

b) The Negligent Performance of a Contract of Service Causing Economic Loss to a Third Party

The rule of privity of contract has encouraged third-party beneficiaries to a contract to sue in tort when a negligent performance of a contract causes them economic loss. Again, the concepts of assumption of responsibility and reasonable reliance are influential in these cases. There is, however, in some cases the added problem of indeterminacy. There may be large numbers of beneficiaries who indirectly or incidentally stand to benefit from the contractual performance of the defendant. This problem of incidental contractual beneficiaries is equally a problem for those who would reform the law of contract. It is difficult to find appropriate language or concepts to determine the range of third-party beneficiaries who ought to be given a personal right to enforce a contract. The courts are, therefore, likely to take into account additional factors in deciding if the service provider owes a duty of care to the plaintiff third party. Consideration may be given to the size of the pool of potential plaintiffs, the end and aim of the contract, and whether or not it was intended that the plaintiff should benefit from the performance of the contract.

The Supreme Court addressed this issue in *B.D.C. Ltd. v. Hofstrand Farms Ltd.*[108] The defendant courier entered into a contract with the

---

107   The issue has arisen in England in *Calvert v. William Hill Credit Ltd.*, [2008] EWCA Civ 1427, where a duty of care was recognized but the claim failed for lack of causation, and in a number of cases in Australia including *Reynolds v. Katoomba RSL All Services Club Ltd.* (2001), 189 A.L.R. 510 (N.S.W.C.A.) where, in the absence of special circumstances, there is no duty of care on gambling operators. For a general discussion of this issue see P. Mitchell, "Problem Gambling and the Law of Negligence" (2010) 18 T.L.J. 1.

108   [1986] 1 S.C.R. 228.

Crown to deliver an envelope from a governmental department to a land registry office by a certain date. Delivery was delayed because of the defendant's negligence. This resulted in certain grants of land not being registered to the plaintiff in sufficient time to allow it to perform a lucrative contract with another party. The plaintiff blamed the courier for the deal falling through. The Court held that the defendant did not owe a duty of care to the plaintiff. The Court observed that the defendant had no knowledge of the contents of the envelope, no knowledge of the plaintiff, and no knowledge of the plaintiff's contract. Consequently, there was no real basis for concluding that the defendant had assumed responsibility to the plaintiff, that the end and aim or intention of the contract was to benefit the plaintiff, or that the plaintiff had acted in reliance on the defendant. At most it might have been foreseen that some person or class of persons had a financial interest in the contents of the envelope and that they might suffer some loss as a result of its late delivery. A duty based on that degree of foreseeability would, however, create severe indeterminacy problems. The Court concluded that there was insufficient proximity between the parties to support a duty of care.

A useful contrast to *B.D.C.* is found in the House of Lords decision in *White v. Jones*,[109] which is typical of a number of "wills cases" that have arisen in the last few years. In *White* the defendant solicitor was retained by the testator to draft and execute a new will designed to distribute his estate to the plaintiffs. The defendant failed to carry out that task in a timely and competent manner and the testator died before the new will was operative. The estate was distributed to other beneficiaries under an earlier will. The House of Lords found that the defendant was liable to the plaintiffs. Even in the absence of any act of reliance by the plaintiffs, the factors in favour of a duty of care were compelling. First, lawyers assume a general responsibility for the drafting and execution of valid wills, and testators, beneficiaries, and the public rely in a general way upon their competence to carry out that task. Second, the direct purpose and intention of a contract to draft a will is to ensure that the testator's estate is, in due course, distributed according to the testator's wishes. Third, the disappointed beneficiaries are members of a limited class of persons who are known by name to the defendant and the extent of the solicitor's liability is controlled by the size of the estate. This allays any indeterminacy concerns. Fourth, practical justice dictates a remedy because the estate cannot sue since

---

109 [1995] 2 A.C. 207 (H.L.) [*White*]. See also *Wilhelm v. Hickson*, [2000] 9 W.W.R. 196 (Sask. C.A.).

it has suffered no loss, and, unless a duty of care is recognized, the persons who have suffered the loss (the disappointed beneficiaries) will have no claim because they were not parties to the contract of professional services. Fifth, recognition of a duty of care may provide some deterrence against poor legal practice.[110]

These two cases indicate the many factors that are influential in deciding if a service provider owes a duty of care to a third person. Nevertheless, the ideas of an assumption of responsibility and reasonable reliance are likely to be found most compelling. They, most comfortably, fill the void of a contractual relationship. The importance of an assumption of responsibility was recognized in *James v. British Columbia*.[111] In that case the Crown had intended to include a clause in a tree farming licence that would have prevented the licensee from closing its mill without the approval of the Crown. The clause was intended to alleviate the concerns of the workers' union about job security. Officials of the Crown negligently omitted to include the protective provision. Subsequently, the licensee closed its mill and the workers lost their jobs. The motions judge characterized the class action as one for the negligent performance of a service causing economic loss. The Crown had made a decision to include such a clause and had, thereby, assumed the responsibility of including it in the licence. It had failed to discharge that responsibility and the class action was certified.[112]

---

110 *White* has not, however, ushered in a more extensive third party liability on solicitors and notaries dealing with wills and estates: see *Hall v. Bennett Estate* (2003), 227 D.L.R. (4th) 263 (Ont. C.A.); *Esser v. Brown* (2004), 242 D.L.R. (4th) 112 (B.C.C.A.); and *Graham v. Bonnycastle*, [2004] A.J. No. 940 (C.A.).

111 [2004] B.C.J. No. 933 (S.C.), appeal dismissed [2005] B.C.J. No. 518 (C.A.).

112 The English cases also reflect the significance of an assumption of responsibility. See *Henderson v. Merrett Syndicates Ltd.* (1994), [1995] 2 A.C. 145 (H.L.) where the defendant managers of underwriting syndicates assumed a responsibility to the members of the syndicate to determine which risks to insure, which insurance risks should be reinsured, and which claims should be settled. They were held liable for the catastrophic losses caused by their negligence. See also *Gorham v. British Telecommunications plc.*, [2000] EWCA Civ 234 (the defendant insurer that undertook pension and life insurance planning for a client was held to assume a responsibility to the client's dependants and was liable for their financial harm on the death of the client); *Her Majesty's Commissioners of Customs and Excise v. Barclay's Bank*, [2006] UKHL 28 (the defendant bank was held not to have assumed a responsibility to a creditor who had obtained freezing orders over money held in accounts at that bank and it was not liable when it negligently allowed the debtor to withdraw money in defiance of the orders); and *West Bromwich Albion Football Club Ltd. v. El Safty*, [2006] EWCA Civ 1299 [*El Safty*] (the defendant surgeon who negligently advised and unsuccessfully treated a knee injury of a professional soccer player was held to owe a duty

c) **Negligent Misrepresentation and Negligent Performance of a Service**

It is not always easy to distinguish between cases that are characterized as negligent misrepresentation cases and those that are characterized as negligent performance of a service cases. Negligent misrepresentations are often the end product of a long period of professional work that is sabotaged by a single negligent error in the course of its performance. Emphasis may be placed on the performance of the task or the erroneous words that are its product. An example of this is *Edgeworth Construction Ltd. v. N.D. Lea & Associates Ltd.*[113] where erroneous plans and specifications for the design and construction of a highway prepared by the defendant engineering firm resulted in loss to the plaintiff contractor who relied on them to its detriment. The Court chose to consider the case as one of negligent misrepresentation, albeit that the negligence arose in the engineering and design process.

There are also cases that do not appear to fit easily into either category. In *Spring v. Guardian Assurance Plc.*,[114] for example, the defendant employer provided a reference for the plaintiff, a former employee. In this reference, the defendant included erroneous and damaging information that prevented the plaintiff from securing employment. The House of Lords held that the provider of a reference owes a duty of care to the person who is the subject of the reference and imposed liability. The defendant had voluntarily assumed responsibility for preparing an accurate reference and the plaintiff depended on the defendant to discharge this important and influential task carefully. The case may be categorized as one of negligent misrepresentation but it is not a case where the misrepresentation was made to the plaintiff. It was provided directly to the prospective employer of the plaintiff. Nor was the loss caused by the plaintiff's reliance on the representation. A similar situation arose in *Haskett v. Equifax Canada Ltd.*,[115] which involved aspects of misrepresentation and the faulty performance of a service. The Ontario Court of Appeal refused to strike out a statement of claim alleging a duty of care owed by credit reporting agencies to those persons on whom they issue credit reports. The loss was triggered when third-party credit suppliers either refused to issue credit to the plaintiffs or increased the cost of credit because of the erroneous reports. The Court

---

of care exclusively to the player and not to the player's employer. He did not assume any responsibility to the employer football club for its financial harm arising from the premature end of the player's career).

113 Above note 96.

114 [1995] 2 A.C. 296 (H.L.) [*Spring*].

115 [2003] O.J. No. 771 (C.A.)[*Haskett*].

relied primarily on the *Anns/Cooper* test.[116] A final example is found in *Hughes v. Sunbeam Corporation (Canada)*.[117] In that case, the defendant tested and approved ionization smoke alarms that were alleged to be inadequate in detecting smoke and smouldering fires in time to allow occupants to escape safely. A class action was brought seeking a refund for the costs of the alarm, its removal, and installation of an effective one. The claim might be characterized as involving either negligent misrepresentation or negligent performance of a service. The Ontario Court of Appeal characterized it as a novel claim and applied the *Anns/Cooper* test. It concluded that the defendant did not owe a duty of care to the plaintiffs. There was insufficient proximity between the parties. The defendant acted for the benefit of the entire public and it was not fair and just to impose liability on the defendant, particularly when the plaintiffs had not paid for the defendant's services. This conclusion was supported by residual policy factors including indeterminacy concerns and a preference to allocate such losses to the manufacturers of the product.

These cases indicate that any approach which uses categories to analyse cases will, inevitably, produce difficulties at the margins. Nevertheless, in the area of economic losses, the advantages of classification probably outweigh the disadvantages of the alternatives of either dealing with all economic cases on the basis of some elusive, all-encompassing general principle or approaching them as isolated single instances that are a law unto themselves. The occasional misfit cases are manageable under the *Anns/Cooper* test and the basic concepts of assumption of responsibility and reliance.

3) Relational Economic Loss

Relational economic loss occurs when the defendant negligently damages the property or person of a third party and, because of the relationship between that property or that person and the plaintiff, the plaintiff suffers pure economic loss. The loss is relational because the plaintiff is at least one step removed from the person who suffers the property damage, personal injury, or death. Relational economic loss flowing from property damage, personal injury, or death gives rise to

---

116 It has been suggested that cases like *Spring* and *Haskett* may represent a new category of duty of care in respect of economic loss, namely Negligent Provision of Incorrect Information about Third Parties: see P. Burns & J. Blom, *Economic Interests in Canadian Tort Law* (Markham, ON: LexisNexis Canada Inc., 2009) at 391.

117 [2002] O.J. No. 3457 (C.A.).

similar policy considerations. They are not, however, controlled by the same legal principles.

a) Relational Economic Loss Arising from Property Damage

Relational economic loss arising from property damage may be contractual or non-contractual. Contractual relational economic loss arises where the defendant has interfered with or damaged the property of a third person with whom the plaintiff has a contractual relationship. The property damage disrupts or interferes with the performance of the contract, causing the plaintiff to lose some economic advantage or benefits. A plaintiff may, for example, have a contractual right to use a *privately*-owned bridge. The bridge may be damaged and temporarily closed because of the defendant's negligence. This may force the plaintiff to use more expensive alternative transportation routes and it may additionally cause a loss of customers and a loss of profit. Non-contractual relational economic loss arises where there is no contract between the property owner and the plaintiff but, nevertheless, damage to the property adversely affects the plaintiff's business interests. For example, the defendant may damage a *public* bridge, which then needs to be temporarily closed for repairs. A number of businesses in the immediate area that depend upon the bridge may suffer economic loss from increased transportation costs and/or a loss of customers.

Claims for both contractual and non-contractual relational economic loss give rise to severe indeterminacy problems. There is the potential for a multitude of claims leading to a burdensome liability that is totally disproportionate to the degree of the defendant's fault. For example, a single act of negligence damaging transportation routes, communication systems, energy distribution systems, or the environment may give rise to many more contractual and non-contractual relational economic loss claims than could be accommodated without severe disruptions to the business world, to liability insurance systems, and to the courts. There is general agreement that strong controls must be placed on recovery for relational economic loss arising from property damage.

i) *Contractual Relational Economic Loss*

In the last few decades, there has been much debate about how the courts should deal with contractual relational economic loss. Broadly speaking, there have been two views. The first is to apply an exclusionary rule that disallows all contractual relational economic loss claims except those that fall into a few exceptional categories of cases where identifiable policy factors strongly support recovery. The other view is that contractual relational economic loss claims should be dealt with on a case-by-case basis and should be allowed where, on the facts, there are no insuperable indeterminacy problems. It is argued that economic loss is not qualitatively different from property damage, and there is no pressing reason to arbitrarily exclude all these claims from the operation of the fault system and its compensatory and deterrent aspirations. All that is needed, on this view, is an adequate control device to keep liability within tolerable limits.

This difference of approach was evident in the Supreme Court decision in *Canadian National Railway v. Norsk Pacific Steamship Co.*[118] In that case, the defendant was the owner of a tug that negligently struck a railway bridge spanning the Fraser River. The bridge, which was owned by Public Works Canada, was closed for several weeks for repair. The plaintiff, Canadian National Railway, enjoyed a sophisticated contractual licence to use the bridge for its rail traffic. The defendant knew that the bridge was used by CN, that it was essential to CN's operation, and that CN was the main user of the bridge. CN sued for the cost of rerouting its trains while the bridge was closed. The plaintiff succeeded in the Supreme Court but the Court did not speak with a single voice. With the exception of one judge, the Court was evenly split between the views of McLachlin J., as she then was, who wrote the leading judgment in favour of the plaintiff, and LaForest J., who wrote a powerful dissenting judgment. Justice Stevenson broke the tie in favour of the plaintiff but he adopted an approach with which no other judge agreed.

Justice McLachlin took a flexible, fact-sensitive, case-by-case approach that relied on the two branches of the *Anns* test to contain indeterminate liability. In her view, however, the first branch of the *Anns* test would be satisfied in the context of relational economic loss only if a much closer relationship of proximity was established between the parties than that arising from foreseeability alone. In contractual relational economic loss claims, a scrupulous examination of the facts must be undertaken to determine if there is sufficient closeness, including physical closeness, circumstantial closeness, causal closeness, and closeness arising from the assumption of responsibility, to support a *prima facie* duty of care.[119] Reference was then made to the second branch of the *Anns* test to determine if the *prima facie* duty of care should be negated on policy grounds. On the facts, McLachlin J. found

---

118 [1992] 1 S.C.R. 1021 [*Norsk*].

119 This approach of McLachlin J. foreshadows her judgment in *Cooper*, above note 86.

sufficient proximity between the parties to support a *prima facie* duty that was not negated by policy concerns.[120]

Justice LaForest held that the exclusionary rule must be applied to contractual relational economic loss claims and no duty of care arises in respect of that loss unless the case falls within narrow exceptional categories, none of which applied to the case at hand. It was not only the indeterminacy concerns that led him to this conclusion. He noted that negligence liability was not required on deterrent grounds in these cases since the owner of the damaged property will always be able to sue the tortfeasor. The issue, therefore, narrowed to a determination of whether or not it was good policy to utilize the most expensive compensatory system yet devised (the fault/liability system) to allocate the plaintiff's loss to the defendant. In his view, there were good reasons not to do so. First, the incremental extension of negligence liability based on proximity would produce much uncertainty and unpredictability when the primary need of business persons and their insurers is certainty. Second, most persons and businesses are able to meet their compensatory needs in more efficient and less expensive ways. They may, for example, be able to channel their foreseeable economic losses to the property owner by appropriately worded terms of their contract. They may also purchase first-party business interruption and loss insurance that is tailored to their particular needs. These reasons were sufficient to support the exclusionary rule and its application to the facts at hand.

Norsk left the law in an unsatisfactory state. Two visions for the development of negligence law in respect of contractual relational economic loss were presented. In many cases, the choice will make no difference to the result of a case, but at the heart of each is a different attitude to these claims. Justice McLachlin's more liberal approach demanded of the defendant compelling reasons why there should not be liability for contractual relational economic loss. Justice LaForest's more cautious approach demanded of the plaintiff compelling reasons why there should be liability for contractual relational economic loss.

The Supreme Court tried to resolve these differences in *Bow Valley Husky (Bermuda) Ltd. v. Saint John Shipbuilding Ltd.*[121] One of the many issues in that case was a claim for contractual relational economic loss suffered by the users of an offshore oil-drilling rig. The rig was built by the defendant, Saint John Shipbuilding Ltd., for Bow Valley Husky

---

120 Justice McLachlin also supported her judgment on the ground that the parties were involved in a joint venture, a concept that is discussed later in this chapter.
121 [1997] 3 S.C.R. 1210 [*Bow Valley*].

(Bermuda) Ltd. A component of the heating system known as thermaclad was supplied by the defendant Raychem. The rig was leased by the owner, Bow Valley Husky (Bermuda) Ltd., to the plaintiffs. During the drilling of an exploratory well, the thermaclad caught fire and, as a result of the fire, the rig was out of service for several months for repairs. During this time, the plaintiffs were obliged, under their contracts, to pay day rates (rental) to the owner and they suffered additional financial losses in respect of contracts with suppliers. The plaintiffs claimed that the defendants had a duty to warn them of the inflammability of the thermaclad and their failure to do so caused them contractual relational economic loss.

The Court recognized that the defendants had a duty to warn the plaintiffs of the risk of fire but it rejected their claim for contractual relational economic loss. In a judgment concurred in by LaForest J. and, on this point, agreed to by the other members of the Court, McLachlin J. sought to accommodate the different views in *Norsk*. First, she held that contractual relational economic loss is recoverable only in special categories of exceptional cases. This amounts to a recognition of a general exclusionary rule subject to exceptions. Second, the exceptional categories of cases currently recognized by the Supreme Court include cases where the plaintiff has some possessory or proprietary interest in the damaged property, general average cases, cases where the defendant and plaintiff are involved in a joint venture, and transferred loss cases.[122] Third, although the categories of exceptional cases are not closed, the Court will not assiduously seek to develop new categories. There must be compelling policy reasons in favour of recognizing a new category. New categories may be recognized in situations where the deterrent effect of the potential liability of the property owner is low or where, despite a degree of indeterminate liability, the plaintiff had no opportunity to allocate the risk of economic loss to the owner of the property, either because of the kind of transaction involved or because of an inequality of bargaining power. Fourth, the approach in *Anns* (or now *Anns/Cooper*) must be used to determine if a new category of exceptional cases should be recognized.

Justice McLachlin held that the case did not fall within any existing exceptional category of cases. It, therefore, fell to be examined under the *Anns* test. First, foreseeability of the economic loss sufficient to establish a *prima facie* duty of care was satisfied on the facts of the case. Second, the policy factors dictated that the *prima facie* duty must be negated. In the Court's opinion, the indeterminacy concerns were in-

---

122 These categories are discussed below.

superable. A number of methods to control extensive liability and to distinguish the plaintiffs' loss from that of others (including confining liability to the users of the rig) were rejected on the grounds that they were not sufficient to meet the indeterminacy problems or they were arbitrary and without legal or social justification. Furthermore, there was no need for additional deterrence since the rig owner sued the defendants, and there had been every opportunity for the plaintiffs to channel their economic losses back to the owner by way of contract because the owners and the users were individual corporate entities of the same corporate conglomerate.

One important consequence of *Bow Valley* is that it has shifted the focus of attention in respect of contractual relational economic loss claims from a search for an appropriate general principle to control liability to an examination of the exceptional categories of cases that are now recognized by the Court. A brief review of those categories will indicate the current scope of recovery for contractual relational economic loss and may provide a guide to categories that may be recognized in the future.[123]

aa. The Plaintiff has a Possessory or Proprietary Interest in the Damaged Property

In most cases of contractual relational economic loss, the plaintiff has no more than a contractual relationship with the property owner. In some cases, however, the plaintiff may, in addition, have some proprietary or possessory interest in the property, making it appear that the plaintiff is the owner in all but name. Since few plaintiffs will have this kind of interest, the indeterminacy concerns created by contractual relational economic loss are allayed. The most common situation is that of a demise or bare boat charter (lease) of a ship. In these cases, the charterer takes complete possession and control of the ship, supplies its own crew, and in essence becomes the *de facto* owner of the ship for the duration of the charter party. If the ship is put out of service because of damage caused by the defendant's negligence, the charterer may sue the defendant directly for the loss of use profits even though the plaintiff is not the owner of the damaged property. There is some uncertainty about the position of time charterers. Time charterers do not take over possession or control of the ship but merely give instructions to the owner's captain and crew to carry goods at the charterers'

---

123 A more detailed description of these categories is found in the judgments in *Norsk*, above note 118, and in Feldthusen, above note 81 at 248–64.

direction. These distinctions may not, however, be sufficient to justify a different solution.

bb. General Average Contribution

In the course of a voyage, a ship may be in peril and the shipowner may incur expenses to save the ship and continue the voyage with minimal disruption. The expenses may include salvage and towing fees, repair costs, pilotage, harbour levies, and the cost of unloading and reloading the ship if that is necessary to complete the repairs. The cargo owners are obliged to contribute to these expenses in what are known as general average contributions. Tort law may bear on this issue when a ship is imperilled by the negligence of another party. For example, a minor collision at sea necessitating repairs may be caused by the negligence of another ship. In those circumstances, the cargo owners may recover the contribution that they have made under the doctrine of general average contribution from the tortfeasor even though they have no possessory or proprietary interest in the ship and their cargo is unharmed. This may be justified on the grounds that the shipowner and the cargo owners are engaged in a joint venture, there are no indeterminacy concerns, and the plaintiffs recover only expenditures that the owner would have been able to recover but for the contribution.

cc. Joint Venture

Joint ventures arise where a number of people use property owned by one of them for a joint business enterprise. When the defendant negligently damages or destroys the property, all of the participants may suffer economic losses. These financial losses are recoverable directly from the tortfeasor by the owner and non-owners of the property. The best example is the "loss of the catch" situation. Commercial fishermen may agree to participate in a commercial fishing expedition with the owner of a trawler. The terms of the agreement may allocate a share of the catch to all involved as their remuneration. An action may be brought by all the participants directly against a tortfeasor who damages and disables the fishing trawler by all the participants. The reasons for allowing this claim mirror those supporting the general average claims.

dd. Transferred Loss

A transferred loss claim arises most commonly in respect of a contract for the sale of goods. The contract may allocate the risk of damage to the buyer before the ownership of the goods passes from the seller. If, during this period, the goods are damaged by the negligence of a third person, the owner may have no claim because she has suffered no loss (the risk being allocated to the buyer) and the buyer may have no claim because he has no ownership in the damaged goods. The buyer's claim for the contractual relational economic loss may be supported on the grounds of fairness, the need for deterrence, and the lack of indeterminacy problems.[124]

Overall, there seems to be little room for any vigorous expansion of these special categories. The exceptions are narrow and predominantly maritime in nature. The Supreme Court now seems to have set its collective face against contractual relational economic loss claims, and a court that has expressed itself to be concerned about the certainty and predictability in the allocation of relational business losses arising from negligently damaged property is unlikely soon to increase the scope of liability.

ee. Pre–*Bow Valley* Authorities

All earlier authorities dealing with contractual relational economic loss should now be reassessed in the light of *Bow Valley*.[125] Special attention must be given to the two earlier decisions of the Supreme Court, neither of which was expressly overruled or doubted by the Court in *Bow Valley*.

The first is *Rivtow Marine Ltd. v. Washington Iron Works*,[126] which, on its facts, is not dissimilar to *Bow Valley*. The Court allowed recovery for a loss of profits caused by the defendant manufacturer's delay in issuing a timely warning of a dangerous defect in a crane installed on a floating barge. The delay in warning forced the plaintiff, who had leased the barge from its owner, to do repairs in the plaintiff's busiest season rather than during the off-season when its loss of profits would have been less. The plaintiff recovered the avoidable loss of profits caused by the defendant's negligence. Both *Rivtow* and *Bow Valley* involve the failure to give warnings to those who have contracted to use vessels manufactured in whole or in part by the defendants. One difference is that the plaintiff in *Bow Valley* sued for the payment of day rates and associated expenses rather than a loss of profits. Nevertheless, the cases are sufficiently alike to have deserved some explanation by the Court in *Bow Valley* of the material points of difference.[127]

---

124 The plaintiffs' argument in *Bow Valley* that its claim was one for transferred loss from the owner was rejected on the grounds that it is confined to physical damage and that the losses of the owners and the plaintiffs were not the same.

125 Above note 121.

126 [1974] S.C.R. 1189 [*Rivtow*].

127 Note that *Rivtow* was referred to approvingly in *Cooper*, above note 86.

The second is *Norsk*.[128] The status of *Norsk* would seem to be in some doubt since *Bow Valley*. It was not included in the list of exceptional categories in *Bow Valley* and it could be regarded as impliedly overruled. However, McLachlin J.'s judgment in *Norsk* also held that the operations of the owner of the bridge and the plaintiff were so closely allied that they were participants in a joint venture. The case may, therefore, be assigned to that exceptional category. Justice LaForest did not agree with her characterization of the relationship. He adopted a more conventional description of a joint venture as a joint undertaking of a commercial enterprise in the nature of a partnership entailing a willingness to share in its profits and losses. A contractual arrangement licensing the use of a bridge was insufficient to meet his criteria. It seems unlikely that McLachlin J.'s interpretation of joint venture will carry the day. The relationship in *Bow Valley* was not characterized as such on arguably stronger facts and in *Design Services v. Canada*,[129] the Supreme Court showed no enthusiasm for broadening the joint-venture exception. It noted that a joint venture is not a general category of duty of care. It applies only where property integral to the joint venture is damaged and a party to the joint venture who has no proprietary interest in the damaged property has suffered economic losses. It could not be relied on in *Design Services* which dealt with a design-build construction tendering process. In that case the main contractor/tenderer lost a tendering competition because of a contractual breach of the tendering rules by the owner. This, in turn, caused economic losses to the team of non-privity potential sub-contractors. The Court held that the sub-contractors could not rely on the joint venture exception to sue the owner in negligence since their loss did not arise from property damage.[130]

ff.   Post–*Bow Valley* Authorities

There has been no significant development in contractual relational economic loss claims since *Bow Valley*. One case, however, presented some interesting issues. In *Fraser v. Westminer Canada Ltd.*[131] the respondent corporation intentionally and tortiously attacked the business reputation and integrity of a business promoter in whose venture the appellants had invested. As a consequence of the attack the business venture failed and the appellants suffered economic harm. The appellants were, therefore, the foreseeable casualties of the respondent's intentional tort to a third party. The Nova Scotia Court of Appeal

---

128 Above note 118.

129 Above note 79.

130 See also *Terpstra Farms Ltd. v. Argue and Associates*, [2010] O.J. No. 235 (S.C.J.).

131 (2003), 228 D.L.R. (4th) 513 (N.S.C.A.).

held that the respondent owed no duty of care to the appellants since there was insufficient proximity between the parties and the potential indeterminacy problems were severe since the appellant investors were not known by the respondent and others with a financial stake in the venture might also be encouraged to seek a remedy.

ii)   Non-contractual Relational Economic Loss

The Supreme Court has not had an opportunity since *Bow Valley* to address non-contractual relational economic loss but there seems little doubt that the exclusionary rule applies. The indeterminacy concerns are even more severe in this class of relational economic loss. The extent of liability for contractual relational economic loss is necessarily restricted to those who have contractual relationships with the property owner. Non-contractual relational economic loss may be suffered by any member of the public who in some way is dependent upon the property of another. *Star Village Tavern v. Nield*[132] is one of a number of cases of non-contractual relational economic loss arising from the interruption of public transportation routes. In that case, the plaintiff suffered a loss of profits from his tavern when a provincial bridge was closed temporarily in order to repair damage to it caused by the defendant's negligence. The plaintiff was one of many businesses that may have been affected adversely by the defendant's conduct. The Court rejected the plaintiff's claim. There is no significant loss of deterrence in these situations since the property owner will, normally, be able to sue for his damage. There will be much less opportunity to channel the losses to the property owner by way of contract but first-party loss insurance is available to cover both contractual and non-contractual relational economic loss.[133]

b)   Relational Economic Loss Arising from Personal Injury or Death

Personal injury or death may also cause relational economic loss to third persons including family members, partners, business associates, employees, and customers. These situations give rise to the same kind of policy concerns as relational economic loss arising from property damage. They have not, however, traditionally been dealt with on the

---

132   (1976), 71 D.L.R. (3d) 439 (Man. Q.B.). This case was referred to in chapter 1.

133   See also *Brooks v. Canadian Pacific Railway Ltd.*, [2007] S.J. No. 367 (Q.B.) (no recovery for economic loss arising from the precautionary evacuation of a town following the derailment of a train carrying toxic chemicals) and *Conestoga Meat Packers Ltd. v. Fehr*, [2007] O.J. No. 3150 (S.C.J.) (no recovery for economic loss arising from a power outage at the plaintiff's hog operation following the defendant's truck striking a hydro pole).

basis of any general principle. Both the common law and legislation have recognized some discrete and narrow categories of contractual and non-contractual relational economic loss claims arising from personal injury or death.

i)   Contractual Relational Economic Loss

The early common law developed a cause of action *per quod servitium amisit* that continues to be applicable in most provinces. In modern terminology, it is an action for contractual relational economic loss arising from the injury of an employee. The claim can be brought by the employer for the loss of services provided by the employee where the employee was injured by a tortfeasor. The action was originally based on the idea that the employer had a proprietary right in his servant. Attitudes to the employment relationship have changed dramatically since then, but the action remains as an exception to the exclusionary rule.

The current scope of the action has not been authoritatively determined by the Supreme Court. It probably applies in respect of all injured employees so long as they remain in the employer's employment after the injury. The employer may recover his own losses including the cost of replacement workers and wages and other benefits paid to the injured employee. The weight of modern authority suggests that the loss of business profits is not recoverable but the point is not conclusively resolved.[134]

The action *per quod servitium amisit* has been abolished in British Columbia.[135] Nevertheless, in *D'Amato v. Badger*,[136] an automobile-repair corporation sued for a loss of profits arising from an injury to a part-owner and employee of the corporation. To circumvent the statute that abolished the old common law action, the plaintiff corporation characterized its action as one in negligence for contractual relational economic loss. The plaintiff, which may have been encouraged by the uncertainty generated by the *Norsk* decision, was unsuccessful in the Supreme Court. The Supreme Court held that the claim could not succeed under either the proximity approach championed by McLachlin J. or as an exception to the exclusionary rule under the approach favoured

---

134 See J. Irvine, "The Action *Per Quod Servitium Amisit* in Canada" (1980) 11 C.C.L.T. 241, and *Canada (Attorney General) v. Livingstone*, [2003] A.J. No. 1638 at paras. 42 & 43 (Q.B.).

135 *Law and Equity Act*, R.S.B.C. 1996, c. 253, s. 63. The action is also abolished in New Brunswick: see *Law Reform Act*, above note 66, s. 1(1).

136 [1996] 2 S.C.R. 1071 [*D'Amato*].

by LaForest J. in *Norsk*.[137] The indeterminacy concerns were sufficient to negate a duty of care. Justice Major, who spoke for the Court, concluded that to allow the claim would invite many further actions by other individuals and corporations and would remove the incentive for plaintiffs to protect themselves by securing first-party insurance to cover foreseeable financial losses or, where possible, to negotiate on the question of who will bear the risk of the loss.[138] This decision may foreshadow the demise of the action *per quod servitium amisit*. The ancient action may not seem consistent with the Court's general approach to relational economic loss.[139]

ii) Non-contractual Relational Economic Loss Arising from Personal Injury or Death

The only kind of non-contractual relational economic loss that is recoverable is that which is suffered by the family members arising out of the death or injury to a relative caused by the defendant's negligence.

aa. Death of a Family Member

Fatal accidents legislation in all provinces allows family members to sue for their loss of financial support caused by the wrongful death of a close relative. Indeterminacy concerns are addressed by the legislation. It carefully defines the range of family members who have claims and the range of losses that are recoverable.[140]

---

137 *D'Amato* was decided before *Bow Valley*.

138 See also *El Safty*, above note 112, where the plaintiff football club sent one of its professional soccer players to the defendant surgeon for advice and treatment of a knee injury. The defendant's negligence ended the player's career. The plaintiff sued in negligence for the economic harm suffered from the loss of the player. The Court held that no duty of care was owed by the physician to the club. In its view a duty was owed exclusively to his patient.

139 One way to synthesize the action *per quod servitium amisit* within modern negligence law in a way which is consistent with *D'Amato* has been suggested by the judge at first instance in *Canada (Attorney General)* v. *Livingstone*, above note 134, appeal allowed [2004] A.J. No. 790 (C.A.) He held that while the *per quod* action existed in Alberta, it was preferable to handle such claims as actions in negligence for contractual relational economic loss. In his view the posited duty of care could stand as an exception to the exclusionary rule because the *Anns* test was satisfied. The harm suffered by the employer was foreseeable and there were no issues of indeterminacy in either the number of claims or amounts payable so long as the remedy did not extend to the recovery of lost profits. The Alberta Court of Appeal did not discuss the point. It sent the matter back to the trial court to reconsider the matter in light of the *Cooper* decision.

140 See chapter 2.

bb. Injury to a Family Member

The ancient common law action *per quod consortium amisit* allowed a husband to recover damages for a total loss of consortium arising from injuries to his wife caused by a tortfeasor. Consortium has two elements, an economic element and an emotional element. The economic element includes the domestic services provided by a wife in the home. The emotional element includes the support, comfort, and affection provided by a wife. The action that covered both kinds of losses was not available to the wife. This blatant sexism has led to two different reforms. Some provinces have abolished the action.[141] The others have extended it to wives. There is some doubt about the scope of the modern action in those provinces where it survives. It probably continues to allow recovery both for loss of domestic services[142] (non-contractual relational economic loss) and for the intangible emotional loss of a spouse. It is also probable that a spouse may recover damages for a partial loss of consortium as well as for its total destruction.

Ontario has extended its fatal accidents legislation to permit claims by close family members of those *injured* by a tortfeasor. They may sue for their own pecuniary loss (non-contractual relational economic loss), such as expenses incurred for the benefit of the injured person and, where domestic and health-care services are provided, the value of those services and lost income.[143]

4) Product Quality Claims

The decision of *Donoghue v. Stevenson*[144] prompted a significant expansion of a manufacturer's liability for personal injury and property damage caused by defective products, but it was not until the decision in *Hedley Byrne & Co. v. Heller & Partners Ltd.*[145] that serious attention was given to the liability of a manufacturer for product quality claims made by non-privity third parties. Some preliminary explanation of product quality claims may be helpful.

The majority of these claims have arisen in respect of the negligent construction of defective buildings. Most commonly the building has a latent defect caused by the negligence of the builder. If the original

---

141 The action has been abolished in British Columbia, Manitoba, New Brunswick, Nova Scotia, Ontario, and Saskatchewan.

142 The claim for loss of domestic services is today more properly framed as being for the loss of homemaking capacity, to be brought by the injured person.

143 *Family Law Act*, above note 36, s. 61(2).

144 Above note 1.

145 Above note 76.

purchaser/owner discovers the defect, a claim for breach of the construction contract may be available against the builder. The building may, however, be sold before the defect is discovered. When the second owner discovers the defect, financial losses may be incurred in carrying out the needed repairs. The second owner cannot sue the builder for breach of contract because he is not a party to the contract between the builder and the first owner. At best the second owner is an incidental third-party beneficiary who has no personal right to sue on the construction contract. A claim for breach of contract by the second owner against the first owner is not likely to be successful because a contract for the sale of a second-hand building does not, normally, contain either an express or implied warranty of quality of construction. The old principle of *caveat emptor* (let the buyer beware) still applies to real estate transactions. These difficulties encourage the plaintiff to ignore the contractual links and to sue the builder directly in negligence.

This appears to be an attractive option given the wrongdoing of an insured builder and the innocence of the subsequent buyer who, normally, will not carry first-party insurance to cover the financial loss arising from latent defects in the premises. Furthermore, if the claim is not recognized, there is a loss of deterrence because the first owner has no loss and no interest in suing the builder.

This claim is, however, conceptually quite different from that recognized in *Donoghue*. A product quality claim seeks to recover compensation for damage to or in the building itself. It is not a claim for damage caused by the building, which might arise, for example, if the building or part of it collapsed and injured a person or property. The key points of difference are that the product quality claim is brought to recover economic loss (the cost of repairs) and the claim is one that traditionally has been available only in contract. It is contractual in nature because it seeks to secure for the second owner the benefit of the bargain between the builder and the first owner. It is, in reality, a claim for the breach of a warranty of quality by a non-contracting party. To allow a tort claim by a subsequent owner against the builder would subvert the contractual rules of privity. This is the conundrum of product quality claims in negligence.

The issue arose in *Winnipeg Condominium Corporation No. 36 v. Bird Construction Co.*[146] The case involved an apartment block built by the defendant contractor that had been sold by the first owner to the plaintiff. Ten years after construction there was concern about the state of stone cladding on the exterior of the building and some modest

---

146 [1995] 1 S.C.R. 85 [*Bird*].

remedial steps were undertaken. These remedial steps proved insufficient and some years later a large slab of cladding fell from the ninth
storey. The entire cladding was replaced at a cost of $1.5 million. The
plaintiff tried to recover this cost from the defendant. The defendant
argued that it owed no duty of care to the plaintiff and the case went to
the Supreme Court on this preliminary issue.

The Court held that the builder did owe a duty of care to the plaintiff. It drew a distinction between product quality defects that create a
real and substantial danger to the occupants of the building and non-
dangerous defects such as poor quality or shoddy construction. The
Court held that the defendant owed a duty of care in respect of dangerous defects. Justice LaForest stated:

> [W]here a contractor (or any other person) is negligent in planning or
> constructing a building, and where that building is found to contain
> defects resulting from that negligence which pose a real and sub-
> stantial danger to the occupants of the building, the reasonable cost
> of repairing the defects and putting the building back into a non-
> dangerous state are recoverable in tort by the occupants.[147]

This duty of care is owed independently of any contractual provisions
or exemptions in the contract of sale between the defendant and the
first owner.

The Court applied the *Anns* test in establishing the duty of care.
The foreseeability of damage to future occupants of the building created sufficient proximity to create a *prima facie* duty of care. The Court
found no compelling policy reasons to negate the duty. Indeterminacy
concerns were not severe. The class of plaintiffs was restricted to the
future occupants of the building. The amount of money payable by the
defendant was restricted to the cost of repairs. The duration of potential
liability was restricted to the useful life of the building. This may be a
considerable period of time, but it will be increasingly difficult to assign
the need for repair to the builder's negligence rather than normal wear
and tear. There were, moreover, several policy factors that strongly supported the imposition of a duty of care, including the encouragement of
preventive measures to avoid future damage to persons or to property,
the deterrence of poor construction, the availability of affordable third-
party liability insurance for builders, and the purchaser's difficulties

---

147   *Ibid*. at 102.

in detecting latent defects, negotiating contractual protection from the vendor, and securing first-party insurance.[148]

a) Dangerous Defects

The *Bird* case has done much to clarify the law in respect of defects that create a real and substantial danger to the occupants of a building. Every new development of negligence law, however, ushers in a new set of issues and the *Bird* decision is no exception. In *Bird* there was a great deal of emphasis on the degree of danger of the defect. This condition was clearly met on the facts of the case. The danger was extreme and, given the fact that part of the cladding had already fallen off the building, the danger was imminent. Some of the occupants might have been killed. This is not, however, the typical situation that will present itself to the courts. The typical case involves a building that has an inadequate foundation which causes it to lean, sag, and crack, or a defective roof that leaks, or poor construction leading to premature rotting of the structure. There is no immediate danger but postponing the repairs will increase their ultimate expense and at some indeterminable time in the future, the building or part of it may collapse. In these cases, it will not be easy to draw the line between dangerous and non-dangerous defects. It appears, however, that the courts will be generous in their interpretation of the requisite danger. In *Roy v. Thiessen*,[149] for example, the Saskatchewan Court of Appeal recognized that *Bird* was applicable in respect of a negligently built house into which water seeped. This posed a potential threat of rot endangering the structural integrity of the house during its natural life span. There was in the Court's view no need for the danger to be "imminent." Indeed such a requirement would defeat the policy of encouraging homeowners to expedite the repair of dangerously defective buildings.[150]

---

148 It should not be overlooked that a municipality may be liable for both dangerous and quality defects in premises where there has been an operational failure of building inspectors to enforce building codes and/or detect defects. See *Neilson v. Kamloops (City of)*, [1984] 2 S.C.R. 2; *Rothfield v. Manalakos*, [1989] 2 S.C.R. 1259; *Ingles v. Tutaluk Construction Ltd.*, [2000] 1 S.C.R. 298; and *Strata Plan NW 3341 v. Delta (Corp.)*, [2002] B.C.J. No. 2142 (C.A.). There is, however, no liability on government for the negligent drafting of building codes. See *Kimpton v. Canada*, [2002] B.C.J. No. 2691 (S.C.). See also section H, below in this chapter.
149 [2005] S.J. No. 195 (C.A.). See also *North Sydney Associates v. United Dominion Industries Ltd.* (2006), 268 D.L.R. (4th) 491 (N.S.C.A.) where it was held that repairs to cracked and missing welds in the roofing joists of a mall were necessary to prevent a collapse of the roof.
150 This issue has also arisen in the "leaking condominium" litigation in British Columbia. In *Strata Plan VR 1534 v. Regent Development Corp.*, [1996] B.C.J. No.

It was also not clear initially if the *Bird* principle extended to dangerous chattels. A strong indication of its applicability to chattels was the reliance by LaForest J., in *Bird*, on the dissenting judgment of Laskin C.J. in *Rivtow Marine Ltd. v. Washington Iron Works*.[151] In that case, Laskin C.J. favoured the imposition of liability on the manufacturer for the costs of repairing a defective and dangerous crane that was affixed to a floating barge leased by the plaintiff. The repairs were prompted when a crane of identical design collapsed, causing a loss of life. This position has been confirmed by the Alberta Court of Appeal in *Plas-Tex Canada Ltd. v. Dow Chemical Ltd.*[152] It was held that the cost of repairing defective and dangerous gas pipelines was recoverable by non-privity third parties from the manufacturer of a defective polyethelene resin used in the manufacture of the pipes. This extension to dangerous chattels also finds support in the well-established practice of manufacturers, particularly in the automobile industry, to recall defective and dangerous products.

b) Non-dangerous Defects

The Supreme Court in *Bird* did not categorically rule out recovery in respect of non-dangerous defects in buildings and products. The issue was deliberately left to be decided in a future case which raised the point directly. The High Court of Australia has, however, dealt with the issue beginning with *Bryan v. Maloney*.[153] In that case the plaintiff was the third owner of a house that was negligently built by the defendant. Soon after the plaintiff purchased the house, cracks appeared in the walls. The cracks were caused by the insufficiency of the foundation. It was not able to withstand the pressure of the expansion and contraction of the clay soil. There was no evidence that the house was in

---

6 (S.C.), it was recognized that liability could be imposed on building trades where negligence had allowed water to enter the main fabric of the building, which caused rot that threatened the integrity of the structure and posed a substantial danger to the health and safety of the occupants. In that case, however, the evidence did not establish the negligence of the defendant roofer.

151 Above note 126.

152 [2004] A.J. No.1098 at para 90. See also *Poulin v. Ford Motor Co. of Canada Ltd.*, [2008] O.J. No. 4153 (C.A.) (application to certify a class action for repair costs against the manufacturer of defective springs in door latches of motor vehicles that would cause doors to open in roll-over and side impact crashes denied on other grounds) and *Brett-Young Seeds Ltd. v. K.B.A. Consultants*, [2006] M.J. No. 121 (Q.B.), var'd on other grounds [2007] M.J. No. 56 (C.A.) (motion to strike pleadings denied in respect of repair costs of dangerous hopper bottom cones to be placed under existing grain bins).

153 (1995), 182 C.L.R. 609 (H.C.A.) [*Bryan*].

danger of collapse. It was purely a case of shoddy construction. Nevertheless, the High Court allowed recovery of the cost of repair against the defendant. The Court, in essence, created a transmissible builder's warranty of reasonable and competent workmanship running with the building to future owners.

The decision of the High Court in *Bryan* alters the conventional boundaries of contract and tort liability much more significantly than the Supreme Court's decision in *Bird*. *Bird* is broadly compatible with the traditional function of negligence law, which is to provide compensation for the consequences of risky or dangerous conduct and to promote accident prevention by encouraging the abatement of future risks of personal or property damage. *Bryan*, on the other hand, protects the reasonable expectations of non-privity third parties in respect of the quality of the premises that they have purchased. This extension of tort law into the heart of contract law was largely prompted by the failure of contract law to modify its privity rules to secure some consumer protection for the purchasers of second-hand houses. This use of tort to supplement the inadequacies of contract law, however, raises some difficult issues.

Tort law has little experience with setting standards, not of reasonable safety, but of reasonable quality. That standard may be set by the initial contract between the builder and the first owner. In that case, the plaintiff would be viewed as a third-party beneficiary whose rights would be coextensive with those of the original purchaser. An alternative approach is to formulate an independent standard of quality on the basis of the reasonable expectations of the reasonable person. Reference would need to be made to all the surrounding circumstances, including the reputation of the builder, the initial price paid for the building, the nature and purpose of the building, and the construction standards and trade practices at the time of construction. One danger with this approach is that, in situations where there is an exemption clause in the first contract of sale, the independent obligation owed by the builder to the plaintiff may be more onerous than that owed by the builder to the first purchaser.[154]

It is also unclear if such a principle applies to all shoddy construction including minor or cosmetic defects or whether it is restricted to serious structural flaws.

---

154 A third approach has been suggested by C. Chisick, "*Winnipeg Condominium Co. No. 36 v. Bird Construction Co.*: The Death of the Contractual Warranty?" (1998) 25 Man. L.J. 393 at 407: "[T]he standard of care would be defined on a case-by-case basis, based on the reasonable expectations of the *subsequent purchaser*" [emphasis added].

Some of these concerns and difficulties may explain why the High Court chose to interpret *Bryan* narrowly in the later case of *Woolcock Street Investments Pty Ltd. v. CDG Pty Ltd.*[155] In that case the High Court considered the extension of the principle in *Bryan* to a commercial building. The issue was whether consulting engineers who had designed the foundations of a warehouse and office building were liable to the second owner for the cost of repairing non-dangerous defects in the foundation. The Court unanimously declined to extend the principle in *Bryan* to the case at hand. The majority of the Court did not, however, adopt a bright line distinction between private dwellings and commercial premises. The majority explained that *Woolcock* differed from *Bryan* on more general criteria. In *Woolcock*, the original owner exercised such control over the construction project that the engineers owed no duty of care to him and, furthermore, the second owner was not in a position of vulnerability, being better placed to negotiate a warranty of quality in the purchase agreement, to obtain an assignment of the original owner's rights and to discover the defects by an inspection of the premises prior to sale. The Court suggested that where a subsequent owner is in a position to look after his own interests he will be expected to do so.[156]

Canadian law remains ambivalent on the issue of shoddy buildings. Some courts have concluded that there is no liability in respect of non-dangerous defects. Others have refused to strike out pleadings alleging non-dangerous defects on the grounds that the issue remains open. *Heinicke v. Cooper Rankin Ltd.*[157] and *Sable Offshore Energy Inc. v. Ameron International Corp.*[158] are illustrative of each position. In *Heinicke*, the plaintiff purchased a new house that had been roofed with untreated pine shakes rather than with the time-tested cedar shingles. The pine shakes proved inadequate to the task and had to be replaced prematurely. An action was brought *inter alia* against the architects who recommended the pine shakes as an acceptable exterior material. The action failed on the grounds that the defective roofing material created no real and substantial danger to the occupants. The Court expressly refused to follow *Bryan* albeit that the plaintiff as a purchaser of resi-

---

155 [2004] HCA 16.
156 The New Zealand courts have allowed recovery for non-dangerous defects in residential property but have drawn a sharp distinction between residential dwellings and commercial premises, see *Te Mata Properties Ltd. v. Hastings District Council*, [2009] 1 N.Z.L.R. 460 (C.A.) and *North Shore Council v. Body Corporate 188529 (Sunset Terraces)*, [2010] 3 N.Z.L.R. 486 (C.A.).
157 [2006] M.J. No. 446 (Q.B.).
158 [2007] N.S.J. No. 246 (C.A.) [*Sable*].

dential real estate was in a vulnerable position being unaware of the unsuitability of untreated pine shakes.[159] In *Sable* the Court declined to strike out pleadings alleging non-dangerous defects arising from the paint used in the construction of the off-shore platforms, on-shore plants and connecting pipelines of a billion dollar natural gas project. It was alleged that the paint had failed to prevent corrosion of the steel infrastructure. The Court held that in spite of the commercial nature of the construction the claim was not obviously unsustainable.

There is likely to be substantial reluctance to extend an obligation of reasonable quality to commercial or consumer chattels. They are subject to a wide range of quality, which is often reflected in the price, and many chattels have a short life and a planned obsolescence. Moreover, some consumer protection legislation provides non-privity consumers with remedies against manufacturers. The Ontario Court of Appeal has dealt with a case that raised some of these issues, including the difficulty in differentiating dangerous defects from ones of quality. In *Hughes v. Sunbeam Corporation (Canada)*[160] the defendant was the manufacturer of ionization smoke alarms. It was alleged that the alarms were incapable of detecting smoke and smouldering fires in time to permit occupants to escape to safety. The Court of Appeal refused to strike out the statement of claim in a class action on the grounds that it disclosed no reasonable cause of action. Although the chattel was not dangerous in itself, *reliance* on a defective smoke alarm was dangerous. The claim was, therefore, consistent with the safety rationale of *Bird*. Nevertheless, the Court recognized that liability was problematic because of a number of factors, including the spectre of indeterminate liability, the unusual nature of the proposed remedy (a refund of the cost of the alarm, its removal, and the installation of a new one), the practicality of discarding the defective product, and the inter-relationship of contract and tort. The Court also recognized that, ultimately, the claim may be more about the *quality* of a twenty-dollar smoke alarm than about a defective product.

H. GOVERNMENTAL LIABILITY

In the early common law, the government or Crown was immune from all tort liability. This was reflected in the maxim that "the King can do

---

159 See also *Sentinel Self-Storage Corp. v. Dyregrov*, [2003] M.J. No. 395 (C.A.), Steel J.A.
160 See above note 117.

no wrong." Eventually a special procedure known as a Petition of Right was used to bring tort actions against the government. Today, federal and provincial legislation have removed the procedural obstacles against bringing tort actions against the government.[161] The legislation recognizes that governments are liable for the torts committed by its officers, employees, and agents. Nevertheless, special care must be taken when suing governments. The pertinent enabling legislation must be addressed, its conditions must be complied with, and other related legislation may impose special procedural rules relating to limitation periods or the giving of notice before commencing an action. Moreover, the removal of procedural obstacles against bringing tort actions against the government has ironically led to the introduction of some common law protections and limitations on governmental liability in negligence. The courts have been particularly concerned about the need to control the extent of governmental liability in negligence for losses caused by the exercise of governmental powers.

Before we address the issue of governmental liability in negligence, it is useful and convenient to make some preliminary reference to the special rules relating to liability for corrupt governmental practices.

1) Corruption and Negligence

Canada is not plagued by the public corruption that is commonplace in some countries. Canada's public servants and officers may make occasional mistakes and blunders and from time to time they may be negligent but in general they are honest. Consequently, most of the litigation centres on allegations of negligence. Nevertheless, tort liability for harm caused by the dishonest and unlawful actions of public officials is well established. The applicable tort is *misfeasance in public office*. The gravamen of the tort is that public officers[162] must carry out

---

161   See Canada *Crown Liability and Proceedings Act*, R.S.C. 1985, c. C-50; Alberta *Proceedings Against the Crown Act*, R.S.A. 2000, c. P-25; British Columbia *Crown Proceeding Act*, R.S.B.C. 1996, c. 89; Manitoba *The Proceedings Against the Crown Act*, R.S.M. 1987, c.P140; New Brunswick *Proceedings Against the Crown Act*, R.S.N.B. 1973, c. P-18; Newfoundland and Labrador *Proceedings Against the Crown Act*, R.S.N.L. 1990, c. P-26; Nova Scotia *Proceedings Against the Crown Act*, R.S.N.S. 1989, c. 360; Prince Edward Island *Crown Proceedings Act*, R.S.P.E.I. 1988, c. C-32; Ontario *Proceedings Against the Crown Act*, R.S.O. 1990, c. P.27; and Saskatchewan *The Proceedings Against the Crown Act*, R.S.S. 1978, c. P-27.

162   The scope of the term "public office" was discussed by the Ontario Court of Appeal in *Freeman-Maloy v. Marsden*, [2006] O.J. No. 1228. The court refused to strike out a statement of claim alleging misfeasance in public office by the President of York University on the grounds that she was not the holder of a

their functions for the public good and exercise their powers in good faith to achieve the purposes for which are given. The ambit of the tort is quite narrow and until recently it was rarely litigated. Towards the end of the last century the tort enjoyed a renaissance and today is much more frequently the subject of litigation. The leading decision is *Odhavji Estate v. Woodhouse*[163] in which the Supreme Court canvassed the traditional scope of the tort and indicated that it has a wider application than previously thought.

Prior to *Odhavji* the tort was understood to deal with two kinds of wrongdoing; the abuse of a *power* that the public official actually possessed and conduct that was knowingly beyond the power or jurisdiction of the public official. The first branch of the tort was commonly referred to as an abuse of statutory powers. It was established where a public officer exercised a statutory power or authority for the purpose of causing harm to the plaintiff (a phenomenon known as targeted malice) or for any other improper purpose, such as to reward friends or to gain personally. The second branch was established where a public officer with actual knowledge of his lack of statutory power or authority acted in a manner that he knew would probably harm the plaintiff. The requirement of knowledge was also probably met when the public officer exhibited a reckless indifference to his authority or to the probable consequences of his act. The decision of the Supreme Court in the famous case of *Roncarelli v. Duplessis*[164] is illustrative of both branches. In that case, the plaintiff's liquor licence was cancelled by the Quebec Liquor Commission at the direction of the defendant premier of the province. This move was made in order to punish the plaintiff for providing bail money to fellow members of the Jehovah's Witness faith who had been charged with offences relating to the distribution of their religious literature. The behaviour of the premier could clearly have been characterized as targeted malice, but the premier had to his knowledge no authority to revoke the licence (that power lay with the Commission) and he knew that harm would be caused to the plaintiff. Consequently, the second branch of the tort was satisfied. If the premier had exercised his own power in revoking the licence, the targeted

---

"public office." The court was of the view that it was sufficient that in exercising her statutory authority to discipline a student she was performing a public function and was subject to public law review. The court was not persuaded that a narrower conception of the term, limiting it to a government official or a person under such direct governmental control as to invite the application of the *Charter of Rights and Freedoms*, should be adopted.

163   [2003] 3 S.C.R. 263 [*Odhavji*].
164   [1959] S.C.R. 121.

malice would have been an essential element to liability under the first branch.

In *Odhavji* the Supreme Court held that the tort was not restricted to these two conventional scenarios. The case involved a police shooting which caused the death of a family member of the plaintiffs. The plaintiffs alleged that the chief of police and other police officers, in breach of their statutory duties, failed to co-operate with the Special Investigations Unit charged with the task of investigating the shooting. The plaintiffs alleged that they had suffered nervous shock as a consequence of the defendants' misfeasance in public office. The defendants moved to strike the statement of claim on the grounds that it disclosed no reasonable cause of action. The Court held that the tort is "broadly based on *unlawful* conduct in the exercise of public functions generally"[165] and is established where a public officer has engaged in deliberate and unlawful conduct in her capacity of a public officer and the public officer was aware both that her conduct was unlawful and that it was likely to harm the plaintiff.[166] Since the plaintiffs alleged these two elements in their statement of claim their case was permitted to proceed.

Although the decision in *Odhavji* has generalized and extended the tort of misfeasance of public office it still requires proof of conscious wrongdoing of public officers. There is no liability merely because an action is *ultra vires* the powers of the officer and good faith discretionary decisions can be made without the anxiety of possible tort liability. The tort of misfeasance in public office may, however, in appropriate cases, be complemented by other torts, such as malicious prosecution, fraud, conspiracy, and intimidation, which also provide protection against the dishonest and deliberate wrongdoing of public officials.

Tort law has a limited power to address judicial corruption. The interest of society in an independent and fearless judiciary generally outweighs competing interests of individual litigants. Judges enjoy a generous judicial immunity from tort liability. There is a complete immunity in respect of all judicial acts done within the court's jurisdiction, and it probably extends to acts beyond the court's jurisdiction where the judge has an honest belief that the act was within the court's jurisdiction.[167] Liability is only likely where a judge acts knowingly in excess of jurisdiction and with malice, a most improbable situation. The

---

165 Above note 163 at para. 17.
166 In the absence of actual knowledge, reckless indifference to the legality of the conduct and its likelihood to cause harm will suffice. See *Three Rivers District Council v. Bank of England (No. 3)*, [2000] 2 W.L.R. 1220 (H.L.).
167 *Sirros v. Moore* (1974), [1975] 1 Q.B. 118 (C.A.).

matter is, however, complicated by some uncertainty as to the meaning of jurisdiction, the relevance of the level of the court, and legislative protections. The lack of a private tort remedy does not, of course, indicate any indulgence of judicial wrongdoing. Judicial councils act as the watchdogs on judicial conduct and judges can be removed from office for serious wrongdoing.

2) Negligence

Most governmental activities and services are carried out under permissive or enabling statutes. The legislation does not normally impose a duty to carry out certain tasks or services. It is written in terms of what the government or public authority may do, not what it must do. The legislation is empowering rather than mandatory because the need and demand for governmental services are infinite and the resources and money of government are finite. Statutory powers permit political and discretionary decisions to be made to determine the allocation of scarce resources, the priority of competing needs, and the manner in which governmental services are delivered. Yet, in a time of activist government, there is no shortage of private citizens alleging that they would have avoided certain losses if the government had acted differently in respect of a matter that has directly and adversely affected them. One vehicle to voice a complaint and possibly secure a remedy for the alleged inadequacy of governmental services is an action in negligence. It may be argued that the government owed a private law duty of care to prevent the loss suffered by the plaintiff. This has required the courts to address the relationship between the private law of negligence and the competent provision of governmental services to its citizens. Fitting the duty of care into this matrix of legislation, political realities, and discretionary decision making has proved to be a difficult task.

Modern Canadian law on governmental liability for the exercise or failure to exercise statutory powers begins with the Supreme Court decision in *Welbridge Holdings Ltd. v. Greater Winnipeg (Municipality of)*.[168] In that case, the defendant municipality passed a zoning bylaw to permit the plaintiff to construct an apartment block. In other proceedings, the bylaw was quashed because of procedural irregularities in the legislative process. This disrupted the plaintiff's plans and caused financial loss. The action against the municipality alleged a failure to take care in the passage of the bylaw. The Court held that no duty of care was owed to any private citizen in respect of the legislative,

---

168 [1971] S.C.R. 957.

judicial, or quasi-judicial functions of government and, since the claim attacked the defendant's legislative and quasi-judicial functions relating to the passage of bylaws, no liability was imposed. On the other hand, it was recognized that a duty of care may be imposed in respect of the administrative, ministerial, or business actions of government where governmental actions more closely resemble private sector activities. The Court's decision in respect of legislative and judicial functions[169] and the general approach of categorizing the governmental function that is the subject matter of the litigation have not changed.

There have, however, been further refinements of the classification of and approach to the administrative functions of government. The legal developments fall into two phases. The first phase, from 1978 and 2000, emphasized a dichotomy between policy decisions and the operational conduct of governmental entities. The second, beginning in 2001 with *Cooper v. Hobart*,[170] maintains this dichotomy as part of the analysis but places much greater emphasis on the legislative framework controlling the activities of the governmental entity and the extent to which the legislative language supports a private duty of care.

The first phase began in 1978 when the House of Lords articulated the dichotomy between policy and operational matters in *Anns v. Merton London Borough Council*.[171] Lord Wilberforce suggested that a distinction must be drawn between administrative functions that are essentially policy or planning in nature, which would not normally be subject to a private law duty of care, and operational matters that normally would be subject to a duty of care. In many situations it is difficult to draw this distinction because governmental decision making and activities often involve both policy considerations and operational conduct. Nevertheless, beyond the margins, the general idea is clear enough. Policy and planning decisions are discretionary decisions normally made at a high level of government dealing with the allocation of resources and the determination of priorities in respect of governmental services. The decisions involve economic, social, and political

---

169 Judges are immune from any liability to litigants in the tort of negligence. This guards the independence of the judiciary and relies on the appeal structure as the appropriate avenue for remedies. In the absence of fraud or bad faith, arbitrators are immune from civil liability, see *Flock v. Beattie*, [2010] A.J. No. 313 (Q.B.). The position of mediators is explored by J. Schulz, "Mediator Liability in Canada: An Examination of Emerging American and Canadian Jurisprudence" (2000) 32 Ottawa L. Rev. 269 and J. Schulz, "Obstacles to Tortious Liability for Mediator Malpractice" (2002) 17 Sup. Ct. L. Rev. (2d) 149.

170 [2001] 3 S.C.R. 537.

171 [1978] A.C. 728 (H.L.).

considerations in deciding which statutory powers will be exercised, when they will be exercised, where they will be exercised, and how they will be exercised. These are uniquely governmental decisions and the remedy for bad government lies in the ballot box, not in the courts. In due course, however, these policy decisions are implemented and governmental services are delivered to the public at an operational level. A private law duty of care may be owed in the performance of these operational functions.

This framework of policy and operational functions of government was adopted by the Supreme Court in *Neilsen v. Kamloops (City of)*,[172] which dealt with a municipality's failure to enforce its bylaws and prevent the completion of a house with defective foundations. A majority of the Court imposed liability on the ground that the matter was largely operational.[173] It also commented on the issue of policy decisions and held that policy decisions are not entirely immune from judicial scrutiny. First, there may be liability for the total failure of the governmental body to consider whether or not the statutory power should be exercised. The holder of the statutory power must seriously address that question. Second, there may be liability for a bad-faith exercise of discretion. This may arise where a decision is made for an improper reason or the decision is one that no reasonable person would have made. Beyond these two instances, however, a policy decision is not justiciable in negligence law.

At each end of the spectrum of governmental functions, the policy/operational dichotomy presents few difficulties. If, for example, the pith and substance of the plaintiff's case is that she has suffered injuries because the government has failed to provide sufficient funds to upgrade a rural highway or because government has failed to fund expensive diagnostic equipment owing to a need to cut back health-care expenditure, she is likely to be unsuccessful. If, on the other hand, the claim centres on injuries caused by the incompetent operation of road construction equipment or by the failure to correctly interpret medical testing at a hospital, it may well succeed. There can be little doubt, however, that at the margins, the line between policy and the operational matters is elusive.

The difficulties were exacerbated by some unevenness of decision making at the Supreme Court level. A useful illustration of this can be found in the comparison of three cases: *Barratt v. North Vancouver*

---

172 [1984] 2 S.C.R. 2.

173 A useful discussion of the operational failure of municipalities to inspect premises and enforce building codes is found in *Rothfield v. Manalakos*, [1989] 2 S.C.R. 1259 and *Ingles v. Tutaluk Construction Ltd.*, [2000] 1 S.C.R. 298.

(District of),[174] Just v. British Columbia,[175] and Brown v. British Columbia (Minister of Transportation & Highways).[176] In each of these cases, a person was injured or killed as a result of an alleged failure of the defendant municipal or provincial government to detect and remedy dangerous highway conditions.

In Barratt the plaintiff was injured when he rode his bicycle into a pothole that had not been fixed by the defendant municipality. The plaintiff argued that the defendant's inspection and repair system was inadequate to discover and address the danger that had caused his injury. The Supreme Court held that the system of inspection and repair was determined by "policy" decisions involving the weighing of costs, benefits, and priorities, which could not be the subject of a private law duty of care to the plaintiff. The Barratt decision signalled a broad interpretation of the term "policy" that was quite protective of public authorities. In Just the defendant province's system of inspection for the discovery and removal of unstable rocks above highways failed to detect a boulder that broke loose and crashed onto the plaintiff's automobile, injuring him and killing his daughter. The lower courts confidently held that the defendant's inspection system was the result of policy decisions and found for the defendant. A majority of the Supreme Court disagreed with that characterization and ordered a new trial to determine if there was negligence. In his leading judgment, Cory J. did not change the conceptual framework of liability, but he did suggest a much narrower interpretation of policy decisions by adopting the more restrictive term true policy decisions and by suggesting that policy decisions normally involve the broad allocation of funding at a high level of government. The system of inspection that the province had implemented was open to judicial scrutiny as an operational matter. He noted, however, that

> [t]he manner and quality of an inspection system is clearly part of the operational aspect of a governmental activity and falls to be assessed in the consideration of the standard of care issue. At this stage, the requisite standard of care to be applied to the particular operation must be assessed in light of all the surrounding circumstances including, for example, budgetary restraints and the availability of qualified personnel and equipment.[177]

---

174 [1980] 2 S.C.R. 418 [Barratt].
175 [1989] 2 S.C.R. 1228 [Just].
176 [1994] 1 S.C.R. 420 [Brown].
177 Just, above note 175 at 1245.

His judgment in *Just* appeared to show a clear preference for a much wider judicial scrutiny of governmental action[178] and a desire to rely on the flexibility of the standard of care to avoid placing an undue burden on government.[179] *Brown* dealt with an automobile accident caused by black ice on a British Columbia highway. At issue was the sufficiency and operation of the defendant's system to deal with such dangers on the highway. The province was, at the time of the accident, operating its summer system of highway inspection and maintenance, which, in comparison to its winter system, involved fewer resources, less equipment, fewer personnel, and reduced hours of operation. The plaintiff challenged the reasonableness of using the summer system in early November. Justice Cory, who wrote the main judgment, noted that policy decisions are not *necessarily* made at the highest level of government. It is the nature of the decision that is the controlling factor and the decision to operate under a summer schedule was a *true policy* decision. It involved political, economic, and social factors and was not subject to a duty of care. The *Brown* case indicated some resilience from the *Just* decision but Cory J. gave no indication that any change was intended.[180]

These cases gave rise to a debate about the adequacy and sufficiency of the policy/operational dichotomy to resolve governmental liability cases in a consistent and fair manner. On the one hand it provided a framework to achieve a reasonable balance between governmental freedom of action and governmental accountability, it permitted certain categories of liability including road maintenance and building inspection to be established, and it permitted a cautious extension of negligence doctrine into the field of governmental activities.[181] On the other hand the unpredictability and uncertainty of the application of the dichotomy at the margins was undeniable and a generous interpretation of "operational" threatened to usher in a very broad scope of governmental liability. The Supreme Court appears to have been persuaded by the latter concerns.

The second phase began in 2001 with the decision in *Cooper v. Hobart*.[182] It introduced additional layers of analysis which have had

---

178 In *Just*, the *Barratt* case was described as one where the Court found the municipality's system to be reasonable. That is not an interpretation that any previous judge had given to *Barratt*.

179 At the retrial the defendant was found liable: see *Just v. British Columbia* (1991), 60 B.C.L.R. (2d) 209 (S.C.).

180 See also *Swinamer v. Nova Scotia (A.G.)*, [1994] 1 S.C.R. 445.

181 See L.N. Klar, *Tort Law*, 4th ed. (Toronto: Carswell, 2008) at 308–11 for a list of cases where the Court characterized the conduct as a policy issue and a list of cases where the conduct was classified as operational.

182 Above note 86.

the effect of significantly slowing the growth and development of governmental liability. *Cooper* dealt with the alleged failure of the governmental regulator of mortgage brokers to exercise his powers and take timely action to prevent a delinquent broker from causing additional financial losses to a large number of investors. The Court introduced and applied the *Anns/Cooper* test of foreseeability, proximity, and residual policy factors. It held that the regulator owed no duty of care to the investors on the grounds that there was no *proximity* between them. The Court indicated that there were a number of factors to be taken into account in determining proximity in novel cases of governmental liability. First, careful consideration must be given to the controlling statute. The duty must be found in the framework and language of the legislation.[183] Second, if a duty is supported by the legislation, it must be determined if that duty is a private duty of care sufficient to found a negligence action or whether it is a duty owed only to the public at large. Third, a private duty of care is unlikely to be recognized if it is inconsistent with other duties, either public or private, falling on the defendant. Fourth, consideration must be given to the closeness and directness of the relationship between the government and the claimant. The Court did not, however, entirely exclude the operational/policy dichotomy from its framework of analysis. It was identified as one of the residual policy factors to be considered after a *prima facie* duty of care has been established.

The *Cooper* analysis presents severe obstacles to claimants. The identification of a duty in legislation which is predominantly permissive in nature is a challenge unto itself and the requisite degree of closeness between the government and a citizen will be difficult to establish unless there is some direct communication or individual interaction between a citizen and the governmental authority. If a *prima facie* duty of care is established the policy/operational issue must still be addressed. *Holtslag v. Alberta*[184] and *Eliopoulos (Minister of Health and Long Term Care)*[185] are illustrative of many decisions since *Cooper*. In *Holtslag* the plaintiffs had used untreated pine shakes as a roofing material on

---

183 This approach appears to be inconsistent with the Supreme Court's rejection of a tort of breach of statutory duty in *Wheat Pool*, above note 69. See L. Klar, "The Tort Liability of the Crown: Back to *Canada v. Saskatchewan Wheat Pool*" (2007) 32 Advocates' Q. 293.

184 (2006), 265 D.L.R. (4th) 518 (Alta. C.A.).

185 [2006] O.J. No. 4400. See also *A.L. v. Ontario (Minister of Community and Social Services)*, [2006] O.J. No. 4673 (C.A.); *Attis v. Canada (Minister of Health)*, [2008] O.J. No. 3766 (C.A.); and *783783 Alberta Ltd. v. Canada (Attorney General)*, [2010] A.J. No. 783 (C.A.).

their homes. They were unsuitable to the task and they deteriorated prematurely. An action was brought against the provincial Director of Building Standards for the breach of an alleged duty of care when issuing product listings authorizing the use of pine shakes for roofing. The Alberta Court of Appeal upheld the trial judge's decision granting a nonsuit on the grounds that no duty of care was owed to the plaintiffs. The Court held that the controlling legislation supported no more than a general duty to the public and, there was no proximity of relationship between the Director and home owners. Furthermore, the plaintiffs were attempting to impose liability for a policy decision. The same factors figured prominently in the Ontario Court of Appeal decision in *Eliopoulos*. In that case the estate of a deceased victim of West Nile Virus alleged that governmental officials owed a duty of care to take reasonable care to prevent the spread of the virus and protect the residents of Ontario from the disease. The Court held that the pertinent legislation contained no more than a general public duty to safeguard the health of residents and there was no proximity of relationship between the government and the deceased. Additionally the claim was characterized as an attack on public health policy, not on any operational matter.

There is, nevertheless, still a significant field of governmental liability remaining after *Cooper*. *Cooper* did not negate any existing category of governmental liability including the established categories of duty of care in respect of the inspection of buildings and road maintenance. Furthermore, the Supreme Court has, since *Cooper*, recognized some additional categories of governmental liability. They include duties of care on the police to both a targeted suspect of criminal wrongdoing[186] and to the family of the deceased victim of a police shooting in respect of an investigation of the incident,[187] a duty on provincial officials to implement a judicial order favourable to the plaintiffs,[188] and a duty on mine inspectors to exercise care for the safety of miners.[189] Lower courts have also fashioned novel duties, either by arguing from analogy from existing categories or applying the *Anns/Cooper* test, where practical justice demands a remedy. A useful example is *Heaslip Estate v. Mansfield*

---

186 *Hill v. Hamilton-Wentworth Police Services*, [2007] S.C.J. No. 91.

187 *Odhavji*, above note 163.

188 *Holland*, above note 71.

189 *Fullowka v. Pinkertons of Canada Ltd.*, [2010] S.C.J. No. 5. The Supreme Court has, however, held that the mere breach of a statutory duty by provincial officials does not generate a private duty of care (*Holland, ibid.*) and that a residential treatment centre for minors and its social workers are under no duty of care to the family of a child in its custody (*Syl Apps Secure Treatment Facility v. B.D.*, [2007] S.C.J. No. 38).

Ski Club Inc.[190] where the Ontario Court of Appeal refused to strike out pleadings alleging the negligence of a governmental air ambulance service for its failure to use available resources to transfer a patient with life-threatening injuries to a hospital that was better equipped to provide the necessary health care. The patient died while being transported by land. The Court held that the facts fell within the existing category recognized in *Just* of a public authority's negligent failure to act in accordance with established policy where it is reasonably foreseeable that a failure to do so will cause physical harm to a person.[191]

It is fair, however, to conclude that the tide of governmental liability which reached its zenith with *Just* has turned and any significant extension of governmental liability in the future is unlikely.

I. PREVENTION OF CRIMINAL VIOLENCE

The tort process has not proved to be effective in responding to the public's concern about criminal violence. Those who suffer injuries as a result of such violence normally have an action in battery[192] against the criminal but the prospects for recovering any money are not good. The criminal may never be apprehended and, if he is apprehended and sued, it is unlikely that any judgment will be paid. The victims of criminal violence may receive some indemnification for related expenses, lost income, and pain and suffering from the criminal injuries compensation schemes but that does not provide the full compensation promised by tort law.

This has led imaginative and innovative lawyers to explore the potential liability of financially viable third parties for the criminal conduct of others. Until recently, courts have resisted the temptation to impose liability on anyone other than the criminal. He is the person primarily responsible for the criminal violence and there has been an understandable reluctance to shift any of that responsibility to someone else. Nevertheless, the expansion of negligence law, the erosion of the nonfeasance immunity, a less rigorous approach to intervening acts,

---

190 [2009] O.J. No. 3185 (C.A.).

191 The Court also applied the *Cooper* test concluding that there was a sufficiently close and direct relationship between the deceased and the governmental authority rendering it just to require the latter to be mindful of the deceased's interests. Furthermore the conduct at issue was predominantly operational in character.

192 Battery lies for the intentional infliction of bodily harm to the plaintiff. See chapter 4.

and a greater willingness to impose liability on governmental institutions has led to a legal environment that encourages and facilitates the liability of third parties who are in a position to prevent crime before it is committed and, thereby, protect the public.

The primary targets for this kind of third-party liability are law enforcement officials. There was already authority imposing liability for damage caused by offenders who escape from custody[193] or who are imprudently and prematurely released from custody.[194] In those cases, however, the offender was already in custody and the defendant was charged with responsibility for his supervision and control. The more contentious cases are those that seek to impose liability on the police for a negligent failure to solve a crime, to warn of a serial offender before the plaintiff suffers loss or to take protective measures to secure the safety of a potential victim of crime. This issue has arisen in three illustrative and contrasting cases, *Hill v. Chief Constable of West Yorkshire*,[195] *Jane Doe v. Metropolitan Toronto (Municipality) Commissioners of Police*,[196] and *Mooney v. British Columbia (A.G.)*.[197] The *Hill* case dealt with a pretrial motion seeking to dismiss a claim on the ground that the defendant owed no duty of care to the plaintiff. *Jane Doe* and *Mooney* were decisions on the merits.

In the *Hill* case, an action was brought by the family of Ms. Hill, the final victim of a serial murderer whose crimes spanned a five-year period. It was alleged that, if the police had exercised reasonable care in the investigation of the crimes, the offender would have been apprehended before Hill was murdered. A number of factors supported the imposition of a duty of care. It was readily foreseeable that any delay in the apprehension of the killer would pose a great threat to other young women including the plaintiff. Furthermore, the duty of care suggested was consistent with the general functions of the police, namely, the efficient investigation of crime, the timely apprehension of criminals, and the protection of the public. It would also promote the compensatory and deterrent functions of negligence law. In spite of this, the House of Lords held that the police owed no duty of care to the plaintiff to apprehend the killer in a timely and efficient manner. It held that there was insufficient proximity between the defendant and the large class of potential victims to support a duty of care and that public policy fa-

---

193 *Dorset Yacht Co. v. Home Office*, [1970] A.C. 1004 (H.L.).
194 See, for example, *Toews v. McKenzie* (1980), 109 D.L.R. (3d) 473 (B.C.C.A.) (no liability on the facts).
195 (1988), [1989] A.C. 53 (H.L.) [*Hill*].
196 (1998), 39 O.R. (3d) 487 (Gen. Div.).
197 [2004] B.C.J. No. 1506 (C.A.) [*Mooney*].

voured police immunity from liability in negligence. There was, in the Court's view, no need for negligence law to provide a deterrent against poor policing. The best endeavours of the police could not be doubted. Furthermore, the imposition of a duty of care might lead to defensive policing, to a flood of claims, and to resources being diverted from the fight against crime to the defence of litigation. Lastly, many policing decisions are of a policy and discretionary nature dealing with the allocation of resources and the priority of investigations, which should not be second-guessed by the courts.

Jane Doe heralded a less conservative approach in Canada. Jane Doe was sexually assaulted by a serial rapist who operated in the vicinity of two Toronto streets. He targeted single white females who lived in apartments to which he gained entrance through the balcony doors. The defendant police, who knew that the sexual assaults would continue until the rapist was apprehended, did not warn women in the area. The Court held that the police owed a duty of care to the plaintiff. She was one of a specific group of women who, to the knowledge of the police, were at specific risk of harm and they had failed to warn her or in some other way protect her. Cause-in-fact was established on the plaintiff's evidence that, had she been warned, she would have taken protective measures that would probably have prevented the sexual assault. The trial judge noted that the decision was consistent with the statutory obligation of the police to protect citizens and that providing warnings to the women at risk would not have compromised the police investigation.[198] She rejected any suggestion that policing was a complicated business in which the courts should refrain from interfering. The *Jane Doe* case may be distinguished from *Hill*. First, the plaintiff in *Jane Doe* was a member of a narrower and more distinct class of persons than those threatened in *Hill*. Second, the issue in *Jane Doe* was one of timely warning. In *Hill* the efficacy and competence of a long police investigation were at issue.

Mooney involved a domestic dispute between the plaintiff and her partner. It escalated into an event of extreme violence during which the plaintiff was traumatized, her daughter was severely injured and her friend was killed. Prior to this event the plaintiff had implored the police to take steps to protect her and her family. Although her partner had a record of violent crime, some of which was directed at the plaintiff, and was under a probation order, the police officer dealing with the matter, in contravention of police policy, took no action. The action

---

198 Liability was also imposed on the police for breaching Ms. Doe's rights under the *Charter of Rights and Freedoms*. See chapter 8.

against the police ultimately failed on the lack of proof of cause-in-fact but the trial judge recognized a duty of care and that position was not contested on appeal. *Mooney* is distinguishable from both *Hill* and *Jane Doe*. Unlike *Jane Doe*, the plaintiff required no warning of the danger she faced. Unlike *Hill* the police knew the identity of the dangerous individual and they knew the identity of the few persons who were most at risk from his conduct. Furthermore, no indeterminate duty to the community at large was posited.[199]

These cases appear to indicate different jurisdictional attitudes to the accountability of the police. The English courts favour a broad immunity based on the policy grounds outlined in *Hill*.[200] The Canadian courts favour an incremental approach calling for a close consideration of the facts, the competing interests of the parties and policy considerations. Such an approach is probably more attuned to the views of Canadian citizens about the accountability of public authorities and to the public's interest in effective policing.[201] It is also preferable to deal with these cases by setting appropriate standards of care sensitive to the competing interests of the parties rather than to assert the absence of a duty of care and the creation of an immunity that inevitably will be subject to exceptions in compelling cases.

Some support for this approach can be drawn from the Supreme Court's decision in *Fullowka v. Pinkerton's of Canada Ltd.*[202] which dealt with the liability of a private security firm. The defendant firm had been retained by the owner of a mine to maintain order during a bitter and at times violent strike. A rogue striker breached security, trespassed into the mine and set off a bomb. The blast killed nine replacement miners. The Court held that the firm owed a duty of care to the replacement miners. The firm had undertaken responsibility for the safety of a well defined and identified group of vulnerable persons who relied on

---

199 Strong support for a private law duty of care in this context is found in M.I. Hall, "Duty, Causation and Third Party Perpetrators: The Bonnie Mooney Case" (2005) 50 McGill L.J. 597. But see *Spencer v. Attorney General*, [2010] N.S.J. No. 640 (S.C.). The plaintiff's husband was arrested by the RCMP for domestic violence and detained overnight. The next day an officer drove him to the family home where he was left to retrieve his belongings. Shortly thereafter he set fire to the house. An application for summary judgment by the defendant officer was successful on the grounds that no duty of care was owed to the plaintiff. There was no foreseeability of property loss and insufficient proximity.

200 See also *Van Colle v. Chief Constable of Hertfordshire Police*, [2008] UKHL 50.

201 See also *Odhavji*, above note 163, recognizing a duty of care on the chief of police to the family of a victim of a police shooting to conduct an inquiry in accordance with statutory obligations under the *Police Services Act*.

202 Above note 189.

the firm to protect their safety. The Court also held that the province owed a duty of care to the miners. The province was under a statutory responsibility for the safety of the mines and its inspectors had, in the course of daily inspections of the mine, developed a close, direct, and personal relationship with this defined group of persons.[203]

There are, of course, other third parties who may be in a position to intervene and prevent the commission of a crime. There may be a duty of care on probation officers in respect of harm caused by a parolee to a third party caused by either the officer's poor decision making, failure to supervise, or failure to warn the third party.[204] A mother who knows that her spouse is sexually abusing her daughter has a duty to protect her daughter if she has the ability and means to act.[205] Physicians, psychiatrists, and other professionals may become aware of the intent of a patient or client to commit a criminal act.[206] A much-discussed decision in this context is the Californian case of *Tarasoff v. Regents of University of California*.[207] In that case, a psychotherapist was sued when his patient murdered Ms. Tarasoff. The patient told the psychotherapist of his murderous intentions, but the psychotherapist did not warn the victim or her family. Foreseeability, the desirability of protecting the victim, and the seriousness of the threat to an identified person supported the existence of a duty of care. The defendant argued that the recognition of a duty to the potential victim would compromise the confidentiality of the professional relationship, have a chilling effect on the openness of the therapeutic process, and lead to practical difficulties such as evaluating the seriousness of the threats and the degree of danger to others. The Court gave priority to the safety and protection of innocent third persons and imposed a duty of care.[208]

---

203 The Court, however, concluded that both the private firm and the province had met the applicable standard of care and the claims failed on that basis.

204 *D.H. v. J.H. (Guardian ad litem of)*, [2008] B.C.J. No. 921 (C.A.) (authorizing a pedophile to live in a building where young children resided) and *D.W. v. Oak Bay (District)*, [2005] B.C.J. No. 2268 (S.C.) (failure to warn a hockey association that a pedophile parolee was coaching minor hockey). See also *Couch v. Attorney-General*, [2008] NZSC 45.

205 *K.K. v. K.W.G.*, [2008] O.J. No. 2436 (C.A.).

206 There may even be exceptional circumstances where a statutory regulator of professionals may be liable. In *V.M. v. Stewart*, [2003] B.C.J. No. 1967 (S.C.), appeal dismissed [2004] B.C.J. No. 1852 (C.A.), a claim that the College of Physicians and Surgeons of British Columbia had failed to investigate and take steps to protect patients after it received information of sexual misconduct by a physician in the course of medical treatment was permitted to proceed.

207 551 P.2d 334 (Cal. 1976).

208 Some support for this view can be derived from the Supreme Court decision in *Smith v. Jones*, [1999] 1 S.C.R. 455 [*Jones*] on the related issue of the solicitor/

There is also considerable room for the development of premises-security litigation. A duty of care may be imposed on the owner or occupier of a building to take reasonable security measures for the protection of the tenants and visitors when he is aware that criminal activity has taken place or is likely to take place either on the premises or in its general vicinity. Careful attention must, however, be paid to each particular case to determine if the appropriate vehicle of liability is negligence law or occupiers' liability law.[209]

J. NEGLIGENT INVESTIGATIONS

The negligent investigation of wrongdoing by either the police or private sector actors such as private investigators may cause substantial harm to suspects including wrongful arrest, wrongful dismissal from employment, and the denial of valid insurance claims. The liability of the police for a negligent investigation was recognized by the Supreme Court in *Hill v. Hamilton-Wentworth Regional Police Services*.[210] The plaintiff was arrested, prosecuted, convicted, and imprisoned for twenty months for a crime he had not committed. He sued the investigating police officers alleging various acts of negligence that had led to his wrongful arrest. The Court recognized that the police owe a duty of care to a "particularized" suspect who is the subject of their investigation. Chief Justice McLachlin, writing for the majority, applied the *Anns/Cooper* test. The foreseeability and proximity requirements of that

---

client privilege. The Court recognized a "public safety exception" to the solicitor/client privilege and, by inference, to the physician/patient duty of confidentiality. The solicitor may inform the appropriate authorities where there is a clear and imminent threat of serious bodily injury or death posed to an identifiable person or class of persons by a client. The Court did not, however, address the issue of a duty to disclose such information to the relevant authorities or to the potential victim or victims.

209   *Q. v. Minto Management Ltd.* (1985), 49 O.R. (2d) 531, aff'd (1986), 57 O.R. (2d) 781 (C.A.), where a landlord was held personally liable for a sexual assault on a tenant by its employee. But see also *Mitchell v. Glasgow City Council*, [2009] A.C. 874, where the House of Lords took a more conservative approach to landlord liability for the wrongdoing of a tenant. In that case, tenant A had acted abusively and threatened to kill tenant B. The landlord met with A and threatened him with eviction if he continued this course of conduct. One hour after the meeting A killed B. The Court held that the landlord owed no duty of care to warn B of the meeting or its purpose since it had assumed no responsibility for the safety of B and it was not aware of any real and immediate threat to A's life.

210   [2007] S.C.J. No. 41.

test were, in her opinion, satisfied, and the *prima facie* duty of care was not negated on the grounds that a duty of care would have a chilling effect on the work of the police or that it would be inconsistent with their quasi-judicial and discretionary decision making. It was also argued that the posited duty of care did not give rise to indeterminacy problems, it was consistent with and reflective of values underlying the *Charter of Rights and Freedoms*, it provided a more adequate remedy than the torts of false imprisonment and malicious prosecution, and it addressed public concerns about the number of wrongful convictions in Canada, some of which have resulted from flawed investigations.[211] The standard of care is that of the conduct of a reasonable police officer *at the time of the investigation.*[212] The conduct of the police officers in *Hill*, in the Court's view, may not have reflected current policing standards but they did meet the standard of care applicable in 1995 when the investigation took place.[213]

The duty to investigate a suspect with due care was extended to the private sector by the Ontario Court of Appeal in *Correia v. Canac Kitchens.*[214] In that case an employer hired the defendant private investigation firm to investigate suspected theft and drug use in the workplace.

---

211 A pathologist may also be under a duty of care to a potential suspect when investigating a suspicious death pursuant to the *Coroners Act*: see *Reynolds v. Kingston (City) Police Services Board*, [2007] O.J. No. 900 (C.A.). See also *Young v. Bella*, [2006] S.C.J. No. 2, recognizing a duty on professors to get their facts straight before reporting a student to child welfare authorities on ill-founded suspicions of child abuse.

212 The Supreme Court's decision in *Hill* is consistent with its earlier decision in *Odhavji*, above note 163, where the Court refused to strike out a claim for psychiatric harm by the family of a person killed in a police shooting alleging that the chief of police of Toronto was under a duty of care to ensure that his officers co-operated fully with and discharged their duties to the Special Investigations Unit in its investigation of the fatal shooting. See also *Wellington v. Ontario*, [2010] O.J. No. 2433 where the Ontario Divisional Court refused to strike out a mother's claim that the Special Investigations Unit owed her a duty of care in the investigation of the fatal police shooting of her son. But see *Thompson v. Sanaach (District) Police Department*, [2010] B.C.J. No. 1239 where the British Columbia Court of Appeal struck out a father's claim that the police owed him a duty of care in investigating his complaint that his estranged wife beat their children with a spatula.

213 The House of Lords took a much more conservative approach in *Trent Strategic Health Authority v. Jain*, [2009] 2 W.L.R. 248, holding there was no duty of care on public health authorities to the owners of a home for elderly persons. A negligent and erroneous inspection led to a precipitous and successful *ex parte* motion to revoke the owner's operating licence. The home was closed and the owners became bankrupt.

214 [2008] O.J. No. 2497 (C.A.).

A series of errors by the investigators led to an innocent, long-term employee being dismissed for cause and immediately being turned over to the police who arrested him on the strength of the private investigation. The defendant's motion for summary judgment on the negligent investigation claim was unsuccessful at the appellate level. The case raised many of the issues that were resolved in *Hill* and the Court found no reason to distinguish the case on the grounds that the defendant was a private investigator. The defendant undertook an investigation of the kind the police would normally perform with the knowledge that the police would be unlikely to undertake their own inquiry. The extent of the duty of careful investigation on private sector actors is, however, not fully settled. The Court in *Correia*, for example, held that there is no duty of care on employers in the investigation of wrongdoing in the workplace and it distinguished *Elliott v. Insurance Crime Prevention Bureau*,[215] which held that a private investigator retained by an insurer was *not* under a duty of care to an insured whose claim for a fire loss was initially rejected by the insurer on the basis of an erroneous report prepared by the investigator. Although much of the reasoning in *Elliott* has been undercut by the decision in *Hill*, it was distinguished in *Correia* on the grounds that the insured had a strong, albeit not complete, remedy against the insurer in contract and that a tort obligation of care on the investigator would threaten the integrity of the discrete contractual links between, the investigator, the insurer, and the insured in a way that would impair the insurer's ability to handle claims in an effective and expeditious manner.

K. EDUCATIONAL MALPRACTICE

The central mission of the public education system is to instill basic academic skills in the students it serves. There are few more important public services. School boards and teachers are, however, largely immune from liability in negligence in respect of their educational responsibilities. They are, of course, under a duty of care in respect of their students' personal safety and property but not in respect of their educational needs and expectations.

The issue of educational malpractice arose initially in the United States.[216] The cases that have been brought before American courts may

---

215 (2005), 236 N.S.R. (2d) 104 (C.A.).
216 See, for example, *Peter W. v. San Francisco Unified School District*, 60 Cal. App. 3d 814 (Ct. App. 1976).

be divided broadly into two groups. The first group involves plaintiffs without identifiable learning disabilities who, nevertheless, have completed their schooling without acquiring basic reading and math skills. The second group deals with plaintiffs who have diagnosable learning disabilities, such as dyslexia, which have not been detected or, if detected, have not been addressed in an appropriate manner. Almost without exception, the claims in both groups of cases have failed at the threshold stage of an absence of a duty of care. A number of reasons have been given by American judges for refusing to entertain actions in either category. First, it is difficult to set the standard of care in order to determine if there is fault. Teaching methods and theories of learning are so diverse that it is not possible to formulate a normative standard. Second, a determination of cause-in-fact presents formidable problems. The failure of a student in a school system may be due to a wide range of social, economic, family, genetic, physical, and environmental factors operating unequally throughout the course of the plaintiff's education. It is difficult to gauge the contribution of poor teaching to the plaintiff's lack of academic skills. Third, the courts ought not to interfere with the educational system or second-guess the full range of budgetary, discretionary, and pedagogical decisions that must be made in the performance of statutory powers. Fourth, administrative procedures to remedy specific concerns and grievances may be available to students and their parents during the plaintiff's schooling. Finally, educational malpractice may unleash a flood of burdensome litigation against school boards that are already under financial pressure. These reasons are certainly sufficient to proceed with caution in respect of educational malpractice claims but they must be weighed against arguments in favour of imposing liability.

School boards and teachers assume a responsibility for the quality of the educational system and for the schooling of children, and both the students and their parents foreseeably and reasonably rely on that system. The failure to educate can have profound economic and emotional consequences, and it is arguable that a plaintiff should at least be given a chance to satisfy the difficult burden of proof in respect of the standard of care and causation and hold the system accountable.

There have been few Canadian cases that have directly addressed the issue of educational malpractice but those that have accept the American view. In *Hicks v. Etobicoke (City) Board of Education*,[217] the

---

217 [1988] O.J. No. 1900 (Dist. Ct.). See also *R.(L.) v. British Columbia* (1999), 180 D.L.R. (4th) 639 (B.C.C.A.), appeal dismissed (*sub nom. Rumley v. British Columbia*) (2002), 205 D.L.R. (4th) 19 (S.C.C.).

Court held that there was no tort of educational malpractice. The same conclusion was reached in *Gould v. Regina (East) School Division No. 77*.[218] In the *Gould* case, the plaintiff was a seven-year-old girl who had suffered stress and anxiety as a result of the defendant's teaching. Justice Matheson relied on the American authorities and struck out the statement of claim alleging negligence as disclosing no reasonable cause of action. He emphasized the difficulty in setting a standard of care in this context and the fact that the distress and anxiety alleged by the plaintiff was not compensable in negligence. This case is, however, distinguishable from the typical educational malpractice case. It focused on the alleged emotional abuse of the plaintiff and the insensitive behaviour of the teacher during one school year. This is different from cases of academic impairment on graduation and prolonged failure to recognize and address the special educational needs of the plaintiff.

In due course, the Supreme Court will address the issue of educational malpractice. The Court may draw a distinction between the two groups of cases that have been addressed by the American courts and look more favourably on those that deal with the failure to diagnose and deal with recognizable learning disabilities.[219] In those cases, there is likely to be less difficulty with the standard of care and causation issues. The evaluation, testing, and placement of children with special needs is often conducted by school psychologists and other experts whose standard of care is more readily ascertainable. Causation may also be established from medical research detailing the impact of the disability on a child's ability to learn. Furthermore, these cases focus on the treatment of a particular child. They do not seek to challenge the integrity and standards of the system. They, therefore, present fewer indeterminacy concerns and they target the operation of the system and not its policy decisions. These are the kinds of cases that are most likely to breach the wall of immunity from negligence liability now enjoyed by our educators.[220]

There is also some evidence that the courts are more willing to recognize a duty of care on institutions of higher education. In *Young v. Bella*,[221] the Supreme Court held a university liable when its administrators

---

218 (1996), [1997] 3 W.W.R. 117 (Sask. Q.B.).

219 See *X (Minors) v. Bedfordshire County Council*, [1995] 2 A.C. 633 (H.L.).

220 See *Phelps v. Hillingdon London Borough Council*, [2000] 3 W.L.R. 776 (H.L.) where a local education authority was found vicariously liable for the negligence of its educational psychologist who failed to diagnose the plaintiff pupil's dyslexia. It also indicated that teachers may owe a duty of care to pupils in respect of their special educational needs.

221 Above note 211.

caused financial and reputational harm to a student when they mishandled an unfounded suspicion that she was a child abuser. They reported her to the child welfare authorities without taking the elementary step of speaking to the student, which would have cleared up the misunderstanding. Furthermore, although most courts decline to recognize a duty of care in respect of purely academic matters, the Manitoba Court of Appeal in *Hozaima v. Perry*[222] recently refused to dismiss an action against the University of Manitoba relating to the evaluation of a dental student's academic performance and her lack of success in the university's internal appeal process.[223]

L. LEGAL MALPRACTICE

On the whole, legal malpractice cases are handled in much the same way as other professional liability cases. There are, however, three situations where special considerations apply. The first relates to the duty of care in the conduct of litigation. The second relates to the liability of lawyers to non-client third parties. The third addresses the concept of informed consent to legal representation.

1) The Duty of Care of a Lawyer in the Conduct of Litigation

In Canada, lawyers owe a duty of care to their clients in respect of all legal tasks that they undertake to perform. There has, however, been a good deal of debate in Commonwealth courts as to whether or not litigators ought to be under a duty of care to their clients in respect of the conduct of civil and criminal litigation. The issue of the *litigator's immunity* or, as it is known in England, the *barrister's immunity* illustrates again the need to balance divergent policy factors and the different manner in which they are balanced over time and between jurisdictions. The modern story of the litigator's immunity begins in 1967 when the House of Lords in *Rondel v. Worsley*[224] confirmed the historic barrister's immunity on the grounds that it was consistent with, and supported by, modern policy considerations. The Court provided a litany of reasons for the immunity. They included:

---

222 [2010] M.J. No. 45.
223 There may also be liability arising from corporate training programs for employees, see *Giesbrecht v. McNeilly*, [2007] M.J. No. 28 (Q.B.).
224 [1969] 1 A.C. 191 (H.L.) [*Rondel*].

i)   The lawyer owes a duty not only to the client but also to the court. When those duties conflict, the duty to the court overrides that owed to the client. This is a reality that may not be appreciated by disappointed clients.

ii) A duty of care may lead to defensive advocacy that may prolong litigation unduly.

iii) All the participants in a trial enjoy an immunity from civil liability and lawyers should not be excluded from that protection.

iv) An action for negligence in the conduct of a trial necessitates a trial within a trial because it must be determined if the defendant lawyer's negligence in the first trial was a cause-in-fact of the plaintiff's loss.

v)   The action in negligence may evolve into a supplementary or collateral appeal process which may bring the administration of justice into disrepute.

vi) Advocacy involves difficult technical and tactical decisions that may have to be made without time for reflection and evaluation.

vii) Lawyers may face a floodgate of claims from dissatisfied and disappointed clients.[225]

The Court held that these reasons cumulatively justified the immunity.

In Canada a litigator's immunity has never been a part of negligence law. Nevertheless, when the issue arose a decade after *Rondel* in *Demarco v. Ungaro*,[226] Krever J. thought it appropriate to review the reasoning in *Rondel* and reconsider the Canadian position. He found the reasons given in *Rondel* for the special protection of litigators more impressive in their number than their cogency in an Ontario context. He observed that there was no empirical evidence that lawyers in Ontario, who had been subject to a duty of care to their clients, had favoured the interests of their clients over their duty to the court. There was also no evidence that there was any prolongation of trials, defensive advocacy, or flood of claims in Ontario. He also noted that the need to relitigate the initial cause of action and the creation of a collateral appeal process may cause some difficulties but none of a magnitude justifying a denial of a remedy to the innocent victims of legal malpractice. Furthermore, the general immunity of the participants in a trial focuses primarily on the freedom from actions in defamation, a protection that is not jeop-

---

225 The House of Lords also included in its reasons the fact that in England there are situations where a barrister may be obliged to represent a client. It is not clear why this would excuse a failure to take care, but, in any event, it is a factor that is not relevant in Canada.

226 (1979), 21 O.R. (2d) 673 (H.C.J.) [*Demarco*].

ardized by an obligation that counsel exercise reasonable skill and care on behalf of her client.

His decision did not, however, ultimately turn upon an evaluation of the reasoning of the House of Lords. It turned on his evaluation of what was in the public interest of the citizens of Ontario. Justice Krever made note of the large number of lawyers in Ontario; the significant expansion of the legal profession; and the number of inexperienced professionals who were in practice, all of whom have a right to appear before all levels of courts and are protected by liability insurance. It was his opinion that in this socio-legal environment, "enlightened, non-legally trained members of the community"[227] would not support an anomalous immunity for litigators. It would be inconsistent with the general accountability of all professionals to their clients, customers, and patients.

Demarco has been followed consistently by Canadian courts and recently it has been approved by the Ontario Court of Appeal in *Wernikowski v. Kirkland Murphy and Ain*.[228] The Court of Appeal emphasized the policy factors that support the Canadian position, including the accountability of litigators, the maintenance of minimum standards of competence of litigators, fairness to plaintiffs, and the integrity of the justice system.

In 2000 the wisdom of the Canadian position was vindicated. The House of Lords in *Arthur J.S. Hall and Co. v. Simons*[229] overruled *Rondel*. The Court discounted the reasons in *Rondel* and placed a premium on the competing policies that have driven Canadian law.[230]

Nevertheless, there is one troubling consequence of the litigator's duty of care. It can give rise to a collateral *civil* challenge to a *criminal* conviction, thereby threatening the consistency, coherence, and integrity of the legal system. This mischief may be avoided by the exercise of the Courts' discretion to strike out proceedings as an abuse of process. There is, however, no uniformity as to how that discretion should be exercised. The Saskatchewan Court of Appeal[231] has adopted the English view that such actions are ordinarily an abuse of process and will be struck out, thereby avoiding both the difficulty of relitigating the

---

227 *Ibid.* at 693.

228 [1999] O.J. No. 4812 (C.A.) [*Wernikowski*].

229 [2000] UKHL 38.

230 The Supreme Court of New Zealand abolished the immunity in *Chamberlains v. Lai*, [2006] N.Z.S.C. No. 70. The High Court of Australia, however, upheld the immunity in *D'Orta-Ekenaike v. Victoria Legal Aid* (2005), 214 A.L.R. 92.

231 *Fisher v. Halyk* (2003), 18 C.C.L.T. (3d) 56. See also *Michaud v. Brodsky*, [2008] M.J. No. 201 (C.A.).

criminal decision in order to establish causation in the civil action and the potential embarrassment of having conflicting judicial decisions on the same matter. The Ontario Court of Appeal[232] has taken a more flexible approach dependent upon the facts of each case. An action may be struck out if, for example, it is brought for an improper purpose or before all avenues of appeal are exhausted or where the question of the lawyer's competence was unsuccessfully litigated in the criminal process. The mere prospect of relitigation will not, however, be a sufficient reason in itself to strike the proceedings. This position is supported by the need to protect plaintiffs who may have been wrongly convicted as a consequence of legal malpractice and by discounting the difficulties of relitigation.

The difficulties faced in suing a litigator should not, however, be minimized. In particular it will be difficult to prove that the lawyer is in breach of the standard of professional care. Some latitude must be given to lawyers; litigation is not a precise science and in hindsight, decisions and tactics may be second-guessed and conclusions may be drawn that alternative approaches might have been more successful. It must be remembered, however, that there is no liability merely for mistakes and errors. The burden of proof on plaintiffs is a difficult one, requiring proof that the legal representation provided to the plaintiff failed to meet reasonable standards and current practices. It will also be difficult to establish the causal link between the negligence and the plaintiff's loss. Nevertheless, if that burden is met, there does not seem to be any compelling policy reason to protect the defendant lawyer.

2) The Duty of Care to Non-client Third Persons

The issue of a duty of care to non-client third persons arises in two different situations. The first relates to situations where a lawyer is representing a client in respect of a transaction or a dispute with another person. That other person, in relation to the contract between the lawyer and her client, is a non-client third person. There may be situations where the lawyer owes a duty of care to that non-client third person as well as to her own client The second situation arises where a lawyer is retained by a client to engineer a transaction that is designed to bestow a benefit on a third person. The lawyer may be sued by the non-client third-party beneficiary if the transaction fails to achieve its purpose because of the lawyer's negligence. Each situation requires separate consideration.

---

232 *Wernikowski*, above note 228.

Lawyers represent their clients in their dealings with third persons in a variety of situations including the negotiation of contracts, the drafting and reviewing of transactional documents, the settlement of disputes, and the conduct of litigation. The third persons may or may not be represented by counsel. In either case the general rule is clear. The lawyer's obligation is to her client alone. Moreover, it is not merely an obligation of reasonable care. There is, additionally, an obligation of fiduciary care entailing the most stringent obligations of loyalty, good faith, and devotion to the best interests of the client, including an obligation to avoid any conflict of interest. It is, therefore, unlikely that a lawyer will be held under a duty of care to any person other than her client. This general immunity in respect of third persons is also supported by the fact that the lawyer has, normally, assumed no responsibility to the non-client third person and it is not reasonable for the non-client to rely on the lawyer for advice or protection. It is generally understood that the lawyer is retained to protect the interests of the client alone. This position is illustrated by the English case of *Gran Gelato Ltd. v. Richcliff (Group) Ltd.*[233] That case dealt with a conveyancing transaction between parties who were both legally represented. The plaintiff took an assignment of a sublease of a commercial property and spent a substantial sum of money developing it. The vendor's solicitors were asked if there were any unusual provisions in the head lease. They replied that there were none. But there was, in fact, a redevelopment break clause that diminished the value of the assigned interest substantially. It was held that the vendor's solicitor owed no duty of care to the purchaser.

There are, however, some exceptional situations where courts may recognize that a lawyer is under a duty of care to a non-client third person. This is more likely if the non-client does not have legal representation of his own. This was the situation in *Granville Savings & Mortgage Corp. v. Slevin.*[234] In that case the plaintiff, Granville, agreed to make a loan to Smith, a client of the defendant solicitor. A condition of the loan was that it be secured by a first charge on property owned by Smith. Granville did not retain legal counsel to protect its interests in this transaction. It was content to hand over the money to the defendant on the understanding that the transaction would be carried out as agreed and that the mortgage would be a first charge on the property. The defendant was negligent in searching the title and what he believed to be a first charge was in fact a sixth charge. When the loan was not

---

233 [1992] Ch. 560 [*Gran Gelato*].
234 [1993] 4 S.C.R. 279 [*Granville*].

repaid, a number of actions were commenced by Granville, including an action in negligence against the defendant. In a short judgment, the Supreme Court reversed the Manitoba Court of Appeal and held that the defendant owed a duty of care to Granville. The Court concluded that there was a special relationship between the defendant lawyer and the plaintiff. The defendant had undertaken a responsibility in respect of the priority of the security and the plaintiff had reasonably relied on this undertaking. It might also be noted that the duty of care did not conflict with the interests of the defendant's client.

There is less likelihood of a duty of care being owed to a non-client third party who is legally represented in the transaction. There may, nevertheless, be special situations where a duty of care is owed. A lawyer may assume some responsibility or undertake to perform some task such as the answering of some questions, the provision of a certificate evidencing some course of conduct, or the giving of an assurance that would not conflict with the lawyer's duty to his own client. Reliance on those undertakings may in the circumstances be reasonable. Indeed, in the light of *Granville*, a case like *Gran Gelato* may be decided differently in Canada.

In addition to these situations, lawyers may also be under some obligation to third persons if they are aware of, or are alerted to, the fact that their client intends to embark on a course of violent or fraudulent conduct.[235] The caselaw is not well developed on this point and it raises difficult issues of duties of affirmative action in favour of third parties and the confidentiality of the lawyer-client relationship. Nevertheless, if the danger to a third party is extreme, the legal framework of negligence is sufficient to establish a duty to take some action such as declining to represent the person, providing a warning to the third person at risk, or reporting the matter to the appropriate authorities.[236]

The second situation arises when lawyers are engaged to engineer a transaction designed to secure some advantage or benefit to a third person. The best examples are "wills cases" where a lawyer, who has been retained by a testator to draft her will, has been held to owe a duty of care to the intended beneficiaries of the will. This is an aspect of the liability for the negligent performance of a contract of service canvassed earlier. In the context of contracts for legal services, it is as yet unclear if this duty extends beyond the wills cases to other kinds of legal

---

235 See *Bowles v. Johnston, Oliphant, Van Buekenhout & Deans*, [1988] 4 W.W.R. 242 (Man. Q.B.).

236 See *Jones*, above note 208, where the Supreme Court recognized a "public safety exception" to the solicitor/client privilege. The Court did not deal with the issue of a duty to warn.

services designed to provide benefits to third persons. There is some indication in the leading decision of *White v. Jones*[237] that wills cases are in a special category and that the principle in those cases may not apply to *inter vivos* transactions. Unlike the wills cases, the client may have a remedy against the lawyer and he may also be in a position to repair the damage caused by the failure of an *inter vivos* transaction.[238] On the other hand, attempts in the past to restrict duties of care to special facts have often proved unsuccessful. If justice demands it, a duty of care is likely to be found.

3) Informed Consent to Legal Representation

Informed consent is a concept that was developed in the area of medical treatment to enhance and protect the patient's right to self-determination and autonomous decision making. The right to informed decision making has not, as yet, extended beyond the medical sphere to other professional relationships such as lawyers and their clients. Lawyers are, however, routinely advising their clients about various courses of action, each of which has its own risks and benefits. The client cannot determine which path of action is most consistent with his personal and financial interests unless full and reliable information is provided by his lawyer. The concept of informed decision making is not only consistent with a lawyer's ethical duties but may well be a legal obligation. This duty may be particularly pertinent in respect of the commencement, conduct, or settlement of litigation. An unsuccessful defendant may, for example, argue that he was not informed by his lawyer of the risk of substantial punitive damages being awarded against him when he decided not to settle the claim against him. The proof of a failure to provide material information of this nature may be negligent. The plaintiff client must, of course, prove cause-in-fact. The modified objective test would probably be used to determine if a reasonable person in the client's particular circumstances would, if properly advised, have chosen a different course of action that would have avoided the adverse consequences suffered by him.

---

237 Above note 109.
238 See *Hemmens v. Wilson Browne*, [1995] Ch. 223 (no liability for a failed gift which the client donor could have remedied).

M. STATUTORY REGULATION OF PROFESSIONAL PERSONS

Most providers of professional services are subject to some form of regulation pursuant to a statutory instrument. Some professions are self-governing and some are governed by public bodies. Generally speaking, the task of the regulator is to set licensing qualifications, develop codes of professional and ethical conduct, monitor compliance, resolve disputes, and, where necessary, penalize delinquent conduct by fines or the suspension or revocation of licences. These regulatory systems are designed to maintain the integrity of the profession and protect the public from unprofessional conduct. Occasionally, a regulator who has detected or has some suspicion of professional wrongdoing fails to act in a timely, effective, and appropriate manner. This may permit the wrongdoer to continue to cause harm to clients or members of the public. These victims may claim that the regulator is liable for not preventing the loss by warning the public of the risk or suspending or revoking the licence of the impugned professional.

The issue of a regulator's liability was considered by the Supreme Court in *Cooper v. Hobart*[239] and *Edwards v. Law Society of Upper Canada*.[240] In each case a regulator, the Registrar of Mortgage Brokers in British Columbia in *Cooper* and the Law Society of Upper Canada in *Edwards*, was sued on the grounds that it failed to act in a timely and responsible manner after receiving information that a member of the regulated profession had acted improperly. As a consequence of this negligence, the plaintiff investors had relied on these professionals and had suffered financial losses. The Supreme Court held that the defendants did not owe a private duty of care to the plaintiffs. Although the plaintiffs fell within the scope of reasonable foresight as likely to suffer harm in the advent of negligence on the part of the defendants, there was no proximity of relationship between the parties. In both cases a close reading of the enabling legislation led the Court to the conclusion that the regulators owed a general duty to the public to ensure the integrity and efficiency of the regulated activities, but there was no *prima facie* duty of care owed to members of the public or to individual clients of the regulated service providers. In any event, the Court held that there were compelling residual policy reasons to negate any private duty. They included problems of indeterminacy, difficulties in rendering the policy and quasi-judicial decisions necessary to suspend

---

239 Above note 86.
240 (2001), 206 D.L.R. (4th) 211 (S.C.C.) [*Edwards*].

a professional service provider, and, in *Cooper*, a reluctance to allocate the losses ultimately to the taxpayer.

Cooper and *Edwards* were given a broad reading by the Ontario Court of Appeal in *Rogers v. Faught*.[241] In that case the plaintiff patient sued the Royal College of Dental Surgeons of Ontario and the College of Dental Hygienists of Ontario in respect of harm done to her temporomandibular joints (TMJs) suffered in the course of having her teeth cleaned. The plaintiff alleged that the defendant colleges had failed to initiate risk management measures, including the introduction of appropriate professional standards and the provision of continuing education, in order to prevent harm to TMJs. The Court chose not to distinguish *Cooper/Edwards* on the basis that the plaintiff's loss in *Rogers* was personal injury. The Court followed *Cooper* and *Edwards* and held that a review of the enabling legislation led to the conclusion that the respective colleges owed a duty to the public rather than to individual patients.[242]

The decision of the Supreme Court to provide an immunity to the regulators of professionals is not surprising. Obstacles to the recognition of a duty of care included the need to establish a duty of affirmative action; the nature of plaintiffs' losses (often economic); and the fact that regulators act under legislative powers in policy, quasi-judicial, and quasi-legislative functions. Nevertheless, a powerful tool to enhance consumer protection and deter sloppy regulators has been withheld. The denial of a duty of care protects not only the regulator who, by oversight, fails to act in a timely manner, but also the regulator who grossly neglects his public duty.[243]

---

241 [2002] O.J. No. 1451 (C.A.).

242 One exceptional case is *V.M. v. Stewart*, above note 206, where the College of Physicians and Surgeons of British Columbia had allegedly failed to investigate and take steps to protect patients after receipt of information of sexual misconduct by a physician in the course of medical treatment. The trial judge distinguished the earlier cases on the basis of the egregious nature of the physician's alleged conduct, the limited class of persons at risk and the nature of the harm and refused to strike out the statement of claim.

243 For a contrasting approach see *Finney v. Barreau du Quebec*, [2004] S.C.J. No. 31 where civil liability was established under the *Civil Code of Quebec*, S.Q. 1991, c. 64 on the defendant Barreau for its very serious carelessness amounting to bad faith in failing to protect the public from the professional misconduct and incompetence of a lawyer.

N. NON-STATUTORY REGULATORY BODIES

The work of statutory regulatory agencies is complemented by a range of private sector commercial and non-commercial regulatory bodies. Members of the public may agree to form an association that regulates an activity in which they all participate. The power of the regulatory body to make and enforce rules derives from the agreement of its members. The function of the body may be both to protect the interests of its members and to protect the interests of some segment of the public. There are a multitude of such organizations involved in a very wide range of activities giving rise to difficulty in determining the existence and scope of any duty of care owed to members and/or a class of the public. A few illustrations will suffice to present the range of circumstances and the issues involved.

Some organizations promote the integrity and competence of service providers. In *Morgis v. Thomson Kernaghan & Co.*,[244] for example, the Ontario Court of Appeal held that the Investment Dealers Association of Canada, an unincorporated voluntary association of securities' dealers owed no duty of care to an investor for financial loss suffered by the misconduct of a member. It was alleged that the association was under a duty to ensure the competence and integrity of its members and respond to complaints in a timely and effective manner. The Court held that albeit that the Association was not a statutory body, its function and responsibilities were sufficiently similar to the statutory regulator considered in *Cooper v. Hobart*[245] to warrant an immunity.

Other organizations focus on the safety of products and services. In *Hughes v. Sunbeam Corporation (Canada)*,[246] the Ontario Court of Appeal held that an independent tester and endorser of a consumer product (smoke alarm) owes no duty of care to the ultimate consumers of the product and was not liable for the cost of replacements. Similarly, the House of Lords held in *Marc Rich & Co AG v. Bishop Rock Marine Co. Ltd.*[247] that a private classification society that regulated the seaworthiness of ships owed no duty of care to the owners of cargo that was lost when the ship sank. The ship had been cleared to sail after an inadequate inspection failed to disclose a cracked hull. These two cases may, however, be contrasted with *Perrett v. Collins*[248] and, more

---

244 [2003] O.J. No. 2504 (C.A.).
245 Above note 86.
246 [2002] O.J. No. 3457 (C.A.).
247 [1996] A.C. 211 (H.L.).
248 [1998] 2 Lloyd's L. Rep. 255 (C.A.).

recently, *More v. Bauer Nike Hockey Inc.*[249] *Perrett* dealt with a flying association that certified the air-worthiness of a kit-set aircraft assembled by its members. A duty of care was owed to a passenger of a member injured in a crash. *More* dealt with the Canadian Standards Association (CSA) which sets minimum impact-resistance standards for ice hockey helmets.[250] The plaintiff, who was wearing a CSA certified helmet, was injured when he fell and hit his head against the boards. It was held that the CSA owed a duty of care to the plaintiff and liabililty may be imposed if unreasonably low standards were set.[251] These cases may be reconciled on the basis of the interests protected. In *More*, *Hughes* was distinguished as an economic loss case and *Marc Rich* dealt with property losses.[252]

There are also bodies that regulate sporting and recreational activities. The English Court of Appeal and the High Court of Australia have both had an opportunity to consider their responsibilities to the participants in these activities. In *Watson v. British Boxing Board of Control*[253] the plaintiff suffered permanent brain injuries when he was knocked unconscious in a boxing match conducted under rules of the British Boxing Board of Control (BBBC). The BBBC was a non-profit corporation that controlled and regulated all professional boxing in the United Kingdom. The plaintiff would have made a good recovery if he had been resuscitated at ringside rather than half an hour later at hospital. The Court found that the BBBC owed a duty of care to the plaintiff and was liable for failing to establish rules requiring that effective resuscitation treatment be available at ringside. There were many factors supporting the conclusion that there was sufficient proximity between the BBBC and the plaintiff to warrant a duty of care. First, the BBBC had complete control and power over professional boxing in the United Kingdom and the plaintiff was one of a determinate class of fighters. Second, the BBBC assumed responsibility for the safety of fighters and the fighters, in turn, relied on the Board's expertise and knowledge in formulating the rules for the sport. Third, boxing is a notoriously dangerous sport and the Board already had in place rules requiring that some med-

---

249 [2010] B.C.J. No. 1954.

250 All players in organized amateur ice hockey in Canada must wear a CSA-certified helmet.

251 The claims against CSA and the manufacturer Bauer failed on other grounds.

252 See also *Colantino (Litigation Guardian of) v. Kuhlmann*, [2006] O.J. No. 903 (S.C.J.), dealing with a claim against the National Spa and Pool Association of Canada that sets design and construction standards for above ground swimming pools.

253 [2001] 2 W.L.R. 1256 (C.A.).

ical assistance be available at ringside. The High Court of Australia came to a different conclusion on weaker facts in *Agar v. Hyde*.[254] The International Rugby Football Board (IRFB) is responsible for determining the rules of rugby. The plaintiffs alleged that they suffered broken necks because the IRFB's rules relating to scrums exposed players to an unreasonable risk of neck injury. However, the defendant was not the IRFB, which, as an unincorporated association, could not be sued as a discrete legal entity. The defendants were members of the Board who had attended the meetings of the IRFB in England. The Court held that the defendants owed no duty of care to individual rugby players. The alleged duty would be owed to all players of rugby worldwide in games that were not under the direct control or supervision of the defendants or the Board. The Board had no power to insure that rugby was played under its rules, and rules could be varied and interpreted at the local level. Moreover, the individual Board members had no power to change the rules set by the IRFB. They could propose changes and vote on them, but a collective decision was necessary to change the rules of the game.

It is not surprising that these cases indicate some unevenness in decision making. They present a perfect storm of contentious issues including obligations of affirmative action, relational liability, the nature of the harm and the nature and function of the body under consideration including the degree of control it exercises, its degree or expertise, the extent of an assumption of responsibility to persons or classes of persons and the extent of reliance by those who suffer harm. A fair conclusion is that judicial caution will be evident and that it will be very difficult to establish the liability of a non-statutory regulator for property loss or financial harm.

FURTHER READINGS

Products Liability

EDGELL, D.F., *Product Liability in Canada* (Toronto: Butterworths Canada Ltd., 2000)

LINDEN, A.M. & B. FELDTHUSEN, *Canadian Tort Law*, 8th ed. (Toronto: Butterworths, 2006) at 599–671

STAPLETON, J., *Product Liability* (London: Butterworths, 1994)

---

254 (2000), 74 A.L.J.R. 1219 (H.C.A.).

WADDAMS, S.M., *Products Liability*, 4th ed. (Toronto: Carswell, 2001)

Informed Consent to Medical Treatment

KATZ, J., "Informed Consent—A Fairy Tale? Law's Vision" (1977) 39 U. Pitt. L. Rev. 137

ROBERTSON, G., "Informed Consent Ten Years Later: The Impact of *Reibl v. Hughes*" (1991) 70 Can. Bar Rev. 423

SCHULTZ, M.M., "From Informed Consent to Patient Choice: A New Protected Interest" (1985) 95 Yale L.J. 219

Human Reproduction

ADJIN-TETTEY, E., "Claims of Involuntary Parenthood: Why the Resistance?" in J.W. Neyers, E. Chamberlin, & S. Pitel, eds., *Emerging Issues in Tort Law* (Oxford and Portland, OR: Hart Publishing, 2007) 85

FOLEY, T., "*Dobson v. Dobson*: Tort Liability for Expectant Mothers?" (1998) 61 Sask. L. Rev. 177

LOVELL, P.A. & R.H. GRIFFITH-JONES, "'The Sins of the Fathers'—Tort Liability for Prenatal Injuries" (1974) 90 Law Q. Rev. 531

SYMMONS, C.R., "Policy Factors in Actions for Wrongful Birth" (1987) 50 Mod. L. Rev. 269

TEFF, H., "The Action for 'Wrongful Life' in England and the United States" (1985) 34 Int'l & Comp. L.Q. 423

Occupiers' Liability

DI CASTRI, J.V., *Occupiers' Liability* (Agincourt, ON: Burroughs, 1991)

LINDEN, A.M. & B. FELDTHUSEN, *Canadian Tort Law*, 8th ed. (Toronto: Butterworths, 2006) at 711–58

OSBORNE, P.H., "*The Occupiers' Liability Act* of Manitoba" (1985) Man. L.J. 177

Breach of Statutory Duty

LINDEN, A.M. & B. FELDTHUSEN, *Canadian Tort Law*, 8th ed. (Toronto: Butterworths, 2006) at 222–49

Pure Economic Loss

BISHOP, W., "Economic Loss in Tort" (1982) 2 Oxford J. Legal Stud. 1

————, "Negligent Misrepresentation through Economists' Eyes" (1990) 96 Law Q. Rev. 360

CANE, P., *Tort Law and Economic Interests*, 2d ed. (Oxford: Clarendon Press, 1996)

FELDTHUSEN, B., *Economic Negligence*, 5th ed. (Scarborough, ON: Carswell, 2008)

————, "Liability for Pure Economic Loss: Yes, But Why?" (1999) 28 U. West. Aust. L. Rev. 84

SMILLIE, J.A., "Negligence and Economic Loss" (1982) 32 U.T.L.J. 231

Governmental Liability

COHEN, D., "The Public and Private Dimensions of the UFFI Problem" (1983–84) 8 Can. Bus. L.J. 309 & 410

FELDTHUSEN, B., *Economic Negligence*, 5th ed. (Scarborough ON: Carswell, 2008) at 261–310

LINDEN, A.M., "Tort Liability of Governments for Negligence" (1995) 53 Advocate 535

SOPINKA, J., "The Liability of Public Authorities: Drawing the Line" (1993) 1 Tort L. Rev. 123

WOODALL, M.K., "Private Law Liability of Public Authorities for Negligent Inspection and Regulation" (1992) 37 McGill L.J. 83

WRUCK, H., "The Continuing Evolution of the Tort of Misfeasance in Public Office" (2008) 41 U.B.C. L. Rev. 69.

Prevention of Crime

CHILDS, S. & P. CEYSSENS, "*Doe v. Metropolitan Toronto Board of Commissioners of Police* and the Status of Public Oversight of the Police in Canada" (1998) 36 Alta. L. Rev. 1000

O'DAIR, R., "Liability in Tort for the Transmission of A.I.D.S.: Some Lessons from Afar and the Prospects for the Future" (1990) Curr. Legal Probs. 219

RANDALL, M., "Sex Discrimination, Accountability of Public Authorities and the Public/Private Divide in Tort Law: An Analysis of *Doe v. Metropolitan Toronto (Municipality) Commissioners of Police*" (2001) 26 Queen's L.J. 451.

Educational Malpractice

FOSTER, W.F., "Educational Malpractice: A Tort for the Untaught?" (1985) 19 U.B.C. L. Rev. 161

PARKER, J.C., "Educational Malpractice: A Tort Is Born" (1991) 39 Clev. St. L. Rev. 301

Lawyers' Malpractice

KLAR, L.N., *Tort Law*, 3d ed. (Toronto: Carswell, 1996) at 359–69

SMITH, G.A., "Liability for the Negligent Conduct of Litigation: The Legacy of *Rondel v. Worsley*" (1982–83) 47 Sask. L. Rev. 211

Statutory Regulation of Professional Persons

HARRIS B., A. CARNES, & Q. BYRNE, eds., *Disciplinary and Regulatory Proceedings*, 3d ed. (Chichester, England: Barry Rose Law Publishers Ltd., 2002) c. 19

Non-governmental Regulatory Agencies

GEORGE, J., "*Watson v. British Boxing Board of Control*: Negligent Rule-Making in the Court of Appeal" (2002) 65 Mod. L. Rev. 106

KIRK, J. & A. TRICHARDT, "*Sports Policy and Liability and Sporting Administrators*" (2001) Aust. L.J. 504

WITTING, C., "Negligent Inspectors and Flying Machines" [2000] Cambridge L.J. 544

CHAPTER 4

INTENTIONAL TORTS

A. INTRODUCTION

The tort of negligence is complemented by a number of independent, named (nominate) torts that deal with the intentional interference with the person, property (land and chattels), and economic interests. The tort of negligence and the intentional torts are, however, divided by more than the degree of culpability of the defendant's conduct. There are significant differences in form, substance, and policy between these two regimes of tortious responsibility. Identification of some of these differences will enhance an understanding of the nature and function of the intentional torts.

The tort of negligence is a modern tort. It is essentially a product of the twentieth century. The basic structure of some of the nominate intentional torts is centuries old. While there was some modification of them in the twentieth century, the general outlines of liability have been clear for a long time.

The tort of negligence is a tort of broad and general application. It focuses primarily on the quality of the defendant's conduct and is, consequently, inherently ubiquitous in its range of application. Most of the intentional torts are quite narrow in scope. They are restricted to closely defined fact patterns and particular categories of damage. This reflects the cautious and incremental development of the early common law, which focused on discrete categories of wrongs with clearly identifiable boundaries.

The tort of negligence is characterized by general principles and the use of highly discretionary concepts such as *reasonableness* and *foreseeability*. The nominate intentional torts are defined by rules that tend to be more precise, narrow, and rigid than the negligence principles. Indeed, some seem to have been elevated to a status akin to statutory provisions.

The tort of negligence underwent a transition in the twentieth century from a limited number of duties of care arising from discrete categories of relationships to an unlimited number of duties arising from a general conception of relationships based on the reasonable foreseeability of harm to others. This process has not occurred in the intentional torts. The courts have been slow in generalizing and integrating the discrete intentional torts into a more coherent and cohesive system of general principles.[1]

The tort of negligence is dynamic, expansionary, and largely reflective of current public attitudes and policies. It displays a vitality and capacity for vigorous growth that is not mirrored in the intentional torts. The intentional torts tend to be static and are, in the main, characterized by convention, orthodoxy, and conservatism. The courts have been slow to discard historical technicalities, and there has been a reluctance to recognize new interests deserving of protection from intentional interference such as the interests in privacy, equality, peace of mind, dignity, and fair market practices. This has prompted some legislatures to fill the void with privacy legislation, human rights codes, and legislation policing the marketplace.

Liability insurance and loss distribution policies are central to the development, operation, and expansion of the tort of negligence. As a rule, liability insurance does not cover intentional damage. Consequently, the intentional torts operate more as a conventional loss-shifting system emphasizing corrective justice and allocating responsibility between the individual litigants. This enhances the punitive, deterrent, and educational functions of the intentional torts and encourages a greater emphasis on the accountability of individual defendants for culpable wrongdoing. The downside of the absence of liability insurance is that the victims of intentional wrongdoing are much less likely to receive adequate compensation for their losses. Consequently, the victims of intentional wrongdoing are forced to place much more reliance on their own first-party (loss) insurance and on governmental

---

1   The only exception is the tort of intentional interference with economic interests by unlawful means, which may lead to an integration of various business torts within a general principle. See section F, below in this chapter.

compensation schemes. The availability of these alternative means of compensation depends greatly on the kind of damage that is suffered. Persons suffering physical injury often have no first-party disability insurance and they therefore need to rely greatly on the no-fault criminal injury compensation schemes or on the social welfare system. Those who suffer intentional property loss or damage will often have first-party insurance and generally will have little need to rely on tort law. Some economic losses suffered by commercial entities may be covered by business interruption insurance. In the business arena, however, defendants who cause economic loss are more likely to be capable of paying damages.

All these characteristics of the intentional torts have a subtle but significant effect on the amount of litigation arising from intentional conduct, on the practical significance of the intentional torts as compensatory vehicles, and on the general vitality of this area of tort law.

B. THE MEANING OF INTENTION

In tort law the culpability of the defendant's conduct is defined with reference to the consequences of that conduct. Negligence is conduct that gives rise to a foreseeable and substantial risk of its consequences. As the likelihood of the consequences increases, the conduct of the defendant may be described first as *grossly negligent* and then as *reckless*.[2] Conduct is not, however, intentional unless the defendant either desires the consequences of his conduct or the consequences are substantially certain to result from the conduct.

The first definition of intentional conduct is intuitive. Intent commonly connotes a subjective desire to cause the consequences of one's actions. When one person stabs another he wants to injure him. The injury is said to be caused with *actual* intent. Conduct is also intentional if the consequences, while not desired, are substantially certain to result from the defendant's conduct. Imagine, for example, a defendant who shot into a crowd of people, hitting and injuring B. He cannot avoid liability for the intentional infliction of harm to B by claiming that he meant to hit C. It was substantially certain that he would injure someone and that is sufficient to make the act intentional. To excuse

---

2   These concepts play no significant role in tort law. At common law they are drawn within the umbrella concept of negligence. There are, however, some legislative provisions that require the proof of gross negligence or recklessness in order to establish a statutory cause of action.

the defendant from liability would reward stupidity and exclude extremely dangerous and morally culpable conduct from the reach of the intentional torts. In such circumstances, the defendant is said to have *constructive* or *imputed* intent.

The definition of intent has been extended further by the concept of *transferred* intent. It arises, for example, where A intends to shoot B but misses and hits C, whom A had no *actual* intention to injure. Sometimes *constructive* intent can be found in such cases, but if it is inapplicable because, for example, it was not known that there was anyone else nearby, A's intent to injure B is transferred to C. This legal fiction is justified on the grounds of the serious moral culpability of the defendant's behaviour and the complete innocence of the plaintiff. As between A and C, the loss, in all fairness, should be allocated to A. It has even been suggested that intention may be transferred from one intentional tort to another.[3] It may apply, for example when A intends to shoot B (a battery) but misses and hits C's automobile (trespass to chattels).

A defendant may be incapacitated from forming the requisite intent by mental disability or infancy. The caselaw does not speak with a single voice but the predominant view is that a defendant is not liable if he did not understand the *nature and quality* of his act.[4] A defendant will, however, be liable if he knew what he was doing but did not know it was wrong.

C. INTENTIONAL INTERFERENCE WITH THE PERSON

There are several individual nominate torts dealing with the intentional interference with the person. Each tort protects the plaintiff from the intentional interference of a discrete personal interest such as bodily security (battery), freedom from threats of violence (assault), liberty (false imprisonment and malicious prosecution), psychological security (intentional infliction of nervous shock), and privacy (the tort of invasion of privacy). A broad protection of the plaintiff's personal integrity and autonomy is achieved by this congregation of torts, each of which has its own elements of liability.

---

3   A.M. Linden & B. Feldthusen, *Canadian Tort Law*, 8th ed. (Toronto: Butterworths, 2006) at 35.

4   *Gerigs v. Rose* (1979), 9 C.C.L.T. 222 (Ont. H.C.J.).

1) Battery

A direct, intentional, and physical interference with the person of another that is either harmful or offensive to a reasonable person is a battery.[5] The tort recognizes a person's right to bodily integrity and personal security. Freedom from physical interference is so highly valued that battery is actionable without proof of damage.[6]

Most of the cases of battery deal with intentional interference that is harmful to the plaintiff. It is a battery to punch, stab, or shoot a person. It is also a battery to interfere physically with another person in a way that is offensive to an ordinary sense of dignity and honour. It is a battery, for example, to cut a person's hair, to spit on a person, to throw a cream pie in a person's face, to push a person away rudely, to take a person's fingerprints, or to hit a person with a snowball. A medical examination and any intimate or sexual contact are also batteries and are actionable unless there is some justification such as the consent of the plaintiff.

Deliberate physical interference that is neither harmful nor offensive is not a battery. It is not, therefore, a battery to tap a person on the shoulder to get her attention or to give a person a congratulatory pat on the back. The status of borderline conduct such as an unsolicited hug or an uninvited social kiss on the cheek depends upon the relationship between the persons, the surrounding circumstances, and the shifting tides of social convention and propriety.

Actual bodily contact is not essential to establish a battery. To grab a person by her clothing or to snatch something from the plaintiff's hand is sufficient. There is not a great deal of authority on the applicability of battery to intangible interference with the person such as being X-rayed, receiving laser treatment, or being subjected to ultraviolet light in a sun-tanning salon, but there is no policy reason to withhold the protection of the battery action from these modern intrusions on one's personal integrity.[7] The plaintiff does not need to be aware of the battery at the time that it takes place. An inappropriate touching or sexual assault of a plaintiff, who is unconscious as a result of illness, intoxication, or an anaesthetic, is actionable as a battery.

Battery is a product of the ancient writ of trespass to the person, a central characteristic of which was the need to prove that the plaintiff's

---

5   A useful discussion of the tort of battery is found in *Non-Marine Underwriters, Lloyds of London v. Scalera*, [2000] 1 S.C.R. 551, McLachlin J., as she then was [*Scalera*].

6   The technical term is that the tort is actionable *per se*.

7   Purists will point out that battery applies only to a physical interference with the person.

injury was caused by a *direct* act. Directness remains an essential requirement for liability not only in battery but in all the intentional torts that trace their origin to the writ of trespass (battery, assault, false imprisonment, trespass to land, and trespass to chattels). In battery, the defendant must directly interfere with the body of the plaintiff.[8] It is not, therefore, a battery to put poison in a person's food or to lay a trap for a person. In those situations, the interference with the plaintiff is not sufficiently immediate upon the defendant's act. Indirect intentional acts probably remain independently actionable under a residual and innominate tort. There is little modern justification for this dichotomy between direct and indirect acts and there are some indications that Canadian courts may, in due course, follow the lead of the American courts and jettison this historical baggage.

A further characteristic of the tort of battery, and the other intentional torts with origins in the writ of trespass, is that, in contrast to the tort of negligence, the burden of proof in respect of the wrongfulness of the defendant's conduct is on the *defendant*.[9] The plaintiff need only prove that the defendant directly interfered with his person in a harmful or offensive way. The defendant then carries the burden of proof that his conduct was neither intentional nor negligent or that some legally recognized defence applies. This reverse onus is justified by the direct causal link between the defendant's antisocial conduct and the violation of the plaintiff's right to personal autonomy. In such circumstances the defendant may fairly be required to establish that the loss was caused without intention or fault.[10]

The rule that the defendant carries the burden of proof to disprove that his conduct was intentional or *negligent* identifies a further historical anomaly of the tort of battery. A person who is injured by a direct *negligent* act may sue either in battery or in negligence. Modern practice is to sue in negligence and to confine battery to intentional acts, but plaintiffs who anticipate difficulty in proving negligence may resort to the technicalities of the tort of battery to secure a more favourable allocation of the burden of proof. It is used most often in shooting and sporting accidents.[11] It may not, however, be used in automobile accident cases where negligence is the only cause of action.[12]

---

8   Linden, above note 3 at 44 states that an indirect act is now actionable in battery. L.N. Klar, *Tort Law*, 4th ed. (Toronto: Carswell, 2008) at 47–48, takes the more conventional view.

9   *Cook v. Lewis*, [1951] S.C.R. 830 [*Cook*].

10   See *Scalera*, above note 5 at 556.

11   See *Cook*, above note 9.

12   Klar, above note 8 at 57.

The defendant's liability in battery is not restricted, as it is in negligence, to the foreseeable consequences of his act. The defendant is liable for all the consequences of his battery.[13] This broader rule of remoteness of damage, which is probably applicable to all of the intentional torts, is justified on the ground that the defendant's conduct, being intentional, carries the stain of moral culpability, which warrants a more extensive responsibility.

The most frequently committed batteries in modern society are acts of criminal violence. Tort litigation, however, holds little promise of compensation for the victims of criminal violence. Many offenders are not apprehended and those who are apprehended are often not worth suing. This has led to the introduction of criminal injuries compensation schemes in all provinces. Under these schemes, some victims of criminal violence receive modest no-fault benefits including an indemnity for related expenses and lost income and compensation for nonpecuniary losses. These schemes do not displace tort liability. They provide an alternative and supplementary compensatory mechanism without extinguishing the tort rights of the victim.

There is one area of criminal violence, however, where there has been a resurgence in the use of the battery action. The survivors of sexual assault, spousal abuse, incest, and child abuse are making increasing use of the tort of battery to hold offenders accountable for their wrongdoing. This is particularly common in respect of intra-family abuse and the abuse of children in institutional, custodial settings. In those situations, there is no problem in identifying the offender and some of the offenders (or their employers) may be able to pay an award of damages. It is important to note, however, that financial compensation is not always the primary motivation for this kind of litigation. The plaintiff may be more interested in securing the accountability of the offender and a public recognition of the extent of the defendant's wrongdoing. There may also be a hope that a public confrontation with the defendant and a judicial recognition of the defendant's responsibility will provide some therapeutic benefits[14] and promote the plaintiff's psychological and emotional recovery from the abuse.[15] These potential advantages of an action in battery must, however, be balanced against the disadvantages, which include the stress and expense of litigation,

---

13 *Bettel v. Yim* (1978), 20 O.R. (2d) 617 (Co. Ct.).
14 See B. Feldthusen, "The Civil Action for Sexual Battery: Therapeutic Jurisprudence?" (1993) 25 Ottawa L. Rev. 203.
15 See Law Commission of Canada, *Restoring Dignity: Responding to Child Abuse in Canadian Institutions* (Ottawa: Minister of Public Works and Governmental Services, 2000).

the emotional burden of recounting and being cross-examined in open court on the wrongdoing of the defendant, and the difficulties in securing payment of the judgment. The survivor of the abuse needs to make an informed decision, after consultation with legal advisers and therapists, as to whether or not litigation is in her best interests.

In cases of incest and other forms of sexual and physical abuse of young children, short limitation periods may present a procedural obstacle to the plaintiff's claim. Most limitation legislation postpones the running of time until the age of majority but the claims of the survivors of childhood abuse may not be brought until much later in adulthood when the true extent of the emotional and psychological harm caused by the abuse is apparent. At that time, limitation periods may, at first sight, appear to have extinguished the cause of action.[16] This issue was addressed by the Supreme Court in *M.(K.) v. M.(H.)*,[17] a case of childhood incest. The Court held that the cause of action, from which time runs, does not arise until the survivor of the incest has a complete and full understanding of both the wrongfulness of the defendant's act and the causal relationship between those acts and the psychological and emotional consequences of the acts in adulthood. Furthermore, the Court held that such complete knowledge is not likely to be acquired by the plaintiff in the absence of some form of professional therapy or counselling. In most provinces, this discoverability principle has been complemented by legislative initiatives that dispense with limitation periods for sexual misconduct, including sexual assault, in carefully defined circumstances.[18]

2) Assault

The word assault is commonly used to describe what in tort law is a battery. Strictly speaking, however, an assault in tort law is the threat of an immediate battery. Any direct and intentional act that causes a

---

16   The time limit for a battery action is often two years from when the cause of action arose.

17   [1992] 3 S.C.R. 6. See also *Novak v. Bond* (1999), 172 D.L.R. (4th) 385 (S.C.C.).

18   For example, Alberta *Limitation Act*, R.S.A. 2000, c. L-12, s. 5(2); British Columbia *Limitation Act*, R.S.B.C. 1996, c. 266, ss. 3(4)(k) & (l); Manitoba *The Limitations of Actions Act*, R.S.M. 1987, c. L150, s. 2.1(2); Newfoundland and Labrador *Limitations Act*, S.N.L. 1995, c. L-16.1, s. 8(2); Northwest Territories *Limitation of Actions Act*, R.S.N.W.T. 1988, c. L-8, s. 2.1(2); Nova Scotia *Limitation Act*, R.S.N.S. 1989, c. 258, s. 5. Nunavut *Limitations of Action Act*, R.S.N.W.T. (Nu.) 1988, c. L-8, s. 2.1(2). Ontario *Limitations Act*, S.O. 2002, c. 24, s. 10; Saskatchewan *Limitation of Actions Act*, R.S.S. 1978, c. L-15, s. 3(3.1); and Yukon *Limitation of Actions Act*, R.S.Y. 2002, c. 139, s. 2(3).

person to apprehend immediate harmful or offensive bodily contact is an assault. It is, for example, an assault to point a gun at a person and threaten to shoot him. Only when the person is shot is there a battery completing the couplet "assault and battery." Assault and battery are, however, independent causes of action. Where a defendant does not execute a threat of imminent contact, there is an assault but no battery. Where the defendant commits a surprise battery from behind, there is no assault because the plaintiff did not anticipate the battery. It must, however, be observed that these technical distinctions are not always honoured by judges and lawyers and reference to a battery as an assault is not infrequent.

The plaintiff must actually apprehend an immediate battery and that apprehension must be reasonable in the circumstances. There is, however, no requirement that the plaintiff be afraid. The tort protects both the brave and the fearful. There is also no need to prove any physical damage. The apprehension of imminent contact is enough.

Threats of future violence will not suffice. There must be a threat of immediate bodily contact. It is not, therefore, an assault to shake your fist at a person from a distance or to threaten to beat him up to-morrow. It is not always easy to draw the line between immediate and future threats. The famous case of *Stephens v. Myers*[19] is illustrative. The defendant advanced on the plaintiff in a threatening manner at a parish meeting. The defendant was intercepted and restrained when he reached the chair next but one to the chair on which the plaintiff was sitting. The Court found that an assault had taken place.

There are a number of subsidiary rules in respect of assault that have been established over the centuries, some of which are in need of re-evaluation and others of which have now been discarded. It has been held, for example, that mere words cannot amount to an assault. This must be doubted in the face of modern communications and technology. There would seem to be no reason to deny a remedy when a person is phoned and told that there is a bomb in her house and it is about to be detonated. It has also been said that passive conduct cannot amount to an assault. It is true that passive conduct does not normally generate an apprehension of immediate violence but there does not seem to be any reason why a person who walks into her home to find a stranger sitting passively with a gun pointed at her should not have a remedy. It was also suggested at one time that the defendant must have the means of carrying out the threat so that threatening to shoot a person with an unloaded gun was not an assault. This view is now thoroughly

---

19   (1830), 4 C. & P. 349, 172 E.R. 735 (N.P.).

discredited and liability will be imposed so long as the plaintiff did not know that the gun was unloaded. All of these situations should be resolved by reference to the intent of the defendant and the reasonableness of the plaintiff's apprehension of an immediate battery rather than by the application of rules derived from ancient decisions on their unique facts.[20]

There has been much written about conditional threats. This flows from the old case of *Tuberville v. Savage*[21] where a man placed his hand on his sword and said, "If it were not assize time, I would not take such language from you." The Court held that this was not an assault. The judgment is clearly correct because the reasonable meaning of the words is, "You are safe from violence because the judges are in town." The case was occasionally misinterpreted to suggest that a conditional threat could not be an assault. That view has been repudiated. "Give me your wallet or I will kill you" is a conditional threat but it, nevertheless, is intended to create an apprehension of immediate violence. The modern view is that a threat of violence coupled with a condition that the speaker has no right to impose, the compliance with which is essential to purchase one's safety, is an assault. There is, for example, an assault when, in the course of a domestic dispute, the defendant spouse declares, "I will kill you if you take me to court."[22] The defendant has no right to require the plaintiff to buy her safety by giving such an assurance. It is a threat of immediate violence because the defendant is attempting to secure an immediate promise that she will not take him to court in the future and violence may reasonably be expected if the assurance is not given. It is less reasonable to interpret it as a threat of future violence that will occur only when the court proceedings are filed.

The award of damages for an assault that is not accompanied by a battery is likely to be modest[23] in the absence of aggravating circumstances or factors that justify an award of punitive damages.[24] Actions

---

20   This approach was taken by the House of Lords in a case of criminal assault. In *R. v. Ireland* (1997), [1998] A.C. 147 (H.L.), it was held that silent telephone calls may be an assault if they give rise to a fear of imminent personal violence.

21   (1669), Mod. Rep. 3, 86 E.R. 684 (K.B.).

22   *Holcombe v. Whitaker*, 318 So.2d 289 (Ala. 1975).

23   See *Santamaria v. James*, [2004] O.J. No. 744 (S.C.J.) where $2,500 was awarded where the defendant insulted, shouted at, and wagged his finger at the plaintiff. See also *Mainland Sawmills Ltd. v. USW Union Local 1-3567*, [2007] B.C.J. No. 2098 (S.C.) [*Mainland Sawmills*], that dealt with nineteen assault claims arising from a violent and threatening confrontation between members of rival trade unions. Damages ranged from $750–$5,000.

24   In *Warman v. Grosvenor*, [2008] O.J. No. 4462 (S.C.J.), general damages of $15,000 and punitive damages of $5,000 were awarded where the defendant

for assault are, in fact, uncommon in modern times.[25] Of much greater practical significance is the fact that an assault justifies the use of reasonable force in self-defence and it is in this context that the issue of assault is most likely to arise.

3) False Imprisonment

The tort of false imprisonment protects a person's individual liberty. A direct intentional[26] imprisonment of another person is a false imprisonment. It is actionable without proof of damage. There must be a complete restriction on the plaintiff's physical liberty. This was established in *Bird v. Jones*.[27] In that case, the plaintiff was partially obstructed from exercising a public right of passage across a bridge. There was nothing, however, preventing him from passing around the obstruction and continuing across the bridge. It was held that a partial obstruction and disturbance of a right of way is not a false imprisonment. There must be a complete detention of the plaintiff.[28] *Bird* has stood unchallenged for 166 years for good reason. It must be remembered that false imprisonment is actionable without proof of damage. It is neither good sense nor good policy to make every obstruction in the modern urban environment actionable. If an obstruction causes damage, a remedy may be available under negligence or public nuisance.

Physical imprisonment in a room or a building is not necessary. A person may be imprisoned on an aircraft, in a motor vehicle, or on a boat. The use of restraints in health-care facilities is a false imprisonment. Imprisonment can also be psychological. This may arise when a suspect is asked to accompany a store detective or a police officer for questioning. If the person goes freely and voluntarily to deal with the matter there is no imprisonment. If, however, the person is intimidated by a show of authority, afraid of the consequences of refusal, apprehends the use of force, or is seeking solely to avoid public embar-

---

assaulted the plaintiff in a sustained campaign of terror waged by online postings and e-mail.

25 The tort of assault may, however, have a future role in addressing the significant problem of bullying, particularly in high schools. Such conduct may well include threats of imminent violence and, on that basis, be actionable. See J. Elvin, "Liability of Schools for Bullying" (2002) 61 Cambridge L.J. 239.

26 There continues to be some doubt on the point, but a direct negligent imprisonment is probably actionable as a false imprisonment or, where there is damage, in negligence.

27 (1845), 7 Q.B.R. 742, 115 E.R. 668 (Q.B.).

28 If the detained person has a reasonable and safe means of escape, he is not imprisoned for the purposes of this tort.

rassment, he may be imprisoned and the defendant will be required to justify the detention on the ground of her legal authority to arrest the person.

There is no Canadian authority on whether or not the plaintiff must be conscious of his imprisonment. The strong protection that the law has traditionally given to personal liberty suggests that an awareness of the confinement is not necessary. This would be consistent with the most recent English authority on the point.[29] Consequently, a remedy is probably available to kidnapped infants and mentally incompetent adults who, because of age or an illness such as Alzheimer's disease, are unaware of their detention.

It should be noted that the word "false" in false imprisonment is misleading. The plaintiff is required only to prove a direct imprisonment. "False" suggests that it was unjustified because of a lack of consent or legal authority to imprison. These are, however, defences that must be proved by the defendant. The defendant also carries the burden of showing that her actions were neither intentional nor negligent.

4) Malicious Prosecution

The tort of malicious prosecution reflects a delicate balance between two important and competing interests. The first interest is the freedom of individual citizens from groundless criminal prosecutions that may result in damage to their reputation, a loss of liberty, and financial loss. The second is the public interest in the effective and uninhibited prosecution of criminal wrongdoing. The tort of malicious prosecution strongly favours the public interest by protecting prosecutors from liability unless the prosecution was brought maliciously and without reasonable and probable cause.

This position was justified historically on the need to encourage private citizens to assist in bringing criminals to justice. In the past, considerable reliance was placed on the assistance of private citizens and the bringing of private prosecutions to enforce the criminal law. It was believed that imposing liability for mistakes or carelessness on the part of private prosecutors might inhibit voluntary and cooperative conduct. Today, of course, the criminal justice system is administered by professional governmental officials such as police officers and government prosecutors. There is less reliance on private citizens and private prosecutions are largely a thing of the past. Nevertheless, the traditional deference paid to prosecutors continues.

---

29   *Murray v. Ministry of Defence*, [1988] 1 W.L.R. 692 (H.L.).

The requirements of malicious prosecution are well established. The plaintiff must prove that the defendant initiated the proceedings against the plaintiff, that the proceedings terminated in the plaintiff's favour, that there was no reasonable and probable cause for the proceedings, that there was malice on the part of the defendant, and that the plaintiff sustained damage.[30] These criteria are notoriously difficult to establish but the courts to date have exhibited little enthusiasm to relax them and widen the scope of liability. Each requirement deserves brief comment.

a) Institution of the Proceedings by the Defendant

The defendant must have instigated the proceedings. This means that the defendant must have been actively instrumental in bringing a prosecution. Laying an information or bringing a charge against the plaintiff is sufficient. Merely providing information to the police is normally not sufficient unless a false report is deliberately given to the police for the purpose of prompting a wrongful prosecution. Malicious prosecution has been restricted to criminal and quasi-criminal proceedings and has not generally been applied to civil litigation. This is explained in part by the serious threat to liberty, reputation, and wealth posed by criminal prosecutions.

b) Termination of the Proceedings in the Plaintiff's Favour

The proceedings must have terminated in the plaintiff's favour. A conviction that has not been set aside forecloses an action in malicious prosecution. It is not, however, necessary that the plaintiff be acquitted on the merits. A discharge at a preliminary hearing, a stay of prosecution, a successful appeal, or an acquittal on a technicality are sufficient to satisfy this element of the cause of action. A malicious prosecution action may also be available in those cases where, after conviction and a long period of imprisonment, new evidence comes to light which exonerates the accused and results in the conviction being set aside.[31]

---

30 See *Nelles v. Ontario*, [1989] 2 S.C.R. 170 at 192–93, Lamer J. [*Nelles*] for a general outline of these principles.

31 These situations are now generally remedied by a negotiated compensation package from government: for example, the settlement between David Milgaard and the government of Saskatchewan. See also, Manitoba, *Commission of Inquiry Regarding Thomas Sophonow, The Inquiry Regarding Thomas Sophonow: The Investigation, Prosecution and Consideration of Entitlement to Compensation* (Winnipeg: Manitoba Justice, 2001).

c) Lack of Reasonable and Probable Cause

It is not easy to prove that the defendant had no reasonable and probable cause to bring the proceedings. The concept has a subjective element, requiring an actual belief in guilt, and an objective element, requiring a rational basis for that belief. The plaintiff must, therefore, prove either the absence of an honest belief in guilt on the part of his accuser or the absence of reasonable grounds for such a belief or the absence of both elements. *Roberts v. Buster's Auto Towing Service Ltd.*[32] is illustrative. In that case, the plaintiff's rental car had been towed to the defendant's compound because of a parking violation. The plaintiff went to retrieve the vehicle, and as he drove out of the exit of the compound, he paused to see if the lane was clear. At that moment an employee of the defendant activated an automatic gate which threatened to hit the car. The plaintiff tried to avoid the gate by driving off but he was unsuccessful and both the gate and the car were damaged. The defendant's employee swore an information alleging that the plaintiff had *wilfully* damaged the gate. Clearly, on the facts, the employee had *neither* an honest belief in the plaintiff's guilt nor any reasonable basis to believe in his guilt.

d) Malice

The defendant must be motivated by malice. Motive is not usually a relevant factor in tort law. An invasion of a protected interest for good or bad reasons is equally wrongful in most circumstances. Malicious prosecution is exceptional in this regard. Malice includes the colloquial notion of spite, ill will, and vengeance but also extends to any improper purpose. The proper purpose of a prosecution is to bring an offender to justice and to enforce the criminal law. Consequently, to instigate a prosecution to secure a private collateral benefit, to coerce a person into a desired course of conduct, or, as in *Roberts*, to shift the blame for causing damage to property to an innocent person is an improper purpose, and constitutes malice in this context.

e) Damage

Malicious prosecution is not actionable without proof of actual damage such as loss of reputation, loss of liberty, or financial loss.[33] In most cases of malicious prosecution there is no difficulty in establishing one or more of these heads of damage unless the baseless prosecution is terminated almost immediately after its commencement.

---

32   (1976), 70 D.L.R. (3d) 716 (B.C.S.C.) [*Roberts*].
33   Financial loss includes the costs of defending the criminal prosecution.

5) Malicious Prosecution and Crown Prosecutors

The application of malicious prosecution to Crown prosecutors was clarified in the recent decision of the Supreme Court in *Miazga v. Kvello Estate*.[34] Towards the end of the twentieth century, the Supreme Court, in *Nelles*,[35] abolished an ancient common law immunity enjoyed by attorneys general and Crown prosecutors. After *Nelles* there were indications that courts might go further and apply the tort to Crown prosecutors in a manner which would enhance their accountability and favour those who were wrongly prosecuted. A number of options were canvassed including drawing an inference of malice from the lack of reasonable and probable cause, substituting recklessness for malice and, most radically, imposing a duty of care on Crown prosecutors[36] These initiatives were opposed by those who argued that policy factors did not support the relaxation of the elements of malicious prosecution. They included the need to protect the independence of Crown prosecutors from political or judicial interference, the difficult discretionary and quasi-judicial decisions required of prosecutors, the chilling effect a broader liability might have on their work, the possibility of a flood of litigation, and the tensions public prosecutors inevitably encounter in balancing their dual, and sometimes competing, responsibilities as advocates for the Crown and as "ministers of justice." The Supreme Court in *Miazga* was swayed by these arguments and it delivered an opinion that is strongly protective of Crown prosecutors. It held that malice remains the central element of the tort. Furthermore, malice will only be found in exceptional cases where the impugned conduct of the Crown prosecutor is so extreme and egregious as to be an abuse or a perversion of the system of criminal justice. Incompetence, lack of professionalism, laziness, recklessness, honest mistake, negligence, or gross negligence will not be sufficient to impose liability[37] The practical consequence of *Miazga* is to foreclose malicious prosecution as a viable

---

34   [2009] S.C.J. No. 51.

35   Above note 30.

36   See *Oniel v. Metropolitan Toronto (Municipality) Police Force*, [2001] O.J. No. 90 (C.A.); *Folland v. Ontario*, [2003] O.J. No. 1048 (C.A.); and *Driskell v. Dangerfield*, [2007] M.J. No. 206 (Q.B.).

37   The Court also held that in assessing a lack of reasonable and probable cause it is the Crown prosecutor's objective and professional assessment of the legal strengths of the case that is significant. The lack of reasonable and probable cause will be found only where the prosecutor did not believe *objectively* that, in the circumstances, proof beyond a reasonable doubt could be established. A lack of personal (subjective) belief in the guilt of the accused will not impair a finding of reasonable and probable cause.

remedy for the wrongly convicted against Crown prosecutors. It will be a rare case where one can secure evidence of a deliberate subversion and abuse of the system of criminal justice.

6) False Imprisonment and Malicious Prosecution

False imprisonment and malicious prosecution are mutually exclusive causes of action. False imprisonment lies in respect of the direct imprisonment of the plaintiff by the defendant. If the imprisonment occurs or is continued after an intervening discretionary decision by a police officer or an official exercising judicial power, the defendant is not liable for false imprisonment. The source of this distinction lies in the fact that false imprisonment derives from the writ of trespass which requires a direct act. Malicious prosecution derives from the action on the case that addresses indirect acts. The case of *Roberts* is again illustrative. The defendant's employee reported the incident with the gate to the police and requested that the police apprehend the plaintiff. The police stopped the plaintiff and detained him at the side of the highway before taking to the police station. This initial detention was a false imprisonment by the *employee* because she directed the police to apprehend the plaintiff and they acted on her behalf.[38] Later the employee swore an information before a justice of the peace who ordered the plaintiff to be held in custody. Since the detention after the laying of the information was at the direction of a judicial officer, the only cause of action against the employee for the continuing detention was malicious prosecution.

7) Malicious Procurement and Execution of a Search Warrant

The tort of malicious procurement of a search warrant is closely related to the tort of malicious prosecution. The foundation of each is the intentional abuse of the processes of the court. The elements of this cause of action were discussed by the Privy Council in *Gibbs v. Rea*.[39] In that case, search warrants were issued on the ground that the plaintiff was suspected of trafficking in drugs or benefiting from the drug trade. The Court held that the plaintiff must establish that the defendant made a successful application for a search warrant, that the defendant had no reasonable and probable cause to make the application (what amounts to reasonable cause depends on the requirements of the legislation

---

38   It was also, of course, a false imprisonment by the police for which they were able to establish the defence of legal authority.

39   [1998] A.C. 786 (P.C.) [*Gibbs*].

controlling the reasons for the grant of the warrant), that the defendant acted with malice, and that the plaintiff suffered damage. The tort was established in *Gibbs* because there was absolutely no evidence suggesting that the plaintiff was, in any way, involved in the drug trade, and the defendant presented no evidence in justification of its actions.

8) Abuse of Process

Malicious prosecution is usually restricted to criminal and quasi-criminal proceedings. The tort of abuse of process is applicable in respect of the improper use of the civil litigation process. This tort is easier to establish than malicious prosecution because the plaintiff does not have to establish either that the proceedings terminated in the plaintiff's favour or that the plaintiff lacked reasonable and probable cause to bring the action. There are four elements of the tort. First, the defendant must have brought the civil action or process. Second, the proceedings must be brought for a collateral and improper purpose. Third, there must be evidence of some overt act or threat, independent of the litigation, designed to secure the defendant's improper purpose. Fourth, the plaintiff must prove damage.

It is noteworthy that the malicious use of the litigation process is not, in itself, actionable. There must in addition be proof of some *overt act*, independent of the litigation, that is designed to advance the defendant's wrongful purpose. Imagine, for example, that two rival employees, Jones and Smith, are in line for a future promotion in a workplace that is not governed by a collective bargaining agreement. Jones makes some uncomplimentary remarks about Smith to some of their fellow employees. Smith seizes on this opportunity to instigate an action in defamation against Jones solely for the purpose of disrupting Jones's chances for the promotion. The collateral purpose is established. Later, Smith says to Jones, "If you drop out of the race for the promotion, your litigation woes are over." This satisfies the requirement of an overt act. If Jones drops out of the race and loses the promotion that would otherwise have been his, he suffers damage and the tort is complete.

The requirement of an overt act has proved to be a significant obstacle to plaintiffs. This has led some courts to dispense with the requirement and to emphasize the inherent wrongfulness of the abuse of the right to litigate. Other courts continue to emphasize the importance of establishing an overt act not merely as compelling evidence of malice but as an essential independent control device on the scope of the action.[40]

---

40 See J. Irvine, "The Resurrection of Tortious Abuse of Process" (1989) 47 C.C.L.T. 217; Klar, above note 8 at 74–76; and *Metrick v. Deeb*, [2003] O.J. No. 2221 (C.A.).

9) Intentional Infliction of Nervous Shock

Liability for the intentional infliction of nervous shock was first recognized in the famous case of *Wilkinson v. Downton*.[41] In that case, the defendant, by way of a practical joke, told the plaintiff that her husband had been seriously injured in an accident and that he was lying in a tavern with both of his legs broken. The defendant's statements were false. The plaintiff became seriously ill from the shock to her nervous system and she suffered serious and permanent physical consequences. The Court imposed liability on the basis of the defendant's constructive intent to shock and harm the plaintiff.

There are three elements that make up the tort of intentional infliction of nervous shock. First, there must be outrageous or extreme conduct. The circulation or communication of false and shocking information, unwarranted accusations of criminal wrongdoing or immorality made to the plaintiff,[42] and threats of future violence and other terrifying conduct are likely to be sufficient to ground liability. A number of cases involve a single shocking event similar to that in *Wilkinson*. Others address a pattern of behaviour such as emotional abuse, cyber-bullying, harassment, and intimidation. In *Clark v. R.*,[43] for example, proof of a pattern of behaviour involving many incidents of sexual harassment of a female police officer by her male colleagues and supervisors, cumulatively causing her nervous shock, was sufficient to impose vicarious liability on the Crown. This application of the tort to a hostile work environment was confirmed by the decision of the Ontario Court of Appeal in *Prinzo v. Baycrest Centre for Geriatric Care*.[44] In that case, liability was imposed in respect of workplace harassment that was described as extreme, insensitive, and in wanton disregard for the plaintiff"s health. Second, there must be proof of actual intent or, as in *Wilkinson*, constructive intent to cause harm of the kind suffered.[45] There are instances where "constructive intent" has been interpreted to include conduct where there was less than a substantial certainty that harm would occur. This tends to muddy the distinction between intentional and negligent conduct. This imprecision at the margins is, however, often inconsequential since liability may be imposed for the

---

41   [1897] 2 Q.B. 57.
42   If such statements were made to third parties, they would be defamatory.
43   [1994] 3 F.C. 323 (T.D.).
44   [2002] O.J. No. 2712 (C.A.) [*Prinzo*]. See also *Correia v. Canac Kitchens*, [2008] O.J. No. 2497 (C.A.) and *Piresferreira v. Ayotte*, 2010 ONCA 384 [*Piresferreira*].
45   This is frequently described in the caselaw as "calculated to produce harm."

negligent infliction of nervous shock.[46] Third, the plaintiff must prove nervous shock which is defined, as it is in the tort of negligence, as a recognizable psychiatric illness or physical harm. Anguish, worry, and emotional distress are insufficient to support an action. This is a significant obstacle for some plaintiffs who have suffered severe emotional distress. For example, in *Radovskis v. Tomm*,[47] the plaintiff mother was unable to secure a remedy from an offender who had committed a serious sexual assault on her five-year-old daughter because she presented no evidence of illness. In recent years, however, there has been some relaxation in the interpretation of nervous shock and, under the cover of conventional doctrine, the courts are edging towards recognizing severe emotional stress as sufficient, particularly where the defendant's conduct is utterly outrageous.

This tort mirrors the tort of negligence in its requirement that the plaintiff must not have a predisposition or susceptibility to shock. The defendant will, however, be liable if his conduct targets a known vulnerability of the plaintiff. Liability was imposed in *Timmermans v. Buelow*,[48] for example, where a landlord sent threatening and harassing eviction letters to a tenant whom he knew to be in a fragile mental state.

There is one situation where the tort of intentional infliction of nervous shock is inapplicable. In *Frame v. Smith*[49] the Supreme Court refused to apply it in the circumstances of marriage breakdown and consequential custody and access disputes. The Court held that the risk of vindictive and extortionate litigation was too high and that these disputes were more appropriately resolved by the sophisticated regime of federal and provincial family law, which provides a wide range of remedies to protect the interests of family members.

10) Privacy

There is no consistent approach to liability for the invasion of privacy in Canada. In some provinces the common law applies. In four provinces, British Columbia, Manitoba, Saskatchewan, and Newfoundland and Labrador, privacy acts have created a statutory tort.[50]

---

46 The distinction is important, however, in the employment context because the employer owes no duty of care to avoid nervous shock to employees. See *Pires-ferreira*, above note 44.

47 (1957), 65 Man. R. 61 (Q.B.).

48 [1984] O.J. No. 2408 (H.C.J.).

49 [1987] 2 S.C.R. 99.

50 British Columbia *Privacy Act*, R.S.B.C. 1996, c. 373; Manitoba *The Privacy Act*, R.S.M. 1987, c. P125; Newfoundland and Labrador *Privacy Act*, R.S.N.L. 1990, c. P-22; Saskatchewan *Privacy Act*, R.S.S. 1978, c. P-24.

a) Common Law

The common law has not developed a discrete and well-defined tort of invasion of privacy. There are a number of reasons for its failure to address adequately the protection of privacy interests. First, privacy is a relatively modern idea, the protection of which was not a priority when the fundamental contours of tort liability were being developed in the common law. Second, privacy is an elusive concept that is to some extent dependent upon personal attitudes and expectations. There is a clear societal consensus about the importance of personal safety but agreement on a normative degree of privacy is much more difficult to find. Some persons live in obsessive secrecy. The lives of others are an open book. Third, the protection of privacy requires a very difficult and delicate balance to be drawn between the interest in privacy and the interest in freedom of information and freedom of expression. There is a profound tension between the personal interest in being left alone and the public interest in being informed. Many people deplore the excesses of intrusive journalism and the tactics of the paparazzi, but they generally support freedom of information legislation and they recognize the great contribution that the mass distribution of information and opinion by modern communication systems makes to the quality of their lives and their ability to make informed political, financial, and personal decisions.[51] Fourth, the common law has been slow to recognize and protect intangible personal losses that are commonly the consequence of a breach of privacy. Transient emotional distress has traditionally generated fears of a flood of litigation, which has dictated judicial caution. Fifth, it is difficult to define the elements of a privacy tort because privacy claims arise in very diverse circumstances ranging

---

51 The Supreme Court has discussed the balance between the individual's right to privacy and the public's right to information in respect of the right to privacy contained in the Quebec *Charter of Rights and Freedoms*: see *Aubry v. Editions Vice-Versa Inc.*, [1998] 1 S.C.R. 591 [*Aubry*]. The defendant published an inoffensive, artistic photograph of the plaintiff sitting on the steps of a public building without the plaintiff's consent. The Court held that, while the taking of the photograph was not a breach of privacy because the plaintiff was in a public place, its publication was a breach of her privacy that was not justified by the public's right to information. The Court observed that each case depends upon the nature of the information and the situation of those concerned. It was pertinent that the plaintiff was not by choice or circumstances a public figure. She was not part of a newsworthy event. Furthermore, her image was not incidental to a photograph of a public building, event, or group of people. In those kinds of situations her privacy right would generally yield to the public's right to information, but in this case the photograph was of her alone, and she had the right to control the publicity given to that image.

from those with territorial or spatial aspects, to those that relate to the person and to those that arise in an informational context.[52] Sixth, there are often difficulties in both establishing the damage caused by the loss of privacy and determining the appropriate quantum of damages to compensate that loss. Finally, the legal response to the protection of privacy in the past few decades has tended to emphasize direct statutory regulation of commercial and governmental activities rather than the development of a common law tort of privacy.[53] Consequently, the law of torts is not well placed to deal with the myriad of privacy issues that will present themselves in this century.

The traditional response to the infringement of privacy has been to rely on the well-established, traditional torts to provide an indirect protection of privacy interests rather than to create an independent tort of privacy. Trespass to land, private nuisance, the intentional infliction of nervous shock, and trespass to chattels are all capable, in certain circumstances, of providing some protection of privacy interests. The person who snoops through another's window may commit a trespass to land. An unauthorized search of another's purse is a trespass to chattels. Constant harassing phone calls may be actionable as a private nuisance. The disadvantage of this approach is that the protection is incomplete, unpredictable, and uncertain. This is an inevitable consequence of using torts that were designed primarily to protect non-privacy interests to perform new tasks.

In the past few decades, however, there are indications of a nascent common law tort of privacy. The first step was the recognition of a remedy for the misappropriation of a person's name or likeness for commercial purposes. It might be argued that this protects the right of publicity of public figures rather than a right to privacy.[54] Nevertheless, it evidenced the inherent power of the common law to address issues similar to that of privacy and encouraged judges to consider seriously arguments in favour of a common law tort of privacy. Courts now routinely refuse to strike out a statement of claim alleging an invasion of privacy on the ground that it discloses no known cause of action. Many of these cases, however, inhabit the fringes of conventional tort liability

---

52 See *R. v. Dyment*, [1988] 2 S.C.R. 417 at para. 417, La Forest J.

53 See, for example, *Privacy Act*, R.S.C. 1985, c. P-21, *Personal Information Protection and Electronic Documents Act*, S.C. 2000, c. 5, and provincial freedom of information and protection of privacy legislation in most provinces (for example, *Freedom of Information and Protection of Privacy Act*, R.S.O. 1990, c. F.31).

54 Misappropriation of personality is dealt with later in this chapter as a tort of intentional interference with economic interests. See section F(1)(d), below in this chapter.

and the pleadings normally include additional allegations of traditional wrongdoing. There are, as yet, only a few decisions on the merits, none of which explores the form, scope, and elements of an independent common law tort of privacy at any great length. Nevertheless, liability has been imposed for the unauthorized taping and publication of a private conversation,[55] the aiming of a surveillance camera into a neighbour's yard,[56] harassment,[57] and the disclosure of a sexual assault on an undercover police officer.[58] In *Somwar v. McDonald's Restaurants of Canada Ltd.*,[59] the court refused to strike out a statement of claim alleging that an employer had invaded the privacy of an employee by obtaining a consumer report containing credit information without his permission. The learned judge concluded that it was not settled law that there was no tort of privacy in Ontario and, furthermore, the time had come to recognize invasion of privacy as a tort in its own right.[60] This view is supported by the decision in *Caltagirone v. Scozzari-Clouthier*,[61] dealing with the non-consensual disclosure to family members that the plaintiff was HIV positive. It was held that, in the absence of consent or a legitimate public interest, the acquisition or disclosure of private information was actionable.[62]

Support for a discrete tort of invasion of privacy may be drawn not only from the authorities referred to but also from other persuasive sources. Section 8 of the *Charter of Rights and Freedoms*[63] protects citizens from unreasonable search and seizure thereby enshrining privacy as a concept worthy of constitutional protection[64] and section 5 of the Quebec *Charter of Human Rights and Freedoms*[65] explicitly recognizes a right to private life. Furthermore, other common law jurisdictions have developed a common law protection of privacy. A tort of invasion

---

55   *Saccone v. Orr* (1981), 34 O.R. (2d) 317 (Co. Ct.).

56   *Lipiec v. Borsa* (1996), 31 C.C.L.T. (2d) 294 (Ont. Gen. Div.).

57   *Roth v. Roth* (1991), 4 O.R. (3d) 740 (Gen. Div.). See also *Palad v. Pantaleon*, [1989] O.J. No. 985 (Dist. Ct.) (harassment of a debtor by creditors). ·

58   *R.(L.) v. Nyp* (1995), 25 C.C.L.T. (2d) 309 (Ont. Gen. Div.).

59   *Somwar v. McDonald's Restaurants of Canada Ltd.* (2006), 263 D.L.R. (4th) 752 (S.C.J.) [*Somwar*]. See also *Shred-Tech Corp. v. Viveen*, [2006] O.J. No. 4893 (S.C.J.).

60   *Somwar, ibid.* at 760 and 763.

61   [2007] O.J. No. 4003 (S.C.J. Small Claims Court).

62   The claim failed on other grounds.

63   Part 1 of the *Constitution Act, 1982*, being Schedule B to the *Canada Act 1982* (U.K.), 1982, c. 11.

64   See *Hunter v. Southam Inc.*, [1984] 2 S.C.R. 145; *R. v. Dyment*, above note 52; and *R. v. Gomboc*, [2010] S.C.J. No. 55.

65   R.S.Q. c. C-12.

of privacy has long been recognized in the United States[66] and although the House of Lords declined to recognize a discrete tort of invasion of privacy[67] it has developed a remedy for the publication of private information by extending the action for breach of confidence.[68] A discrete tort of invasion of privacy has been established in New Zealand for the disclosure of private facts where there is a reasonable expectation of privacy and disclosure of the information would be highly offensive to a reasonable person[69] and in Australia the High Court has opened the way to the recognition of a tort of privacy.[70]

b) The Privacy Acts of British Columbia, Manitoba, Newfoundland and Labrador, and Saskatchewan

In British Columbia, Manitoba, Newfoundland and Labrador, and Saskatchewan, a statutory tort of privacy has been created. The Saskatchewan *Privacy Act*[71] is representative of the legislation in the other provinces in both form and substance. The centrepiece of the Saskatchewan Act is section 2, which declares that it is a tort to violate, wilfully and without claim of right, the privacy of another. The tort is actionable without proof of damage. Privacy is not exhaustively defined but section 3 describes conduct that, in the absence of consent, is *prima facie* evidence of a violation of privacy. The surveillance of others, listening to or recording private conversations, using another's name or likeness for commercial purposes, and making use of personal documents such as diaries and letters are included. Section 6 states that a person is entitled to the degree of privacy that is reasonable in the circumstances. Relevant factors in that assessment include the nature and impact of the defendant's conduct, the relationship between the parties, and any apology or offer of amends made by the defendant. Some guidance on the range of protection provided by the Act can be drawn from the relatively few cases in Saskatchewan and the other provinces

---

66   American tort law has recognized four categories of a tort of invasion of privacy, namely intrusion into a person's seclusion or solitude or private affairs; public disclosure of embarrassing private facts; placing a person in a false light in the public eye; and misappropriation of a person's name or likeness. See W. Prosser, "Privacy" (1960) 48 Cal. L. Rev. 383 at 389.

67   *Wainwright v. Home Office*, [2004] 2 A.C. 406 (H.L.).

68   *Campbell v. Mirror Group Newspapers Ltd.*, [2004] 2 A.C. 457 (H.L.). See also *McKennit v. Ash*, [2006] EWCA 1714.

69   *Hosking v. Runting*, [2005] 1 N.Z.L.R. 1 (C.A.) and *Andrews v. Television New Zealand Ltd.*, [2009] 1 N.Z.L.R. 220 (H.C.).

70   *Australian Broadcasting Corporation v. Lenah Game Meats Pty. Ltd.* (2001), 76 A.L.J.R. 1.

71   Above note 50.

with comparable legislation. A number of situations have been considered, including the disclosure of personal and private information, surveillance, media coverage of private figures, and harassing behaviour. First, the disclosure of personal information has been found to be an invasion of privacy in a number of cases. The unauthorized publication of the health status of an employee to persons who had no legitimate interest in that information was held to be a breach of privacy, for which the defendant escaped liability only because the disclosure was not wilful.[72] The publication of the name of a victim of crime that was subject to a court-ordered publication ban,[73] and the unauthorized release for television broadcast of a videotape of tunnel-graft surgery designed to secure an artificial hairpiece, were also held to be invasions of privacy.[74] The only aberrant decision is one in which the circulation of a topless photograph of the female plaintiff by a male acquaintance in whose possession the photograph was mistakenly left was held not to be an invasion of privacy.[75] Second, surveillance may be actionable. The legitimacy of surveillance depends on the kind of surveillance, its location, and the legitimate interests of the defendant. There are, however, two situations where there is little debate. First, the use of hidden video cameras or peep holes to surreptitiously watch and/or record intimate and personal activities in a bathroom or bedroom are not only actionable but may warrant punitive damages.[76] Eavesdropping and/or the recording of private telephone conversations are also a clear violation of privacy.[77] Second, the observation and photographing of persons who are in a public place, such as a municipal park, is not normally actionable because there is generally no reasonable expectation of privacy in such places.[78] There is more debate where there is video surveillance of private or quasi-private locations. Video surveillance directed at the

---

72 *Peters-Brown v. Regina District Health Board* (1996), [1997] 1 W.W.R. 638 (Sask. C.A.).

73 *F.(J.M.) v. Chappell* (1998), 158 D.L.R. (4th) 430 (B.C.C.A.).

74 *Hollinsworth v. BCTV* (1998), [1999] 6 W.W.R. 54 (B.C.C.A.). The television broadcaster was not, however, held liable. It did not wilfully and without claim of right invade the plaintiff's privacy, because it believed the plaintiff had consented to the broadcast.

75 *Milton v. Savinkoff* (1993), 18 C.C.L.T. (2d) 288 (B.C.S.C.).

76 *L'ee v. Jacobson* (1992), 87 D.L.R. (4th) 401 (B.C.S.C.), rev'd (1994), 120 D.L.R. (4th) 155 (B.C.C.A.). See also *Malcolm v. Fleming*, [2000] B.C.J. No. 2400 (S.C.) and *L.A.M. v. J.E.L.I.*, [2008] B.C.J. No. 1612 (S.C.).

77 *Ferguson v. McBee Technologies Inc.*, [1988] 6 W.W.R. 716 (Man. C.A.) and *Watts v. Klaemt*, [2007] B.C.J. No. 980 (S.C.).

78 *Lord v. Canada (Attorney General)* (2000), 50 C.C.L.T. (2d) 206 (B.C.C.A.).

plaintiff's house and backyard[79] and video surveillance directed at the entrance of the plaintiff's suite in an apartment block[80] were held to be breaches of privacy largely because of the insufficiency of the defendant's interest in the surveillance. More latitude was given to an insurer who conducted video surveillance of an insured who was receiving disability benefits. It was held that it was permissible not only to conduct video surveillance of her activities in public places, but also, and more controversially, to capture her activities on video by means of a long-range lens aimed at the uncovered windows of her well-lit home.[81] Latitude has also been given to private investigators who embark on a pattern of following and watching to the distress of the plaintiff. Such conduct is permissible so long as the employer of the investigator has a legitimate interest to protect and the investigator's conduct is reasonable and discreet.[82] When an investigation intrudes into areas unrelated to its legitimate purpose, privacy may be violated.[83] Third, there are instances where a private citizen has become involuntarily involved in a newsworthy event. Media coverage of the event may place the person in the public spotlight without his consent. These situations present a clash of interests between privacy and freedom of information and the public interest. There are few cases on point but the television coverage of a scuffle in the course of a labour dispute was held not to be a violation of privacy because it was a newsworthy event that took place during the day at a public location.[84] Finally, harassing conduct may also amount to a breach of privacy. Harassment of a newly married couple by an ex-girlfriend of the husband was held to be a breach of privacy.[85]

A wide range of defences set out in section 4 of the Act seeks to balance the right to privacy with other legitimate interests. They include consent, the exercise of a lawful right of defence of person or property, legal authorization, reasonable police investigation, reasonable news gathering, and the publication of information that is either in the public interest or fair comment on a matter of public interest or would be a privileged communication within the law of defamation.

---

79   *Wasserman v. Hall*, [2009] B.C.J. No.1932 (S.C.).

80   *Heckert v. 5470 Investments Ltd.* (2008), 62 C.C.L.T. (3d) 249 (B.C.S.C.).

81   *Milner v. Manufacturer's Life Insurance Co.*, [2006] B.C.J. No. 2787 (S.C.).

82   *Davis v. McArthur* (1970), 17 D.L.R. (3d) 760 (B.C.C.A.) (surveillance of spouse suspected of adultery) and *Druken v. R.G. Fewer and Associates Inc.*, [1998] N.J. No. 312 (S.C.T.D.) (insurer investigating a claim).

83   *Insurance Corporation of British Columbia v. Somosh* (1983), 51 B.C.L.R. 344 (S.C.).

84   *Silber v. British Columbia Broadcasting System Ltd.* (1985), 25 D.L.R. (4th) 345 (B.C.S.C.). See also the discussion of this issue in *Aubry*, above note 51.

85   *Pateman v. Ross* (1988), 68 Man. R. (2d) 181 (Q.B.).

The Act authorizes a broad range of remedies. An award of damages, an injunction, an accounting for profits that have accrued as a consequence of the violation of privacy, and orders for the surrender of articles or documents that have been secured through a violation of privacy are all available.

The *Privacy Acts* are not a panacea but they do provide some protection of privacy and they are likely to be useful and influential in the development of the common law in those provinces without a statutory tort.[86]

11) Discrimination

In the early 1980s, some courts were attracted to the idea of a tort of discrimination which would complement the protection of equality found in federal and provincial human rights legislation. The protection of equality interests, like privacy, requires a balance to be drawn with other legitimate interests. For example, the interest in freedom from discrimination must be balanced against the interest in freedom of contract which is a characteristic of a competitive marketplace. In the case of equality, however, the existing legislative schemes provide a blueprint for the balancing of those interests. Tort law could, therefore, with relative ease, provide a supplementary or alternative remedy which would be consistent with those available under the legislative regimes. The issue reached the Supreme Court in *Seneca College of Applied Arts & Technology v. Bhadauria*.[87] In that case, the plaintiff was a woman of East Indian origin who made several applications for teaching positions at the defendant college. Despite being well qualified for the positions, she was not even given an interview. She claimed that this was due to her ethnic origin and she brought a tort action against the college. An application to strike out the statement of claim as disclosing no cause of action was successful at first instance, but the Ontario Court of Appeal held that the plaintiff had a common law right not to be discriminated against because of her ethnic origin, which was independent of statutory obligations and remedies. This decision was in turn reversed by the Supreme Court. It held that the Ontario *Human Rights Code*[88] provided a comprehensive and exhaustive vehicle for protection against discrimination and there was no need to recognize and develop a complementary tort remedy. The decision has been regretted by some. An

---

86   For a useful discussion of the general concept of privacy, see R. Bruyer, "Privacy: A Review and Critique of the Literature" (2006) 43 Alta. L. Rev. 553.

87   [1981] 2 S.C.R. 181 [*Seneca College*].

88   R.S.O. 1990, c. H.19.

independent tort of discrimination would have had certain advantages. The processing of complaints under human rights codes depends to a degree upon the resources, energy, and discretion of the governmental bureaucracy charged with enforcing the code. Tort actions are commenced and controlled by the plaintiff. Furthermore, compensatory remedies may be more generous under the tort system. The decision in *Seneca*, however, only excludes tort actions that are based directly on a breach of the human rights code or the policies found therein. An action based on an independent tort such as an assault or intentional infliction of nervous shock may be brought albeit that the impugned conduct is also a breach of the code.[89]

12) Stalking

In recent years there has been a great deal of public attention and concern directed to the issue of stalking. Broadly speaking, stalking occurs when a person knowingly or recklessly harasses another person in a manner that leads that other person to fear for her own safety. Such conduct is prohibited under section 264(1) of the *Criminal Code*[90] (the term criminal harassment is used), but there is no independent common law tort of stalking providing a civil remedy for the subject of the stalking against the offender.

The subjects of stalking may resort to the conventional heads of tortious liability. A stalker, in the course of his activities, may commit a number of torts such as assault, battery, the intentional infliction of nervous shock, trespass to land, private nuisance, or defamation for which liability may be imposed. The use of traditional torts does not, however, capture the full extent of the wrongful conduct. It focuses attention on the various discrete acts of the stalker which may appear relatively insignificant when examined in isolation from the complete pattern of behaviour. The only area of tort law that promises a holistic remedy is the nascent common law tort of privacy and the statutory tort under the privacy acts. Although it is not always characterized as

---

89   It has been argued that the ruling in *Seneca College* is out of step with the increased emphasis on the protection of human rights in other areas of the law and that the time is ripe for a reconsideration of the decision. See L. Chartrand, "The Crumbling Wall of *Bhadauria*: If Not Today, Tomorrow" in S. Rodgers, R. Ruparelia, & L. Belanger-Hardy, eds., *Critical Torts* (Markham, ON: Lexis Nexis, 2009) at 107. Some support for this position is found in a comment by Binnie J. in *Honda Canada Inc. v. Keays*, [2008] S.C.J. No. 40 at para. 119 that the development of tort law was not "frozen forever" by *Seneca College*.

90   R.S.C. 1985, c. C-46.

such, stalking is a substantial and unreasonable invasion of another's privacy. This was recognized in the case of *Pateman v. Ross*,[91] where a young woman, who was unable to accept either the termination of her relationship with the plaintiff or his subsequent marriage to another woman, embarked on a course of harassing conduct aimed at the plaintiff, his wife, and family. The trial judge had no hesitation in concluding that the conduct was a violation of the Manitoba *Privacy Act* and awarded an injunction against the defendant.

Although it is not beyond the power of the common law to develop a general tort of stalking,[92] it is more likely that legislative initiatives will extend the civil remedies for stalking. In Manitoba, for example, *The Domestic Violence and Stalking Prevention, Protection and Compensation and Consequential Damage Amendments Act*[93] contains a panoply of civil remedies for both stalking and domestic violence, including a tort of stalking actionable without proof of damage.

13) Harassment

There is no conventional or clear distinction between stalking and harassment and the terms are often used interchangeably. The dichotomy drawn here is between harassing conduct that causes a person to fear for her own safety (stalking) and harassing conduct that is seriously annoying, distressing, pestering, and vexatious (harassment). Harassment may include some minor sexual harassment, some forms of bullying, harassment by creditors or governmental officials, and abusive or racist communications, all of which may be disturbing and upsetting but not frightening. Harassment, so described, may not fall within any of the traditional torts although harassing telephone calls to one's home

---

91 *Pateman v. Ross* (1988), 68 Man. R. (2d) 181 (Q.B.).
92 In England, concern about stalking led to the recognition of a nascent tort of harassment. In *Khorasandjian v. Bush*, [1993] Q.B. 727 (C.A.) [*Khorasandjian*], for example, the English Court of Appeal upheld an injunction to prohibit a classic case of stalking of a young woman who lived with her parents. The tort of harassment (the English court used the terminology of harassment rather than stalking) was based on the principles of private nuisance and the intentional infliction of nervous shock. This development in tort law was, however, subsequently overtaken by passage of the *Protection from Harassment Act 1997* (U.K.), 1997, c. 40, which created both criminal and civil remedies for stalking. This legislative initiative was one of the reasons that subsequently led the House of Lords to overrule *Khorasandjian* in *Hunter v. Canary Wharf Ltd.*, [1997] A.C. 655 and to put an end to the tort of harassment. It is possible, of course, that *Khorasandjian* will find more fertile soil in Canada.
93 S.M. 1998, c. 41.

may be a nuisance and some harassment may be a breach of privacy. In extreme circumstances, harassment may be actionable as an intentional infliction of nervous shock.[94]

There is not a great deal of authority addressing the issue of a discrete tort of harassment. The issue has, however, arisen in cases dealing with the conduct of debt collection agencies that is not only persistent and unpleasant but also in breach of consumer protection legislation,[95] the persistent and hostile conduct of a neighbour,[96] the bitter aftermath of a failed romantic relationship,[97] and hostilities among employees in the workplace.[98] Most of these cases involve a series of disparate incidents some of which may satisfy an existing head of tort liability. The harm, however, arises from the accumulation of incidents that globally can best be described as harassment. Many courts doubt the existence of a discrete tort of harassment.[99] Nevertheless, several courts appear to be inclined to fashion a remedy where the conduct is outrageous or completely unacceptable in light of reasonable standards of civil discourse, the conduct is deliberately targeted at the plaintiff and the plaintiff suffers severe mental distress. Some courts find a previously recognized tort on which to base liability; some accept that a mixture of tortious and non-tortious acts are sufficient to remedy all the harm without a close analysis of each incident, some find a remedy in consumer protection legislation, and some seem prepared to recognize a nascent tort of harassment. From a policy perspective, there appear to be few arguments against the recognition of a discrete tort of harassment. The defendant's interest in free speech would not be unduly compromised and plaintiffs would be protected from outrageous and extreme behaviour. Such a tort may play a salutary role in respect of cyber-bullying and extreme racist and homophobic speech. The weakness of the current situation is that it produces uncertainty, uneven decision making, and confusion with the tort of infliction of nervous shock which requires more than severe mental distress.

There has been a good deal of debate and commentary about sexual harassment in the workplace and the role of civil liability in respect of

---

94   See *Prinzo*, above note 44 (harassment of an employee by her employer during the performance of the contract of service).
95   *Total Credit Recovery (B.C.) Ltd. v. Roach*, [2007] B.C.J. No. 804 (S.C.) and *Unilever Canada Inc. v. Crosslee Trading Co.* (2006), 151 A.W.C.S. (3d) 200 (Fed. Ct.).
96   *Garrett v. Mikalachki*, [2000] O.J. No. 1326 (S.C.J.) and *Rathmann v. Rudka*, [2001] O.J. No. 1334 (S.C.J.).
97   *Pilon v. Nahri*, [2006] O.J. No. 2640 (S.C.J.).
98   *Mainland Sawmills*, above note 23.
99   *Prince George (City) v. Reimer*, [2010] B.C.J. No. 146 (S.C.).

such conduct.[100] In *Chapman v. 3M Canada Inc.*,[101] an action for sexual harassment in the workplace was struck out as disclosing no cause of action. The Ontario Court of Appeal affirmed the decision of the lower court, which had applied the reasoning of the Supreme Court in *Bhadauria* and held that the Ontario *Human Rights Code* provided an exhaustive and exclusive scheme of adjudication and redress for such claims and there is no room for the development of an independent tort of sexual harassment. A further obstacle to tort remedies for sexual harassment in the unionized workplace was created by the Supreme Court decision in *Weber v. Ontario Hydro*,[102] which excludes tort actions from employment disputes arising under a collective bargaining agreement governing the parties. These disputes must be resolved under the labour arbitration process.

An alternative approach was taken in *Lajoie v. Kelly*,[103] a case dealing with sexual harassment in a non-unionized work place. The Court recognized an independent tort of sexual harassment and imposed civil liability albeit that the conduct was a breach of the *Human Rights* Code[104] of Manitoba. In defining the tort, the trial judge adopted the words of the Supreme Court in *Janzen v. Platy Enterprises Ltd.*[105] describing sexual harassment as "any sexually oriented practice that endangered an individual's continued employment, negatively affects his/her work performance, or undermines his/her sense of personal dignity." This definition was wide enough to cover both the hostile work environment situation that arose in *Lajoie* and the quid pro quo situations where benefits and other advantages are tied to sexual favours.[106]

---

100 G. Demeyere, "Common Law Actions for Sexual Harassment: The Jurisdiction Question Revisited" (2003) 28 Queen's L.J. 637 and T. Witelson, "Retort: Revisiting *Bahdauria* and the Supreme Courts Rejection of a Tort of Discrimination" (1998–99) 10 N.J.C.L. 149.

101 (1995), 24 C.C.L.T. (2d) 304 (Ont. Gen. Div.), aff'd (1997), 37 C.C.L.T. (2d) 319 (Ont. C.A.). See also *Allen v. C.F.P.L. Broadcasting Ltd.* (1995), 24 C.C.L.T. (2d) 297 (Ont. Gen. Div.); and *Nicholas v. Mullin* (1998), 199 N.B.R. (2d) 219 (Q.B.).

102 [1995] 2 S.C.R. 929.

103 [1997] 3 W.W.R. 181 (Man. Q.B.).

104 S.M. 1987–88, c. 45.

105 [1989] 1 S.C.R. 1252.

106 Some legislatures have also taken additional measures to combat harassment in the work place. See *Occupational Health and Safety Amendment Act* (*Violence and Harassment in the Workplace*), S.O. 2009, c. 23.

14) Defences to the Intentional Interference with the Person

There are a number of defences to the torts of intentional interference with the person. Most of the defences (consent, self-defence, defence of a third person, defence of property, discipline, legal authority, and illegality) are complete defences, but provocation and contributory negligence are partial defences that dictate a reduction in damages. There are also two concepts, mistake and duress, which traditionally have not been treated as either a complete or a partial defence. The burden of proof to establish complete and partial defences is on the defendant.

a)   Complete Defences

i)   Consent

There are occasions where it is in the interests of an individual to agree to an intentional interference with her person. It may secure some desirable personal, material, emotional, or economic benefit. Consequently, the law recognizes the right of an individual to exercise her autonomy and consent to the intentional interference with her person. People commonly consent to a variety of batteries, including medical care, haircutting, body piercing, tattooing, and sexual contact. Travelling in an elevator or an aircraft necessitates consenting to an imprisonment, and elite athletes who agree to random drug testing consent to an invasion of their privacy.

Consent may be express, or it may be implied from the conduct of the plaintiff. Consent to a routine dental examination may, for example, be implied from sitting in a dental chair and opening one's mouth. The conduct must be such that a reasonable person would be led to believe that the plaintiff was consenting to the interference. Consent must be freely and voluntarily given. A consent given under the influence of drugs or given as a consequence of violence or a threat of violence is invalid. Other serious forms of duress may also invalidate consent.

In most situations, a consent may be revoked. A consent given to a dentist to extract a tooth does not prevent a patient from changing her mind. The revocation may be a breach of a contract for dental services for which the dentist may have a remedy but the legal power of the patient to revoke her consent is unfettered. There are, however, some situations where public convenience, safety, and expense temporarily negate the power to revoke a consent freely given. For example, the consent to be imprisoned for the duration of a non-stop commercial flight, an ocean cruise, or a frightening carnival ride is, in the absence of special circumstances such as serious illness, irrevocable.

Issues of consent arise most often in cases of battery. There are four situations where it arises with particular frequency: interpersonal violence, contact sports, medical treatment, and sexual relationships.

aa. Interpersonal Violence

Not all interpersonal disputes are settled with reason and civility. Occasionally, differences are settled by violence. Where the parties have consented to fight, the loser will not be able to sue in battery for the injuries suffered. Each person has consented to the batteries inflicted by the other. Consequently, when hockey players mutually drop their gloves or bar patrons accept invitations "to step outside" to settle differences or gangs agree to fight each other, they all waive their right to bodily security. The courts will, however, carefully assess the scope of the mutual consent of the parties and where it is exceeded, by the use of a weapon or by the administration of a beating to a defeated foe, liability will be imposed.

bb. Contact Sports

Contact sport involves the intentional interference with the person of another which, outside the sporting arena, would result in liability for battery. Players are protected from liability by the implied consent of all the participants to physical interference that is an integral part of the sport. There are, of course, limits to the immunity of players from civil liability. The privilege to play a contact sport is not a licence to inflict serious harm on an opponent. A line must be drawn between bodily contact that is an expected part of the game and that which is not.

In Canada, there is a difference in judicial opinion on the appropriate legal analysis to achieve a fair compromise between the nature of the game and the safety of the players. One approach, based on the tort of battery, has been championed by the Manitoba Court of Appeal. Its approach is to classify all bodily contact in sport as *prima facie* a battery. The burden of proof is then on the defendant to establish that the plaintiff impliedly consented to that battery. As a general rule, it has been held that an implied consent extends to all batteries other than those where the defendant intends to cause injury in contravention of the rules of the sport. Both a breach of the rules and an intention to injure are required to exceed the implied consent.[107] *Agar v. Canning*[108]

---

107 Courts that have adopted the battery/implied consent approach may describe the nature of conduct to which the player has not consented in somewhat different terms (for example, intent to cause serious injury in breach of the rules, reckless disregard for safety in breach of the rules, intent to injure, and so on).

108 (1965), 54 W.W.R. (N.S.) 302 (Man. Q.B.), aff'd (1966), 55 W.W.R. (N.S.) 384 (Man. C.A.) [*Agar*].

and *Temple v. Hallem*,[109] both of which are decisions of the Manitoba Court of Appeal, are illustrative. In *Agar*, a hockey player was held liable for a vicious slash across the plaintiff's face which indicated an intent to cause serious injury in violation of the rules of the game. In *Temple*, the plaintiff was injured when the defendant, who was trying to score a run in a mixed-league recreational softball game, slid into her as she guarded home plate. The Court held that the defendant was not liable because he did not intend to injure her and sliding, even in a professional way, was not prohibited by the league rules.

The other approach has been used by the British Columbia Court of Appeal. It is based, not on a battery analysis, but on basic negligence principles. It incorporates the issue of acceptable and agreed risk into the application of the standard of care that players in the particular sport owe to one another. An illustrative case is *Zapf v. Muckalt*.[110] In that case, the defendant checked the plaintiff into the boards from behind in the course of a Junior A hockey game. The plaintiff was rendered a quadriplegic. The Court formulated the defendant's obligation in negligence terminology:

> What would a reasonable competitor, in his place, do or not do? The words "in his place" imply the need to consider the speed, the amount of body contact and the stresses in the sport, as well as the risks the players might reasonably be expected to take during the game, acting within the spirit of the game and according to the standards of fair play. A breach of the rules may be one element in that issue but not necessarily definitive of the issue.[111]

Since the defendant's conduct was at worst reckless and at best careless, liability was imposed.

The use of negligence principles, rather than battery, to draw the line between acceptable and unacceptable conduct on the sporting fields and arenas of Canada is probably more pro-plaintiff in sentiment and may be more in tune with the growing public concern about safety in sports, which is evidenced by rule changes providing better protection for players and by the mandating of protective equipment in organized sport at all levels. Liability in negligence not only makes a more significant contribution to accident prevention in sport but also facilitates needed compensation to the victims of sporting accidents. The more pro-defendant stance of the Manitoba Court of Appeal may

---

109 (1989), 58 D.L.R. (4th) 541 (Man. C.A.).
110 (1996), 142 D.L.R. (4th) 438 (B.C.C.A.).
111 *Ibid.* at 446, citing *Unruh (Guardian ad litem of) v. Webber* (1994), 112 D.L.R. (4th) 83 at 96 (B.C.C.A.).

reflect greater judicial concern for the chilling effect that a more extensive liability may have on amateur sport and a reluctance to expose young uninsured people[112] to large damage awards.

It is convenient to note here that negligence principles are generally applicable to a variety of other claims that may arise from sporting endeavours, including the liability of coaches, umpires, and organizers to players, and the liability of players and owners of facilities to spectators.[113]

cc. Medical Treatment

Medical treatment is an actionable battery unless the attending health-care professional has secured the patient's consent.[114] Every competent adult patient controls her health care by exercising an unfettered power to consent to treatment, to refuse treatment, to give a conditional consent to treatment, or to revoke a consent previously given. An excellent example of the power of battery law to protect a patient's right to make autonomous decisions in her own interests is found in the trial judgment in *Allan v. New Mount Sinai Hospital*.[115] A surgical patient warned the attending anaesthetist not to insert a needle in her left arm because "he would have nothing but trouble there." The defendant anaesthetist ignored her request and inserted an intravenous needle into her left arm. In the course of the surgery, the needle slipped out of the vein and she suffered a severe allergic reaction when anaesthetic was released into the surrounding tissue. The defendant was found liable in battery for ignoring the patient's specific prohibition against use of her left arm and neither his competence nor his good faith provided any excuse. The trial judge spoke of the importance of consent.

> Without a consent, either written or oral, no surgery may be performed. This is not a mere formality; it is an important individual right to have control over one's own body . . . . It is the patient, not the doctor, who decides whether surgery will be performed, where it will be done, when it will be done and by whom it will be done.[116]

---

112 It should not be overlooked that some young people may have liability insurance under their own homeowners' or tenants' policies or those of their parents.

113 See *Henderson v. Hockey Canada*, [2010] M.J. No. 24 (Q.B.).

114 Some provinces have legislation relating to consent to medical treatment: see, for example, Ontario *Health Care Consent Act, 1996*, S.O. 1996, c. 2, Sch. A, s. 10.

115 (1980), 28 O.R. (2d) 356 (H.C.J.), rev'd on another point (1981), 33 O.R. (2d) 603 (C.A.).

116 *Ibid.* at 364 (H.C.J.).

Hospital administrators are particularly sensitive to the need to prove the patient's consent to treatment and it is common practice to use a variety of written consent forms. These forms provide useful evidence of consent but they are not conclusive of the issue. The court must be convinced of the reality of consent, and consideration will be given to the mental capacity of the patient, the language of the form, the explanations given to the patient, and the circumstances surrounding the signing of the form to determine if the consent is genuine. Sometimes careful consideration must be given to the wording of these forms to determine if collateral or extended procedures in the course of surgery are within the scope of the patient's written consent. General words permitting a surgeon to do anything that is advisable or in the patient's best interests are probably not, in themselves, effective other than in situations of unforeseen complications closely associated with the planned procedures.

A patient retains the right to revoke his consent at any time before or during a medical procedure. Requests to stop a procedure must not be brushed aside as expressions of pain or anxiety. The physician must comply with the revocation of consent immediately unless to do so would threaten the life of the patient or pose immediate and serious problems to the patient's health.[117]

The failure to provide information about the risks and benefits of surgery or other invasive procedures does not invalidate the patient's consent so as to permit an action in battery. It was settled in *Reibl v. Hughes*[118] that, in those situations, negligence is the appropriate cause of action. Battery applies only where there is no consent to the surgery at all, where the terms of the consent have been clearly exceeded, or where the nature and character of the surgery have been misrepresented.

Some persons may not have the capacity to consent. The issue arises, most often, in respect of persons under the age of majority and those who suffer from a mental illness.

There is no set age at which a young person has the capacity to consent to medical treatment. The common law rule is that a mature minor has the power to consent to or refuse medical treatment. Maturity, in this context, means that the minor has the capacity and intelligence to understand the nature of the proposed medical treatment, the risks and potential benefits of it, and the risks of refusing it. A good illustration of the application of the mature minor rule is found in the Alberta Court

---

117 See *Ciarlariello v. Schacter*, [1993] 2 S.C.R. 119.
118 [1980] 2 S.C.R. 880.

of Appeal decision in *C.(J.S.) v. Wren*.[119] In that case, the parents of a sixteen-year-old sought an injunction to prevent her from terminating her pregnancy. The Court concluded that she was a normal, intelligent sixteen-year-old who had sufficient understanding to make up her own mind free of parental restraint.[120]

Mental illness may also impair the capacity of a patient to understand the nature of the proposed medical intervention and its risks and benefits. If the patient does not have the capacity to consent, a substitute decision maker may act. At common law, a close family member probably has the power to make medical decisions that are either consistent with the patient's past wishes or are good-faith determinations of the patient's best interests. In some provinces, legislation resolves any doubt by detailing the selection of substitute decision makers and the principles on which they must act.[121]

A person may wish to control the course of his health care when he is no longer able to communicate his wishes because of future mental or physical incapacity. The incapacity may arise gradually in the course of a debilitating illness or suddenly from a stroke or an unanticipated accident that leaves the victim unconscious. A person may, for example, seek to prohibit the use of blood products, to prevent the use of heroic resuscitation and life-prolonging measures, or, in some other way, to dictate the course of future treatment. In some provinces, this process is now regulated by legislation that recognizes and formalizes written advance directives either in the form of an instructional directive declaring the patient's treatment preferences or in the form of a proxy directive that appoints a substitute decision maker to make treatment decisions on the patient's behalf.[122]

---

119   (1986), 76 A.R. 115 (C.A.). See also *Van Mol (Guardian ad litem of) v. Ashmore* (1999), 168 D.L.R. (4th) 637 (B.C.C.A.). Some provinces have legislation that relates to the power of minors to consent to medical treatment: see, for example, New Brunswick *Medical Consent of Minors Act*, S.N.B. 1976, c. M-6.1; and British Columbia *Infants Act*, R.S.B.C. 1996, c. 223, s. 17.

120   An extensive discussion of the mature minor rule may be found in *A.C. v. Manitoba (Director of Child and Family Services)*, [2009] S.C.J. No. 30. The case dealt with the constitutionality of provisions of the *Child and Family Services Act*, C.C.S.M. c. C80, permitting court-ordered, life-saving medical treatment of a minor under the age of sixteen where both the minor and her parents refused to consent on religious grounds. The legislation was held to be constitutional so long as the power was exercised with reference to the minor's capacity for mature and independent judgment and the need to balance the minor's autonomy interest and society's interest in the protection of the children.

121   See, for example, *Health Care Consent Act*, above note 114.

122   See, for example, Nova Scotia *Medical Consent Act*, R.S.N.S. 1989, c. 279. See also B. Sneiderman, J.C. Irvine, & P.H. Osborne, *Canadian Medical Law: An Introduc-*

There are still some circumstances, however, where common law principles apply. Not all provinces have advance directive legislation and, even in those provinces that do, a patient may carry informal instructions that do not comply with the statutory formalities. In those circumstances, reference must be made to *Malette v. Shulman*,[123] which was decided by the Ontario Court of Appeal prior to that province's advance directive legislation. In that case, the plaintiff was involved in a car accident. She was not conscious when she was admitted to hospital but she did have an undated signed card in her purse indicating that she was a member of the Jehovah's Witness faith who did not want any blood administered to her under any circumstances. The defendant physician ignored the directive and administered blood in the reasonable belief that it was necessary to preserve her health and possibly to save her life. The Court held that the written card was clear, limited in scope, and unequivocal. The tenets of her faith were well known in the community, the authenticity of the card had not been challenged, and her calculated decision to reject the use of blood in her medical treatment ought to have been honoured. The defendant was held liable in battery even though he had acted in good faith and the treatment may, indeed, have saved her life.

The Court also noted that a physician who follows the directions contained in a card cannot be found liable if the card no longer reflects the true wishes of the plaintiff. Physicians must, therefore, be alert to any evidence that the card is not a reliable reflection of the patient's wishes. The card may be old, it may contain unclear or extravagant instructions, or it may claim membership in unknown sects or cults. When a physician has reasonable grounds to believe the card to be invalid, she may provide treatment to preserve the life or health of the patient.

dd. Sexual Relationships
Any sexual or intimate physical contact is a battery unless there is a free and voluntary consent to it.[124] Consent secured by force or threats

---

tion for Physicians, Nurses and Other Health Care Professionals, 3d ed. (Toronto: Carswell, 2003) at 599–633.

123 (1990), 72 O.R. (2d) 417 (C.A.).

124 It has been argued that in cases of sexual battery only *actual* affirmative consent should be valid. Constructive consent based upon the assumption a reasonable person would draw from the conduct of the plaintiff would be insufficient. See E. Adjin-Tettey, "Protecting the Dignity and Autonomy of Women: Rethinking the Place of Constructive Consent in the Tort of Sexual Battery" (2006) 39 U.B.C. L. Rev. 3.

of force is invalid. Consent is also invalid where there is a gross inequality of power between the two people and the stronger person has exploited the vulnerability of the weaker person to secure a consent to intimate acts. In *Norberg v. Wynrib*,[125] for example, a physician took advantage of a young woman patient who was addicted to painkillers. Rather than treat her addiction, he initiated an arrangement where he provided painkillers in exchange for sexual favours. A majority of the Supreme Court held that there was a power-dependency relationship between the defendant and the plaintiff and that the defendant had exploited the plaintiff's vulnerability to secure her consent. Her consent was therefore invalid. This principle is equally applicable in cases of incest and the sexual abuse of young persons by teachers, coaches, or religious leaders where the defence of consent may be raised.

A consent may also be vitiated by fraud. The courts have traditionally drawn a distinction between fraud as to the nature and character of the bodily interference, which does negate the plaintiff's consent, and fraud as to collateral matters, which does not negate the consent. Consequently, it was held that the consent of a naive young woman, who was tricked by a choir master into believing that the act of sexual intercourse was a form of voice training, was inoperative.[126] She did not understand the nature of the act. On the other hand, a consent to sexual intimacy is valid even though it may have been secured by fraudulent misrepresentations of the defendant's marital status, wealth, or degree of affection for his partner. These are collateral matters and any remedy must be sought in fraud or negligence.[127]

It is not yet clear how the courts will approach the issue of fraudulent representations of freedom of sexually transmitted diseases and fraudulent concealment of sexually transmitted diseases. In these situations, there is not normally any mistake about the nature and character of the act of intimacy but there is a lack of understanding of the grave risk arising from the contact. One way of dealing with this is to hold that the ignorance of the danger is sufficient to vitiate the consent and warrant the imposition of liability in battery for all of its consequences. This approach was taken by the Supreme Court in the context

---

125 [1992] 2 S.C.R. 226.

126 *R. v. Williams*, [1923] 1 K.B. 340 (C.A.).

127 These claims are, however, rarely successful. See L. Wolfson & A. Himel, "Broken Promises, Broken Hearts: Intrafamilial Tort and Contract Claims" (2002) 25 Advocates' Q. 441. But see *Raju v. Kumar*, [2006] B.C.J. No. 630 (S.C.) (liability in deceit for the defendant's dishonest misrepresentations of love, fidelity, and intent to have children made to the plaintiff in order to persuade her to marry him and thereby gain access to Canada from Fiji).

of the criminal law. The accused in *R. v. Cuerrier*[128] was charged with two counts of aggravated assault. He was alleged to have engaged in unprotected sexual intercourse with the complainants without disclosing that he was HIV positive. The complainants, who had not tested HIV positive, claimed that they would not have consented to sexual intercourse if they had known of the health status of the accused. The Court held that fraud vitiates the consent it secures when there is concealment of a "significant risk of serious bodily injury" to the consenting person. This principle is readily transferable to tort law and is applicable where the defendant fraudulently conceals that he is HIV positive or suffers from a venereal disease. Resort may also be had to the tort of negligence. There is clear liability for negligent misrepresentations that cause foreseeable physical injury or illness. The *concealment* of a sexually transmitted disease may also be actionable in negligence on the basis that there is a special relationship between sexual partners which imposes a duty of affirmative action to take reasonable steps to protect each other from disease. This idea of informed consent to sexual relationships is broadly analogous to the doctrine of informed consent to medical treatment.[129]

ii) Self-Defence

A person is permitted to use reasonable force to repel actual violence (a battery) or a threat of immediate violence (an assault).[130] The reasonableness of the force is determined by a consideration of all the surrounding circumstances, including the nature of the attack, the size and strength of the opponent, the force needed to repel the attack, the use of weapons, and the availability of non-violent means of defence. The privilege is entirely defensive in nature. It does not permit unnecessary violence, it does not permit punishment of the attacker, and it does not sanction disproportionate violence. Nevertheless, a deadly attack may be met with deadly force.

The defendant is not required to measure the force with nicety. A delicate calibration of the precise force needed for one's defence is not expected in the face of violence or the threat of immediate violence, and the defendant does not lose the protection of the defence merely because more serious injuries were caused than, in retrospect, were technically necessary to repel the attack.

---

128 [1998] 2 S.C.R. 371.

129 Fraudulent statements relating to the absence of sexually transmitted diseases may also be actionable in the tort of deceit.

130 See, for example, *Wackett v. Calder* (1965), 51 D.L.R. (2d) 598 (B.C.C.A.).

iii) Defence of a Third Person

A privilege to use reasonable force to defend a third person from violence or the threat of immediate violence has been recognized. This is not surprising given the general attitude to, and approval of, rescuers. The factors taken into account in determining the reasonableness of the force mirror those considered in determining self-defence. *Gambriell v. Caparelli*[131] is an exemplary case. The defendant's son and the plaintiff got into a brawl in a back lane. The defendant, who did not speak English, feared that her son was being choked. The fight ended when she hit the plaintiff over the head with a garden cultivator. In the particular circumstances of the case, more moderate conduct may well have been insufficient to protect her son. The action in battery against her was dismissed.[132]

iv) Defence of Property

In some circumstances the possessor of land may use physical force to protect his property from unlawful entry (trespass) by another. When the unlawful entry is peaceable, the possessor must first request the trespasser to leave the premises. If the trespasser refuses to comply with the request to leave, reasonable force may be used to eject him from the property. The possessor is not required to make a preliminary request that the trespasser leave where the entry is forcible or is such as to create a fear of immediate violence. Force may be used only for the purpose of removing the intruder. If the intruder resists, force may be increased as required to eject the trespasser. Under no circumstances, however, may a possessor use deadly force or deliberately cause serious injury to a trespasser who will not leave the property. The protection of property interests does not warrant causing death or serious injury. The possessor must justify that kind of force on the basis of either self-defence or the defence of a third party.

The law is less clear in respect of injuries caused by mechanical devices and other stratagems designed to protect property and to deter intruders. A thicket of intersecting principles bears on this issue, including the privilege to defend one's property, occupiers' liability rules, rules about the liability for animals such as guard dogs, and the rules about consent, contributory negligence, and illegality. Until this tangle is sorted out by an authoritative court, the best guide is reasonableness. The use of barbed wire, guard dogs, fences with spikes, and stone

---

131 (1974), 7 O.R. (2d) 205 (Co. Ct.).

132 The defence is not restricted to the defence of a family member, see *Babiuk v. Trann*, [2005] S.J. No. 41 (C.A.), aff'g [2003] S.J. No. 614 (Q.B.) (defence of a teammate in a rugby game).

walls with jagged glass embedded on top will in most cases be regarded as reasonable deterrence, and intruders will not be able to recover for the minor injuries caused by them. The use of punitive or retributive devices such as spring guns, electrically charged wire fences, vicious attack dogs, and other devices that seriously threaten life and limb are normally unreasonable and liability may be imposed. The marginal cases require a careful consideration of all the relevant factors, including the time of day of the intrusion, the nature and purpose of the intrusion, the danger and degree of concealment of the protective device, the nature of the land use being protected, the motive of the possessor of the land, and any posted notices warning of the protective system.

v) Discipline
The law continues to recognize a privilege on the part of parents and teachers to use reasonable force to discipline children. The defendant must prove that the force was used solely for the purposes of correction and that the force was objectively reasonable. The defence mirrors section 43 of the *Criminal Code* which provides the same protection against criminal prosecution. The corporal punishment of children is a contentious issue. There are those who support the privilege of parents to use appropriate and measured force in the correction of their children's behaviour. Others suggest that it is not a very effective way to influence the behaviour of children, that a ban on corporal punishment might assist in reducing child abuse and that it is an indefensible anomaly in a country that has abolished the corporal punishment of all adults including the most serious criminals. There is much less support for the privilege of a teacher to use corporal punishment and that is reflected in the policies of school boards.

Unsuccessful attempts have been made to repeal section 43 and, in 2004, an attempt was made in *Canadian Foundation for Children, Youth and the Law v. Canada (Attorney General)*[133] to have the provision declared in violation of the *Charter of Rights and Freedoms*.[134] The section withstood the challenge but the Supreme Court gave section 43 a very narrow interpretation. Parents may use minor corrective force of a transitory and trifling nature but there is no protection of any force applied to a child under two or to a teenager. There are no circumstances in which degrading, inhuman, and harmful conduct is allowed and the use of objects or blows to the head are always unreasonable. Teachers may use reasonable force only to remove a child from a classroom or to

---

133 [2004] S.C.J. No. 6.
134 Above note 63.

secure compliance with instructions. This narrow reading of the provision which is a reasonable compromise between the opposing views seems equally applicable to the common law defence in tort law.

Captains of ships and aircraft also have a privilege to exercise reasonable force to secure the safety of their ship or aircraft or its passengers. This privilege probably arises only when the ship is at sea or the aircraft is in the air. In those situations, the police are not available to secure order and the captains are permitted to act in their stead. The privilege is particularly important in respect of disorderly and intoxicated passengers on aircraft.

vi) Necessity

Courts are reluctant to sanction an intentional interference with the person on the ground of necessity. Nevertheless, there are occasions where interference with the person can be justified on the ground that it will achieve a benefit which outweighs the wrong to such an extent that the wrong must be forgiven. Examples include the provision of emergency medical treatment to maintain the life or health of an unconscious patient and the reasonable restraint of patients in health-care facilities who, because of mental or physical incapacity, are a danger to themselves or others. The defences of self-defence and defence of a third party are also loosely related to the concept of necessity but in those situations the plaintiff is also a wrongdoer.

vii) Legal Authority

The defence of legal authority is now largely statutory in nature. Tort law has adopted various statutory provisions designed to protect governmental officials and private citizens from criminal liability in the administration of the criminal justice system. This legal authority is found in a range of statutes including the *Criminal Code*[135] and is used primarily to protect officials from liability in battery and false imprisonment actions. One issue that arises frequently is the authority of private citizens and police officers to make arrests without warrants. An arrest is a false imprisonment that the defendant often attempts to justify on the ground of legal authority. The power of a private citizen to arrest another person without a warrant is limited. She is permitted to arrest a person who is found committing an indictable offence, or a person who she believes on reasonable grounds has committed a criminal offence and is both escaping arrest and being freshly pursued by persons who have lawful authority to arrest the person. An owner or

---

135 Above note 90.

possessor of land can also arrest a person whom she finds committing a criminal offence on her land.[136] This places a significant burden on private citizens, including store detectives attempting to combat shoplifting, in justifying an arrest. It is warranted by the high priority given in Canada to the freedom of the person and freedom from wrongful detention. Police and other peace officers enjoy more generous powers. They may arrest a person who has committed an indictable offence or who, on reasonable grounds, they believe has committed or is about to commit an indictable offence. They may also arrest a person who is found committing a criminal offence.[137]

A more extensive consideration of the defence of legal authorization cannot be undertaken here,[138] but careful consideration must be given to a range of statutory privileges and complementary common law protections when the torts of intentional interference with the person, such as battery, and torts of intentional interference with property, such as trespass to chattels and trespass to land, are committed in the exercise of functions related to the administration of criminal justice.

viii) Illegality: Ex Turpi Causa Non Oritur Actio

There are some old decisions suggesting that a claim for the intentional interference with the person may be defeated by the illegality or immorality of the plaintiff's conduct at the time when the tort was committed. The defence has now fallen into disuse and disrepute. The Supreme Court observed in *Norberg v. Wynrib*[139] that the defence is applicable only in rare circumstances. This position was further clarified in *Hall v. Hebert*,[140] where the Court restricted the defence to situations where the imposition of liability would permit the plaintiff to profit from wrongdoing, evade a criminal sanction,[141] or would, in some other way, undermine the integrity of the legal system. It does not apply to a claim for compensatory damages for bodily injury.

b) Partial Defences

i) Provocation

Provocation is conduct closely related in time to the tortfeasor's act, which would cause a reasonable person to lose his self-control and act

---

136 *Ibid.*, s. 494. For a discussion of the alternative interpretations of s. 494, see *Parlee (Guardian ad litem of) v. Port of Call Holdings Ltd.*, [2000] B.C.J. No. 698 (S.C.).

137 *Criminal Code, ibid.*, s. 495(1).

138 See Klar, above note 8 at 143–49 and Linden, above note 3 at 97–104.

139 Above note 125.

140 [1993] 2 S.C.R. 159.

141 See *British Columbia v. Zastowny*, [2008] S.C.J. No. 4.

out of anger and frustration. It arises most frequently in respect of actions for battery. Provocative conduct includes not only speech such as insults, abusive language, blasphemous taunting, and the use of racial or ethnic slurs but also conduct such as obscene gestures, adulterous actions, acts of betrayal, and outrageous conduct targeted at a close family member of the defendant. Conduct that creates a fear of immediate violence will not normally be characterized as provocation because an assault gives rise to the right of self-defence and the propriety of the defendant's conduct will be assessed on that basis.

Provocation provides only a partial defence to the intentional interference with the person. This is a wise policy. A complete defence would tend to promote violence. There would be no incentive to exercise self-control and restraint in the face of provocative conduct. Nevertheless, it is common experience that, if you are abusive to others and taunt them, they may react violently, and Canadian courts are in agreement that there should be some reduction in damages where the plaintiff is partially to blame for the violence. There is no agreement, however, on the manner in which the reduction of damages is to be made. In the 1970s the prevalent approach championed by the Courts of Appeal of Manitoba[142] and Ontario[143] was that provocative conduct justified withholding aggravated and punitive damages but did not justify any reduction of compensatory damages. This approach emphasized the compensatory function of tort law and indicated an unwillingness to reduce compensation to the plaintiff. More recently, the Courts of Appeal of Alberta,[144] Newfoundland,[145] British Columbia,[146] and Nova Scotia[147] have favoured, additionally, a reduction in compensatory damages by the degree to which the plaintiff is responsible for the loss. This approach, which treats provocation similarly to contributory negligence, emphasizes corrective justice between the litigants and recognizes that where both have acted wrongfully, an award of full compensatory damages unduly discounts the plaintiff's degree of responsibility. In respect of intentional torts, where liability insurance plays such a minimal role, the latter view has much to commend it.

---

142 *Check v. Andrews Hotel Co.* (1974), 56 D.L.R. (3d) 364 (Man. C.A.).
143 *Shaw v. Gorter* (1977), 16 O.R. (2d) 19 (C.A.); *Landry v. Patterson* (1978), 22 O.R. (2d) 335 (C.A.).
144 *Kuehn v. Hougen*, [1997] A.J. No. 982 (C.A.).
145 *Hurley v. Moore* (1993), 112 Nfld. & P.E.I.R. 40 (Nfld. C.A.).
146 *Bruce v. Coliseum Management Ltd.* (1998), 165 D.L.R. (4th) 472 (B.C.C.A.).
147 *Nichol v. MacKay*, [1999] N.S.J. No. 323 (C.A.).

ii) Contributory Negligence

The issue of contributory negligence is clearly allied to that of provocation but it is a wider concept, operating wherever the plaintiff has failed to take reasonable steps for her own safety. Whether or not damages may be reduced on the ground of contributory negligence depends upon the language of the applicable apportionment legislation. The apportionment legislation has been construed quite liberally and, where it allows apportionment on the basis of the "fault" of each of the parties, it has, in some cases, been applied to the intentional torts. A good example is *Berntt v. Vancouver (City of)*.[148] The plaintiff was injured in a riot that followed the seventh-game loss of the Vancouver Canucks in the 1994 Stanley Cup final. The plaintiff was shot by a rubber bullet fired by a police officer. The police officer was, in the circumstances, unable to legally justify the shooting. Nevertheless, the plaintiff's damages were reduced by 75 percent on the ground of his contributory negligence. He was an eager participant in the riot and had incited the crowd. Some legislation, however, allows apportionment only on the basis of the "negligence" of each party, which makes its extension to the intentional torts problematic.

c) Inoperative Defences

i) Mistake

Mistake is not a defence to the intentional interference with the person. It is no defence, for example, that a surgeon cut off the wrong leg because he was labouring under an innocent and reasonable misapprehension. This is clearly good policy. It provides a powerful incentive to exercise great caution before intentionally interfering with another person. The only exception relates to the defences of self-defence and defence of a third person. Those situations demand that the plaintiff be permitted to respond immediately to what she honestly and reasonably believes to be a threat of immediate violence without first inquiring into, or investigating the validity of, that belief.[149]

ii) Duress

Proof that the defendant was coerced or forced by others to interfere intentionally with the person of the plaintiff is not a defence. The policy

---

148 [1997] 4 W.W.R. 505 (B.C.S.C.), new trial ordered (1999), 174 D.L.R. (4th) 403 (B.C.C.A.).

149 This issue was discussed at length in the House of Lord's decision in *Ashley v. Chief Constable of Sussex Police*, [2008] UKHL 25. The Court ruled that the belief of the defendant in an imminent attack must be not only honest but also reasonable.

of the law is that coercion and pressure must be resisted even when severe consequences may flow from a refusal to submit. This may seem harsh but any other rule would tend to promote violence by providing protection to those who bend to the will of a third party and injure the plaintiff.

15) Remedies

The primary remedy for the intentional interference with the person is damages. Compensatory damages are calculated in the same manner as injury and fatality claims in negligence. The only added dimension to an award of damages under the intentional torts is the greater possibility of *aggravated damages* or *punitive damages*.

Aggravated damages are essentially compensatory in nature. They recognize that the malicious, high-handed, and outrageous nature of the defendant's conduct may add a degree of humiliation, loss of dignity, and embarrassment to the plaintiff. Aggravated damages may be incorporated into, and inflate the award of, general damages or may be awarded as a discrete amount.

There is no clearer recognition of the deterrent and punitive function of tort law than the power of judges to award *punitive damages*. Punitive damages may be awarded where the conduct of the defendant is so outrageous, socially unacceptable, or intolerable that it warrants strong deterrence and is deserving of punishment in excess of that inherent in the compensatory award.[150] Punitive damages are most common in respect of sexual batteries and other criminal violence. Courts are, however, reluctant to award punitive damages if the defendant has received a criminal sentence for the conduct that is the subject of the tort claim. Overall punitive damages for intentional interference with the person tend to be moderate and rarely exceed $100,000.[151]

D. INTENTIONAL INTERFERENCE WITH LAND: TRESPASS TO LAND

Trespass to land provides a remedy for the direct, intentional (or negligent), and physical interference with land in the possession of the plaintiff. It is actionable without proof of damage. Trespass to land is

---

150 For the principles applicable to the awarding of punitive damages, see *Whiten v. Pilot Insurance Co.* (2002), 209 D.L.R. (4th) 257 (S.C.C.).
151 Klar, above note 8 at 119.

committed in three ways. First, and most commonly, it is a trespass to enter personally onto land in possession of the plaintiff without permission. This covers a broad range of situations, including persons who break and enter, adults who mistakenly walk through a door marked "no admission," and young children who, lacking an acute sense of private property, wander wherever their curiosity or interest may take them. Second, it is a trespass to place objects on the plaintiff's property. To kick a ball onto the property of the plaintiff, to deliver parcels to the wrong address, or to dump garbage onto the land of another person are acts of trespass. Trespass to land by leaving or placing an object on the land is referred to as a *continuing trespass*, which gives rise to new causes of action each day until the object is removed. The advantage of this principle is that the plaintiff's trespassory remedies are protected from limitation periods and subsequent possessors may also have a remedy. Third, a trespass may arise when the possessor revokes a visitor's permission or licence to be on the property. If the visitor does not leave the property within a reasonable time, he becomes a trespasser and reasonable force may be used to eject him. This arises most commonly when disorderly patrons and fans are ejected from bars and sporting events.

The formulation of trespass to land as a direct physical interference with land in the possession of the plaintiff allows the tort to protect a number of diverse interests. It was initially designed to protect landholders from violent intrusion or eviction from their land. The development of a civil remedy reduced the likelihood of violence and protected the possessor's interest in the peaceful enjoyment of his property. In modern tort law, trespass to land plays a much more sophisticated role. First, it protects the possessor's interest in freedom of land use. The power to control entry onto land facilitates the use and development of it in accordance with the possessor's desires and interests. A possessor of land is not required to accommodate others who may have a reasonable need or desire to enter his land. Second, trespass to land plays a conventional compensatory and deterrent role when an intruder damages land or destroys premises. Third, trespass to land plays an important role in the protection of privacy interests. The slightest intrusion into a person's home or apartment gives rise to trespassory remedies. That a person's home is his castle is, in no small part, due to the tort of trespass to land. Finally, trespass to land is an adjunct of the law of real property. It plays a role in the determination of competing land claims and the settlement of boundary disputes. It also provides protection to the possessor against the acquisition of prescriptive easements over his property as a result of twenty years of continuous trespassing in derogation of the possessor's rights. The trespassory conduct may be trivial and harmless, such as a technical but permanent invasion of airspace or the use of land as a pedestrian right of way. Nevertheless, the tort of trespass to land allows the possessor to assert his proprietary rights and prevent the establishment of a prescriptive easement.[152] The capacity of the tort of trespass to complement property law is enhanced by the fact that trespass to land is actionable without proof of damage and also by the fact that mistake is no defence.

1) Elements of Liability

There are a number of essential elements to the tort of trespass to land. The intrusion onto the land must be direct. This requirement is common to all torts of trespass. *Mann v. Saulnier*[153] provides a good illustration. The defendant in that case built a perpendicular fence on the boundary line between his and the plaintiff's property. In the course of time and weathering, the fence leaned marginally over the boundary line and into the plaintiff's airspace. It was held that there was no liability in trespass to land because the intrusion was not direct.[154] The element of directness diminishes the power of trespass to land to deal with some environmental pollution. Oil spills that wash onto the plaintiff's land, waste that is carried down rivers to the plaintiff's land, and herbicides, pesticides, and airborne pollutants that drift in the wind to the plaintiff's land are likely to be regarded as indirect interferences with land.[155] Damage caused by indirect interference may be actionable as a nuisance.

The defendant's interference with land must be *intentional* or *negligent*. The burden of proof is, however, on the defendant. The plaintiff needs to prove only a direct interference with land. The defendant must then show a lack of intention or negligence. In practice, trespass to land is restricted to intentional interference because negligent interference will normally be pleaded in the tort of negligence. It is not necessary to show that the defendant intended to do a wrongful act against the plaintiff possessor. The intention to intrude on, or interfere with, land

---

152 Easements cannot be acquired by prescription in all provinces: see, for example, Alberta *Law of Property Act*, 2000, c. L-7, s. 69(3) and British Columbia *Land Title Act*, R.S.B.C. 1996, c. 250, s. 24.

153 (1959), 19 D.L.R. (2d) 130 (N.B.S.C.A.D.).

154 Additionally, there was no intentional act or negligence on the part of the defendant.

155 See *Smith v. Inco Ltd.*, [2010] O.J. No. 2864 (S.C.J.). The emission of nickel particles from a refinery which contaminated the plaintiffs' land was held to be an indirect interference.

that is, in fact, in the possession of the plaintiff is sufficient. Mistake is no defence. The old case of *Basely v. Clarkson*[156] is illustrative. The defendant was held liable in trespass to land for innocently mowing the plaintiff's grass in the belief that it was his own.

As noted above, trespass to land, like other torts of trespass, is actionable without proof of damage. Every unauthorized intrusion onto the plaintiff's land, no matter how trivial or fleeting, is actionable.

The defendant's interference with the land must be *physical*. There is some unevenness in the cases as to what is and what is not a physical intrusion but the requirement excludes smog, chemical fumes, smoke, noise, odour, and probably vibrations. This is another requirement that hampers the tort of trespass to land from dealing with some kinds of environmental pollution. The tort of nuisance may provide a remedy.

Trespass to land does not protect title to, or ownership of, land. It protects *actual possession* of land. Possession is a difficult and fluid concept of property law. It is based on the idea of occupation and control of land coupled with the intention to exclude other persons. The possessor is one who exercises exclusive occupation of land, such as an owner in occupation of his land or a tenant occupying under a lease. An owner of leased property cannot as a general rule sue in trespass because he has surrendered his possession of the land to the tenant for the term of the lease. A person who only has a licence to be on the property, such as a live-in nanny, a guest in a hotel room, and the holder of season's tickets to a seat at the theatre, does not have sufficient possession to exercise trespassory remedies. The emphasis on possession rather than ownership derives from the early function of trespass to land to minimize violence by protecting the person in actual possession of the land against forcible intrusion or eviction. So strong was that policy that even a person in wrongful possession of land has the protection of the remedies for trespass to land against all intruders other than an owner who enters on the strength of his right to immediate possession. In technical language, the defendant may not raise a *jus tertii* (a right in a third person) in defence to an action for trespass to land.

An owner who is out of possession but who has a right to immediate possession has a number of remedies that are loosely allied to the trespass action. First, the owner may, on the strength of his title, bring an action for the recovery of land. This was formerly known as an action of *ejectment*. Second, if the owner can make a peaceable entry onto the land, a request may be made of the person in wrongful possession to leave and, if there is no compliance with that request, reasonable

---

156 (1681), 3 Lev. 37, 83 E.R. 565 (C.P.).

force may be used to eject that person. Third, when a person with a right to immediate possession enters the land and takes possession, he is deemed, under the doctrine of *trespass by relation*, to have been in possession since the right to immediate possession arose. This allows an action for damages (known as *mesne profits*) to be brought for damage suffered during the period of wrongful occupation, including economic loss from the loss of use of the land, damage to, or deterioration of, the land, and the costs of regaining possession.

2) Defences to the Intentional Interference with Land

There are three important defences to trespass to land: consent, necessity, and legal authorization.

a) Consent

There is no liability in trespass to land where the possessor has consented to another entering his land. Consent to enter property is commonly known as a *licence*. A licence may be express or implied,[157] contractual or gratuitous, and given to an individual, a group, or the world. When a licence is given for a particular purpose, an abuse of that purpose may terminate the licence. For example, the licence of a housesitter is likely terminated if the premises are used as a crack house or a gambling establishment.

Gratuitous licences are revocable at will but there is some doubt surrounding the revocability of a contractual licence for a particular purpose and for a limited duration. The situation most commonly arises in respect of contractual licences to see theatrical performances, movies, and sporting events. The conventional view is that, in the absence of misconduct or any breach of management rules by the licensee, his licence is irrevocable.[158] Imagine, for example, that a contractual licence to see a movie is revoked by the owner in breach of the contract. The licensee refuses to leave the theatre and reasonable force is used to eject him. The owner will be liable in battery on the grounds that the licence could not be revoked, the licensee never became a trespasser, and no privilege to use reasonable force to remove him arose.

A few provinces have legislation that empowers a court to issue a judicial licence in narrow circumstances. It arises where a house is built so close to the boundary line that its owner cannot carry out repairs

---

157 An extensive discussion of the indicia of an implied licence is found in *Montreal Trust v. Williston Wildcatters Corp.*, [2004] S.J. No. 541 (C.A.).

158 *Davidson v. Toronto Blue Jays Baseball Ltd.* (1999), 170 D.L.R. (4th) 559 (Ont. Gen. Div.).

without entering the adjoining property. If the adjoining owner refuses to give a licence to enter his property, an application may be made for an order permitting entry for the purpose of effecting the repairs.[159]

b) Necessity

A trespass to land may be justified on the grounds that a situation of danger and emergency arose and it was necessary to commit a trespass to land to prevent harm to the public, the trespasser, the possessor of the land, or a third party which significantly outweighed the damage or loss caused to the innocent plaintiff.[160] Illustrations of each situation are, respectively, the destruction of premises to prevent the spread of fire to an urban area (public benefit), trespassing on the land of another to prevent a spread of fire onto the trespasser's own land (trespasser's benefit), trespassing on land to extinguish a fire on the possessor's land to prevent more extensive damage to the possessor's land (possessor's benefit), and trespassing on land to save the life of a stranger drowning in the possessor's swimming pool (third party's benefit). The wrongful acts must be prompted by imminent peril and must be necessary in the light of the advantage to be gained and the absence of other available options.

There is, however, no consensus on whether necessity is a complete or an incomplete defence. A complete defence negates all liability and allocates the loss to the innocent plaintiff. An incomplete defence excuses the wrongfulness of the act, disallows any self-help remedy to eject the trespasser, and prevents an award of nominal or punitive damages, but it also requires the defendant to pay compensation for any damage caused to the plaintiff. It is unlikely that either view will be suitable for all situations and the extent of protection is likely to be tailored to the particular circumstances of each case.[161]

c) Legal Authorization

There are a wide range of circumstances where entry onto land is statutorily authorized. This arises most frequently in respect of the administration of criminal justice. Entry for the purposes of executing a

---

159 See, for example, *Property Law Act*, R.S.B.C. 1996, c. 377, s. 34.

160 Klar, above note 8 at 154, lists these four situations.

161 See L. Klar, "The Defence of Private Necessity in Canadian Tort Law" in *Issues in Legal Scholarship*, Vincent v. Lake Erie Transportation Co. and the Doctrine of Necessity 2005: Article 3, online: www.bepress.com/ils/iss7/art3, for an analysis of the cases and an argument against the application of the defence where the defendant in an emergency damages the property of the plaintiff while making self-help efforts to protect his more valuable property or life.

warrant for the arrest of a person or a warrant to search premises are two examples where trespass to land will be protected by legal authorization. There is also a range of other legislation which permits public officials to enter premises for a variety of purposes, including determining land valuation for taxation purposes and checking compliance with health regulations and building codes.

A special protection is provided to the possessor where a person who enters onto property with legal authority abuses or exceeds his authority. The doctrine of *trespass ab initio* applies and the entry is deemed to be wrongful from the moment of entry. The abuse of a contractual licence may terminate it from the point at which the abuse occurs but the doctrine of *trespass ab initio* does not apply.

3) Remedies

A range of remedies are available to the possessor of land. An action for damages may be brought, but if the intrusion is trivial and causes no substantial damage to the land or loss of privacy, damages are likely to be nominal.[162] Where actual loss has been caused, damages are not restricted to the reasonably foreseeable consequences of the loss. The defendant is probably liable for all the direct consequences of the trespass. In *Turner v. Thorne*,[163] for example, the defendant was liable for the personal injuries of the plaintiff who fell over boxes that had been mistakenly delivered and left in his garage. Flagrant acts of trespass in knowing disregard of the possessor's rights may warrant an award of punitive damages.

A plaintiff may seek injunctive relief from both continual acts of trespass and continuous acts of trespass, such as leaving chattels on the land of the plaintiff or building premises or other structures that intrude over the boundary line. An injunction is an equitable remedy that is granted at the discretion of the court. The court may order a *prohibitory* injunction dictating that the defendant cease continual acts of trespass or a *mandatory* injunction to take positive steps to terminate a continuous trespass, such as requiring the dismantling and removal of a building intruding across a boundary line. An injunction may be withheld if damages would be an adequate remedy or where the trespass is trivial and an injunction would create a substantial hardship

---

162 Nominal damages are a small sum of money awarded to indicate that the rights of the plaintiff have been infringed. They can be awarded only in torts that are actionable without proof of damage, and they are most commonly used where trespass to land is used to settle boundary disputes.

163 [1960] O.W.N. 20 (H.C.).

to the defendant. Injunctive relief may also be available in exceptional circumstances for threatened acts of trespass.

These judicial remedies may not, however, be suitable where there are temporary and minor acts of trespass which demand a prompt and inexpensive response. In these circumstances, the possessor may resort to either a self-help remedy or a prosecution under petty trespasses legislation. The self-help remedy is the privilege to use reasonable force to remove a trespasser if she does not leave the premises after the landholder has asked her to. The petty trespasses acts, which are found in most provinces, make trespass to land an offence punishable by a small fine.[164] This provides for a more timely and effective punishment and deterrence of trespassers. Some acts also allow a small award of damages to be made upon conviction under the act.[165]

4) Trespass to Land and Shopping Malls

There has been some debate over whether or not the traditional rules of trespass to land should be applied to modern shopping malls. Shopping malls are privately owned and the owner normally remains in possession of all areas, both inside and outside the mall, which are not leased to retailers and service providers. In order to facilitate business, the owner extends an unrestricted invitation or licence to the public to enter the mall. This broad invitation to the public does not make the mall public property but it does attach to the mall some of the characteristics of public property and it distinguishes the premises from the private nature of a personal residence or business office. The public character of a mall does, for example, preclude the owner from excluding or removing a member of the public in contravention of human rights legislation. This quasi-public character of the land use does not, however, prevent the owner from removing a person from the premises for any other reasons. Trespass to land does not require the landholder to have a good reason or indeed any reason to exclude a person from his property.

This rule was challenged in the case of *Harrison v. Carswell*.[166] Mrs. Carswell was an employee of a tenant in a suburban shopping mall. The employees of the tenant, a food retailer, were on strike and Carswell participated in a peaceful informational picket line on the sidewalk outside her employer's premises. She was approached by the owner

---

164 See, for example, Manitoba *The Petty Trespasses Act*, R.S.M. 1987, c. P50.
165 See, for example, Ontario *Trespass to Property Act*, R.S.O. 1990, c. T.21, s. 12.
166 (1975), [1976] 2 S.C.R. 200 [*Harrison*].

of the shopping mall and informed that picketing was not permitted anywhere in the mall and she was invited to move to a distant public sidewalk beyond the boundaries of the complex. When she refused and continued picketing, she was charged and convicted under the Manitoba *Petty Trespasses Act*.[167] A majority of the Supreme Court upheld the conviction and confirmed the right of a private property owner to control his property and to exclude any person from it. The majority view does have the merit of certainty and predictability. Nevertheless, Laskin C.J.C. wrote a strong dissenting judgment. He chided the majority for failing to modify ancient principles to accommodate modern land use and balance the competing interests of the mall owner and members of the public. In his view, the modern shopping mall was so far removed from the paradigm of private property that some restriction on the owner's power of exclusion was appropriate. He was of the opinion that a member of the public could be excluded only for legitimate reasons such as disorderly conduct, illegitimate activities, or other activities that interfered with the effective, profitable, and peaceable operation of the mall. There was, in his opinion, no right to exclude a peaceful and lawful picketer from the property. The mall owner's right to exclude persons was, in his view, coextensive with his ability to provide a good reason for doing so.

The majority decision in *Harrison* prompted the Manitoba legislature to make a limited union-friendly amendment to the *Petty Trespasses Act* to protect informational picketers outside shopping malls from prosecution. It permits the distribution of true statements, outdoors, on private property to which the public is normally given access. The general principle, however, remains in effect and has been used, for example, to exclude a successful gambler from a horse-racing track.[168]

Harrison was, of course, decided before the passage of the *Charter of Rights and Freedoms*.[169] The *Charter* does not apply directly to private disputes but the Supreme Court has spoken of the importance of developing the common law in a way that is consistent with, and reflective of, the freedoms and values embodied in the *Charter*.[170] It is intriguing to speculate on how recognition in the *Charter* of the freedoms of expression, peaceful assembly, and association might have affected the judgment of the majority in *Harrison*. The judgment of Laskin C.J.C. is more protective of those interests. The current situation is further complicated in respect of prosecutions under petty trespasses

---

167 Above note 164.
168 *Russo v. Ontario Jockey Club* (1987), 62 O.R. (2d) 731 (H.C.J.).
169 Above note 63.
170 For a further discussion of the *Charter* and tort law, see chapter 8.

acts because legislation is directly subject to *Charter* scrutiny. It seems unlikely, therefore, that the last word has been spoken on this issue. As Laskin C.J.C. observed, shopping malls are taking on the character of the public markets[171] and main streets of a former era. They are not just commercial locations. They are locations for public intercourse in all of its various aspects, and the ancient principles that currently control access to them are likely to be challenged again.

5) Trespass to Airspace

There is an old Latin maxim of the common law (*cujus est solum ejus est usque ad coelum*) which suggests that the possessor of the surface of land also has possessory rights to all that lies below the surface and to all the airspace above it. That maxim warranted little attention and gave rise to few disputes for centuries. It was only with the advent of air travel in the twentieth century that it became necessary to balance the interests of the possessor of land to his airspace with the legitimate interests of others in the use of that airspace. The new principles to achieve this balance of interests have not as yet been fully and authoritatively worked out but it appears that the courts are differentiating among three kinds of interference in airspace: permanent intrusion into airspace at a relatively low level, temporary intrusion into airspace by means other than by aircraft, and intrusion by aircraft.

There is a great deal of judicial consistency in respect of permanent low-level intrusions into airspace by signs, billboards, hydro lines, and parts of buildings which project over the plaintiff's property. Intrusions of this nature are actionable trespasses to land, and compensatory and injunctive relief are available without proof of damage.[172] Some municipalities take advantage of this rule and levy an "intrusion fee" on retailers who put up advertising signs that project over public sidewalks.

The law relating to the temporary intrusion into airspace by means other than by aircraft has developed largely in respect of cases dealing with the use of cranes on construction sites. It is not uncommon in the construction of high-rise buildings for the booms of construction cranes on top of the structure to swing through the airspace of the adjacent owner. Construction companies normally secure a licence to use the neighbour's airspace but sometimes the negotiations for a licence are not successful. An adjacent owner may, for example, attempt to exploit a strong bargaining position and demand an excessive sum

---

171 *Harrison*, above note 166 at 210.
172 See, for example, *Didow v. Alberta Power Ltd.* (1988), 88 A.R. 250 (C.A.) [*Didow*].

for the privilege of using his airspace. In that situation, the contractor may be tempted to proceed without a licence, thereby prompting the neighbour to sue for trespass to airspace. There is some unevenness in the judicial response to this issue. Some courts have held the intrusion to be a trespass and have issued an immediate injunction prohibiting the use of the crane in a wrongful manner.[173] Some courts have taken the same position but have suspended the operation of the injunction until completion of the building project.[174] Another option is to remedy the intrusion by an award of damages which may be calculated nominally or on the basis of a reasonable charge for a licence. Other courts have suggested that such an intrusion ought not to be regarded as a trespass at all and that the appropriate remedy is in negligence and nuisance, both of which require proof of damage.[175] The weight of authority, however, is that the intrusion into airspace by the boom of a crane is a trespass. This permits an appropriate remedy to be sensitively tailored to the surrounding circumstances of the individual case, including the reasonableness of the plaintiff's behaviour in refusing to give permission.

There is also a variety of possible approaches in respect of intrusion by aircraft. One approach is that intrusion by aircraft is not a trespass at all and that the landowner is restricted to a remedy in negligence or nuisance. The second approach is that intrusion by aircraft is a trespass subject to a privilege of reasonable and legitimate flight.[176] This approach requires a balance to be drawn between the interests of the surface owner and the use of the incumbent airspace by others. Most recreational, military, and commercial flight would be privileged but flight for the purpose of photographing private property, spraying a powerful insecticide over an urban area, testing military weapons, advertising products or services, or conducting surveillance may give rise to some difficult issues.[177] The third view, which probably represents the current Canadian position,[178] is that trespassory remedies are available only for intrusion by aircraft within the surface owner's zone of

---

173 See, for example, *Lewvest Ltd. v. Scotia Towers Ltd.* (1981), 126 D.L.R. (3d) 239 (Nfld. S.C.T.D.).

174 See, for example, *Woollerton & Wilson Ltd. v. Richard Costain Ltd.*, [1970] 1 W.L.R. 411 (Ch.).

175 *Didow,* above note 172.

176 There is some support for this view in *Atlantic Aviation Ltd. v. Nova Scotia Light & Power Co.* (1965), 55 D.L.R. (2d) 554 (N.S.S.C.).

177 This approach, which seeks to balance the interests of the surface possessor with those of others who seek to use the airspace, echoes the approach of Laskin C.J.C. in *Harrison.*

178 See *Didow,* above note 172.

effective possession. Effective possession is an elusive concept but the general idea is that it extends to a height necessary to protect the plaintiff's current or future enjoyment, comfort, or use of land. The zone of effective possession will in most cases be no more than a few hundred feet above the ground. Above that, the remedy must be sought in negligence or nuisance.[179]

E. INTENTIONAL INTERFERENCE WITH CHATTELS

There are four nominate intentional torts protecting interests in chattels:[180] trespass to chattels, detinue, conversion, and the action on the case to protect an owner's reversionary interest. Each has a discrete, though overlapping, role in the protection of interests in chattels. In *practice* each tort is commonly associated with a different form of interference with chattels. The typical case of trespass to chattels is that of intentional damage to a chattel in the physical control of the plaintiff. Detinue typically applies where the defendant refuses to return the plaintiff's chattel to her. Conversion commonly applies where the defendant has taken the plaintiff's chattel. The action on the case to protect the owner's reversionary interest applies to permanent damage to the plaintiff's chattel which occurred when the chattel was in the possession of someone else. These are, however, gross generalizations and the definition of each tort is not restricted to these typical situations. Moreover, a single fact situation may give rise to a number of causes of action. The plaintiff may choose the most advantageous remedy. These nominate torts are supplemented by replevin and the recaption of chattels, which are procedures designed to secure the timely return of chattels that have been wrongly taken or detained by another person.

1) Trespass to Chattels

Trespass to chattels is the oldest of the torts of intentional interference with chattels. It applies where the defendant directly and intentionally

---

179 For a subterranean trespass to land, see *Austin v. Rescon Construction (1984) Ltd.* (1987), 45 D.L.R. (4th) 559 (B.C.S.C.), var'd as to damages (1989), 57 D.L.R. (4th) 591 (B.C.C.A.). See also *Star Energy Weald Basin Limited v. Bocardo SA*, [2010] UKSC 35, dealing with drilling for oil under the claimant's land.
180 Chattels include all property other than land.

(or negligently[181]) interferes with a chattel in the possession of the plaintiff. Trespass to chattels protects possession rather than ownership. Indeed, a person in wrongful possession may bring an action in trespass against anyone except an owner with a right to immediate possession. This emphasis on possession reflects the fact that the main priority of the early common law was to minimize violence. The law sought to prevent violent confrontations over the possession of chattels where title lay in the hands of an owner out of possession who was not exercising his ownership rights. The solution was found in protecting the person who had physical control (possession) of the chattel. An owner out of possession such as a bailor of a chattel for a fixed term cannot, therefore, sue in trespass.[182]

Any direct interference with a chattel is actionable, including damage, destruction, taking, or movement of it. In practice, trespass is most commonly used where a chattel has been damaged or where there has been some minor unauthorized use or movement of the chattel. The destruction or taking of chattels is usually remedied by the tort of conversion or the tort of negligence. Knowledge that the interference is wrongful is not required. Mistake is no defence.

It is not clear if trespass to chattels continues to be actionable without proof of damage. One view is that the traditional rule plays a useful role in preventing people from touching valuable art and museum pieces and in providing a remedy for the unauthorized moving or temporary use of chattels. The other view is that unless goods are taken, damage should be an essential element of liability since there is no pressing policy need to protect a dignitary interest in the inviolability of chattels.

The remedy for trespass to chattels is an award of damages. The measure of damages for a damaged chattel is the reduction in its market value or the cost of repairs where that is less. The market value of the chattel is the appropriate measure for the taking or destruction of a chattel.

Canadian courts have not yet dealt with the application of trespass to chattels to online interference with computer systems. A variety of interesting issues will arise including the meaning of property, the novelty of intangible interference, and whether harm should be an

---

181 The burden of proof is on the defendant to prove an absence of intention and negligence. In practice the tort of negligence will be used to remedy damage caused by a direct negligent act.

182 This rule is, however, qualified by the concept of vicarious possession. This allows an owner to sue when his employee, agent, or bailee at will has possession of his chattel.

essential element of online trespass. The American courts that have begun to grapple with these issues have agreed that trespass to chattels provides an appropriate framework for analysis. The leading case is *Intel Corp. v. Hamidi*.[183] In that case the defendant was a disgruntled former employee of the plaintiff corporation. He sent mass e-mails that were critical of the plaintiff to thousands of the plaintiff's employees. The plaintiff sought an injunction to put a stop to this on the grounds that the defendant's unauthorized use of its server was a trespass to chattels. An injunction was granted both on summary judgment and on appeal but the California Supreme Court reversed these decisions. It held that direct harm to the chattel was an essential element of trespass to chattels in California. In *Hamidi*, therefore, no tort was committed because there was no evidence that there was any *significant* impairment in the operation, value, or processing capacity of the plaintiff's server. The nature and degree of harm sufficient to complete the tort was not fully resolved but the Court did not favour earlier decisions where injunctions had been issued to prevent the use of the plaintiff's server for sending bulk e-mail[184] and to prevent the accessing of information that was available to the public from the plaintiff's website[185] on the basis of minimal harm to the plaintiff's computing system and/ or indirect harm to business interests. The *Hamidi* decision may be seen, therefore, as one that favours freedom of access and use of online systems and diminishes the protection of the operators of those systems unless there is a substantial degradation in their storage or processing capacity. *Hamidi* also challenges the wisdom of the view that trespass to chattels is actionable *per se*. If harm is not needed to maintain online trespass in Canada some form of privilege of reasonable access or implied consent to the use of computer systems will need to be developed.[186]

2) Detinue

An action in detinue is available where a person with a right to the immediate possession of a chattel has requested[187] its return from a

---

183 71 P.3d 296 (Ca. Sup. Ct. 2003).

184 *Compuserv Inc. v. Cyber Promotions Inc.* 962 F. Supp. 1015 (S.D. Ohio 1997).

185 *eBay Inc. v. Bidder's Edge Inc.* 100 F. Supp. 2d 1085 (N.D.Cal. 2000).

186 For a very useful discussion of some of these issues see W. Adams, "There is No There There: *Intel Corp. v. Hamidi* and the Creation of New Common Law Property Rights Online" (2004) 40 Can Bus. L.J. 87.

187 The unauthorized possession of another's chattel, in itself, is not wrongful. It becomes wrongful when the defendant denies the plaintiff's right to it. Con-

defendant who has possession of the chattel or who had possession of it but lost it as a result of a wrongful act.[188] The tort protects the plaintiff's right to the chattel and focuses on the defendant's denial of the plaintiff's rights by refusing to return it. A demand for the chattel by the plaintiff and a refusal by the defendant to return it are normally essential components of the cause of action. The demand alerts the defendant to the plaintiff's claim to the chattel and provides an opportunity for the defendant to return it to its rightful owner and, thereby, avoid liability. It is probably not necessary to make a demand if it is clear that the defendant is determined to keep the chattel, thereby making a request futile.

Unlike trespass and conversion, detinue may be remedied by an order for the return of the chattel. The most common remedy for detinue is a judicial order that the defendant *either* give up the chattel *or* pay for its value and pay damages for its detention. Alternatively, a court may award damages for the value of the chattel and damages for its detention. Less commonly, an order may be made for the return of the chattel with damages for its detention.[189] This order is appropriate where the chattel is not easily replaceable, such as an heirloom, jewellery, or unique industrial or commercial equipment or machinery.

Since the essence of the tort is the refusal to return the chattel, an action may be defeated by the defendant returning the chattel before judgment is given. Furthermore, since the tort is a continuing one arising out of the persistent failure of the defendant to comply with the request to return the chattel, damages for the value of the chattel are assessed at the time of judgment rather than the date of the initial refusal to return it. This may be contrasted with the general rule in conversion that damages are assessed at the time of the conversion.

3) Conversion

Conversion is the most recent of the three main torts providing protection against the intentional interference with chattels. Nevertheless, it has proved to be an expansionary and flexible concept that now encompasses many situations that, at an earlier time, were the predominant preserve of trespass to chattels or detinue. There are three central

---

sequently, a bailee who merely continues in possession after the term of a bailment has expired is not acting wrongfully until he denies the bailor's right to it.

188 For example, a bailee who lost possession of the chattel as a consequence of an intentional or negligent act.

189 The three forms of the remedy for detinue are set out in *General & Finance Facilities Ltd. v. Cooks Cars (Romford) Ltd.*, [1963] 1 W.L.R. 644 (C.A.).

elements to the tort of conversion. First, it protects persons who are in possession of chattels or who have a right to the immediate possession of chattels. Second, it is restricted to the intentional interference and dealing with chattels. Conversion is not, for example, available for the negligent damage or destruction of chattels. Third, an act of conversion is one that so seriously interferes with the plaintiff's rights to the chattel that the defendant may, in fairness, be required to pay its full value.[190] The payment of damages equivalent to the full value of the chattel is said to effect a forced judicial sale of the chattel to the defendant. This explains why orders for the return of the chattel are not made in a conversion action. The defendant is treated as if he had bought the chattel and he can keep it.

The concept of a forced sale is also the safest guide in the multitude of marginal cases where a determination must be made if the interference with a chattel is sufficiently serious to be a conversion. A good rule of thumb is to consider the degree of interference with the chattel and assess whether or not it is fair and reasonable that the defendant be forced to pay the full market value for it.

Chattels may be converted in a number of ways. The most frequent form of conversion is probably the taking of chattels in the course of criminal activity such as break and entry, shoplifting, and car theft. For obvious reasons, criminal taking rarely gives rise to tort litigation. The intentional *destruction* of a chattel is also clearly a conversion. The unauthorized *disposition* of another's chattel by way of sale or pledge is a conversion. The intentional disposition of chattels is made at one's peril. Mistake is no defence to conversion. Consequently, both an innocent seller of stolen goods and the innocent purchaser to whom they are transferred are both liable in conversion. There are some exceptions to this rule, the most important of which include some commercial situations where a non-owner of goods is empowered to transfer a good title to an innocent purchaser.[191] Nevertheless, the transferor remains liable in conversion. Certain ministerial dealings with goods by those who are not principals to a transaction affecting rights in the goods are also protected. For example, persons packing, storing, or carrying goods for another in ignorance of that person's lack of title and with no knowledge that they are participating in a transaction involving the unauthorized

---

190 J.G. Fleming, *The Law of Torts*, 9th ed. (Sydney: LBC Information Services, 1998) at 60–61.

191 The most common examples are the doctrines of apparent authority and apparent ownership, sale or pledge by a mercantile agent under the Factors legislation, and the power of sellers and buyers in possession to pass good title under sale of goods legislation.

transfer of title to the goods are not liable in conversion.[192] An involuntary bailee who surrenders a chattel to a non-owner is also protected from liability in conversion if reasonable care is taken and an honest belief is held that the transferee is the true owner. A great deal of difficulty is encountered in deciding if the *temporary taking, movement*, or *use* of a chattel is a conversion. All the surrounding circumstances must be considered, including the duration of the interference, the kind of interference, the purpose of the interference, and the amount of damage inflicted. The most useful test is whether or not the interference is sufficiently serious to warrant a forced sale of the chattel to the defendant. The classic case on this point is *Fouldes v. Willoughby*.[193] In that case, the plaintiff and two of his horses boarded the defendant's ferry. Before it departed, a dispute arose and the defendant asked the plaintiff to remove himself and his horses from the ferry. When the plaintiff refused, the defendant led the horses off the ferry and turned them loose. The Court held that the defendant was not liable in conversion. The interference with the plaintiff's rights was not of sufficient seriousness to require the defendant to pay for the horses. At most there had been a trespass to chattels. A similar issue arises where another person's umbrella is used to run an errand in the rain, where a motor vehicle that is blocking an entrance is pushed out of the way, or where a person reads another's newspaper or uses a neighbour's tools or sports equipment. If the interference is of short duration and the chattel is returned unharmed, it is unlikely to be held to be a conversion.

Conversion may also be committed by *refusing to comply with a request to return* a chattel to its rightful owner. It is in this situation that conversion intrudes on the traditional domain of detinue. However, in conversion, unlike detinue, a single cause of action arises when the defendant refuses to return the chattel, damages are calculated at the time of the conversion, and the only remedy is an award of damages. The plaintiff may choose the more advantageous action. There are also some situations, such as where a bailee has *negligently* lost the chattel, where the owner has no claim in conversion and must sue in detinue or negligence.

There is some debate about the assessment of damages in conversion and detinue. The theory behind each tort leads to a different date of assessment of the market value of the chattel. The act of conversion obliges the defendant to pay for the chattel. Consequently, when the act of conversion occurs, the plaintiff must mitigate his loss by promptly

---

192 *Hollins v. Fowler* (1875), L.R. 7 H.L. 757 (H.L.).
193 (1841), 8 M. & W. 540, 151 E.R. 1153 (Ex. Ct.).

replacing it. Damages are assessed, therefore, at the time of the conversion or, at the latest, when the plaintiff is aware of the conversion. Detinue is a continuing wrong and the cause of action may be defeated by a return of the chattel at any time before judgment. Damages are thus assessed at the date of the trial. This disparity in valuation dates has led to the guideline that detinue is the tort of choice on a rising market and conversion is preferable on a falling market. There has been some support for bridging the gap by awarding in conversion any increase in the value of the goods as consequential damages or by awarding the plaintiff the highest value of the converted goods between the time of conversion and the trial. This would lessen the evil of having remedies dependent on procedural technicalities, and it would assist plaintiffs who cannot afford to replace chattels at the time of the conversion.

4) The Action on the Case to Protect the Owner's Reversionary Interest

The emphasis in trespass to chattels, detinue, and conversion on the protection of possession or the right to immediate possession fails to address the interest of an owner without either possession or a right to immediate possession. That situation arises most frequently in respect of an unexpired bailment for a fixed term. In that situation, the bailor has neither possession nor a right to immediate possession. The action on the case to protect the owner's reversionary interest arises where the chattel has been destroyed or permanently damaged by the intentional or negligent act of the defendant. The classic authority is *Mears v. London & South Western Ry. Co.*,[194] where the defendant negligently caused serious damage to a barge that was owned by the plaintiff but leased to a third party. The plaintiff succeeded on proof of permanent damage to the plaintiff's reversionary interest. This action is rarely used in Canada because permanent damage or destruction most commonly arises, as it did in *Mears*, as a consequence of negligence and the action is brought in negligence.

5) An Illustrative Case: *Penfold's Wines Pty. Ltd. v. Elliott*

The High Court of Australia decision in *Penfold's Wines Pty. Ltd. v. Elliott*[195] provides an excellent illustration of both the discrete range of each of the nominate torts and the incomplete protection of chattels

---

194 (1862), 11 C.B.N.S. 850, 142 E.R. 1029 (C.P.).
195 (1946), 74 C.L.R. 204 (H.C.A.).

from intentional interference. In that case, the plaintiff sold its wine to customers in returnable bottles that remained in the ownership of the plaintiff.[196] The defendant hotel keeper refilled some of these bottles with his own wine when customers brought them to him. The plaintiff objected to its bottles being used in this manner. In the absence of any general principle prohibiting the intentional interference with another's chattels, the plaintiff was obliged to fit the defendant's conduct into an established head of tort liability. This proved to be an impossible task.

The plaintiff could not sue in trespass to chattels. It had surrendered possession (but not ownership) of the bottles to its customers who had temporarily given possession of them to the defendant for the purpose of filling them with wine. Detinue did not apply because the plaintiff had made no demand of the defendant for its bottles. The defendant was not liable in conversion. He had not acted in defiance of the plaintiff's ownership rights, nor was the use of the bottles to hold wine a sufficient interference with the plaintiff's chattels to warrant a forced judicial sale to the defendant. The action on the case to protect the owner's reversionary interest was not available because the bottles had not been damaged or destroyed. The High Court concluded that the defendant's actions were not tortious.

6) The Recovery of Chattels

Only the tort of detinue holds out the prospect of recovering a chattel. The other torts are remedied in damages. This deficiency in the common law has been overcome, to some degree, by the use of *replevin* and the self-help remedy of *recaption* of chattels.

a) Replevin

Replevin is not a tort. It is a procedure that permits the speedy and effective recovery of a chattel subject to an ultimate judicial resolution of the dispute. The general idea is to maintain the status quo ante until the matter can be judicially resolved. In all provinces, there are either statutes or rules of court which outline the procedure and the requirements that must be met to secure an order of replevin. Normally, a plaintiff with a right to immediate possession must allege that the chattel was wrongfully taken, or wrongfully detained, by the defendant. The court may then order seizure of the chattel and its return to the plaintiff. The plaintiff may be ordered to post security to protect the

---

196 The words "This bottle remains the property of Penfold's Wines Ltd." were embossed on the bottles.

defendant from any loss if the plaintiff's claim turns out to be without merit. The recovery of the chattel is followed by a hearing of the claim on the merits and a final determination is made of the respective rights of the litigants.

b) Reception of Chattels

The law recognizes a limited right of self-help in the recovery of chattels. A person who has a right to the immediate possession to a chattel, which is stronger than the right of the person in possession, may, without legal process, physically take back the chattel. There is uncertainty, however, as to the extent of wrongdoing that the law will tolerate to achieve the reception of a chattel. The recaptor may find it necessary to use physical force or intrude onto the land of the recaptee to get his chattel back and consequently may be faced with an action for battery or trespass to land brought by the recaptee. There is not a lot of authority dealing with this issue. This is not surprising given the extralegal nature of the process and the wrongful act of the recaptee in taking or retaining the chattel.

Understandably, there is some reluctance in permitting physical force (a battery) to be used to recapture chattels. Nevertheless, a person may use reasonable force to recapture a chattel that has been wrongfully taken from him.[197] If, for example, an owner sees a person stealing his bicycle, he may use reasonable force to get it back. If the owner was not permitted to do so, he may never see his bicycle again and he may be left bereft of any effective remedy. Greater licence is given in respect of trespass to land. Chattels are commonly on the land of the recaptee and the reception remedy would be unduly restricted if the recaptor was not permitted to enter the land to get them back. The recaptor may trespass on the land to recapture a chattel that was either wrongfully taken from him or, where the possession of the recaptee was initially lawful, a request for its return has been denied, provided that the entry is peaceable, and the recapture is carried out without any breach of peace.[198]

7) Defences

The defences to the intentional interference with chattels largely mirror the defences that are applicable to the other intentional torts. The

---

197 There is authority in Ontario that suggests that physical force is not permitted in any circumstances: see Ontario Law Reform Commission, *Study Paper on Wrongful Interference with Goods* by R.L. Simmonds & G.R. Stewart, with the assistance of D.P. Paciocco (Toronto: Ontario Law Reform Commission, 1989) at 69*ff*.

198 *Devoe v. Long*, [1951] 1 D.L.R. 203 (N.B.S.C. (A.D.)).

defence of consent and that of legal authorization are most commonly raised. The sale, bailment, and gift of chattels are all consent-driven transactions that defeat any action for conversion. Legal authority arises frequently in the administration of the criminal law. In very narrow circumstances, necessity may also be available.

8) Distress Damage Feasant

A special self-help remedy known as *distress damage feasant* may justify a defendant's refusal to deliver up a chattel to the person with a right to immediate possession to it. An occupier of land may seize a chattel that is unlawfully on his land and has caused or is causing damage. The requirement of damage is essential because the power to seize the chattel is given solely for the purpose of securing payment of compensation for the loss caused. The remedy is most commonly associated with the impoundment of trespassing cattle that have caused damage to crops but it is not restricted to that situation. It may apply, for example, in respect of damage caused by an aircraft that makes an unauthorized landing on the occupier's land, and to harm caused by motor vehicles that have been parked illegally on the occupier's land.[199] The chattel must be on the land at the time of seizure and there is no right of sale, merely a right to retain the chattel until the compensation is paid.

F.   INTENTIONAL INTERFERENCE WITH ECONOMIC INTERESTS

There are a number of nominate torts collectively referred to as *economic torts* or *business torts* that deal, primarily, with the intentional interference with economic interests.[200] The law of torts has exhibited a great deal of caution in this area. A free market economy invites spirited and robust competition and intentionally causing economic harm to rivals is in most circumstances perfectly legitimate. Tort law has, therefore, defined wrongful business activities quite narrowly. A tort remedy is available only for serious misconduct that disrupts the efficient operation of the marketplace. The nominate torts fall into two categories, those that deal with deceptive market practices such as *deceit, injurious*

---

199 See *Barbour v. University of British Columbia*, [2009] B.C.J. No. 617 (S.C.).

200 A detailed discussion of liability for economic loss in tort law is found in P.T. Burns & J. Blom, *Economic Interests in Canadian Tort Law* (Markham, ON: Lexis Nexis Canada, 2009).

falsehood, passing-off, and *misappropriation of personality*, and a more amorphous group that deals with improper market practices. The latter group includes *conspiracy, intimidation, inducement to breach a contract*, and *intentional interference with economic interests by unlawful means*. These torts focus on the illegitimacy of combined coercion, competition by unlawful means, and the deliberate interference with contractual rights.[201]

1) Deceptive Practices

Tort law provides significant protection against deceptive practices in the marketplace. This is supported by a number of policy factors, including ideas of fundamental fairness, a judicial antipathy to those who have secured an unjust enrichment at the expense of another by deception, and the goal of promoting an efficient marketplace. At the heart of the torts of deceit, injurious falsehood, passing-off, and misappropriation of personality is the simple moral proposition that you must not advance your business interests by lying. You must not lie about the nature or quality of the property or services that you offer to customers (deceit); you must not lie disparagingly about the business or trade of others (injurious falsehood); you must not lie that the goods or services that you are selling are those of another (passing-off); and you must not lie that your goods or services are endorsed or used by an identified person (misappropriation of personality). In spite of the centrality of the general concept of honesty in business dealings and the protection of both competitors and consumers from falsehood, each tort has its own rules and boundaries. This is explained in part by the historical development of the torts and in part by the fact that only deceit deals with lies that are directed at the plaintiff. In the other torts the plaintiff is harmed by lies directed at third persons.

a) Deceit
Deceit is established whenever a person has made a fraudulent statement that intentionally causes another person to rely on it to her detriment.[202] Most of the cases deal with economic loss arising from fraudulently induced contracts but deceit is not restricted to those loss-

---

201 The role of tort law as a regulator of free market practices has diminished with the increase in legislative and administrative controls. Federal and provincial legislation complements tort law in the areas of competition, copyright, patents and trademarks (federal), and corporations, securities, labour relations, business practices, and consumer protection (provincial).

202 *Pasley v. Freeman* (1789), 3 Term. Rep. 51, 100 E.R. 450 (K.B.).

es and may extend to property damage and personal injury.[203] There are four essential elements to an action in deceit: misrepresentation, fraud, reliance, and damage.

A misrepresentation may be made verbally, in writing, or by conduct. The misrepresentation must normally be one of past or present fact. Statements of opinion, law and prediction, and vague and boastful sales commendations ("puffs") are not normally sufficient because the representation must be of a kind on which a reasonable person would rely. As a general rule, there must be some positive statement or conduct although half-truths, active concealment, and the failure to correct an honest misrepresentation that is later found to be untrue may also be sufficient.[204] There is no liability for a failure to disclose facts within one's possession unless there are special circumstances such as a fiduciary relationship between the parties or where the vendor of land knows of serious latent defects in the property which are not easily discoverable by the purchaser and are such as to make the property dangerous or uninhabitable.[205]

The misrepresentation must be made fraudulently. The meaning of fraud was authoritatively decided in the House of Lords decision in *Derry v. Peek*.[206] In that case, the directors of a tramway company issued a prospectus representing that their company had legislative permission to use steam power. In fact, the right to use steam power was conditional on the consent of the Board of Trade, which the directors mistakenly assumed was a mere formality. The Board did not give its consent and the company ultimately went into liquidation. The plaintiff, who bought shares on the strength of the prospectus, sought to recover his losses. The Court held that the misrepresentation was not made fraudulently. Fraud requires proof of dishonesty. It is satisfied by proof either that the defendant knew that the statement was untrue (a lie) or that the defendant made the statement recklessly, not knowing if the statement was true or false and, therefore, without a belief in its truth. Since the directors had an honest though mistaken belief in the truth of the statement, they could not be held liable in deceit.

---

203 The extent to which deceit will be applied to inter-family falsehoods, such as a misrepresentation by a wife to her former husband that her children were fathered by him, has not been fully explored. A useful discussion of the issue is found in the High Court of Australia decision in *Magill v. Magill*, [2006] HCA 51.

204 See Klar, above note 8 at 670–71.

205 See J. Irvine, "Annotation to *Sevidal v. Chopra*" (1987) 41 C.C.L.T. 181; and Klar, above note 8 at 672.

206 (1889), 14 App. Cas. 337 (H.L.).

The defendant must intend that the plaintiff will rely on the fraudulent misrepresentation and the plaintiff must in fact rely on it.[207] The requirement that the defendant intends that the plaintiff will rely on the misrepresentation addresses the problem of potentially indeterminate liability in deceit.[208] It does not require the statement to be made to the plaintiff but it does require proof that the defendant either desired the plaintiff to rely on it or there was a substantial certainty that he would rely on it in the manner that caused the damage. The requirement of actual reliance addresses the need for causation between the fraudulent misrepresentation and the loss. There can be no liability where the plaintiff knows that the representation is untrue or decides to rely, not on the representation, but on his own inquiries or judgment.

The plaintiff must prove actual damage caused by reliance on the fraudulent misrepresentation. Damages are awarded to put the plaintiff in the position he would have been in if the misrepresentation had not been made, not to place him in the position he would have been in if the representation was true. There is some doubt about whether the rule of remoteness of damage in deceit is reasonable foreseeability or directness. Since moral turpitude is central to deceit, the wider rule of direct consequences would seem to be appropriate.[209]

Deceit has always been a difficult tort to prove because of its central element of dishonesty. Courts are reluctant to make a finding of serious moral guilt in the absence of compelling evidence. Moreover, care must be taken in alleging fraud because an unsubstantiated allegation of fraud may lead a court to impose a higher award of costs against the unsuccessful plaintiff.

The difficulty in proving fraud and the relatively narrow scope of the tort prompted legal initiatives over the course of the twentieth century which lessened the need for plaintiffs who suffer economic harm as a consequence of misrepresentations to rely on deceit. In tort law, liability for false statements has been expanded by recognition of liability for negligent misrepresentations under *Hedley Byrne*.[210] In the law of contract, pre-contractual statements, whether they are fraudulent, negligent, or innocent, are more likely now to be construed as contractual warranties, the breach of which triggers damages designed to put the plaintiff in the position she would have been in if the statement had been true. Furthermore, most provinces have consumer protection and

---

207 *Kelemen v. El-Homeira*, [1999] A.J. No. 1279 (C.A.).

208 The leading case on this point is *Peek v. Gurney* (1873), L.R. 6 H.L. 377.

209 See *Doyle v. Olby (Ironmongers) Ltd.*, [1969] 2 Q.B. 158 (C.A.) and *Smith New Court Securities Ltd. v. Scrimgeour*, [1997] A.C. 254.

210 *Hedley Byrne & Co. Ltd. v. Heller & Partners Ltd.*, [1964] A.C. 465 (H.L.).

business practices legislation that provide a wide range of remedies for false representations made in the course of consumer transactions.

b) Injurious Falsehood

Injurious falsehood grew out of slander of title and slander of goods to provide a more general protection against certain false statements that injure another in his trade or business.[211] Slander of title is made out where a defendant makes false statements that a person does not own his land, thereby preventing that person from leasing or selling it. Slander of goods developed by analogy to protect against false statements in respect of both the ownership and the quality of the plaintiff's goods. Eventually, the tort of injurious falsehood emerged to protect against a broad range of false statements which are disparaging of the plaintiff's trade, business, or property in a way that leads other persons not to deal with him. The essential elements of injurious falsehood are: a false statement made of or concerning the plaintiff's business, trade, or property, publication of that statement to a third person, malice, and actual pecuniary loss. Justification is a defence to the action.

The plaintiff must prove a false statement was made of, or concerning, the plaintiff's trade, business, or property. Unlike defamation, which protects a person's reputation, injurious falsehood protects a person's business and commercial interests.[212] The false statement may be about the quality of the plaintiff's products or services, the competence of his employees, the ownership of property, or the scope, nature, location, legality, viability, or existence of the plaintiff's business operation.

There must be proof that the disparaging statement was made to a third person. The gist of injurious falsehood is that the plaintiff is damaged by the impact of the false statements on his current or future customers. The plaintiff will not be able to establish that his losses were caused by the defendant's statements in the absence of proof that third parties were aware of them.

The false statement must be made maliciously. There is some uncertainty as to the meaning of malice in this context. There is no difficulty with statements that the defendant knows are untrue and are made with spite, ill will, and the intention to damage the plaintiff. The problem is in determining the minimal content of the term. It is prob-

---

211 Fleming, above note 190 at 778.

212 Nevertheless, there is a substantial overlap between the two torts because an attack on a person's business may reflect poorly on his character and an action can be brought by a corporation for harm to its good name. It is normally advantageous to frame an action in defamation because the falsity of the statement is presumed, damage is presumed, and there is no need to prove malice.

ably sufficient that the defendant knew that the statement was false or was reckless as to whether the statement was true or false[213] and the damage was intended or was the natural and probable result of the publication.[214]

Damage to the plaintiff's trade, business, or property interests is required. Evidence of broken contracts or the loss of long-term customers is clearly sufficient. Greater difficulty is presented where there is only a general decline of revenues in a business that has a casual and transient customer base. In that situation, the plaintiff must show clearly that the losses were caused by the defendant's statements and not by extraneous business contingencies.

The defence of justification is available to the defendant but the requirement of malice limits its scope so severely that it is hard to imagine where it could be invoked successfully.

There are many injurious statements that cause injury to trade or business which are not protected by injurious falsehood. There is no liability on a defendant who makes false factual claims about his own goods or services with the intention of drawing customers away from the plaintiff, and a wide latitude is also given to extravagant and boastful "puffing" by defendants about their own goods and services and their superiority to the competition. A defendant may also make disparaging statements about a competitor's products which are true, regardless of his motive.[215]

c)   Passing-Off

Passing-off protects the goodwill of the plaintiff's business from misrepresentations made by the defendant that his goods or services are those of the plaintiff. This classic definition of passing-off has been extended incrementally in recent years but it continues to identify the three traditional components of the passing-off action: the existence of goodwill in the plaintiff, a misrepresentation made to the public, and

---

213 *Manitoba Free Press Co. v. Nagy* (1907), 39 S.C.R. 340.

214 For a useful discussion of common law authorities on this and other aspects of injurious falsehood, see *Palmer Bruyn & Parker Pty Ltd. v. Parsons* (2001), 76 A.L.J.R. 1631 (H.C.A.).

215 The common law tort of injurious falsehood is complemented by s. 7(a) of the *Trade-Marks Act*, R.S.C. 1985, c. T-13 which states "no person shall make a false or misleading statement tending to discredit the business wares or services of a competitor." A range of remedies is set out in s. 53 of the Act. The primary advantage of s. 7(a) is that proof of malice is not required. There may also be a remedy for misrepresentations of a competitor's pricing and services made in comparison advertising under s. 52 of the *Competition Act*, R.S.C. 1985, c. C-34. See *Maritime Travel Inc. v. Go Travel Direct.Com Inc.*, [2009] N.S.J. No. 177 (C.A.).

actual or threatened damage caused by the diversion of customers or injury to the plaintiff's reputation.[216]

Passing-off protects the plaintiff's proprietary interest in the goodwill of his business. Goodwill is the power to attract customers and to retain the loyalty of existing customers. It is acquired by quality goods or services which are identified by their distinctive name or mark. The name or mark may include any symbols, logos, images, packaging, design artwork, or other trade insignia which are, in the public's mind, distinctive of, and associated with, the plaintiff's products. Descriptive words may qualify where they have become exclusively associated with the plaintiff's product and have thereby achieved a technical secondary meaning.

The gravamen of the passing-off action is a misrepresentation by the defendant that damages the plaintiff's goodwill. The classic case is that of a trader who uses the plaintiff's name, mark, or other trade insignia to mislead consumers that his goods are those of the plaintiff. This is known as a source misrepresentation. A maker of a new cola drink may not, for example, market it as "Pepsi."[217] Most source misrepresentations are, however, more subtle. They seek to create an illusion by use of other trade indicia of the plaintiff's products that the defendant's goods and services are those of the plaintiff. The defendant usually intends to deceive consumers but it is sufficient that the misrepresentation is likely to cause confusion in the mind of the typical casual customer who is not prone to make close inspections of products. The misrepresentation must also be material in the sense that it led customers to make purchases that they would not otherwise have made.

Passing-off now extends beyond source misrepresentations to a wide range of misrepresentations that damage the plaintiff's goodwill. Passing-off applies where the defendant has misrepresented the plaintiff's goods as being of a higher quality than that assigned to them by the plaintiff.[218] It applies where the defendant falsely claims some connection to the plaintiff, which damages the plaintiff's goodwill. It also extends to reverse passing-off where the defendant claims that the

---

216 See *Ciba-Geigy Canada Ltd. v. Apotex Inc.*, [1992] 3 S.C.R. 120 for a useful discussion of the principles of passing-off.

217 Passing-off is known as the law of unregistered trade-marks. The registration system under the *Trade-marks Act*, above note 215, complements the tort of passing-off and offers certain advantages. See D. Vaver, *Intellectual Property Law: Copyright, Patents, Trade-marks* (Concord, ON: Irwin Law, 1997) at 177–79. Passing-off still remains important where there is no statutory protection or a mark has not been registered.

218 *Spalding & Bros. v. A.W. Gamage Ltd.* (1915), 113 L.T. 198 (H.L.).

plaintiff's goods or services are his. The most significant extension of passing-off, however, is to quality misrepresentations where the defendant falsely claims that his product has a quality which is uniquely associated with that of the plaintiff or a class of plaintiffs. Protection has been given to geographic place names where the producers in that area have a reputation for a distinctive quality product. It is not, therefore, permissible to market *Spanish* champagne.[219] Consumers will not be confused about the source of the product but they may be deceived that it is as good as the real thing from France and the goodwill of the producers of champagne may be damaged. Protection has also been given to the Dutch producers of Advocaat,[220] a high-quality alcoholic beverage with a reputation for quality ingredients. The defendant was restrained from marketing an inferior product under the name English Advocaat. In general, these extensions of passing-off remain faithful to the classic model of the tort, namely, a *misrepresentation* causing *damage* to the plaintiff's *goodwill*.

The third element of passing-off is actual or threatened damage to the plaintiff's goodwill caused by diverting customers or injuring the plaintiff's business reputation. Actual damage is remedied by an award of damages and/or an injunction. Threatened damage is sufficient to warrant an injunction if the plaintiff stands to suffer irreparable damage in the absence of intervention.

Although the primary role of passing-off is to protect the plaintiff's goodwill, other factors exercise some influence in borderline cases. In particular, courts are alert to the tendency of the tort to support monopolistic practices, the power of the tort to protect consumers from bogus goods and services, and the interest of consumers in price competition and a wide selection of goods and services.[221] These factors played a role in the Supreme Court's decision in *Consumers Distributing Co. v. Seiko Time Canada Ltd.*[222] Seiko watches are manufactured in Japan and are marketed under a system of authorized distributors and dealers that must comply with a particular marketing strategy, including specifications as to packaging, information, international product guarantees, and after-sales service. The plaintiff was the authorized

---

219 *Bollinger v. Costa Brava Wine Co.* (1959), [1960] Ch. 262. There is, however, no liability if there is no confusion among consumers: see *Institut national des appellations d'origine des vins & eaux-de-vie v. Andres Wines Ltd.* (1991), 74 O.R. (2d) 203 (C.A.).

220 *Erven Warnink BV v. J. Townend & Sons (Hull) Ltd.*, [1979] A.C. 731 (H.L.).

221 J.C. MacInnis, "Commercial Morality and Passing-Off: A Model for a Modern Tort" (1998) 30 Can. Bus. L.J. 415.

222 [1984] 1 S.C.R. 583.

distributor of Seiko watches in Canada. The defendant lawfully secured a supply of Seiko watches from an unofficial source outside Canada and marketed them independently. The plaintiff sought to exclude this competition by bringing an action in passing-off. It is important to note that, when the action reached the Supreme Court on appeal, the defendant was in compliance with an injunction directing it to give notice to the public that it was not an authorized dealer and that the plaintiff's international guarantee did not apply to sales by the defendant. The appeal focused on the defendant's failure to comply with a second injunction that prohibited the defendant from selling or advertising Seiko watches anywhere in Canada. The Supreme Court held that, in light of the defendant's compliance with the first injunction, there was no longer any confusion in respect of the source or quality of the plaintiff's product. It therefore allowed the defendant's appeal in respect of the second injunction. In the Court's view, the defendant may have taken advantage of the goodwill of the Seiko name and of the demand for its product but, given the compliance with the first injunction, there was no misrepresentation to the public, an essential element of the tort. The defendant had merely marketed the watches in a different way. The Court was reluctant to permit a manufacturer to secure a monopoly over the distribution and selling of its product by adopting a particular marketing strategy. It was also in the consumers' interest to be able to choose between buying only the watch at a lower price and buying the whole package at a higher price.

The extension of passing-off to quality misrepresentations and the abandonment of the requirement that the litigants must share a common field of commercial activity have opened up further avenues of development. Two areas that test the limits of passing-off are the protection of character merchandising and protection of businesses from dilution misrepresentations. There has been difficulty in satisfying the traditional requirements of passing-off in both these areas. Unauthorized character merchandising arises where a trader uses the plaintiff's cartoon figure or fictional movie or television character to sell products or services.[223] The requisite misrepresentation is that the defendant is licensed to use the character. There may, however, be difficulty in showing damage to the plaintiff's goodwill.[224] The tort may also apply to dilution misrepresentations where a producer of a famous high-quality product such as Pentax or Cartier objects to *any* use of its name even though there is no actual or potential damage to their goodwill (Pentax

---

223 The use of a person's real name or persona is protected by the tort of misappropriation of personality.

224 H. Carty, "Character Merchandising and the Limits of Passing-Off" (1993) 13 Legal Stud. 289.

Shoes). The business is, in fact, objecting to the misappropriation of the plaintiff's name or mark itself in a way that may diminish its exclusivity and cachet.[225] An extension of passing off into these areas suggests an evolution of the tort from one that protects the plaintiff's goodwill to one that prevents the misappropriation of a character or a name.

d) Misappropriation of Personality

Misappropriation of personality, which was first recognized by the courts of Ontario,[226] protects the right of a person to control the use of her name and likeness for commercial purposes. The tort provides a remedy for both ordinary persons and public figures but it applies most frequently where a defendant seeks to promote her goods or services by deceiving the public that a public figure or celebrity endorses or uses them. The tort may incidentally protect consumers from deceptive practices but its primary function is to protect the plaintiff's goodwill in her name and personality.

The requirements of the tort are the intentional use of the plaintiff's name or likeness or other recognizable aspect of her personality such as her voice or visual image, the unauthorized use of same to promote the defendant's commercial interests, and damage. Damages are normally assessed on the fair market value of the use of the plaintiff's name or likeness. This is commonly referred to as the "lost user fee." Injunctive relief is also available. Furthermore, unlike defamation, the cause of action survives the death of the celebrity to the advantage of the deceased's estate.

It has been recognized that this tort must balance the plaintiff's interest in protecting a valuable proprietary asset arising from her notoriety and the public interest in freedom of expression and freedom of information. Consequently, the tort does not protect a person from being the subject of some journalistic, biographical, or informational publication that, broadly speaking, is in the public interest.[227] The primary purpose of the tort is to protect the plaintiff's right to publicity by preventing the unauthorized commercial exploitation of the plaintiff's personality.[228]

---

225 H. Carty, "Dilution and Passing-Off: Cause for Concern" (1996) 112 Law Q. Rev. 632.

226 *Krouse v. Chrysler Canada Ltd.* (1974), 1 O.R. (2d) 225 (C.A.); *Athans v. Canadian Adventure Camps Ltd.* (1977), 17 O.R. (2d) 425 (H.C.J.).

227 See the trial judgment in *Gould Estate v. Stoddart Publishing Co.* (1996), 30 O.R. (3d) 520 (Gen. Div.), aff'd on other grounds (1998), 39 O.R. (3d) 545 (C.A.).

228 *Horton v. Tim Donut Ltd.* (1997), 45 B.L.R. (2d) 7, aff'd (1997), 104 O.A.C. 234 (C.A.).

A tort of misappropriation of personality is also found in the privacy acts of British Columbia, Manitoba, Saskatchewan, and Newfoundland and Labrador. The general thrust of the statutory language is similar to that of the common law tort. However, in most jurisdictions the statutory cause of action does not survive the death of the person[229] and, during her lifetime, it is actionable without proof of damage. The assignment of this tort to privacy legislation indicates that the tort, in fact, protects two interests, a commercial interest in the exploitation of one's name or likeness and a privacy interest in not having one's name or likeness used for commercial purposes. The common law tort emphasizes the first interest and the privacy acts emphasize the second. Both, however, are probably couched in sufficiently general terms to provide a remedy in either situation.

2) Improper Market Practices

In tort law, the limits to proper market practices are drawn by the nominate torts of conspiracy, intimidation, inducement to breach a contract, and the intentional interference with economic interests by unlawful means. The scope and development of these torts have been profoundly influenced by the landmark 1898 House of Lords decision in *Allen v. Flood*.[230] In that case, the defendant trade union official threatened to call employees out on a *lawful* strike unless their employer *lawfully* dismissed the plaintiff. The employer complied with this threat and the plaintiff sued the defendant. The jury found that the defendant's action was malicious, being motivated purely to punish the plaintiff for some past anti-union conduct of which the defendant disapproved. The case provided the Court with an opportunity to establish some general principle of liability for the unjustified infliction of economic harm, such as one imposing liability for the *intentional* infliction of economic loss without justification,[231] for the *malicious* infliction of economic loss, for the infliction of economic loss through *unfair market practices*, or for causing loss by *abuse of the right* to participate or compete in the marketplace. Instead, the Court chose to give free rein to the zealous pursuit of self-interest in the marketplace and held that, in the absence

---

229 The position in Manitoba is not clear. The legislation does not address this point.

230 [1898] A.C. 1 (H.L.) [*Allen*].

231 There was some early authority favouring such a tort: see *Keeble v. Hickeringill* (1707), 11 East. 574n, 103 E.R. 1127 (K.B.). It found fertile soil only in the United States, where it evolved into the *prima facie* tort doctrine based on the intentional interference with economic interests without justification. See *Tuttle v. Buck*, 119 N.W. 946 (Minn. 1909).

of one of the established economic torts, no liability could be imposed merely because the economic loss was caused *intentionally*, *maliciously*, or *unfairly*. Since the defendant in *Allen* had not committed any nominate economic tort and had not used any other illegal means, he was not liable. No degree of bad faith, malicious conduct, or unfairness could make conduct that was lawful in itself, unlawful. More than any other case, *Allen* impeded the development of a coherent and principled approach to improper market practices. As a consequence of *Allen*, the courts, throughout most of the twentieth century, focused largely on defining the scope of the discrete economic torts without the guidance or active pursuit of any coherent general principle.

a) Conspiracy

The tort of conspiracy deals with situations where two or more persons have entered into and acted upon an agreement to cause economic loss to another person. There are two branches of conspiracy: conspiracy to damage the plaintiff by lawful means (simple conspiracy), and conspiracy to damage the plaintiff by unlawful means.[232]

i) Simple Conspiracy

Simple conspiracy arises where two or more persons agree to use *lawful* means for the predominant purpose of causing economic loss to the plaintiff. The agreement may be express or implied, formal or informal, contractual or non-contractual, but it must show an intention to act together in planned, concerted action to damage the plaintiff. The tort is complete once the conspirators have acted pursuant to the agreement and have thereby caused harm to the plaintiff. It is not easy to reconcile this tort with the decision in *Allen* because conduct that, according to *Allen*, would not be actionable if undertaken by a single entity, is rendered wrongful by the mere fact of combination and an *illegitimate motive*. This "magic of combination" is probably consistent with an intuitive sense of fair play. Harsh competition, one on one, is acceptable, but to act in concert to the detriment of a single person is often unfair. This rationale does not always apply in the modern marketplace because single entities such as multinational corporations may exercise much greater economic power than many smaller entities in combination. Nevertheless, the tort is too well entrenched to be affected by the loss of its early *raison d'être*.

---

232 A useful discussion of conspiracy is found in P. Burns, "Civil Conspiracy: An Unwieldy Vessel Rides a Judicial Tempest" (1982) 16 U.B.C. L. Rev. 229.

The central element of liability in simple conspiracy is proof that the defendants' *predominant* purpose was to injure the plaintiff rather than to promote their own legitimate interests. A liberal interpretation of predominant purpose has allowed the courts to give free rein to most competitive practices and great latitude to the activities of organized labour. This pattern was set in two landmark House of Lords cases: *Mogul Steamship Co. v. McGregor Gow & Co.*[233] and *Crofter Hand Woven Harris Tweed Co. v. Veitch*.[234] In the *Mogul* case, the defendants were a cartel of shipping companies that enjoyed a monopoly over the carriage of tea between China and England. They forced the plaintiff, a rival shipper, out of business by a variety of legal, but unfair, trade practices such as boycotting agents who did business with the plaintiff and predatory pricing. The Court held the defendant was not liable in conspiracy because the predominant purpose of the agreed action was not to injure the plaintiff but to advance their own economic interests. Initially, the courts were less generous in their assessment of the purpose of the activities of organized labour but this was reversed in the *Crofter* decision. It dealt with the production of tweed cloth on the Isle of Lewis. The plaintiff mill owners had secured a competitive advantage over traditional businesses by importing yarn from the mainland rather than relying on the local crofters. The defendants, who were officials of a union to which the local crofters and stevedores belonged, imposed a total embargo on the import of yarn and brought the plaintiffs' production to a halt. No unlawful means were used. The Court held that there was no actionable conspiracy because the defendants were pursuing their own economic interests and their predominant purpose was to protect the livelihood of the union members, not to injure the plaintiffs.

The result of these two decisions is that the tort of simple conspiracy has made no substantial inroads upon either the principle or the spirit of *Allen*. The courts have shown no great enthusiasm for using the tort to police the fairness of business or labour practices. It is only in cases of spiteful, vengeful, or vindictive conduct where the predominant purpose is to injure the plaintiff that liability will be imposed. This kind of mean-spirited and ruthless exercise of power to inflict harm is not common. It has, consequently, been left to legislatures to control monopolistic market practices. The Canadian *Competition Act*,[235] for example, prohibits conspiracies designed to lessen competition unduly. Most industrial action does not amount to a simple conspiracy because

---

233 [1892] A.C. 25 (H.L.).
234 [1942] A.C. 435 (H.L.).
235 R.S.C. 1985, c. C-34.

its predominant purpose is to improve the working conditions of union members. Some provinces have gone further and have legislated immunities for concerted action in a trade dispute where the acts, if done by a single person, would not be actionable.[236]

Simple conspiracy may be alleged by corporations when groups of private citizens organize boycotts, informational pickets, or demonstrations to exert economic pressure on them to change their conduct or policies in respect of the environment, labour practices, or some other social issue.[237] The intriguing aspect of these cases is that the defendants are not normally acting in their own self-interest. They are acting in what they perceive to be the public interest and are asserting their right of free speech to influence corporate activity. The issue arose in *Daishowa Inc. v. Friends of the Lubicon*.[238] The defendant, Friends of the Lubicon, was a political action group that organized a consumer boycott of the plaintiff's paper products in protest of the plaintiff's logging operations on lands in Alberta claimed by the Lubicon Cree. Members of the group approached the customers of the plaintiff and requested their co-operation in refusing to purchase the plaintiff's products. If the customer refused, an informational picket was set up outside the customer's place of business to enlist the support of their patrons and to put pressure on the customers of the plaintiff. The Friends of the Lubicon were successful and the plaintiff lost many customers. The plaintiff sought an injunction against their conduct on the basis of a number of business torts, including simple conspiracy. The Court held that simple conspiracy was not established because the predominant purpose of the defendant's conduct was not to injure the plaintiff but

---

236 See, for example, Saskatchewan *The Trade Union Act*, R.S.S. 1978, c. T-17, s. 28: "An act done by two or more members of a trade union, if done in contemplation or furtherance of a trade dispute, shall not be actionable unless the act would be actionable if done without any agreement or combination."

237 Litigation brought by corporations to combat this kind of damaging political action are commonly known as SLAPP suits (Strategic Law Suits Against Public Participation). These lawsuits are not usually based solely on simple conspiracy. They commonly allege defamation, other business torts and other tortious and illegal acts. The suits place a significant financial and emotional burden on political activists. See C. Tollefson, "Strategic Lawsuits and Environmental Politics: *Daishowa Inc. v. Friends of the Lubicon*" (1996) 31 J. Can. Stud. 119. See also *Fraser v. Saanich (District)*, [1999] B.C.J. No. 3100 (S.C.). Steps have been taken in some provinces to control SLAPPs. In 2009 the Quebec legislature passed Bill 9, *An Act to Amend the Code of Civil Procedure to Prevent Improper Use of the Courts and Promote Freedom of Expression and Citizen Participation in Public Debate*. Legislation has also been recommended in the *Report of the Anti-SLAPP Advisory Panel* to the Attorney General of Ontario in October 2010.

238 (1998), 39 O.R. (3d) 620 (Gen. Div.).

to focus attention on an important public issue and to provide support for the Lubicon Cree. The absence of self-interest was not sufficient to warrant the imposition of liability.

ii) Conspiracy to Injure by Unlawful Means

A conspiracy to injure by unlawful means arises where two or more persons agree to act unlawfully and either the predominant purpose of the activity is to harm the plaintiff *or* the conduct is directed at the plaintiff and the defendants should have known that harm was likely to result.[239] The tort is complete once the conspirators have acted on the agreement and have harmed the plaintiff. The elements of combination, unlawful activity, and the intent or likelihood of damage provide strong grounds for imposing liability. In the context of this and most other business torts, the term *unlawful activity* gives rise to some uncertainty but it includes criminal conduct, independent tortious acts, breach of contract, breaches of legislation such as labour relation statutes or the *Competition Act*,[240] and other civil wrongs.

The importance of the tort should not, however, be overestimated because the emphasis on independently illegal conduct and intent to injure suggests that the individual conspirators will often each be liable on some other basis. However, where the illegal act is not in itself a tort if done by one person (for example, the breach of some statutes), resort may be made to conspiracy to injure by unlawful means.[241]

iii) Defences to Conspiracy

The defence of justification is available to the defendants but, given the elements of the tort, it is unlikely to play a significant role. In simple conspiracy the issue of justification is largely addressed by a consideration of the defendant's predominant purpose, which is central to establishing liability. Conspiracy to cause damage by unlawful means is not normally susceptible of justification.

b) Intimidation

Intimidation was recognized as a discrete and independent tort in 1964 in the House of Lords decision of *Rookes v. Barnard*.[242] It is now well es-

---

239 The leading Canadian decision is *Canada Cement Lafarge Ltd. v. British Columbia Lightweight Aggregate Ltd.*, [1983] 1 S.C.R. 452.

240 Above note 235.

241 The unlawful act need not be independently actionable by the claimant. See *Total Network SL v. Her Majesty's Revenue and Customs Commissioners*, [2008] UKHL 19.

242 [1964] A.C. 1129 (H.L.) [*Rookes*].

tablished that intimidation arises where the defendant either threatens to use unlawful means to coerce a third person to damage the plaintiff or threatens unlawful acts that directly compel the plaintiff to act to his detriment. The former situation is known as three-party intimidation and the latter as two-party intimidation. The gravamen of each is the threat of an unlawful act.

i) Three-Party Intimidation

Three-party intimidation is best illustrated by the case of *Rookes*. In that case, the plaintiff, an employee of BOAC (now British Airways), resigned his membership in his union. In an attempt to maintain a closed shop, the defendant union officials, some of whom were also employees of BOAC, threatened BOAC with strike action unless the plaintiff's employment was terminated. The strike action would have been in breach of a no-strike clause in the defendants' employment contract. BOAC submitted to this coercion and lawfully[243] terminated the plaintiff's employment. The Court held that the essential elements of three-party intimidation—coercion by threats of unlawful conduct, an intention to injure the plaintiff, and damage—were established.

The intimidation must involve threats of unlawful acts, and the person against whom the threats are aimed must submit to the pressure and act against the plaintiff. An unconditional threat is not intimidation. Nor is it intimidation if the subject of the threat withstands the pressure and refuses to act against the plaintiff. If the defendant makes good on the threat, some independent action in tort or contract will normally be available to the threatened person. Initially, it was thought that the threatened acts needed to be criminal wrongs or independent torts, but since *Rookes* it is clear that a threatened breach of contract is sufficient.[244]

ii) Two-Party Intimidation

In three-party intimidation, the plaintiff is not the person who is threatened but the person who suffers the loss. In two-party intimidation, the plaintiff is both the person who is threatened and the person who suffers the loss. The essential ingredients of two-party intimidation are coercion by threats of unlawful acts, an intention to injure, and damage. For example, a person may be coerced into closing his business

---

243 The plaintiff did not, therefore, have an action against his employer.

244 The tort of three-party or two-party intimidation is not, however, committed if "a party to a contract asserts what he reasonably considers to be his contractual right": see *Central Canada Potash Co. v. Saskatchewan* (1978), [1979] 1 S.C.R. 42 at 87, Martland J. [*Central Canada Potash*].

by threats of violence or property damage. There is some debate about the applicability of two-party intimidation where the defendant threatens to break a contract with the plaintiff.[245] An action for anticipatory breach of contract and other contractual remedies are available to the plaintiff and the wisdom of making every threatened breach of contract an independent tort has been doubted.[246]

iii) Defences to Intimidation

Justification is recognized as being a defence to intimidation but, given the requirement of threats of illegal activity, it plays a limited role. Some narrow scope may be found for it in cases where the wrongdoing is relatively minor and the purpose of the threat is to achieve some compelling and beneficial social purpose.

c) Inducement to Breach a Contract

The primary means of transferring property and services in a market economy is by way of a contract. It is not surprising, therefore, that tort law has supplemented and reinforced the protection of contractual relationships provided by the law of contract. The modern protection of contractual rights in tort law begins with the case of *Lumley v. Gye*.[247] In that case, Miss Wagner, niece of the German composer, was under an exclusive contract to sing in the plaintiff's theatre. The defendant persuaded her to break her contract with the plaintiff and to sing at his theatre. The defendant was held liable for directly inducing Miss Wagner to break her contract with the plaintiff even though the plaintiff had a claim for breach of contract against Miss Wagner.[248]

Since *Lumley*, there has been a great deal of judicial activity broadening the protection of contractual relationships. Three discrete branches of the tort of inducement to breach a contract have been recognized: direct inducement to breach a contract, indirect inducement to breach a contract, and interference with a contract by unlawful means without causing breach.[249] The three torts protect existing contractual rights. They do not protect anticipated or planned commercial arrangements.

---

245 Klar, above note 8 at 698.
246 *Central Canada Potash*, above note 244 at 87, Martland J.
247 (1853), 2 E. & B. 216, 118 E.R. 749 (Q.B.) [*Lumley*].
248 It is an unusual tort because the defendant is liable for participating in a wrong that he could not commit himself.
249 A useful discussion of inducement to breach a contract in all its forms is found in *Garry v. Sherritt Gordon Mines Ltd.* (1988), 45 D.L.R. (4th) 22 (Sask. C.A.) [*Garry*].

i)   Direct Inducement to Breach a Contract

Any direct inducement to breach a contract is actionable. The essential elements of the tort are a direct inducement to breach the contract, knowledge of the contractual link on the part of the defendant, an intention to secure a breach of contract, and damage. Justification is a defence.

The defendant must directly induce a breach of contract. Any conduct that evidences an intention to encourage, persuade, cajole, or convince a person to breach her contract is sufficient. In *Lumley*, for example, the defendant offered Miss Wagner more money to sing for him.[250] Examples of other direct inducements include words of encouragement, threats, incentives, entering into contractual arrangements with another person which, to the knowledge of the defendant, are incompatible with the person's contractual obligations to the plaintiff, and giving reasons why another party should breach her contract. There is, however, no liability for merely providing information about various options, including breach, so long as it is given in a dispassionate and neutral manner and does not seek, even in a subtle way, to pressure or encourage the contracting party to breach her contract.

The courts have been sensitive to the position of lawyers and other professional advisers acting in the course of their professional duties. A lawyer may advise a client of the possibility and consequences of a breach of contract and a physician may discuss the inadvisability of continuing stressful employment without liability. The client or patient is, of course, liable for breach of contract if she chooses to commit a breach of contract. Special leniency has also been extended to the directors of corporations who decide in good faith that it is not in the best interests of their corporation to perform a contract. They are protected from personal liability as long as they are acting "bona fide within the scope of their authority and in the interests of the corporation."[251] The plaintiff's remedy lies in an action for breach of contract against the corporation.

The defendant must have knowledge of the contractual relationship that is broken. In *Lumley*, for example, the defendant knew of the contract because he was the manager of a rival opera company. He knew that Miss Wagner would have to breach her contract if she were to leave the plaintiff and sing for him. Knowledge of the precise terms of the

---

250   D.A. Howarth, *Textbook on Tort* (London: Butterworths, 1995) at 474.

251   *Said v. Butt*, [1920] 3 K.B. 497. For an excellent discussion of the wider issue of the tortious liability of corporate directors, officers, and employees, see B. Welling, "Individual Liability for Corporate Acts: The Defence of Hobson's Choice" (2000) 12 Sup. Ct. L. Rev. (2d) 55.

contract need not be known but the defendant must be aware that his conduct will result in the breach of a contractual relationship. Wilful blindness to the existence of the contract may also be sufficient but there is no general obligation on a prospective contractor to inquire actively if proposed contracts will result in the breach of existing contractual arrangements between the negotiating party and a third party.

The defendant must have an intention to secure a breach of contract. There is, however, no need to prove that the defendant intended to harm the plaintiff. The defendant is, as appears to have been the case in *Lumley*, often motivated more by a desire to advance his own interests than to damage those of the plaintiff. This is not a defence when those interests are advanced by deliberately securing a breach of contract.[252] One Canadian decision[253] suggests that there may be liability for a direct *negligent* inducement to breach a contract but it has gathered little support.[254] The general view is that such cases are better resolved within the tort of negligence in a manner that is consistent with the developing liability for the negligent infliction of economic loss.[255]

The tort is actionable on proof of damage which, in most cases, is the loss of the contractual bargain. The loss is also recoverable by the plaintiff against the contract breaker.[256] There may, however, be advantages to suing in tort. In tort, damages are "at large," which permits the court to take into account the conduct of the defendant and to compensate for any loss of commercial reputation by the plaintiff. The tort action is also advantageous where the contract breaker is insolvent, where punitive damages that are available only in contract in limited circumstances[257] are warranted, or where there are procedural obstacles to the contract action.

Justification is a defence to the direct inducement to breach of contract, but there is little useful modern authority.[258] What there is sug-

---

252 In the recent decision of *SAR Petroleum Inc. v. Peace Hills Trust Co.*, [2010] N.B.J. No. 104 (C.A.) [*SAR*], the requisite intention was described as a desire to cause a breach of contract as an end in itself or as a means to an end.

253 *Nicholls v. Richmond (Township of)* (1983), 145 D.L.R. (3d) 362 (B.C.C.A.).

254 See *SAR*, above note 252 at para. 51, Robertson J.A.: "negligent conduct is not actionable."

255 See Klar, above note 8 at 683.

256 The plaintiff may not, however, recover double damages.

257 See *Whiten v. Pilot Insurance Co.*, above note 150.

258 The landmark authorities are *Glamorgan Coal Co. v. South Wales Miner's Federation*, [1903] 2 K.B. 545 (C.A.), aff'd (*sub nom. South Wales Miners' Federation v. Glamorgan Coal Co.*) [1905] A.C. 239 (H.L.); *Brimelow v. Casson*, [1924] 1 Ch. 302; and *Hill (Edwin) & Partners v. First National Finance Corp.* (1988), [1989] 1 W.L.R. 225 (C.A.).

gests, first, that it has a narrow scope (which is not surprising given the public interest in the integrity of contractual links); second, that the absence of malice or bad faith is insufficient to establish the defence; and third, that a scrupulous consideration must be given to all the surrounding circumstances. Clearly the most pertinent factor is the motive and objective for procuring the breach of contract and whether the object to be achieved by the breach warrants excusing the wrongdoing. Attention is also paid to the kind of contract breached; the relationship between the defendant, the contract breaker, and the plaintiff; and the kind of inducement used.

The issue of justification may arise where the defendant directly induces a breach of contract to promote his own interests, the interests of the contract breaker, or the public interest. Justification on the ground of the defendant's self-interest is normally a non-starter unless the defendant is protecting equal and competing contractual or property rights of his own.[259] Imagine, for example, that a vendor sold the same piece of land to A and to B. To protect his contractual rights, A takes steps against the vendor to secure his performance of the contract. This results in the vendor breaking his contract with B. A will not be liable for inducement to breach a contract.[260]

Some old authorities suggest that the defence of justification may be made out where the defendant persuades a person to break a contract that is particularly harsh or immoral or otherwise disadvantageous to the contract breaker. Today, there is much less reason to encourage paternalistic and meddling defendants to induce a breach of contract in the name of altruism for the contracting party. Modern contract law and consumer and labour protection legislation provide contracting parties with generous remedies in respect of agreements that are disadvantageous on the grounds of mistake, misrepresentation, pressure, unconscionability, or public policy. Contracting parties may be given information about available legal remedies but a direct inducement to breach the contract is unlikely to be excused on the ground that it was for the contract breaker's good.

Finally, a defendant may seek to excuse his conduct on the ground that it was in the public interest. Justification in the public interest may be established where the breach of contract has been induced by a regulatory agency or disciplinary body charged with the responsibility for policing the safety or integrity of certain activities such as professional

---

259 See *Johnson Waste Management v. BFI Canada Inc.*, [2010] M.J. No. 331 (C.A.) and *SAR*, above note 252.

260 Fleming, above note 190 at 764.

conduct, provided that there were no more reasonable alternatives to achieve their laudable goal. A law society, for example, would not be liable to the client of a professional who could no longer honour his retainer because he had been found guilty of professional misconduct and forbidden from the further practice of law. The issue may also arise where a defendant directly induces a breach of contract between a corporation and a customer for political or social reasons such as concern about the corporation's exploitation of Third World labour, its desecration of the environment, or its failure to adopt policies of equality in the workplace. The courts are more reluctant to excuse the wrongdoing on these grounds. There are sufficient *legal* avenues to promote social and political views, to apply pressure legally, and to publicize one's causes.

Justification is not susceptible of precise or predictable guidelines. The situations in which the issue arises are so diverse and fact-specific that each requires a careful examination of the individual circumstances to determine whether or not the motive, object, and reason for inducing a breach of contract should excuse the defendant.

ii) Indirect Inducement to Breach a Contract

The foundation principle in *Lumley v. Gye* has been extended to include indirect inducements to breach a contract. The courts have, however, taken care to keep the liability for indirect inducement to breach a contract within reasonable limits. This has been achieved, in large part, by requiring that the indirect inducement is by independently illegal means and that the breach of contract is a necessary consequence of the defendant's illegal act. The other requirements of knowledge of the contract, an intention to cause a breach of the contract, and damage mirror those of the parent tort.[261] It is, nevertheless, important to emphasize the requirement of intention. Although the means may be indirect, the aim and target of the conduct must always be to secure a breach of contract.

The key to the tort of indirect inducement to breach a contract is the requirement of conduct that is independently illegal. This contrasts with direct inducement, which is, in itself, an illegal act. The emphasis on illegal means in this branch of the tort is necessary to prevent it from making accepted market practices illegitimate. Examples of such practices would be cornering the market in a particular commodity and thereby forcing other suppliers to breach their contracts with cus-

---

261 *Thomson (D.C.) & Co. v. Deakin*, [1952] Ch. 646 (C.A.); and *Garry*, above note 249.

tomers, or calling a legal strike that causes the employer to default on contracts with its customers.[262]

Indirect inducement to breach a contract by unlawful means can arise in a variety of ways, including stealing tools from a contractor which are essential to the performance of a contract with a third party, the physical restraint or intentional injury of a contracting party in order to cause a breach of contract, the direct inducement of employees to break their contract with their employer in order to prevent the employer from performing a contract with the plaintiff, and breach of contract by a supplier to cause the purchaser to default on a contract with a subpurchaser.

The requirement that the breach of contract is a necessary consequence of the indirect inducement emphasizes the importance of causation. Given that the conduct inducing the breach is indirect and sometimes quite remote from the damage, clear proof is required to show that the contractual default was caused by the defendant's illegal conduct and that the breach was unavoidable.

Justification plays an even more minor role in this branch of the tort, given the emphasis on the need to show an illegal act.[263]

iii) Interference with a Contract by Unlawful Means without Causing Breach

Canadian courts adopted[264] the view of Lord Denning, expressed in *Torquay Hotel Co. v. Cousins*,[265] that liability extends to "a case where a third person *prevents* or *hinders* one party from performing his contract, even though it be not a breach."[266] To establish liability, there must be proof of the defendant's knowledge of the contract, an intent to interfere with the contractual performance by illegal means, and economic harm. The novelty of this branch of the tort is the absence of a breach of contract. It applies to all situations where the performance of the contract has been interfered with, but is particularly pertinent to the situation where an induced breach of contract is excused by a valid and appropriately worded exemption clause. It is difficult to find a good reason to excuse the defendant because of the fortuitous presence of an

---

262 Fleming, above note 190 at 760–61.
263 See *Verchere v. Greenpeace Canada*, [2004] B.C.J. No. 864 (C.A.) (illegal interference with contractual relations of logging employees by protesters not justified by their laudable motives to save the rain forest).
264 See P. Burns, "Tort Injury to Economic Interests: Some Facets of Legal Response" (1980) 58 Can. Bar Rev. 103 at 119.
265 [1969] 2 Ch. 106 (C.A.).
266 *Ibid.* at 138.

exemption clause of which the defendant was not aware. This branch of the inducement tort is, however, unlikely to survive as an independent head of liability. Recent authority favours its absorption within the tort of intentional interference with economic interests by unlawful means with which it has greater affinity.[267]

d) Intentional Interference with Economic Interests by Unlawful Means

It was noted earlier that in *Allen v. Flood*[268] the House of Lords declined to formulate any general, all-embracing principle in respect of improper or unacceptable market practices. In lieu thereof, the nominate torts have developed as discrete categories of liability. It has, however, become apparent that there is a fundamental unity to most of these pockets of tortious liability which is largely consistent with the spirit of *Allen*. With the exceptions of the anomalous tort of simple conspiracy and the tort of direct inducement to breach a contract, all of the torts require proof of both an *intention* to harm the economic interests of the plaintiff *and independently illegal conduct* by the defendant. Indeed, if one characterizes the wrongfulness of a person who directly induces a breach of contract as intentional conduct that causes *another* to commit an illegal act (the breach of contract), there is an even greater unity among the discrete heads of liability.[269] This commonality has led to the emergence of a general tort of intentional interference with economic interests by unlawful means. Its essential elements are: an intention to injure the plaintiff's economic interests; an interference in those interests by illegal or unlawful means; and economic harm. This tort, consequently, remains true to the spirit of *Allen* because it continues to define the limits of freedom of competition and the pursuit of economic self-interest by the *legality* of the means used. There has, however, been some unevenness in the manner in which these elements of the tort have been interpreted by Canadian courts. The Ontario Court of Appeal sought to resolve some of the uncertainty in *Alleslev-Krofchak v. Valcom Ltd.*[270] First, the intent element was described, not as the predominant purpose[271] of the defendant, but simply as an intent to cause harm either

---

267 See *Alleslev-Krofchak v. Valcom Ltd.*, [2010] O.J. No. 3548 at para. 95 where the Ontario Court of Appeal expressed the view that nothing less than a breach of contract will satisfy the inducement tort.

268 Above note 230.

269 T. Weir, *Economic Torts* (Oxford: Oxford University Press, 1997) at 29–30.

270 Above note 267.

271 See *Reach M.D. v. Pharmaceutical Manufacturers Association of Canada* (2003), 65 O.R. (3d) 30 (C.A.).

as an end in itself or as a means to an end, such as enriching oneself or others. Second, the meaning of unlawful means was clarified. The Court rejected the wide definition of "any act that one is not at liberty to do." It preferred a much tighter definition of unlawful means, and in so doing the Court narrowed the scope of the tort. It began by noting that the tort applies in three-party scenarios where the defendant has caused economic harm to the plaintiff through the instrumentality of a third party. Furthermore, the defendant's unlawful conduct must be actionable by the third party, or would have been actionable if the third party had suffered harm.[272] Finally, the circumstances must be such that the plaintiff cannot sue the defendant directly under some other head of liability. If a direct action can be brought by the plaintiff against the defendant, there is no need of assistance from the unlawful interference tort. The Court paid less attention to the third element of economic harm but it probably includes any interference with trade, business relationships, or livelihood and interference with business expectancies and prospective economic advantages, so long as there is a causal connection between the unlawful means and the loss suffered.[273]

The centrality of unlawful conduct in the torts relating to improper marketing practices suggests that the tort of intentional interference with economic interests by unlawful means has considerable potential to achieve some integration and rationalization of the conventional heads of liability and to establish a more principled development of the nominate torts. A significant step has been taken in that direction by the House of Lords in its decision in *OBG Ltd. v. Allan*.[274] In that case the Court examined the relationship between intentional interference with economic interests by unlawful means and the tort of direct inducement to breach a contract and its progeny, indirect inducement to breach a contract and interference with a contract by unlawful means without causing breach. The Court redrew the map in respect of these torts. In its opinion the tort of inducement to breach a contract should be confined to its original formulation under *Lumley v. Gye*. There was, in its view, an essential difference between direct inducement to breach a contract which was characterized as an accessory tort and the other branches of the tort which were based on the independently unlawful

---

272 It should be noted, however, that one month after *Alleslev-Krofchak*, a differently constituted panel of the Ontario Court of Appeal in *Barber v. Vrozos* [2010] O.J. No. 3607 stated that the unlawful means requirement was met by proof that the act was one that the defendant was "not at liberty to do." No reference was made to *Alleslev-Krofchak*.

273 See *Flintoft v. Quai*, [2004] O.J. No. 4227, 27 C.C.L.T. (3d) 308 (S.C.J.).

274 [2007] UKHL 21.

conduct of the defendant. The latter two branches should be subsumed within the broader tort of intentional interference of economic interests by unlawful means.[275]

FURTHER READINGS

Intentional Interference with the Person

ALEXANDER, E.R., "Tort Liability of Children and Their Parents" in D. Mendes da Costa, ed., *Studies in Canadian Family Law*, vol. 2 (Toronto: Butterworths, 1972) 845

ATRENS, J.J., "Intentional Interference with the Person" in A.M. Linden, ed., *Studies in Canadian Tort Law* (Toronto: Butterworths, 1968) 378

CRAIG, J.D.R., "Invasion of Privacy and *Charter* Values: The Common-Law Tort Awakens" (1997) 42 McGill L.J. 355

FELDTHUSEN, B., "The Canadian Experiment with the Civil Action for Sexual Battery" in N.J. Mullany, ed., *Torts in the Nineties* (North Ryde, NSW: LBC Information Services, 1997) c. 10

HANDFORD, P.R., "Tort Liability for Threatening or Insulting Words" (1976) 54 Can. Bar Rev. 563

KLAR, L., "Intentional and Negligent Trespass: It is Time to Clarify the Law" (2004) 28 The Advocates' Q. 410

MANITOBA LAW REFORM COMMISSION, *Report on Stalking* (Winnipeg: Manitoba Law Reform Commission, 1997)

PICHER, P., "The Tortious Liability of the Insane in Canada . . . With a Comparative Look at the United States and Civil Law Jurisdictions and a Suggestion for an Alternative" (1975) 13 Osgoode Hall L.J. 193

PROSSER, W.L., "Insult and Outrage" (1956) 44 Cal. L. Rev. 40

SLADE, C., "Intentional Infliction of Mental Suffering: Reconsidering the Test for Liability" (2008) 34 Advocates' Q. 322

---

275 The Ontario Court of Appeal's decision in *Alleslev-Krofchak* is sympathetic to this approach.

SOPINKA, J., "Malicious Prosecution: Invasion of *Charter* Interests: Remedies: *Nelles v. Ontario*: *R. v. Jedyack*: *R. v. Simpson*" (1995) 74 Can. Bar Rev. 366

TRINDALE, F., "The Modern Tort of False Imprisonment" in N.J. Mullany, ed., *Torts in the Nineties* (North Ryde, NSW: LBC Information Services, 1997) c. 8

Intentional Interference with Chattels

FLEMING, J.G., *Law of Torts*, 9th ed. (Sydney: LBC Information Services, 1998) c. 4

GREEN, S. & J. RANDALL, *The Tort of Conversion* (Oxford: Hart Publishing, 2009)

ONTARIO LAW REFORM COMMISSION, *Study Paper on Wrongful Interference with Goods*, by R.L. Simmonds & G.R. Stewart, with the assistance of D.P. Paciocco (Toronto: Ontario Law Reform Commission, 1989)

PROSSER, W.L., "The Nature of Conversion" (1957) 42 Cornell L. Rev. 168

WARREN, E.H., "Qualifying as Plaintiff in an Action for a Conversion" (1936) 49 Harv. L. Rev. 1084

Intentional Interference with Land

IRVINE, J., "Some Thoughts on Trespass to Air Space" (1986) 37 C.C.L.T. 99

LOADER, L., "Trespass to Property: Shopping Centres" (1992) 8 J. L. & Social Pol'y 254

MAGNET, J.E., "Intentional Interference with Land" in L.N. Klar, ed., *Studies in Canadian Tort Law* (Toronto: Butterworths, 1977) 287

Intentional Interference with Economic Interests

BAGSHAW, R., "Can the Economic Torts Be Unified?" (1998) 18 Oxford J. Legal Stud. 729

BURNS, P., "Civil Conspiracy: An Unwieldy Vessel Rides a Judicial Tempest" (1982) 16 U.B.C. L. Rev. 229

———, "Tort Injury to Economic Interests: Some Facets of Legal Response" (1980) 58 Can. Bar Rev. 103

BURNS, P. & J. BLOM, *Economic Interests in Canadian Tort Law* (Markham, Ont.: Lexis Nexis Canada, 2009)

CARTY, H., *An Analysis of the Economic Torts* (Oxford: Oxford University Press, 2001)

————, "Character Merchandising and the Limits of Passing Off" (1993) 13 Legal Stud. 289

————, "Dilution and Passing Off: Cause for Concern" (1996) 112 Law Q. Rev. 632

————, "Intentional Violation of Economic Interests: The Limits of Common Law Liability" (1988) 104 Law Q. Rev. 250

HEYDON, J.D., *Economic Torts*, 2d ed. (London: Sweet & Maxwell, 1978)

KAIN, B. & A. ALEXANDER, "The 'Unlawful Means' Element of the Economic Torts: Does a Coherent Approach Lie Beyond *Reach*?" in Hon. T.L. Archibald & Hon. R.S. Echlin, eds., *Annual Review of Civil Litigation, 2010* (Toronto: Thomson Carswell, 2010) 33.

MACINNIS, J.C., "Commercial Morality and Passing-Off: A Model for a Modern Tort" (1998) 30 Bus. L.J. 415

RICHARDSON, G., "Interference with Contractual Relations: Is *Torquay Hotel* the Law in Canada?" (1983) 41 U.T. Fac. L. Rev. 1

WEIR, T., *Economic Torts* (Oxford: Clarendon Press, 1997)

STRICT LIABILITY

A. INTRODUCTION

The distinguishing feature of the strict liability torts is that there is no need to prove that the defendant was guilty of any wrongful (intentional or negligent) conduct. In the absence of defences, proof that the defendant caused the plaintiff's loss in the manner prescribed is sufficient to impose liability. Strict liability does not play a significant formal role in modern Canadian tort law. Historically, the evolution of the common law of torts has been from strict liability to fault liability. Consequently, the remaining areas of strict liability tend to be ancient and few in number. Moreover, those torts of strict liability that do survive were eroded in the course of the twentieth century by the relentless expansion of the tort of negligence.

The torts of strict liability include the rule in *Rylands v. Fletcher*, liability for fire, the scienter action for damage caused by dangerous animals, and cattle trespass. It is also conventional to include in this list vicarious liability even though it is not a discrete tort. It imposes a strict liability for the torts of others with whom the defendant has a particular relationship.

These few remnants of true strict liability do not, however, tell the full story of strict liability in Canadian tort law. The formal decline of the discrete strict liability torts has been matched by a rise in a *de facto* strict liability under the guise of strict standards of care within the tort of negligence. This is particularly evident in the fields of motor-vehicle accidents, product accidents, and accidents arising from dangerous activities. This is not entirely surprising because strict liability continues to have some functional attraction in modern tort law. It can optimize both the deterrent and the compensatory impact of tort law by demanding exceptional care and expanding the range of persons who receive compensation. It can improve the administrative efficiency of tort law by eliminating the often difficult task of determining fault. It can also be used to create an enterprise liability, which allocates the full losses generated by a particular activity or enterprise (such as manufacturing, railroad or air transportation, or nuclear power operations) to that activity or enterprise. An enterprise liability facilitates the distribution of losses and may achieve some market deterrence.

Canadian judges are not immune to these ideas. They have not, however, been willing to embrace strict liability formally or theoretically and to utilize it openly as a general basis for the allocation of modern accident losses. Canadian judges are much more comfortable utilizing the discretion embodied in the standard of reasonable care in the tort of negligence to impose a strict standard of care where appropriate rather than changing the theoretical framework of tort law.

There is, therefore, a paradox in the Canadian law of torts in respect of strict liability. On the one hand, the courts have shown no willingness either to expand existing heads of strict liability or to create new heads of strict liability. On the other hand, there is a willingness, in certain situations, to impose a covert strict liability under the guise of applying traditional negligence principles.[1]

B. THE RULE IN *RYLANDS V. FLETCHER*

The litigation in *Rylands v. Fletcher*[2] gave rise to the most significant rule of strict liability in tort law. The case dealt with an earthen water reservoir that failed and flooded the plaintiff's coal mine. The reservoir had been built by contractors on land occupied by the defendant. The contractors were negligent. They built the reservoir over disused mine shafts that led to the plaintiff's mining operation. The contractors, however, were not sued and, because they were not employees of the defendant,

---

1   One possible explanation of this phenomenon is that the traditional strict liability torts do not apply strict liability to the activities and circumstances that Canadian judges believe most deserve it, such as products liability, motor-vehicle accidents, and ultra-hazardous activities.

2   (1868), L.R. 3 H.L. 330, aff'g (*sub nom. Fletcher v. Rylands*) (1866), L.R. 1 Ex. 265 (Ex. Ch.) [*Rylands*].

he was not vicariously liable for their negligence.[3] The plaintiff's claim, therefore, depended on the recognition of a strict liability for the escape of water. Although the courts at this time were increasingly attracted to fault as the basis of tort liability, the Exchequer Chamber, in a unanimous judgment delivered by Blackburn J., imposed a strict liability on the defendant. The Court may have been influenced by a number of reservoir failures in England a few years earlier which caused significant loss of life and property,[4] but Blackburn J., typically, made no reference to those events. He drew on the ancient strict liability for damage caused by dangerous animals, cattle trespass, and some early nuisance cases to fashion a general principle of strict liability. He stated:

> We think that the true rule of law is, that the person who for his own purposes brings on his lands, and collects and keeps there anything likely to do mischief if it escapes, must keep it in at his peril, and, if he does not do so, is prima facie answerable for all the damage which is the natural consequence of its escape. He can excuse himself by shewing that the escape was owing to the plaintiff's default; or perhaps that the escape was the consequence of vis major, or the act of God.[5]

The House of Lords dismissed the defendant's appeal but, in the course of his judgment, Lord Cairns introduced the concept of a *non-natural* use of land. He emphasized that no liability could be imposed for the *natural* run-off of water from higher land to the lower land. In *Rylands*, however, the defendant had collected water artificially and a strict liability was appropriate for this *non-natural* use of land. This concept of non-natural use has played a central role in the evolution of the tort.

The rule in *Rylands v. Fletcher*, as originally formulated, was a strict liability tort of considerable scope and it was applicable to a wide range of land use. It was inevitable, therefore, that there would be some tension between this special rule of strict liability and the emerging tort of negligence. The rule in *Rylands v. Fletcher*, in fact, proved to be no match for the burgeoning tort of negligence and, in the twentieth century, it was progressively restricted both by a modification of its essential elements of liability and by a proliferation of defences. It now operates within a narrow compass and rarely leads to a liability that could not have been established under the torts of nuisance or negligence.

---

3   No claim was available in trespass to land because the intrusion was indirect, and private nuisance was not available at that time because there was an isolated escape of water.

4   A.W.B. Simpson, "Legal Liability for Bursting Reservoirs: The Historical Context of *Rylands v. Fletcher*" (1984) 13 J. Legal Stud. 209.

5   *Rylands*, above note 2 at 279–80.

1) Elements of Liability

To establish liability under the rule in *Rylands v. Fletcher*, the plaintiff must show a non-natural use of land, an escape of something likely to do mischief from the land, and damage.

a) Non-natural Use of Land

A non-natural use of land is an essential element of strict liability in the rule in *Rylands v. Fletcher*. Today, however, non-natural use has a different meaning from that initially ascribed to it by Lord Cairns. It no longer means artificial, foreign, or not arising in the course of nature. It means dangerous, extraordinary, special, and of no general benefit to the community. The pivotal case in this development was *Rickards v. Lothian*,[6] which dealt with the escape of water from a domestic plumbing system. The water escaped from a basin in a lavatory in an upper floor of the defendant's building to a lower floor, which was occupied by the plaintiff. The Privy Council held that the principle of strict liability was not applicable in these circumstances. The Court defined a non-natural use of land as a "special use [of land] bringing with it increased danger to others, and must not merely be the ordinary use of the land or such a use as is proper for the general benefit of the community."[7] The defendant's plumbing system was not special, dangerous, extraordinary, or detrimental to the community.

The seeds of future confusion and uncertainty about the meaning of non-natural use were sown in this case because there is no consistency among the descriptive terms—special, dangerous, extraordinary, and without general benefit to the community. Moreover, the factors listed in *Rickards* have received different degrees of emphasis from different judges at different times. It is now clear, however, that the one consistent factor in determining whether or not a land use is non-natural is the creation of an increased danger. The other factors play a more erratic role in decision making in the more marginal cases. This emphasis on danger is wise because it provides a defensible justification for the imposition of a strict liability. Nevertheless, the concept of non-natural use continues to be elusive and difficult to apply.

The cases indicate that there are two general categories of non-natural use: land use that has a great magnitude of danger independent of the particular circumstances of the case, and land use that is not always dangerous but is so in the particular circumstances of the case.

---

6   [1913] A.C. 263 (P.C.) [*Rickards*].
7   *Ibid.* at 280.

The first category includes uses of land that are commonly regarded by the public as dangerous in themselves. They include the storage of water in bulk; the manufacture and use of explosives; fumigation with poisonous gas; the bulk storage or transportation of natural gas, propane, dangerous chemicals, or gasoline; the storage or use of nuclear materials; and the storage or use of dangerous biological agents. In this category, there is little debate about the element of non-natural use and, consequently, there are few reported cases. These land uses are in almost all circumstances highly dangerous and they fully warrant the application of strict liability. The high degree of danger usually trumps any of the other *Rickards* factors to the contrary.

The second category includes uses of land that do not carry the same degree of danger. In this category of cases a more balanced consideration is given to all the relevant factors set out in *Rickards*, including the degree of danger of the land use, the utility and normality of the land use, and the circumstances of time and place. In this category it is difficult to predict what is and what is not a non-natural use of land. *Mihalchuk v. Ratke*[8] and *Gertsen v. Metropolitan Toronto (Municipality of)*[9] illustrate the point. In *Mihalchuk*, the defendant farmer sprayed herbicide on his land from an aircraft. Some of the herbicide drifted onto the plaintiff's land and damaged the plaintiff's crops. The Court held that the spraying of herbicide in this manner was a non-natural use of the defendant's land and liability was imposed. The Court emphasized that spraying herbicide from the air was an unusual operation at that time. The neighbours gathered to watch it take place. The use of an aircraft and the mixture of oil and herbicide also increased the danger of the herbicide drifting onto the plaintiff's crops. There was much less chance of drifting from the normal method of spraying by boom from a tractor. In *Gertsen* the defendant municipality disposed of garbage in a landfill adjacent to a residential area. As the organic material decomposed, it produced methane gas which drifted onto the plaintiff's property and accumulated in his garage. The gas ignited when he started his car and he was injured. The Court found that this was a non-natural use of land. Special emphasis was placed upon the time, place, and circumstances of the land use. The landfill was located in a small ravine in a residential neighbourhood and there was no compelling public need to have used this particular area. These decisions are typical of cases in this category of non-natural use. They are highly

8   (1966), 57 D.L.R. (2d) 269 (Sask. Q.B.) [*Mihalchuk*].
9   (1973), 2 O.R. (2d) 1 (H.C.J.) [*Gertsen*].

fact-specific and involve a juggling of the various *Rickards* factors in no fixed pattern. They have little precedential value.[10]

The emphasis on the normality, utility, context, and circumstances of the land use in this second category of non-natural use tends to blur the distinction between the strict liability under the rule in *Rylands v. Fletcher* and the tort of negligence. A special land use that is dangerous because of the circumstances of time and place is likely to be found to be a negligent use of land. The rule in *Rylands v. Fletcher*, therefore, takes on some of the characteristics of a fault regime and is transformed into a loose fault-based liability. This is evidenced by the fact that in both *Mihalchuk* and *Gertsen*, the defendant was also found liable in negligence. The most dramatic illustration of this coalescence of the second category of non-natural use and the tort of negligence is found in *Aldridge v. Van Patter*.[11] The case dealt with an accident on a stockcar race track. One of the cars went out of control and crashed through a light fence into an adjacent park where it injured the plaintiff. It was held that the race track was a non-natural use of land and liability was imposed under the rule in *Rylands v. Fletcher*. Emphasis was placed on the facts that it was a dirt track that produced a great deal of dust, the cars were travelling at high speed, the track was not banked, and there was no substantial barrier or fence around the track. The defendant was also held liable in negligence. The finding of negligence was supported by the same factors that had supported the conclusion that it was a non-natural use. There is in the judgment, however, no cross-reference or any indication of relationship between the independent findings of liability.

The uneven evolution in the interpretation of non-natural use has left a residue of inconsistent cases, some of which may no longer be reliable. It has on occasion been applied to seemingly normal activities that in most circumstances generate no special, increased danger, such as a flagpole, a carnival ride, street Christmas decorations, painting operations on a bridge, and, most improbably, the activities of a group of gypsies.[12] The lack of consistency in the interpretation of non-natural use may be traced to the cobbling together of disparate factors in the definition of non-natural use in *Rickards* and differing judicial attitudes to strict liability.

---

10 An exception is the consistent line of authority since *Mihalchuk* favouring strict liability for damage caused by the aerial spraying of chemicals, notwithstanding the fact that such operations are now common.

11 [1952] O.R. 595 (H.C.J.).

12 See A.M. Linden & B. Feldthusen, *Canadian Tort Law*, 8th ed. (Toronto: Butterworths, 2006) at 535–36.

b) The Escape of Something Likely to Cause Mischief

The escape of something likely to cause mischief from land controlled by the defendant has always been an essential element of the rule of *Rylands v. Fletcher*. There are two components to this element: mischievous things and escape. The former is largely superfluous now that the concept of non-natural use carries the connotation of special danger. Consequently, there are few occasions where the component of mischief warrants independent consideration. The same cannot be said for the requirement of an escape from the land occupied by the defendant.

Although the requirement of an escape from land in the occupation of the defendant has on occasion been construed quite liberally,[13] it remains an essential element to liability. Most cases deal with a single escape of a harmful element but modern authority suggests that it extends to situations where harm has been caused by multiple escapes of elements such as toxic chemicals and refinery emissions.[14]

The only serious challenge to the escape requirement was made in the case of *Read v. J. Lyons & Co.*[15] In that case, the plaintiff was a government inspector who was carrying out her duties in the defendant's munitions factory in the middle of the Second World War. A high-explosive shell detonated and she was injured. Being unable to prove negligence, she relied on the rule in *Rylands v. Fletcher*. The defendant argued that strict liability was inapplicable on the facts because the plaintiff was on the defendant's land. The plaintiff's argument appealed to both logic and policy. It was argued that, if the reason for strict liability is the ultra-hazardous nature of the activity, the defendant should, logically, be responsible for all the losses arising from the non-natural use of land and not just for losses arising beyond the property. Furthermore, a maintenance of the escape requirement would result in greater protection being given to the property interests of a neighbour than to the personal security interests of a visitor to the defendant's premises. Preferring property interests to the interest in personal safety does not appear to be good policy. The rule of strict liability, it was argued, should rest solely on the ultra-hazardous nature of the activity rather than on the location of the plaintiff. The impressive logic and good

---

13 Both Linden, *ibid.* at 627–28, and L.N. Klar, *Tort Law*, 4th ed. (Toronto: Carswell, 2008) at 560–62, point out that the requirement has been given a liberal interpretation in Canada, and is satisfied by an escape from one part of a building to another and from pipes, cables, and tanks controlled by the defendant.

14 See *Cambridge Water Co. v. Eastern Counties Leather Plc.*, [1994] 2 A.C. 264 (H.L.) (toxic chemicals) and *Smith v. Inco. Ltd.*, [2010] O.J. No. 2864 (S.C.J.) (nickel emissions).

15 [1947] A.C. 156 (H.L.) [*Read*].

sense of the argument did not fall on sympathetic ears. The House of Lords displayed an ill-concealed hostility to the whole concept of strict liability and insisted on the requirement of an escape from the defendant's premises. The Court's policy preference for fault as the general touchstone of tort liability was advanced by keeping the rule in *Rylands v. Fletcher* within narrow parameters.

The refusal of the House of Lords in *Read* to extend strict liability to all losses generated by a non-natural use of land effectively marginalized the rule in *Rylands v. Fletcher*. It was left without any consistent or coherent policy rationale. Occasionally, Canadian courts have flirted with the idea of a broad responsibility for all losses generated by ultrahazardous activities, but the need to establish some sort of an escape continues to be an essential and confining component of liability.

In retrospect, *Read* was the wrong case at the wrong time to promote and develop a broader-based doctrine of strict liability for dangerous activities. At the time the case was decided, fault as a basis of civil liability was in the ascendancy. Strict liability was discounted as an anachronism, an idea whose time had passed. Furthermore, the Second World War produced a catastrophic loss of life, health, and property, almost all of which went uncompensated. Mrs. Read was one casualty of the war effort. This was not a good time to claim that the manufacturer of munitions essential to the war effort owed her a more stringent duty than reasonable care.

c) Damage

The rule in *Rylands v. Fletcher* is actionable only on proof of harm to the plaintiff. Most of the cases deal with damage to neighbouring land but harm to chattels is also recoverable. The House of Lords has held that personal injury losses are not recoverable under the rule in *Rylands v. Fletcher*, since the tort, in its view, applies solely to adjust property losses between neighbours.[16] That view has been rejected by Canadian courts as is illustrated by both *Gertsen* and *Aldridge*. The English view may be historically and doctrinally defensible but the Canadian view is better policy since it extends strict liability protection to the more significant interest, that of security of the person. There is a dearth of authority in respect of the recovery of pure economic loss caused, for example, by the escape of toxic fumes, radiation, or harmful biological agents. The risk of indeterminate liability may prompt judicial caution as it has in negligence law.

---

16   See *Transco plc v. Stockport Metropolitan Borough Council*, [2004] 1 All E.R. 589 (H.L.).

There has been little discussion in Canada about the appropriate rule of remoteness of damage under the rule in *Rylands v. Fletcher.* Justice Blackburn in *Rylands* spoke vaguely of liability for the "natural consequences" of the escape of something likely to cause mischief. The imposition of strict liability may suggest that liability should extend to all the direct consequences of an escape, whether foreseeable or not, but the decision of the House of Lords, in *Cambridge Water Co. v. Eastern Counties Leather Plc.,*[17] has thrown some doubt on that proposition. The defendant in that case had for many years operated a tannery. In the course of its operation, chemicals used in the tanning process had occasionally spilled on the ground. These chemicals had, over the years, percolated down into the underground water aquifers, polluting the water. The plaintiff, whose business involved drawing water from these aquifers for the purpose of supplying drinking water to the public, suffered loss as a consequence of the pollution. At the time the chemicals were spilled, it was not foreseeable that they would have an adverse impact on the underground water. The House of Lords held that the defendant's business was a non-natural use of land but there was no liability for the unforeseeable consequences of the escape of chemicals. The adoption of reasonable foreseeability as the remoteness rule does, however, further erode the strength of strict liability and moves the tort another step closer to the tort of negligence.

2) Defences

The application of the rule in *Rylands v. Fletcher* has been substantially diminished by numerous defences. Some of the defences, including act of God and default of the plaintiff, were established in the case of *Rylands v. Fletcher.* Others, such as consent and the act of a third person, seem to have been borrowed from the nineteenth-century law of negligence. Collectively the defences reflect the lack of any consistent theory of strict liability and a fundamental ambivalence about the intensity of the strict liability established in *Rylands v. Fletcher.* The courts have not, therefore, been eager to reduce the number of defences or to restrict them in any significant manner. This is in marked contrast to the erosion of the defences to the negligence action.

a) Consent

There is no liability where the plaintiff either expressly or impliedly consented to the defendant's non-natural use of land. In this context,

---

17   [1994] 2 A.C. 264 (H.L.).

consent has been interpreted loosely. It appears to be sufficient that the plaintiff knew of the dangerous use of land and entered or remained in a place of danger. Taking possession of land that is adjacent to a known non-natural land use or leasing a part of a building in which the defendant conducts a non-natural use seems to be sufficient to establish the consent of the plaintiff. In *Peters v. Prince of Wales Theatre (Birmingham) Ltd.*,[18] for example, the plaintiff leased part of a building from the defendant. The plaintiff knew that the building had a sprinkler fire-prevention system. Taking possession with knowledge of the system was sufficient to establish the defence of consent when a malfunction caused flooding damage to the plaintiff. This emphasis on consent to the physical risk of damage is reminiscent of the way voluntary assumption of risk was defined in nineteenth-century negligence law. By way of contrast, modern negligence law interprets the defence strictly, requiring proof that the plaintiff agreed to consent to both the physical and the legal risk of damage and thereby abandoned legal recourse in respect of damage caused by a lack of care. If that approach was applied to the rule in *Rylands v. Fletcher*, it would be necessary to show that the plaintiff agreed to bear the loss arising from any accidental failure to prevent a damaging escape from the non-natural use of land, a much more difficult task.

b) Mutual Benefit

It is well accepted that the general benefit or utility of the defendant's land use is relevant in deciding if the land use is non-natural. The Supreme Court has, for example, been unwilling to regard a municipal sewer system as a non-natural use of land.[19] There is less agreement, however, on whether or not proof that the plaintiff benefited from the defendant's land use is an independent defence. The older cases, which support that view, commonly dealt with situations where the plaintiff and defendant shared the use of premises and the plaintiff suffered loss from activities that today would not be regarded as a non-natural use of land. The mutual benefit defence may, therefore, have developed as an early recognition that strict liability is not applicable to the ordinary use of land. The more modern view is that mutual benefit is not an independent defence. At most it is an evidentiary factor in establishing the defence of consent because it is, normally, not possible to take a benefit from the land use without having the degree of knowledge and

---

18 [1943] 1 K.B. 73 (C.A.).
19 *Tock v. St. John's (City) Metropolitan Area Board*, [1989] 2 S.C.R. 1181.

acceptance of the land use which is conventionally sufficient to establish the defence of consent.

c) Default of the Plaintiff

No liability arises where the escape is caused by the default of the plaintiff. The defence mirrors the nineteenth-century negligence rule that contributory negligence of the plaintiff is a complete bar to an action. Legislation has since introduced apportionment into negligence law but the drafters of that legislation do not appear to have intended that it apply to strict liability.[20] Consequently, default of the plaintiff continues to be a complete bar to liability under the rule in *Rylands v. Fletcher*.[21]

d) Act of a Stranger and Act of God

These two defences are grouped together because each excludes liability where the escape is caused by a particular kind of unforeseeable intervening act. To this extent they operate in a way that is similar to intervening acts (*novus actus interveniens*) in negligence law. Where the escape is caused by the deliberate and unforeseeable act of a person over whom the defendant has no control, such as a trespasser, or by a natural event of such intensity that no reasonable person could be expected to foresee it and guard against it, there is no liability under the rule in *Rylands v. Fletcher*. A common element of the two situations is that the intervening events that cause the loss are so unforeseeable that the defendant could not have guarded against them and he is, therefore, totally free of negligence. In theory a "no negligence" defence is incompatible with strict liability, the purpose of which is to allocate losses on the basis of cause alone. Its acceptance indicates the general ambivalence towards strict liability and the modern tendency to blur the line between strict liability and fault liability.

e) Statutory Authority

Some of the land use that is subject to the rule in *Rylands v. Fletcher* is authorized by legislation. It is most common in respect of public services carried on by government and public bodies. Typically, the legislation is permissive in nature and does not expressly indicate how it affects the strict liability of the service provider. That task has been

---

20 The legislation normally applies to the situations where the defendant is negligent or at fault.

21 Some flexibility on this issue may be signalled by the Supreme Court decision in *Bow Valley Husky (Bermuda) Ltd. v. Saint John Shipbuilding Ltd.*, [1997] 3 S.C.R. 1210. In a negligence action governed by maritime law, the Court changed the common law to permit apportionment.

left to the judiciary. In the nineteenth and early-twentieth centuries, the courts were quite protective of statutorily authorized land use. To-day, the pendulum is swinging back in favour of plaintiffs and there is a greater willingness to impose liability. The defendant is normally a better loss distributor and there is more sympathy for the idea that the public should pay for individual losses caused by activities and services from which the whole community benefits.

The current scope of the defence is quite narrow. First, careful con-sideration must be given to the enabling legislation to determine if the land use is authorized. The defendant must then prove that the damage caused was an inevitable and unavoidable consequence of the author-ized activity. It is not sufficient to show that reasonable care was taken. It must be shown that it was practically impossible to avoid the damage.

It may be argued that statutory authorization should not be a de-fence at all. There is, quite apart from the loss distribution point men-tioned earlier, the argument that it is always within the legislature's power to expressly immunize an activity from tort liability and, if the legislature fails to take that step, it indicates that the full tort rights of citizens are not affected. This would also be consistent with the broader responsibility of government in respect to operational matters in the tort of negligence. This view has not, however, been adopted by the courts either with respect to the rule in *Rylands v. Fletcher* or nuisance.

3) The Rule in *Rylands v. Fletcher*, Negligence, and Nuisance

The rule in *Rylands v. Fletcher*, negligence, and nuisance are not mutually exclusive causes of action. Plaintiffs commonly allege liability under all three heads of liability. It is indeed an unusual case where liability under the rule in *Rylands v. Fletcher* is not sustainable under alternative causes of action. This has led to much discussion about its place in modern tort law. A number of views compete for acceptance. First, there are those who would abolish the rule in *Rylands v. Fletcher* on the grounds that it serves little practical purpose and that the torts of negligence and nuis-ance are adequate to the task. This was the approach of the High Court of Australia in *Burnie Port Authority v. General Jones Pty Ltd.*[22] It abol-ished the rule in *Rylands v. Fletcher* on the grounds that it was fraught with difficulty and uncertainty, replete with arbitrary qualifications and exceptions, and was devoid of defensible principle or policy. The second approach is to marginalize the rule in *Rylands v. Fletcher* as a subspecies

---

22   (1994), 179 C.L.R. 520.

of nuisance law dealing with property losses caused by isolated escapes from neighbouring property. This view has gained the approval of the House of Lords, most recently in *Transco plc v. Stockport Metropolitan Borough Council*.[23] The House of Lords not only restricted claimants to those with a proprietary interest in the land, it also narrowed the concept of non-natural use by requiring proof that the use is both extraordinary and exceptionally dangerous. The third view is that the rule in *Rylands v. Fletcher* ought to be emancipated from the qualifications and exceptions that confine it and be replaced with a modern tort that imposes strict liability for all losses generated by abnormally dangerous activities.[24] A template for such a tort is found in the American doctrine of abnormally-hazardous activities.[25] An attractive aspect of this option is that it creates an enterprise liability which internalizes the losses of dangerous activities and also draws a defensible line between negligence and strict liability on the basis of the degree of danger of the activity.

C. FIRE

Many centuries before the rule in *Rylands v. Fletcher* was formulated, there was, in the common law, a special action on the case imposing strict liability on an occupier of land for damage caused by the escape of a fire under his control. The intensity of that strict liability is a matter of debate, but it was probably not applicable to a fire started by an act of God or the act of a stranger, since fires arising from those sources could not be characterized as fires under the occupier's control. In 1774 the *Fires Prevention (Metropolis) Act*[26] was passed. The Act sought to relieve occupiers from liability for fires that began accidentally on their land. Its general purpose was to inject some degree of fault as an essential element of liability for the escape of fire, but it was poorly drafted and its interpretation has been the subject of a great deal of unresolved debate.

The special action for the escape of fire has long since been overtaken by more modern tort principles and is no longer of any consequence in Canada. Liability for the escape of fire must now be established on one of the standard heads of tort liability such as the rule in *Rylands*

---

23 Above note 16.
24 Linden, above note 12 at 540–44 argues strongly in favour of strict liability for abnormally dangerous activities, "free of the historical restraints of non natural use, escape and mischief."
25 *Restatement, Torts (Second)*, §§ 519 & 520.
26 (U.K.), 14 Geo. III, c. 78, s. 86.

v. Fletcher, negligence, or nuisance. The application of modern principles has, however, been complicated by the fact that the *Fires Prevention (Metropolis) Act* or its equivalent remains *in force* in all provinces west of Quebec. The courts have, therefore, felt obliged to interpret an ancient statute that was designed to modify a common law action that is no longer of any consequence in Canada. Predictably, the courts have not allowed the statute to interfere with the modern principles of loss allocation. The statute has been simply construed as protecting a defendant from liability wherever that is consistent with modern tort principles. In terms of its power to shape liability for the escape of fire, the legislation is a dead letter.

Strict liability for the escape of fire may now be established under the rule in *Rylands v. Fletcher*. Consideration must, of course, be given as to whether the fire arose in respect of a non-natural use of land. Fires for heating, cooking, or other domestic purposes are unlikely to be considered as amounting to a non-natural use. Opinion is divided on the use of fire for agricultural purposes. Liability also extends to fires that arise spontaneously from a land use that qualifies as a dangerous fire hazard.

The tort of negligence also imposes a heavy responsibility for damage caused by the escape of fire. Stringent standards of care coupled with the generous use of circumstantial evidence facilitate the imposition of liability on occupiers in respect of fires that are negligently lit or escape because of a lack of continuing vigilance or control. There is some degree of covert strict liability under the guise of the application of the tort of negligence. An occupier is also held liable for the negligence of his employees, independent contractors, and guests. An occupier is even under a duty to take reasonable steps to control or extinguish a fire arising on his land from any source, including an act of a stranger or an act of God. The latter situation arose in the Australian case of *Goldman v. Hargrave*[27] where a landowner failed to take sufficient measures to extinguish a fire caused by a lightning strike in a gum tree. The tree was felled but the fire was not put out. A few days later it spread and damaged the plaintiffs' land.

The tort of private nuisance is often overlooked in respect of liability for the escape of fire. Nevertheless, the infliction of damage by the escape of fire from a neighbouring property may amount to a nuisance. Private nuisance may apply to a single escape of fire, and negligence is not an essential element of liability unless the fire arises from the act of a stranger or an act of God.

---

27   [1967] 1 A.C. 645 (P.C.).

D. THE SCIENTER ACTION (LIABILITY FOR HARM CAUSED BY DANGEROUS ANIMALS)

1) The Elements of Liability

Under the scienter action, the keepers of dangerous animals are strictly liable for injuries and harm caused by them.[28] Scienter, which means knowledge, is the central element of this cause of action. The plaintiff must prove not only that the animal was dangerous but also that the keeper knew that the animal was dangerous. For the purposes of this action, animals are divided into two classes: animals *ferae naturae* and animals *mansuetae naturae*.[29]

Animals *ferae naturae* are those that are considered, by their nature, to be dangerous to people. They include such animals as tigers, elephants, wolves, and bears. These animals are conclusively deemed to be dangerous and their keepers are conclusively presumed to know that such animals are dangerous. A keeper is strictly liable even though the injury may not have been of the kind that led the courts to categorize the animal as *ferae naturae*.

Animals *mansuetae naturae* are by their nature harmless to people and include domesticated farm animals and cats and dogs. A normally harmless animal may, however, have shown a dangerous propensity to cause damage of the kind suffered by the plaintiff. In those circumstances, the keeper is strictly liable under the scienter action if he was aware of its dangerous nature before it attacked the plaintiff.

In recent years, an additional element has been introduced into the scienter action. Some courts now require proof that the animal that caused the injury escaped from the *control* of the defendant keeper.[30] This requirement operates to protect defendants whose animals have been caged or tethered at the time that the plaintiff was injured. In *Maynes v. Galicz*,[31] for example, the scienter action was held to be inapplicable in respect of a caged wolf. The plaintiff child was bitten on the hand when she ventured too close to the cage. This additional requirement is another example of the pervasive influence of fault doctrine on the torts of strict liability. Proof that the animal remained under the control of the keeper is another way of saying that the keeper took

---

28 In Manitoba the common law actions of scienter and cattle trespass (section E in this chapter) have been replaced with a comprehensive regime of strict liability for damage caused by *all* animals, *Animal Liability Act*, S.M. 1998, c. 8.
29 The classification of animals is a question of law.
30 See J. Irvine, "Case Comment on *Lewis v. Oeming*" (1983) 24 C.C.L.T. 2.
31 (1976), 62 D.L.R. (3d) 385 (B.C.S.C.).

reasonable care in respect of the animal. Consequently, once control becomes an issue, the focus is drawn to the defendant keeper's conduct and the adequacy of the control exercised. The adequacy of the control depends upon the foreseeability of danger in the circumstances and the measures that the keeper took to avoid that risk of injury. The strict liability for dangerous animals is thereby adulterated by demanding a determination of the reasonable care of the keeper.

The application of the scienter action to the modern phenomenon of a wild life safari park where visitors drive among dangerous animals was clarified in *Cowles v. Balac*.[32] In that case the automatic window of the plaintiff's car was inadvertently lowered allowing a Bengal tiger to enter the vehicle and attack the occupants. The trial judge held that although the tiger was controlled within the boundaries of the park and the occupants of the vehicle were intended to be caged within their vehicle the tiger was, for the purposes of the scienter tort, out of control and liability was imposed for the serious injuries suffered.

The rule of remoteness of damage in the scienter action has not been authoritatively established. The cases seem evenly divided between a directness rule and foreseeability. The use of the foreseeability rule introduces fault concepts into the equation but it is consistent with the rule that the defendant is responsible only for injuries of a kind that the animal *mansuetae naturae* had shown a propensity to cause.

2) Defences

There are a number of defences to the scienter action. To a large extent, they mirror the defences in the rule in *Rylands v. Fletcher*. Four of the defences—default of the plaintiff, consent, trespass of the plaintiff, and illegality—address common concerns and often overlap. They withhold the advantage of strict liability from the plaintiff where he is, for one reason or another, undeserving or to some degree blameworthy.

a)   Default of the Plaintiff
There is no liability if the injury is the result of the plaintiff's fault. This mirrors the nineteenth-century common law rule in negligence where contributory negligence was a complete bar to an action. It has been applied most frequently where the plaintiff entered an animal's cage, came too close to the animal, or attempted to feed or pet the animal. Some of these situations may now be similarly resolved on the ground that there has been no loss of control of the animal by the keeper. This

---

32   [2005] O.J. No. 229 (S.C.J.), aff'd [2006] O.J. No. 4177 (C.A.).

position is out of step with current policies that do not favour the allocation of all personal injury losses to a careless plaintiff, and it seems a particularly harsh result in the scienter action, based as it is on the defendant's knowledge of the danger of his animal. Apportionment is a much fairer result but the provincial apportionment legislation was not written with strict liability torts in mind.[33]

b) Consent

Consent is established where the plaintiff has voluntarily exposed herself to the risk of injury by the animal. Placing oneself in harm's way with knowledge of the danger posed by the animal is probably sufficient. This, too, reflects the defence of voluntary assumption of risk as it was interpreted in nineteenth-century negligence law and is closely related to the defence of default of the plaintiff. Where the plaintiff is injured as a result of coming too close to an animal, cleaning the cage of a dangerous animal, or petting an animal, the defences appear to be interchangeable. In negligence law, the defence of voluntary assumption of risk has been restricted severely, and an agreement between the plaintiff and the defendant that the former accepts both the physical and the legal risk of injury must be established by the defendant. These negligence principles do not appear to have intruded into the scienter action as yet.

c) Trespass by the Plaintiff

There is no liability if the defendant was trespassing at the time of the injury. The defence, which is consistent with those of default of the plaintiff and consent, reflects the old common law rule that the occupier of premises is under no obligation to a trespasser other than not to intentionally or recklessly injure her. That minimal obligation to trespassers, however, no longer represents the law. At common law and under provincial occupier's liability legislation, the standard of care is, in all but exceptional circumstances, much higher, being generally one of common humanity or reasonable care. It is not clear how these changes will affect the scienter action.

d) Illegality (*Ex Turpi Causa Non Oritur Actio*)

At the time of the injury, the plaintiff may have been involved in some illegal or wrongful act. For example, a dog that is known to be dangerous may bite a burglar. The conventional view is that the illegality of

---

33 Nevertheless, the common law is exhibiting more flexibility in the use of apportionment in cases not controlled by legislation: see above note 21.

the plaintiff's act is a complete defence to the scienter action. There is, however, generally no need to rely exclusively on the illegality defence in the scienter action. The other defences of default of the plaintiff, consent, or trespass of the plaintiff will normally render the same result. There is also doubt about the current status of the illegality defence because the Supreme Court has largely abolished the defence in respect of personal injury actions in negligence and intentional torts.[34] It is not yet clear what effect that will have on the scienter action.

e)   Deliberate Act of a Stranger and Act of God

Neither defence is firmly established in the scienter action but its close affinity to the rule in *Rylands v. Fletcher* suggests that the defendant may not be liable if the escape of the animal was caused by the deliberate act of a stranger or an act of God. Both defences require proof that the animal escaped because of an intentional act of a stranger or a natural phenomenon that was utterly unforeseeable and so could not reasonably be guarded against. The defences, therefore, operate to exculpate a defendant who can establish a complete lack of fault. It is not, however, immediately apparent why, in a regime of strict liability, an innocent plaintiff, rather than the innocent keeper of the animal, should bear the loss from unforeseeable circumstances. This explains why there continues to be doubt about the applicability of the two defences in the scienter action.

3) Dogs

At common law a dog is classified as a harmless animal (*mansuetae naturae*). A plaintiff must, therefore, establish that his injuries were caused by a dog that had previously displayed a propensity to cause such injuries and that the defendant keeper of the dog knew of its dangerous propensity.[35] This scheme of responsibility may well have been appropriate in a rural and agricultural society but urbanization, the increase in dog ownership, and the danger that some popular breeds of dogs pose to both children and adults have led some provincial legislatures to impose a heavier responsibility on the keepers of dogs. The legislation is not uniform. It commonly relieves the plaintiff of the burden of proving that the dog has previously shown a dangerous propensity about which the keeper knows.[36] There is some uncertainty whether

---

34   *Hall v. Hebert*, [1993] 2 S.C.R. 159.
35   See, for example, *Richard v. Hoban* (1970), 3 N.B.R. (2d) 81 (S.C.A.D.).
36   See, for example, *Newfoundland Dog Act*, R.S.N. 1990, c. D-26, s. 8.

this creates a strict liability or whether it merely shifts the burden of proof to the defendant to establish the lack of scienter. Ontario has taken the more straightforward approach of imposing an express strict liability for injuries caused by dogs, subject to a reduction in damages for the contributory negligence of the plaintiff.[37]

4) The Scienter Action and Negligence

The scienter action and negligence are not mutually exclusive causes of action. A plaintiff who is unsuccessful under the scienter action may still establish that her injuries were caused by the negligence of the keeper of the animal. Some judges seem to prefer to use negligence principles, particularly in the not infrequent cases where some apportionment of the loss reflecting the plaintiff's contributory negligence appears to be appropriate.

E. CATTLE TRESPASS

1) Elements of Liability

An owner of cattle is strictly liable for damage caused by the escape of his cattle onto land in the possession of the plaintiff.[38] The term "cattle" has been defined expansively. It extends to most farm animals such as cows, sheep, goats, horses, pigs, and ducks. It does not include cats and dogs, probably because it has never been customary to fence in cats and dogs and landowners have been willing to accept the annoyance of occasional intrusion by them. The plaintiff is, normally, an occupier of neighbouring land and the most common complaint is damage to or destruction of crops. Liability does, however, extend to other forms of damage which flow from the trespass, including damage to land, chattels, other animals, personal injury to occupiers, and, possibly, personal injury to non-occupiers.

There are some exceptions to the strict liability of cattle trespass. When cattle escape onto adjoining land while they are being driven along a highway[39] or cause injury to motorists and passersby when they

---

37   Ontario *Dog Owners' Liability Act*, R.S.O. 1990, c. D.16, s. 2. The same principle is applied to all animals in Manitoba under the *Animal Liability Act*, above note 28.

38   See, for example, *Acker v. Kerr* (1973), 2 O.R. (2d) 270 (Co. Ct.).

39   *Goodwyn v. Cheveley* (1859), 4 H. & N. 631, 157 E.R. 989 (Ex.).

escape from adjoining land onto the highway,[40] liability must be established in negligence.[41]

2) Defences

Most of the defences to cattle trespass mirror those found in the scienter action.

a) Default of Plaintiff

There is no liability where the cattle escape onto the plaintiff's land because of the plaintiff's negligence. The plaintiff may, for example, forget to close a gate between her property and that of the defendant. There is, however, no duty on the part of the plaintiff to fence her land to keep cattle out. Cattle trespass is based broadly on the owner's duty to fence cattle in.

b) Consent

Consent to the intrusion of cattle is a complete defence. This is most likely to arise where the plaintiff has given a licence to the defendant to graze cattle on the plaintiff's land.

c) Deliberate Act of a Stranger and Act of God

It is doubtful that these defences are applicable to cattle trespass. The reason is that their recognition would severely restrict the scope of strict liability because the escape of fenced cattle is likely to arise from deliberate acts of strangers or from severe natural phenomena such as floods, ice storms, blizzards, and tornadoes.

3) Distress Damage Feasant

In some situations a self-help remedy is available to deal with cattle trespass. It is known as *distress damage feasant*.[42] It empowers the plaintiff to impound the straying cattle and to hold them as security for the damage that has been caused by them. The cattle must be returned when compensation is paid.

---

40   *Fleming v. Atkinson*, [1959] S.C.R. 513.
41   Negligence is available as an alternative cause of action for damage caused by escaping cattle.
42   This self-help remedy is not restricted to cattle. It may be applied to other chattels trespassing on land. The remedy is, however, designed to provide security for compensation for damage caused by the chattel. Most chattels do not cause damage to land.

4) Legislation

There is a great deal of provincial and municipal legislation and regulation relating to the control and responsibility of owners of agricultural livestock. It may modify or abrogate the ancient regimes of tort liability for cattle and must, therefore, be given careful attention.[43]

F. VICARIOUS LIABILITY

Vicarious liability is not a discrete tort. It describes the responsibility that one person may have for the torts of another because of the relationship between them. Vicarious liability is described as strict because it requires no proof of personal wrongdoing by the person subject to it. The establishment of the requisite relationship between the defendant and the tortfeasor is the key to vicarious liability. It does not displace the personal liability of the tortfeasor. It merely provides the plaintiff with an alternative defendant who is more likely to be solvent, to have liability insurance, or to be able to spread the loss in some other way. The most common relationship giving rise to vicarious liability is that of master and servant or, in more modern language, that of employer and employee. Vicarious liability also applies to the relationship of principal and agent. These two relationships may be contrasted with those of employer and independent contractor, parent and child, bailor and bailee, and trustee and beneficiary, which do not normally give rise to vicarious liability.

1) Employer and Employee (Master and Servant)

An employer is strictly liable for the torts of her employees committed within the course of their employment. The vicarious liability of an employer has been justified on two broad policy grounds: the provision of a just and practical remedy and the deterrence of future harm.[44] The imposition of liability is just because the employer has created an enterprise which creates a risk of employee wrongdoing. Those risks should be borne by the enterprise. The imposition of liability is practical because the employer normally has deeper pockets than the employee and/or is in a better position to spread the loss through liability insurance or the pricing of goods and services. Vicarious liability serves

---

43   See, for example, Alberta *Stray Animals Act*, R.S.A 2000, c. S-20; British Columbia *Livestock Act*, R.S.B.C. 1996, c. 270; Ontario *Pounds Act*, R.S.O. 1990, c. P.17.

44   *Bazley v. Curry*, [1999] 2 S.C.R. 534 at 553 & 554.

a deterrent function by transferring the loss to employers and thereby encouraging them to adopt accident prevention measures including risk management and to improve methods of selecting, training, and supervising workers.

a) Employees and Independent Contractors

The primary test to distinguish an employee from an independent contractor is the control test.[45] An employee is a person who is under the direct control and supervision of the employer who is empowered to tell the employee how, when, and where to do the work. Waiters, retail clerks, construction workers, agricultural workers, industrial workers, and bus drivers are typically employees. Independent contractors are not under the employer's control. They are hired to complete a particular task and are controlled by the terms of their contract with the employer, not by the personal instructions of the employer. Plumbers, accountants, automobile repairers, builders, and painters typically operate as independent contractors. The control test is not, however, easy to apply in a modern economy. It is, for example, difficult to accommodate professional and highly skilled employees within the control test. Their skills and expertise may be far superior to those of their employer and it is unrealistic to suggest that the employer can direct them as to how to do their work. Furthermore, those who are conventionally thought of as independent contractors may, under the terms of their contract of service, be subject to very close control by the person who hires them. The control test has therefore been supplemented by other tests. The "entrepreneur test" amplifies the factors to be taken into account in addition to control, including consideration of the ownership of tools, the chance of profit, and the risk of loss. Independent contractors conventionally own their own tools and their ultimate reward depends on the success of their business.[46] The "organization test" concentrates on the degree to which the worker is integrated into the employer's business enterprise. An employee is commonly integrated into the employer's business. An independent contractor is usually a discrete and independent business.[47] The "enterprise test" takes a more functional approach imposing vicarious liability where the employer controls the activities of the worker, where he is in a position to reduce the loss,

---

45   *Performing Right Society Ltd. v. Mitchell & Booker (Palais de Danse) Ltd.*, [1924] 1 K.B. 762.

46   *Montreal (City of) v. Montreal Locomotive Works Ltd.* (1946), [1947] 1 D.L.R. 161 (P.C.).

47   *Stevenson, Jordan & Harrison Ltd. v. MacDonald & Evans* (1952), 1 T.L.R. 101 (C.A.).

where he benefits from the activities of the worker, and where the true cost of the product or service should fairly be allocated to the enterprise providing it.[48] The Supreme Court reviewed each of these approaches in *671122 Ontario Ltd. v. Sagaz Industries Canada Inc.*[49] It concluded that there was no one conclusive test. The Court called for a close examination of the total relationship and an approach which synthesized many of the factors found in the various nominate tests. Justice Major stated:

> The central question is whether the person who has been engaged to perform the services is performing them *as a person in business on his own account* [or on account of his employer]. In making this determination, the level of control the employer has over the worker's activities will always be a factor. However, other factors to consider include whether the worker provides his or her own equipment, whether the worker hires his or her own helpers, the degree of financial risk taken by the worker, the degree of responsibility for investment and management held by the worker, and the worker's opportunity for profit in the performance of his or her tasks.[50]

Justice Major also cautioned that the relative weight given to these and other relevant factors would depend upon the facts and circumstances of each case.[51]

The approach outlined in *Sagaz* has not been restricted to commercial entities. In *K.L.B. v. British Columbia*,[52] for example, a majority of the Supreme Court concluded that foster parents are not employees of the provincial government. A majority of the Court noted that foster parents enjoy a considerable degree of independence and discretion in meeting the goals of foster care and concluded that the government did not exercise sufficient control over the daily activities of the foster parents for them to be regarded as employees. They were acting on their own account not on account of the government.

Occasionally the courts have had to address the problem of the "borrowed servant." It arises where an employer allows another business to second temporarily one of its employees. There is a factual presumption that the general employer remains vicariously liable for the torts of the borrowed servant but ultimately it is a question of who has

---

48   R. Flannigan, "Enterprise Control: The Servant-Independent Contractor Distinction" (1987) 37 U.T.L.J. 25.

49   [2001] 2 S.C.R. 983 [*Sagaz*].

50   *Ibid.* at 1005 [emphasis added].

51   See also *Belton v. Liberty Insurance Co. of Canada* (2004), 72 O.R. (3d) 81 (C.A.) at para. 11 where Juriansz J.A. articulated five principles modelled on *Sagaz*.

52   [2003] 2 S.C.R. 403.

control of the employee. Relevant factors in this determination include the nature and duration of the secondment, who has the power of dismissal, who pays the employee, and whose equipment and tools are being used to do the work. The leading case is *Mersey Docks & Harbour Board v. Coggins & Griffiths (Liverpool) Ltd.*,[53] where the defendant hired out a crane and its operator to a stevedoring company involved in unloading ships. The House of Lords adopted the control test and concluded that the operator was not an employee of the stevedoring company. The stevedoring company could direct the operator of the crane to perform certain tasks but it did not have any power over the manner in which the crane was operated or over the operator himself.[54] The problem of the borrowed servant is to some degree a product of the conventional assumption that an employee can have only one employer. An employee had, therefore, to be assigned to either the general or the temporary employer. The Supreme Court has, however, recently recognized that an employee may have more than one employer. In *Blackwater v. Plint*[55] both the federal government and a church were found to be the joint employers of an employee who abused a student in a residential school run by them. Consequently, if both the general employer and the temporary employer have some degree of control over the temporary employee it will no longer be necessary to make a choice between them. The borrowed servant issue will be restricted to the less likely scenario of one or the other having full control over the employee at the time of her wrongful act.

Remuneration is not an essential element of an employment relationship for the purposes of vicarious liability. Volunteers working for charitable organizations, public institutions, and sporting associations may be employees. Volunteers are normally under the direct supervision and control of the employer and are acting on account of the organization rather than on their own account.

---

53   [1947] A.C. 1 (H.L.).
54   In *Biffa Waste Services Ltd. v. Maschinenfabrik Ernst Hese GmbH*, [2008] EWCA Civ 1257, the English Court of Appeal indicated that the plaintiff carried a heavy burden to prove the transfer of control from the general employer to the temporary employer.
55   [2005] S.C.J. No. 58. The Court assessed contribution between the defendants at 75 percent to Canada and 25 percent to the church. This assessment was not made on the basis of comparative fault because vicarious liability does not depend upon the wrongdoing of an employer. The Court differentiated the degree of responsibility of the defendants on the degree of control and supervision exercised by them and their comparative power to have prevented the harm. See also *Viasystems (Tyneside) Ltd. v Thermal Transfer (Northern) Ltd.*, [2005] EWCA Civ 1151.

Drawing the distinction between an employee and an independent contractor will continue to challenge the Courts. The continuing re-organization of the economy exacerbates the difficulties. The long-term employment relationship epitomizing ongoing and personal control of workers is giving way to contracting out, term positions, casual work, and employment relationships where employer and worker are linked only by computer. Future innovative hiring and work relationships will present increasing challenges to the traditional concepts. It is likely, however, that the courts will mould the principles of vicarious liability to these new relationships because the strong policy factors that support them are unlikely to diminish.

b)   The Course of Employment

An employer is not liable for all the torts of its employees. There must be some connection between the wrongdoing and the employment relationship. This requirement is captured by the rule that the tort must have been committed in the course of employment. The employer is not, therefore, liable for torts committed by the employee at home or in sporting and recreational activities.

The phrase "course of employment" has not, however, been interpreted narrowly. It covers most tortious acts that are broadly incidental or related to the employment function. Any wrongful or unauthorized mode of carrying forward the employment function is normally within the course of employment. Conduct that is unrelated to, and distinct from, the employment function is not within the course of employment. An illustration can be drawn from the activities of a nurse in a hospital setting. Routine negligence ranging from medication errors, failing to report a patient's symptoms, and lapses in sterile procedures are all unauthorized and wrongful modes of performing the nursing function and the employer hospital will be vicariously liable. Conduct that is independent of the normal nursing function, such as negligence when acting as a private nurse on days off, involving a patient in a fraudulent commercial venture, and carrying out techniques that are clearly to be performed solely by physicians, are outside the course of employment.

Employers sometimes give clear instructions or prohibitions in respect of the employment function. When a tort is committed as a result of the employee failing to follow those directions, the employer may argue that the tortfeasor was not acting in the course of her employment. The courts have addressed this issue by drawing a distinction between prohibitions about how the work is to be done and prohibitions about what work is to be done. Express prohibitions relating to the manner in which the work is to be done do not insulate the employer from vicarious liability. If this was not the case, employers would defeat the doctrine of vicarious liability by issuing express prohibitions against any wrongful or negligent conduct in the workplace. Prohibi- · tions and directions that seek to define the sphere of employment or the nature of the task or work to be carried out will normally protect the employer from vicarious liability. The line between the two is not always easy to draw. In *Canadian Pacific Railway Co. v. Lockhart*,[56] the defendant employer issued an express prohibition against the use of uninsured motor vehicles when employees were on company business. The employee, a carpenter who worked at different locations throughout Toronto, used his own uninsured car to drive to job sites. His negligent driving injured the plaintiff. The Privy Council held that the instruction related to his conduct within the course of employment. It did not limit the sphere of employment or the task to be carried out. The employee was not forbidden from driving a car, merely from driving one that was uninsured. The defendant employer was liable to the plaintiff.

It is difficult to establish the employer's liability for the intentional wrongdoing of an employee. Deliberate wrongdoing is intuitively outside the employee's scope of employment. Nevertheless, employers have been held liable for both intentional and criminal acts of their employees. There are cases where bar owners have been held liable for batteries committed by their employees against patrons.[57] Vicarious liability has also been found where employees have stolen the property of customers and have committed fraudulent acts solely for their personal benefit.[58] A security company has been found liable for the arson of one of its guards, which damaged the property that he was supposed to protect.[59]

In 1999 the Supreme Court addressed the issue of intentional wrongdoing in two cases of sexual assault of children by employees of non-profit organizations. In *Bazley v. Curry*,[60] the employer ran two residential facilities for emotionally troubled children between the ages of six and twelve. The role of the employees was to act as substitute

---

56   [1942] A.C. 591 (P.C.).

57   See, for example, *Evaniuk v. 79846 Manitoba Inc.* (1990), 68 Man. R. (2d) 306 (Q.B.). This case was discussed in chapter 1.

58   See, for example, *Lloyd v. Grace, Smith & Co.*, [1912] A.C. 716 (H.L.).

59   *British Columbia Ferry Corp. v. Invicta Security Services Corp.* (1998), 167 D.L.R. (4th) 193 (B.C.C.A.). But see *Royal Bank of Canada v. Intercom Security Ltd.*, [2005] O.J. No. 4700 (S.C.J.).

60   Above note 44.

parents to the children. They were responsible for the physical and emotional well-being of the children and they were involved in such intimate activities as bathing the children and putting them to bed. One of the employees committed a series of sexual assaults against the plaintiff in the residence. Justice McLachlin, as she then was, speaking for the whole Court, held that the employer was vicariously liable for the sexual assaults that took place. The Court chose to de-emphasize the conventional terminology of "scope of employment" and "unauthorized modes of doing authorized tasks." It favoured a two-step approach. A court must first determine if the situation is controlled by unambiguous precedent, in which case it must be applied. In the absence of such authority, the decision turns on policy considerations supporting vicarious liability generally, namely, the provision of a just and practical remedy and the deterrence of future harm. As a general rule, these policy factors support the principle that the employer is liable where the employee is placed in a position that creates or enhances the risk of the wrongful act. It is not sufficient that the employer provided the *opportunity* for the wrongdoing. The employer's enterprise and the power given to the employee must have materially increased the risk of the wrongdoing. This provides a sufficiently close connection between the employment and the wrongful act to justify the employer's responsibility. The relevant factors to be taken into account in applying this test include the opportunity afforded the employee to abuse his power, the extent to which the wrongful act may have furthered the employer's aims, the extent to which the act was related to friction, confrontation, or intimacy inherent in the employer's enterprise, the extent of the power conferred on the employee in relation to the victim, and the vulnerability of potential victims to the wrongful exercise of the employee's power. In *Curry* the test was clearly satisfied. The employer authorized the employee to undertake a parental, intimate, and nurturing role that materially increased the risk of abuse.

The scope of the Court's ruling in *Curry* was brought into sharper focus by its decision in the companion case of *Jacobi v. Griffiths.*[61] In that case the employee was the program director for a Boys' and Girls' Club that provided recreational after-school activities for children who lived in the community. The employee developed a friendship with the plaintiff brother and sister, which led to a series of sexual assaults, most of which took place after-hours in the employee's home. The Court was unable to agree on the application of the test outlined in *Curry* to these facts. The majority, in a decision written by Binnie J., distinguished

---

61   [1999] 2 S.C.R. 570 [*Griffiths*].

Curry and refused to impose vicarious liability on the employer. It emphasized the importance of a strong connection between the enterprise risk and the sexual assaults. The nature of the employment must have significantly increased the risk of sexual assaults. In its view, the employer provided access to the plaintiffs and the opportunity to commit the sexual assaults but there was not a sufficiently strong connection between the kind of risk created and the nature of assault to warrant vicarious liability. The role of the program director was to establish a rapport with the children, to be their friend, and to provide adult mentoring. It was not to develop a parental, intimate, or nurturing relationship similar to that in *Curry*. The majority was also influenced by a concern that a finding of vicarious liability would threaten to impose an undue burden on all non-profit organizations whose activities involve some interaction between adult employees and children and would be inconsistent with current judicial opinion on the limits of vicarious liability for sexual abuse. In her dissenting opinion, McLachlin J. held that the facts of the case fell comfortably within the scope of the principle in *Curry*. She emphasized the role of the club in providing care and protection for vulnerable children, the power and influence engendered by the position held by the employee, and his ability to build a trusting and intimate relationship from that position. In her view, the employer had sufficiently increased the risk of sexual assault to warrant a finding of vicarious liability.

The Supreme Court has considered the strong connection[62] test in a number of subsequent cases. Vicarious liability has been imposed on a Roman Catholic Episcopal Corporation for the sexual abuse of child parishioners by one of its priests[63] and on both the federal government and the United Church of Canada for the sexual abuse of children by an administrator and a dormitory supervisor of a residential school for Aboriginal children.[64] In contrast liability was not imposed on the employer of a worker hired as a baker, boat driver, and odd-jobs person who sexually assaulted a child in a residential school for Aboriginal children albeit that he had a residence on the school grounds,[65] nor on a school board for sexual abuse of a third grade day school student by

---

62   A number of other adjectives are used in the Supreme Court cases including close, sufficient and strong and direct connection but strong is the predominant descriptor and most reliably captures the essence of the test.

63   *John Doe v. Bennett*, [2004] 1 S.C.R. 436.

64   *H.L. v. Canada (A.G.)*, [2005] 1 S.C.R. 401 (administrator) and *Blackwater v. Plint*, [2005] S.C.J. No. 58 (dormitory supervisor).

65   *E.B. v. Order of the Oblates of Mary Immaculate in the Province of British Columbia*, [2005] S.C.J. No. 61.

the school janitor.[66] These cases indicate that much depends upon the nature of the power and authority attendant on the employee's position and the degree to which they are enabled to use that authority to insinuate themselves into the intimate lives of their victims.[67]

While the majority of cases deal with the sexual misconduct of employees the approach in *Curry* is equally applicable to other kinds of wrongdoing including fraudulent acts by employees of financial/investment businesses which cause economic loss to customers and clients. Courts have commonly imposed vicarious liability on these businesses either on the basis of the strong connection test or on the basis of a principal's liability for the acts of its agent where those torts are committed within the scope of the agent's authority.[68]

2) Principal and Agent

The relationship of principal and agent is one where the principal empowers the agent to act on her behalf in such a way as to affect her legal relationship with others. The agent is most commonly authorized to make contracts and transfer property on behalf of the principal. The general rule is that the principal is vicariously liable for the torts of her agent committed within the scope of her actual or apparent authority. Most of the cases involve fraudulent misrepresentations in respect of contracts entered into by agents but there are numerous cases dealing with a wide range of torts for which the principal has been held liable. It should be pointed out that many agents are also employees. In those circumstances, plaintiffs often rely on the vicarious liability of the employer since the phrase "course of employment" is normally broader than "scope of authority." When an agent is an independent contractor, reliance must be placed on the agency rules of vicarious liability.

---

66   *E.D.G. v. Hammer*, [2003] 2 S.C.R. 459. The Supreme Court in *Griffiths*, above note 61, approved the decision of the British Columbia Supreme Court in *Hammer* rejecting the vicarious liability of the school board. That point was not, therefore, argued before the Supreme Court in *Hammer*. The vicarious liability of an employer for sexual abuse of a student by a teacher remains unclear. See *H.(S.G.) v. Gorsline*, [2004] A.J. No. 593 (C.A.). (no vicarious liability) and *Doe v. Avalon East School Board*, [2004] N.J. No. 426 (S.C.T.D.) (vicarious liability).

67   Compare *T.W. v. Seo*, [2005] O.J. No. 2467 (C.A.) where an employer was found vicariously liable for sexual assault on a patient by an ultrasound technician, and *P.S. v. R.H.M.*, [2006] B.C.J. No. 504 (C.A.) where a landlord was not found to be vicariously liable for the sexual assault of a tenant by an employee repairman.

68   For example, *Thiessen v. Mutual Life Assurance Co.*, [2001] B.C.J. No. 1849 (S.C.), var'd [2002] B.C.J. No. 2041 (C.A.), leave to appeal to S.C.C. dismissed, [2002] S.C.C.A. No. 454.

Agency also forms the basis of liability in partnership law. The partnership firm and all other partners are liable for the tortious acts of partners acting in the ordinary course of the firm's business or within the scope of their authority.

3) Statutory Vicarious Liability

The rules of vicarious liability have been modified legislatively in respect of the owners of motor vehicles. The purpose is to extend the common law vicarious liability of the owner of the motor vehicle for the torts of employees who are driving the vehicle in the course of employment to members of the owner's family, and in some provinces, to any persons who are driving the motor vehicle with the owner's consent. The Ontario legislation,[69] for example, makes the owner liable for all damage caused by the negligent operation of his motor vehicle on a highway unless the motor vehicle was in the possession of some person without the owner's consent. Although the wording of the provincial legislation is not uniform, the general policy is clear. It is to allocate accident losses caused by authorized drivers to the owner of the motor vehicle who has ultimate control over the use of the vehicle and has liability insurance.

4) Independent Contractors

An independent contractor is normally a discrete business entity that is independent from the employer who hires it. It is able to take its own risk management and accident prevention measures and arrange for appropriate liability insurance. A person who employs an independent contractor to perform services or undertake tasks on his behalf is not, therefore, ordinarily liable for the torts committed by the contractor carrying out the work.

The employer does, however, have some personal duties in respect of independent contractors, including a duty of care in selecting and hiring the independent contractor and a duty of care to supervise the contractor to the extent that is reasonable, having regard to the technicality of the work.[70] The employer may in exceptional circumstances

---

69   *Highway Traffic Act*, R.S.O. 1990, c. H.8, s. 192(2).

70   In *K.L.B. v. British Columbia*, above note 52, for example, the Supreme Court recognized the direct liability of government for a negligent failure to assess potential foster parents and to monitor carefully the home environment when a placement was made.

be under a duty to check that the independent contractor has liability insurance to protect third parties.[71]

a)   Non-delegable Duties

There are some truly exceptional circumstances where the employer is subject to statutory and common law duties of care that are non-delegable. In those circumstances, the work may be delegated to an independent contractor but the employer remains fully responsible for the failure of the contractor to take care in its performance. A non-delegable duty resting on the employer is not merely a duty to take care. It is a duty to ensure that care is taken. The concept of a non-delegable duty is a useful device that allows a court to advance the policies supporting vicarious liability to independent contractors when the circumstances suggest that it is appropriate to do so.

There are a number of discrete and diverse categories of non-delegable duties. They include strict statutory duties to do a positive act, and duties of care both on employers to maintain a safe work environment, and on bailees in respect of chattels entrusted to them. An employer is also liable where an independent contractor's wrongful conduct has created a public or private nuisance, has failed to maintain the lateral support of adjacent land, and has caused harm in the performance of extra-hazardous activities including fire. Courts have been content to list these duties without attempting to identify any underlying principle or policy that justifies the imposition of strict liability on the employers of independent contractors in these situations.

The leading case on non-delegable duties is *Lewis (Guardian ad litem of) v. British Columbia*.[72] In that case, the defendant province hired an independent contractor to remove protruding rocks from a cliff-face above a highway. The work was carried out negligently by the contractor, and a rock that ought to have been removed fell onto the highway, killing a motorist. The province argued that since the work was delegated to an independent contractor it was not liable. The Court disagreed holding that the province was under a non-delegable duty of care and was liable because care had not been taken. Justice Cory focused on the legislative provisions imposing various obligations on the defendant and concluded that the legislation indicated that the duty

---

71   This intriguing issue has arisen in England in cases involving personal injury caused by under-insured independent contractors. See *Gwilliam v. West Hertfordshire Hospitals N.H.S. Trust*, [2002] EWCA Civ 1041 and *Naylor v. Payling*, [2004] EWCA Civ 560.

72   [1997] 3 S.C.R. 1145 [*Lewis*]. See also *Mochinski v. Trendline Industries Ltd.*, [1997] 3 S.C.R. 1176.

to carry out maintenance on the highway was non-delegable. He found additional support for this conclusion in a number of policy factors, including the vulnerability of the driving public arising from the fact that it is in no position to know if the work of a contractor has been done satisfactorily, the reasonable expectation of the public that the province is ultimately responsible for highway safety, and the practical difficulties in determining which contractor was responsible for the work in question. Justice McLachlin (as she then was) wrote a concurring opinion in which she began to explore the idea that the disparate categories of non-delegable duties are instances of some broader principle. She observed that the existence of a non-delegable duty depended on the nature of the relationship between the parties, the nature and extent of the duty, and the propriety of holding the defendant liable for the wrongful conduct of the independent contractor. This appeared to herald a more principled approach to the categories of non-delegable duty around such concepts as the degree of risk in the work to be performed by the contractor or the employer's assumption of responsibility for the conduct of the contractor. A rationalization of non-delegable duties around some general principle might, moreover, lead to a more robust role for the concept.

Lewis encouraged further litigation and in subsequent Supreme Court cases dealing with the abuse of children, it was argued that non-delegable duties of care were owed by provincial governments to children in foster homes,[73] by school boards to students,[74] and by the federal government to residential school students[75] to protect them from institutional sexual or physical abuse. These arguments were not met with success. Lewis was read narrowly as a case that turned on the applicable statutory language at issue. The Court, therefore, examined the applicable statutes and concluded that they did not impose non-delegable duties to ensure the safety of children. The "child abuse" cases suggest that there is little likelihood of the development of a broader range of non-delegable duties or that there will be any change in conventional doctrine such as the rule in *Yepremian v. Scarborough General Hospital*.[76] In that case it was held that a hospital does not owe a non-delegable duty of care to its patients and is, therefore, not liable for the negligence

---

73   *K.L.B. v. British Columbia*, above note 52, and *M.B. v. British Columbia*, [2003] 2 S.C.R. 477.

74   *E.D.G. v. Hammer* above note 66.

75   *Blackwater v. Plint*, above note 64.

76   (1980), 28 O.R. (2d) 494 (C.A.).

of physicians who have privileges to practice there. They are independent contractors and the hospital is not liable for their negligence.[77]

The responsibility of an employer in respect of a non-delegable duty is confined to wrongful acts in the performance of the task or work that the independent contractor was hired to do. The employer is not liable for collateral or casual acts of negligence.[78] This is another elusive concept. It is designed to impose a narrower responsibility than the phrase "course of employment" used in respect of employees. Nevertheless, the negligent act must be quite discrete and severable from the assigned task before the employer escapes responsibility.

5) Liability of the Employee or the Agent

The rules of vicarious liability in respect of employers and principals do not prevent an action being brought against the employee or agent personally.[79] The rules of vicarious liability are designed to secure the responsibility of the employer and the principal, not to exonerate the tortfeasor. Moreover, the doctrine of indemnification allows an employer to seek reimbursement from an employee on whose behalf it has been found vicariously liable.[80] A similar result may arise from the fact that employers and employees and principals and agents are joint tortfeasors. This allows both to be sued and permits the employer or principal to seek contribution from the employee or agent tortfeasor under the applicable apportionment legislation. Indemnification and contribution claims against employees are likely to be subrogated claims brought in the name of the employer by the employer's insurer to recoup the amount paid out under the policy of insurance. This process of reallocating the loss from the employer's insurer to the employee has been undermined and questioned by the Ontario Court of Appeal in *Douglas v. Kinger (Litigation guardian of)*.[81] The case dealt with a subrogated claim brought by the employer's insurer against a thirteen-year-old employee whose negligence caused substantial fire damage to his employer's property. The case was not technically one of

---

77   Residents and interns are, however, likely to be classified as employees, see, for example, *Guay v. Wong*, [2008] A.J. No. 1552 (Q.B.).

78   J.G. Fleming, *The Law of Torts*, 9th ed. (Sydney: LBC Information Services, 1998) at 437.

79   As a general rule this is so even if the employee is carrying out services in performance of a contract between his employer and the plaintiff; see *London Drugs Ltd. v. Kuehne & Nagel International Ltd.*, [1992] 3 S.C.R. 299.

80   *Lister v. Romford Ice & Cold Storage Co.*, [1957] A.C. 555 (H.L.).

81   2008 ONCA 452.

vicarious liability because the employee had not caused harm to a third party and it was resolved in favour of the plaintiff on the grounds that in the particular circumstances of the case he owed no duty of care to his employer. Nevertheless, the Court criticized the indemnification rule and indicated that its survival was due more to the common practice of insurers in refraining from exercising it than to any sound policy foundation.

There continues to be some doubt about the personal liability of an employee for a negligent misrepresentation causing economic loss made in the course of performing a contract of service between his employer and the plaintiff. In *Edgeworth Construction Ltd. v. N.D. Lea & Associates Ltd.*,[82] the Supreme Court held that only the employer of engineers who negligently prepared plans and specification for the design and construction of a highway was liable to the plaintiff contractor who relied on them to its detriment. Other cases have distinguished *Edgeworth* and have imposed liability on the employee provided that the requisite elements for liability for negligent misrepresentation, including reasonable and foreseeable reliance, can be established against the employee.[83]

6) Direct Liability of Employers and Principals

Vicarious liability does not exclude the direct and personal liability of an employer or principal for the breach of a personal duty owed directly to the plaintiff. Liability may arise, for example, where an employer has authorized or instigated an employee to commit a tortious act, or has failed to train or supervise an employee, or has requested that an employee carry out tasks that are beyond his abilities and expertise.[84]

---

82   [1993] 3 S.C.R. 206. See also *Williams v. Natural Life Health Foods Ltd.*, [1998] 2 All E.R. 577, where the House of Lords held that a director of a contracting company could not be liable for a negligent misrepresentation unless he assumed personal liability for the statement and the requisite reliance was established.

83   *Strata Plan No. VR 1720 v. Bart Developments Ltd.*, [1999] 53 B.C.J. No, 382 (S.C.), appeal dismissed [2000] B.C.J. No. 363 (C.A.). See also *NBD Bank, Canada v. Dofasco Inc.*, [1999] O.J. No. 4749 (C.A.) and *Sophie's Gold and Gift Shop Ltd. v. Lloyd's Underwriters, Lloyd's, London*, [2001] B.C.J. No. 1730 (S.C.).

84   In *Griffiths*, above note 61, for example, the Supreme Court sent the case back to trial to determine if there was any fault-based liability on the employer for the sexual assaults of the employee on the plaintiffs. See also *White v. Canada (Attorney General)*, [2002] B.C.J. No. 1821 (S.C.), appeal dismissed [2003] B.C.J. No. 442 (C.A.).

There is also the concept of a *negligent hiring*, which is more developed in the United States than it is in Canada. It arises where the employer of an employee, agent, or independent contractor fails to take appropriate care, such as seeking references or doing background checks in the hiring process, and employs a person who is unfit for the position or task. The advantage of framing the action in this way is that it may avoid some of the restrictions of vicarious liability. Imagine, for example, that an employee commits a sexual assault on a customer or client which is held to be outside the scope of employment. If the employment created an opportunity for the assault, liability may be based on the failure to do background checks that would have disclosed past sexual misconduct of a similar nature. A personal duty of care in the selection of personnel is particularly warranted where the employee will be in a position of trust dealing with the finances of the employer's customers, or in a position of authority and power over vulnerable persons such as children.

FURTHER READINGS

The Rule in *Rylands v. Fletcher*

EHRENZWEIG, A.A., "Negligence without Fault" (1966) 54 Cal. L. Rev. 1422

FLETCHER, G.P., "Fairness and Utility in Tort Theory" (1972) 85 Harv. L. Rev. 537

JONES, W.K., "Strict Liability for Hazardous Enterprise" (1992) 92 Colum. L. Rev. 1705

KEETON, R.E., "Conditional Fault in the Law of Torts" (1959) 72 Harv. L. Rev. 401

MURPHY, J., "The Merits of *Rylands v. Fletcher*" (2004) 24 Oxford J. Legal Stud. 643

NEYERS, J., "A Theory of Vicarious Liability" (2005) 43 Alta. L.R. 287

NOLAN, D., "The Distinctiveness of *Rylands v. Fletcher*" (2005) 121 Law Q. Rev. 421

SIMPSON, A.W.B., "Legal Liability for Bursting Reservoirs: The Historical Context of *Rylands v. Fletcher*" (1984) 13 J. Legal Stud. 209

Liability for Animals

KING JR., J.H., "A Goals-Oriented Approach to Strict Tort Liability for Abnormally Dangerous Activities" (1996) 48 Baylor L. Rev. 341

MANITOBA LAW REFORM COMMISSION, *Report on Tort Liability for Animals* (Winnipeg: Manitoba Law Reform Commission, 1992)

Vicarious Liability

FLANNIGAN, R., "Enterprise Control: The Servant-Independent Contractor Distinction" (1987) 37 U.T.L.J. 25

MURPHY, J., "Juridical Foundations of Common Law Non-Delegable Duties" in J.W. Neyers, E. Chamberlain, & S.G.A. Pitel, eds., *Emerging Issues In Tort Law* (Oxford: Hart Publishing, 2007) 369

STEVENS, R., "Non-Delegable Duties and Vicarious Liability" in J.W. Neyers, E. Chamberlain, & S.G.A. Pitel, eds., *Emerging Issues in Tort Law* (Oxford: Hart Publishing 2007) 331

CHAPTER 6

NUISANCE

A. INTRODUCTION

There are two torts of nuisance: private nuisance and public nuisance. Other than their name, they do not have a great deal in common. Private nuisance protects people from interference with the use, enjoyment, and comfort of their land. Public nuisance primarily protects the public in the exercise of rights that are common to all citizens, such as the right of passage on public highways and navigable rivers. A common trait of each tort is the elusive nature of the term "nuisance" and the difficulty in defining the limits of its application.

B. PRIVATE NUISANCE

A person's interest in the integrity, security, enjoyment, and use of land is protected by the torts of trespass to land, the rule in *Rylands v. Fletcher*, negligence, and private nuisance. Trespass to land is available in respect of any direct and physical intrusion onto land that is in the possession of the plaintiff. It is actionable without proof of damage. The rule in *Rylands v. Fletcher*[1] provides a remedy for damage caused by the escape of something likely to do mischief from a neighbour's non-natural use

---

1 (1868), L.R. 3 H.L. 330, aff'g (*sub nom. Fletcher v. Rylands*) (1866), L.R. 1 Ex. 265 (Ex. Ch.).

of land. Negligence is available in respect of all physical damage to land caused by a failure to take care. Private nuisance is applicable to indirect physical or intangible interference with property and all direct interference that is not physical.[2] Private nuisance is most frequently used to deal with noise, odour, fumes, dust, and smoke that emanate from the defendant's land and interfere with the plaintiff's use, enjoyment, and comfort of land. Private nuisance is not actionable unless the interference is unreasonable and the plaintiff has suffered some damage.

The primary function of private nuisance is to draw an appropriate balance between the defendant's interest in using land as he pleases and the plaintiff's interest in the use and enjoyment of land. Although some fault concepts have crept into the private nuisance action, it is still, in the main, a tort of strict liability. Liability does not depend upon the nature of the defendant's conduct or on any proof of intention or negligence. It depends, primarily, upon the nature and extent of the interference caused to the plaintiff.

Not every interference with the comfort and enjoyment of property is a nuisance. In both urban and rural areas there must be a good deal of give and take between neighbours and a degree of tolerance of the reasonable and beneficial activities of others. The limits of tolerance are reached when the defendant's activity causes an unreasonable interference with the plaintiff's use, enjoyment, and comfort of land. This discretionary concept allows courts to tailor their decisions sensitively to the particular circumstances of the case. The advantage of a high degree of fact sensitivity and flexibility is, however, offset by a related degree of uncertainty and unpredictability, leading some commentators to despair of finding a workable and predictable guide to decision making.[3] One useful starting point is to distinguish between conduct that causes *physical and material* damage to the plaintiff's land and conduct that interferes with the plaintiff's *enjoyment and comfort* of land.

1) Physical Damage to Land

The courts take a strict approach to the infliction of physical damage to the plaintiff's property. The infliction of physical damage is, in

---

2   In some situations private nuisance may provide a remedy for a series of direct physical intrusions, such as the continual intrusion of golf balls from a neighbouring golf course. See *Carley v. Willow Park Golf Course Ltd.*, [2002] A.J. No. 1174 (Q.B.).

3   William Prosser described the law of nuisance as an "impenetrable jungle": see W.P. Keeton, ed., *Prosser and Keeton on the Law of Torts*, 5th ed. (St. Paul, MN: West, 1984) at 616.

almost all circumstances, regarded as an unreasonable interference with the plaintiff's use and enjoyment of land. Consequently, damage to the paintwork of buildings and chattels on the land caused by the discharge of pollutants, structural damage to premises caused by vibrations, crop damage caused by the drift of herbicide sprayed on the defendant's property, water damage to the basement of a house caused by a blocked drain on the defendant's land, damage caused by the escape of fire from the defendant's land, and damage to trees and shrubs caused by polluting fumes from the defendant's factory are all actionable. There is no need for continual interference with the property. An isolated incident causing physical damage may be sufficient. In *Tock v. St. John's (City) Metropolitan Area Board*,[4] for example, the Supreme Court imposed liability in private nuisance when a blockage of the defendant's sewer drains and a heavy rainfall combined to flood the basement of the plaintiff's house.

The proof of physical damage is not conclusive of the issue of unreasonable interference. If the damage is trivial it may not be beyond the bounds of reasonable tolerance. There is also no liability where physical damage has arisen solely as a result of the abnormal sensitivity of the plaintiff's land use. This proposition was established in *Robinson v. Kilvert*.[5] The defendant's business of manufacturing paper boxes in the cellar of a building required a hot, dry environment. Although the heat was never more than eighty degrees Fahrenheit, it damaged a quantity of high-quality paper used in the plaintiff's business on the ground floor. The Court held that there was no liability in private nuisance. The heat would not have affected the ordinary use of land. The plaintiff's damage arose solely from the abnormal delicacy and sensitivity of his business. The ruling in this case may reflect an early reluctance to hold a defendant liable for unforeseeable damage. This may explain why *Robinson* has not been followed in subsequent cases where the defendant knew of the plaintiff's sensitive operation and with malice or spite deliberately caused damage. Such a situation arose in *Hollywood Silver Fox Farm v. Emmett*.[6] The defendant real estate developer concluded that a sign indicating the proximity of the plaintiff's silver fox farm to his residential real estate development was detrimental to its commercial success. The defendant asked the plaintiff to take it down. When the plaintiff refused to remove it, the defendant tried to persuade him to change his mind by discharging shotguns

---

4   [1989] 2 S.C.R. 1181 [*Tock*].
5   (1889), 41 Ch. D. 88 (C.A.) [*Robinson*].
6   [1936] 2 K.B. 468.

near the plaintiff's farm. The defendant knew that the loud noise would disrupt the breeding season of the plaintiff's extremely nervous and temperamental animals. The defendant argued that in normal circumstances the discharge of firearms is not an unreasonable interference with the enjoyment of land and the plaintiff's loss arose solely from the hypersensitivity of silver foxes in the breeding season. Nevertheless, the defendant was found liable in private nuisance. The defendant's knowledge of the plaintiff's sensitive land use, combined with the malicious nature of the defendant's conduct, made the interference unreasonable. One Canadian court has pushed this exception further and imposed liability in the absence of malice. The defendant was held liable for failing to take reasonable care by suspending the blasting of stumps on his land while the plaintiff's fur-bearing animals were breeding. The defendant, at no inconvenience to himself, could have suspended the blasting for a month and avoided causing damage to the plaintiff.[7]

2) Interference with Enjoyment and Comfort of Land

A landholder is required to be much more tolerant of occasional interference in her comfort and enjoyment of land. The courts take a fairly robust approach to the extent of give and take that is required, particularly in an urban environment. All citizens must tolerate a certain level of noise, odour, and pollution. In order to prove a private nuisance, the plaintiff must show an interference that in all the circumstances of the case is unreasonable to the ordinary person. No protection is given to fastidious or delicate sensibilities.[8] The circumstances relevant to deciding if the interference is unreasonable include the character of the neighbourhood, the intensity of the interference, the duration of the interference, the time of day and the day of the week of the interference, the zoning designation of the area, the utility of the defendant's activity, the nature of the defendant's conduct, and the sensitivity of the plaintiff. None of these factors is conclusive but they do deserve some further comment.

a) The Character of the Neighbourhood
Nuisance is a relative concept dependent to a large extent on the kind of neighbourhood where the activity takes place. There is a famous distinction drawn in an old English case between Belgrave Square, a quiet residential area of London, and the industrial area of Bermondsey. The

---

7   *MacGibbon v. Robinson*, [1953] 2 D.L.R. 689 (B.C.C.A.).
8   *Walter v. Selfe* (1851), 4 De G. & Sm. 315, 64 E.R. 849 at 852.

Court observed that "what would be a nuisance in Belgrave Square would not necessarily be so in Bermondsey."[9] Every city has its Belgrave Squares and its Bermondseys and the noise and smells that are tolerable in an industrial and commercial area may be excessive in a residential neighbourhood. The standard of tolerance may also be different in a rural area compared with that of an urban environment. The smells of some agricultural operations that may be reasonable in a rural environment may be intolerable in an urban residential area, and a reasonable level of noise in the city may be too much for a rural area. Those who live in a remote cottage area may have a reasonable expectation of even greater peace and quiet.

b)   The Intensity of the Interference

There is no liability for the occasional loud noise, the transient bad smell, the periodic barking of a dog, or the smoke from a barbecue. The interference must be of sufficient intensity to be intolerable to the ordinary Canadian citizen. The kinds of smells that amount to nuisances have, for example, been described as "nauseating," "sickening," "very offensive," and "absolutely horrible."[10] More scientific evidence can now be brought in respect of noise. The decibels may be counted and public health standards may be used as a guide to tolerable limits. Those limits are not, however, conclusive of the issue. In *Sutherland v. Canada (Attorney General)*[11] the trial judge held that aircraft noise arising from the operation of a new runway at Vancouver International Airport amounted to a private nuisance. The court held that consideration must be given not only to the scientific noise metrics evidence but also to the subjective evidence of the noise and its effect on the plaintiffs who lived below the flight path.[12]

c)   The Duration of the Interference

Reasonable people are tolerant of quite a significant interference with their enjoyment of land if the interference is temporary and short-lived. The occasional loud party next door, the noise and dust from a construction site, and the repair of residential roads are normally in the realm of the tolerable. When the interference is persistent and long-term, the tolerable may become intolerable. Many of the cases where

9   *Sturges v. Bridgman* (1879), 11 Ch.D. 852 at 865.
10   See, for example, *Appleby v. Erie Tobacco Co.* (1910), 22 O.L.R. 533 (C.A.).
11   [2001] B.C.J. No. 1450 (S.C.), rev'd on other grounds [2002] B.C.J. No. 1479 (C.A.).
12   See also *Suzuki v. Munroe*, [2009] B.C.J. No. 2019 (S.C.) where considerable reliance was placed on the "decibel count" of a neighbour's air-conditioning unit.

private nuisance has been established deal with long-lasting incompatible land uses.

d) The Time of Day and the Day of the Week

The time of day when the interference takes place is particularly relevant to the acceptable level of noise. In a residential area it is reasonable to expect less noise at night than during the day. Most people work during the day and sleep at night.[13] Noise in the early hours of the morning leading to broken sleep patterns is a particular concern.[14] Those who work nights are out of step with conventional patterns and they cannot demand the same degree of quiet for their sleep. The day of the week has also been regarded as a relevant factor. Courts have taken judicial notice of the fact that many people like to sleep late on weekends and early morning noise on those days, even the ringing of church bells,[15] may be regarded as a nuisance.

e) Zoning Designation

The twentieth century witnessed a massive growth in the governmental control of land use by means of municipal zoning, building regulations, environmental legislation, and other land use and public health legislation and regulations. This has diminished the importance of private nuisance in adjusting and resolving land-use conflict. Canadian courts have not, however, recognized compliance with zoning bylaws or other rules or regulations controlling land use as a defence to an action in private nuisance. It is a factor in determining both the character of the neighbourhood and the standard of tolerable interference but it is not conclusive of the issue. This is a wise policy. Compliance with zoning regulations does not guarantee that the defendant's use of land is not an unreasonable interference with that of a neighbour.

---

13   See, for example, *Walker v. Pioneer Construction Co. (1967) Ltd.* (1975), 8 O.R. (2d) 35 (H.C.J.), where the noise from the defendant's asphalt plant was held to be a nuisance at night but not during the day.

14   See *Popoff v. Krafczyk*, [1990] B.C.J. No. 1935 (S.C.) where the squawking of the defendant's macaws daily between 5:00 a.m. and 6:00 a.m. was held to be a nuisance.

15   See the Australian decision in *Haddon v. Lynch*, [1911] V.L.R. 5 (S.C.), aff'd [1911] V.L.R. 230 (F.C.), where an injunction was awarded to restrain the ringing of church bells until after 9 a.m. on Sundays. See also *Laing v. St. Thomas Dragway*, [2005] O.J. No. 254 (S.C.J.) where an injunction was issued to prohibit motor vehicle racing before 1 p.m. on Sundays.

f)   The Utility of the Defendant's Conduct

A defendant may not defend an action in private nuisance on the basis that the defendant's use of land is generally beneficial to the public. Nevertheless, the utility of the activity is likely to have some bearing on the standards of tolerance of reasonable persons and, where liability is imposed, it may have an influence on the ultimate remedy. Trains, planes, and automobiles, industrial and commercial activities, emergency vehicles, the construction and repair of infrastructure, and agricultural operations are all productive of some level of interference with the enjoyment of land. They are also indispensable activities in a modern society and courts are acutely aware of the need to avoid decisions that are disruptive of, or incompatible with, essential operations and beneficial societal activities. Courts have, for example, been particularly cautious in respect of agricultural operations such as hog farming and other animal husbandry that carry an unavoidable odour and industries upon which many persons depend for their livelihood. Conversely, a stricter view may be taken towards purely recreational and sporting activities with less vital social benefit. A court may, for example, be less favourably inclined to rock concerts, loud music in residential areas, all-night revelry, and the continual intrusion of golf balls from a neighbouring golf course.

g)   The Nature of the Defendant's Conduct

The primary focus in a private nuisance action is the impact of the defendant's activities on the plaintiff's enjoyment of property. Nevertheless, the nature of the defendant's conduct is not ignored. Decision making in private nuisance is influenced to some degree by the comparative assessment of the reasonableness of the conduct of the parties. The courts are, for example, less likely to protect the land use of a defendant who acts unreasonably and is motivated by a desire to cause annoyance, discomfort, and inconvenience to the plaintiff than one that is conducted prudently for a laudable purpose. *Christie v. Davey*[16] is an illustrative case. The plaintiff, a music teacher, lived in a semi-detached house next to the defendant. The defendant objected to the sound of the music coming from the plaintiff's premises. He protested by hammering and banging trays on the common wall between the two residences. This was done maliciously to annoy the plaintiff and interfere with his vocation. An injunction was issued to prohibit it. The judge observed that he might have taken a different view of the matter if both litigants were entirely innocent.

---

16   [1893] 1 Ch. 316.

h)   The Sensitivity of the Plaintiff

There is no liability if the plaintiff is abnormally sensitive to the defendant's land use. The standard is that of the reasonable and ordinary resident in the geographic area and the rule in *Robinson v. Kilvert*[17] applies equally to interference with the enjoyment and comfort of land. No protection is given to abnormally light sleepers or those who suffer from allergies. There is also no protection available for abnormally sensitive commercial activities such as a special illuminated advertising sign that was adversely affected by flood lighting of the defendant's property.[18] Once a nuisance is established, however, the defendant must take the plaintiff as he finds him and will probably be liable for the full extent of his loss.

3) Non-intrusive Nuisances

The most common form of private nuisance is one that emanates from the defendant's land, crosses the plaintiff's boundary, and intrudes onto the plaintiff's land, causing material damage or a loss of enjoyment or comfort to the plaintiff. Nuisance by noise, smoke, water, fumes, chemicals, and odour take this form. Not all nuisances are of this kind. An unreasonable interference with land may occur without any intrusion onto the plaintiff's land. The usual principles of private nuisance are applicable in these cases, but courts are more reluctant to intervene when there is no tangible or intangible invasion of the plaintiff's property.

There are few circumstances where physical damage to property can be inflicted without some intrusion. The best example is the decision in *Pugliese v. Canada (National Capital Commission)*.[19] In that case, the defendant's construction of a sewer collector lowered the water table under the plaintiffs' land. This caused the plaintiffs' land to subside, which, in turn, resulted in damage to their houses. The defendant was held liable in private nuisance even though the damage was caused by the removal of water rather than the invasion of some substance onto the property. This case is consistent with the strong protection provided by private nuisance in respect of physical damage.

There is much greater reluctance to impose liability for non-intrusive conduct that interferes with the enjoyment and comfort of land. These cases pose a much greater threat to the defendant's freedom of land use. There is, for example, generally no liability for blocking the

---

17   Above note 5.

18   *Noyes v. Huron & Erie Mortgage Corp.*, [1932] O.R. 426 (H.C.J.).

19   (1977), 17 O.R. (2d) 129 (C.A.), var'd [1979] 2 S.C.R. 104.

plaintiff's view or for preventing the entry of sunlight onto the plaintiff's land. There is also no liability for blocking or changing the circulation of air to the plaintiff's property.[20] No protection is given to aesthetics. A neighbour's property may be extremely ugly either because of general disrepair and untidiness or because of the architecture, the vivid colour of the paintwork, or the assortment of statues, garden gnomes, and fla- mingoes in the yard. The courts have wisely avoided becoming art crit- ics and the arbiters of good taste. Nuisance has also seldom been used to provide protection against non-intrusive breaches of privacy. Liabil- ity has been imposed for large numbers of *intrusive* harassing telephone calls,[21] but there was no liability for spying on the plaintiff's horse- racing track in order to provide radio broadcasts of the races,[22] and an initiative in England to use private nuisance to protect a person from stalking near her home proved to be unsuccessful.[23] A court has also refused to give a remedy to plaintiffs who were fearful of their safety and their property values when an isolation hospital was constructed in their neighbourhood.[24] A similar response is likely to those who object to a properly run group home for the mentally ill, juvenile offenders, or prisoners in a pre-release program.

Some non-intrusive interferences with the comfort and enjoyment of land are actionable. The use of a residential house for prostitution, which gave rise to an increase in both vehicular traffic and the number of undesirable persons in the area, has been held to be a nuisance even though there was no intrusive interference with the plaintiff's prop- erty.[25] A non-intrusive nuisance may also be found in respect of "spite fences" where a defendant, for no reason other than to cause distress and annoyance to a neighbour, builds a high fence to block sunlight, a view, or the circulation of air. The issue has not arisen in Canada, pos- sibly because of municipal regulations controlling the height of fences, but in the United States courts have been willing to treat such non- intrusive conduct as a nuisance. The spiteful nature of the landowner's conduct was influential in finding a non-intrusive nuisance in *White v.*

20 Any significant future reliance on the sun or the wind to generate energy may lead to a reconsideration of the absence of a right to sunlight and airflow.

21 *Motherwell v. Motherwell* (1976), 1 A.R. 47 (S.C.A.D.).

22 *Victoria Park Racing and Recreation Grounds Co. v. Taylor* (1937), 58 C.L.R. 479 (H.C.A.).

23 *Hunter v. Canary Wharf Ltd.*, [1997] A.C. 655 (H.L.) [*Canary*], disapproving *Khorasandjian v. Bush*, [1993] Q.B. 727 (C.A.).

24 *Shuttleworth v. Vancouver General Hospital* (1927), 38 B.C.R. 300 (S.C.).

25 *Thompson-Schwab v. Costaki*, [1956] 1 W.L.R. 335 (C.A.).

Leblanc.[26] The landowner deliberately positioned a commercial high-way trailer on his property to block the sea view from his neighbour's property in order to prevent the neighbour from selling his house at market value. Although a view is generally not protected the trailer could have been conveniently and easily been parked elsewhere on the property. A similar issue arose in the context of a public nuisance in *Manitoba (A.G.) v. Campbell.*[27] In that case an injunction was issued to force a farmer to dismantle a seventy-four-foot steel tower on his own property that was in line with the runway of an adjoining airport. The tower served no purpose other than to maliciously disrupt night land-ings at the airport. The tower was erected on the day before the effect-ive date of a planning order that was designed to control the height of adjacent structures so that flight paths were not interfered with.

Liability was also imposed in *Nor-Video Services Ltd. v. Ontario Hydro,*[28] where the operations of the defendant's electrical power in-stallations disrupted the reception and transmission of television sig-nals of the plaintiff cable television company. The plaintiff's case was strengthened by the defendant's earlier assurances that there would be no interference with the signals, by its failure to take reasonable steps that would have avoided the interference, and by its failure to honour a promise to attend promptly to any interference that might arise. The case provides a nice contrast to the House of Lords decision in *Hunter v. Canary Wharf Ltd.*[29] It arose out of the construction of Canary Tower, an 830-foot high-rise, in London. The building interfered with the tele-vision reception of householders in the area for a period of three years before the problem was resolved. They sued for damages, claiming that the enjoyment of their property had been impaired. The Court con-cluded that the building was not a private nuisance. The defendant had a right to build on his land in accordance with land-planning regula-tions, and the blocking of television signals was analogous with the blocking of light, air, or view. It was felt that freedom of land use would be unduly hampered by recognizing the plaintiffs' claim.

It is perhaps no coincidence that in the four cases of non-intru-sive nuisance that have been referred to — *Thompson, White, Campbell,* and *Nor-Video* — the defendant's conduct, in addition to causing an unreasonable interference with the enjoyment of plaintiffs' land, was either illegal, malicious, or negligent. Furthermore, in *Canary* there

---

26   [2004] N.B.J. No. 384 (Q.B.).

27   (1983), 24 Man. R. (2d) 70 (Q.B.), var'd [1985] 4 W.W.R. 334 (Man. C.A.) [*Camp-bell*].

28   (1978), 19 O.R. (2d) 107 (H.C.J.).

29   Above note 23.

was judicial speculation that the result might have been different if the construction of the Tower was in contravention of land-use control legislation. It may be reasonable to conclude that the motive and the nature of the conduct of the defendant have special relevance to the issue of non-intrusive interferences with the enjoyment and comfortable use of land.[30]

4) Malice

The role of malice on the part of the defendant has already been referred to. It is a factor to be taken into account in deciding if there is a nuisance and it may tip the balance in favour of the plaintiff where the competing land uses are, apart from that factor, evenly balanced. Some reference must, however, be made in this context to the famous case of *Bradford Corporation v. Pickles*.[31] In that case, the defendant extracted subterranean water that would otherwise have flowed to the use and advantage of the plaintiff municipality. The defendant's conduct was held to be malicious. It was motivated by a desire to force the plaintiff to buy his land at an extravagant sum. Nevertheless, the House of Lords held that the defendant had an absolute legal right to the water and the presence of a bad motive could not make the exercise of that legal right unlawful. It declined to recognize any general principle that rights are given for beneficial and appropriate purposes and that the abuse of rights for antisocial purposes is actionable. It is not easy to integrate *Bradford* into the modern law of private nuisance. One explanation is that *Bradford* dealt solely with the defendant's proprietary right to extract water in circumstances where the plaintiff had no competing right to the continuing flow of underground water from above. Since the plaintiff had no protected interest in the water, there was no need to qualify or balance the defendant's exercise of his right of extraction with any right of the plaintiff. Nuisance law does, however, recognize rights of neighbours in respect of most other kinds of interference such as by noise and smells, and in those situations malice becomes relevant in balancing the competing rights. Another factor that may have been of some influence was that *Bradford* was an early case of a non-intrusive nuisance.

---

30 See also *Ontario (A.G.) v. Dieleman* (1994), 20 O.R. (3d) 229 (Gen. Div.), additional reasons (1995), 22 O.R. (3d) 785 (Gen. Div.).

31 [1895] A.C. 587 (H.L.).

5) Coming to the Nuisance

In the landmark case of *Sturges v. Bridgman*,[32] the noise and vibrations of the defendant's commercial operation caused no undue interference with his neighbours until the plaintiff physician built consulting rooms near the boundary of their two properties. The plaintiff argued that there was an unreasonable interference with his use of land. The defendant claimed that his land use was first in time, that it had caused no problem for many years, and that the plaintiff was the author of his own misfortune by coming to the nuisance. The Court refused to give priority to the defendant's first land use and issued an injunction. The principle taken from the decision, that it is no defence that the plaintiff came to the nuisance, is sometimes questioned and sometimes creates unfairness.[33] Nevertheless, it is probably good policy. Society and land use are always in a state of change and flux and it is reasonable to demand some degree of readjustment and accommodation of existing land use to a changing neighbourhood. It does not seem wise to protect pockets of ancient land use that have become incompatible with a changing neighbourhood or modern land-use patterns.

6) Standing

Careful consideration must be given to two questions: Who may be sued in private nuisance and who may sue in private nuisance? Centuries of judicial attention have not, unfortunately, achieved the degree of certainty that one might have anticipated. This is in large part due to the modern trend in nuisance law to extend both the range of persons who may be liable for a private nuisance and the range of plaintiffs eligible to sue in private nuisance. Consequently, the rules about who may be sued and who may sue are in some flux.

a) Defendants
The creator of a nuisance is always liable for it. In most nuisance cases the creator of the nuisance is the possessor of land on which the nuisance arises. Liability may, however, also be imposed on a person who creates a nuisance on the land of another or on public property.[34]

---

32   Above note 9.

33   See *Miller v. Jackson*, [1977] Q.B. 966 (C.A.), where Denning M.R. expressed unhappiness with the rule and refused to apply it where a cricket ground was transformed into a nuisance when residential houses were built too close to the ground.

34   See *Susan Heyes Inc. v. Vancouver (City)*, [2009] B.C.J. No. 1046 (S.C.) where a contractor created a private nuisance on a city street.

A possessor of land may, in addition to nuisances arising from her own positive conduct, be responsible for nuisances on her land created by a stranger, a predecessor in title, or an act of nature. But liability for the failure to abate or remove such a nuisance depends upon a finding of negligence. The intrusion of fault into this situation is consistent with the normal judicial caution exhibited in situations of nonfeasance. The courts are sensitive to the fact that a nuisance created by a trespasser or an act of nature is thrust upon the defendant and strict liability may impose too heavy a burden on her. The leading case is *Sedleigh-Denfield v. O'Callaghan*.[35] In that case, a nuisance was created on the defendant's land by a third party. The House of Lords held that, where a possessor knows or ought to know of the nuisance, he must take reasonable steps to abate it. In *Sedleigh-Denfield* the defendant had known of the unauthorized drainage work on his land for three years but had failed to take an elementary step to prevent the flooding that damaged the plaintiff.

The principle in *Sedleigh-Denfield* was extended to nuisances arising naturally on the land of the defendant in *Goldman v. Hargrave*.[36] Prior to that case, landholders enjoyed an immunity from liability when the natural condition of their land damaged their neighbours. This was central to the decision in *Rylands v. Fletcher*, where the House of Lords distinguished the escape of a non-natural collection of water in a reservoir, for which there was a strict liability, from the natural run-off of water for which there was no liability at all. In *Goldman*, a gum tree standing on the defendant's property in Western Australia burst into flames when it was struck by lightning. The defendant felled the tree and left it to burn itself out. Before the fire died out, the weather conditions changed and an increase in both the temperature and the wind revived the fire. It spread to the plaintiffs' properties where it caused damage. The defendant sought to distinguish *Sedleigh-Denfield* on the ground that it dealt with a man-made hazard. The Privy Council, however, held that there was no difference in principle between a natural hazard and an artificial hazard. If the defendant knows or ought to know of a natural or man-made hazard not of his making arising on his land, he is under a duty to take reasonable care to remove it or abate it. The Court also held that, since the duty was one of affirmative action in the face of a hazard not of the defendant's making, a modified objective standard of care was appropriate. The defendant is required to take only those steps that are reasonable in the light of the defend-

---

35   [1940] A.C. 880 (H.L.) [*Sedleigh-Denfield*].
36   [1967] 1 A.C. 645 (P.C.).

ant's physical and material resources and personal circumstances. The defendant was held liable for failing to extinguish the fire.[37]

b) Plaintiffs

The conventional view is that private nuisance is a tort to land and is actionable only by those who enjoy proprietary rights or an interest in land. Those with proprietary rights sufficient to sue in private nuisance include an owner in possession, a tenant, an owner out of possession if the nuisance causes permanent damage that would affect his reversionary interest, and, possibly, a licensee with exclusive possession of the land. *Gleneagles Concerned Parents Committee Society v. British Columbia Ferry Corporation*[38] is illustrative. In that case, a non-profit society of concerned parents of school children applied for an injunction to prevent the extension of the defendant's ferry terminal until an environmental assessment was completed. It was argued that the extension would create a nuisance in respect of the school. The court held that the society had no standing to sue in private nuisance as it had no propriety interest in the school property.

The restriction of the action in private nuisance to those with proprietary rights creates few problems in respect of actual property damage but it does cause difficulty in respect of both interference with the comfort and enjoyment of the land and personal injuries that may be suffered by permanent residents such as family members who do not have proprietary rights. Some Canadian courts have broadened the conventional rule in order to provide a remedy for family members and other permanent occupants without proprietary rights. In *Motherwell v. Motherwell*[39] an injunction was issued to protect the spouse of the owner of the family home who was harassed by constant telephone calls, and in *MacNeill v. Devon Lumber Co.*[40] the New Brunswick Court of Appeal upheld an award of damages to the children of the joint owners of the family home in respect of the annoyance and discomfort of dust from the defendant's mill. These cases extend private nuisance

---

37 The principle in *Sedleigh-Denfield* has on occasion been extended unduly and applied in circumstances where the defendant created the nuisance. See L.N. Klar, *Tort Law*, 4th ed. (Toronto: Carswell, 2008) at 732–34. For a discussion of the responsibilities of landlord and tenant in respect of a nuisance arising from the disrepair of the leased premises and for a nuisance created by the tenant, see A.M. Linden & B. Feldthusen, *Canadian Tort Law*, 8th ed. (Toronto: Butterworths, 2006) at 82–83.

38 [2001] B.C.J. No. 668 (S.C.).

39 Above note 21.

40 (1987), 82 N.B.R. (2d) 319 (S.C.A.D.). See also *Saelman v. Hill*, [2004] O.J. No. 2122 (S.C.J.).

beyond its traditional focus on property rights to a more general and personal protection of the enjoyment of life of the permanent occupiers of homes and apartments.

This approach was, however, rejected by the House of Lords in *Hunter v. Canary Wharf Ltd.*[41] The action for the disruption of television signals was brought not only by owners and tenants of residential dwellings but also by their spouses, partners, children, and other relatives who shared the home but had no rights to the property. The Court emphasized that in its view private nuisance is a tort to land rather than to the person and held that, even if the disruption of television signals was a nuisance, only those with proprietary rights could sue. While some courts have followed *Hunter*[42] there are indications that the Canadian approach will withstand the English critique. In the course of its decision in *St. Lawrence Cement Inc. v. Barrette*,[43] the Supreme Court commented on the similarities between Quebec law and the common law action in private nuisance and expressed the opinion that liability should not be restricted to those with proprietary rights.

7) Defences

The four main defences to an action in private nuisance are statutory authorization, statutory immunity, consent, and prescription.

a) Statutory Authority

The defence of statutory authority was established in the nineteenth century to protect legislatively approved public and private enterprises and activities that were in the public interest and for the public good. The authorizing legislation itself rarely spoke clearly on the issue of tortious liability arising from the activity, but judicial policy favoured protecting fledgling industries, municipalities, public utilities, and other undertakings approved of by the legislature. In the twentieth century, judicial attitudes changed and there is now less enthusiasm for policies that shelter legislatively approved activities from tortious liability. There is much greater support for the view that the loss caused by a beneficial and authorized enterprise should be allocated to the enterprise so that the loss may ultimately be spread among the community that benefits from it, rather than to private persons or businesses who are often less able to spread the loss.

---

41 Above note 23.

42 See *Sutherland v. Canada (Attorney General)*, [2001] B.C.J. No. 1450 (S.C.), rev'd on other grounds [2002] B.C.J. No. 1479 (C.A.).

43 [2008] 3 S.C.R. 392 at para. 83.

The Supreme Court re-examined the scope of the defence in two cases, *Tock v. St. John's (City) Metropolitan Area Board*[44] and *Ryan v. Victoria (City of)*.[45] *Tock* contains an extensive but inconclusive discussion of the defence. *Ryan* rather tersely brought some certainty to the issue. In *Tock* the basement of the plaintiff's house was flooded when the defendant municipality's storm sewer became blocked in the course of a heavy rainfall. The storm sewer was constructed and maintained under statutory authority. The Court agreed that the defence of statutory authority must be construed narrowly but there was no agreement on the appropriate principles to achieve this. Justice Wilson sought to largely negate the defence by confining it to statutory authority that gave no discretion to the defendant as to the time, location, or performance of the authorized activity. Since almost all modern legislation is discretionary in respect of the performance of the activity, the defence would be largely inapplicable. If the defence was *prima facie* applicable, the defendant carried the further burden of proving that the nuisance was inevitable in spite of every reasonable step being taken to avoid it. Justice LaForest called for an open consideration of who should bear the loss. All the surrounding circumstances, including the utility of the authorized conduct, the degree of interference with private rights, and the availability and cost of preventive measures must be considered, but, as a general rule, it was reasonable to allocate material damage resulting from isolated and infrequent occurrences to defendants, and ordinary and diffuse disturbances to reasonable comfort to plaintiffs. Justice Sopinka held to the more conventional view that the defence applied to all authorized activities but the defence was not made out unless it was established that the nuisance was an inevitable consequence of the activity. Each of these approaches led to the conclusion that the defence was inapplicable in *Tock* but no judge was able to command a majority of the Court in support of his or her judgment.

A period of uncertainty followed *Tock*, which was finally resolved by the unanimous decision of the Court in *Ryan*. *Ryan* was a case of *public* nuisance, dealing with railway tracks running down the centre of a city street. The tracks were dangerous because the flangeway gap running along the inside edge of the tracks was wide enough to trap the tires of motorcycles, thereby creating a risk of accidents of the kind suffered by the plaintiff. The defendant railway company argued that it was not liable because the railway track was statutorily authorized and it had complied with all rules and regulations in respect of it. The

44   Above note 4.
45   [1999] 1 S.C.R. 201 [*Ryan*].

Court held that the tracks were a public nuisance and, on the facts, the statutory authorization was no defence. It summarily repudiated the approaches of Wilson and LaForest JJ. and endorsed the judgment of Sopinka J. In its view, to establish the defence of statutory authority, the defendant must prove that it was practically impossible to avoid creating a nuisance. It is not sufficient to show that reasonable care has been taken. The nuisance must be shown to be an inevitable and unavoidable result of the authorized activity. Since the flangeway gap could have been narrowed to prevent the accident, the defence failed.[46]

b)   Statutory Immunity

It is ironic that, at a time when the defence of statutory authority is receiving a narrow interpretation, provincial legislatures have selected certain beneficial land uses for complete immunity from the tort of private nuisance. This legislation has been prompted largely by the conflict between agricultural operations in rural areas and expanding urban communities, new residential developments in rural areas, hobby farms, and cottage developments. The first Act of this kind was the *Nuisance Act*[47] of Manitoba. The Act was passed in response to a successful action against a hog producer in respect of the odour produced by his operation. The plaintiff, who owned a nearby residential property, secured an injunction and an award of damages.[48] The government of the day disapproved of the decision and sought to prohibit the private nuisance action from being used in this manner by passage of the *Nuisance Act*.[49] It protects all businesses (including urban operations) from liability in nuisance for odour unless the plaintiff can prove a breach of provincial land-use control statutes and regulations. This legislation was followed ten years later by the *Farm Practices Protection Act*,[50] which singles out agricultural operations for a broader protection

---

46   For a case where the defence was established, see *Sutherland v. Canada (Attorney General)*, [2002] B.C.J. No. 1479 (C.A.) [*Sutherland*].

47   R.S.M. 1987, c. N120.

48   *Lisoway v. Springfield Hog Ranch Ltd.*, [1975] M.J. No. 188 (Q.B.).

49   It is interesting that legislation was deemed necessary in light of the fact that Canadian judges have, on the whole, been sympathetic to farming interests. There is even some authority suggesting that proof that the nuisance arose from a normal act of animal husbandry is a complete defence: see J. Irvine, "Case Comment: *Metson v. R.W. DeWolfe Ltd.*; The Changing Face of Nuisance, and *Rylands v. Fletcher*" (1980) 14 C.C.L.T. 225.

50   S.M. 1992, c. 41. All provinces have similar legislation: for example, Ontario *Farming and Food Production Act*, 1998, S.O. 1998, c. 1, s. 2; and British Columbia *Farm Practices Protection (Right to Farm) Act*, R.S.B.C. 1996, c. 131, s. 2. For a useful discussion of the *Farming and Food Production Act*, see *Pyke v. Tri Glo Enterprises Ltd.*

than that provided by the *Nuisance Act*. An agricultural operation that complies with normal farm practices and legislative land-use control laws cannot be held liable in nuisance for any odour, dust, dirt, smoke, or any similar disturbance. The Act also established a Farm Practices Protection Board with dispute settlement and enforcement functions in respect of abnormal or illegal land use. The action for private nuisance is restricted to situations where the agricultural activity is not protected by the legislation and the bureaucratic settlement procedures have been unsuccessful in resolving the dispute. It may be noted that the Act does not extend to nuisances such as fire, flood, or the drift of agricultural chemicals that cause physical damage to property.[51]

c) Consent

The defence of consent arises infrequently in cases of nuisance. It is sometimes referred to as the defence of *consent and acquiescence*, but if the latter term suggests that tacit approval by standing by in the face of a nuisance is sufficient to establish the defence, it would be misleading. It appears that there must be strong evidence of approval or active encouragement of the defendant's nuisance-generating activity. *Kacsmarik v. Demenlenaere*[52] is illustrative. In that case, the defendant asked the plaintiff to close the windows of his greenhouse while the defendant was spraying herbicide in the adjacent fields. The plaintiff agreed to do so but inexplicably opened the windows before the danger to his greenhouse broccoli seedlings had passed. The court held that the plaintiff had consented to the activity and had indicated to the defendant that he was willing to protect himself.

d) Prescription

A privilege to commit a nuisance may in some provinces be acquired by prescription. The defendant must establish that the nuisance (not merely the activity) has continued, uninterrupted, for twenty years, that the plaintiff has known of the nuisance for that period of time, and that the plaintiff has not sued on it or taken any other steps to prevent it.[53]

(2001), 55 O.R. (3d) 257 (C.A.). See also J. Kalmakoff, "The Right to Farm: A Survey of Farm Practices Protection Legislation in Canada" (1999) 62 Sask. L.R. 226.

51   Express immunities from liability in nuisance may be found in other statutes such as those negating liability for the malfunction of municipal sewage systems. See, for example, the *Local Government Act*, R.S.B.C. 1996, c. 323, s. 288.

52   [2002] P.E.I.J. No. 15 (S.C.).

53   These privileges are known as easements. The technicalities involved in their acquisition are best left to texts on real property.

e)   Contributory Negligence

Contributory negligence does not feature in most private nuisance cases. The plaintiff is, normally, not in a position to move away or avoid the nuisance and the courts have not required plaintiffs to take steps such as building protective structures, keeping windows closed, or taking other measures to mitigate the consequences of the defendant's action. Furthermore, it is no defence that the plaintiff came to the nuisance. In the rare instances where the plaintiff is found guilty of contributory negligence, there may be some apportionment of damages if the language of the applicable contributory negligence legislation permits it.

8) Remedies

The remedy of choice in private nuisance for a continuing interference with the plaintiff's land is an injunction. Damages are also available and are most suitable where there has been a single damaging event such as a fire or damage by water. There is also a limited self-help remedy permitting the plaintiff to abate a nuisance.

a) Injunction

An injunction is the usual remedy in private nuisance actions. The continuing nature of most nuisances and the contemplation of prospective damage makes damages an inadequate remedy. The courts have a broad discretion not only in deciding if an injunction should be issued but also in deciding its terms. Consideration is given to all the surrounding circumstances, including the social utility of the defendant's activities, the conduct of the parties, the nature of the continuing loss, and the overall public interest. An injunction may be *prohibitory*, requiring the complete cessation of the defendant's activity, or it may be *mandatory*, requiring positive steps to be taken to adjust the defendant's activity so as to abate the nuisance. The implementation of an injunction may be postponed to allow the defendant to make changes to his activities. *Interlocutory* injunctions may be issued after the filing of a statement of claim and before a trial on the merits, when intervention is needed quickly because of the damage that is being caused to the plaintiff. The plaintiff is normally required to show that his claim raises a serious question to be tried, that he will suffer irreparable harm in the absence of injunctive relief, and that the balance of convenience between the litigants favours the plaintiff. A *quia timet* injunction may be given to prevent *anticipated* damage so long as that damage is imminent and the damage, if suffered, would be substantial and irreparable.

b) Damages

In some cases a plaintiff may not seek injunctive relief. If, for example, the nuisance has terminated, an award of damages for past losses will provide a complete remedy. In other cases, damages may be awarded in addition to, or in lieu of, an injunction. Damages in addition to an injunction are awarded for past losses. Damages in lieu of an injunction are given for both past and *future* losses. Courts are reluctant to give damages in lieu of an injunction because it amounts to a compulsory purchase by the defendant of a privilege to continue the wrongful interference with the plaintiff's interests. Generally speaking, they are available only where the harm is small, where adequate damages are easily estimated, and where an injunction would create intolerable hardship for the defendant.

Damages are available for a broad range of losses, including physical damage to property, interference with enjoyment and amenities of the land, damage to chattels on the land, economic loss, and, probably, diminution in the value of land and personal injuries. The gradual acceptance of the view that nuisance is not solely a tort to land supports its extension to personal injuries. Liability is restricted to the reasonably foreseeable consequences of the nuisance. This is another example of the gradual intrusion of negligence principles into the ancient tort of private nuisance.

c) Abatement

Abatement is a self-help remedy that has fallen into some judicial disfavour. There is less need to exercise self-help today. The machinery of the modern civil justice system provides sufficient and timely remedies to deal with most eventualities. Caution is also dictated by the risk that self-help may prompt a violent response from the creator of the nuisance.

It is most appropriate where a trivial nuisance may be abated by an act outside the wrongdoer's land. It has long been recognized, for example, that a neighbour may trim back branches or roots of trees that intrude across the boundary.[54] The abator is not required to give notice to the landowner before action is taken *outside* the wrongdoer's land. There is also a privilege to enter the wrongdoer's property. Self-help in this manner is most appropriate where the nuisance can be quickly and easily abated without undue disruption of the wrongdoer's activities. Unblocking a drain to prevent imminent flooding, extinguishing an

---

54 The right to cut back roots and branches arises even though no damage sufficient to support an action for damages has been suffered. The reason for this anomaly is probably that the intrusion is closely analogous to a trespass to land, though not technically actionable as such because the entry is indirect.

uncontrolled fire, or preventing the spread of sewage onto the plaintiff's land may fall into this category. Notice of entry is normally required unless there is an emergency where the life or property of the abator is threatened. The abatement must always be reasonable and there must be no unnecessary damage caused to the land.

C. PUBLIC NUISANCE

Public nuisance is not primarily a tort concept. A public nuisance is a crime for which public remedies including injunctive relief at the behest of the attorney general are available. A public nuisance may, however, also have tortious consequences if it causes special damage to an individual person. In those situations, a private action for damages or an injunction may be available to the injured person. The central issues in public nuisance are its definition and the various public and private remedies that are available. Both have generated difficulty.

1) The Definition of a Public Nuisance

The common law definition of a public nuisance has found its way into the *Criminal Code*[55] as a common nuisance. Section 180(2) of the *Criminal Code* states:

> [E]very one commits a common nuisance who does an unlawful act or fails to discharge a legal duty and thereby
> (a) endangers the lives, safety, health, property or comfort of the public; or
> (b) obstructs the public in the exercise or enjoyment of any right that is common to all the subjects of Her Majesty in Canada.

This definition captures the common law meaning of public nuisance and illustrates the extreme generality of the concept. It covers a wide range of eclectic activities and it is very difficult to give the concept greater clarity and precision than is found in section 180(2). Some further guidance is, however, provided by the recognition that public nuisances generally fall into two broad categories.[56]

The first category includes interferences with the rights and interests of the public which all persons share in common. The classic examples of public nuisances in this category include obstructing a

---

55   R.S.C. 1985, c. C-46.
56   R.A. Buckley, *The Law of Nuisance*, 2d ed. (London: Butterworths, 1996) at 67.

public highway with a stalled motor vehicle, barriers, protest marches, excavations or heavy smoke, blocking access to a public park, blocking a navigable waterway, destroying a provincial forest, polluting a river or stream, polluting the air with smoke and fumes, obstructing a public sidewalk with temporary structures, demonstrators or line-ups of people, selling food that is unfit for human consumption, and running a bawdy house. These are all instances of either an interference with public rights of way or an interference with the public's interest in property, safety, health, or comfort. It is not, however, every trivial interference with the public's rights that amounts to a public nuisance. A degree of tolerance and a spirit of give and take is as necessary in this context as it is in private nuisance. Consideration must be given to all the surrounding circumstances, including the utility of the defendant's conduct, the nature and extent of the interference with the public's rights and interests, and the burden of avoiding or abating the nuisance. A temporary obstruction of a street to deliver goods, the closure of a highway to carry out repairs, and the partial obstruction of a sidewalk with construction scaffolding are unlikely to amount to a public nuisance. In this category of public nuisance there is less emphasis on the number of persons directly affected. An obstruction of the highway or the pollution of a river may directly affect only a few people but, nonetheless, the right of the public to passage on that highway and the right of the public to fish in that river have been infringed and the courts are not hesitant to find a public nuisance.

The second category of public nuisance arises from a widespread interference with the use and enjoyment of private land. In this situation, a public nuisance arises where the defendant's activities have created a multiplicity of *private* nuisances that may be remedied either by each landowner as a private nuisance or, cumulatively, by public remedies as a public nuisance.[57] The primary problem in this category of cases is to decide, in the particular circumstances, how many private nuisances make a public nuisance. One approach suggests that a combination of private nuisances become a public nuisance when they affect a "class" of persons or a "neighbourhood."[58] There is no precision in these terms but the cases seem to suggest that a combination of somewhere around ten private nuisances is normally sufficient. Another view suggests that there is a public nuisance where the interference with private property is so widespread in its range and so indiscriminate in its effect that it

---

57   See *Sutherland*, above note 46 at para. 27.
58   *Attorney General v. P.Y.A. Quarries Ltd.*, [1957] 2 Q.B. 169 at 184 (C.A.), Romer L.J.

may reasonably be characterized as a public responsibility[59] that should be remedied by governmental rather than private action.

In most cases the two approaches will lead to the same result. A public nuisance has, for example, been recognized where a quarry caused dust, noise, and vibrations to many landowners over a widespread area[60] and where the operation of a training centre for ultralight aircraft caused high noise levels and disturbed residents in a rural area.[61] In *Ontario A.G. v. Orange Productions Ltd.*,[62] an injunction was issued where a planned rock concert, in the light of past experience, was likely to be plagued by excessive numbers of people, noise, dust, lack of sanitation, and rowdy conduct, all of which would interfere with the enjoyment of the neighbouring landowners. In each of these three cases, a substantial number of persons were affected and governmental intervention was warranted to stop the public nuisance.

These two categories may not exhaustively describe all public nuisances but they do identify the situations that arise most frequently and they also indicate that the term covers both situations that bear little relationship to the tort of private nuisance and situations where the public nuisance arises from a multiplicity of private nuisances.

2) Remedies

Both public and private remedies are available for a public nuisance. Public remedies include a criminal prosecution under section 180 of the *Criminal Code*, an action by the attorney general for an injunction and/or damages, and a relator action where the attorney general empowers a private citizen to seek an injunction in the name of the attorney general. The most common public remedy, and normally the remedy of choice for those affected by a continuing public nuisance, is an injunction secured by the attorney general.

Private tort remedies arise in two ways. Where the public nuisance arises from a combination of discrete private nuisances, the individual occupiers may personally bring an action for an injunction or damages relying on the tort of private nuisance. All other kinds of public nuisances give rise to an independent action for damages (or an injunction) for members of the public who suffer *special or particular damage* as distinct from the inconvenience and loss suffered by members of the public generally. The restriction of private tort actions to those who

---

59   *Ibid.* at 191, Denning L.J.
60   *Ibid.*
61   *Manitoba (A.G.) v. Adventure Flight Centres Ltd.* (1983), 22 Man. R. (2d) 142 (Q.B.).
62   [1971] 3 O.R. 585 (H.C.J.).

have suffered special damage acts as a control device to prevent a flood of private actions brought by every member of the public who has suffered similar and often trivial losses. Consequently, a member of the public who has been inconvenienced by an obstruction of the highway has no claim, but a person who suffered personal injury from the obstruction does have a claim for her special damage. In this context, personal injury, damage to property, depreciation in the value of land, loss of business, and economic loss qualify as special and particular damage so long as the loss is foreseeable and is not suffered by the public at large.

The conventional view in Canada is that greater damage of the same kind as that suffered by the public generally does not qualify as special and particular damage. A distinction has been drawn between harm that is merely of a greater *degree* than that suffered by the general public and harm that is of a different kind from that suffered by the general public. This rule was applied in *Hickey v. Electricity Reduction Co. of Canada.*[63] In that case, the plaintiffs were commercial fishermen whose livelihood was adversely affected by the pollution of Placentia Bay, Newfoundland. The pollution arose from the discharge of toxic chemicals into the bay by the defendant. The plaintiffs' claim for damages failed on the grounds that the defendant's actions had interfered with the rights of all citizens to fish in the bay. The plaintiffs' loss, while greater in degree, was essentially of the same kind. A similar approach was taken in *Stein v. Gonzales*[64] where the plaintiffs, owners of a hotel and an apartment block, sued the defendant prostitutes who congregated on the street and caused a loss of business. The Court refused to award damages. It was held that many businesses in the area had suffered business losses as a result of the defendants' activities and the plaintiffs' losses were not of a different kind.

There is some support for a more liberal approach that would allow an action for damages for those who have suffered more serious loss than that caused to the general public. This would appear to address sufficiently the indeterminacy issue and would enhance the power of the tort of public nuisance to address pollution of the environment. Indeed, the time may be ripe to dispense with the terminology of kind and degree completely and allow a claim for damages for actual physical or economic loss.

There is some uncertainty about the relationship between the private action for damages in public nuisance and negligence. Negligence

---

63   (1970), 2 Nfld. & P.E.I.R. 246 (Nfld. S.C.).
64   (1984), 14 D.L.R. (4th) 263 (B.C.S.C.).

is not an essential element of public nuisance but it has intruded noticeably in two situations involving personal injuries. The first deals with the complete or partial collapse of structures and buildings above or adjacent to a public highway or sidewalk. The requirement that negligence be proved has been explained on a number of grounds including the affinity of these cases with other highway accident cases, the analogy with the *Sedleigh-Denfield v. O'Callaghan*[65] principle which requires proof of negligence in respect of a private nuisance that does not arise from the defendant's positive act, and, more broadly, that negligence is required in cases where any damage is an inadvertent result of conduct that is not in itself a public nuisance.[66] The second situation involves collisions with parked or stalled motor vehicles blocking or creating an obstacle on the highway. There has been a trend to resolve these personal injury cases on the basis of negligence. This trend did not, however, receive any support from the Supreme Court decision in *Ryan v. Victoria (City)*.[67] In that case, as we have seen, the plaintiff was injured when the wheel of his motorcycle became wedged in the flangeway gap at the inner edge of the defendant railway's tracks, which ran down the centre of a city street. The Court held that the unduly wide flangeway gap was an unreasonable interference with the public's right of access and constituted a public nuisance. The defendant was liable for the plaintiff's special damage.

3) Public Nuisance and Environmental Protection

Public nuisance has not played a major role in environmental protection. There are a number of reasons for this. Attorneys general have not aggressively pursued public nuisance remedies and private persons, who have no standing to exercise remedies available to government, rarely suffer the kind of special damage necessary to support a private tort action. There are, however, some indications that the current concern for the environment may lead to a revitalized role for public nuisance.

Some support for that view may be drawn from the Supreme Court decision in *British Columbia v. Canadian Forest Products*.[68] It dealt with the negligent destruction by fire of a vast tract of provincial forest including environmentally sensitive areas. The government sought to

---

65 Above note 35.
66 Klar, above note 37 at 720–21.
67 Above note 45.
68 [2004] 2 S.C.R. 74. See A. Lintner, "Trees Left Standing: A Case Comment on *British Columbia v. Canadian Forest Products Ltd.* (2003) 49 C.E.L.R. (N.S.) 34.

recover damages for its loss. There had been some doubt about the attorney general's right to sue for damages for a public nuisance but the Court confirmed that the government may recover damages for environmental harm in both negligence and public nuisance.[69] Damages may be awarded for commercial losses, restorative costs and for the loss of "use," "passive use," and "intrinsic value"[70] suffered by the public prior to complete restoration of the environment.

This case may foreshadow other adjustments to enhance the power of public nuisance to secure compensation for environmental degradation and to deter conduct which is harmful to the environment. First, the standing rule might be altered to permit, at the discretion of the court, public interest organizations or persons acting on behalf of the public to bring an action for damages for environmental harm where the attorney general has declined to do so.[71] Second, the private tort action for special damage might be made available to those members of the public who have suffered harm which is of the same kind as that suffered by the community but of a greater degree. Finally, where there are a large number of private nuisances creating a public nuisance greater resort may be had to *class* actions in private nuisance thereby avoiding the need to prove special damage. In *Smith v. Inco Ltd.*,[72] for example, a class action was brought by 7000 owners of residential properties in the City of Port Colborne to recover the reduction in value of their properties caused by the publicity given to findings that their properties were contaminated by nickel deposits migrating from the defendant's refinery. Liability was imposed in both private nuisance and under the rule in *Rylands v. Fletcher.*

---

69   *Ibid.* at 114–15, paras. 81 & 82.

70   The terms use, passive use, and intrinsic value are well understood in environmental law. They describe different aspects of the benefits derived from the environment including the direct use made of it by the public, the general and indirect enjoyment of the environment by persons, and the inherent value of the ecosystem beyond its use to humans. There are several methodologies for assessing damages for each of these heads of damage. See, M. Olszynski, "The Assessment of Environmental Damages Following the Supreme Court's Decision in *Canfor*" (2005) 15 J. Envtl. L. & Prac. 23.

71   Some provinces have eased the standing rule in public nuisance permitting private citizens to sue in limited circumstances, see *Environmental Bill of Rights, 1993*, S.O. 1993, c. 28, s. 103.

72   [2010] O.J. No. 2864 (S.C.J.). See also, *Roberts v. Canadian Pacific Railway Co.*, [2006] B.C.J. No. 2905 (S.C.) where a class action in nuisance brought by landowners for the emission of coal dust from trains was not certified on the grounds that the class was too wide and there were insufficient common issues.

FURTHER READINGS

BILSON, B., *The Canadian Law of Nuisance* (Toronto: Butterworths, 1991)

BUCKLEY, R.A., *The Law of Nuisance*, 2d ed. (London: Butterworths, 1996)

FAIETA, M.D., "Civil Liability for Environmental Torts" (2004) Annual Review of Civil Litigation 21

HOGG, P.W., "Torts — Nuisance — Defence of Statutory Authority: *Tock v. St. John's Metropolitan Area Board*" (1990) Can. Bar Rev. 589

McLAREN, J.P.S., "Nuisance in Canada" in A.M. Linden, ed., *Studies in Canadian Tort Law* (Toronto: Butterworths, 1968) 320

PROSSER, W.L., "Private Action for Public Nuisance" (1966) 52 Va. L. Rev. 997

PUN, G.S. & M.I. HALL, *The Law of Nuisance in Canada* (Markham, ON: LexisNexis, 2010).

TROMANS, S., "Nuisance — Prevention or Payment?" (1982) 41 Cambridge L.J. 87

CHAPTER 7

DEFAMATION

A. INTRODUCTION

The interest of persons in protecting their good reputations was recognized early in the development of the common law and it continues to receive strong protection under the tort of defamation. This is in marked contrast to the response of tort law to most other intangible personal interests. Tort law has been very slow, for example, in developing remedies for breach of privacy, harassment, and emotional distress, and it has "passed" on the issue of discrimination. There are a number of reasons why reputation is one of the few dignitary interests that has received special protection.[1] Some are historical. The invention of the printing press prompted the development in the common law of strong criminal and civil laws to combat seditious and blasphemous libel,[2] which was perceived as a serious threat to the public order and to the Crown.[3] The high value placed on reputation by the English elite classes and the desire to minimize violence, particularly by duelling, as

---

1 Battery, assault, and private nuisance protect dignitary interests to some degree.
2 At common law, defamation was actionable as libel (written defamation) and slander (verbal defamation). The extent to which this dichotomy remains in the Canadian law of defamation is dealt with later in this chapter.
3 J.G. Fleming, *An Introduction to the Law of Torts*, 2d ed. (Oxford: Oxford University Press, 1985) at 196. Libel continues to be a crime in Canada: see *Criminal Code*, R.S.C. 1985, c. C-46, ss. 296–301.

a means of defending one's honour were also factors. Canadian judges have maintained the high priority that has traditionally been given to the protection of reputation. This is explained in part by the pivotal role of reputation in the protection of personal dignity, status, prestige, and power; by the sensitivity of judges to the importance of reputation in their own professional careers; by the extensive economic harm that can flow from an attack on a person's reputation; by the power of modern systems of mass communication to disseminate defamatory statements to large numbers of persons; and by the need to encourage persons of integrity to enter and continue in public service. The protection of reputation does, however, impinge on other highly valued interests such as freedom of expression and freedom of the press, both of which are protected by the *Charter of Rights and Freedoms*. Freedom of speech guards against oppressive and abusive governmental actions, protects the free exchange and testing of political ideas, facilitates a search for truth, enhances the efficient operation of the marketplace, supports a flourishing artistic community, and maximizes the flow of information essential for individual, social, and political decision making. It is the foundation of a vibrant and free democracy. Defamation law strikes a balance between these competing interests. An unduly assiduous protection of reputation may diminish the flow of important information and may lead news media outlets to be overly cautious in publishing investigative journalism in the public interest.[4] An unduly robust protection of freedom of expression and freedom of the press may be very destructive of a person's hard-earned and unblemished reputation for integrity and honesty. The law of defamation has traditionally favoured the protection of reputation over free-speech interests and, to a significant degree, modern Canadian defamation law continues to reflect this bias. Recently, however, the Supreme Court has begun a gradual recalibration of defamation law in favour of free speech. It has been influenced by reform in other common law jurisdictions and by the failure of traditional doctrine to reflect sufficiently the constitutional recognition of freedom of expression and freedom of the press in the *Charter*.[5]

---

4   This phenomenon is known as "libel chill."

5   See *Grant v. Torstar Corp.*, [2009] S.C.J. No. 61, and the discussion of the defence of responsible communication on a matter of public interest in section E(4), below in this chapter.

B. THE GENERAL FRAMEWORK OF THE TORT OF DEFAMATION

The tort of defamation balances the interest of individuals in their reputation with the public interest in free and unfettered speech in an unusual way. The courts have chosen a low threshold for the establishment by the plaintiff of a *prima facie* cause of action in defamation. Any communication that would cause the plaintiff to lose respect or esteem in the eyes of others is likely to be held to be defamatory. Consequently, few cases of defamation are fought over whether or not the defendant's words are defamatory. In itself, this would, of course, be an intolerable restriction of free speech. The daily newspapers, television programs, radio talk shows, political discourse, and the casual conversations of Canadians contain many statements that impair the reputation of others and diminish the esteem in which persons are held by others. The balance in favour of free speech is restored by a number of defences. These defences are designed to permit the vigorous exchange of information, ideas, criticism, and views that are essential in a modern democracy. One or more of the defences is usually central to most defamation litigation and they are pivotal in drawing an appropriate balance between the competing values of reputation and free speech. This framework does, however, tend to load the dice in favour of the plaintiff and the protection of reputation because the defendant carries the burden of proving some justification or privilege to legitimize his defamatory statement.

It may also be noted that defamation is a difficult and technical area of the Canadian law of torts. In part, this is due to the immense diversity of speakers, meanings, and contexts of spoken and written words and the difficulty of drawing an appropriate balance between reputation and free speech, and in part it is due to the early entrenchment of some legal principles that do not operate easily or well in modern conditions, to the interplay among ancient common law principles, to the relationship between the common law and reforming provincial legislation,[6] to

---

6   All Canadian provinces have defamation acts: see Alberta *Defamation Act*, R.S.A 2000, c. D-7; British Columbia *Libel and Slander Act*, R.S.B.C. 1996, c. 263; Manitoba *Defamation Act*, R.S.M. 1987, c. D20; New Brunswick *Defamation Act*, R.S.N.B. 1973, c. D-5; Newfoundland and Labrador *Defamation Act*, R.S.N.L. 1990, c. D-3; Nova Scotia *Defamation Act*, R.S.N.S. 1989, c. 122; Ontario *Libel and Slander Act*, R.S.O. 1990, c. L.12; Prince Edward Island *Defamation Act*, R.S.P.E.I. 1988, c. D-5; Saskatchewan *Libel and Slander Act*, R.S.S. 1978, c. L-14; Northwest Territories *Defamation Act*, R.S.N.W.T. 1988, c. D-1; and Yukon Territories *Defamation Act*, R.S.Y. 2000, c. 52. These statutes operate as a gloss on fundamental

complex rules of procedure, and to the division of tasks between judge and jury. Only the general principles, concepts, and themes of defamation law are canvassed here.[7]

C. THE ELEMENTS OF THE CAUSE OF ACTION

1) A Defamatory Statement

A defamatory statement is one that reduces the esteem or respect in which the plaintiff is held by others in the community. The test for defamation is an objective one. It is sufficient to prove that the statement would have the effect of lowering esteem or respect for the person in the minds of persons variously described as "right-thinking members of society"[8] or "reasonable or ordinary members of the public."[9] There is no need to prove that the statement was false or that there was any actual loss of esteem by another individual. It is no defence that those who heard the defamatory statement did not, in fact, think less of the plaintiff or that they knew the statement to be untrue or did not believe it. This lessens the plaintiff's burden of proof by dispensing with the need to bring evidence about who heard the statement, who believed it, and who had knowledge of its untruth. These questions may be relevant in the assessment of damages but not in the determination of liability.

Liability in defamation is strict. The plaintiff is not required to prove that the defendant intended to defame the plaintiff or that the defendant failed to take reasonable care in ascertaining the truth of the statement. It is also no defence that the defendant was unaware of the defamatory meaning of the words he used or that the defendant did

---

common law principles making relatively modest reforms. Their more important contributions include the abolition or modification of the distinction between libel and slander, the introduction of some special defences and protections in favour of media defendants, and some procedural innovations.

7   The niceties of defamation law can be pursued at a variety of levels. The general treatises on tort law, including L.N. Klar, *Tort Law*, 4th ed. (Toronto: Carswell, 2008) and A.M. Linden & B. Feldthusen, *Canadian Tort Law*, 8th ed. (Toronto: Butterworths, 2006), provide an excellent introduction. Monographs by R. McConchie & D. Potts, *Canadian Libel and Slander Actions* (Toronto: Irwin Law, 2004) and R. Brown, *Defamation Law: A Primer* (Toronto: Carswell, 2003) provide a more detailed account. The most detailed and authoritative text is R. Brown, *The Law of Defamation in Canada*, 2d ed. (Scarborough, ON: Carswell, 1994).

8   *Sim v. Stretch*, [1936] 2 All E.R. 1237 at 1240 (H.L.), Lord Atkin.

9   *Color Your World Corp. v. Canadian Broadcasting Corp.* (1998), 38 O.R. (3d) 97 at 106 (C.A.), Abella J.A.

not intend the words to refer to the plaintiff. Nor is it a defence that the defendant merely repeated what he had been told by a reliable and authoritative source.

The concept of a defamatory statement extends beyond oral or written words to include movies, cartoons, drawings, billboards, and photographs. Indeed, any communication that would lead ordinary Canadian citizens to think less of the plaintiff is defamatory.[10] Defamatory statements may include allegations of dishonourable conduct such as dishonesty, malingering, fraud or criminal activity, disparaging remarks about a person's character, integrity, competence in his profession or trade, fitness for public office, allegations of ties to disreputable organizations, and allegations that cause a person to be shunned, ridiculed, hated, pitied, or held in contempt, such as allegations of racism, venereal disease, poverty, and immorality. Allegations that the plaintiff broke any of the ten commandments or committed any of the deadly sins are also defamatory. "[A]lmost all uncomplimentary comment is defamatory."[11]

Defamatory statements must, however, be distinguished from statements of abuse and blasphemous statements made in anger. Such statements may be distressing and annoying and they may be embarrassing when they are heard by third persons but they are not normally perceived as being damaging to the plaintiff's reputation.

One of the tests of a defamatory statement is whether or not the statement tends to lower the plaintiff in the eyes of the "right-thinking members of society." Occasionally this has led courts to take a very idealistic view of societal attitudes. In one case, for example, it was held not to be defamatory to allege that a member of a golf club informed the police of the presence of illegal gambling machines on the club's premises.[12] The allegation certainly lowered the plaintiff in the esteem of fellow club members, particularly those who enjoyed gambling, but the Court took the lofty view that no "right-thinking" person would think less of a person for informing the police of illegal activities. Most courts, however, use the more generous standard of the ordinary person, which promotes decision making that is more reflective of the typical Canadian citizen and actual societal attitudes. The ordinary person test is more compatible with the conventional wisdom that it is defamatory to allege that a person is the survivor of incest or sexual assault, that a person has cancer, or that a person is gay or a lesbian, albeit that

---

10   No action in defamation can, however, be brought to protect the reputation of deceased persons.

11   Klar, above note 7 at 753.

12   *Byrne v. Deane*, [1937] 1 K.B. 818 (C.A.).

there is no reason to think less of such a person. Defamation law deals with statements that do, in fact, tend to lower the reputation of people in the estimation of ordinary people, not with how people ought to react or with the idealized norms of political and social correctness.

It is increasingly difficult to formulate the views and attitudes of the ordinary Canadian citizen in our diverse and multicultural society. Consequently, statements that tend to lower a person in the estimation of members of a segment of society may be defamatory. It may be defamatory, for example, to allege that a member of a religious community has broken dietary laws or has received forbidden medical treatment that has lowered her in the estimation of the members of that community. The plaintiff must, however, be lowered in the eyes of members of a respectable segment of society. An allegation of a failure to commit a sufficient number of crimes may diminish a person's esteem among gang members or among a criminal underclass but no action for defamation is available to protect antisocial or criminal repute.

Normally, the courts assess the natural and ordinary meaning of words in determining their defamatory nature. Consideration may also be given to evidence of slang or colloquial meanings that may not be immediately apparent to everyone. As well, there are situations where apparently innocent words can, by the introduction of evidence of extrinsic facts, be shown to have a defamatory meaning. This is known as a true innuendo. For example, to say that Jones is paid well to play football is an apparently innocent statement. It may even suggest that Jones is a good football player. However, if evidence is adduced to show that Jones plays in a university conference that prohibits the payment of players, the statement is shown to allege wrongdoing and dishonesty on his part. The proof of the extrinsic facts translates the apparently innocent words into words with a clear defamatory content.[13]

A corporation may bring an action in defamation. It does not have a reputation in the personal sense but it has a business reputation which may be defended from attacks that it is corrupt, that it is a vehicle for fraud, or that it ignores pollution controls. Federal, provincial, and local governments may not, however, bring an action in defamation against their critics. Democratic values including free speech require the widest freedom to comment on governments. One may attack a democratically elected government as corrupt, incompetent, or a failure without fear of civil action. This immunity does not, however, apply to attacks on individual public officials or those elected to public office who may seek vindication in an action for damages.

---

13   See, for example, *Tolley v. J.S. Fry & Sons Ltd.*, [1931] A.C. 333 (H.L.).

2) Reference to the Plaintiff

The defamatory statement must be one that may reasonably be understood as referring to the plaintiff. The plaintiff may be identified by name, description, or context. Evidence of surrounding circumstances and extrinsic facts may be adduced to show the connection. The test is whether a reasonable person acquainted with the plaintiff would believe that the words referred to him. There is no need to prove that any person did, in fact, understand the statement as referring to the plaintiff. There is also no need to prove any intent or negligence in making reference to the plaintiff or to prove that the defendant knew or ought to have known of the plaintiff. In one famous case, a newspaper publisher was held liable when an author of an article in the paper made a defamatory remark about a fictional character (Artemus Jones) with the same name as the plaintiff lawyer.[14]

Defamation of a group or class of persons presents special problems. The key issue is whether or not the words can reasonably be interpreted as referring to and defaming each individual member of the group. The size of the group, the extravagance of the statement, the context of the statement, and any words of qualification must be taken into account. It is not, however, easy to determine when defamatory words said of a group impair the reputation of individual members of the group. To say, for example that "all law students cheat" is clearly not actionable by all law students individually. The statement is made of too large a group of persons. It is grossly extravagant and it would be understood by reasonable persons to be a gross exaggeration and generalization that could not seriously be taken to refer to each and every law student in Canada. However, to say that all law students who are members of a small seminar class or a study group cheat may have an adverse impact on the reputations of individual members of the class and may, therefore, be actionable.[15]

---

14   *E. Hulton & Co. v. Jones* (1909), [1910] A.C. 20 (H.L.).

15   The rules relating to group defamation eliminate defamation as an effective remedy to minority groups subject to hate propaganda. Some jurisdictions have sought to overcome this absence of protection legislatively. See, for example, Manitoba *Defamation Act*, above note 6, s. 19(1), which permits a person belonging to a race, a person professing a religious creed, or a person of any sexual orientation to seek an injunction to prevent the circulation of libellous statements that expose persons belonging to that race, religious creed, or sexual orientation to hatred, contempt, and ridicule such as to raise unrest or disorder among the people.

3) Publication

Defamation protects reputation. It is, therefore, essential that the de-famatory statement be published to a third person who heard it or read it and understood it.[16] Publication of the statement is the actionable wrong. Consequently, to call another a liar and a crook to his face, be-yond the hearing of any third person, is not actionable in defamation. It may cause a good deal of distress to the person accused of such conduct and it may diminish his self-esteem but there is no loss of esteem in the eyes of others and his *reputation* is not impaired.

Publication does not entail any formal disclosure to large numbers of persons. Publication to a single person is sufficient. Indeed, each time a defamatory statement is communicated or repeated, a new cause of action arises. In general, there are good reasons for this rule. Each publication further erodes the plaintiff's reputation and the originator of the defamatory material may be judgment-proof. The production and publication of books, magazines, movies, and theatrical produc-tions involves many sequential publications as the project moves from its creator through the production and distribution processes. These publishers are now treated as joint tortfeasors all of whom must be joined in one cause of action. There is little support for the American one-publication rule operating from the time of general release of the defamatory work, to avoid jurisdictional and limitation problems aris-ing from subsequent distribution, sales, or performance of the defama-tory material.

The rules about publication have been qualified to avoid an in-tolerable burden on innocent mechanical distributors of publications containing defamatory material. A distinction is drawn between the producers and the *innocent disseminators* of widely distributed print or visual defamatory material. News vendors, book distributors and re-tailers, libraries, video stores, and, in some circumstances, printers are not liable if they have no knowledge of any defamatory content in the material and no reason to be suspicious that the material contained defamatory material and if they have exercised reasonable and prac-tical steps to vet the material.[17] The liability of innocent disseminators, therefore, depends upon proof of fault.

The strict liability for defamation is also alleviated to some degree by the requirement that the publication must be intentional or due to a lack of care, such as leaving defamatory material where others may see

---

16   It probably does not, however, have to be understood in a defamatory sense: see Klar, above note 7 at 759.

17   *Vizetelly v. Mudie's Select Library Ltd.*, [1900] 2 Q.B. 170 (C.A.).

it or making verbal defamatory statements in circumstances where it is foreseeable that others may overhear the conversation.[18] An accidental publication is not actionable.

A defendant is not normally responsible for the republication of a defamatory statement by another person. There are, however, exceptional circumstances, including those where the republication was authorized or intended by the defendant or where the republication of the statement was likely to occur. In those circumstances it is reasonable that the original publisher continues to bear some continuing responsibility.

D. LIBEL AND SLANDER

At common law, defamatory statements are categorized as either libel or slander. Originally, the distinction turned on whether the communication was written (libel) or verbal (slander). Libel is viewed as the more serious form of defamation because of its permanence, the greater likelihood that it was premeditated, and its capacity for wider dissemination. It is actionable without proof of special damage. Slander is, in contrast, more likely to be transient and impromptu and its publication is limited to those within hearing distance of the defendant. As a general rule, it is actionable only on proof of special damage. This has proved to be a difficult distinction to apply with the advent of modern communications such as radio, film, television, facsimile transmission, e-mail, and Internet postings. Happily, many provinces, including Alberta, Manitoba, New Brunswick, Nova Scotia, and Prince Edward Island, have legislatively abolished the distinction between libel and slander. In those provinces all defamatory statements are actionable without proof of special damage. In the provinces that maintain the distinction, there has been some adjustment in the traditional meaning of libel to accommodate modern circumstances. In general, emphasis is now placed on visibility and permanence as the primary characteristics of libel so as to include film, e-mail, and other computer communications. There has also been some legislative reform categorizing television and radio broadcasts as libel.[19]

The only significant substantive difference between libel and slander that remains in the common law relates to the proof of damage. As noted above, damage is presumed in libel, and in slander special damage must be proved by the plaintiff. Special damage includes any ma-

---

18   See, for example, *McNichol v. Grandy*, [1931] S.C.R. 696.
19   See, for example, Ontario *Libel and Slander Act*, above note 6, ss. 1(1) and 2.

terial or financial loss. It does not include embarrassment or emotional distress caused by the slanderous imputation. There are, however, four categories of slanderous statements which, because of their seriousness, are actionable without proof of such damage. They include imputations of criminal wrongdoing of sufficient seriousness to warrant imprisonment, the imputation of unchastity in a woman, the imputation of an infectious or contagious disease that might cause a person to be avoided or shunned, and statements that reflect adversely on a person's character with respect to her trade, profession, or business.

E. DEFENCES

The pivotal role of the defences in defamation is evidenced by the fact that every day in Canada many critical and derogatory things are said and written about others in all manner of print publications, radio, and television broadcasts and in social and political dialogue without exposing the speaker to liability in defamation. In the absence of the defences to defamation, it would be necessary to cleanse all public and private speech of uncomplimentary comments and statements. This would not only demand an intolerable burden of self-censorship but would also impose an unreasonable restriction on one's freedom to voice dissent, criticism, or outrage, to promote unpopular social or political views, to voice opinion both wrongheaded and sensible, and to be involved in the spirited and robust dialogue that is the hallmark of a healthy democracy. A heavy burden is, therefore, placed on the defences of justification, privilege (both absolute and qualified), fair comment on matters of public interest, responsible communication on a matter of public interest, and consent to protect the important value of free speech and restore an appropriate balance between the protection of reputation and free speech.

1) Justification

Proof that the defamatory statement is true is a complete defence to liability in defamation. A person is always permitted to speak the truth about another no matter how painful or damaging the truth may be. The reason that is most commonly given for this defence is that defamation protects the plaintiff's reputation, and if the plaintiff's reputation is damaged by the truth, it is a reputation that is unwarranted and unworthy of protection by the law of defamation.

It is not necessary to establish the literal truth of each and every word or phrase used by the defendant but there must be proof that the words are substantially true in respect of their defamatory meaning. The claim of justification does carry some risks because a failure to substantiate a claim of justification may warrant an increase in damages.

The defence of justification may operate harshly in respect of a citizen of good repute whose reputation is damaged by the revelation of youthful indiscretions or past misconduct that are no longer indicative of his character or integrity. A person who makes such statements without reason other than to cause anguish, distress, and embarrassment may be accused of abusing the right of free speech. The common law does not, however, investigate the motives of those who damage others by disclosing true facts. To this extent, priority is given to robust free speech. Such conduct is better classified as a breach of privacy arising from the publication of personal information that is not in the public interest. It may be actionable under the privacy acts of British Columbia, Manitoba, Newfoundland, and Saskatchewan, or under the nascent common law tort of privacy.

2) Privilege

There are certain occasions when the public interest in promoting full and frank communication between individuals takes precedence over the protection of an individual's reputation. These are referred to as occasions of privilege, and defamatory statements are not actionable. The privilege attaches to certain occasions, not to particular speakers or messages. As a general proposition, the occasion must be one where it is necessary, in the public interest, to speak candidly, without impediment or inhibition and without the threat of potential liability for statements that damage the reputation of others. The privilege may be absolute or qualified. Absolute privilege provides a complete immunity from liability for defamation even if the statement is made with malice. Qualified privilege is destroyed by malice but protects *bona fide* and honest statements.

a) Absolute Privilege

An absolute privilege arises when the occasion justifies the complete pre-eminence of free speech and the full eclipse of the plaintiff's interest in the protection of his reputation. These occasions, which are in the main designed to facilitate the operations of all branches of government, are quite well defined and are, understandably, held in tight check by the courts.

The privilege extends to all statements made in the course of parliamentary proceedings and statements made in the provincial legislatures. Reports of these legislative proceedings and the meetings of its constituent committees are subject to a qualified privilege both at common law and under the defamation acts.

An absolute privilege also extends to all statements made by the parties, witnesses, counsel, and the judge in the course of judicial proceedings. Statements made between counsel and client in preparation of, and in contemplation of, litigation are subject to absolute privilege, as are communications between counsel and potential witnesses and the reports submitted by potential witnesses in preparation for trial. Reports of judicial proceedings are subject to an absolute privilege if the strict conditions of the provincial defamation acts are complied with, and they are accorded a qualified privilege under the common law. The protection of reports of both judicial and legislative proceedings is justified by the public's legitimate interest in institutions of government.

Communications on official business between high executive officials of state such as cabinet members and the highest level of the civil service are absolutely privileged; the privilege may also extend to the senior levels of the military and the police. Finally, communications between spouses are similarly privileged to protect the confidentiality of the marital relationship. In each of these situations there is a vital public interest in candid and uninhibited communications.

b) Qualified Privilege

The occasions of qualified privilege are more difficult to define. There is no tightly drawn list of discrete occasions to which the privilege attaches, and the multitude of diverse situations found in the cases do not suggest clear and predictable rules. A couple of points should be kept in mind. First, qualified privilege is not extended lightly. There must be a compelling public policy reason to permit honest defamatory statements to be made at the expense of the plaintiff's reputation. That reason must be found in the public utility and social desirability of uninhibited and candid communication free from the threat of legal action. Secondly, occasions of qualified privilege are defined by the correlative concepts of duty and interest between the parties to the communication. Normally, there must be some reciprocity of these concepts between those who are privy to the communication, such as a moral, social, or legal duty to speak to someone with a legitimate interest to receive the information, a legitimate interest in giving information to someone with a duty to receive it, or a legitimate interest in providing this information to someone with a mutual interest in receiving it.[20] These concepts are not only sufficiently loose and discretionary to accommodate the multitude

---

20   See, for example, *Adam v. Ward*, [1917] A.C. 309 (H.L.).

of situations that arise but they also allow the privilege to be crafted to special relationships, special occasions, and for special purposes. They also allow the courts to control the scope of the privilege in order to accommodate legitimate needs appropriately while minimizing the scope of potential damage to the reputation of others. Ultimately, however, the question is whether or not the interest in free speech ought to be given priority over the interest in individual reputation.

A few examples will suffice to illustrate the process. A qualified privilege extends to erroneous communications from a parent to an adult child about the disreputable conduct of the person he intends to marry. There is a moral duty on the part of a parent to protect an immediate member of her family, and her son has a legitimate interest in receiving it. The privilege would not, however, extend to a communication of that information to the parent's friends or business associates. Neither duty nor interest is present. Furthermore, a qualified privilege is not enjoyed by a stranger who volunteers information of that kind. The interest of the son remains unchanged but the stranger has no social or moral duty to tell him. The situation becomes more complicated when the allegation of disreputable conduct is made by a distant relative, a close friend, or an employer. The court must assess current notions of moral and social obligation. A qualified privilege also arises when a law professor agrees, at the request of a student, to write a letter of reference to a potential employer of the student. The professor has a moral duty to write it and the future employer has a legitimate interest in a candid assessment of the applicant. The privilege does not, however, extend to communications with other people. A qualified privilege may also arise on the basis of common or mutual interest between groups or associations of people such as business associates, creditors of a single debtor, shareholders and directors of a corporation, members of trade and professional associations, religious congregations, and service clubs. The privilege covers communications that relate to issues of common concern to the members of the group. A qualified privilege also extends to a person who has been subjected to an attack on his reputation. He has a clear interest in responding to the attack and restoring his reputation. There is a moral duty on those who have heard of or read the initial attack to listen to or read the response so that matters may be set straight and the reputation of the victim may be restored.

In all of these situations, a qualified privilege may be justified as essential to facilitate business, professional, and social relationships and as being broadly in the public interest. These exemplary instances might be multiplied but it would serve little purpose since each case turns on its own facts and circumstances.

Normally, an occasion of qualified privilege protects a communication to a limited number of persons but a publication to the world may be privileged. A person may, for example, respond to an attack on his reputation made by the media through the media. Furthermore, members of Parliament, who have an absolute privilege on the floor of the House of Commons, enjoy a qualified privilege to make public statements outside the House relating to the conduct of governmental officials.[21] This can be justified on the grounds that the member has a public duty to inform the electorate, and citizens have a legitimate interest in the affairs of government.

The news media do not, however, enjoy a qualified privilege in reporting the news. The Supreme Court, in a number of decisions in the mid-twentieth century, held that the media do not have a moral or social duty to report on matters of public interest.[22] The media had to rely on the defences of justification, fair comment, or the tightly crafted statutory and common law privileges given to reports of judicial and legislative proceedings and of some public committees. Towards the end of the last century this position was beginning to fall out of favour and courts gradually began to recognize that a qualified privilege may attach to some media reports on matters of high public importance.[23] This development was, however, largely overtaken by the recent recognition by the Supreme Court of the defence of "responsible communication on a matter of public interest."[24] This provides the media with more generous protection in respect of factual errors and allows the issue to be resolved more transparently and directly.[25]

The defence of qualified privilege is lost if the defendant abuses it. This can arise in a number of ways. The defamatory communication must not be published to those who do not have a legitimate interest or duty to receive the communication. There is no privilege in respect of defamatory statements that are not relevant to, or in furtherance of, the purpose for which the privilege is given. The defence is also lost on proof of malice. There is no protection for defamatory statements

---

21   See, for example, *Stopforth v. Goyer* (1979), 23 O.R. (2d) 696 (C.A.).
22   *Globe & Mail Ltd. v. Boland*, [1960] S.C.R. 203; *Banks v. Globe & Mail Ltd.*, [1961] S.C.R. 474.
23   See *Leenen v. Canadian Broadcasting Corporation* (2001), 6 C.C.L.T. (3d) 97 and *Campbell v. Jones*, [2002] N.S.J. No. 450 (C.A.).
24   See section 4, below in this chapter.
25   The defence of qualified privilege does, however, have certain advantages since it is defeated only by the proof of malice by the plaintiff. Under the defence of responsible communication on a matter of public interest, the defendant must prove due diligence in ascertaining the veracity of the statement.

that are known to be untrue or are made with reckless disregard for the truth. Malice also includes not only communications that are motivated by spite, ill will, and hatred but also those motivated by other improper purposes.

3) Fair Comment on a Matter of Public Interest

The defence of fair comment on a matter of public interest provides a vital degree of protection for the robust discussion of matters in the public domain. It is a key concept in restoring the balance between free speech and freedom of the media on the one hand, and reputation on the other. There are a number of elements to the defence which require amplification.

First, the statement must be one of comment or opinion and be interpreted as such by the ordinary reader or listener. The defence does not extend to factual statements. The distinction is important because it allows the reader or listener to recognize that the statement is a subjective assessment or opinion of the defendant with which one may agree or disagree. To say that X is immoral is a statement of fact that must be justified. To describe accurately X's conduct and declare it to be immoral is opinion or commentary. Second, the comment must be based on a substratum of true facts which are expressly or impliedly stated by the defendant, are known by the plaintiff, or are so well known to the public as to be notorious. Third, the comment must be made on a matter of public interest. The term public interest is defined neither as a matter that the public needs to know nor as a matter in which the public has an interest. The former is unduly restrictive and the latter extends to matters of minimal public importance such as mere curiosity in the private lives of prominent persons. The law steers a middle path defining a matter of public interest as one in which the public or a segment of the public has a legitimate interest or concern. Legitimate interest has not, however, been construed narrowly. It includes more than just governmental actions and the conduct of public officials. It extends to all public affairs and events, including the arts, sports, religion, lifestyles, business ventures, and the public conduct of persons who, through choice or circumstances, become public figures. Indeed, most of the topics that are the subject of reputable newspapers, television broadcasts, radio talk shows, and online discussion sites fall comfortably within the definition of public interest, The defence applies only to the public dimension of the topics under discussion. It is a matter of legitimate public interest, for example, to discuss the performance of a public official in the discharge of his public duties but defamatory statements about his relationship with his children must be justified. Fourth, the comment must be fair. This does not, however, mean that the comment must be reasonable or balanced. Fair in this context means honest. There are two tests of honesty that have competed for recognition in this context; a subjective test and an objective test. The subjective test asks whether the defendant had an actual honest belief in the view expressed. The objective test asks if the comment was one that an honest person could make on the proven facts, however prejudiced, obstinate, or exaggerated his views may be. In 1978, in *Cherneskey v. Armadale Publisher's Ltd.*[26] the Supreme Court adopted the subjective test requiring the defendant to prove that he truly believed what he was saying. This test was criticized on a number of grounds. First, it is the more restrictive of the two tests and does not give sufficient weight to freedom of expression. Second, it does not harmonize well with the fact that the defence of fair comment may be defeated by proof that the defendant acted with malice. A true belief in the comment leaves little room for a finding of malice. Third, it creates problems for secondary publishers such as media outlets and websites that provide a public forum for the comments of others. Newspaper proprietors, for example, may not agree with the views expressed in some letters to the editor or in op-ed pieces, but it would be a disservice to the community to suppress them.[27] Fourth, there are circumstances in which, for valid reasons, persons express opinions in which they have no belief. A debater may assert an opinion which he does not believe and a talk-show host may play the devil's advocate expressing a view contrary to his own in order to stir up controversy and to prompt a robust response from his listeners. It was this latter situation which led the Supreme Court to re-examine the subjective test in *WIC Radio Ltd. v. Simpson.*[28] In that case the plaintiff, Simpson, was a well-known activist who strenuously opposed the introduction of materials dealing with homosexuality into the public schools' curriculum. In the course of a radio broadcast the defendant talk-show host expressed the defamatory opinion that the plaintiff condoned violence against homosexuals. At trial, however, he testified that he had no honest belief in that view. He could not, therefore, satisfy a subjective test of fairness. It was, however, in the Court's view, an opinion that could honestly have

---

26   *Cherneskey v. Armadale Publisher's Ltd.* (1978), [1979] 1 S.C.R. 1067].

27   After the decision in *Cherneskey* some of the provinces, including Alberta, Manitoba, New Brunswick, and Ontario passed legislation protecting the publication of another's opinion contrary to the publisher's beliefs if the comment is one that an honest person might hold.

28   [2008] S.C.J. No. 41.

been expressed on the proven facts by a person with prejudiced, exaggerated, or obstinate views. The Court reversed *Chernesky*, adopted the objective test, and held that the defence was established. The Court was influenced by some of the weaknesses of the subjective test alluded to above and the desire to promote the *Charter* value of freedom of speech. The concept of fairness does, therefore, provide a great deal of latitude for vigorous and harsh criticism on public issues even where the criticism may have serious economic and professional consequences for its target. Finally, the defence of fair comment is lost if the plaintiff proves malice on the part of the defendant. Malice includes spite, ill-will, and ulterior motive. The adoption of the objective test of fairness reinvigorates malice as a discrete element of the defence. The honesty of the defendant's beliefs is now a factor in determining malice.

4) Responsible Communication on a Matter of Public Interest

The defence of responsible communication on a matter of public interest was established by the Supreme Court in *Grant v. Torstar Corp.*[29] It was prompted in large part by the recognition of the difficult burden carried by news media publishers who, despite care in establishing the veracity of their reporting on a matter of public interest, nevertheless include a defamatory statement of fact. Under the law before *Grant*, such statements had to be justified unless some privilege was established. Consequently, a publisher needed not only to have confidence in the truth of the story but also to have confidence in his ability to prove its truth. This generated a degree of caution on the part of the media. That caution could be exploited by the powerful, the wealthy, and the privileged who would seek to suppress any anticipated uncomplimentary coverage by threatening court action. Important matters of public interest might, therefore, go unreported because of the "libel chill" cast by conventional principles. *Grant* provided an opportunity for the Supreme Court to recalibrate the tort of defamation to provide additional protection for freedom of speech and to further protect robust discussion on matters of public interest without unduly sacrificing the interest in reputation.

Grant dealt with a story in the *Toronto Star* which reported on the plaintiff's plans to extend his private three-hole golf course on his lakefront estate to nine holes. The local residents objected to these plans on environmental grounds. The story also reported the suspicions of

---

29   [2009] S.C.R. No. 61.

some of the residents that the plaintiff was improperly exercising political influence behind the scenes to secure governmental approval for this venture. At trial, the defendant was unable to establish the defence of justification or fair comment. Damages were assessed at $1.4 million. The Court of Appeal ordered a new trial to allow the defendant to argue the defence of "responsible journalism on a matter of public interest" which had recently been recognized by that Court.[30] The Supreme Court agreed that the case should be retried but it reformulated the defence recognized by the Court of Appeal more broadly as one of "responsible communication on a matter of public interest." In establishing this defence, the Court relied on two arguments; one of principle and one based on jurisprudence. The argument of principle was grounded in the constitutional protection of free speech and freedom of the media in the *Charter*, and the chilling effect defamation law had on the robust debate on matters of public interest. The Court emphasized the essential role of free speech in the functioning of our democratic institutions, in the pursuit of truth through the exchange of ideas and information, and in the self-realization of individuals. It concluded that the law did not give sufficient weight to the constitutional value of free expression. The jurisprudential argument was based on the appellate decisions in other common law jurisdictions that had adjusted their defamation laws to more fully protect freedom of speech. The most robust protection of free speech is provided in the United States.[31] A public figure cannot recover in defamation unless the plaintiff can prove "actual malice," meaning knowledge of the falsity of the statement or reckless indifference to the truth. The Australian High Court has recognized a generic privilege for all widely broadcast statements of information and opinion dealing with governmental and political matters affecting the citizens, provided that the defendant acted reasonably, which includes having a reasonable belief in the truth of the statement, taking reasonable steps to verify the statement, giving the target of the defamatory statement a chance to respond, and publishing that response unless it is impractical or unnecessary to do so.[32] New Zealand developed a qualified privilege for all statements made about the actions and qualities of

---

30   *Cusson v. Quan*, [2007] O.J. No. 4348 (C.A.).

31   *New York Times Co. v. Sullivan*, 376 U.S. 254 (1964). For a useful outline of subsequent US Supreme Court decisions dealing with the scope and range of the decision in *Sullivan*, see J.C.P. Goldberg & B.C. Zipursky, *Torts* (Oxford: Oxford University Press, 2010) at 320–29.

32   *Lange v. Australian Broadcasting Corporation* (1997), 189 C.L.R. 520. Some Australian states have since passed defamation acts which incorporate a more generalized public interest defence.

those currently or formerly elected to parliament, and those with immediate aspirations to such office, so far as those actions and qualities directly affect or affected their capacity (including their personal ability and willingness) to meet their public responsibilities.[33] Like other occasions of qualified privilege the defence is defeated by proof of malice. In the United Kingdom, the House of Lords focused initially on the need to provide additional protection to conventional media outlets for their reporting on matters of public interest. It formulated the defence of "responsible journalism on a matter of public interest."[34] The key concept of "responsible conduct" is assessed on a slate of factors including the steps taken to determine the veracity of the statement, the reliability of sources, the seriousness of the allegation, the degree of public interest, and any opportunity afforded to the plaintiff to put forth his side of the story. It was this approach which was first embraced by the Ontario Court of Appeal[35] and now forms the basis of the broader defence of responsible communication on a matter of public interest.

There are two essential elements to the defence. First, the statement must be on a matter of public interest. Public interest is defined in this context, as it is in the fair comment defence, as meaning legitimate public interest. Second, the defendant must have acted responsibly in making the communication. On this point, the Court offered a list of factors similar to those offered by the House of Lords to examine the conduct of the defendant. They are designed to test the degree of diligence and responsibility exercised in the investigation, writing, and fact-checking of the story. Consideration must be given to the seriousness of the allegation and the degree of harm that may be caused by it, the degree of public importance of the matter, the urgency of publication, the status and reliability of the defendant's sources, whether the plaintiff's side of the story was sought and accurately reported, whether the inclusion of the defamatory statement was justifiable, and any other

33   *Lange v. Atkinson*, [2000] 3 N.Z.L.R. 385 (C.A.).

34   *Reynolds v. Times Newspapers Ltd.*, [2001] 2 A.C. 127; *Jameel v. Wall St. Journal Europe*, [2006] UKHL 44. In *Seaga v. Harper*, [2008] UKPC 9, the defence was extended to publications on matters of public interest in any medium.

35   *Cusson*, above note 30, was also appealed to the Supreme Court and was decided at the same time as *Grant*. The plaintiff *Cusson* was a member of the Ontario Provincial Police who, without permission of the OPP, went with his dog to New York soon after 9/11 to assist in the search-and-rescue effort. His actions were heralded as heroic until the defendant published a series of articles that alleged that he had misrepresented himself to the American authorities and had interfered with the rescue work. The Supreme Court ordered a new trial to permit the defendant to establish the defence of responsible communication on a matter of public interest. See *Quan v. Cusson*, [2009] S.C.J. No. 62.

relevant considerations.[36] The application of these factors will pose some challenges. In evaluating the conduct of those in the conventional news media proof of standard journalistic practices will be of assistance. Greater difficulty will be encountered in measuring the conduct of those using less traditional and less formal forms of communication such as online news outlets, blogs, message boards, and websites.

5) Reportage

The defence of reportage was clarified in *Grant*. The general proposition is that every publication of a defamatory statement is a new cause of action and it is no defence that the defendant was repeating statements made by third parties. It applies when the public interest lies in the fact that the statement was made rather than in its truth. A fair report of the statement will be protected provided that it attributes the statement to a person, it indicates that its truth has not been verified, it sets out both sides of the dispute fairly, and it provides the context in which the statement was made.

This might apply, for example, to a report that a prime minister in a news conference accused the leader of the opposition of theft. The public interest lies in the fact that the accusation was made, and so long as the other provisos were met the report would be protected.

6) Consent

Consent by the plaintiff to publication of the defamatory statement is a complete defence. This defence arises only in unusual circumstances but it may arise where the plaintiff has agreed to go on television or radio to discuss and refute defamatory allegations or rumours circulating about him. Publication of those statements by the media in the course of the broadcast would clearly not be actionable so long as the discussion adhered to an agreed subject matter.[37]

7) Apology and Retraction

Apology and retraction are partial defences that operate to mitigate damages. An apology is recognized at common law as a mitigating factor in the award of damages and this has now been codified by provincial

---

36   See *Hansen v. Tilley*, [2010] B.C.J. No. 2112 (C.A.) for a useful discussion of the factors and their application to the facts.

37   See, for example, *Syms v. Warren* (1976), 71 D.L.R. (3d) 558 (Man. Q.B.).

legislation. There are also special statutory provisions relating to apologies by newspapers and broadcasters.

Retraction is a statutory concept that applies only to newspapers and broadcasters. If there has been a full and complete retraction in compliance with the strict statutory requirements, liability is restricted to the plaintiff's actual damage.

These partial defences are of particular importance to the media, given the strict liability at common law for mistaken and innocent defamation.

F. REMEDIES

The primary remedy for defamation is an award of damages. Damages in defamation are "at large," meaning that once liability is established, damages are not restricted to the actual loss proved by the plaintiff. This is important because it may be difficult to prove the actual loss suffered as a result of a widely circulated defamatory statement. For example, it may be difficult for a business person who was wrongfully accused of fraudulent business practices to quantify precisely the financial loss suffered as a result of the loss of customers or business opportunities. The quantum of damages depends upon a variety of factors, including the nature and seriousness of the defamatory communication, the extent of publication and circulation of the defamatory material, the motivation and conduct of the defendant, the reputation of the plaintiff and whether or not the reputation was warranted, and the extent of the damage caused to the plaintiff. The conduct of the defendant may also warrant an award of aggravated damages or punitive damages.

Awards of damages for defamation can be high. In *Hill v. Church of Scientology of Toronto*,[38] the Supreme Court upheld an award of $1.6 million in compensatory, aggravated, and punitive damages in respect of the defamation of the plaintiff lawyer relating to the performance of his professional duties. It is worthy of note that this award far exceeds any award of non-pecuniary damages for catastrophically injured accident victims. Those damages are currently capped at $300,000. There is, however, no cap on general damages for defamation even though the interest in personal safety would seem more compelling than the interest in reputation.

Injunctive relief to prevent the publication of a libel is available only in exceptional circumstances because of the threat to freedom of speech.

---

38   [1995] 2 S.C.R. 1130 [*Hill*].

G. CYBER-DEFAMATION

The Internet is not a defamation-free zone. The fundamental elements to establish a cause of action and the enumerated defences apply equally to electronic communications made by e-mail, texting, and tweeting and to statements found on websites, chat rooms, message boards, and blogs. The magic of the common law process is that it allows fundamental principles to be developed and applied to new technologies and circumstances. This process is not, however, free from contention or challenges and Canadian courts have begun to address some of the issues arising from cyber-defamation. The authoritative resolution of these issues at the highest level has yet to occur but it is possible to identify some of the issues, canvas alternative resolutions, and sense the current judicial mood.

There was some suggestion initially that the courts might take a more robust view of online communications and be less inclined to find statements to be defamatory because of freedom of expression interests, the anonymity of many communicators, a general willingness of Internet users to discount the veracity of online banter, and the group characteristics of those using various Internet sites. The courts, however, have not been attracted to that view. Cyber-communications are treated in the same way as communications made by more conventional means. Indeed, online defamation may be viewed more seriously given the potential for very wide publication, the longevity of some postings, and the significant harm that may follow.[39]

A number of cases have considered some novel issues relating to the publication of defamatory statements. The first relates to the conventional rule requiring proof by the plaintiff that the defamatory statement was communicated to a third person. This may pose problems in cyberspace where e-mail may be deleted without being read and the proof of "hits" on a website or notice board does not, in itself, prove that the offensive words were read.[40] One alternative is to apply a rebuttable presumption of publication if Internet-users have accessed the particular site. The second issue relates to the liability of third parties

---

39 See *Best v. Weatherall*, [2010] B.C.J. No. 716 (C.A.) where the Court reversed the trial judge's conclusion that an e-mail which was otherwise defamatory was not given the context of a typically robust public debate among those who lived on Salt Spring Island.

40 *Crookes v. Newton*, [2009] B.C.J. No. 1832 (C.A.) [*Crookes*], leave to appeal to the S.C.C. granted, [2009] S.C.C.A. No. 448 and argued in December 2010 (judgment reserved). The location of the reader may also be important in determining which court has jurisdiction to deal with the case.

such as Internet service providers (ISPs) and other intermediaries for the defamatory content in third-party communications facilitated by their service. Technically every republication creates a new cause of action. Many of these intermediaries can shelter under the innocent dissemination rule by arguing that they are mere conduits for the communications. Liability may arise, however, if they play a more active role in moderating or monitoring websites or in refusing to remove defamatory material once it is drawn to their attention.[41] A third issue relates to the use of hyperlinks contained in one communication to a site which contains defamatory material. The inclusion of the link is not, in itself, a publication of the defamatory material, but if the reason for including the hyperlink is to bring attention to the defamatory material, to encourage the reader to access the site, or to endorse or adopt the defamatory words, liability may ensue.[42] The fourth issue arises from difficulties in identifying anonymous persons who have sent defamatory communications. Identification may not be possible without the co-operation of ISPs or other intermediaries. They may not be helpful, citing the privacy and freedom of expression interests of the originators of the communication. There appears to be a growing consensus, however, that a court order requiring the intermediary to identify the source of the statement will be made when the plaintiff is able to establish a *prima facie* case of defamation and a consideration of the competing interests of reputation, privacy, and free speech makes it appropriate.[43] The final issue relates to the alleged unfairness of the multiple publication rule which regards each downloading of defamatory material as an independent cause of action thereby retriggering the commencement of limitation periods. The courts may in due course adopt a single publication rule.[44]

Cyber-defamation may also increase the judicial use of injunctions. Courts are traditionally reluctant to use injunctive relief in the area of

---

41 *Carter v. B.C. Federation of Foster Parents Assn.*, 2005 BCCA 398. In the United States, s. 230 of the *Communications Decency Act of 1996* states that "no provider or user of an interactive computer service shall be treated as the publisher or speaker of any information provided by another information content provider."

42 *Crookes*, above note 40.

43 *Warman v. Wilkins-Fournier*, 2010 ONSC 2126 (Div. Ct.) See also *Mosher v. Coast Publishing Ltd.*, [2010] N.S.J. No. 211 (S.C.) (newspaper ordered to identify persons who posted comments anonymously on a newspaper's news website) and *York University v. Bell Canada Enterprises*, [2009] O.J. No. 3689 (S.C.J.) (ISP ordered to disclose information about an e-mail user).

44 A single publication rule is favoured in the United States.

defamation because of the degree to which freedom of expression may be affected. Cyber-defamation, however, may remain on a website for an eternity and be accessed by a limitless number of persons. One can expect, therefore, a much greater use of injunctions requiring defamatory material to be deleted by defendants, forbidding defendants from making future online reference to the plaintiff, or in other ways utilizing the flexibility of the various forms of injunctive relief.[45]

H. DEFAMATION AND NEGLIGENCE

The commonly held view was that the tort of defamation was the exclusive basis for claims of harm to reputation. You could not, for example, avoid the technicalities of the tort of defamation by "dressing up" your case as an action in negligence. This orthodoxy was considered by the Supreme Court in *Young v. Bella*,[46] a negligence action brought by a student in social work against the university in which she was enrolled. The student was erroneously suspected of being a child abuser. The source of the suspicion was an inadequately footnoted research paper submitted to her professor. These suspicions could have been allayed by speaking with the student. The university officials chose instead to report their suspicions to child protection authorities. This report became known in police and social worker circles and it was not discredited until a child protection official interviewed the student two years later. By that time her reputation and career plans were significantly harmed. The university argued that the case was one of defamation and it was protected by qualified privilege. The Court, however, upheld liability in negligence on the grounds that the university was under a pre-existing duty of care to the student and the harm suffered was not exclusively to her reputation. The earlier cases calling for a mutual exclusivity between the torts were explained as cases where there was no pre-existing duty of care. Furthermore, in the Court's opinion, freedom of expression and the policies underlying qualified privilege could be taken into account in determining the appropriate standard of care.

---

45   For example, *McLeod (Masluk McLeod Gallery) v. Sinclair*, [2008] O.J. No. 5242 (S.C.J.). Courts are likely, however, to continue to be very reluctant to issue interlocutory injunctions.

46   (2005), 261 D.L.R. (4th) 516 (S.C.C.).

FURTHER READINGS

BARENDT, E., *et al.*, *Libel and the Media: The Chilling Effect* (Oxford: Clarendon Press, 1997)

BOIVIN, D.W., "Accommodating Freedom of Expression and Reputation in the Common Law of Defamation" (1997) 22 Queen's L.J. 229

BROWN, R., *Defamation Law: A Primer* (Scarborough, ON: Carswell, 2003)

————, *The Law of Defamation in Canada*, 2d ed. (Scarborough, ON: Carswell, 1994)

DOWNARD, P., *Libel*, 2d ed. (Markham, ON: Lexis Nexis Canada, 2010)

MCCONCHIE, R. & D. POTTS, *Canadian Libel and Slander Actions* (Toronto: Irwin Law, 2004)

POTTS, D., *Cyberlibel: Information Warfare in the 21st Century?* (Toronto: Irwin Law, 2011)

WEILER, P.C., "Defamation, Enterprise Liability, and Freedom of Speech" (1967) 17 U.T.L.J. 278

WILLIAMS, J.S., *The Law of Libel and Slander in Canada*, 2d ed. (Toronto: Butterworths, 1988)

CHAPTER 8

RELATIONSHIPS

A. INTRODUCTION

Tort law does not operate in a legal vacuum. There are other important areas of private and public law which control the relationship of persons to one another and to private and public institutions. The conventional divisions and classifications of the legal system inevitably give rise to interrelationships and overlap between discrete areas of the law which need to be resolved. These difficulties are exacerbated by the fact that there are often no sharp and distinct boundaries between the various regimes of responsibility. At the margins they tend to shade the one into the other, each using similar concepts to resolve conflicts that arise between litigants. In this chapter the reader is alerted in a summary way to some of the relational issues arising in the field of tort law and the general principles that bear on those issues. In particular, consideration is given to the private law regimes of contract law, fiduciary law, the law of restitution, and the action for breach of confidence and the public law constitutional principles found in the *Canadian Charter of Rights and Freedoms*.

B. PRIVATE LAW

Many civil obligations arise from the relationships between people. Tortious obligations of reasonable care arise from the relationships of proximity, of reasonable reliance, and of assumption of responsibility. Contractual obligations arise from exchange transactions, promissory reliance, and the receipt of promised benefits. Fiduciary obligations arise from relationships of trust, confidence, and dependence. Restitutionary obligations arise where one person has secured an unjust enrichment at the expense of another. Confidential relationships arise when one person has entrusted secrets or private information to another. It is not uncommon, however, for a relationship to satisfy the definition of more than one of these legal constructs. Each legal characterization of the relationship may or may not generate similar obligations. A good example is found in the relationship of solicitor and client. The relationship may be characterized as a relationship of proximity, as a contractual relationship, as a fiduciary relationship or as a confidential relationship. Each of these characterizations is sufficient to establish an obligation of care and prudence on the part of the solicitor. Each characterization of the relationship may, however, generate different legal consequences for a breach of that common duty of care because the rules relating to procedures and remedies in tort, contract, fiduciary law and confidentiality are not uniform. A further complication arises where the obligations on the solicitor generated by the characterization of the relationship differ. The obligations of a solicitor as a fiduciary and confidant are, for example, more extensive than her duty of care in negligence. It is, therefore, necessary to have some mechanism to determine which set of rules should govern the parties.

1) Contract Law and Tort Law

There are many relationships in which a duty to use reasonable care arises from both the proximate and the contractual nature of the relationship between the parties. The situation commonly arises in relationships between professionals and their clients, but it may also arise in other situations. The content of the duty of care, whether it is analysed as tortious care or as contractual care flowing from an implied term of the contract, is normally the same and the choice of one cause of action or the other is normally of no practical significance. In a few situations, however, the choice between tort and contract does make a difference. The rules relating to the measure of damages, limitation periods, remoteness of damage, conflict of laws, and punitive damages are not the same in contract and tort. One or other may be more advantageous to the plaintiff.

There was in the 1970s a great deal of debate as to how cases such as these ought to be resolved. There were two competing views. The theory of *mutual exclusivity* proposed that, since the parties had chosen to enter a contractual relationship, the action must be brought in contract and the dispute must be resolved exclusively by the application of contractual rules. The alternative theory of *concurrence of actions* permitted the plaintiff to make a full and free choice among the alternative causes of action in contract and tort and to select the cause of action that was most advantageous to her. After some initial hesitation, the Supreme Court adopted the theory of concurrence of actions. In *Central Trust Co. v. Rafuse*[1] the Court held that, in circumstances where the facts supported a cause of action for negligence against a solicitor in both tort and contract, the plaintiff enjoyed an unfettered choice of causes of action or could sue concurrently in both causes of action and ultimately choose the remedy that was most advantageous to her. The rule of concurrence of actions is, however, subject to an important qualification. If the contract between the parties contains a term, normally an exemption clause, which limits or negates the obligation of care that would normally arise between the parties, the contract governs the relationship and it cannot be evaded by the subterfuge of suing in tort.

In most situations, the choice of actions is between an implied contractual duty of care arising out of a contract of services and the mirror-image duty of care arising from the proximity of the parties. The issue of interrelationship has, however, also arisen frequently in respect of negligent misrepresentations made between the parties to a contract. The misrepresentations may be pre-contractual, made in the negotiations leading up to the contract, or they may be post-contractual, made after the contract is made and before or during the performance of the contract. The principles of contract law relating to misrepresentations have long been settled and for a period of time it was unclear how the liability for negligent misrepresentations arising from *Hedley Byrne & Co. Ltd. v. Heller & Partners Ltd.*[2] would operate in a contractual context. It is now clear that the rule of concurrence also applies to negligent misrepresentations, and if the elements necessary for tort liability for a negligent misrepresentation are established, the plaintiff may choose that remedy so long as it is not limited or negated by the terms of the contract.[3]

The Supreme Court's strong commitment to the theory of concurrence of actions is further evidenced by its decision in *BG Checo International Ltd. v. British Columbia Hydro & Power Authority.*[4] The Court

---

1   [1986] 2 S.C.R. 147 [*Rafuse*].
2   [1964] A.C. 465 (H.L.).
3   *Queen v. Cognos Inc.*, [1993] 1 S.C.R. 87.
4   [1993] 1 S.C.R. 12.

dealt with an unusual situation arising from a construction contract. The owner had assured the contractor that certain land had been cleared in order to facilitate the construction work. The Court found that the statement was not only a pre-contractual negligent misrepresentation but it was also an express term of the construction contract. It was argued by the defendant that an express term of the contract could give rise only to a claim for breach of contract, and the plaintiff had no right to formulate a claim in tort in order to take advantage of the tort rules relating to the assessment of damages. The Court rejected that argument, holding that the principle in *Rafuse* was not restricted to a concurrence between duties of care in negligence and duties of care arising from *implied* contractual obligations. It was open to the plaintiff to frame its action in negligence.

2) Fiduciary Law and Tort Law

A fiduciary relationship is an equitable concept that arises where a person (the beneficiary) has placed such reliance, confidence, power, and trust in the hands of another (the fiduciary) that the fiduciary may reasonably be expected to act with the utmost care, loyalty, and good faith towards the beneficiary. The fiduciary is required to set self-interest aside and to act, in the matter at hand, in the interests of the beneficiary. There are a number of nominate categories of relationships that have been characterized as fiduciary. They include the relationships of trustee and beneficiary, solicitor and client, religious leader and follower, physician and patient, parent and child, and principal and agent.

The relationship between a fiduciary and a beneficiary may also be contractual and it is likely to be sufficiently proximate to generate a *prima facie* duty of care. In such circumstances, the plaintiff often prefers to sue for breach of fiduciary duty. There are a number of reasons for this. First, fiduciary relationships give rise to strict obligations on the fiduciary. They include a duty of loyalty, a duty to act in good faith and in the interest of the beneficiary, a duty to avoid a position of conflict of duty and interest, and a duty not to profit at the expense of the beneficiary. These obligations are generally more stringent than those arising in tort and contract and they may elevate the standard of conduct required of the defendant. It is also easier to establish that the defendant owed positive obligations to act for the benefit of the plaintiff if he is a fiduciary. Second, the characterization of the defendant's conduct as a breach of fiduciary duty may secure a more generous limitation period for the commencement of an action. Third, the remedies for breach of a fiduciary obligation are in some instances more generous than those for breach of contract or tortious wrong-doing. The assessment of equitable compensation, for example, may be more generous than an award of damages for breach of contract or in tort. The courts seek to restore the plaintiff fully to the position he would have been in but for the breach of the fiduciary duty. To achieve this goal, the limitations applicable to the assessment of damages in tort and contract, including causation rules, remoteness of damage principles, and contributory negligence, may be applied more loosely or not at all. Additionally, a court may force the defendant to disgorge gains that have been secured from the breach of fiduciary duty and may be more willing to use the full range of equitable remedies.

There has been much less controversy in respect of the rules relating to situations that give rise to a concurrence of tort, contract, and fiduciary claims. The rule of concurrence of causes of action giving rise to a full and free choice to the plaintiff is applicable. In *Canson Enterprises Ltd. v. Boughton & Co.*,[5] for example, the Supreme Court recognized that the plaintiff, who was a client of the defendant solicitor, could pursue claims for breach of contract, negligence, and breach of the solicitor's fiduciary duties concurrently and could choose the remedy most advantageous to him.

Until recently, the concurrence of causes of action between tort and fiduciary law was not very common because fiduciary relationships were largely contained within the nominate relationships. The categories of fiduciary relationships are not, however, closed and the Supreme Court has recognized that *ad hoc* fiduciary relationships can arise in any relationship where a careful examination of the facts indicate sufficient elements of power, discretion, and influence on the part of the "fiduciary" and reliance, vulnerability, trust, and confidence on the part of the "beneficiary" to support the conclusion that the fiduciary must act selflessly in the interests of the beneficiary in the matter at issue.[6] This has allowed the extension of fiduciary law beyond the nominate relationships to a range of personal and commercial relationships that were previously controlled largely by contractual or tort principles. In the latter part of the last century, the Supreme Court made quite robust use of fiduciary law in situations that had in the past often been controlled by tort law. A few cases will illustrate the Court's approach.

In *Norberg v. Wynrib*,[7] the Supreme Court dealt with the professional misconduct of the defendant physician who took advantage of a female

---

5   [1991] 3 S.C.R. 534.
6   *Hodgkinson v. Simms*, [1994] 3 S.C.R. 377.
7   [1992] 2 S.C.R. 226.

patient who was addicted to painkillers. The defendant maintained her addiction by supplying the drugs she so desperately needed, in exchange for sexual favours. The majority of the Court relied on tort and contract principles to fashion a remedy for the plaintiff. However, McLachlin J., as she then was, chose to emphasize the fiduciary nature of the physician-patient relationship. Hitherto, the only fiduciary obligation that was understood as arising from the physician-patient relationship was that of confidentiality. Her ladyship, however, identified fiduciary care as central to the whole relationship of physician and patient. The concept of fiduciary care, embodying the notion of selflessly acting in the best interests of the patient, captured most fully the nature of the defendant's wrongdoing and supported a more generous award of damages than that calculated by the majority under contract or tort principles. The characterization of the physician-client relationship as a fiduciary relationship was also central to the Court's decision in *McInerney v. MacDonald*,[8] which held that a patient must be given complete access to the information contained in her medical records. The Court has also emphasized the fiduciary nature of the relationship between parent and child. In *M.(K.) v. M.(H.)*[9] a father's incestuous relationship with his daughter was regarded as a breach of his fiduciary duty.

The concept of fiduciary relationships also intruded into commercial relationships. In *Hodgkinson v. Simms*, for example, the defendant was an accountant specializing in real estate tax shelter investments. The plaintiff stockbroker relied heavily on the defendant and, following his advice, invested in a number of real estate tax shelters. Unknown to the plaintiff, the defendant had a profitable relationship with the land developers in whose projects the plaintiff invested. He received commissions for every investment made. The plaintiff discovered this situation of divided loyalty after the real estate market collapsed and he lost heavily on his investment. The defendant argued that the plaintiff's losses were caused not by his failure to disclose his interests in the transactions but by the general downturn of the property market. A majority of the Supreme Court found that there was a power/dependency relationship between the parties, and the total reliance of the plaintiff on the defendant and the influence the defendant had over the plaintiff supported the conclusion that, unlike many advisory relationships, this relationship was fiduciary in nature. The defendant was in breach of his fiduciary duty in failing to disclose his financial interest in the investments. The majority allowed the plaintiff to recover his complete

---

8   [1992] 2 S.C.R. 138.
9   [1992] 3 S.C.R. 6.

loss on the ground that, if the appropriate disclosure had been made, he would not have made the investment and would not have suffered the loss. In its view, the same result could be reached for breach of contract. The minority held that the relationship was not a fiduciary one. The only remedy was for breach of contract and, in its opinion, under contract principles, the entire investment loss was not recoverable. The case illustrates the two main attractions of characterizing a claim as one for breach of fiduciary duty, namely, the intensification of obligations and the extensiveness of remedies.[10]

Since the turn of the century, the robust application of fiduciary law and the development of *ad hoc* fiduciary duties has slowed. The Supreme Court has both clarified and narrowed the essential elements of an *ad hoc* fiduciary relationship and has defined more closely the kind of wrongdoing that gives rise to a breach of such a relationship. *Galambos v. Perez*[11] and *K.L.B. v. British Columbia*[12] are illustrative. In *Galambos*, the Court dealt with relationship between a lawyer and an employee who loaned the lawyer's firm substantial sums of money. The Court held that they were not in a conventional relationship of lawyer and client in respect of the loan and, moreover, there was no *ad hoc* fiduciary relationship between them. The Court emphasized that a power/dependency relationship and reliance by the weaker party did not, of themselves, create an *ad hoc* fiduciary relationship. The focus of analysis must be on the alleged fiduciary and the essential question is whether that person expressly or impliedly undertook the responsibility of acting with loyalty to the other person. Furthermore, the fiduciary must have discretionary power to affect the other party's interests. These tests were not met in *Galambos*.[13] The nature of the wrongdoing

---

10   For an interesting example of the use of fiduciary law to overcome impediments to tortious responsibility, see *Lafrance v. Canada (Attorney-General)*, [2003] O.J. No. 1046 (C.A.). In that case, the Ontario Court of Appeal refused to strike out a statement of claim against the federal government by second generation survivors of residential school abuse. The claim was based on an alleged fiduciary obligation on the government to protect successive generations of Aboriginal people from the destruction of culture, language, and status that inhered in the policy to assimilate them into white, Christian Canadian Society. The tort claim could not succeed because of the nature of the harm and a lack of duty of care to those not born until many years after the implementation of the policy.

11   [2009] S.C.J. No. 48.

12   [2003] S.C.J. No. 51 [*K.L.B.*].

13   See also *Reference re Broome v. Prince Edward Island*, [2010] S.C.J. No. 11. The provincial government that provided some funding for a privately-owned and operated residential home for orphans was not under a fiduciary duty to them and was not responsible for the abuse they suffered in the facility. The province had no power or control over how the home was run.

sufficient to support fiduciary remedies was addressed in *K.L.B.* In that case, the Court recognized that the Superintendent of Child Welfare was in a fiduciary relationship with children who were removed from their parents and placed in a foster home where they were abused. It was argued that this was a breach of the Superintendent's fiduciary duty to the children because the placement was not, in retrospect, in the best interests of the children. The Court noted that the liability of a fiduciary is not strict and, furthermore, that in this context the application of a "best interests of the child" test was unworkable. The Court declared that the essence of fiduciary wrongdoing is a breach of trust and there must be some evidence of disloyalty or the promotion of one's interests at the expense of those of the beneficiary in order to establish liability. Since there was no evidence that the Superintendent had harmed the children by any act of disloyalty or conduct which favoured governmental interests over those of the children there was no breach of fiduciary obligation.[14]

3) Restitution and Tort Law

Restitution and tort law are less likely to intersect and overlap than other areas of the law. Restitution is based on the concept of unjust enrichment. A remedy is provided where the defendant has been unjustly enriched at the expense of the plaintiff. A plaintiff who, for example, has paid money in the mistaken belief that it is owed to the defendant may recover that sum. Restitution is not based on the commission of any wrong by the defendant. It focuses on the restoration of a benefit received by the defendant which, in justice, ought to be repaid to the plaintiff. Tort law, contract law, and fiduciary law, on the other hand, emphasize the defendant's commission of a wrong and the defendant's obligation to pay the plaintiff for the loss caused by that wrong. Tort law rarely provides remedies that restore benefits to the plaintiff. Consequently, these two areas of private law tend to operate independently of each other. Nevertheless, plaintiffs sometimes have a choice between an action in tort and one in restitution. This arises under the doctrine of waiver of tort. It operates where a person has made a monetary gain or secured a benefit as a consequence of the commission of a tort. The plaintiff may elect to waive the tort and sue in restitution to compel payment of that sum. This may arise, for example, in respect of money secured by fraud. The plaintiff may sue in deceit or waive the tort and

---

14   There was, however, liability in negligence for the failure to adequately assess, control, and monitor the foster-home environment.

sue in restitution. The same choice arises where a defendant converts the plaintiff's chattel and later sells it for more than its value on the date of conversion. The plaintiff may waive the less advantageous tort claim (damages in conversion are normally the value of the chattel at the date of conversion) and sue in restitution to recover the full proceeds of the sale. Tort claims and restitution claims are mutually exclusive. A plaintiff may commence an action in both but ultimately, an election must be made between the causes of action.

There has been a good deal of debate recently about the scope and nature of waiver of tort.[15] First, it is not clear if the doctrine is restricted to intentional torts such as conversion and deceit or whether it extends to torts such as negligence and nuisance. Second, it is not clear if all the elements of the tort must be established or whether a breach of a tortious obligation such as a negligent act which causes no *loss* to the plaintiff but secures a benefit for the defendant is sufficient. Third, it is not clear if all the technical elements of an action in restitution, namely an enrichment of the defendant, a corresponding deprivation of the plaintiff, and a lack of any juristic reason for the enrichment must be established by the plaintiff or whether the commission of a tort and securing a benefit therefrom is sufficient in itself to found a claim.

4) Breach of Confidence and Tort Law

The action for breach of confidence is available when three elements are established namely, the information disclosed is confidential, it is communicated in confidence, and the information is misused by the person to whom it was communicated. The action has been variously described as an action in tort, restitution, contract, property, law and as an equitable action. It is more commonly regarded as an action *sui generis*. The action protects two kinds of confidential information, commercial and personal. The former category covers information such as trade secrets, secret formulae, customer lists, and secret information shared among those involved in a joint commercial venture. The remedy sought is frequently restitutionary in nature forcing the defendant to disgorge of benefits secured by the misuse of the information and an injunction to prevent its further misuse. This category of confidentiality fits most comfortably with contract and restitutionary law but it has a weak link to the business torts for improper conduct in the market place. It is the

---

15   *Serhan Estate v. Johnson and Johnson*, [2006] O.J. No. 2421 (Div. Ct.); *Pro-Sys Consultants Ltd. v. Microsoft*, [2006] B.C.J. No. 3035 (S.C.); *Reid v. Ford Motor Co.*, [2006] B.C.J. No. 993 (S.C.); and *Heward v. Eli Lilly & Co.*, [2007] O.J. No. 404 (S.C.J.).

latter category that has a closer affiliation with tort law. It may arise where a person confides personal information to another who betrays that confidence and tells third persons. The remedy sought is normally damages for the harm caused by the disclosure and an injunction to prevent further circulation of the information. The action for breach of confidence is, therefore, positioned to protect some privacy interests in provinces without privacy acts. Its scope, however, is limited to the realm of private information and initially it was necessary to show a confidential relationship between the plaintiff and the defendant. Recently, however, the action has attained greater prominence and scope in the field of privacy in England. This was achieved by abandoning the requirement of a confidential *relationship* and attaching liability to the use of information that a reasonable person would regard as confidential, howsoever that information may have been acquired. It has been held by the House of Lords, for example, that it was a breach of confidence for a newspaper to publish photographs of the supermodel Naomi Campbell leaving a meeting of Narcotics Anonymous.[16]

The focus in Canada has been more on the nascent common law tort and the statutory torts of privacy than on a reinvigorated action for breach of confidence but such actions may have an important if small role to play. For example, Naomi Campbell is a public figure who was photographed in a public place and could not, therefore, rely on the common law or the privacy acts. On other facts there may be alternative causes of action. The privacy acts have rejected any theory of mutual exclusivity and it is likely that the common law will permit a concurrence of actions.

C. PUBLIC LAW

1) The *Charter of Rights and Freedoms* and Tort Law

The *Canadian Charter of Rights and Freedoms* has, so far, had relatively little impact on the law of torts. There are three ways in which tort litigation may be affected by the *Charter*. First, there are some cases where the *Charter* is directly relevant and applicable. Second, since the *Charter* is the repository of the fundamental values and principles of Canadian law, it informs and influences the development of tort law. Third, the *Charter* is the basis for the development of discrete constitutional torts.

---

16   *Campbell v. MGM*, [2005] 1 A.C. 593 (H.L.).

a) Direct Application to a Common Law Tort Action

The *Charter of Rights and Freedoms* is rarely directly applicable to tort litigation. This is because the *Charter* applies to governmental action[17] and, unless there is a substantial governmental connection in the case, the *Charter* is inapplicable.[18] Most common law tort litigation between private litigants will not have a sufficient governmental connection to make the *Charter* directly applicable. There may, exceptionally, be a sufficient governmental connection if a legislative enactment is an integral part of the common law cause of action or if there is a statutory defence to that cause of action. One of the parties may argue that the pertinent legislation is in breach of the *Charter* and is unconstitutional. Such a finding would directly affect the common law tort litigation.[19]

There may also be a sufficient governmental connection if one of the parties to a common law tort action (not based on a breach of *Charter* rights) is an official or an organ of government. There does not, however, appear to be a great deal of enthusiasm for this possibility because it risks the development of inconsistent tort principles applicable to governmental and non-governmental litigants.[20]

b) Indirect Application

The indirect application of the *Charter* to Canadian tort law has been recognized expressly by the Supreme Court. The Court has observed that the application, interpretation, and development of the common law must be informed by, and be consistent with, the fundamental constitutional values enshrined in the *Charter*.[21] To this extent, the *Charter* is relevant to tort law. In the latter years of the twentieth century, there was little indication that the *Charter* would play a significant role in reshaping and reformulating tort doctrine. In more recent years, reliance on *Charter* values is more common. The change in attitude is most striking in the law of defamation where there is tension between the

---

17   Section 32(1) of the *Charter* declares that it applies "to the Parliament and government of Canada in respect of all matters within the authority of Parliament . . ." and "to the legislature and government of each province in respect of all matters within the authority of the legislature of each province."

18   *R.W.D.S.U. v. Dolphin Delivery Ltd.*, [1986] 2 S.C.R. 573 [*Dolphin Delivery*].

19   A similar issue arose in respect of a claim for damages arising from a breach of the *Charter* in *Prete v. Ontario* (1993), 16 O.R. (3d) 161 (C.A.), where it was held that legislation establishing a very restrictive limitation period did not protect the Crown from liability. As a general rule, limitation of actions legislation will, however, apply to *Charter* claims, see *Alexis v. Toronto Police Service Board*, [2009] O.J. No. 5170 (C.A.).

20   L.N. Klar, *Tort Law*, 4th ed. (Toronto: Carswell, 2008) at 8.

21   *Dolphin Delivery*, above note 18 at 603, McIntyre J.

Charter values of free speech and freedom of the press and the jealous protection of reputation found in tort doctrine. The Supreme Court initially applied the conventional common law principles, holding that they maintained an appropriate balance between reputation and free speech.[22] In this century that balance has been altered in favour of free speech by loosening the requirements of the defence of fair comment in *WIC Radio v. Simpson*[23] and, more significantly, by recognizing the defence of "responsible communication on a matter of public interest" in *Grant v. Torstar Corp.*[24] In each of these decisions the Court was influenced by the importance of the constitutional right to free speech embodied in the *Charter*. The *Charter* was also referred to in *Hill v. Hamilton-Wentworth Regional Police Services*[25] where the Court held that the police owe a duty of care in the investigation of a particularized suspect of criminal wrongdoing. There is, therefore, some evidence that the Supreme Court is making increasing use of the *Charter* in novel tort cases, which address the protection of *Charter* values.

c) Constitutional Torts

A more fertile avenue of development for civil liability arising out of the *Charter* lies in the development of constitutional torts. Constitutional torts may arise when a government official or entity of government breaches a person's *Charter* rights. The basis for such a claim is found in section 24(1) of the *Charter*, which empowers a court to award a remedy that is "appropriate and just in the circumstances" to anyone whose *Charter* rights or freedoms have been violated. The scope and interpretation of the section 24(1) remedy and the relationship with the private law remedies under the law of torts was addressed by the Supreme Court in *Vancouver (City) v. Ward*.[26] In that case, the police violated the plaintiff's *Charter* rights by mistakenly and without cause both arresting and strip-searching him and impounding his automobile. He made a claim for damages under section 24(1). The Court set out a template for analyzing and applying the subsection. First, the Court noted that section 24(1) provides to the Courts a very broad discretion in crafting appropriate remedies for breach of the *Charter*. Second, an award of damages is often appropriate since it is a well recognized and conventional judicial remedy for the vindication of a claimant's rights, and can be quantified in a way which is fair to both the claimant and

---

22   *Hill v. Church of Scientology*, [1995] 2 S.C.R. 1130.
23   [2008] S.C.J. No. 41.
24   [2009] S.C.J. No. 61.
25   [2007] S.C.J. No. 41.
26   [2010] S.C.J. No. 27.

the state. Third, in assessing the propriety and fairness of an award of damages, a functional approach is to be adopted. The claimant must establish that damages would achieve the goals of either *compensation* for harm including mental distress, *vindication* of the claimant's *Charter* rights, or *deterrence* of state officials from similar conduct in the future. Fourth, damages may be refused on the grounds that adequate remedies already exist in the law or that they would unduly hamper good governance, such as the exercise of the legislative and policy functions of government. Fifth, state action pursuant to legislation that is later found to be unconstitutional is not subject to a section 24(1) remedy. Finally, the award of damages will generally be both moderate and conventional, albeit subject to some variation on the basis of the seriousness of the breach and/or the degree of harm to the claimant. The Court upheld the trial judge's award of $5,000 for the strip-search but concluded that damages were not appropriate for the impoundment of the motor vehicle.

The Court also sought to clarify the relationship between the constitutional remedy and tort remedies which protect similar interests such as false imprisonment, malicious prosecution, and battery. First, the Court distinguished constitutional damages from damages under tort law. The section 24(1) remedy is an independent action imposing strict liability directly on the state. It is not a vicarious liability for the wrongdoing of individual state officials and state officials are not personally liable. Any wrongdoing by the official such as an intentional, malicious, or bad faith *Charter* breach, is relevant to the quantum of damages, not to the issue of liability. Second, the claimant is not required to exhaust tort remedies before seeking a section 24(1) damages remedy and, furthermore, concurrent actions may be brought. Third, there is no opportunity for double indemnity. If the claimant has received tort damages sufficient to meet the goals of compensation, vindication, and deterrence, an award under section 24(1) may not be fair or appropriate. Finally, and most elusively, the Court noted that, in determining the propriety of constitutional damages, reference may be made to and guidance sought from the "practical wisdom" embodied in conventional tort doctrine.

FURTHER READINGS

BURROWS, A.S., "Contract, Tort and Restitution—A Satisfactory Division or Not?" (1983) 99 Law Q. Rev. 217

FARQUHAR, K., "*Hodgkinson v. Simms*: The Latest on the Fiduciary Principle" (1994) 29 U.B.C. L. Rev. 383

HADDEN, T., "Contract, Tort and Crime: The Forms of Legal Thought" (1971) 87 Law Q. Rev. 240

ROSS, J., "The Common Law of Defamation Fails to Enter the Age of the *Charter*" (1996) 35 Alta. L. Rev. 117

TETTENBORN, A.M., *An Introduction to the Law of Obligations* (London: Butterworths, 1984)

THE CANADIAN LAW OF TORTS IN THE TWENTY-FIRST CENTURY

At the beginning of the twentieth century, no judge or lawyer could have foreseen the substantial expansion and evolution of the Canadian law of torts that would take place in the following hundred years. We are not in any better position today to predict what the next hundred years will bring. Nevertheless, there are certain trends and themes in Canadian tort law that are likely to be influential in its development and evolution in the twenty-first century. These themes include the centrality and dominance of the tort of negligence, the dynamism and expansionary nature of the tort of negligence, the incremental drift towards a greater generalization and integration of tort rules, the reform and modernization of tort law, the dominance of the compensatory function of tort law, and the rise of alternative and supplementary legal and non-legal compensatory and deterrent mechanisms that threaten to marginalize and diminish the importance of tort law. Not all of these themes are discrete phenomena and not all of them point in the same direction, but they each warrant some attention in anticipating the future path of Canadian tort law.

A. THE CENTRALITY OF THE TORT OF NEGLIGENCE

In the twentieth century the tort of negligence blossomed into the dominant field of tort liability. Virtually all activities that carry a risk of personal injury or property damage are now subject to the general duty of care, and the courts continue to expand liability to new interests, activities, and losses. The dominance of the tort of negligence is also indicated by the extent of the intrusion of fault concepts into other areas of tort law. The strict liability torts have, for example, been heavily diluted by fault concepts, most notably in the definition of non-natural use in the rule in *Rylands v. Fletcher*,[1] the requirement of a loss of control of the animal in the scienter action, and in the interpretation of the defences. The torts of trespass to person, chattels, and land have been transformed from torts of strict liability to torts requiring proof of wrongdoing. The tort of nuisance exhibits some characteristics of fault liability. This is most apparent in the principles controlling the responsibility of a landowner for a private nuisance created by a third party, the remoteness of damage rule (foreseeability), and the uneven trend towards fault in respect of personal injuries caused by a public nuisance on the highway. Some areas of tort law, such as defamation, have withstood the rising tide of fault liability. Nevertheless, the twentieth century was the century of the tort of negligence and its influence will be felt long into this century.

B. THE DYNAMISM OF THE TORT OF NEGLIGENCE

The dominance of the tort of negligence is due, in part, to the expansionary forces unleashed by *Donoghue v. Stevenson*,[2] *Hedley Byrne & Co. Ltd. v. Heller & Partners Ltd.*,[3] and *Anns v. Merton London Borough Council*.[4] No other area of Canadian tort law has displayed the vitality of negligence law, and while *Cooper v. Hobart*[5] has slowed its advance, there is little evidence to suggest that its capacity for growth is spent. Further growth in the amount of litigation and the scope of liability may be expected in a number of areas.

First, there will be cutting edge cases in areas such as product design, governmental services, educational services, crime prevention, business activities and health care. The recent history of the tort of

---

1 (1868), L.R. 3 H.L. 330, aff'g (*sub nom. Fletcher v. Rylands*) (1866), L.R. 1 Ex. 265 (Ex. Ch.).

2 *M'Alister (or Donoghue) v. Stevenson*, [1932] A.C. 562 (H.L.) [*Donoghue*].

3 [1964] A.C. 465 (H.L.).

4 [1978] A.C. 728 (H.L.).

5 [2001] 3 S.C.R. 537.

negligence has been one of incremental expansion and that is likely to be its foreseeable future. There are also a number of current activities that have not felt the full impact of negligence liability. The extent of the responsibility of many persons such as religious leaders, mediators, counsellors, therapists, adoption counsellors, and computer technicians and service providers has yet to be tested.

Second, current litigation in respect of prenatal injuries and defective medical products such as breast implants and heart valves may herald a substantial increase in negligence liability in the general area of biotechnology, including medicine and genetic engineering. At the frontiers of medical science there are special risks and the potential for mass disasters. The tort principles relating to professional liability, products liability, prenatal injuries, and wrongful birth may foster further extensions of negligence liability in this area.

Third, there is likely to be an increase in mass "toxic tort" claims arising from injuries and illness caused by chemical compounds, toxic products, and environmental pollution. There has been more experience of these claims in the United States. The victims of asbestos, Agent Orange, radiation, tobacco, defective pharmaceuticals, and environmental pollution have all turned to the American courts to seek compensation. The Canadian tort system is protected from some of these claims by the workers' compensation schemes and the lack of strict liability for defective products. Nevertheless, Canada is not immune to toxic disasters, and the greater availability of modern class actions facilitates mass claims. Potential claimants include not only those persons who suffer illness or injury from exposure to toxic compounds but also exposed persons who must undergo periodic medical testing to check for the onset of illness and those who suffer from disease phobia from the fear of future illness. The extent of liability will depend, in part, upon the willingness of courts to rework causation and burden of proof principles in favour of plaintiffs and the future judicial evaluation of commercial and industrial practices in respect of the design, manufacture, handling, and storage of toxic elements and products.[6]

Fourth, there is likely to be a substantial growth in respect of liability for the gathering, evaluation, and communication of information. The importance of accurate information is already recognized by the liability for economic loss caused by negligent misrepresentations. One area of substantial growth is in the obligation to *volunteer* beneficial

---

6   For some of the current difficulties, see *Guimond Estate v. Fiberglas Canada Inc.* (1999), 207 N.B.R. (2d) 355 (S.C.T.D.), aff'd [1999] N.B.J. No. 525 (C.A.) (allegations of illness arising from the use of styrene in the fiberglass boat-building industry).

information for the advantage of others. The source of this possible expansion is found in the combination of duties to provide accurate information with the burgeoning duties of affirmative action and the growth of fiduciary duties, both of which erode the nonfeasance immunity and require persons to act in the interests of others with whom they have a special relationship. The convergence of these several principles suggests a more extensive responsibility for volunteering beneficial information to assist those with whom one has a personal, professional, or business relationship.

Fifth, negligence law will also be a contributor in the burgeoning field of cyber-torts. The courts will be called upon to determine the extent of duties of care on the manufacturers of hardware and software, the responsibilities of users, and the standard of care in respect of software to protect against viruses, hackers, and others intent on cyber-wrongdoing. These cases are also likely to raise extensive issues of jurisdiction, conflicts of law, enforcement, and the extent of recoverable loss. It might be noted, however, that there are many cyber-issues that will come within the scope of other torts.[7]

Sixth, there is likely to be an increase in liability arising from the spread of illness. Transmission of diseases such as HIV and Hepatitis C have already been the subject of litigation. The SARS emergency and the prospect of other new and virulent, virus-related illness opens new vistas of potential litigation. The severe nature of these illnesses, the lack of potent remedies, the potential for rapid spread among the community, the need for prompt and efficient containment and quarantine measures, and consequential economic dislocation support the imposition of stringent duties of protective care on a wide range of persons, including government officials, health care professionals, businesses, and private individuals. A moment's reflection on the SARS crisis and the H1N1 influenza pandemic identifies a few of the issues that will arise: the liability of airline and airport operators; the efficacy of measures taken by public health officials to contain the spread of the virus; the obligation of individuals who know or suspect that they have been exposed to the illness or have contracted the illness; the standard of care owed when health care institutions and professionals are overwhelmed by epidemics and pandemics; the efficacy of infection control

---

7   They include e-mail harassment; cyber-stalking; online hate speech and defamation; the liability of Internet service providers for the wrongs of third parties; invasions of privacy, including employer monitoring of e-mail and the secret monitoring of websites; identification theft and other kinds of fraud; online impersonation; unauthorized intrusions on websites; the spoliation of computer evidence; and harm caused by spamming, hacking, and viruses.

in health care and other institutions; the quality and safety of protective products such as masks, gowns, and goggles; the responsibility of service industries to protect the public; and the personal responsibility of each citizen to take protective measures against contracting the disease.

Finally, there is likely to be greater use of the negligence action as a political weapon to achieve social change. Such litigation, while based on wrongdoing, is designed primarily to create a heightened public awareness of grievances in the expectation that the resulting political pressure will produce either some governmental response, such as an enhanced settlement process or increased safety regulations, or some private sector adjustment of delinquent behaviour. This process is encouraged and facilitated by the use of class actions. The success of the litigation may be less important than the achievement of a wider agenda. This phenomenon is illustrated by litigation that has captured the attention of the public in North America in recent years. Actions have been brought against the manufacturers and distributors of firearms, tobacco companies, and fast food businesses for harm caused by their lawful products; against governments for failing to take stronger steps to protect citizens from pollution; against casinos for not protecting compulsive gamblers from the consequences of their addiction; against airlines for air-travel related thrombosis; against the Canadian government by Serbian nationals seeking reparation for damage inflicted in military action; and against film and television producers by the naïve and the unsophisticated who attempt, unsuccessfully, to replicate the computer-enhanced feats of action heroes and professional athletes. Much of this litigation has been unsuccessful, but its initiation and the attendant publicity has had a corrective effect on the conduct of those targeted by it.

C. GENERALIZATION AND INTEGRATION

In the twentieth century, tort law drifted incrementally and erratically towards greater generalization and integration. Narrow categories of liability controlled by rules of a low degree of abstraction and discretion, in some instances, gave way to broad and unifying principles. The best example, of course, is *Donoghue*, where Lord Atkin emancipated the duty of care from specific relationships and brokered a general conception of relationships giving rise to a duty of care known as the neighbour principle. It set the model for negligence principles of a high degree of abstraction which carry a great deal of discretion and facilitate flexible and sensitive decision making. This process is also evident in the coalescence of the torts dealing with improper market practices around the concept of intentional interference with economic interests by unlawful means, and in the generality of the nascent tort of privacy. There is also an echo of this process in the insinuation of negligence concepts into other areas of tort law.

The trend to generalization and integration has not, however, been universal. The nominate torts dealing with the intentional interference with the person have proved to be resistant to this process. This is due partly to their antiquity and partly to the lack of cases reaching the appellate level. The tort of conversion has played some role in the integration of the torts dealing with the interference with chattels, but no overriding principle such as one imposing liability for the wrongful interference with chattels has emerged.[8] The torts of strict liability have maintained their narrow discrete categories. To some degree, this is the result of the judicial policy of containing strict liability within narrow boundaries. A general principle of strict liability for ultra-hazardous activities would invite a considerable expansion in the scope of strict liability. There has also been no integration in the torts of trespass to land and private nuisance, and defamation remains anchored in its special rules.

Nevertheless, the drift towards generality and the development of synthesizing principles can be expected to be a feature of Canadian tort law in this century. That path has been followed by other mature legal systems and has led to the American Law Institute's Restatement of Torts[9] in the United States and to the codification of tort law in Quebec, France, and Germany, all of which evidence, to a greater or lesser degree, broad and general principles.

D. REFORM AND MODERNIZATION

In the latter part of the twentieth century, the Supreme Court paid a lot of attention to the reform and modernization of tort law. This was long overdue. Tort law carried a great deal of historical baggage into the

---

8   See Ontario Law Reform Commission, *Study Paper on Wrongful Interference with Goods* by R.L. Simmonds & G.R. Stewart, with the assistance of D.P. Paciocco (Toronto: Ontario Law Reform Commission, 1989).

9   American Law Institute, *Restatement of the Law: Torts — Second* (St. Paul, MN: American Law Institute, 1965).

twentieth century and much has been done, in an incremental way, to adjust tort law to modern Canadian realities.

Not surprisingly, much of the change has taken place in the tort of negligence. The Supreme Court has developed an authoritative frame-work—first under the *Anns/Kamloops* principle and now under *Anns/ Cooper*—for the determination of a duty of care. It has also provided guidance on other foundational elements of the tort of negligence, such as causation, proof of fault, and remoteness of damage. The Court has also reworked the defences to negligence liability to promote the compensatory policies of modern tort law. The defence of voluntary assumption of risk has been narrowed and, for all practical purposes, the defence of illegality has been eclipsed. The Court has also played a strong role in reforming the assessment of damages rules in personal injury and fatality litigation. A number of more specific issues have also been addressed, such as product warnings, product quality, breach of statutory duty, informed consent to medical treatment, governmental liability, and liability for economic loss.

There is, however, a great deal of work left to be done in this century. The rules relating to the negligent infliction of nervous shock are unsatisfactory. The law relating to the intentional interference with chattels is unduly complex. The torts of intentional interference with the person are replete with oddities and anachronisms ranging from concepts such as directness and the reverse onus of proof of wrongdoing to the failure to provide sufficient protection of dignitary interests such as equality and freedom from both harassment and mental distress. The further development of the nascent tort of privacy is needed in those jurisdictions without privacy acts and clarification of the relationship between the tort of intentional interference with economic interests by unlawful means and the other business torts is desirable. The rule in *Rylands v. Fletcher* should either be generalized to all ultra-hazardous activities or abolished. The rules relating to the strict liability for damage caused by animals should be rationalized and integrated around some general principle of strict liability or fault. The rules of vicarious liability are in need of further attention on issues ranging from the exclusion of all independent contractors from its scope to the lack of any unifying principle explaining the non-delegable duties of care. Some further recalibration of defamation in favour of freedom of speech may be desirable.

Most of the responsibility for the future shape of tort law rests with the Supreme Court. The provincial legislatures may make some contribution, as they have in the past, most notably in the fields of occupiers' liability and privacy. The pace of judicial reform depends, to a large extent, on the kinds of cases that are appealed to the Supreme Court and upon the Court's declared policy to reform the common law in an incremental manner, leaving fundamental reform to the legislatures. Nevertheless, the Supreme Court has embarked on the task of developing a modern Canadian law of torts that is largely independent of other common law jurisdictions and this work will continue in the twenty-first century.

E. THE TRIUMPH OF COMPENSATION AND LOSS DISTRIBUTION POLICIES

Throughout most of the twentieth century, the conventional wisdom was that the central and largely equal functions of tort law were the compensation of harm and the deterrence of wrongful conduct. It is now apparent that there is a substantial imbalance between these functions. The prevalence of liability insurance, the popularity of loss distribution policies, and the pro-plaintiff bias of the judiciary, particularly in personal injury cases, has led to a much greater emphasis on compensation as the predominant function of tort law. The capacity of tort law to influence personal conduct has diminished and the primary responsibility for public safety has shifted to statutory regulation and the criminal law. Tort law has some residual deterrent power but it is haphazard and uneven in its impact.

This evolution has wrought a fundamental change in the tort system. It has evolved from a fault system that was designed to burden the defendant with the consequences of his own wrongdoing to a fault/insurance system that burdens the public, or a segment of the public, with the consequences of the defendant's wrongdoing. This transformation has occurred without any conscious decision of any judge, legislator, or policy maker. Nevertheless, the reality is inescapable. In general, tort law no longer deals (other than as a formality) with the question of whether the defendant should pay. It deals with the question of whether the public should pay. In practice, there are two ultimate outcomes of almost all tort actions for damages. The loss is allocated to the public or to the plaintiff.

This reality has not, however, penetrated formal tort rules, which continue to be premised on the assumption that defendants pay awards of damages out of their own pockets. This profound disconnection between loss-shifting rules and loss-spreading realities presents a fundamental challenge to the judiciary in this century. There are a number of possible approaches to the conundrum.

First, the tort system may continue as it has in the past, supported by a belief that while it may not perform any one of its functions well, it is, nevertheless, a beneficial legal institution, and by a conviction that neither socialized universal no-fault schemes nor systems requiring citizens to protect themselves from accidental losses with first-party insurance offer better alternatives. The loss-shifting system backed by extensive liability insurance will remain substantially intact and this century will witness an incremental expansion of tort liability fuelled by late twentieth-century judicial policies.

Second, the courts may resile from their current expansionary tendencies, with their emphasis on compensation and loss distribution policies, and, in their place, they may emphasize tort law as a system of personal responsibility for wrongdoing. This would demand both a greater fidelity to concepts such as reasonable care, cause-in-fact, and reasonable foreseeability and a greater emphasis on the innate morality of the other functions of tort law, such as accountability, corrective justice, deterrence, and punishment. The tort system may be brought under tighter control and some of the consequences of late twentieth-century judicial activism may be reversed. There may be some contraction in the scope of duties of affirmative action, in governmental liability, in the extent of secondary liability of deep pocket third persons for the wrongdoing of others, and in the extent of the intrusion of tort law into the traditional areas of contract law. Defences may be reinvigorated to reflect more closely the comparative responsibility of the litigants. Greater use may be made of punitive damages. Defendants would, of course, continue to protect themselves with liability insurance but there might be less emphasis on loss distribution policies in the development of tort doctrine and judicial decision making.

Third, courts may recognize and embrace fully the integration of tort liability rules and liability insurance systems into a symbiotic fault/insurance system. They may more self-consciously model tort rules with reference to the patterns of insurance (both liability and first-party insurance), to the capacity of defendants as a class to distribute loss, and to the power of plaintiffs as a class to protect themselves with first-party insurance and other compensatory mechanisms. The courts may undertake a more open examination of tort rules to determine how they should operate in this century given all we know about the operation of the tort system. This may include not only an evaluation of the kinds of losses that should be borne by various activities but also the basis (fault or strict liability) on which that allocation should be made. This would usher in a more radical change to the tort process but it would not be entirely inconsistent with modern trends. The narrow scope of recovery in negligence for relational economic loss and for economic loss caused by auditors to non-privity third persons who rely on their work has been influenced by a more open discussion of how those losses should ultimately be allocated. The restriction of the defence of voluntary assumption of risk and the many other changes to tort rules to facilitate the compensation for personal injuries have been driven by considerations of loss distribution. The narrowing of the defence of statutory authority in private nuisance indicates a preference for public institutions and ultimately the public to bear most of the losses generated by their activities. Greater emphasis on these sorts of questions may lead to an expansion or a contraction of the current scope of tort liability. In the absence of sufficient alternative accident compensation schemes, personal injury losses might continue to be spread by the tort/insurance system. Indeed, liability may be expanded in some areas. Products liability may evolve into a tort of strict liability allocating the full cost of defective products to manufacturers and ultimately to the purchasers of their products. Courts may also be willing to impose a more stringent fault liability on health-care professionals to facilitate the broader compensation of victims of medical accidents. Courts may be less eager to follow these kinds of policies in the area of property damage. A contraction of liability leaving greater scope for the operation of first-party insurance may be favoured. The decision of the Newfoundland Court of Appeal[10] to relax the standard of care on volunteer firefighters indicates a preference to allocate more of the risk of fire damage to property owners and their insurers. Victims of relational economic loss may continue to be encouraged to protect themselves. These kinds of considerations may also be useful in determining how losses arising from defective biotechnology, toxic products, pollution, and informational deficits should be allocated in the future.

It is not clear how the courts will respond to the challenges posed by the triumph of compensation and loss distribution policies but the coherence, integrity, and, possibly, the survival of the tort system may depend upon it.

---

10   *Hammond v. Wabana (Town of)* (1998), 170 Nfld. & P.E.I.R. 97 (Nfld. C.A.).

F. THE MARGINALIZATION OF TORT LAW

At the dawn of a new millennium, two competing visions of the future of the Canadian law of torts present themselves. Many of the trends that have been identified in this chapter promise a modern and robust tort system ready to face the challenges of the twenty-first century. Nevertheless, there is a darker vision that anticipates the growing marginalization of tort law and a diminution in both its vitality and the role it plays in Canadian society. Three phenomena threaten the significance of tort law, namely, the inaccessibility of tort remedies, the tort reform movement and the growth of alternative compensatory and accident prevention mechanisms.

The first phenomenon is a practical issue of access to justice. The expense of civil litigation, the rules relating to court costs, the complexities of civil procedure, the uncertainties of tort doctrine, the unpredictability of judicial decision making in many situations, the slow pace of civil process, the absence of legal aid for the middle class, and the emotional toll exacted on litigants by the adversary process all conspire to cause severe accessibility problems. There have been some initiatives that have provided some relief, such as procedural reform, the increased use of mediation, the increased availability of class actions, and the greater use of contingency fee arrangements, but many viable tort claims are not litigated. This presents a significant challenge to Canadian tort law and if solutions are not found, Canadian tort law will become increasingly remote from the citizens it is designed to serve.

The second phenomenon presents a more direct threat to some of tort law's pro-plaintiff rules. It is the influence of the tort reform movement which began in the United States. Tort reform is a legislative response designed to repeal tort rules which are perceived as too pro-plaintiff and unduly burdensome to defendants. It is motivated by the belief that tort law creates too great a burden on business, government, and the insurance industry. Almost all American states have passed legislation introducing caps on non-pecuniary damages and punitive damages, changing joint and several liability to proportionate liability, or reducing limitation periods. In Australia the tort reform recommendations of the Ipp Committee[11] have been implemented by all state and territorial governments. The legislation narrows the scope of potential tort liability and limits the quantum of damages that may be awarded. It is designed to reduce the cost of the tort system in the area of personal

---

11 Commonwealth of Australia, Panel of Eminent Persons, *Review of the Law of Negligence Report* (Canberra: Department of Treasury, 2002).

injury and death. Cumulatively these reforms have significantly curtailed the Australian tort system. Canada has, however, been largely immune from these influences. In 2002 the British Columbia government released a consultation paper entitled *Civil Liability Review*. This paper suggested that it may be an appropriate time to reign in tort liability by introducing pro-defendant reforms of limitation periods, joint and several liability and non-delegable duties of care, and by making more extensive use of structured settlements. Insurers and some professional associations have also lobbied for similar initiatives. Legislative implementation of such an agenda would be a significant restraint on tort liability and would impact adversely on plaintiffs' remedies.

The third phenomenon threatening the vitality of tort law is the increasing number of cheaper and more efficient compensatory and accident prevention mechanisms that have supplemented or replaced the tort process. When the functions of tort law are achieved by superior alternatives, tort law is diminished.

The trend is most evident in the field of personal injury compensation. The important role of governmental no-fault plans, social welfare, and first-party life and disability insurance in compensating accident victims was alluded to in chapter 1. Tort law has been ousted from the workplace and its role in respect of automobile accidents has been diminished. The injuries arising from criminal violence are more likely to be compensated by criminal injury compensation schemes than by tort law. It has been estimated that only about 10 percent of accidental injury is now actionable under the tort system.[12] This trend is likely to continue. A no-fault plan has been recommended for the victims of medical accidents.[13] The diminution of tort law as a compensatory mechanism is matched by its loss of vitality in accident prevention. This task has been largely assumed by government and is achieved by a wealth of quasi-criminal rules and regulations controlling most activities that carry a risk of personal or property damage.

This diminution of the role of tort law in the field of personal injury may also create pressure for fundamental legislative reform of all public schemes of compensation. There are at least two models of reform. First, all public compensation vehicles, including tort law, might be replaced with a universal no-fault accident compensation scheme similar to that operating in New Zealand. No-fault schemes promise greater efficiency,

---

12   B. Feldthusen, "If This Is Torts, Negligence Must Be Dead" in K.D. Cooper-Stephenson & E. Gibson, eds., *Tort Theory* (North York, ON.: Captus Press, 1993) at 394 and 401.

13   Conference of Deputy Ministers of Health, *Liability and Compensation in Health Care* (Toronto: University of Toronto Press, 1990) (Chair: J. Robert S. Pritchard).

a broader range of persons compensated, and accident prevention initiatives that may be as effective as tort law. The second possibility is the
abolition of all public mechanisms of compensation, including tort law,
leaving citizens to secure their own private life and disability insurance to protect themselves from accidents. Those accident victims who
failed to do so would fall under the social welfare system and would be
treated in the same way as victims of illness, congenital disability, and
other misfortune.

The marginalization of tort law is also evident in respect of the damage, theft, or destruction of property. The insurance of property on a
first-party basis is so prevalent, particularly in respect of theft of chattels
and fire losses, that little reliance is placed on the tort system. Furthermore, the trespassory remedies of damages and injunctions are seldom
used for the wrongful entry onto land. It is more often dealt with by calling the police, by self-help, or by laying a charge under petty trespasses
legislation. The importance of private nuisance has diminished. Many
land-use disputes are resolved under municipal bylaws, land-use regulations, and environmental controls, or under specialized legislation, such
as farm practices legislation, which replace the tort of nuisance with
administrative dispute resolution procedures. Other problems such as
rowdy parties and loud music are frequently resolved by the police. Public nuisances are often resolved by governmental action.

The business torts have been supplemented by a wealth of legislation controlling improper practices in the marketplace, and consumers probably rely more on consumer protection and business practices
legislation than tort law for remedies for defective products and services. The importance of passing-off has been diminished by the system
of registration of trademarks. Injurious falsehood has a statutory twin
that sweeps away the limiting concept of malice.[14]

Tort law has also been marginalized in respect of the protection of
dignitary interests. The initiative has been seized by the legislatures
in dealing with privacy and equality. The one tort that does strongly
protect the dignitary interest of reputation (defamation) is so complex
and so expensive to litigate that it has little significance for ordinary
Canadians. Defendants in defamation cases are often media outlets and
plaintiffs are often lawyers, politicians, and celebrities, many of whom
have other ways of clearing their names.

---

14 See *Trade-marks Act*, R.S.C. 1985, c. T-13, s. 7, which states that "no person
    shall . . . make a false or misleading statement tending to discredit the business,
    wares or services of a competitor." There is some doubt about the constitution-
    ality of the provision.

The marginalization of tort law has, in some fields, been supported by the Supreme Court. In *Seneca College of Applied Arts & Technology v. Bhadauria*[15] the Court held that no tort action was available in respect of disputes that fall within the jurisdiction of human rights codes. In *Weber v. Ontario Hydro*[16] the Court declined to entertain tort claims arising from employment disputes where the parties are governed by a collective bargaining agreement. The parties must resolve their dispute under the labour arbitration process. Workers' compensation legislation has been interpreted in a way that bars workers from suing physicians in respect of medical treatment of their work-related injuries,[17] and tort remedies have been limited in the field of family breakdown and custody disputes.[18]

This supplementation and replacement of tort law is not a new phenomenon. Tort law has never operated in splendid isolation from other institutions that have similar aspirations as tort law. Nor is it suggested that tort law is in imminent danger of disappearing. Nevertheless, there are signs that tort law is in decline.

The Canadian law of torts has been likened to a Gothic cathedral dedicated to "individual autonomy, individual dignity, individual responsibility and individual worth."[19] It is, indeed a marvellous structure that has been built with the intellectual and emotional energy of lawyers and judges on a foundation of personal responsibility for one's wrongdoing. This structure has, however, been adulterated by the triumph of loss distribution policies. It has been diminished by accessibility problems. It is attacked by "tort reformers." It has been marginalized by alternative compensatory and accident prevention mechanisms. It remains to be seen if the future witnesses a spiritual revival in the cathedral or whether its congregation continues to dwindle and its utility continues to diminish.

---

15   [1981] 2 S.C.R. 181.
16   [1995] 2 S.C.R. 929.
17   *Kovach v. British Columbia (Workers' Compensation Board)*, [2000] S.C.J. No. 3 and *Lindsay v. Saskatchewan (Workers' Compensation Board)*, [2000] S.C.J. No. 4.
18   *Frame v. Smith*, [1987] 2 S.C.R. 99.
19   A.M. Linden & B. Feldthusen, *Canadian Tort Law*, 8th ed. (Toronto: Butterworths, 2006) at 32.

FURTHER READINGS

BELL, P.A. & J. O'CONNELL, *Accidental Justice: The Dilemmas of Tort Law* (New Haven, CT: Yale University Press, 1997)

BELOBABA, E.P., *Products Liability and Personal Injury Compensation in Canada: Towards Integration and Rationalization* (Ottawa: Consumer and Corporate Affairs Canada, 1983)

CANE, P., *The Anatomy of Tort Law* (Oxford: Hart Publishing, 1997)

CONAGHAN, J. & W. MANSELL, *The Wrongs of Tort* (London: Pluto Press, 1993)

FELDTHUSEN, B., "If This Is Torts, Negligence Must Be Dead" in K.D. Cooper-Stephenson & E. Gibson, eds., *Tort Theory* (North York, ON: Captus Press, 1993) 394

HUBER, P.W., *Liability: The Legal Revolution and Its Consequences* (New York: Basic Books, 1988)

ISON, T.G., *The Forensic Lottery: A Critique on Tort Liability as a System of Personal Injury Compensation* (London: Staples Press, 1967)

KLAR, L., "Downsizing Torts" in N.J. Mullany & A.M. Linden, eds., *Torts Tomorrow: A Tribute to John Fleming* (North Ryde, NSW: L.B.C. Information Services, 1998)

KOENIG, T.H. & M.L. RUSTAD, *In Defense of Tort Law* (New York: New York University Press, 2001)

LEWIS, R., "Insurance and the Tort System" (2005) 25 L.S. 85

LINDEN, A.,"Viva Torts" (2005) High Tech L.J. 139

LITTLE, J.W., "Up with Torts" (1987) 24 San Diego L. Rev. 861

STAPLETON, J., "Tort, Insurance and Ideology" (1995) 58 Mod. L. Rev. 820

SUGARMAN, S.D., "Doing Away with Tort Law" (1985) 73 Cal. L. Rev. 558

———, "Serious Tort Law Reform" (1987) 24 San Diego L. Rev. 795

———, "Rethinking Tort Doctrine: Visions of a Restatement (Fourth) of Torts (2002) 50 U.C.L.A. L. Rev. 1

GLOSSARY

Abatement: A self-help remedy to remove a nuisance from which the abator suffers.

Abuse of process: The use of civil process in furtherance of an improper motive.

Accident: An unexpected or untoward event that causes injury to another, or conduct that no reasonable person would foresee as creating a risk of injury to others.

Act of God: An extraordinary natural phenomenon that is beyond the foresight of a reasonable person and could not therefore be guarded against.

Actio per quod consortium amisit: A Latin expression for a common law action originally available only to a husband (now extended to wives) for the loss of personal and domestic services arising from an injury caused by the tortfeasor to a spouse.

Actio per quod servitium amisit: A Latin expression for a common law action brought by an employer for the loss of services of an employee injured by a tortfeasor.

Action: *See* cause of action.

Action on the case: A cause of action originating from the writ of trespass on the case. A feature of the writ was that the circumstances of the case were set out in it. Trespass on the case evolved into a number of nominate and innominate torts that are characterized by the need to prove fault and damage.

Actionable *per se*: An expression indicating that a tort is complete without proof of damage. It is applicable to the torts of trespass.

Assault: An intentional act causing another reasonably to anticipate immediate harmful or offensive bodily contact. Also used loosely to refer to the intentional injury of a person.

Bailment: A delivery of goods by one person (the bailor) to another (the bailee) for some purpose after which the goods are to be returned to the bailor.

Balance of probabilities: A standard of proof satisfying a judge or jury that the facts at issue probably occurred as alleged. Sometimes referred to as a preponderance of the evidence or a 51 percent likelihood of occurrence.

Battery: The intentional and direct interference with the body of another that is either harmful or offensive.

Burden of proof: The obligation to produce evidence to prove facts necessary to establish a cause of action or a defence. It normally rests on the person who asserts a particular matter.

Cause of action: A factual situation, the existence of which entitles a person to bring legal proceedings against another person and secure a remedy.

Cause-in-fact: The factual link between one person's actions and another person's damage.

Charterparty: A contract under which an owner leases a ship to another (the charterer) for the carriage of goods.

Chattels: All movable property; goods.

Class action: An action brought by one person as a representative of many persons with similar claims.

Confidentiality: An obligation to keep information secret.

Conspiracy: An agreement by two or more persons to carry out legal acts, the predominant purpose of which is to injure the plaintiff, or an agreement by two or more persons to injure another by illegal acts.

Continuing trespass: A trespass to land by wrongfully leaving or placing a chattel on the land of another. It gives rise to daily actions in trespass to land until the chattel is removed.

Contribution: A principle applicable where two or more defendants are jointly and severally liable. When the judgment is paid by one of the defendants, reimbursement (contribution) may be sought from the other defendant(s) in an amount proportionate to his (their) responsibility.

Contributory negligence: The failure of a plaintiff to take care for her own safety which contributes to her loss.

Conversion: The intentional interference with the right of another to a chattel which is of sufficient seriousness to require the interferer to pay for the chattel.

Damages
- *Compensatory*: A monetary remedy designed to restore the plaintiff to the position he would have been in but for the tortfeasor's conduct.
- *Aggravated*: A monetary remedy designed to compensate for the humiliation, distress, or embarrassment resulting from the tortfeasor's vicious, malicious, or shocking conduct.
- *Punitive (exemplary)*: A monetary remedy in addition to compensatory damages designed to punish the tortfeasor for his malicious, high- handed, or outrageous conduct.
- *Contemptuous (derisory)*: A monetary remedy in the smallest denomination to indicate that a tort has been technically committed but, in the opinion of the judge, the action should not have been brought because the plaintiff has suffered no real loss. It is usually applicable only in defamation actions.
- *Conventional*: A monetary remedy in the form of a single lump sum payable equally to all claimants without reference to their individual losses.
- *Nominal*: A small monetary remedy designed to indicate that, although the plaintiff has suffered no harm, a tort has been committed and the rights of the plaintiff have been infringed. Only applicable in torts that are actionable *per se*.
- *Non-pecuniary*: A monetary remedy designed to compensate an injured person's pain, suffering, permanent loss of mental or physical capacity, and loss of expectation of life.
- *Pecuniary*: A monetary amount designed to compensate the cost of future care of an incapacitated plaintiff and the loss of earning capacity.

Defamation: A communication that leads an ordinary person to think less of another person.

De minimis: A Latin expression meaning that the law does not concern itself with trifles.

Detinue: A tort arising from the refusal to return a chattel after a demand has been made for it by a person with a right to the immediate possession of it.

Distress damage feasant: A self-help remedy that permits a possessor of land to impound a chattel which is wrongfully on his land as security for the payment of compensation for damage caused by it.

Duress: Coercion or compulsion to force another person to do some act.

Duty of care: The legal obligation to exercise care in favour of the plaintiff and her interests.

Easement: A right enjoyed by a person over his neighbour's property, such as a right of way.

Enterprise liability: The general concept of allocating all losses generated by a business, activity, or institution to that entity by means of strict liability.

Estate: The property and rights of any kind enjoyed by a deceased at the time of his death.

***Ex turpi causa non oritur actio*:** A Latin phrase loosely translated as "no cause of action can arise from a base cause," which indicates that no action in tort is permitted if it would undermine the integrity of the legal system. It is a defence in rare cases such as where an award of damages would enable a plaintiff to avoid a criminal sanction or profit from wrongdoing.

False imprisonment: A direct and intentional confinement of a person within tangible or intangible boundaries.

Fiduciary: A person occupying a position of trust *vis-à-vis* another person.

First-party insurance: A contract of insurance under which the insurer, in exchange for the insured's promise to pay premiums, promises to pay the insured compensation for loss arising from the happening of a given event.

Fraud: An untrue statement of fact that the speaker either knows to be untrue or is consciously indifferent as to whether it be true or false. A statement made without an honest belief in its truth.

Gross negligence: Conduct that carries a high degree of risk.

Harassment [as used in this book]: Conduct that is seriously annoying, distressing, and disturbing to another person but does not cause that person to fear for her own safety.

Indivisible damage: Damage caused by two or more persons no distinct part of which can be assigned to the conduct of any one person.

Inducement to breach a contract: Persuasion, encouragement, or coercion of a contracting party intended to secure a breach of her contract with a third party.

Injunction: A discretionary court order to do or not to do something. An injunction may be *mandatory* (requiring a positive course of action), *prohibitory* (requiring the cessation of some activity), *interlocutory* (an interim injunction before trial), and *quia timet* (issued before any damage has been suffered).

Injurious falsehood: An untrue and malicious statement made to a third party disparaging another person's business or property.

Intention: Conduct that produces consequences which are desired by the actor or are substantially certain to occur.

Inter alia: A Latin phrase meaning among other things.

Inter vivos: A Latin phrase meaning from one living person to another.

Invitee: A visitor in whom an occupier of land has an economic interest.

Joint and several liability: All tortfeasors are collectively and individually liable for the plaintiff's loss. The plaintiff may choose which tortfeasor against whom to execute his judgment.

Jus tertii: A Latin phrase for "a right in a third person." A normally unsuccessful plea made by a tortfeasor in respect of an action for trespass to land or chattels indicating that the plaintiff's possession was wrongful *vis-à-vis* a third person.

Liability insurance: A contract under which the insurer, in exchange for premiums paid by the insured, undertakes to protect the insured from legal liability of a kind and to an extent set out in the policy.

Libel: Originally, a defamatory statement in written form. The term now extends to defamatory statements in visible and permanent form.

Licence: Permission to be on the land of another.

Limitation of action: The time period in which a plaintiff must commence a tort action. The various time periods are set out in provincial *Limitation of Actions* legislation and other statutes.

Malice: To act with a bad or improper motive.

Malicious prosecution: A baseless, improper, and unsuccessful prosecution of the plaintiff which causes actual damage to him.

Market deterrence: The general concept of allocating accident costs to the producers of those accidents so that the costs of accidents are internalized in the price of a product or activity. It is anticipated that the high cost of dangerous products and services will lead consumers to purchase cheaper (safer) products and services, thereby creating incentives to reduce accidents.

Mesne profits: Damages for the loss of use of land, damage to land, and the cost of recovering land awarded to an owner of land who recovers possession from a trespasser.

Misappropriation of personality: The unauthorized use of the name or likeness of a person in order to sell one's goods or services.

Misfeasance: An act or the failure to act which creates a risk of harm to another person.

Misfeasance in public office: Intentional conduct of a public official in abuse of her power, or knowingly beyond the scope of her jurisdiction, causing damage to the plaintiff.

Mitigation of loss: Steps that a plaintiff might reasonably be expected to take to minimize the damage or loss caused by the tortfeasor.

Necessity: A defence alleging that the tortfeasor's conduct should be excused on the grounds that he acted in an emergency and the benefit gained by his wrongful act outweighed the harm suffered by the plaintiff.

Negligence: A tort based on careless conduct or conduct that creates a reasonably foreseeable risk of harm.

Nervous shock: Psychiatric damage giving rise to physical consequences or a recognized psychiatric illness caused by a sudden and unexpected traumatic event.

No-fault compensation: Compensation based on the condition or need of an incapacitated person rather than on the proof that the loss was caused by the wrongdoing or tort of another person.

Nonfeasance: The failure to confer a benefit or an advantage on another person.

Nonsuit: The dismissal of a claim on the grounds that there is insufficient evidence to support the claim.

Novus actus interveniens: A Latin term for an intervening unforeseeable event that occurs after the defendant's negligent act and operates to precipitate or worsen the plaintiff's loss. The defendant is not liable for the loss precipitated or aggravated by such an event.

Nuisance (private): Conduct that interferes unreasonably with the use, enjoyment, and comfort of land.

Nuisance (public): Conduct that unreasonably interferes with the exercise of public rights or endangers the lives, property, or comfort of the public.

Occupier: A person with actual control of premises or land.

Occupiers' liability: A common law or statutory tort controlling the liability of occupiers of land or premises for harm caused to their visitors.

Passing-off: A misrepresentation that goods or services sold by one person are those of another or that they have a quality associated with those of the other person.

Personal injury: The term is used in tort law to include traumatic injury, illness, and nervous shock.

Pleadings: The process of a formal exchange of written documentation between the litigants defining the contested issues of fact, and, to a lesser extent, law, giving rise to the dispute between the parties.

Policy: A term that refers to the judicial analysis of the social costs and benefits of a legal principle or a judicial decision.

Possession of chattels: Physical control of a chattel.

Possession of land: Actual occupation of land coupled with the intention to control entry.

Prescription: The doctrine of land law under which persons secure an interest in land by acts of user or the lapse of time.

Proportionate liability: Two or more tortfeasors are responsible only for their proportionate share of liability.

Recklessness: Conduct that exposes others to a very high risk of injury.

Remoteness of damage: A rule that determines if the damage suffered by the plaintiff is sufficiently proximate to the tortfeasor's conduct to justify the imposition of liability.

Res ipsa loquitur: A Latin phrase meaning that the "facts speak for themselves." A kind of circumstantial evidence of negligence arising from the occurrence of an accident of unknown cause that does not normally happen without the negligence of a person.

Restitutio in integrum: A Latin phrase meaning the restoration of an injured person to the position she was in before the tortfeasor's conduct.

***Rylands v. Fletcher* (the rule in):** A tort of strict liability for damage caused by the escape of something likely to do mischief from a non-natural (dangerous) use of land.

Scienter action: The Latin word for knowledge. A common law action imposing strict liability for damage caused by animals that the owner knows to be dangerous.

Several concurrent tortfeasors: Two or more tortfeasors whose independent tortious acts are causes-in-fact of indivisible damage.

Several liability: Where two or more tortfeasors independently cause the same harm to the plaintiff and each is individually liable for the plaintiff's loss.

Slander: An oral defamatory communication.

Strict liability: Tort liability based solely on the causation of damage rather than proof of the defendant's intent or negligence.

Sui generis: A Latin phrase meaning a class unto itself.

Thin-skull rule: The principle that requires a tortfeasor to take his victim as he finds him and to compensate him to the full extent of his injuries even though they may be more serious than expected because of the plaintiff's pre-existing conditions, predispositions, and vulnerabilities.

Tort: A civil wrong remedied primarily by an award of damages.

Tortfeasor: A person who has committed a tort.

Toxic torts: A label used when conventional heads of tortious liability are used to remedy harm caused by chemicals or products such as Agent Orange or asbestos.

Trespass: A term deriving from the ancient writ of trespass that provided a civil remedy for direct damage to person and property.

Trespass ab initio: A principle that deems a person who enters land as of right to be a trespasser from the moment of entry if she abuses or exceeds her licence while on the property.

Trespass to chattels: The direct and intentional interference with a chattel in the possession of another.

Trespass to land: A direct and intentional intrusion on land in the possession of another.

Trespass by relation: A principle that deems a person with a right to the immediate possession of land to have been in possession of the land from the time the right arose once he has regained possession of it.

Trespasser: A person who enters land without permission of the possessor or remains on land after the permission of the possessor is revoked.

Vicarious liability: The liability of one person for the torts of another because of the nature of the legal relationship between them, for example, employer and employee.

Volenti non fit injuria: A Latin phrase meaning that "no injury can be done to a willing person." A defence based on the plaintiff's consent to injury without legal recourse against the person who caused it.

Volition: The capacity consciously to control and direct bodily movement.

Warranty: A strict contractual promise; a guarantee.

TABLE OF CASES

INDEX

ABOUT THE AUTHOR

Philip H. Osborne is a professor of law at the University of Manitoba where he teaches the law of torts and the law of contracts. He is a co-author of *Canadian Medical Law: An Introduction for Physicians, Nurses and Other Health Care Practitioners*, 3d ed. (with J.C. Irvine and B. Sneiderman).